CONTEXTUALIZING ISRAEL'S SACRED WRITINGS
ANCIENT LITERACY, ORALITY, AND LITERARY PRODUCTION

SBL PRESS
Ancient Israel and Its Literature

Thomas C. Römer, General Editor

Editorial Board

Suzanne Boorer
Marc Brettler
Victor H. Matthews
Benjamin D. Sommer
Gale Yee

Number 22
Contextualizing Israel's Sacred Writings:
Ancient Literacy, Orality, and Literary Production

CONTEXTUALIZING ISRAEL'S SACRED WRITINGS
ANCIENT LITERACY, ORALITY,
AND LITERARY PRODUCTION

edited by

Brian B. Schmidt

SBL Press
Atlanta, Georgia

CONTEXTUALIZING ISRAEL'S SACRED WRITINGS
ANCIENT LITERACY, ORALITY,
AND LITERARY PRODUCTION

Copyright 2015 by SBL Press

All rights reserved. No part of this work may be reproduced or transmitted in any form or by any means, electronic or mechanical, including photocopying and recording, or by means of any information storage or retrieval system, except as may be expressly permitted by the 1976 Copyright Act or in writing from the publisher. Requests for permission should be addressed in writing to the Rights and Permissions Office, Society of Biblical Literature, 825 Houston Mill Road, Atlanta, GA 30329 USA.

Library of Congress Cataloging-in-Publication Data

Contextualizing Israel's sacred writings : ancient literacy, orality, and literary production / edited by Brian Schmidt.
  pages cm. — (Society of biblical literature : ancient Israel and its literature ; volume 22)
 "The present volume has its origins in the International Conference on Orality and Literacy in the Ancient World ... held in Ann Arbor in the Summer of 2012"—Introduction
  Includes bibliographical references and index.
  ISBN 978-1-62837-118-5 (pbk. : alk. paper) — ISBN 978-1-62837-119-2 (ebook) — ISBN 978-1-62837-120-8 (hardcover : alk. paper) 1. Literacy—Religious aspects—Judaism—Congresses. 2. Oral tradition—Congresses. 3. Bible. Old Testament—Criticism, interpretation, etc.—Congresses. I. Schmidt, Brian B., editor.
  BM538.L58C66 2015
  221.6—dc23
                                                        2015019542

Printed on acid-free, recycled paper conforming to ANSI/NISO Z39.48-1992 (R1997) and ISO 9706:1994 standards for paper permanence.

CONTENTS

Abbreviations   vii

Introduction
    Brian B. Schmidt   1

    1. EPIGRAPHIC INDICATIONS OF LITERACY AND ORALITY
             IN ANCIENT ISRAELITE SOCIETY

Levantine Literacy ca. 1000–750 BCE
    André Lemaire   11

Literacy in the Negev of the Late Monarchical Period
    Nadav Na'aman   47

Scribal Curriculum during the First Temple Period: Epigraphic Hebrew and Biblical Evidence
    Christopher A. Rollston   71

Memorializing Conflict: Toward an Iron Age "Shadow" History of Israel's Earliest Literature
    Brian B. Schmidt   103

Let the Stones Speak! Document Production by Iron Age West Semitic Scribal Institutions and the Question of Biblical Sources
    Jessica Whisenant   133

    2. THE INTERFACE OF ORALITY AND LITERACY IN THE HEBREW BIBLE

Orality, Textuality *and* Memory: The State of Biblical Studies
    David M. Carr   161

The Performance of Oral Tradition in Ancient Israel
    Robert D. Miller II   175

Text Criticism as a Lens for Understanding the Transmission of
    Ancient Texts in Their Oral Environments
    Raymond F. Person Jr.   197

Oral Substratum, Language Usage, and Thematic Flow in the Abraham-
    Jacob Narrative
    Frank H. Polak   217

Royal Letters and Torah Scrolls: The Place of Ezra-Nehemiah in
    Scholarly Narratives of Scripturalization
    Elsie Stern   239

3. Aspects of Orality and Literacy in Ancient Israel in Comparative Perspective

The "Literarization" of the Biblical Prophecy of Doom
    James M. Bos   263

What if There Aren't Any Empirical Models for Pentateuchal
    Criticism?
    Seth L. Sanders   281

Scripturalization in Ancient Judah
    William M. Schniedewind   305

Hebrew Culture at the "Interface between the Written and the Oral"
    Joachim Schaper   323

Subject Index   341

Ancient Sources Index   368

ABBREVIATIONS

ÄAT	Ägypt und Alten Testament
ABS	Archaeology and Biblical Studies
ADAJ	Annual of the Department of Antiquities of Jordan
ADPV	Abhandlungen des Deutschen Palästina-Vereins
AfO	*Archiv für Orientforschung*
AIL	Ancient Israel and Its Literature
AJA	*American Journal of Archaeology*
AJP	*American Journal of Papyrology*
AMD	Ancient Magic and Divination
ANEM	Ancient Near East Monographs
AOAT	Alter Orient und Alten Testament
AoF	*Altorientalische Forschungen*
ArelG	*Archiv für Religionsgeschichte*
ASA	Annales du service des antiquties
ASOR	American Schools of Oriental Research
ATANT	Abhandlungen zur Theologie des Alten und Neuen Testaments
AuOr	*Aula Orientalis*
BA	*Biblical Archaeologist*
BAAL HS	Bulletin d'Archéologie et d'Architecture Libanaises, Hors-Série
BAR	*Biblical Archaeology Review*
BASOR	*Bulletin of the American Schools of Oriental Research*
BAAL HS	*Bulletin d'Archéologie et d'Architecture Libanaises, Hors-Série*
BBR	*Bulletin for Biblical Research*
BEATAJ	Beiträge zur Erforschung des Alten Testaments und des antiken Judentum
BEStud	Brown Egyptological Studies
BibInt	Biblical Interpretation
BibOr	*Biblica et Orientalia*

BN	*Biblische Notizen*
BO	*Bibliothetica Orientalis*
BSOAS	Bulletin of the School of Oriental and African Studies
BWANT	Beiträge zur Wissenschaft vom Alten und Neuen Testament
BZAW	Beihefte zur Zeitschrift für die Altestamentliche Wissenschaft
CHANE	Culture and History Ancient Near East
CIPOA	Cahiers de l'Institut du Proche-Orient ancien du Collège de France
CM	Cuneiform Monographs
DMOA	Documenta et Monumenta Orientis Antiqui
EBR	Encyclopedia of the Bible and Its Reception
ErIsr	*Eretz Israel*
FAT	Forschungen zum Alten Testament
Gibson, *TSSI*	John C. L. Gibson, *Textbook of Syrian Semitic Inscriptions*. 4 volumes. Oxford: Clarendon, 1971–2009
HAHE	Handbuch der althebräischen Epigraphik
HBAI	Hebrew Bible Ancient ISrael
HEO	Hautes études orientales
HKAT	Handkommentar zum Alten Testament
HO	Handbuch der Orientalistik
HSCP	Harvard Studies in Classical Philology
HSM	Harvard Semitic Monographs
HSS	Harvard Semitic Studies
HTR	*Harvard Theological Review*
HUCA	*Hebrew Union College Annual*
IAA	Israel Antiquities Authority
IDB	The Interpreters Dictionary of the Bible
IEJ	*Israel Exploration Journal*
IES	Israel Exploration Society
IOS	Israel Oriental Studies
JAJSup	Journal of Ancient Judaism Supplements
JANER	*Journal of Ancient Near Eastern Religions*
JANES	*Journal of Ancient Near Eastern Studies*
JAOS	*Journal of the American Oriental Society*
JBL	*Journal of Biblical Literature*
JCS	*Journal of Cuneiform Studies*
JESHO	*Journal of the Economic and Social History of the Orient*
JHS	*Journal of Hellenic Studies*
JNES	*Journal of Near Eastern studies*
JPOS	*Journal of the Palestine Oriental Society*

JR	*Journal of Religion*
JSOT	*Journal for the Study of the Old Testament*
JSOTS	*Journal for the study of the Old Testament Supplements*
KAI	*Kanaanaeische und aramaeische Inschriften*. Herbert Donner and Wolfgang Röllig. 2nd ed. Wiesbaden: Harrassowitz, 1966–1969
KTAH	Key Themes in Ancient History
LAI	Library of Ancient Israel
LAPO	Litteratures anciennes du Proche Orient
LHBOTS	Library of Hebrew Bible Old Testament Studies
MUSJ	Melanges de l'Universite Saint-Joseph
NEA	*Near Eastern Archaeology*
NEAEHL	*The New Encyclopedia of Archaeological Excavations of the Holy Land*. Edited by Ephraim Stern. 4 vols. Jerusalem: Israel Exploration Society & Carta; New York: Simon & Schuster, 1993
OEBA	*The Oxford Encyclopedia of the Bible and Archaeology* (Oxford Encyclopedias of the Bible). Edited by Danial M. Master. 2 volumes. Oxford: Oxford University Press, 2013
OHBS	*Oxford Handbook of Biblical Studies*. Edited by J. W. Rogerson and Judith M. Lieu. Oxford: Oxford University Press, 2008
OBO	Orbis biblicus et orientalis
OHBS	Oxford Handbook of Biblical Studies
OLA	Orientalia lovaniensia analecta
Or	*Orientalia (NS)*
OTS	Old Testament Studies
PEFQS	*Palestine Exploration Fund Quarterly Statement*
PEQ	*Palestine Exploration Quarterly*
RA	*Revue d'assyriologie et d'archéologie orientale*
RB	*Revue biblique*
REJ	*Revue des etudes juives*
RelSRev	*Religious Studies Review*
RSF	*Rivista di studi fenici*
SAAS	State Archives of Assyria Studies
SEL	*Studi epigraphici e linguistici*
SHAJ	*Studies in the History and Archeology of Jordan*
SHCANE	Studies in the History and Culture of the Ancient Near East
SJLA	Studies in Judaism in Late Antiquty
ST	*Studia theologica*

TA	*Tel Aviv*
ThTo	*Theology Today*
ThZ	*Theologisches Zeitschrift*
UF	*Ugarit-Forschungen*
VT	*Vetus Testamentum*
VTSup	Vetus Testamentum Supplements
WAW	Writings from the Ancient World
WSS	Avigad, Nahman and Benjamin Sass, *Corpus of West Semitic Stamp Seals*. Jerusalem: Israel Academy, IES, Institute of Archaeology, 1997
WUNT	Wissenschaftliche Untersuchungen zum Neuen Testament
ZA	*Zeitschrift für Assyriologie*
ZABR	*Zeitschrift für altorientalische und biblische Rechtgeschichte*
ZAS	*Zeitschrift für aegyptische Sprache und Altertumskunde*
ZAW	*Zeitschrift für die alttestamentliche Wissenschaft*
ZDPV	*Zeitschrift des deutschen Palästina-Vereins*

INTRODUCTION

Brian B. SCHMIDT

From a contemporary Western perspective, it is at the same time both obvious and profound that literacy in the ancient Near Eastern and Mediterranean theaters emerged in a predominantly oral world. The implications of that reality, however, have made only sporadic and gradual inroads into the modern study of early Israelite society, the Hebrew Bible and the relevance of orality and literacy for the actual historical composition of biblical literature. Nonetheless, a run of volumes in recent years resulting from conferences, colloquia and symposia, various edited and authored books and articles, along with a variety of publications in dictionaries and encyclopedias, epitomize the (re)surge(nce) of interest in orality's intersection with ancient literacy. Along with these, a number of publications on primary sources, oral and written, some new, some previously known but newly treated, have invigorated efforts, and authors working on the primary sources exemplify more than ever an increasing self-consciousness with regard to the relevance of their data to the broader issues of cross-cultural literacy and orality.

Yet expert opinion has failed to garner any kind of consensus on a wide spectrum of topics from definitions employed, data examined, questions posed, social reconstructions offered and the dates, loci, and productions conjectured, even collateral evidence considered and analogies invoked. Various theories applied and prospective implications proposed are in flux (e.g., literacy's and orality's juncture with human cognition and social complexity). What does verge on a developing consensus is that widespread ancient Levantine, and Mediterranean, literacy was not the direct and immediate outcome of the alphabet's invention or its implementation. From its beginning literacy's distribution involved a complex, open-ended process impacted at varying times by a wide range of convergent and contingent political, social, and historical factors. Moreover, the notion is gaining ground in recent literature that such factors as political and social stability, urbanizing or centralizing tendencies, economic mobilization and the vernacularization of writing fostered a West Semitic scribal world in which "ethnicizing" literatures could be produced and transmitted. Furthermore, in the case of ancient Israelite tradition, and irrespective of biblical literature's first written recording, Hebrew was continuously used and biblical texts were preserved well beyond the demise of the Israelite and Judahite polities of the eighth and sixth centuries BCE. Lastly, with the demonstrable rejection of the "great divide thesis," researchers are increasingly recognizing that an orality-literacy continuum, the ongoing interaction of orality and literacy, the influence of oral aesthetics and multiformity on the production as well as the transmission and reception of texts, and writing's crucial role as a mnemonic device, all characterized ancient Levantine discourse. Throughout, and within the context of a predominantly oral world, writing remained the primary prerogative of elite society—that of scribes as well as their patrons.

The volume's contributions fall along three identifiable, yet broadly interrelated, trajectories: those that primarily explore the ever expanding epigraphic database for indications of the oral and the written in ancient Israelite society, those that first and foremost mine the Hebrew Bible for examples of the interface between orality and literacy, and those that integrate both of the above in pursuing specific questions such as scripturalization, the oral and textual dimensions of composition as it pertains to biblical poetry, prophecy and narrative and their antecedents, the dialectic between the oral and the written, and the ultimate autonomy of the written in early Israel.

Epigraphic Indications of Literacy and Orality in Ancient Israelite Society

Andre Lemaire seeks to elucidate the evidence for writing from the first millennium as it relates to the dating of the earliest biblical texts and he does so in response to recent statements that writing in more complex forms only emerged in the late eighth century context and that before then, such traditions were transmitted orally. Lemaire reviews the evidence from the Levant spanning 1000–750 BCE. At the earlier end of this continuum, we have Phoenician dedication inscriptions used for the purpose of marking ownership of objects widely distributed throughout the Levant. Then Lemaire surveys those of the later Aramaean kingdoms, Phoenicia, Palestine, and Moab. The inventory from Palestine is sparse, which raises the question of the political and economic situation in Cisjordan, while the sudden appearance of writing in Moab in the second half of the ninth and first half of the eighth centuries coincides with the inscribed stelae produced by the Aramaean kingdoms. In sum, the epigraphic database reveals a strong contemporary scribal tradition in Samaria and Tyre after 800 BCE. With the Deir Alla and Kuntillet Ajrud plaster inscriptions we have confirmation of literary Aramaic and Phoenician traditions that were being copied in the first half of the eighth century. The original text (or "sepher") mentioned in the Balaam text from Deir Alla, "seems at least to date in the ninth or tenth centuries BCE," so "the beginning of a literary tradition in Israel and Judah in the ninth and tenth century is certainly not impossible."

Nadav Na'aman explores the epigraphic data that have been retrieved from archaeological excavations from Negev fortresses and cities of the eighth to sixth centuries BCE and what those data can convey with regard to the levels and distribution of literacy. The maintenance and compensation of state employees located at the fortresses were regularly recorded and dispensed on location using the cheapest writing medium, ostraca, in order to control expenses. In the exceptional case of Arad, the temple administration also required payment and maintenance for the priests and personnel. Bullae suggest that many of these writings were drafts of final form papyrus documents. The ostraca from the fortresses point to state officials as clerks of a sort, whereas Arad's temple requiring priests and administrators suggests scribes with higher levels of literacy at this unique early eighth-century site. The sapiental text from Horvat 'Uza of the seventh–sixth centuries also presupposes a scribe of higher training and ability. Priests, high royal officials, and military commanders enjoyed a higher level of literacy in Judah while low-ranking soldiers and lower-class individuals were illiterate. The distribution of inscriptions in domestic contexts at Horvat 'Uza may suggest that local inhabitants between the elites and the lower classes enjoyed a level of literacy somewhere in the middle.

For Christopher Rollston, sources indicate that scribalism was a lofty profession that required a level of dedication and effort that spanned several years. It was also comprised of hierarchies, though privately scribes produced a range of texts. Yet education took place in small numbers often in domestic contexts among elites, not in public buildings. In early Israel, the high caliber of the Old Hebrew script, the synchronic and diachronic consistency in letter morphology, stance and (often) ductus, and the fact that distinct scripts were regionally developed reflects a significant investment aimed at producing a proper form of writing. The curriculum included orthographic conventions, hieratic numerals, and standardized epistolary formulae. Though small, it was sophisticated and capable of educating in an erudite and standardized manner. Rollston rejects the notion that scribes worked primarily outside the aegis of the state in guilds. The evidence points instead to the palace or state, and in particular the military and economic sectors. A biblical text like the Rab-Shaqeh story in 2 Kings 18 indicates that Judean scribes learned Aramaic as part of their formal training. Finally, Rollston describes the overall curriculum as, "a complex collection of texts from widely different periods," showing "significant dependence on foreign literature and foreign traditions" that had "traveled far and wide" in oral, aural, and written forms.

Brian Schmidt narrates a history of literary production of length in the southern, inland Levant in three phases. The state-scribal development phase spanned the first half of the ninth century. Literature of length remained exclusively oral as requisite infrastructural, technological, material production, and media procurement sectors were early on reemerging from more rudimentary stages of development. Aspiring to emulate Assyria however, Levantine polities initiated enhancements and adaptations to scribal apparatuses and writing systems, as well as the production if not procurement of media materials. During the conflict-affective phase spanning the ninth century's second half, an inland polity or two reached the threshold of producing lengthy literature, but arrival of protracted, repeated, and ever-intensifying conflicts severely disrupted implementation. Six intraregional conflicts with Assyria spanning fifteen years from the mid-ninth century to its latter third were followed by six or more devastating interregional conflicts with Aram-Damascus, Moab, and Ammon dominating over Israel and Judah for the final thirty years of the late ninth century. Redirection, depletion, and exhaustion of substantial human and material resources resulted in a prolonged interruption in lengthy literary-text production among Levantine polities lasting forty years or more. Moreover, the interregional conflicts shifted instability and destruction onto home soil. This only exasperated previous resource losses, inhibited cultural expression and further proliferated postponement of lengthy literary production for the vanquished. Yet near the ninth century's end, during the royal prerogative phase, the victors fashioned unique monumental products of elite emulation and context-specific forms comprising lengthy literary texts. While suspension of written literature of length continued for the vanquished, production would emerge in the following centuries with the return of local stability, stimulus, and industry.

Jessica Whisenant's contribution reviews the epigraphic data across the Levant in order to identify the socio-historical processes and periods that informed the written composition of those works that later made up the Hebrew Bible. She surveys the Iron Age II Levantine evidence before drawing down her focus to the Iron II period in Israel and the Transjordan as the more immediate context for assessing the data in late Iron II Judah. Provisionally, the last was the most likely context in which the earliest texts that eventuated into the books of the Hebrew Bible were produced. Whisenant concludes that at best one can talk about works produced in this period and context that served as *sources* for the various books that later came to make up the Hebrew Bible. By the eighth century, monumental inscriptions that preserved military and construction activities of the royalty were written down along with brief ritual and incantatory texts and prophetic oracles. For various practical and propagandistic purposes, state scribes sometimes left epigraphs at locations on contested border areas such as Deir Alla, Horvat 'Uza, or Kuntillet Ajrud. These along with such hypothetical (though highly plausible) texts as king lists and annals may have led to the production of a chronistic written tradition that strengthened Jerusalem's primacy, uniting the region around a single royal dynasty and a single cultic tradition conveying a unique, dual emphasis on the people as well as on the royalty.

The Interface of Orality and Literacy in the Hebrew Bible

For David Carr, the variations among biblical manuscripts can provide insights into the transmission process and the purpose of their tradents. Carr proposes a "third way," namely, the way of memory. The memory he has in view is not exclusively tied to an oral context or mindset. He illustrates this by citing examples of textual variants that can be correlated with any one of the three: literacy, orality, or memory. When a textual tradition is carried in the mind, memorized and then reproduced, it comprises what Carr refers to as a "memory variant," such as the exchange of one synonym for another. Memory variants, "made sense" to tradents as they strove in their "effort after meaning" and as such they constituted good variants. Carr notes that scribes often relied on memory and rarely consulted actual scrolls when recording brief quotes. Writing served the internalizing of tradition in order that one might memorize and perform it. In the case of biblical literature, we have evidence, even the combination, of textual, oral, and memory variants in the specific formation of long-duration literary-theological texts. Carr also proposes that emendation of the text should be seen as restoration rather than the change of text. Finally, Carr views memory variants as indicators of memory's operation in a multiform early manuscript and quotation tradition of the Hebrew Bible. In such cases, written biblical texts served to support memorization or internalization of tradition and facilitated oral performance.

Robert Miller first offers a review of orality-literacy research and its ongoing impact on biblical studies with a particular focus on the Goody-Ong dichotomy where the role of memory in orality is supposedly sacrificed in favor of the development of analytical and logical skills that literacy provides. He then reiterates the notion that orality and literacy frequently and intensively exist alongside each other in many societies and Israel and Judah are no exceptions. Since their literature began "predominantly oral," one can apply performance critical tools to passages in the Hebrew Bible that may be orally derived. He highlights the determinative role of social convention in performance, but also qualifies this in quoting Vaz de Silva's view of performance that is, "shaped by the interplay between individually generated variations and community-enacted selection mechanisms." For Miller ethnography is also crucial to the reconstruction of practices performed in cases where we have no directly accessible contexts. As for Israelite oral performance, he highlights the analogies between it and Icelandic Skaldic and Eddic poetry. He then explores the postbattle celebrations in the Hebrew Bible including commemorative ballads that were sung and accompanied by dance. On the matter of performance criticism and historical investigation, Miller underscores the role of genre in oral performance and endorses research on collective memory as the next fruitful approach in exploring oral performance in ancient Israel.

Raymond Person takes up the Parry-Lord insight on multiformity of oral traditions by invoking current text critical scholarship in other ancient and medieval literature such as Homeric, Old English poetic, and medieval Arabic prose scholarship. He concludes that such texts reflect a cultural acceptance of the type of multiformity attested in oral traditions which also influenced scribal praxis in transmitting texts; no one instantiation is an exact replication of the tradition. Yet each text, just like each performance of an oral bard, is a faithful representation, although not a full iteration of that tradition. Person adds to the process the *Tendenz* toward expansion identified by scholars working in these various textual traditions. Although such expansions are organic to the traditions, he concludes that these literatures evince performative and compositional traits in the transmission processes that approximate oral processes. When viewed together or conjointly they are reflective of a broader collective memory. Following a review of recent Dead Sea Scrolls scholarship's more nuanced view that every copy of an authoritative text is representative of the broader tradition, Person explores 2 Sam 12:26–31 and 1 Chr 20:1b–3. He similarly suggests that while both texts are imperfect instantiations of a broader more inclusive mental text located in the collective memory of the community, each is nonetheless a faithful representation thereof. Yet the shorter Chronicles text might be closer to the earliest written forms of the tradition, while Samuel represents an expansion.

Frank Polak proposes that the tales of the patriarchal narratives reflect an underlying oral–epic substratum that formed the basic structure for the narratives in their present written form. The unity of the overarching patriarchal narrative was preserved in this oral–epic substratum while repetition and contradiction find their origins in the various oral and text-based narrators within the tradition. For Polak, the Genesis 12–35 narrative formed a "large-scale narrative platform" for various narrators who maintained the stabilized narrative content (or *fabula*) as well as the plot (or *syuzhet*), but who produced variants, continuations and expansions of the basic elements of *fabula*. The platform was to a large extent defined by the oral performance. This finds verification in the number of explicit syntactic constituents, subordinate clauses, and noun groups within a given constituent. The Abraham and the Jacob narratives comprise a discourse profile Polak characterizes as a "lean brisk style" or LBS, which manifests basic features of spontaneous spoken language. The Deuteronomistic corpus is characterized by the "intricate elaborate style" or IES, which is representative of written discourse. The IES presupposes the advanced scribal education and chancery of the eighth century BCE, whereas the former approximates an earlier oral performance of poetry and narrative or "oral-derived literature." Polak proposes three avenues to explain the oral-written interface in the patriarchal narrative: literary design, stylistic profile and redactional process. When the style is high on the LBS scale, dictation by an oral narrator might be in view or a text composed by an orator or a writer well versed in oral performance. When the style is high on the IES scale, the connection is less direct as when general oral style is used rather than a specific performance.

Elsie Stern observes that in Ezra-Nehemiah (E-N) written scrolls are identified as reference points for torah and as an authorizing strategy within the text. Yet the meaning and content of written torah in E-N is not scripturalized. The content is neither identical to extant pentateuchal texts nor is it determinative of authoritative discourse. These articulations of torah within E-N as compositions of torah are expressive of an oral-literary mode. Within this modality, they are audience and context specific articulations that are grounded in received material preserved textually and orally, that has been internalized by the authorized tradents. They are not new inventions. While the content of written torah in E-N is often omitted, the identity of the tradents is not. The tradents are identified as articulators of torah, not interpreters or even brokers of it. This narrative pattern places E-N's representation of torah at the intersection of the book's two central propositions. Ezra, Nehemiah, and their compatriots are the unquestioned and unchallenged sources of torah and the torah that they generate is the only legitimate law of the land. As such torah functions to counter challenges to the right of the returnee community to claim local authority in postexilic Yehud.

Aspects of Israelite and Biblical Orality and Literacy in Comparative Perspective

James Bos explores the initial textualization of the oracle of doom genre in ancient Judah. Bos proposes that such were most likely composed in writing in the seventh or sixth centuries either following the destruction of the north in 721 BCE as Judahite prophets predicted Israel's defeat and/or reflected upon it *ex eventu*, or in the context of a later intra-Judahite conflict between a pro-Babylonian elite faction ensconced in the northern Benjaminite region and a pro-Egyptian faction in Jerusalem. This conflict eventually led to Judahites predicting the downfall of other Judahites. In the first case, the Judahite perspective on Israel's fall, such oracles did not constitute doom oracles per se, but were oracles against a foreign nation (e.g., OAN). Yet such could have served as conceptual and generic models for later Judahite *ex eventu* doom oracles against other Judahites following Jerusalem's fall in 586. In the second scenario, early written *predictive* oracles approximated a turning inward, or a turning on its head, of the oracle against foreign nations. The former scenario, Israel's destruction as viewed from a Judean viewpoint, might have also been an influencing factor on the alienated Judahites' later pronouncements against their fellow Judahites. Once Jerusalem was in fact destroyed, such oracles attracted supplementary literary elaboration and spawned additional doom oracles that were *ex eventu*.

Seth Sanders seeks to answer the question: are there pre-Hellenistic Near Eastern literary examples of the Pentateuch's interweaving of parallel narrative variants? Based on an analysis of the Primary History, Sanders concludes that there are no such parallels and that this provides a crucial clue for locating its composition within a relative chronological history. Highlighting the Primeval History and the Pentateuch's preference for comprehensiveness over coherence, Sanders suggests that such "literary value" led to subsequent attempts by early Jewish commentators unfamiliar with them to harmonize and reconcile apparent contradictions. Sanders employs the literary topos of the flood in order to illustrate how the coherent Gilgamesh flood episode closely resembles the layers of the flood story as attested in the Priestly and non-Priestly sources. The Genesis flood account's interweaving of two parallel variant plots "seems alien to the whole of ancient Near Eastern narrative art....," where sequential or serial expansion or addition ruled the day. The interweaving of Genesis in two preexisting coherent sources depicts a very different literary and conceptual strategy of composition and results in incoherence. This situates the Pentateuch's comprehensiveness and incoherence within the larger relative chronological history of ancient Hebrew literature. He proposes a three-stage development from a "dominant" value of coherence to one of comprehensiveness and incoherence to a dialectical response that returned to coherence through the work of harmonization and conflation emerging in the Hellenistic period.

William Schniedewind explains how the Judean literary corpus gained authoritative religious status or scripturalization, while the great epics and mythic traditions of Mesopotamia, Syria, and Greece did not. Biblical texts do not derive their religious authority from their origins in other precedent literature on which they depended such as Gilgamesh or from their supposed origins in the temples, since the palace scribal apparatus was more prominent in the preexilic period. Neo-Assyrian texts indicate that they could be dictated by the gods and written down by scribes. Something similar obtains with the composition of texts like the Josianic reforms and Deuteronomy or Exodus 24. Revelation is manifested in three ways in ancient Judah: through the use of divine writing, the adoption of the messenger formula for God, and the use of ritual magic used in treaties. The royal messenger formula was adopted under Assyrian influence as a way of endowing written texts with royal authority, and through the writing prophets, with divine authority. Similarly, ritual magic of the treaty blessings and curses and in magical rituals informed the composition of a text like Deuteronomy 27–29, Joshua 8, and Numbers 5. Huldah's prophecy came to Josiah in the form of a letter carried by a messenger that invoked the written treaty curses derived from ritual magic. All of these elements comprised authoritative forms of Neo-Assyrian writing. The Josianic reform narrative thus scripturalizes the scroll and embodies some of the earliest illustrations of the scripturalization process.

For Joachim Schaper, writing's practice increased significantly from the eighth century onwards. The emerging prominence of writing is a direct outgrowth of the increased division of labor in Israelite and Judahite societies. The palaeo-Hebrew script developed as a move toward uniformity in style by institutionalized Israelite scribes. It was not an expression of nationalism. Writing's effects on individuals and on social relations of production were profound. In the Hebrew Bible, conceptualizations of conversation and speech were projected onto the perceived discourse between the deity and humanity creating a sense of immediacy as when Moses communicated with YHWH, "face-to-face, as a man speaks to his friend." Writing shifts language from the aural to the visual domain making possible a different kind of introspection that restructures consciousness. The biblical rhetorical strategy of addressing readers together with the imagined audience in the world of the text created the sense of a unified group of listeners. Written texts served the auxiliary purpose of providing the basis for literate Israelites to "perform" texts on significant occasions (cf. Nehemiah 8). Both the written and the spoken word took on magical properties in ritualized performance. Jeremiah 36 and the Mari texts indicate that prophets dictated messages to scribes. Prophecy transformed into a more text-centered phenomenon and ceased to exist as an oral/aural activity. Schaper concludes that the dialectic between the written and the oral persisted, but an ever-increasing autonomy and veneration (or fetishization) of writing in the context of an oral society eventually dominated.

The present volume has its genesis in the International Conference on Orality and Literacy in the Ancient World held in Ann Arbor during the summer of 2012 and organized by University of Michigan professor and chair of the Department of Classical Studies, Ruth Scodel. Papers presented in Ann Arbor at panel sessions devoted to biblical and Levantine studies have been combined here with others solicited subsequently for their timeliness and relevance to the topics of orality and literacy in the pre-Hellenistic southern Levant and in the Hebrew Bible.

I wish to express my sincere appreciation to Professor Scodel, to all those who participated in the planning, organization and the day-to-day, "hands on" support in making the conference an immense success and to the Departments of Near Eastern Studies and Classical Studies at the University of Michigan for their generous funding of the conference. I also want to convey my gratitude to the colleagues who contributed to the volume as it evolved in its postconference permutations. Including their research alongside an already compelling core of articulations has, with creative and rigorous tones, given voice to a series of crucial issues that would not have been possible otherwise. Finally, and most importantly, this volume would have not seen the light of day without the patience and diligence of all my fellow contributors and the incomparable expertise of Dr. Billie Jean Collins, friend, colleague, and indispensible technical editor who, by all good fortune, oversaw this project to its completion.

Brian B. Schmidt
Ann Arbor, MI

LEVANTINE LITERACY CA. 1000–750 BCE

André LEMAIRE

THE PROBLEM OF LITERACY IN THE LEVANT AT THE BEGINNING OF THE FIRST millennium BCE has been much discussed during the last ten years, especially in connection with the dating of the earliest biblical texts. For instance, according to Israel Finkelstein, "Writing in Judah commenced in the late ninth century, but at that time was sporadic and did not include complex texts; scribal activity gained prominence only in the late eighth century and more so in the seventh century BCE. Therefore pre-late 8th century materials must have been transmitted orally."[1] Before coming back to this point, it is useful, first, to try to understand the problem of literacy itself, specifically, from an epigraphic and historical point of view.

Although the evidence is very limited and its dating and interpretation sometimes debated, we are not "working with no data." To appreciate these data better, it may be useful to distinguish two periods: ca. 1000–850 and ca. 850–750 BCE.

ALPHABETIC INSCRIPTIONS FROM CA. 1000–850 BCE

For this period,[2] we have no unequivocal Aramaic inscriptions, but several "Canaanite" ones come from the central and southern Levant.

---

1. Israel Finkelstein, "Geographical and Historical Realities behind the Earliest Layer in the David Story," *SJOT* 27 (2013): 135.
2. The dating of most of the inscriptions is approximate and the "ca." is meaningful. The date of 850 is especially approximate: actually the main historical change in the Levant is probably connected with the reign of Hazaël (ca. 843–805/3 BCE) and several small inscriptions dated to the middle of the ninth century can be located either in the first period or in the following one.

PHOENICIA

According to most epigraphers and as I have summarized elsewhere,[3] we have now five royal inscriptions and six kings of Byblos from the tenth century:

Aḥirom ca. 1000 BCE
Ittobaal ca. 990/980
Yeḥimilk ca. 970/960
Abibaal ca. 945
Elibaal ca. 924
Shipitbaal ca. 900

Because these inscriptions are without a clear archaeological context, their dating has been questioned and Benjamin Sass has proposed to date them "around the last third of the ninth century."[4] A comparison with other Phoenician inscriptions historically dated from this period, such as the Kulamuwa inscription, show that Sass's dating is palaeographically very unlikely.[5] Actually, with Alan Millard, it would be very difficult to "envisage

---

3. André Lemaire, "West Semitic Epigraphy and the History of the Levant during the 12th–10th Centuries BCE," in *The Ancient Near East in the 12th–10th Centuries BCE: Culture and History*, ed. Gershon Galil et al., AOAT 392 (Münster: Ugarit-Verlag, 2012), 292–93.

4. Israel Finkelstein and Benjamin Sass, "The West Semitic Alphabetic Inscriptions, Late Bronze II to Iron IIA: Archaeological Context, Distribtion and Chronology," *HBAI* 2 (2013): 202; see already Benjamin Sass, *The Alphabet at the Turn of the Millennium: The West Semitic Alphabet ca. 1150–850 BCE. The Antiquity of the Arabian, Greek, and Phrygian Alphabets* (Tel-Aviv: Emery and Claire Yass Publications in Archaeology, 2005), 48–49, 73. This dating is based on the hypothesis "that the script of the Byblos inscriptions (among others cut in stone) is artificial or archaizing" (p. 16). Such a general hypothesis is unlikely, especially if one takes the small Byblos inscriptions into account.

5. See also Christopher A. Rollston, "The Dating of the Early Royal Byblian Phoenician Inscriptions: A Response to Benjamin Sass," *Maarav* 15 (2008): 57–93; idem, *Writing and Literacy in the World of Ancient Israel*, ABS 11 (Atlanta: Society of Biblical Literature, 2010), 24–27. For a detailed palaeographic analysis, see R. G. Lehmann, "Calligraphy and Craftsmanship in the Aḥīrōm Inscription: Considerations on Skilled Linear Flat Writing in Early First Millennium Byblos," *Maarav* 15 (2008): 119–64; Maria Giulia Amadasi Guzzo, "'Alphabet insaisissable' Quelques notes concernant la diffusion de l'écriture consonantique," in *Bible et Proche-Orient: Mélanges André Lemaire*, vol. 1, ed. Jean-Marie Durand and Josette Elayi, Transeuphratène 44 (Paris: Gabalda, 2014), 74–76; Christopher A. Rollston, "The Iron Age Phoenician Scripts," in *"An Eye for Form". Epigraphic Essays in Honor of Frank Moore Cross*, ed. Jo Ann A. Hackett and Walter E. Aufrecht (Winona Lake, IN: Eisenbrauns, 2014), 72–99.

kings of Byblos dedicating statues of dead pharaohs to their goddess."[6] More precisely, studies of the Abibaal and Elibaal inscriptions, as well as of an Ugaritic text, reveal that these pharaoh statues were ordered by the Byblian kings to be put in their own main temple following the coronation of a new pharaoh.[7] So the Abibaal and Elibaal inscriptions are well connected with Egyptian history and, unless the Egyptian chronology of this period is to be totally revised, they should be dated in the second half of the tenth century BCE.

Besides these monumental inscriptions, the Byblos excavations have produced a dozen small inscriptions on stone (the Ahirom graffito,[8] tablet,[9] weight?[10]), bronze ("spatula"[11]), and clay (cones,[12] potsherds[13]). The palaeographic dating of these inscriptions may only be approximate: tenth or even eleventh century BCE.

We now have more than sixty inscribed arrowheads.[14] They are all unprovenanced except one; most however come from the territory of Leba-

---

6. Alan Millard, "Scripts and Their Uses in the 12th–10th Centuries BCE," in Galil et al., *The Ancient Near East in the 12th–10th Centuries BCE*, 408.

7. André Lemaire, "La datation des rois de Byblos Abibaal et Elibaal et les relations entre l'Egypte et le Levant au Xe siècle av. notre ère," *CRAI* (2006): 1697–716.

8. *KAI* 2; Reinhard G. Lehmann, Text 1.2: "Die Inschrift(en) des Aḥīrōm-Sarkophags und die Schachtinschrift des Grabes V in Jbeil (Byblos)," in *Dynastensarkophage mit szenischen Reliefs aus Byblos und Zypern* (Mainz: von Zabern, 2005), 39–54.

9. Maurice Dunand, *Fouilles de Byblos I. 1926–1932* (Paris: Geuthner, 1939), 95–96: no. 1452, pl. XXXI; André Lemaire, *Les écoles et la formation de la Bible dans l'ancien Israël*, OBO 39 (Fribourg: Editions universitaires; Göttingen: Vandenhoeck & Ruprecht, 1981), 11, 88, n. 21.

10. Hélène Sader, "An Inscribed Weight from Byblos," in *Atti del V Congresso internazionale di Studi Fenici e Punici, Marsala-Palermo, 2–8 octobre 2000*, I, ed. A. Spano Giammellaro (Palermo: Universita degli studi di Palermo, Facolta di lettere e filosofia, 2005), 47–51; André Lemaire, "'Ozibaal de Byblos?,'" in *Ritual, Religion and Reason: Studies in the Ancient World in Honour of Paolo Xella*, ed. Oswald Loretz et al. AOAT 404 (Münster, Ugarit-Verlag, 2013), 289–96. The hesitation of Finkelstein and Sass ("West Semitic Alphabetic Inscriptions," 172, n. 118, 219: no. 67) regarding the Byblian origin of this object is perplexing.

11. *KAI* 3; Ryan Byrne, "The Refuge of Scribalism in Iron I Palestine," *BASOR* 345 (2007): 20; Rollston, *Writing and Literacy*, 20.

12. Maurice Dunand, *Fouilles de Byblos II, 1933–1938. 1. Texte* (Paris: Geuthner, 1954), no. 7765, 9400, 10470, 10478, 11671, 11687; Frank Moore Cross and P. Kyle McCarter, "Two Archaic Inscriptions on Clay Objects from Byblus," *RSF* 1 (1973): 3–8; Javier Teixidor, "An Archaic Inscription from Byblos," *BASOR* 225 (1977): 70–71; Gibson, *TSSI* 3:12; Finkelstein and Sass, "West Semitic Alphabetic Inscriptions," 209, 217.

13. Dunand, *Fouilles de Byblos I*, nos. 1450, 2927, 3317; *Fouilles de Byblos II*, nos. 9608, 10469; André Lemaire, "West Semitic Epigraphy," 292, n. 12.

14. See most recently Gaby Abousamra, "Cinq nouvelles pointes de flèches inscrites," in Durand and Elayi, *Bible et Proche-Orient*, 47–56.

non. Most of them can also be approximately dated to the eleventh century; the latest ones however could be ca. 1000 or early tenth century BCE. Some of them are probably connected with Byblos.[15]

Three other proto-Phoenician bronze inscriptions probably date to the tenth century. BCE. They are incised on the outer rim of a cup/bowl:
1. The inscription KS.PSḤ.BN ŠMʿ, "cup of Pasiaḥ son of Shamaʿ," found in a tomb in Kefar Veradim.[16]
2. The inscription KS ŠMʿ.BN LʾMN, "cup of Shamaʿ son of Liamon," found in a tomb in Tekke, near Knossos.[17]
3. The unprovenanced inscription KS ʾBʾBŠ, "cup of Ababash," (around 900 BCE?).[18]

Several other Phoenician inscriptions might be added to this list:

4. A Tell Kazel inscription of two lines on the outer rim of a large bowl probably dates to the tenth century or around 900 BCE.[19]
5. A Sarepta sherd with an inscription painted before firing is difficult to date: twelfth–tenth centuries BCE?
6. A Rosh Zayit sherd with a fragmentary ink inscription is probably connected with the Phoenician culture[20] and was found in a radiocarbon dated layer: 895–835 BCE[21] and might well date to the middle of the ninth century.

---

15. André Lemaire, "West Semitic Epigraphy," 293–94; Lemaire, "Ozibaal de Byblos?," 289–96.

16. Yardeni Alexandre, "A Fluted Bronze Bowl with a Canaanite-Early Phoenician Inscription from Kefar Veradim," in *Eretz Zafon. Studies in Galilean Archaeology*, ed. Tzevi Gal (Haifa: Israel Antiquities Authority, 2002), 65*–74*; "A Canaanite Early Phoenician Bronze Bowl in a Iron Age IIA–B Burial Cave at Kefar Veradim, Northern Israel," *Maarav* 13 (2006): 7–41; Lemaire, "West Semitic Epigraphy," 296; Finkelstein and Sass, "West Semitic Alphabetic Inscriptions," 161–62: no. 17.

17. H. W. Catling, "The Knossos Area, 1974–1976," *JHS* 97 (1977): 11–14; Maurice Sznycer, "L'inscription phénicienne de Tekke, près de Knossos," *Kadmos* 18 (1979): 89–93; Emile Puech "Présence phénicienne dans les îles à la fin du IIe millénaire," *RB* 90 (1983): 374–91; Lemaire, "West Semitic Epigraphy," 296. The date proposed by Frank Moore Cross ("Newly Found Inscription in Old Canaanite and Early Phoenician Scripts," *BASOR* 238 [1980]: 15–17) is probably somewhat early.

18. Sotheby Sale Catalogue April 21, 1975 (London), 62; Sznycer, "L'inscription phénicienne de Tekke," 92: n. 1; Lemaire, "West Semitic Epigraphy," 296, n. 35.

19. Eric Gubel, "The Phoenician Temple at Tell Kazel (Ṣumur)," *BAAL HS* 6 (2009), 459; Finkelstein and Sass, "The West Semitic Alphabetic Inscriptions," 199, n. 209.

20. Zvi Gal and Yardeni Alexandre, *Horbat Rosh Zayit. An Iron Storage Fort and Village*, IAA Report 8 (Jerusalem: Israel Antiquities Authority, 2000), 133–34.

21. Israel Finkelstein and Eliazer Piasetzky, "Radiocarbon, Iron IIA Destructions and the Israel-Aram Damascus Conflicts in the 9th Century B.C.E.," *UF* 39 (2007), 266.

7. A few fragmentary inscribed sherds from tenth- to ninth-century BCE Hazor are probably Phoenician (or possibly Aramaic?).[22] Their dating is approximate.
8. A fragmentary inscription incised on a sherd from Tell el-'Orēme/Kinneret might be Phoenician[23] and date to the early ninth century BCE[24] but this is uncertain.
9. A funerary inscription from Cyprus, now in the Nicosia Museum can be palaeographically dated to the early ninth century BCE.[25]
10. The earliest nonprovenanced funerary stele, probably from the cemetery of Tyre al-Bass, with the inscription LŠM‘, could well be dated to the end of the tenth century as proposed by H. Sader[26] but an early ninth-century BCE date cannot be excluded.

PHILISTIA AND JUDEAN SHEPHELAH

The excavations of Tell eṣ-Ṣafi/Gath brought to light several small inscriptions clearly dated before the destruction of the city by Hazael ca. 820–810 BCE.[27] The sherd 821141 preserves a Canaanite inscription incised after firing on the outside of a bowl fragment. It was found in stratum 4 and the inscription might be dated to the late eleventh or tenth century BCE.[28]

---

22. Bernard Delavault and André Lemaire, "Les inscriptions phéniciennes de Palestine," *RSF* 5 (1979), 1–39, esp. nos. 8–11, 14, 16; Joseph Naveh, "The Epigraphic Finds from Areas A and B," in *Hazor III/IV.* Part 2: *Text*, ed. Amnon Ben-Tor (Jerusalem: Magnes, 1989), 346–47; Sass, *The Alphabet at the Turn of the Millennium*, 85–86; Finkelstein and Sass, "The West Semitic Alphabetic Inscriptions," 171.
23. André Lemaire, review of *Handbuch der hebräischen Epigraphik* I, II/A, III, by J. Renz, *BiOr* 54 (1997): 162.
24. Volkmar Fritz, *Kinneret. Ergebnisse der Ausgrabungen auf dem Tell el-'Orēme am See Genezaret 1982–1985*, ADPV 15 (Wiesbaden: Harrassowitz, 1990), 118, Taf. 41C, 101,1: Taf. IV,3; Johannes Renz and Wolfgang Röllig, *Die Althebräischen Inschriften I. Text und Kommentar*, HAHE I (Darmstadt: Wissenschaftliche Buchgesellschaft, 1995), 65; Finkelstein and Sass, "The West Semitic Alphabetic Inscriptions," 168.
25. *KAI* 30; Olivier Masson and Maurice Sznycer, *Recherches sur les Phéniciens à Chypre*, HEO 3 (Geneva: Droz, 1972), 14; Emile Puech, "Remarques sur quelques inscriptions phéniciennes de Chypre," *Semitica* 29 (1979): 19–26; J. C. L. Gibson, *Textbook of Syrian Semitic Inscriptions III. Phoenician Inscriptions* (Oxford: Clarendon, 1982), 28–30.
26. Hélène S. Sader, *Iron Age Funerary Stelae from the Lebanon*, Cuadernos de arqueologia mediterranea 11 (Barcelona: Bellaterra 2005), 42–43: stele 16.
27. André Lemaire, "Hazaël de Damas, roi d'Aram," in *Marchands, diplomates et empereurs. Études sur la civilisation mésopotamienne offertes à Paul Garelli*, ed. D. Charpin and F. Joannès (Paris: Editions Recherche sur les Civilisations, 1991), 103.
28. Aren M. Maeir et al., "A Late Iron Age I / Early Iron Age IIA Old Canaanite Inscription from Tell eṣ-Ṣâfî/Gath, Israel: Palaeography, Dating, and Historical-Cultural

Three other short inscriptions incised before firing on a jar (747028/1: L'B; 450313/1: RP' or 'G') and one in red ink (1491025: 'B'/TM) were found in stratum A3 and probably date to the middle/late ninth century BCE.[29]

About 8–9 km southwest of Tell eṣ-Ṣafi/Gath, the excavations of Tell Zayit brought to light an inscription incised on a limestone boulder. This inscription is essentially an abecedary. It was dated to the mid-tenth century by the *editio princeps*[30] but this early date has been criticized by Rollston (late tenth or very early ninth century),[31] as well as by Finkelstein, Sass, and Singer-Avitz (ninth century). Actually the length of the vertical strokes does not seem to fit a tenth-century BCE dating and the inscription is more probably early ninth century.[32]

Tell el-Farʿah South, about 22 km south of Gaza, has preserved a potsherd inscribed with ink: L'DNN, perhaps "(Belonging) to our lord." Since it was found in debris, the dating can only be palaeographically approximated.[33] It has been widely discussed; it could date to the ninth century BCE.[34]

Significance," *BASOR* 351 (2008): 39–71; A. M. Maeir (ed.), *Tell es-Safi/Gath I: Report on the 1996–2005 Seasons*, ÄAT 69 (Wiesbaden: Harrassowitz, 2012), 30–32, 64; Lemaire, "West Semitic Epigraphy," 300; Finkelstein and Sass, "The West Semitic Alphabetic Inscriptions," 159–60.

29. Maeir, *Tell es-Safi/Gath I*, 31–32 and *Tell es-Safi/Gath II*, pl. 14.13.6; Finkelstein and Sass, "The West Semitic Alphabetic Inscriptions," 164, 166. Aren M. Maeir and Esther Eshel, "Four Short Alphabetic Inscriptions from Late Iron Age IIa Tell eṣ-Ṣafi/Gath and Their Implications for the Development of Literacy in Iron Age Philistia and Environs," in *"See, I will bring a scroll recounting what befell me" (Ps 40:8): Epigraphy and Daily Life from the Bible to the Talmud Dedicated to the Memory of Professor Hanan Eshel*. JAJSup 12 (Göttingen: Vandenhoeck & Ruprecht, 2014), 69–88, 205–10.

30. Ron E. Tappy, et al., "An Abecedary of the Mid-Tenth Centuruy B.C.E. from the Judean Shephelah," *BASOR* 344 (2006): 5–46; Ron E. Tappy and P. Kyle McCarter, eds., *Literate Culture and Tenth-Century Canaan: The Tel Zayit Abecedary in Context* (Winona Lake, IN: Eisenbrauns, 2008).

31. Christopher A. Rollston, "The Phoenician Script of the Tel Zayit Abecedary and Putative Evidence for Israelite Literacy," in Tappy and McCarter, *Literate Culture and Tenth Century Canaan*, 89.

32. Lemaire, "West Semitic Epigraphy," 300.

33. On the limits of palaeographic dating, see, e.g., William M. Schniedewind, "Problems in the Palaeographic Dating of Inscriptions," in *The Bible and Radiocarbon Dating, Archaeology, Text and Science*, ed. Thomas Levy and Thomas Higham (London: Equinox, 2005), 405–12.

34. Lemaire, "West Semitic Epigraphy," 298. Discussions: Gunnar Lehmann and Tammi J. Schneider, "Tell el-Farah (South) 1999 Ostracon," *UF* 31 (1999): 251–54; "A New Ostracon from Tell el-Farʿah (South)," *NEA* 63 (2000): 113; Ernst Axel Knauf and H. M. Niemann, "Zum Ostracon 1027 vom Tell Fara Süd (Tell el-Fāriʿ/Tel Šaruḥen)," *UF* 31 (1999): 247–50; "Weitere Überlegungen zum neuen Ostrakon 1027 vom Tell el-Faraʿ Süd," *BN* 109 (2001): 19–20; Bob Becking and Jan A. Wagenaar, "Personal Name or Royal Epithet? A Remark on Ostracon 1027 from Tell el-Farʿah (South)," *BN* 107–8 (2001),

A few other inscriptions were found in the periphery of Philistia. Leaving aside the 'Izbet Ṣarṭah ostracon, probably to be dated to the eleventh century BCE,[35] the Gezer tablet, lacking archaeological context as it does, can be paleographically dated to late tenth century BCE.[36]

Farther south, the excavations of Beth-Shemesh have brought to light a few early alphabetic inscriptions. The 1930 "Beth-Shemesh ostracon," written with ink,[37] was thought to be found in the Late Bronze Age level[38] but this is not clear and it is still considered "unstratified" by I. Finkelstein and B. Sass. The date of this probable list of names can only be very approximate to the eleventh century BCE,[39] perhaps even 1000 BCE since it appears palaeographically close to the Khirbet Qeiyafa ostracon.[40] The excavations by Bunimovitz and Lederman, have recovered a fragmentary game board found in an Iron IIB pit and inscribed with ḤNN, "Ḥanan."[41] Palaeographically, it "probably dates in the second half of the tenth or very beginning of the ninth century BCE"[42] but, based as it is on only two different letters, Ḥ and N, this dating is far from certain. A third early alphabetic inscription was found in 2001 and published in 2011. Unfortunately it was (again!) found in a pit so that its dating can only be approximated: pre-level 3 (beginning "in the second half of the tenth century BCE"[43]). The *editio princeps* proposed a date ca. 1150 BCE[44] but comparisons with the 'Izbet Ṣarṭah and Khirbet Qeiyafa ostraca reveal that a later date in the eleventh century BCE would not be palaeographically impossible.[45]

12–14; Ernst Axel Knauf and Hermann Michael Niemann, "Tell el-Far'ah South Ostracon 1027 and a New Identification for the Site," *UF* 43 (2011): 273–82; Finkelstein and Sass, "The West Semitic Alphabetic Inscriptions," 172.

35. Ibid., 298–99.
36. Renz, *Die althebräischen Inschriften 1*, 31; Lemaire, "West Semitic Epigraphy," 299–300.
37. Elihu Grant, "Découverte épigraphique à Beth-Šemeš," *RB* 39 (1930), 401–2.
38. Elihu Grant and Georges E. Wright, *Ain Shems Excavations (Palestine) V* (Haverford, 1939), 46.
39. Lemaire, "West Semitic Epigraphy," 298
40. Finkelstein and Sass, "The West Semitic Alphabetic Inscriptions," 298.
41. Shlomo Bunimovitz and Zvi Lederman, "Beth Shemesh: Cultural Conflict on Judah's Frontier," *BAR* 23.1 (1997): 48, 75–77.
42. Lemaire, "West Semitic Epigraphy," 301.
43. Shlomo Bunimovitz and Zvi Lederman, "The Early Israelite Monarchy in the Sorek Valley: Tel Beth-Shemesh and Tel Batash (Timnah) in the 10th and 9th Centuries BCE," in *"I Will Speak the Riddles of Ancient Times": Archaeological and Historical Studies in Honor of Amihai Mazar*, ed. Aren M. Maeir and Pierre de Miroschedji (Winona Lake, IN: Eisenbrauns, 2006), 419.
44. P. Kyle McCarter, Shlomo Bunimovitz and Zvi Lederman, "An Archaic *Ba'l* Inscription from Tel Beth-Shemesh," *TA* 38 (2011): 179–93.
45. A date as late as the middle of the tenth century, as proposed by Finkelstein and

About 7 km northwest of Beth-Shemesh, the excavations of Tel Batash/ Timnah brought to light a fragmentary inscription incised on the rim of a bowl from stratum IV: B]N.ḤNN[.[46] This inscription seems paleographically contemporaneous to the Beth-Shemesh inscription ḤNN, that is, the late tenth without excluding the early ninth century BCE.[47]

About 6 km south of Beth-Shemesh and 12 km east of Tell eṣ-Ṣafi/Gath, the excavations of Khirbet Qeiyafa retrieved an inked ostracon that is dated from the archaeological context to 1000 BCE.[48] Although its reading is still uncertain, as is its classification (Canaanite, Judean Hebrew, Philistian?), and though its general interpretation is much discussed,[49] there is apparently a consensus regarding its approximate date.[50]

Sass, "The West Semitic Alphabetic Inscriptions," 157, seems difficult.

46. George L. Kelm and Amihai Mazar, "Tel Batash (Timna) Excavations: Third Preliminary Report (1984–1989)," in *Preliminary Reports of ASOR-Sponsored Excavations, 1982–1989*, BASORSup 27 (Baltimore: Johns Hopkins University Press, 1991), 55–56; Renz, *Die althebräischen Inschriften I*, 30; George L. Kelm and Amihai Mazar, *Timnah: A Biblical City in the Sorek Valley* (Winona Lake, IN: Eisenbrauns, 1995), 111.

47. Lemaire, "West Semitic Epigraphy," 301.

48. H. Misgav et al., in *Khirbet Qeiyafa*, Vol. 1: *Excavation Report 2007–2008*, ed. Yosef Garfinkel, and Saar Ganor (Jerusalem: Israel Exploration Society/Institute of Archaeology, 2009).

49. See the essays of Gershon Galil, "The Hebrew Inscription from Khirbet Qeiyafa/ Netaʿim," *UF* 41 (2009): 193–242; William H. Shea, "The Qeiyafa Ostracon: Separation of Powers in Ancient Israel," *UF* 41 (2009): 601–10; Bob Becking and Paul Sanders, "De inscriptie uit Khirbet Qeiyafa: Een vroege vorm van sociaal besef in oud Israël?," *Nederlands Theologisch Tijdschrift* 64 (2010): 238–52; Yosef Garfinkel, Saar Ganor, and Michael G. Hasel, "The Contribution of Khirbet Qeiyafa to Our Understanding of the Iron Age Period," *Bulletin of the Anglo-Israel Archaeological Society* 28 (2010): 47–49; Emile Puech, "L'ostracon de Khirbet Qeyafa et les débuts de la royauté en Israël," *RB* 117 (2010): 162–84; Bob Becking and Paul Sanders "Plead for the Poor and the Widow: The Ostracon from Khirbet Qeiyafa as Expression of Social Consciousness," *ZABR* 17 (2011): 133–48; Alan R. Millard, "The Ostracon from the Days of David Found at Khirbet Qeiyafa," *Tyndale Bulletin* 62 (2011): 1–13; Christopher A. Rollston, "The Khirbet Qeiyafa Ostracon: Methodological Musings and Caveats," *TA* 38 (2011): 67–82; Aharon Demsky, "An Iron Age IIA Alphabetic Writing Exercise from Khirbet Qeiyafa," *IEJ* 62 (2012): 186–99; Gérard Leval, "Ancient Inscription Refers to Birth of Israelite Monarchy," *BAR* 38.3 (2012): 41–43, 70; Christopher A. Rollston, "What's the Oldest Hebrew Inscription?," *BAR* 38.3 (2012): 32–40, 66, 68; William M. Schniedewind *A Social History of Hebrew*, The Anchor Yale Bible Reference Library (New Haven: Yale University Press, 2013), 65–66.

50. Whether it is called Late Iron I or Early Iron IIA: Lily Singer-Avitz, "The Relative Chronology of Khirbet Qeiyafa," *TA* 37 (2010): 79–83; Israel Finkelstein and Eliazer Piasetzky, "Khirbet Qeiyafa: Absolute Chronology," *TA* 37 (2010): 84–88; Yosef Garfinkel and Hoo Goo Kang, "The Relative and Absolute Chronology of Khirbet Qeiyafa: Very Late Iron Age I or Very Early Iron Age IIA?," *IEJ* 61 (2011): 171–83; Ayelet Gilboa, "Cypriot Barrel Juglets at Khirbet Qeiyafa and Other Sites in the Levant: Cultural Aspects

Central Cisjordan/Early Judah/Israel

The mountains of Judah seem to have produced a few small inscriptions from the tenth century or the early ninth century BCE:
- An incised inscription of four letters: LŠDḤ on a potsherd from a tomb northeast of Manaḥat, 4 km southwest of Jerusalem. Its dating is based on paleography and can only be very approximate: eleventh century or around 1000 BCE.[51]
- In 2012, in Jerusalem, the Ophel excavations of Elat Mazar recovered a fragmentary alphabetic inscription incised below the rim of a pithos coming from a fill beneath an Iron IIA floor. The pithos has been provisionally dated to the "early(?) Iron Age IIA" while the inscription, the letters of which are apparently written from left to right: "appear to belong to the eleventh-tenth centuries BCE."[52] The meaning of this inscription is still uncertain and remains widely discussed.[53]
- Three ink inscriptions with ḤMŠ, "five," written on jugs each(?) containing a silver hoard have been found at Es-Semuʻ/Eshtemoa, 15 km south of Hebron. They are paleographically dated to the ninth century[54] It is difficult to specify whether the early or late ninth century is to be preferred but the vertical *mem* with final horizontal line? could be an indication of an early ninth-century date.[55]

---

and Chronological Implication," *TA* 39 (2012): 133–49; Lily Singer-Avitz, "Khirbet Qeiyafa: Late Iron Age I in Spite of It All," *IEJ* 62 (2012): 177–85.

51. Lawrence E. Stager, "An Inscribed Potsherd from the Eleventh Century," *BASOR* 194 (1969): 45–52; John Landgraf, "The Manaḥat Inscription," *Levant* 3 (1971): 92–95; Lemaire, "West Semitic Epigraphy," 301; Finkelstein and Sass, "The West Semitic Alphabetic Inscriptions," 164, n. 62.

52. Eilat Mazar, David Ben-Shlomo, Shmuel Aḥituv, "An Inscribed Pithos from the Ophel, Jerusalem," *IEJ* 63 (2013), 39–49, esp. 45.

53. See, for instance, Gershon Galil, "With More on the Jerusalem Inscription," on the website *Zwinglius Redivivus* July 12 and 29, 2013; Galil, "'*yyn ḥlq*' The Oldest Hebrew Inscription from Jerusalem," *Bulletin of the Anglo-Israel Archaeological Society* 31 (2013): 11–16; Reinhard G. Lehmann and Anna Elise Zernecke, "Bemerkungen und Beobachtungen zu der neuen Ophel-Pithosinschrift," *KUSATU* 15 (2013): 437–50; Alan R. Millard, "The New Jerusalem Inscription—So What?" *BAR* 40.3 (2014): 49–53.

54. Renz, *Die althebräischen Inschriften*, 65–66; Lemaire, "West Semitic Inscriptions," 280. For the dating of the jewelry hoard, see Benjamin Sass, "An Iron Age I Jewelry Hoard from Cave II/3 in Wadi el-Makkuk," *ʻAtiqot* 41.2 (2002), 32, n. 11 ("in the ninth or early eighth century"); David Hamidović, "L'inscription du pithos de l'Ophel à Jérusalem," *Semitica* 56 (2014), 137–49.

55. With the same criterion of the shape of the M, the earliest Arad ostraca, especially no. 76, are probably to be dated to the second half—rather than to the first half—of the ninth century BCE and will be mentioned in the next group.

- About 15 km north of Jerusalem, the excavations of Khirbet Raddana have brought to light a fragmentary inscription incised on a jar handle to be read vertically ’ḤL/P/R(?). It is a surface find and its archaeological and palaeographic dating can only be very approximate: twelfth to the eleventh centuries BCE.[56] Actually a comparison with some of the Khirbet Qeiyafa ostracon *aleph*s[57] could suggest a date as late as 1000 BCE.
- Farther north, at Khirbet Tannin about 7 km southwest of Jenin, another surface find of a fragmentary incised inscription, probably to be read NMŠ can only be very approximately dated to the twelfth or eleventh centuries BCE with a preference for the late eleventh century[58] or around 1000 BCE as now indicated by a comparison with the Khirbet Qeiyafa ostracon.
- Another fragmentary inscribed potsherd, found on the surface of Sheikh Shible, north of Dothan, is later but difficult to date precisely since only the *aleph* is clear: perhaps around 900[59] or the first half of the ninth century BCE.
- An inscription: ’Ḥ’B, incised on a jar handle, has been found on the surface of Tell el-Hamme on the border of the Beth-Shean Valley (c. 1974–1972).[60] The palaeographic dating is approximate: in the ninth century BCE. It could well be second quarter of this same century and the name that of king Ahab. However this is far from certain.

---

56. Lemaire, "West Semitic Epigraphy," 302.

57. Finkelstein and Sass, "The West Semitic Alphabetic Inscriptions," 160.

58. André Lemaire, "Notes d'épigraphie nord-ouest sémitique. 7. Tesson inscrit de Khirbet Tannin," *Semitica* 35 (1985) 13–15; Adam Zertal, *The Manasseh Hill Country Survey.* Vol. 1: *The Shechem Syncline*, CHANE 21.1 (Leiden: Brill, 2004), 174–76: no. 59; Lemaire, "West Semitic Epigraphy," 302.

59. André Lemaire, "Notes d'épigraphie ouest-sémitique. 4. Tessons inscrits du territoire de Manassé," *Semitica* 32 (1982), 16–17; Zertal, *Manasseh Hill Country Survey*, 85–87: no. 1; Lemaire, "West Semitic Epigraphy," 302, n. 87.

60. Ram Gophna and Yosef Porat, "The Survey of Ephraim and Manasse," in *Judaea, Samaria and the Golan: Archaeological Survey 1967–68*, ed. Moshe Kochavi (Jerusalem: Archaeological Survey of Israel/Carta, 1972), 214; Renz, *Die althebraischen Inschriften*, 47; Lemaire, "West Semitic Epigraphy," 279; Amihai Mazar and Shmuel Aḥituv, "Inscriptions from Tel Reḥov and Their Contribution to the Study of Writing and Literacy during the Iron Age IIA," in *Amnon Ben-Tor Volume*, ed. Hillel Geva and Alan Paris, Eretz-Israel 30 (Jerusalem: Israel Exploration Society, 2011), 311 (Hebrew), 154*; Finkelstein and Sass, "The West Semitic Alphabetic Inscriptions," 172; Shmuel Aḥituv and Amihai Mazar, "The Inscriptions from Tel Reḥov and Their Contribution to the Study of Script during Iron Age IIA," in Eshel and Levin, *Epigraphy and Daily Life*, 39–68, 190–203.

- In the Jordan Valley, about 5 km south of Beth-Shean, the excavations directed by Amihai Mazar have found preserved several fragmentary inscriptions from the tenth or early ninth century BCE:[61] actually, according to the excavators, three strata are to be considered here (Stratum VI: tenth century; Stratum V: late tenth/early ninth century; Stratum IV: ninth century until ca. 840/830 BCE) which produced ten inscriptions:
  1. The sherd 104028 (stratum VI) presents two small letters written with ink: 'Y, the second letter being very uncertain.
  2. An incision on the shoulder of a jar (7498/10; stratum VIB): MT' (twice) with clear but perhaps archaic letters, especially the *mem*.
  3. The letter *Lamed* incised on sherd 75109/99 (stratum VIB).
  4. A fragmentary incised inscription on sherd 23138 (stratum VB). The reading of the third letter is uncertain and seems to have been corrected. It could be read B, Ḥ or M so that the whole inscription could be read LNḤM[, LNB'[[62] or, rather, LNMŠ[,[63] since there is only a small fragmentary trace of the fourth letter.
  5. The inscription LNMŠ was clearly incised after firing on the shoulder of a jar from stratum V (no. 84730/4). This inscription can be compared to the one found in Tel 'Amal (*infra*).
  6. The inscription LŠQY NMŠ, "(Belonging) to the cup/bearer Nemesh/Nimshi,"[64] was incised after firing on the shoulder of a jar from stratum IV.
  7. The inscription 'LṢDQ ŠḤLY, "Elṣadaq (son of) Shaḥali," has been incised before firing on the shoulder of a jar (104274) from stratum IV.
  8. A fragmentary inscription M'[..]'M, perhaps to be completed M'NR'M, "Ma'anra'am,"[65] has been incised after firing on the shoulder of a jar (46129/1) from stratum IV.
  9. The inscription L'LYŠ', "(Belonging) to Elyasha'" was written with red ink on a sherd (94443) from stratum IV.

---

61. Amihai Mazar, "Three 10th–9th Century B.C.E. Inscriptions from Tēl Reḥōv," in *Saxa Loquentur: Studien zur Archäologie Palästinas/Israel. Festschrift für Volkmar Fritz*, ed. Cornelius G. den Hertog et al., AOAT 302 (Münster, 2003), 171–84; André Lemaire, "West Semitic Inscriptions," 280–81; Mazar and Aḥituv, "Inscriptions from Tel Reḥov," 300–316 (Hebrew), 154*.

62. Ibid., 302.
63. Lemaire, "West Semitic Epigraphy," 303.
64. Ibid., 281.
65. Ibid., 280.

10. The letter B was incised before firing on a thick sherd from stratum IV.

One may note that the date of the inscriptions NMŠ (nos. 4, 5, and perhaps 6) could correspond to the name of the grandfather of king Jehu (2 Kgs 9:2, 14) and the inscription 'LYŠ' to the name of the prophet "Elisha" (1 Kgs 19:16–19) but these identifications are at best conjectural.

One may also note that another fragmentary inscribed sherd was already found in 1939 on the surface of Tell eṣ-Ṣarem (= Tel Rehov).[66] The pottery was incised before firing but the inscription with apparently remains of seven letters is still enigmatic since only three letters seem clear enough for identification (Š, ʿ, and M) but which are not on the same line. The vertical M and the ʿ with a dot inside it could be dated to the twelfth to eleventh centuries BCE or around 1000 BCE (compare the vertical M of no. 2 above).

About 5 km west of Beth-Shean, the salvage excavations of Tel 'Amal/Nir David brought to light a complete jar inscribed LNMŠ which is palaeographically very similar to no. 5 of Tel Rehov (above) and probably dates to 900 BCE. Both inscriptions probably preserve the name of the same owner, who could have been the grandfather of King Jehu (ca. 841–814).

One may emphasize that this list of Levantine alphabetic inscriptions from ca. 1000–850 is tentative because of the approximation of most of the datings. Thus far for this period, we have no commemorative monumental inscriptions and the monumental inscriptions we do have come from Byblos which are building or dedication inscriptions. We have neither bureaucratic texts nor Syrian-Aramaic inscriptions from this period.[67] That does not mean that we have no inscriptions and that alphabetic writing did not exist outside Byblos. As in Byblos itself, we have now quite a number of small inscriptions mainly on bronze and pottery but also on stone (the funerary stelae from Tyre el-Bass, the Gezer tablet, the Beth-Shemesh game board, the Tel Zayit abecedary). Taking into account the fact that the discovery of inscriptions is always a matter of chance, the variety of the kinds of inscription and of the places where they have been found reveal, at least, that the alphabetic script

---

66. R. B. Kallner, "Two Inscribed Sherds," *Qedem* 2 (1945): 11–14; Eliezer L. Sukenik, "Note on the Sherd From Tell eṣ-Ṣarem," *Qedem* 2 (1945): 15; Lemaire, "West Semitic Epigraphy," 302; Finkelstein and Sass, "The West Semitic Alphabetic Inscriptions," 160–61.

67. Is this connected with the fact that there are not many excavations of Iron Age sites in Syria? One has to be very cautious about using the *argumentum a silentio*! As is obvious above, many inscriptions dating from the early period have been discovered just in the last fifteen years or so.

was used in most regions of the Levant, especially for indicating the ownership of vessels.

WEST SEMITIC INSCRIPTIONS CA. 850–750 BCE

From the beginning of this period, the Aramaic and Transjordanian kingdoms produced several important monumental inscriptions. Because of the abundance of the inscriptions, we shall develop our remarks on the second half of the ninth century without going into details for the following half century.

ARAMAIC KINGDOMS (CA. 850–800 BCE)

Damascus

Several Aramaic inscriptions are clearly to be related to Hazael's reign in Damascus (ca. 843–805/3 BCE).[68] This is the case with two bronze horse forehead ornaments found in Samos and Eretria with the inscription ZY NTN HDD LMR'N ḤZ'L MN 'MQ BŠNT 'DH MR'N NHR, "That which Hadad gave to our lord Ḥazael from 'Umq in the year that our lord crossed the river."[69] Two ivory inscriptions also mention Ḥazael: the first was found at Arslan Tash[70] and the second, fragmentary, at Nimrud,[71] both in north-

---

68. Lemaire, "Hazaël de Damas," 91–108.
69. Helmut Kyrieleis and Wolfgang Röllig, "Ein altorientalischer Pferdeschmuck aus dem Heraion von Samos," *Mitteilungen des Deutschen Archäologischen Instituts. Athenische Abteilung* 103 (1988): 37–75; François Bron and André Lemaire, "Les inscriptions araméennes de Hazaël," *RA* 83 (1989): 35–44; Israel Eph'al and Joseph Naveh, "Hazael's Booty Inscription," *IEJ* 39 (1989): 192–200; Alan R. Millard, "The Hazael Booty Inscriptions," *COS* 2.40:162; Lemaire, "West Semitic Inscriptions," 283.
70. *KAI* 232; Wolfgang Röllig, "Alte und neue Elfenbeininschriften," *Neue Ephemeris für semitische Epigraphik* 2 (1974): 37–64; John C. L. Gibson, *Textbook of Syrian Semitic Inscriptions* II (Oxford: Clarendon, 1975), 4–5; Emile Puech, "L'ivoire inscrit d'Arslan Tash et les rois de Damas," *RB* 88 (1981): 544–62; Lemaire, "West Semitic Inscriptions," 283.
71. M. E. L. Mallowan, *Nimrud and Its Remains* II (London: Collins, 1966), 598–99; Millard, "The Hazael Booty Inscriptions," *COS* 2.40:162–63. These inscriptions are probably contemporaneous to the small Nimrud Aramaic incisions on bricks: Alan R. Millard, "Aramaic at Nimrud on Clay, Potsherds, Bricks and Ivories," in *New Light on Nimrud: Proceedings of the Nimrud Conference 11th–13th March 2002*, ed. John E. Curtis et al. (London: British Institute for the Study of Iraq, 2008), 267–70, esp. 268; John E. Curtis, "The British Museum Excavations at Nimrud in 1989," in Curtis, *New Light on Nimrud*, 61–63.

ern Mesopotamia. However the main Aramaic composition is reflected in the now famous fragments of the Tel Dan stele discovered in 1993 and 1995.[72] Although Hazael is not mentioned in these fragments because the beginning of the inscription is missing, it is generally agreed now that Ḥazael commissioned this stele.[73]

This site also produced a small inscription incised on a vase: LṬB[Ḥ]Y', "(Belonging) to the butchers."[74] Farther south, two other Aramaic inscriptions are also probably to be dated to the second half of the ninth century BCE: LŠQY', "(Belonging) to the cup bearer" (Ein-Gev)[75] and LŠ'WL, "(Belonging) to Shaul" (Tell Deir Alla)."[76] These three inscriptions can only be approximately dated to the middle of the ninth century BCE.[77] They could probably also have been presented in the previous group.

Hamath

Found in the same context as the Hazael inscriptions (*supra*) and a Neo-Hittite inscription with the name Urhilina,[78] a few ivories from Nimrud mention the place names ḤMT, "Hamath," and L'Š, "Lu'ash," as well as the dedication formula ZY HQRB ..., "that offered ...." Although a date in the first half of the eighth century is also possible, these inscriptions probably date from the second half of the ninth century BCE.[79]

---

72. Avraham Biran and Joseph Naveh, "An Aramaic Stele Fragment from Tel Dan," *IEJ* 43 (1993): 81–98; Biran and Naveh, "The Tel Dan Inscription: A New fragment," *IEJ* 45 (1995): 1–18.

73. See especially André Lemaire, "The Tel Dan Stela as a Piece of Royal Historiography," *JSOT* 81 (1998): 3–14; Hallvard Hagelia, *The Tel Dan Inscription: A Critical Investigation of Recent Research on Its Palaeography and Philology*, Acta Universitatis Upsaliensis 22 (Uppsala: Uppsala Universitet, 2006), 122–23; Elena Vismara, "Implicazioni storiche dell'iscrizione di Tel Dan," in *Florilegio filologico linguistico. Haninura de Bon Siman a Maria Luisa Mayer Modena*, ed. C. Rosenzweig et al., Acta et studia 4 (Milan: Cisalpino, 2008), 193–206; Shmuel Aḥituv, *Echoes from the Past: Hebrew and Cognate Inscriptions from the Biblical World* (Jerusalem: Carta, 2008), 466–73; Hallvard Hagelia, *The Dan Debate: The Tel Dan Inscription in Recent Research* (Sheffield: Sheffield Phoenix, 2009), 43.

74. Nahman Avigad, "An Inscribed Bowl from Dan," *PEQ* 100 (1968): 42–44.

75. Benjamin Mazar, "Ein Gev Excavations in 1961," *IEJ* 14 (1964): 1–49; Gibson, *TSSI* 2:5 ("probably belonging to the first half of the 9. cent.").

76. André Lemaire, "Notes d'épigraphie ouest-sémitique," *Syria* 61 (1984), 254–55.

77. According to Mazar and Aḥituv, "Inscriptions from Tel Reḥov," 310, the inscription LŠQY' and the jar bearing this inscription are similar to the inscription and pottery of Stratum IV in Tel Reḥov.

78. Both kings, Hazael and Urhilina, were contemporary with the Assyrian king Shalmaneser III (858–824).

79. Alan R. Millard, "Alphabetic Inscriptions on Ivories from Nimrud," *Iraq* 24

Southwest of Aleppo, the excavations of Tell Afis revealed a fragment of a basalt stele with remains of seven lines and the probable mention of ḤZ'[L], "Hazael" (line 6'). This fragment is likely contemporary with the Tel Dan stele and dates to the last third of the ninth century BCE.[80]

At Hamath itself, unless they are strongly archaizing, a few graffiti on bricks (*Aram Graf* 13, 16?, 18, 45–47[81]) could date from the ninth century BCE.

Beit-Gush (Arpad)

The kingdom of Beit-Gush (Arpad) was an important Aramaean kingdom in northern Syria in the second half of the ninth century and in the first half of the eighth century BCE. Although it is difficult to be precise, a few Aramaic inscriptions from this region may date from the end of the ninth century:

- The famous Milqart stele with a dedicatory inscription of four lines.[82]
- The syntagma BYT GŠ, "Beit Gush," is engraved on the rim of an ivory pyxis[83] with the possible phrase LMLK BYT GŠ, which is similar to the MLK BYT DWD in the Tel Dan stele.
- Three Aramaic seals, at the least,[84] could be dated to the end of the ninth century or around 800 BCE:[85] "L*H*KL 'BD 'BRM," "(Belonging) to *He*kal servant of Abiram," LNRŠ' 'BD 'TRSMK, "(Belonging) to Nurshî servant of 'Atarsumki" and ḤTM BRQ 'BD 'TRŠMN, "Seal of Baraq servant of 'Atarshamain."

(1962): 42; Wolfgang Röllig, "Alte und neue Elfenbeininschriften," *Neue Ephemeris für semitische Epigraphik* 2 (1974): 47–48; Lemaire, "West Semitic Inscriptions," 284.

80. Maria Giulia Amadasi Guzzo, "Area 1: il frammento di stele in basalto con iscrizione," in *Tell Afis (Siria) 2002/2004*, ed. Stephania Mazzoni et al. (Pisa: Universita di Pisa, 2005), 21–23; K. Lawson Younger, "Some of What's New in Old Aramaic Epigraphy," *NEA* 70 (2007): 139.

81. Benedikt Otzen, "Appendix 2. The Aramaic Inscriptions," in *Hama: fouilles et recherches; 1931–1938*. 2.2: *Les objets de la période dite syro-hittite (Âge du Fer)*, ed. Paul J. Riis and Marie-Louise Buhl (Copenhagen: Copenhague Fondation Carlsberg, 1990), 287, 289, 292, 311–12.

82. The most likely reading of line 2 seems to have been proposed by Emile Puech, "La stèle de Bar-Hadad à Melqart et les rois d'Arpad," *RB* 99 (1992): 311–34, but his historical interpretation does not seem convincing.

83. Emile Puech, "Un ivoire de Bît-Guši (Arpad) à Nimrud," *Syria* 55 (1978): 163–69.

84. See also perhaps *WSS*, no. 832.

85. Lemaire, "West Semitic Inscriptions," 285.

Gozan/Guzana (Beit Bahian)

The Aramaean kingdom of Guzana was located near a spring of the Habur River in Upper Mesopotamia. Two monumental Aramaic inscriptions were found there that are to be dated to the second half of the ninth century BCE:[86]

- The famous bilingual Assyro-Aramaic statue of King Hadadyis'i with an Aramaic inscription of twenty-three lines.[87]
- The "altar" inscription with a probable dedicatory inscription from Tell Halaf.[88]

Sam'al

The kingdom of Sam'al, east of the Amanus, is famous for the excavations of its capital (Zincirli) and its monumental inscriptions from the second half of the ninth century to the second half of the eighth century BCE. The local archaic Aramaic dialect, Sam'alian, is already attested by the small Kulamuwa inscription on a gold amulet case dating to the second half of the ninth century,[89] as well as possibly by the Ördekburnu stele. However it is worth noting that the monumental Kulamuwa inscription (ca. 825 BCE) was composed in Phoenician, probably because, at the beginning of his reign, Kulamuwa was more or less a vassal of the kingdom of Que (Cilicia).[90]

---

86. Because of the idiosyncratic palaeography of this inscription, Frank Moore Cross ("Palaeography and the Date of the Tell Fakhariyeh Bilingual Inscription," in *Solving Riddles and Untying Knots. Biblical, Epigraphic, and Semitic Studies in Honor of Jonas C. Greenfield*, ed. Seymour Gitin et al. [Winona Lake, IN: Eisenbrauns, 1995], 393–409) and Joseph Naveh ("Proto-Canaanite, Archaic Greek, and the Script of the Aramaic Text on the Tell Fakhariyah Statue," in *Ancient Israelite Religion: Essays in Honor of Frank Moore Cross*, ed. Patrick D. Miller et al. [Philadelphia; Fortress, 1987], 101–14) were tempted to date it in the eleventh century or to 1000 BCE but the historical interpretation fits a date in the second half of the ninth century. The idiosyncratic palaeography may be explained by a peripherial scribal tradition separated from the main Aramaic scribal tradition by the integration of Guzana in the Assyrian Empire.

87. Ali Abou-Assaf, Pierre Bordreuil, Alan R. Millard, *La statue de Tell Fekherye et son inscription bilingue assyro-araméenne*, Etudes Assyriologiques (Paris: ADPF, 1982); Alan R. Millard, "Hadad-Yith'i," *COS* 2.34:153–54.

88. Guido Dankwarth and Christa Müller, "Zur altaramäischen 'Altar' Inschrift vom Tell Halaf," *AfO* 35 (1988): 73–78; Dirk Schwiderski, *Die alt- und reichsaramäischen Inschriften 2. Texte und Bibliographie*, Fontes et Subsidia ad Biblia pertinentes 2 (Berlin: de Gruyter, 2004), 197.

89. André Lemaire, "SMR dans la petite inscription de Kilamuwa (Zencirli)," *Syria* 67 (1990): 323–27; Josef Tropper, *Die Inschriften von Zincirli*, ALASP 6 (Münster: Ugarit-Verlag, 1993), 50–3.

90. *KAI* 24; Gibson, *TSSI* 3:30–39; K. Lawson Younger, "The Kulamuwa Inscription," *COS* 2:30:147–48.

PHOENICIA (CA. 850–800 BCE)

Thus far we do not have any Byblos inscriptions from the second half of the ninth century, but some of the inscribed funerary stelae from southern Phoenicia, especially from the cemetery of Tyre al-Bass, are probably from this period[91] as are a few inscriptions on funerary jars.[92]

Two Phoenician inscriptions from Cyprus are probably also from this period:
- A funerary monumental inscription, now in the Nicosia museum (7/8 lines).[93]
- An inscription incised on a bowl from the Astarte temple in Kition with a probable date around 800 BCE.[94]

Farther west, in Sardinia, the enigmatic Nora stele[95] probably dates from this period.[96]

PALESTINE (PHILISTIA, ISRAEL, JUDAH; CA. 850–800 BCE)

As we have seen above, some of the inscriptions which were placed in the period spanning 900–850 BCE could be dated to the middle of the ninth

---

André Lemaire, "Les langues du royaume de Sam'al aux IXe–VIIIe s. av. J.-C. et leurs relations avec le royaume de Qué," in *La Cilicie: espaces et pouvoirs locaux (2e millénaire av. J. -C. - 4e siècle ap. J.–C.)*, ed. Eric Jean, Ali M. Dinçol, and Serra Durugönül, Varia Anatolica 13 (Paris: de Boccard, 2001), 185–93.

91. Sader, *Iron Age Funerary Stelae*, 101–2, esp. no. 7 (*tav*), 36 (*mem*); Gaby Abousamra and André Lemaire, *Nouvelles stèles funéraires phéniciennes / New Phoenician Funerary Stelae* (Beirut: Kutub, 2014), nos. 1–3.

92. For instance Pierre Bordreuil, "Epitaphe d'amphore phénicienne du 9e siècle," *Berytus* 25 (1977): 159–61.

93. *KAI* 30; Masson and Sznycer, *Recherches sur les Phéniciens à Chypre*, 13–20; Emile Puech, "Remarques sur quelques inscriptions phéniciennes de Chypre," *Semitica* 29 (1979): 19–26; Gibson, *TSSI* 3:28–30.

94. Emile Puech, "Le rite d'offrande de cheveux d'après une inscription phénicienne de Kition vers 800 avant notre ère," *RSF* 4 (1976): 11–21; Maria Giulia Amadasi Guzzo and Vassos Karageorghis, *Fouilles de Kition III. Inscriptions phéniciennes* (Nicosia: Department of Antiquities / Zavallis Press, 1977), 149–60

95. See the latest essays of Phillip C. Schmitz, *The Phoenician Diaspora: Epigraphic and Historical Studies* (Winona Lake, IN: Eisenbrauns, 2012), 15–31, and Nathan Pilkington, "A Note on Nora and the Nora Stones," *BASOR* 365 (2012): 45–51.

96. *KAI* 46; Gibson, *TSSI* 3:25–28; Frank Moore Cross, "The Oldest Phoenician Inscription from Sardinia: The Fragmentary Stele from Nora," in *"Working with No Data": Semitic and Egyptian Studies Presented to Th. O. Lambdin* (Winona Lake, IN: Eisenbrauns, 1987), 65–74; Maria Giulia Amadasi Guzzo, *Iscrizioni fenicie e puniche in Italia* (Rome: Libreria dello stato, 1990), 41–42.

century and appear here. This is especially the case for the inscriptions from Tel Reḥov stratum IV.

It is appropriate to mention here a few of the Hebrew ostraca from Arad stratum XI (no. 76–79, 80?) or XII (no. 81).[97]

The epigraphic inventory for this period seems poor. Is this to be connected with the political and economical downturn of Cisjordan during the period?

MOAB (CA. 850–800 BCE)

Contrasting with the situation in Cisjordan, Moabite epigraphy is well attested for this period.[98] Two fragments of monumental inscriptions on stone were found at El-Kerak[99] and at Dhibân[100] and a third one from Khirbet el-Mudeyine dating to the second half of the ninth or the first half of the eighth century BCE.[101] These three inscriptions are very fragmentary.

The famous Mesha stone is likewise fragmentary since the bottom is missing but it contains the partial remains of thirty-four lines and is still today one of the longest monumental Northwest Semitic inscriptions. It is probably to be dated about 810 BCE,[102] at the end of the long and successful reign of Mesha.[103]

---

97. One may note that the palaeographic dating of ostraca 78–80 is somewhat uncertain and the traces of 81 are apparently only a few ciphers.

98. Erasmus Gass, *Die Moabiter: Geschichte und Kultur eines ostjordanischen Volkes im 1. Jahrtausend v. Chr.*, ADPV 38 (Wiesbaden: Harrassowitz, 2009), 5–75.

99. William L. Reed and Fred V. Winnett, "A Fragment of an Early Moabite Inscription from Kerak," *BASOR* 172 (1963): 1–9; Gibson, *TSSI* 1:83–84.

100. Roland A. Murphy, "A Fragment of an Early Moabite Inscription from Diban," *BASOR* 125 (1952): 20–22.

101. Michael Weigl, "Eine Inschrift aus Silo 4 in Ḫirbet el-Mudēyine (Wādī eṭ-Ṯemed, Jordanien)," *ZDPV* 122 (2006): 31–45.

102. André Lemaire, "Notes d'épigraphie nord-ouest sémitique," *Syria* 64 (1987): 210–14.

103. André Lemaire, "La stèle de Mésha et l'histoire de l'ancien Israël," in *Storia e tradizioni de Israele: Scritti in onore di J. Alberto Soggin*, ed. Daniele Garrone and Felice Israel (Brescia: Paideia, 1991), 143–69; Manfred Weippert, "Mesa und der Status von 'ganz Dibon,'" in Ninow, *Wort und Stein*, 323–28; André Lemaire, "The Mesha Stele and the Omri Dynasty," in *Ahab Agonistes: The Rise and Fall of the Omri Dynasty*, ed. Lester L. Grabbe, LHBOTS 421 (London: T&T Clark, 2007), 135–44; Lemaire, "West Semitic Inscriptions," 287–92; Nadav Na'aman, "Royal Inscriptions versus Prophetic Story. Mesha's Rebellion according to Biblical and Moabite Historiography," in Grabbe, *Ahab Agonistes*, 145–83; Shuichi Hasegawa, *Aram and Israel during the Jehuite Dynasty* (Berlin: de Gruyter, 2012), 103–5; André Lemaire, "Un siècle et demi de guerre en Transjordanie (c. 882–732)," *SHAJ* 11 (2013): 47–54; Manfred Weippert, "Mōšiʻs Moab," in *Bible et*

The palaeographic dating of inscribed seals is always approximate. However two Moabite seals can be dated to the second half of the ninth century or around 800 BCE because of their palaeographic similarity to the Mesha stele: The seal inscribed L'BDḤWRN[104] and the seal inscribed LKMŠ'R.[105]

The sudden appearance of the use of writing in Moab seems to be contemporary with the first inscribed stele from the Aramaean kingdoms (see above). Actually, Moab was probably allied to Hazael, king of Damascus, in his wars against Israel and Juda. One may also note that both the Mesha inscription and the Tel Dan fragments are apparently aniconic and engraved with cursive letters. Both of them presuppose that there were people able to read them. They contain royal historiographic propaganda with a main theme, namely, victorious war. The Mesha stele, however, reveals that construction projects were also an important theme of written royal propaganda.

First Half of the Eighth Century BCE

As is well known by West Semitic epigraphers, after 800 BCE the number of West Semitic inscriptions clearly increases. For instance, we may mention important monumental inscriptions from the kingdom of Sam'al (Ördekburnu,[106] Hadad,[107] Katumuwa[108]), from Arslan Tash,[109] Sfiré,[110]

Proche-Orient. Mélanges André Lemaire, vol. 3, ed. Jean-Marie Durand and Josette Elayi, Transeuphratène 46 (Paris: Gabalda, 2014), 133–51.

104. *WSS*, no. 1041.

105. Robert Deutsch and Michael Heltzer, *Windows to the Past* (Tel Aviv-Jaffa: Archaeological Center Publications, 1997), 59–61.

106. André Lemaire and Benjamin Sass, "La stèle d'Ördekburnu: vers la solution d'une énigme de l'épigraphie ouest-sémitique," *CRAI* (2012): 227–40; Lemaire and Sass, "The Mortuary Stele with Sam'alian Inscription from Ördekburnu near Zincirli," *BASOR* 369 (2013): 57–136.

107. *KAI* 213; Tropper, *Die Inschriften von Zincirli*.

108. Dennis Pardee, "A New Aramaic Inscription from Zincirli," *BASOR* 356 (2009): 51–71; K. Lawson Younger, "Two Epigraphic Notes on the New Katumuwa Inscription from Zincirli," *Maarav* 16 (2009): 159–79; André Lemaire, "Le dialecte araméen de l'inscription de KTMW (Zencirli, VIIIe s. av. n. è.)," in *In the Shadow of Bezalel: Aramaic, Biblical, and Ancient Near Eastern Studies in Honor of Bezalel Porten*, ed. Alejandro F. Botta (Leiden: Brill, 2013), 145–50.

109. Wolfgang Röllig, "Die Inschriften des Ninurta-bēlu-uṣur, Statthalters von Kār-Salmānu-ašarēd. Teil I," in *Of God(s), Trees, Kings, and Scholars: Neo-Assyrian and Related Studies in Honour of Simo Parpola*, ed. M. Luukko, StOr 106 (Helsinki: Finnish Oriental Society, 2009), 265–78.

110. *KAI* 222–224; André Lemaire and Jean-Marie Durand, *Les inscriptions araméennes de Sfiré et l'Assyrie de Shamshi-ilu*, HEO 20 (Geneva: Droz, 1984); Joseph A. Fitzmyer, *The Aramaic Inscriptions of Sefire*, BibOr 19 (Rome: Pontifical Biblical Institute, 1995).

Afis,[111] Amman[112] as well as the funerary Phoenician stelae from Tyre al-Bass.[113] While people continued using Aramaic and Moabite inscribed seals during this period, the phenomenon of inscribed seals is for this period also clearly attested in Israel, as the famous seal LŠMʿ ʿBD YRBʿM, "(Belonging) to Shemaʿ servant of Jeroboam" demonstrates,[114] while a few incisions on stone[115] and vases[116] from Khirbet el-Qôm (Judah) might also date from this period.

One must emphasize that besides more numerous incised inscriptions on stone or vases, we now have more and more ink on pottery and plaster inscriptions, especially in the southern Levant. More than a century ago, the American excavations of Sebastieh/Samaria brought to light more than one hundred Hebrew ostraca to be dated in the first half of the eighth century, probably under the reigns of Joash and Jeroboam II.[117] These ostraca are related with some kind of royal administration and reveal a flourishing scribal tradition.[118] The inscriptions from Kuntillet Ajrud date also from

---

111. *KAI* 202; André Lemaire, "Joas de Samarie, Barhadad de Damas, Zakkur de Hamat. La Syrie-Palestine vers 800 av. J.-C.," in *Avraham Malamat Volume*, ed. Shmuel Aḥituv and Baruch A. Levine, ErIsr 24 (Jerusalem: Israel Exploration Society, 1993), 148*–57*; see also a fragmentary inscribed sherd [']LWR: Sebastiana Soldi, "Aramaeans and Assyrians in North-Western Syria: Material Evidence from Tell Afis," *Syria* 86 (2009): 104–5.

112. Siegfried H. Horn, "The Amman Citadel Inscription," *BASOR* 193 (1969): 2–13; Frank Moore Cross, "Epigraphic Notes on the Ammān Citadel Inscription," *BASOR* 193 (1969): 13–19; Walter E. Aufrecht, *A Corpus of Ammonite Inscriptions*, ANETS 4 (Lewiston NY: Mellen 1989), 154–63; Aufrecht, "Ammonite Texts and Language," in *Ancient Ammon*, ed. Burton MacDonald and Randall W. Younker, SHCANE 17 (Leiden: Brill, 1999), 163–88; *KAI* 307; Walter E. Aufrecht, "Ammonite Inscriptions," *COS* 2.24–26:139–40; Aḥituv, *Echoes from the Past,* 357–62. A date in the first half of the eighth century palaeographically fits better than a date in the late ninth century BCE.

113. H. Sader, *Iron Age Funerary Stelae from Lebanon* (2005), no. 2, 17, 51 (?); Abousamra and Lemaire, *Nouvelles stèles funéraires phéniciennes*, nos. 4–7(?).

114. *WSS* 2.

115. See funerary inscription 3 dating to the middle of the eighth century: André Lemaire, "Les inscriptions de Khirbet el-Qôm et l'ashérah de YHWH," *RB* 84 (1977): 599–603; Renz, *Die althebräischen Inschriften*, 202–11.

116. See André Lemaire, "Khirbet el-Qôm and Hebrew and Aramaic Epigraphy," in *Confronting the Past. Archaeological and Historical Essays on Ancient Israel in Honor of William G. Dever*, ed. Seymour Gitin et al. (Winona Lake, IN: Eisenbrauns, 2006), 232; Lemaire "West Semitic Inscriptions," 280.

117. G. A. Reisner et al., *Harvard Excavations at Samaria 1908–1910* (Cambridge, 1924) 1:227–46; II, pl. 55; André Lemaire, *Inscriptions hébraïques I. Les ostraca*, LAPO 9 (Paris: Cerf, 1977), 21–81; Renz, *Die althebräischen Inschriften*, 79–109; Aḥituv, *Echoes from the Past*, 258–310; Matthieu Richelle, *Le royaume d'Israël dans la première moitié du VIIIe siècle avant notre ère* (thesis, E.P.H.E. Paris, 2010) 1:24–206.

118. We should mention here the problem of the interpretation of "over 170 clay

this period[119] and there, "the scribal work was executed with confidence, if not flamboyance."[120] This is true for the Hebrew Inscriptions as well as for the Phoenician inscriptions on plaster:[121] they reveal a strong contemporary scribal tradition not only in the kingdom of Samaria but also probably in the kingdom of Tyre.[122]

The same fully developed scribal tradition is attested by the plaster inscriptions from Tell Deir Alla in the middle Jordan Valley.[123] Although their reading is often difficult and tentative,[124] they are clearly dated to the first half of the eighth century BCE by the archaeological context and radiocarbon dating. Although their language has been much discussed, there is more and more agreement that they represent some kind of archaic Arama-

---

bullae" discovered near the Gihon spring in Jerusalem: they could date "to the early eighth century and perhaps even to the late ninth century." They are uninscribed but "some have the fine parallel lines of a papyrus sheet" (Ronnie Reich and Eli Shukroun, "Recent Discoveries in the City of David, Jerusalem," *IEJ* 57 [2007]: 156). They are probably connected with royal administration and were apparently printed in Jerusalem and tied to legal documents (Yuval Goren and Shira Gurwin, "Royal Delicacy: Material Study of Iron Age Bullae from Jerusalem," *The Old Potter's Almanack* 18 [2013], 2–9) but any discussion must await their detailed publication.

119. André Lemaire, "Date et origine des inscriptions hébraïques et phéniciennes de Kuntillet 'Ajrud," *SEL* 1 (1984): 131–43; Ze'ev Meshel, ed., *Kuntillet 'Ajrud (Horvat Teman): An Iron Age II Religious Site on the Judah-Sinai Border* (Jerusalem: Israel Exploration Society, 2012), 61–69, 134–35.

120. Meshel, *Kuntillet 'Ajrud (Horvat Teman)*, 134.

121. For these inscriptions, see also Nadav Na'aman, "The Inscriptions of Kuntillet 'Ajrud Through the Lens of Historical Research," *UF* 43 (2011): 299–324; Erhard Blum, "Die Wandinschriften 4.2 und 4.6 sowie die Pithos-Inschrift 3.9 aus *Kuntillet 'Aǧrūd*," *ZDPV* 129 (2013): 21–54; André Lemaire, "Remarques sur les inscriptions phéniciennes de Kuntillet 'Ajrud," *Semitica* 55 (2013): 83–99; Shmuel Aḥituv, "Notes on the Kuntillet 'Ajrud Inscriptions," in Eshel and Levin, *Epigraphy and Daily Life*, 29–38, 185–87.

122. A few Phoenician ink inscriptions on funerary jars that appeared on the market could come from the cemetery of Tyre al-Bass and date from this period; see bibliography in Gaby Abousamra, "Un nouveau cratère avec une inscription phénicienne," *KUSATU* 10 (2009): 173–96; Abousamra, "Trois nouvelles jarres phéniciennes inscrites," in *Phéniciens d'Orient et d'Occident. Mélanges en l'honneur de Josette Elayi*, ed. André Lemaire, Cahiers de l'Institut du Proche-Orien du Collège de France 2 (Paris: Maisonneuve, in press).

123. Jean Hoftijzer and Gerrit van der Kooij, *Aramaic Texts from Deir 'Alla*, DMOA 11 (Leiden: Brill, 1976).

124. See the essays of Erhard Blum, "Die Kombination I der Wandinschirft vom Tell Deir 'Alla. Vorschläge zur Rekonstruktion mit historisch-kritischen Anmerkungen," in *Berührungspunkte. Studien zur Sozial- und Religionsgeschichte Israels und seiner Umwelt. Festschrift für Rainer Albertz*, ed. Rainer Albertz et al., AOAT 350 (Münster: Ugarit-Verlag, 2008), 573–601; Erhard Blum, "Israels Prophetie im altorientalischen Kontext," in *"From Ebla to Stellenbosch": Syro-Palestinian Religions and the Hebrew Bible*, ed. Izak Cornelius and Louis C. Jonker, ADPV 37 (Wiesbaden: Harrassowitz, 2008), 81–114.

ic.[125] Furthermore these long plaster inscriptions, written in black and red ink within a red frame were very probably copied from a literary manuscript on leather or papyrus.[126] This explains the title in red ink for combination 1: "The Text/Book of Balaam son of Beor, the seer-man of the gods (SPR BLʿM BR BʿR ʾŠ.ḤZH.ʾLHN)." If we have here a copy of one or two literary texts, this explains that the language is not Aramaic as spoken or written in the first half of the eighth century BCE. The original book of Balaam was composed earlier but it is difficult to specify the precise date of the composition of this original[127] since we have no other archaic Aramaic text that is earlier with which to compare. Recently E. Puech has dated with certainty the original text from the end of the second millennium BCE.[128] It is difficult to be so certain but a date in the ninth century during the reign of Hazael[129] is likely. A date in the tenth century BCE, when Hadad apparently founded the kingdom of Damascus,[130] is also possible and might provide a better historical context.[131] Whatever the exact date was of the original of the Balaam narrative found at Tell Deir Alla, an epigrapher can only agree with Manfred Weippert, more than twenty years ago: "That there was no 'real' literary activity in Palestine prior to the middle of the eighth century B.C. is a hypothesis[132] that has been definitively called in question by the

---

125. See, for instance, Jean Hoftijzer and Gerrit van der Kooij, eds., *The Balaam Text from Deir 'Alla Reevaluated* (Leiden: Brill, 1991), 48, 87, 97, 105, 163; Tropper, *Die Inschriften von Zencirli*, 301–6.

126. See already Alan R. Millard, "An Assessment of the Evidence for Writing in Ancient Israel," in *Biblical Archaeology Today: Proceedings of the International Congress on Biblical Archaeology, Jerusalem, April 1984*, ed. Janet Amitai (Jerusalem: Israel Exploration Society, 1985), 307.

127. André Lemaire, "Les inscriptions sur plâtre de Deir 'Alla et leur signification historique et culturelle," in Hoftijzer and Van der Kooij, *The Balaam Text*, 50; Erhard Blum, "Israels Prophetie im altorientalischen Kontext," in Cornelius and Jonker, *From Ebla to Stellenbosch*, 95; Blum, "Die Kombination I der Wandinschirft," 598.

128. Emile Puech, "Balaʿam and Deir ʿAlla," in *The Prestige of the Pagan Prophet Balaam in Judaism, Early Christianity and Islam*, ed. George H. van Kooten and Jacques van Ruiten (Leiden: Brill, 2008), 44: "certainly in the second millennium."

129. Lemaire, "Hazaël de Damas," 91–108.

130. See André Lemaire, "Les premiers rois araméens dans la tradition biblique," in *The World of the Aramaeans I. Biblical Studies in Honour of Paul-Eugène Dion*, ed. P. M. Michèle Daviau et al., JSOTSup 324 (Sheffield: Scheffield Academic Press, 2001), 129–34.

131. On the connection between the use of alphabetic writing and political programs, see, e.g., Seth L. Sanders, "What Was the Alphabet For? The Rise of Written Vernaculars and the Making of Israelite National Literature," *Maarav* 11 (2006): 25–26; Sanders, "Writing and Early Iron Age Israel: Before National Scripts, Beyond Nations and States," in Tappy and McCarter, *Literate Culture and Tenth Century Canaan*, 97–112.

132. This hypothesis was argued on the basis of archaeology by David W. Jamieson-Drake, *Scribes and Schools in Monarchic Judah: A Socio-Archaeological Approach*,

plaster texts from Deir 'Allā although the Mesha inscription could already have taught us a similar lesson."[133]

What can we conclude from this brief and provisional[134] epigraphic survey of Levantine West Semitic inscriptions at the beginning of the first millennium BCE?

1. Although the evidence is very fragmentary and the discovery of inscriptions always a matter of chance,[135] we have several monumental and royal inscriptions from the tenth century BCE in Byblos and, at the same time, several small, short and/or fragmentary inscriptions on stone and vases not only in Byblos but also in Palestine (Philistia, Shephelah, Central Cisjordan): the number and dispersion of these small inscriptions makes it likely that West Semitic writing was employed among local people of a elite? standing[136] who could have their name written on objects belonging to them with, eventually, the writing of the name of the deceased on his funerary stele (Tyre al-Bass).

2. This prestige use of writing seems to go on in the first half of the ninth century BCE with a development in the second half of this century: at this later period, prestige writing is often used in monumental and royal commemorative inscriptions at the service of royal propaganda, at least in the Aramean and Moabite kingdoms. Such a use supposes that there were local people able to read them. Although it is difficult to specify who these people were, one may think at least of people closely associated with the palace.

3. From the first half of the eighth century BCE, we have clear evidence of the diffusion of the use of writing with the development

---

JSOTSup 109 (Sheffield: Almond, 1991) but with a flawed methodology (literacy based solely on archaeology apart from the epigraphic evidence) and many lacunae and inconsistencies in dealing with the archaeological data, see the review by André Lemaire in *JAOS* 112 (1992): 707–8. This position is taken up again, for Judah, by Finkelstein, "Geographical and Historical Realities," 135.

133. Manfred Weippert, "The Balaam Text from Deir 'Allā and the Study of the Old Testament," in Hoftijzer and van der Kooij, *The Balaam Text From Deir 'Alla*, 177.

134. Any *status quaestionis* about the West Semitic inscriptions and scribal activity in the first quarter of the first millennium BCE is provisory since it is open to new discoveries as rightly emphasized by Finkelstein and Sass, "West Semitic Alphabetic Inscriptions," 149–50, 174–75, 188.

135. See esp. Alan R. Millard, "The Knowledge of Writing in Iron Age Palestine," in *"Lasset uns Brücken bauen ...," Collected Communications to the XVth Congress of the International Organization for the Study of the Old Testament, Cambridge, 1995*, ed. Klaus-Dietrich Schunck and Matthias Augustin, BEATAJ 42 (Frankfurt: Lang, 1998), 33–39.

136. For Iron I, see Ryan Byrne, "The Refuge of Scribalism in Iron I Palestine," *BASOR* 345 (2007): 22–23.

of royal administration. There are different scribal traditions with evidence of professional scribes using ink writing according to this local scribal tradition. One may guess that they learnt their profession in some kind of royal school for future scribes in the service of the royal administration.

4. From the plaster inscriptions of Tell Deir Alla and probably from those of Kuntillet Ajrud we have evidence of literary Aramaic and Phoenician traditions copied in the first half of the eighth century BCE. The date of the original of these literary traditions is difficult to specify but, for the "Text/Book of Balaam son of Beor, the seer of the gods," it seems at least to date in the ninth or tenth century BCE.

We must emphasize that these results are "minimal," based on the evidence we have now and that come down to us by chance. Most of the contemporary inscriptions disappeared with time and this is especially true of all the ink inscriptions on papyrus or leather that could have been used for archives in administration or literary tradition.

From this epigraphic evidence, one may conclude that the beginning of a literary tradition in Israel and Judah in the ninth and tenth century is certainly not impossible. The affirmation that "pre-late eighth century materials *must* have been transmitted orally"[137] appears to be an *a priori* assumption that does not take into account all the epigraphic evidence we now have from Levantine inscriptions. People in the Levant neither waited until the late eighth century to use West Semitic writing[138] nor to write documents and literary traditions. This does not diminish the importance of orality[139] for this early period but explains how certain historical traditions from this period may have been transmitted to us after being written down with the advantages and disadvantages of any literary tradition, especially the possibility of additions and revisions.

---

137. Finkelstein, "Geographical and Historical Realities," 135.

138. Cf. Millard, "Knowledge of Writing," 38: "The paucity of epigraphic remains from the tenth and ninth centuries does not denote an absence of writing, it is a phenomenon common across the Fertile Crescent and is explicable as an archaeological accident."

139. For the interplay of orality and literacy in Antiquity, see, e.g., Carr, *Writing on the Tablet of the Heart*; Stuart Weeks, "Literacy, Orality, and Literature in Israel," in *On Stone and Scroll. Essays in Honour of Graham Ivor Davies*, ed. James K. Aitken, Katharine J. Dell, and Brian A. Mastin, BZAW 420 (Berlin: de Gruyter, 2011), 465–78.

References

Abou-Assaf, Ali, Pierre Bordreuil, and Alan R. Millard. *La statue de Tell Fekherye et son inscription bilingue assyro-araméenne.* Etudes Assyriologiques. Paris: ADPF, 1982.
Abousamra, Gaby. "Cinq nouvelles pointes de flèches inscrites." Pages 47–57 in *Bible et Proche-Orient I.* Edited by Jean-Marie Durand and Josette Elayi. Transeuphratène 44. Paris: Gabalda, 2014.
———. "Un nouveau cratère avec une inscription phénicienne." *KUSATU* 10 (2009): 173–96.
———. "Trois nouvelles jarres phéniciennes inscrites." Pages 31–41 in *Phéniciens d'Orient et d'Occident: mélanges Josette Elayi.* Edited by André Lemaire. CIPOA 2. Paris: Maisonneuve, 2014.
Abousamra, Gaby, and André Lemaire, *Nouvelles stèles funéraires phéniciennes.* Beirut: Kutub, 2014.
Aḥituv, Shmuel. *Echoes from the Past. Hebrew and Cognate Inscriptions from the Biblical World.* Jerusalem: Carta, 2008.
———. "Notes on the Kuntillet 'Ajrud Inscriptions." Pages 29–38, 185–87 in *"See, I will bring a scroll recounting what befell me" (Ps 45:8): Epigraphy and Daily Life from the Bible to the Talmud Dedicated to the Memory of Professor Hanan Eshel.* Edited by Esther Eshel and Yigal Levin. JAJSup 12. Göttingen: Vandenhoeck & Ruprecht, 2014.
Aḥituv, Shmuel, and Amihai Mazar. "The Inscriptions from Tel Reḥov and Their Contribution to the Study of Script during Iron Age IIA." Pages 39–68, 190–203 in *See, I will bring a scroll recounting what befell me" (Ps 45:8): Epigraphy and Daily Life from the Bible to the Talmud Dedicated to the Memory of Professor Hanan Eshel.* Edited by Esther Eshel and Yigal Levin. JAJSup 12. Göttingen: Vandenhoeck & Ruprecht, 2014.
Alexandre, Yardeni. "A Canaanite Early Phoenician Bronze Bowl in an Iron Age IIA–B Burial Cave at Kefar Veradim, Northern Israel," *Maarav* 13 (2006): 7–41.
———. "A Fluted Bronze Bowl with a Canaanite-Early Phoenician Inscription from Kefar Veradim." Pages 65*–74* in *Eretz Zafon: Studies in Galilean Archaeology.* Edited by Zvi Gal. Haifa: Israel Antiquities Authority, 2002.
Amadasi Guzzo, Maria Giulia. "'Alphabet insaisissable': Quelques notes concernant la diffusion de l'écriture consonantique." Pages 67–87 in *Bible et Proche-Orient. Mélanges André Lemaire,* vol. 1. Edited by Jean-Marie Durand and Josette Elayi, Transeuphratène 44. Paris: Gabalda, 2014.
———. "Area 1: il frammento di stele in basalto con iscrizione." Pages 21–23 in *Tell Afis (Siria) 2002/2004.* Edited by Stephania Mazzoni et al. Pisa: Universita di Pisa, 2005.
———. *Iscrizioni fenicie e puniche in Italia.* Rome: Libreria dello stato, 1990.
———. "Mise à jour bibliographique des inscriptions publiées dans Kition III (1977)." Pages 204–15 in *Kition dans les textes.* Edited by Marguerite Yon. Kition-Bambula V. Paris: Editions Recherches sur les civilisations, 2004.
Amadasi Guzzo, Maria Giulia, and Vassos Karageorghis. *Fouilles de Kition III. Inscriptions phéniciennes.* Nicosia: Department of Antiquities and Zavallis Press, 1977.

Aufrecht, Walter E. "Ammonite Texts and Language." Pages 163–88 in *Ancient Ammon*. SHCANE 17. Edited by Burton MacDonald and Randall W. Younker. Leiden: Brill, 1999.

———. *A Corpus of Ammonite Inscriptions*. ANETS 4. Lewiston NY: Mellen, 1989.

Avigad, Nahman. "An Inscribed Bowl from Dan." *PEQ* 100 (1968): 42–44.

Avigad, Nahman, and Benjamin Sass. *Corpus of West Semitic Stamp Seals* (= WSS). Jerusalem: Israel Academy / IES / Institute of Archaeology, 1997.

Becking, Bob, and Paul Sanders. "De inscriptie uit Khirbet Qeiyafa: Een vroege vorm van sociaal besef in oud Israël?" *Nederlands Theologisch Tijdschrift* 64 (2010): 238–52.

———. "Plead for the Poor and the Widow: The Ostracon from Khirbet Qeiyafa as Expression of Social Consciousness." *ZABR* 17 (2011): 133–48.

Becking, Bob, and Jan A. Wagenaar. "Personal Name or Royal Epithet? A Remark on Ostracon 1027 from Tell el-Far'ah (South)." *BN* 107–8 (2001): 12–14.

Biran, Avraham, and Joseph Naveh. "An Aramaic Stele Fragment from Tel Dan." *IEJ* 43 (1993): 81–98.

———. "The Tel Dan Inscription: A New fragment." *IEJ* 45 (1995): 1–18.

Blum, Erhard. "Die Kombination I der Wandinschrift vom Tell Deir 'Alla. Vorschläge zur Rekonstruction mit historisch-kritischen Anmerkungen," Pages 573–601 in *Berührungspunkte. Studien zur Sozial- und Religionsgeschichte Israels und seiner Umwelt: Festschrift für Rainer Albertz*. Edited by Ingo Kottsieper, Rüdiger Schmitt, Jakob Wöhrle. AOAT 350. Münster: Ugarit-Verlag, 2008.

———. "Israels Prophetie im altorientalischen Kontext." Pages 81–114 in *"From Ebla to Stellenbosch": Syro-Palestinian Religions and the Hebrew Bible*. Edited by Izak Cornelius and Louis C. Jonker. ADPV 37. Wiesbaden: Harrassowitz, 2008.

———. "Die Wandinschriften 4.2 und 4.6 sowie die Pithos-Inschrift 3.9 aus *Kuntillet 'Aǧrūd*," *ZDPV* 129 (2013): 21–54.

Bordreuil, Pierre. *Catalogue des sceaux ouest-sémitiques inscrits de la Bibliohtèque Nationale, du Musée du Louvre et du Musée biblique de Bible et Terre Sainte*. Paris: Bibliothèque nationale, 1986.

———. "Epitaphe d'amphore phénicienne du 9ᵉ siècle." *Berytus* 25 (1977): 159–61.

Bron François, and André Lemaire. "Les inscriptions araméennes de Hazaël." *RA* 83 (1989): 35–44.

Bunimovitz Shlomo, and Zvi Lederman. "Beth Shemesh: Cultural Conflict on Judah's Frontier." *BAR* 23.1 (1997): 42–49, 75–77.

———. "The Early Israelite Monarchy in the Sorek Valley: Tel Beth-Shemesh and Tel Batash (Timnah) in the 10th and 9th Centuries BCE." Pages 407–27 in *"I Will Speak the Riddles of Ancient Times": Archaeological and Historical Studies in Honor of Amihai Mazar*. Edited by Aren M. Maeir and Pierre de Miroschedji. 2 volumes. Winona Lake, IN: Eisenbrauns, 2006.

Byrne, Ryan. "The Refuge of Scribalism in Iron I Palestine." *BASOR* 345 (2007): 1–31.

Carr, David M. *Writing on the Tablet of the Heart. Origins of Scripture and Literature*. Oxford: Oxford University Press, 2005.

Catling, H. W. "The Knossos Area, 1974–1976," *JHS* 97 (1977): 11–14

Cross, Frank Moore. "Epigrafic Notes on the Ammān Citadel Inscription,"*BASOR* 193 (1969): 13–19.

———. *Leaves from an Epigrapher's Notebook.* Winona Lake, IN: Eisenbrauns, 2003.
———. "Newly Found Inscriptions in Old Canaanite and Early Phoenician Scripts." *BASOR* 238 (1980): 1–20.
———. "The Oldest Phoenician Inscription from Sardinia: The Fragmentary Stele from Nora." Pages 65–74 in *"Working with No Data": Semitic and Egyptian Studies Presented to Th. O. Lambdin.* Edited by D. M. Colomb. Winona Lake, IN: Esenbrauns, 1987.
———. "Palaeography and the Date of the Tell Fakhariyeh Bilingual Inscription." Pages 393–409 in *Solving Riddles and Untying Knots. Biblical, Epigraphic, and Semitic Studies in Honor of Jonas C. Greenfield.* Edited by Ziony Zevit, Seymour Gitin, Michael Sokoloff. Winona Lake, IN: Eisenbrauns, 1995.
Cross, Frank Moore, and P. Kyle McCarter. "Two Archaic Inscriptions on Clay Objects from Byblus." *RSF* 1 (1973): 3–8.
Curtis, John E. "The British Museum Excavations at Nimrud in 1989." Pages 57–64 in *New Light on Nimrud: Proceedings of the Nimrud Conference 11th–13th March 2002.* Edited by John E. Curtis, Henrietta McCall, Dominique Collon, Lamia al-Gailani Werr. London: British Institute for the Study of Iraq, 2008.
Dankwarth, Guido, and Christa Müller. "Zur altaramäischen 'Altar' Inschrift vom Tell Halaf." *AfO* 35 (1988): 73–78.
Delavault, Bernard, and André Lemaire. "Les inscriptions phéniciennes de Palestine." *RSF* 5 (1979): 1–39.
Demsky, Aharon. "An Iron Age IIA Alphabetic Writing Exercise from Khirbet Qeiyafa." *IEJ* 62 (2012): 186–99.
Deutsch, Robert, and Michael Heltzer. *Windows to the Past.* Tel Aviv-Jaffa: Archaeological Center Publications, 1997.
Donner, Herbert, and Wolfgang Röllig. *Kanaanäsiche und aramäische Inschriften* (= *KAI*), I–III. 5th edition. Wiesbaden: Harrassowitz, 2002.
Dunand, Maurice. *Fouilles de Byblos I. 1926–1932.* Paris: Geuthner, 1939.
———. *Fouilles de Byblos II, 1933–1938. 1. Texte.* Paris: Adrien Maisonneuve, 1954.
Durand, Jean-Marie, and Josette Elayi eds. *Bible et Proche-Orient: Mélanges André Lemaire.* 3 volumes. Transeuphratène 44–46. Paris: Gabalda, 2014.
Eph'al, Israel and Joseph Naveh. "Hazael's Booty Inscription." *IEJ* 39 (1989): 192–200.
Eshel, Esther, and Yigal Levin, eds. *"See, I will bring a scroll recounting what befell me" (Ps 40:8): Epigraphy and Daily Life from the Bible to the Talmud Dedicated to the Memory of Professor Hanan Eshel.* JAJSup 12. Göttingen: Vandenhoeck & Ruprecht, 2014.
Finkelstein, Israel. "Geographical and Historical Realities behind the Earliest Layer in the David Story." *SJOT* 27 (2013): 131–50.
Finkelstein, Israel, and Eliazer Piasetzky. "Radiocarbon, Iron IIa Destructions and the Israel-Aram Damascus Conflicts in the 9th Century BCE." *UF* 39 (2007): 261–76.
———. "Khirbet Qeiyafa: Absolute Chronology." *TA* 37 (2010): 84–88.
Finkelstein, Israel, and Benjamin Sass. "The West Semitic Alphabetic Inscriptions, Late Bronze II to Iron IIA: Archaeological Context, Distribution and Chronology." *HeBAI* 2 (2013): 149–220.

Fitzmyer, Joseph A. *The Aramaic Inscriptions of Sefire.* BibOr 19. Rome: Pontifical Biblical Institute, 1995.
Fritz, Volkmar. *Kinneret: Ergebnisse der Ausgrabungen auf dem Tell el-'Orēme am See Genezaret 1982–1985.* ADPV 15. Wiesbaden: Harrassowitz, 1990.
Gal, Zvi, and Alexandre Yardenna. *Horbat Rosh Zayit. An Iron Storage Fort and Village.* IAA Report 8. Jerusalem: IAA, 2000.
Gass, Erasmus. *Die Moabiter: Geschichte und Kultur eines ostjordanischen Volkes im 1. Jahrtausend v. Chr.* ADPV 38. Wiesbaden: Harrassowitz, 2009.
Galil, Gershon. "The Hebrew Inscription from Khirbet Qeiyafa/Neṭa'im." *UF* 41 (2009): 193–242.
———. "With More on the Jerusalem Inscription." *Zwinglius Redivivus* July 12 and 29, 2013. http://zwingliusredivivus.wordpress.com/2013/07/29/gershon-galil-with-more-on-the-jerusalem-inscription/.
Garfinkel, Yosef, and Hoo-Goo Kang. "The Relative and Absolute Chronology of Khirbet Qeiyafa: Very Late Iron Age I or Very Early Iron Age IIA?" *IEJ* 61 (2011): 171–83.
Garfinkel, Yosef, Saar Ganor, and Michael G. Hasel. "The Contribution of Khirbet Qeiyafa to Our Understanding of the Iron Age Period," *Bulletin of the Anglo-Israel Archaeological Society* 28 (2010): 39–54.
Gibson, John C. L. *Textbook of Syrian Semitic Inscriptions II.* Oxford: Clarendon Press, 1975.
———. *Textbook of Syrian Semitic Inscriptions III. Phoenician Inscriptions.* Oxford: Clarendon, 1982.
Gilboa, Ayelet. "Cypriot Barrel Juglets at Khirbet Qeiyafa and Other Sites in the Levant: Cultural Aspects and Chronological Implication." *TA* 39 (2012): 133–49.
Gophna, Ram, and Yosef Porat. "The Survey of Ephraim and Manasse." Pages 195–241 in *Judaea, Samaria and the Golan: Archaeological Survey 1967–68.* Edited by Moshe Kochavi. Jerusalem: Archaeological Survey of Israel; Carta, 1972.
Goren, Yuval, and Shira Gurwin. "Royal Delicacy: Material Study of Iron Age Bullae from Jerusalem," *The Old Potter's Almanack* 18 (2013): 2–9.
Grant, Elihu. "Découverte épigraphique à Beth-Šemeš." *RB* 39 (1930): 401–2.
Grant, Elihu, and Georges Ernest Wright. *Ain Shems Excavations (Palestine) V.* Haverford, PA: Haverford College, 1939.
Gubel, Eric. "The Phoenician Tempel at Tell Kazel (Ṣumur)." *Bulletin d'Archéologie et d'Architecture Libanaises, Hors-Série (BAAL HS)* 6 (2009): 453–68.
Hagelia, Hallvard. *The Dan Debate: The Tel Dan Inscription in Recent Research.* Sheffield: Sheffield Phoenix, 2009.
———. *The Tel Dan Inscription: A Critical Investigation of Recent Research on Its Palaeography and Philology.* Acta Universitatis Upsaliensis 22. Uppsala: Uppsala Universitet, 2006.
———. "What is the Problem with the Tel Dan Inscription?" *KUSATU* 15 (2013): 109–23.
Hallo, William W., and K. Lawson Younger. *The Context of Scripture.* 3 volumes. Leiden: Brill, 1997–2002.
Hamidović, David. "L'inscription du pithos de l'Ophel à Jérusalem." *Semitica* 54 (2014): 136–49.

Hasegawa, Shuichi. *Aram and Israel during the Jehuite Dynasty*. BZAW 434. Berlin: de Gruyter, 2012.
Hoftijzer, Jean, and Gerrit van der Kooij, *Aramaic Texts from Deir 'Alla*. DMOA 19. Leiden: Brill, 1976.
———. eds. *The Balaam Text from Deir 'Alla Reevaluated: Proceedings of the International Symposium Held at Leiden, 21–24 August 1989*. Leiden: Brill, 1991.
Horn, Siegfried H. "The Amman Citadel Inscription." *BASOR* 193 (1969): 2–13.
Jamieson-Drake, David W. *Scribes and Schools in Monarchic Judah: A Socio-Archaeological Approach*. JSOTSup 109. Sheffield: Almond, 1991.
Kallner, R. B. "Two Inscribed Sherds." *Qedem* 2 (1945): 11–14.
Kelm, George L., and Amihai Mazar. "Tel Batash (Timna) Excavations: Third Preliminary Report (1984–1989)." Pages 47–67 in *Preliminary Reports of ASOR-Sponsored Excavations, 1982–1989*. BASORSup 27. Baltimore: Johns Hopkins University Press, 1991.
———. *Timnah: A Biblical City in the Sorek Valley*. Winona Lake, IN: Eisenbrauns, 1995.
Knauf, Ernst Axel, and Hermann Michael Niemann. "Zum Ostracon 1027 vom Tell Fara Süd (Tell el-Fariʿ/Tel Šaruḥen)." *UF* 31 (1999): 247–50.
———. "Tell el-Farʿah South Ostracon 1027 and a New Identification for the Site." *UF* 43 (2011): 273–82.
———. "Weitere Überlegungen zum neuen Ostrakon 1027 vom Tell el-Faraʿ Süd." *BN* 109 (2001): 19–20.
Kyrieleis, Helmut, and Wolfgang Röllig. "Ein altorientalischer Pferdeschmuck aus dem Heraion von Samos." *Mitteilungen des Deutschen Archäologischen Instituts. Athenische Abteilung* 103 (1988): 37–75.
Landgraf, John. "The Manaḥat Inscription." *Levant* 3 (1971): 92–95.
Leval, Gérard. "Ancient Inscription Refers to Birth of Israelite Monarchy." *BAR* 38.3 (2012): 41–43, 70.
Lehmann, Gunnar, and Tammi T. J. Schneider. "Tell el-Farah (South) 1999 Ostracon." *UF* 31 (1999): 251–54.
———. "A New Ostracon from Tell el-Farʿah (South)." *NEA* 63 (2000): 113.
Lehmann, Reinhard G. "Calligraphy and Craftmanship in the Aḥīrōm Inscription: Considerations on Skilled Linear Flat Writing in Early First Millennium Byblos." *Maarav* 15 (2008): 119–64.
———. *Dynastensarkophage mit szenischen Reliefs aus Byblos und Zypern: Text 1.2* Mainz: von Zabern, 2005.
Lehmann, Reinhard G., and Anna Elise Zernecke. "Bemerkungen und Beobachtungen zu der neuen Ophel-Pithosinschrift." *KUSATU* 15 (2013): 437–50.
Lemaire, André. "La datation des rois de Byblos Abibaal et Elibaal et les relations entre l'Egypte et le Levant au Xe siècle av. notre ère." *CRAIBL* (2006): 1697–716.
———. "Date et origine des inscriptions hébraïques et phéniciennes de Kuntillet 'Ajriud." *SEL* 1 (1984): 131–43.
———. "Le dialecte araméen de l'inscription de KTMW (Zencirli, VIIIe s. av. n. è.)." Pages 145–50 in *In the Shadow of Bezalel: Aramaic, Biblical, and Ancient Near Eastern Studies in Honor of Bezalel Porten*. Edited by Alejandro F. Botta. CHANE 60. Leiden: Brill, 2013.

———. *Les écoles et la formation de la Bible dans l'ancien Israël*. OBO 39. Fribourg: Editions universitaires; Göttingen: Vandenhoeck & Ruprecht, 1981.

———. "Hazaël de Damas, roi d'Aram." Page 91–108 in *Marchands, diplomates et empereurs: Etudes sur la civilisation mésopotamienne offertes à Paul Garelli*. Edited by D. Charpin and F. Joannès. Paris: Editions Recherche sur les Civilisations, 1991.

———. *Inscriptions hébraïques I. Les ostraca*. LAPO 9. Paris: Cerf, 1977.

———. "Les inscriptions de Khirbet el-Qôm et l'ashérah de YHWH." *RB* 84 (1977): 595–608.

———. "Les inscriptions sur plâtre de Deir 'Alla et leur signification historique et culturelle." Pages 33–57 in *The Balaam Text From Deir 'Alla Re-Evaluated*. Leiden: Brill, 1991.

———. "Joas de Samarie, Barhadad de Damas, Zakkur de Hamat. La Syrie-Palestine vers 800 av. J.-C." Pages 148*–57* in *Avraham Malamat Volume*. Edited by Shmuel Aḥituv and Baruch A. Levine. ErIsr 24. Jerusalem: Israel Exploration Society, 1993.

———. "Khirbet el-Qôm and Hebrew and Aramaic Epigraphy." Pages 231–38 in *Confronting the Past: Archaeological and Historical Essays on Ancient Israel in Honor of William G. Dever*. Edited by Seymour Gitin, J. E. Wright, J. P. Dessel. Winona Lake, IN: Eisenbrauns, 2006.

———. "Les langues du royaume de Sam'al aux IXe–VIIIe s. av. J.-C. et leurs relations avec le royaume de Qué." Pages 183–93 in *La Cilicie: espaces et pouvoirs locaux (2e millénaire av. J.-C. - 4e siècle ap. J.-C.)*. Edited by Eric Jean, Ali M. Dinçol, and Serra Durugönül. Varia Anatolica 13. Paris: de Boccard, 2001.

———. "The Mesha Stele and the Omri Dynasty." Pages 135–44 in *Ahab Agonistes: The Rise and Fall of the Omri Dynasty*. Edited by Lester L. Grabbe. LHBOTS 421. London: T&T Clark, 2007.

———. "Notes d'épigraphie nord-ouest sémitique. 7. Tesson inscrit de Khirbet Tannin." *Semitica* 35 (1985): 13–15.

———. "Notes d'épigraphie nord-ouest sémitique." *Syria* 64 (1987): 293–316.

———. "Notes d'épigraphie ouest-sémitique. 4. Tessons inscrits du territoire de Manassé," *Semitica* 32 (1982), 15–17.

———. "Notes d'épigraphie ouest-sémitique." *Syria* 61 (1984): 251–56.

———. "'Ozibaal de Byblos?" Pages 289–96 in *Ritual, Religion and Reason: Studies in the Ancient World in Honour of Paolo Xella*. Edited by Oswald Loretz, Sergio Ribichini, Wilfred G. E. Watson, José A. Zamora. AOAT 404. Münster: Ugarit-Verlag, 2013.

———. "Les premiers rois araméens dans la tradition biblique." Pages 113–43 *The World of the Aramaeans I: Biblical Studies in Honour of Paul-Eugène Dion*. Edited by P. M. Michèle Daviau, John W. Wevers, and Michael Weigl. JSOTSup 324. Sheffield: Sheffield Academic Press, 2001.

———. "Remarques sur les inscriptions phéniciennes de Kuntillet 'Ajrud." *Semitica* 55 (2013): 83–99.

———. Review of David W. Jamieson-Drake, *Scribes and Schools in Monarchic Judah: A Socio-Archaeological Approach*. *JAOS* 112 (1992): 707–8.

———. Review of Johannes Renz, *Handbuch der hebräischen Epigraphik* I, II/A, III, 1995. *BiOr* 54 (1997): col. 161–166.

———. "SMR dans la petite inscription de Kilamuwa (Zencirli)." *Syria* 67 (1990): 323–27.
———. "La stèle de Mésha et l'histoire de l'ancien Israël." Pages 143–69 in *Storia e tradizioni de Israele. Scritti in onore di J. Alberto Soggin*. Edited by D. Garrone and F. Israel. Brescia: Paideia, 1991.
———. "The Tel Dan Stela as a Piece of Royal Historiography." *JSOT* 81 (1998): 3–14.
———. "Un siècle et demi de guerre en Transjordanie (c. 882–732)." *SHAJ* 11 (2013): 47–54.
———. "West Semitic Epigraphy and the History of the Levant during the 12th–10th Centuries BCE." Pages 291–307 in *The Ancient Near East in the 12th–10th Centuries BCE. Culture and History*. Edited by Gershon Galil, Ayelet Gilboa, Aren M. Maeir, Dan'el Kahn. AOAT 392. Münster: Ugarit-Verlag, 2012.
Lemaire, André, and Jean-Marie Durand. *Les inscriptions araméennes de Sfiré et l'Assyrie de Shamshi-ilu*, HEO 20 (Geneva: Droz, 1984)
Lemaire, André, and Benjamin Sass. "The Mortuary Stele with Sam'alian Inscription from Ördekburnu near Zincirli." *BASOR* 369 (2013): 57–136.
———. "La stèle d'Ördekburnu: vers la solution d'une énigme de l'épigraphie ouest-sémitique." *CRAI* (2012): 227–40.
Maeir, Aren M., ed. *Tell es-Safi/Gath I: Report on the 1996–2005 Seasons*. ÄAT 69. Wiesbaden: Harrassowitz, 2012.
Maeir, Aren M., and Esther Eshel. "Four Short Alphabetic Inscriptions from Late Iron Age IIa Tell eṣ-Ṣafi/Gath and Their Implications for the Development of Literacy in Iron Age Philistia and Environs." Pages 69–88, 205–10 in *"See, I will bring a scroll recounting what befell me" (Ps 45:8): Epigraphy and Daily Life from the Bible to the Talmud Dedicated to the Memory of Professor Hanan Eshel*. Edited by Esther Eshel and Yigal Levin. JAJSup 12. Göttingen: Vandenhoeck & Ruprecht, 2014.
Maeir, Aren M., Alexander Zuckerman, Stefan Jacob Wimmer, and Aaron Demsky. "A Late Iron Age I/Early Iron Age IIA Old Canaanite Inscription from Tell eṣ-Ṣâfî/Gath, Israel: Palaeography, Dating, and Historical-Cultural Significance." *BASOR* 351 (2008): 39–71.
Mallowan, Max E. L. *Nimrud and Its Remains* II. London: Collins, 1966.
Masson, Olivier, and Maurice Sznycer. *Recherches sur les Phéniciens à Chypre*. Hautes Etudes Orientales 3. Genève: Droz, 1972.
Mazar, Amihai. "Three 10th–9th Century B.C.E. Inscriptions from Tēl Reḥōv." Pages 171–84 in *Saxa Loquentur: Studien zur Archäologie Palästinas/Israel. Festschrift für Volkmar Fritz*. Edited by Cornelius G. den Hertog, Ulrich Hübner, and Stefan Münger. AOAT 302. Münster: Ugarit-Verlag, 2003.
Mazar, Amihai, and Shmuel Aḥituv. "Inscriptions from Tel Reḥov and Their Contribution to the Study of Writing and Literacy during the Iron Age IIA." Pages 300–316 (Hb), 154*, in *Amnon Ben-Tor Volume*. Edited by Hillel Geva and Alan Paris. ErIsr 30. Jerusalem: Israel Exploration Society, 2011.
Mazar, Benjamin. "Ein Gev Excavations in 1961." *IEJ* 14 (1964): 1–49.
Mazar, Eilat, David Ben-Shlomo, and Shmuel Aḥituv. "An Inscribed Pithos from the Ophel, Jerusalem." *IEJ* 63 (2013): 39–49.

McCarter, P. Kyle Shlomo Bunimovitz, and Zvi Lederman. "An Archaic *Ba'l* Inscription from Tel Beth-Shemesh." *TA* 38 (2011): 179–93.
Meshel, Ze'ev, ed. *Kuntillet 'Ajrud (Horvat Teman). An Iron Age II Religious Site on the Judah-Sinai Border*. Jerusalem: Israel Exploration Society, 2012.
Millard, Alan R. "Alphabetic Inscriptions on Ivories from Nimrud." *Iraq* 24 (1962): 41–51.
———. "Aramaic at Nimrud on Clay, Potsherds, Bricks and Ivories." Pages 267–70 in *New Light on Nimrud: Proceedings of the Nimrud Conference 11th–13th March 2002*. Edited by John E. Curtis, Henrietta McCall, Dominique Collon, Lamia al-Gailani Werr. London: British Institute for the Study of Iraq, 2008.
———. "An Assessment of the Evidence for Writing in Ancient Israel." Pages 301–312 in *Biblical Archaeology Today: Proceedings of the International Congress on Biblical Archaeology, Jerusalem, April 1984*. Edited by Janet Amitai. Jerusalem: Israel Exploration Society, 1985.
———. "The Knowledge of Writing in Iron Age Palestine." Pages 33–39 in *"Lasset uns Brücken bauen ...," Collected Communications to the XVth Congress of the International Organization for the Study of the Old Testament, Cambridge, 1995*. Edited by Klaus-Dietrich Schunck and Matthias Augustin. BEATAJ 42. Frankfurt: Lang, 1998.
———. "The Ostracon from the Days of David Found at Khirbet Qeiyafa." *Tyndale Bulletin* 62 (2011): 1–13.
———. "Scripts and Their Uses in the 12th–10th Centuries BCE." Pages 405–12 in *The Ancient Near East in the 12th–10th Centuries BCE. Culture and History*. Edited by Gershon Galil, Ayelet Gilboa, Aren M. Maeir, and Dan'el Kahn. AOAT 392. Münster: Ugarit-Verlag, 2012.
Misgav Haggai, Yosef Garfinkel, and Saar Ganor. "Chapter 14. The Ostracon." Pages 243–57 in *Khirbet Qeiyafa*, Vol. 1: *Excavation Report 2007–2008*. Edited by Yosef Garfinkel and Saar Ganor. Jerusalem: Israel Exploration Society/Institute of Archaeology, 2009.
Murphy, Roland A. "A Fragment of an Early Moabite Inscription from Diban." *BASOR* 125 (1952): 20–23.
Na'aman, Nadav. "Royal Inscriptions versus Prophetic Story. Mesha's Rebellion according to Biblical and Moabite Historiography." Pages 145–83 in *Ahab Agonistes: The Rise and Fall of the Omri Dynasty*. Edited by Lester L. Grabbe. LHBOTS 421. London: T&T Clark, 2007.
———. "The Inscriptions of Kuntillet 'Ajrud Through the Lens of Historical Research." *UF* 43 (2011): 299–324.
Naveh, Joseph. "The Epigraphic Finds from Areas A and B." Pages 346–47 in *Hazor III–IV. Text*. Edited by A. Ben-Tor. Jerusalem: Israel Exploration Society, 1989.
———. "Proto-Canaanite, Archaic Greek, and the Script of the Aramaic Text on the Tell Fakhariyah Statue." Pages 101–14 in *Ancient Israelite Religion: Essays in Honor of Frank Moore Cross*. Edited by Patrick D. Miller, Paul D. Hanson, S. Dean McBride. Philadelphia: Fortress, 1987.
Otzen, Benedikt. "Appendix 2. The Aramaic Inscriptions." Pages 266–318 in *Hama: fouilles et recherches; 1931–1938*. 2.2: *Les objets de la période dite syro-hittite (Âge du Fer)*. Edited by Paul J. Riis and Marie-Louise Buhl. Copenhagen: Copenhague Fondation Carlsberg, 1990.

Pardee, Dennis. "A New Aramaic Inscription from Zincirli." *BASOR* 356 (2009): 51–71.
Pilkington, Nathan. "A Note on Nora and the Nora Stones." *BASOR* 365 (2012): 45–51.
Puech, Emile. "Balaʻam and Deir ʻAlla." Pages 25–47 in *The Prestige of the Pagan Prophet Balaam in Judaism, Early Christianity and Islam*. Edited by George H. van Kooten and Jacques van Ruiten. Leiden: Brill, 2008.
———. "Les inscriptions hébraïques de Kuntillet ʻAjrud." *RB* 121 (2014): 161–94.
———. "Un ivoire de Bît-Guši (Arpad) à Nimrud." *Syria* 55 (1978): 163–69.
———. "L'ivoire inscrit d'Arslan Tash et les rois de Damas." *RB* 88 (1981): 544–62.
———. "L'ostracon de Khirbet Qeyafa et les débuts de la royauté en Israël." *RB* 117 (2010): 162–84.
———. "Présence phénicienne dans les îles à la fin du IIe millénaire." *RB* 90 (1983): 365–95.
———. "Remarques sur quelques inscriptions phéniciennes de Chypre." *Semitica* 29 (1979): 19–26.
———. "Le rite d'offrande de cheveux d'après une inscription phénicienne de Kition vers 800 avant notre ère." *RSF* 4 (1976): 11–21.
———. "La stèle de Bar-Hadad à Melqart et les rois d'Arpad." *RB* 99 (1992): 311–34.
Reed, William, and Fred V. Winnett. "A Fragment of an Early Moabite Inscription from Kerak." *BASOR* 172 (1963): 1–9.
Reich, Ronny, and Eli Shukroun. "Recent Discoveries in the City of David, Jerusalem." *IEJ* 57 (2007): 153–69.
Reisner, George A., Clarence S. Fischer, and David G. Lyon. *Harvard Excavations at Samaria 1908–1910*. Cambridge: Harvard University Press, 1924.
Renz, Johannes. *Die Althebräischen Inschriften I. Text und Kommentar*. Handbuch der althebräischen Epigraphik I. Darmstadt: Wissenschaftliche Buchgesellschaft, 1995.
Richelle, Matthieu. *Le royaume d'Israël dans la première moitié du VIIIe siècle avant notre ère*. Thesis, Ecole Pratique des Hautes Etudes. Paris, 2010.
Röllig, Wolfgang. "Alte und neue Elfenbeininschriften." *Neue Ephemeris für semitische Epigraphik* 2 (1974): 37–64.
———. "Die Inschriften des Ninurta-bēlu-uṣur, Statthalters von Kār-Salmānu-ašarēd. Teil I." Pages 265–78 in *Of God(s), Trees, Kings, and Scholars: Neo-Assyrian and Related Studies in Honour of Simo Parpola*. Edited by M. Luukko. StOr 106. Helsinki: Finnish Oriental Society, 2009.
Rollston, Christopher, A. "The Dating of the Early Royal Byblian Phoenician Inscriptions: A Response to Benjamin Sass." *Maarav* 15 (2008): 57–93.
———. "The Iron Age Phoenician Scripts." Pages 72–99 in *"An Eye for Form": Epigraphic Essays in Honor of Frank Moore Cross*. Edited by Jo Ann Hackett and Walter E. Aufrecht. Winona Lake, IN: Eisenbrauns, 2014.
———. "The Khirbet Qeiyafa Ostracon: Methodological Musings and Caveats." *TA* 38 (2011): 67–82.
———. "The Phoenician Script of the Tel Zayit Abecedary and Putative Evidence for Israelite Literacy." Pages 61–96 in *Literate Culture and Tenth-Century Canaan: The Tel Zayit Abecedary in Context*. Edited by R. E. Tappy and P. K. McCarter. Winona Lake, IN: Eisenbrauns, 2008.

———. *Writing and Literacy in the World of Ancient Israel*. ABS 11. Atlanta: Society of Biblical Literature, 2010.

———. "What's the Oldest Hebrew Inscription?" *BAR* 38.3 (2012): 32–40, 66, 68.

Sader, Hélène. *Iron Age Funerary Stelae from the Lebanon*. Cuadernos de arqueologia mediterranea 11. Barcelona: Bellaterra, 2005.

———. "An Inscribed Weight from Byblos." Pages 47–51 in *Atti del V Congresso internazionale di Studi Fenici e Punici, Marsala-Palermo, 2–8 octobre 2000*, I. Edited by A. Spano Giammellaro. Palermo: Universita, 2005.

Sanders, Seth L. "What Was the Alphabet For? The Rise of Written Vernaculars and the Making of Israelite National Litertature." *Maarav* 11 (2006): 25–26.

———. "Writing and Early Iron Age Israel: Before National Scripts, Beyond Nations and States." Pages 97–112 in *Literate Culture and Tenth Century Canaan: The Tel Zayit Abecedary in Context*. Edited by Ron E. Tappy and P. Kyle McCarter. Winona Lake, IN: Eisenbrauns, 2008.

Sass, Benjamin. *The Alphabet at the Turn of the Millennium. The West Semitic Alphabet ca. 1150–850 BCE. The Antiquity of the Arabian, Greek and Phrygian Alphabets*. Occasional Publication 4. Tel-Aviv: Emery and Claire Yass Publications, 2005.

———. "An Iron Age I Jewelry Hoard from Cave II/3 in Wadi el-Makkuk." *'Atiqot* 41/2 (2002): 32.

Schmitz, Phillip C. *The Phoenician Diaspora: Epigraphic and Historical Studies*. Winona Lake, IN: Eisenbrauns, 2012.

Schniedewind, William M. "Problems in the Palaeographic Dating of Inscriptions." Pages 405–12 in *The Bible and Radiocarbon Dating, Archaeology, Text and Science*. Edited by Th. Levy and Th. Higham. London: Equinox, 2005.

———. *A Social History of Hebrew: Its Origins Through the Rabbinic Period*. New Haven: Yale University Press, 2013.

Schwiderski, Dirk. *Die alt- und reichsaramäischen Inschriften 2. Texte und Bibliographie*. Fontes et Subsidia ad Biblia pertinentes 2. Berlin: de Gruyter, 2004.

Shea, William H. "The Qeiyafa Ostracon: Separation of Powers in Ancient Israel." *UF* 41 (2009): 601–10.

Singer-Avitz, Lily. "Khirbet Qeiyafa: Late Iron Age I in Spite of It All." *IEJ* 62 (2012): 177–85.

———. "The Relative Chronology of Khirbet Qeiyafa." *TA* 37 (2010): 79–83.

Soldi, Sebastiano. "Aramaeans and Assyrians in Northwestern Syria: Material Evidence from Tell Afis." *Syria* 86 (2009): 97–118.

Stager, Lawrence E. "An Inscribed Potsherd from the Eleventh Century." *BASOR* 194 (1969): 45–52.

Sukenik, Eliezer L. "Note on the Sherd From Tell eṣ-Ṣarem." *Qedem* 2 (1945): 15.

Sznycer, Maurice. "L'inscription phénicienne de Tekke, près de Knossos." *Kadmos* 18 (1979): 89–93.

Tappy, Ron E., and P. Kyle McCarter, eds. *Literate Culture and Tenth-Century Canaan: The Tel Zayit Abecedary in Context*. Winona Lake, IN: Eisenbrauns, 2008.

Tappy, Ron E., P. Kyle McCarter, Marilyn J. Lundberg, and Bruce Zuckerman. "An Abecedary of the Mid-Tenth Centuruy B.C.E. from the Judean Shephelah." *BASOR* 344 (2006): 5–46.

Teixidor, Javier. "An Archaic Inscription from Byblos." *BASOR* 225 (1977): 70–71.
Tropper, Josef. *Die Inschriften von Zincirli*. ALASP 6. Münster: Ugarit-Verlag, 1993.
Vismara, Elena. "Implicazioni storiche dell'iscrizione di Tel Dan." Pages 193–206 in *Florilegio filologico linguistico: Haninura de Bon Siman a Maria Luisa Mayer Modena*. Edited by Claudia Rosenzweig, Anna Linda Callow, Vermundo Brugnatelli, Francesco Aspesi. Acta et studia 4. Milano: Cisalpino, 2008.
Weeks, Stuart. "Literacy, Orality, and Literature in Israel." Pages 465–78 in *On Stone and Scroll. Essays in Honour of Graham Ivor Davies*. Edited by James K. Aitken, Katherine J. Dell, and Brian A. Mastin. BZAW 420. Berlin: de Gruyter, 2011.
Weigl, Michael. "Eine Inschrift aus Silo 4 in *Ḥirbet el-Mudēyine* (*Wādī eṯ-Ṯemed*, Jordanien)." *ZDPV* 122 (2006): 31–45.
Weippert, Manfred. "The Balaam Text from Deir ʿAllā and the Study of the Old Testament." Pages 151–84 in *The Balaam Text From Deir ʿAlla Re-Evaluated*. Edited by Jean Hoftijzer and Gerrit van der Kooij. Leiden: Brill, 1991.
———. "Mesa und der Status von 'ganz Dibon.'" Pages 323–28 in *Wort und Stein: Studien zur Theologie und Archäologie. Festschrift für Udo Worschech*. Edited by Friedbert Ninow. Beiträge zur Erforschung der antiken Moabitis 4. Frankfurt: Lang, 2003.
———. "Mōšiʿs Moab." Pages 133–51 in *Bible et Proche-Orient: Mélanges André Lemaire*, vol. 3. Edited by Jean-Marie Durand and Josette Elayi, Transeuphratène 46. Paris: Gabalda, 2014.
Younger, K. Lawson. "Some of What's New in Old Aramaic Epigraphy." *NEA* 70 (2007): 139–46.
———. "Two Epigraphic Notes on the New Katumuwa Inscription from Zincirli." *Maarav* 16 (2009): 159–79.
Zertal, Adam. *The Shechem Syncline*. Vol. 1 of *The Manasseh Hill Country Survey*. CHANE 21.1. Leiden: Brill, 2004.

LITERACY IN THE NEGEV IN THE LATE MONARCHICAL PERIOD

Nadav NA'AMAN

MODERN BIBLICAL-HISTORICAL RESEARCH HAS FOCUSED EXTENSIVELY ON the spread of literacy in the kingdom of Judah and the extent of literateness among the elite and inhabitants of the kingdom. Whereas scholars had once sought to derive some information about these matters from the biblical texts, today it is clear that intrabiblical references are of very limited value for investigating the diffusion and extent of literacy in the kingdom. The bulk of the data concerning the development of writing and the dissemination of literacy come from archaeological excavations conducted for over a century in what had been Judah's territory. Such data help us establish the latest possible date for the adoption of alphabetical writing in Judah's royal court, the stages in the spread of literacy in the kingdom's capital and peripheral cities, and the development of the administration in Judah's territory.

First, however, we must consider what these archaeological findings can tell us about the level of literacy of those who wrote these inscriptions. Royal letters and decrees, state administration, juridical decisions, religious instructions, and literary works were all written on papyrus (or parchment), which have long since perished. Hence, clearly, archaeology can shed light neither on their production nor on their distribution among the central cities and elite of the kingdom. The only sources available for research are those inscriptions written on nonperishable material, in particular clay, made by various persons for various purposes. Hence, the investigation must start by collecting all the data available for research and sorting the epigraphic findings according to function. Only then can we attempt to establish their significance for evaluating the degree and kind of literacy among the inhabitants of the kingdom.

We must keep in mind that the ability to write simple texts does not necessarily indicate full literacy. Scientific literature written over the last two decades on the problem of literacy in ancient Israel and Judah has demonstrated the need to clearly distinguish between a basic knowledge of the alphabet alongside the ability to read and write simple texts, on the one hand, and professional scribes' ability to compose official administrative, juridical and religious texts and literary works, on the other.[1] Since all works written on papyri have perished, the scanty remains available today represent "secondary" productions of writing. These works mainly reflect what people of different professions and classes wrote on available artifacts in various places within the kingdom.

The district selected for research is the biblical Negev, that is, the Beersheba Valley. The reasons for the selection are obvious. First, many central First Temple sites located in the Negev region have been excavated extensively. The dry climate in the region helps preserve the ink, so that a relatively large number of inscriptions have been discovered in the excavated sites. Second, the Negev district suffered two major destructions during the course of the eighth through early sixth centuries BCE: one by the Assyrians in 701 and the second by the Babylonians and Edomites around 587 (or slightly earlier).[2] The two destruction levels enable us to separate the eighth-century inscriptions from those of the late seventh and early sixth century. By comparing the number and contents of the inscriptions written in each period, we can estimate the pace at which literacy spread in the Negev and attempt to draw conclusions about the situation in other districts of the kingdom.

A Survey of the Monarchical Period Inscriptions Unearthed in the Negev

The point of departure for the discussion is a systematic presentation of the inscriptions discovered in the Beersheba Valley in the monarchical period, emphasizing the nature of the sites (cities versus fortresses), the dates of the inscriptions (eighth versus seventh and early sixth century BCE), their tech-

---

1. See for example, André Lemaire, "Writing and Writing Materials," *ABD* 6:999–1008, with earlier literature; Ian Young, "Israelite Literacy: Interpreting the Evidence," *VT* 48 (1998): 239–53, 408–22; David M. Carr, *Writing on the Tablet of the Heart: Origins of Scripture and Literature* (Oxford: Oxford University Press, 2005), 111–73, with earlier literature; Karel van der Toorn, *Scribal Culture and the Making of the Hebrew Bible* (Cambridge, MA: Harvard University Press, 2007), 75–108; Christopher A. Rollston, *Writing and Literacy in the World of Ancient Israel: Epigraphic Evidence from the Iron Age*, ABS 11 (Atlanta: Society of Biblical Literature, 2010), 127–35.

2. For dating the destruction of the Negev settlements slightly before 587 BCE, see Nadav Na'aman, "Textual and Historical Notes on Eliashib's Archive from Arad," *TA* 38 (2011): 88–90.

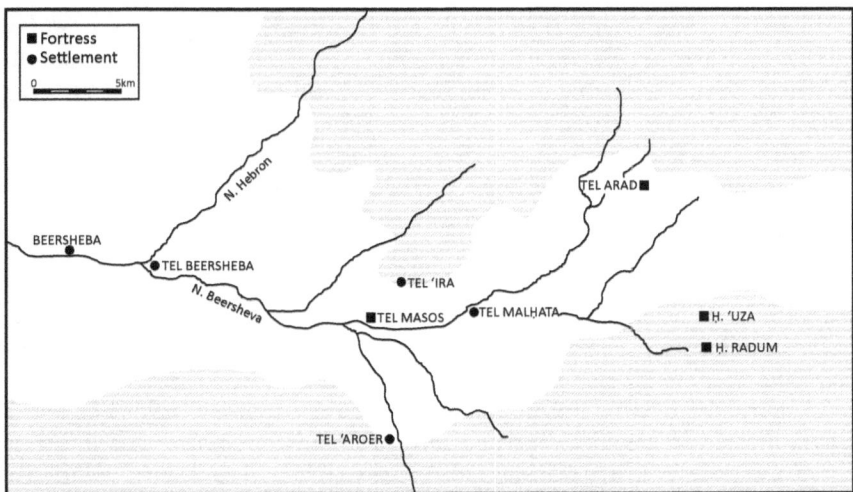

nique of writing (inked inscribed versus incised inscriptions), as well as their form and content.

TEL ARAD

Tel Arad is located in the eastern Beersheba Valley, about 30 km east-northeast of the modern city of Beersheba. It covers an area of about 2.5 dunams (4 dunams = 1 acre) and was fortified from the ninth century through the early sixth centuries BCE. Stratum XI represents the ninth-century fortress, Strata X–VIII the eighth-century one, and Strata VII–VI the seventh and early sixth-century one. Over a hundred Hebrew inscriptions were discovered at the site, comprising the largest corpus of inscriptions discovered so far in the kingdom of Judah.

To begin with, Aharoni ascribed six fragmented ink-inscribed ostraca and one incised inscription on the shoulder of a jug to Stratum XI (nos. 76–81, 93).[3] Assuming that his dating is accurate and these ostraca indeed originated from Stratum XI, they are the earliest discovered to date in the kingdom of Judah.

---

3. Yohanan Aharoni, *Arad Inscriptions*, JDS (Jerusalem: Israel Exploration Society, 1981), 98–101; Johannes Renz, *Die althebräischen Inschriften*. Part 1: *Text und Kommentar*, eds. Johannes Renz and Wolfgang Röllig, Handbuch der althebräischen Epigraphik, 1; Darmstadt: Wissenschaftliche Buchgesellschaft, 1995), 40–47.

Furthermore, about thirty-five ostraca (nos. 41–74, 87) and twelve incised inscriptions (nos. 89–92, 94–95, 98, 100–104) dated to the eighth century have been discovered at Arad, many of them in the temple and nearby area.[4] The ostraca are short, and most of them comprise administrative records recording personal names and numbers or symbols of commodities. A remarkable exception is no. 40, which is a long (fifteen lines) letter. Initially, Aharoni attributed the ostracon to Stratum VII, but in the final publication of the Arad inscriptions he ascribed it to Stratum VIII.[5] However, the ostracon is exceptional in the epigraphic corpus of Strata X–VIII and shares with no. 24 of Stratum VI its script, contents, and author's name (an officer named Malkiyahu). I therefore concur with Dobbs-Allsopp et al. that "this ostracon refers to the same general situation reflected in Arad 24."[6]

Lastly, over forty ink-inscribed ostraca (nos. 1–40, 88, 111) and a single incised inscription on a potsherd (no. 99) were discovered in Strata VII–VI at Arad. Clearly, incised inscriptions almost disappeared in the seventh century, and the local inhabitants mainly used ink for writing. Another remarkable new element is the appearance of letters of various lengths that are not attested in Strata X–VIII. Most of the letters were sent to Eliashib, the fortress commander (nos. 1–18, 24), and few others were dispatched to other officials (nos. 21, 40, 111).[7] Eliashib's surviving archive at Arad, which includes about nineteen letters and three personal seals,[8] is not an isolated find. Collections of bullae, which had originally belonged to small, private

---

4. Aharoni, *Arad Inscriptions*, 75–97, 102, 105–8, 110–11, 114–18; Renz, *Die althebräischen Inschriften*, 67–74, 111–22, 145–65.

5. Aharoni, *Arad Inscriptions*, 70–74 and n. 1.

6. Frederick W. Dobbs-Allsopp et al., *Hebrew Inscriptions: Texts from the Biblical Period of the Monarchy with Concordance* (New Haven: Yale University, 2005), 69–70; Nadav Na'aman, "Ostracon No. 40 from Arad Reconsidered," in *Saxa loquentur. Studien zur Archäologie Palästinas/Israels. Festschrift für Volkmar Fritz zum 65. Geburtstag*, ed. Cornelius G. den Hertog, Ulrich Hübner, and Stefan Münger, AOAT 302 (Münster: Ugarit-Verlag, 2003), 199.

7. For the Arad letters, see Aharoni, *Arad Inscriptions*, 11–38, 46–49, 70–74, 103–4; Anson F. Rainey, "Three Additional Texts," in Aharoni, *Arad Inscriptions*, 124–25; André Lemaire, *Inscriptions hébraïques*, vol. 1: *Les ostraca* (Paris: Cerf, 1977), 155–84, 188–95, 207–9, 220–21; Dennis Pardee, *Handbook of Ancient Hebrew Letters: A Study Edition* (Chico: Scholars, 1982), 24–67; Renz, *Die althebräischen Inschriften*, 353–93, 401–2; Dobbs-Allsopp et al., *Hebrew Inscriptions*, 5–41, 47–53, 69–74, 98–100, 106–7; Shmuel Aḥituv, *Echoes from the Past: Hebrew and Cognate Inscriptions from the Biblical Period. Selected and Annotated*, trans. A. F. Rainey (Jerusalem: Carta, 2008), 92–133, 142–45, 152–53; Stefan Wimmer, *Palästinisches Hieratisch: Die Zahl- und Sonderzeichen in der althebräischen Schrift*, ÄAT 75 (Wiesbaden: Harrassowitz, 2008), 26–59; Na'aman, "Eliashib's Archive," 83–93, with earlier literature.

8. Aharoni, *Arad Inscriptions*, 119–20.

archives and used to seal documents and which survived long after the papyri perished, were found in late seventh through early sixth century Judahite strata.[9] These lost archives, including the Ya'ush archive uncovered at the gate of Level II at Lachish,[10] are unattested in the kingdom of Judah before the latter half of the seventh century BCE and provide clear evidence for the spread of writing throughout the kingdom.

Beside the letters possibly sent to Arad from nearby places, the scribes operating in the fortress of Strata VII–VI produced administrative records with personal names and numbers or symbols of commodities (nos. 22–23, 25–39, 110, 112).

An exceptional inscription is no. 88, which deserves special attention. Several studies have already been dedicated to this unique ostracon, which I suggest restoring as follows:[11]

'ny mlkty bk[l 'šr 'wth npšy]
'mṣ zrʿ w[......... ky]
mlk mṣrym l[' yṣ' .....]

"I reigned over a[ll? that my heart? desired?]. Strengthen the arms and [.... for] the king of Egypt did n[ot? come out? ...]."

> Line 1: For the restoration, see 2 Sam 3:21; 1 Kgs 11:39: *wmlkt bkl 'šr t'wh npšk*, "you will reign over all that your heart desires."
>
> Line 2: After *'mṣ zrʿ* ("Strengthen the arms") we may expect a second encouraging expression like "and make your loins strong" or "and fortify your power mightily" (compare Nah 2:2; Ps 89:22; Prov 31:17).

My restoration of the inscription rests on the assumption that this is a copy of a royal letter, distributed among the secondary towns and for-

---

9. Yohanan Aharoni, *Investigations at Lachish. The Sanctuary and Residency (Lachish V)*, Publications of the Institute of Archaeology, 4 (Tel Aviv: Gateway, 1975), 19–22; Nahman Avigad, *Hebrew Bullae from the Time of Jeremiah: Remnants of Burnt Archive*, trans. R. Grafman (Jerusalem: Israel Exploration Society, 1986); Yair Shoham, "Hebrew Bullae" in *Excavations at the City of David 1978–1985 Directed by Yigal Shiloh*, vol. 6: *Inscriptions*, ed. Donald T. Ariel, Qedem 41 (Jerusalem: Hebrew University of Jerusalem, 2000), 29–57.

10. See recently Renz, *Die althebräischen Inschriften*, 405–37; Dobbs-Allsopp et al., *Hebrew Inscriptions*, 299–328; Aḥituv, *Echoes from the Past*, 56–88, with earlier literature.

11. For discussions of *Arad 88*, see Renz, *Die althebräischen Inschriften*, 302–4, with earlier literature; Dobbs-Allsopp et al., *Hebrew Inscriptions*, 98–100, with earlier literature; Simon B. Parker, "Did the Authors of the Books of Kings Make Use of Royal Inscriptions," *VT* 50 (2000): 364–65; André Lemaire, "Prophètes et rois dans les inscriptions ouest-sémitiques (ixe–vi^e siècle av. J.-C.)," in *Prophètes et rois: Bible et Proche-Orient*, ed. André Lemaire (Paris: Cerf, 2001), 111; Aḥituv, *Echoes from the Past*, 152–53.

tresses of the kingdom, Arad included. The king of Judah opens his letter with a statement that all is well with him. He then orders his commanders to strengthen their forces because the king of Egypt did not come out of his country to assist Judah against Babylonia. If this is indeed the case, the letter refers to Judah's rebellion against Babylonia and to the vain hope of the Judahite king (either Jehoiachin or Zedekiah) that Egypt would come to his aid. In this situation, the king orders his commanders to prepare for the impending Babylonian or Edomite assault and to fortify their places.

Based on the evidence of the ostraca from Lachish, I have previously described how official messages were spread among the commanders and officials of the kingdom of Judah and emphasized that the distribution of messages was confined to one topic: the spread of news about the current situation.[12] The Lachish ostraca are dated to the late monarchic period and illustrate the concrete situation on the eve of the kingdom's downfall. With all due caution, I suggest that no. 88 provides another example of the way messages relating to the current situation were distributed among the towns of Judah in the late monarchic period.

Horvat ʿUza (Khirbet Ghazzeh)

The fortress of Horvat ʿUza is located about 10 km southeast of the fortress of Arad, on the southeastern border of the Beersheba Valley. The site was excavated over the course of seven seasons and thirty-four inscriptions were unearthed in the excavations.[13] The fortress was surrounded by a wall and covers an area of about 2.1 dunams. As no eighth century pottery was discovered in the excavations and the site has only one stratum. Beit-Arieh concluded that it was built during the seventh century and destroyed by the Edomites in the early sixth century BCE.[14]

Except for two inscriptions written on a complete jar, all the inscriptions unearthed at Horvat ʿUza are ink-inscribed ostraca written on jar fragments. All ostraca were written in the Hebrew script, except for one that was written in the Edomite script. All the inscriptions uncovered in the fortress were distributed throughout the domestic quarter and the gate area, whereas no

---

12. Nadav Naʾaman, "The Distribution of Messages in the Kingdom of Judah in Light of the Lachish Ostraca," *VT* 53 (2003), 169–80.

13. Itzhaq Beit-Arieh, "Epigraphic Finds," in *Horvat ʿUza and Horvat Radum: Two Fortresses in the Biblical Negev*, ed. Itzhaq Beit-Arieh, Monograph Series of the Institute of Archaeology of Tel Aviv University, 25 (Tel Aviv: Institute of Archaeology, 2007), 122–87.

14. Itzhaq Beit-Arieh and Bruce C. Cresson, "Stratigraphy and Architecture," in Beit-Arieh, *Horvat ʿUza*, 15–29.

inscription was discovered in the partially excavated western side of the fortress.[15]

Horvat 'Uza was a Judahite border fortress that supervised the movement of people along the southeastern Negev-Aravah route. Travellers and caravans moving along this road must have passed the fortress and have left their mark on the documents unearthed at the site. Three inscriptions indicate this: a short letter left by a Judahite merchant to his agent/partner (no. 2),[16] a memorandum of a secret conversation held between the unnamed scribe and a person referred to by a Phoenician name (Ba'al-'amar), probably a merchant (no. 5),[17] and registration of the toll paid to a Judahite official (Ahiqam) by three Judahites, probably merchants, who lived in Moladah, Rptn and Makkedah (no. 10).[18] An Edomite ostracon, sent by a man named *lmlk* to *blbl*, probably his agent in the place (no. 7), supplies further evidence regarding the site's role on the road leading from Judah to Edom.[19]

Many ostraca are fragmentary and their original function cannot be established. A number of inscriptions include personal names and numbers or symbols of commodities recording the distribution of commodities to the personnel of the fortress (nos. 6, 11, 21, 22, 29, 34). Lists of persons and their parents were also written for some administrative purpose, although their exact function remains unknown (nos. 3, 4, 12, 14, 17, 18, 27, 28).

Two ink inscriptions discovered in the excavations were written on large fragments of an intact jar (nos. 23, 24).[20] The inscriptions record two hierarchical lists of officers who served at the fortress. Comparison of the two lists shows that many names are common to both, whereas some names appear only in one list. Since the inscriptions were written on an intact jar, about half of which has been restored, we can assume that the jar was in use in the last days of the fortress and the commanders list must have recorded the hierarchy of the officers serving in the fortress shortly before it was destroyed by the Edomites.

---

15. For the map of ostraca distribution, see Beit-Arieh, "Epigraphic Finds," 180.

16. For the interpretation of the ostracon, see Nadav Na'aman, "A New Look at the Epigraphic Finds from Horvat 'Uza," *TA* 39 (2012): 216–17.

17. For the interpretation of the ostracon, see Na'aman, "New Look," 217–18.

18. For the interpretation of the ostracon, see Na'aman, "New Look," 218–19.

19. For the interpretation of the Edomite ostracon, see Beit-Arieh, "Epigraphic Finds," 133–7; Aḥituv, *Echoes from the Past*, 350–54; Na'aman, "New Look," 214–16, with earlier literature.

20. Beit-Arieh, "Epigraphic Finds," 160–68; Dobbs-Allsopp et al., *Hebrew Inscriptions*, 527–36; Aḥituv, *Echoes from the Past*, 168–73; Na'aman, "New Look," 220–21, with earlier literature.

A unique ostracon was discovered in a small cell of the gatehouse's front room (no. 1).[21] It is written on the inside surface of a fragment of a late Iron Age burnished bowl. I previously dedicated a detailed study to this ostracon and will not repeat my conclusions here.[22] I posit that the genre of the composition is sapiential and that it shares with the biblical sapiential literature the motifs of the power of words, the danger of an offended ruler and the possible turn of a person's fortune. However, God does not play any role in the plot, and in this regard the composition differs considerably from the biblical sapiential literature. Similar literary works were probably written on perishable material (namely, papyrus) and did not survive. The text is an original work of the late First Temple period, and its preservation is a matter of sheer luck. The text provides a glimpse into the situation in Judah before the consumption of all perishable materials due to human and natural causes.

Horvat Radum (Khirbet Umm Redim)

Horvat Radum is located on the edge of a plateau, about 2.5 km southeast of Horvat 'Uza. It dominates the route leading from the latter fortress to the Aravah. The small fortress, covering an area of a half dunam (its inner dimension is 17.5 × 18.5 m), was excavated for a month in 1989. A wall surrounded the site, and a tower was built in its center. Its construction was dated to the second half of the seventh century and its destruction to the early sixth century BCE.[23]

Four ostraca were discovered in the fortress: one well preserved, recording a short list of names (no. 1) and the other three fragmentary and difficult to read.[24] At the beginning of line 2 of ostracon no. 2 appears a sign that is

---

21. Itzhaq Beit-Arieh, "A Literary Ostracon from Horvat 'Uza," *TA* 20 (1993): 55–63; idem, "Epigraphic Finds," 122–27; Frank Moore Cross, "A Suggested Reading of the Horvat 'Uza Ostracon," *TA* 20 (1993): 64–65; André Lemaire, "Épigraphie palestinienne: Nouveaux documents II – décennie 1985–1995," *Henoch* 17 (1995): 221–22; Graham Davies "Some Uses of Writing in Ancient Israel in the Light of Recently Published Inscriptions," in *Writing and Ancient Near Eastern Society: Papers in Honour of Alan R. Millard*, ed. Piotr Bienkowski, Christopher Mee, and Elizabeth Slater, LHBOTS 426 (London: T&T Clark, 2005), 157–58; Dobbs-Allsopp et al., *Hebrew Inscriptions*, 521–27; Aḥituv, *Echoes from the Past*, 173–77.

22. Nadav Na'aman, "A Sapiential Composition from Horvat 'Uza," *Hebrew Bible and Ancient Israel* 2 (2013): 221–33.

23. Itzhaq Beit-Arieh and Bruce C. Cresson, "Horvat Radum: Stratigraphy and Architecture," in Beit-Arieh, *Horvat 'Uza*, 303–17; Liora Freud, "Horvat Radum: Pottery and Small Finds," in Beit-Arieh, *Horvat 'Uza*, 318–22.

24. Itzhaq Beit-Arieh, "Horvat Radum: Epigraphic Finds," in Beit-Arieh, *Horvat 'Uza*, 323–26.

similar to the *bath*-signs in the Arad inscriptions. If this relationship indeed exists, the ostracon might have recorded distribution of wine jars.

TEL MALHATA (TELL EL-MILH)

Tel Malhata is located in the Beersheba Valley, about 20 km east of modern Beersheba and 10 km southwest of Tel Arad. The site was first excavated in the years 1967 and 1971[25] and again for seven excavation seasons in the years 1990 to 2000.[26] The mound covers an area of some 18 dunams, of which an area of about one dunam was excavated. The city of Stratum IV was built at the beginning of the eighth century BCE. It was fortified by a massive wall with an inner fortress in the southern part of the mound and was destroyed by the Assyrians in about 701 BCE. The city of Stratum III was rebuilt and fortified during the seventh century along the lines of the earlier city. It was utterly destroyed in the early sixth century, possibly by the Edomites, and was never again resettled as an urban center.

The inscriptions from Tel Malhata have not yet been published.[27] Liora Freund, who is currently working on the publication of the excavation report, kindly sent me the chapter on the Tel Malhata inscriptions that Prof. Itzhaq Beit Arieh wrote before his untimely death.[28] I did not consult photographs of the inscriptions, and my analysis rests on this chapter alone.

According to Beit-Arieh's report, eighteen diverse inscriptions have been uncovered in the Iron Age strata of Tel Malhata. Of this corpus, thirteen were ink-inscribed ostraca and five incised on potsherds. All the ostraca were fragmentary and faded, and four are illegible, with no more than scattered identifiable letters. All legible ostraca were written in the Edomite script (nos. 1–8), whereas five of the incised inscriptions were written in Hebrew. All the Edomite ostraca were uncovered in Stratum III (the seventh century BCE), and no ostracon is safely attributed to Stratum IV (a few ostraca whose loci is

---

25. Moshe Kochavi, "Malhata, Tel," *NEAEHL*, 3:934–36.
26. Itzhaq Beit-Arieh, "Malhata, Tel," in *NEAEHL* 5:1917–18; idem, "Excavations at Tell Malhata: An Interim Report," in *The Fire Signals of Lachish: Studies in the Archaeology and History of Israel in the Late Bronze Age, Iron Age, and Persian Period in Honor of David Ussishkin*, ed. Israel Finkelstein and Nadav Na'aman (Winona Lake, IN: Eisenbrauns, 2011), 17–32.
27. See Beit-Arieh, "Excavations at Tell Malhata," 28, 31; Itzhaq Beit-Arieh and Shmuel Aḥituv, "Half.quarter.*glt* – An Inscription from Tel Malhata," *Amnon Ben-Tor Volume*, ed. Joseph Aviram et al., ErIsr 30 (Jerusalem: Israel Exploration Society, 2011), 73–76 (Hebrew).
28. I wish to express my gratitude to Ms. Liora Freud for sharing with me the unpublished manuscript. Itzhaq Beit-Arieh ("Epigraphic Finds") and Ada Yardeni ("An Aramaic Ostracon") authored chapter 5.

insecure are attributed to Strata IV–III). One of the incised inscriptions (no. 17) is dated to the eighth century (Stratum IV), one to Stratum III (no. 16) and the loci of the others are insecure, but generally dated to Strata IV–III (nos. 14–15, 18).

The majority of the Edomite ostraca are administrative documents recording the numbers of people and names of fathers and their sons (nos. 2–3, 5–8). Five of them (nos. 3, 5–8) were discovered in a large pillared building of Stratum III, which must have functioned as a local administrative centre. One ostracon (no. 1) records five personal names, and another (no. 4) is a fragmentary letter. As far as I can determine, no ostracon records the distribution of commodities to the local inhabitants.

Tel ʿAroer (Khirbet ʿArʿara)

Tel ʿAroer is located about 22 km southeast of modern Beersheba and 8 km west-southwest of Tel Malhata, on a main road that led from the Beersheba Valley to the Aravah. The site was excavated in the years 1975–1982. Parts of the mound, as well as extramural buildings, were unearthed in the excavations.[29] The fortified site is located on a natural hill and covers an area of about 20 dunams. Of the three late Iron Age strata unearthed in the excavations, Stratum IV is dated to the eighth century and was destroyed in about 701. Strata III–II are dated to the seventh century, having been destroyed by the Edomites in the early sixth century BCE.

The excavations yielded four Hebrew ostraca, two Hebrew incised sherds, one Edomite ostracon and two south Arabian incised inscriptions.[30] Two of the Hebrew ostraca include one word: a personal name *pšḥr* (Pashḥur) and the letters *qr*. The two others are fragmentary and incomprehensible.[31]

---

29. Avraham Biran, "Aroer (in Judea)," *NEAEHL* 1:89–92; Yifat Thareani, *Tel ʿAroer: The Iron Age II Caravan Town and the Hellenistic–Early Roman Settlement. The Avraham Biran (1975–1982) and Rudolph Cohen (1975–1976) Excavations*, Annual of the Nelson Glueck School of Biblical Archaeology/Hebrew Union College–Jewish Institute of Religion 8 (Jerusalem: Nelson Glueck School of Biblical Archaeology, 2011).

30. Avraham Biran and Rudolph Cohen, "Aroer, 1977," *IEJ* 27 (1977): 251 and pl. 38; André Lemaire, "Notes d'épigraphie nord-ouest Sémitique," *Semitica* 30 (1980): 19–20; Renz, *Die althebräischen Inschriften*, 165–66, with earlier literature; Yifat Thareani, "Hebrew Inscriptions," in Thareani, *Tel ʿAroer*, 223–24, with earlier literature; Joseph Naveh, "An Edomite Inscription," in Thareani, *Tel ʿAroer*, 227; Nahman Avigad and Benjamin Sass, "South Arabian Inscriptions," in Thareani, *Tel ʿAroer*, 228.

31. Renz (*Die althebräischen Inschriften*, 14, 165–66) erroneously dated the ostraca from Tel ʿAroer to the second half of the eighth century. Most of the ostraca from the Beersheba Valley, including the two dated ostraca from Tel ʿAroer, are to be dated to the seventh century. The undated ostraca from Tel ʿAroer should also be dated to the same era.

The four-line Edomite ostracon is incomprehensible. Two of the four ostraca are dated to the late seventh or early sixth century (Stratum IIA), and the loci of two others are unknown. One incised inscription is dated to the early seventh century (Stratum III), and the second is undated.

TEL MASOS (KHIRBET EL-MSHASH)

Tel Masos is located in the Beersheba Valley, about 12 km east of modern Beersheba and 6 km west of Tel Malhata. A small late Iron Age fortress was discovered in a small mound located about 200 m from the main Iron I–IIA site. The excavators observed four building phases, but since the site is badly eroded, it was difficult to estimate the area of the fortress and the nature of its fortifications.[32]

Three Hebrew ostraca were found in the fortress and a fourth in the nearby site. Two ostraca are illegible, and the two others (nos. 1, 3) record four and five personal names respectively, mostly alongside the names of their parents.[33] The line ends of both ostraca are missing; hence, it is unclear whether numbers or commodity symbols accompanied the personal names.

TEL 'IRA (KHIRBET GHARRA)

Tel 'Ira is located on a spur of the Hebron hills that overlooks the Beersheba Valley, about 3 km northeast of Tel Masos and 4 km northwest of Tel Malhata.[34] The 25-dunam site is located on a high hill and is surrounded on all sides by a 1.60- to 1.80-m-high wall. Stratum VII is dated to the eighth century and was partly destroyed in about 701 BCE.[35] The city of Stratum

---

32. Hartmut N. Rösel, "Die Architektur," in *Ergebnisse der Ausgrabungen auf der Khirbet el-Mšāš (Tel Māśōś) 1972–1975. Part 1: Textband*, ed. Volkmar Fritz and Aharon Kempinski, Abhandlungen des Deutschen Palästinavereins (Wiesbaden: Harrassowitz, 1983), 123–26; Orna Zimhoni, "The Pottery," in Fritz and Kempinski, *Khirbet el-Mšāš*, 127–29.

33. For Tel Masos inscriptions, see Volkmar Vritz, "Die Ostraka," in Fritz, and Kempinski, *Khirbet el-Mšāš*, 133–37; Renz, *Die althebräischen Inschriften*, 334–36; Dobbs-Allsopp et al., *Hebrew Inscriptions*, 377–79; Ahituv, *Echoes from the Past*, 164–65.

34. Itzhaq Beit-Arieh, "'Ira, Tel," NEAEHL 2:642–66; id., *Tel 'Ira: A Stronghold in the Biblical Negev*, Monograph Series of the Institute of Archaeology of Tel Aviv University 15 (Tel Aviv: Institute of Archaeology, 1999).

35. For dating Stratum VII at Tel 'Ira to the eighth century BCE, see Lily Singer-Avitz, "Beersheba–A Gateway Community in Southern Arabian Long-Distance Trade in the Eighth Century BCE," *TA* 26 (1999), 56; idem, "Arad: The Iron Age Pottery Assemblages," *TA* 29 (2002), 159, 182.

VI was rebuilt in the seventh century and was entirely destroyed in the early sixth century BCE.

Three ink-inscribed ostraca and four incised sherds have been discovered in the excavations.[36] The incised sherds, all consisting of one word (apparently personal names), were discovered in Stratum VII. One ostracon discovered outside the city wall is a fragmented letter,[37] and a second, ascribed to Stratum VI, is an ink jar label with the names of a person and his father.[38]

A third four-line ostracon, ascribed to Strata VII–VI, opens with the words *mpqd brkyhw* (line 1) and is followed by three personal names (lines 2–4).[39] Scholars transliterated the first word *mipqād* and translated line 1 as either "roll call: Berachiah" or "muster of Berachiah."[40] However, a census/muster always includes many people, which does not fit the short list of three/four men. I suggest rendering line 1 *mupqād brkyhw*, "incumbent: Berachiah." Compare 2 Chr 34:12: "Over them was set (*mupqād*) Jahath and Obadiah the Levites." See also 2 Kgs 12:12; 22:5, 9; 2 Chr 34:10, 17. An identical structure appeared at Horvat 'Uza no. 10: the headline "Paid to Ahiqam, son of Meshulam" is placed on top, and the names of the three persons who paid him are written below.[41] Ostracon no. 1 records that Berachiah was in charge of the three persons, whose names are registered in lines 2–4.

---

36. Beit-Arieh, "The Hebrew Inscriptions," in Beit-Arieh, *Tel 'Ira*, 402–11.

37. Beit-Arieh, "Hebrew Inscriptions," 405–6; Dobbs-Allsopp et al., *Hebrew Inscriptions*, 199.

38. Beit-Arieh, "Hebrew Inscriptions," 406–7; Dobbs-Allsopp et al., *Hebrew Inscriptions*, 199–200.

39. The published photograph does not support Demsky's rendering *mpqd* in line 3. The second letter differs from the /p/ in line 1 and the fourth letter is /r/, as indicated by its comparison to the /r/ and /d/ in line 1. See Aaron Demsky, "The MPQD Ostracon from Tel 'Ira: A New Reading," *BASOR* 345 (2007): 33–38. Demsky was followed by Aḥituv, *Echoes from the Past*, 179–80.

40. Itzhaq Beit-Arieh, "A First Temple Census Document," *PEQ* 115 (1983): 105–8; idem, "Hebrew Inscriptions," 402–5; Avigdor Hurowitz, "How Were the Israelites Counted? Numbers 1:2 and the Like in the Light of a New Inscription from Tel 'Ira," *Beer-Sheva* 3 (1988): 59–61 (Hebrew); Baruch A. Levine, "'The Lord Your God Accept You' (2 Samuel 24:23): The Altar Erected by David on the Threshing Floor of Araunah," ErIsr 24 (*Avraham Malamat Volume*) (Jerusalem: Israel Exploration Society, 1993), 124–25 (Hebrew); Renz, *Die althebräischen Inschriften*, 252; Dobbs-Allsopp et al., *Hebrew Inscriptions*, 197–98. Yosef Garfinkel ("The Meaning of the Word *MPQD* in the Tel 'Ira Ostracon," *PEQ* 119 [1987], 19–23) translated it "guard."

41. Na'aman, "New Look," 218–19.

Tel Beersheba (Tell es-Seba')

Tel Beersheba is located near the confluence of Nahal Hebron (Wadi Khalîl) to Nahal Beersheba (Wadi Seba'), about 4 km east-northeast of the modern city of Beersheba. Although the city was already constructed in the Iron Age 1, inscriptions were discovered only in Stratum II, dating to the late eighth century BCE. At that time, Tel Beersheba was a fortified, well-planned royal city that covered an area of 11.5 dunams and functioned as the major administrative centre of the Negev district. Stratum II was destroyed by the Assyrians in about 701 BCE and following that destruction, it was abandoned for hundreds of years.[42]

Three ink-inscribed ostraca and six incised inscriptions on complete pots and sherds have been discovered in the excavations.[43] The incised sherds included only one or two words, which designated either the owners, the function ("sacred") or the capacity of the vessel ("one-half royal jar").[44] Of the three ink-inscribed ostraca, ostraca no. 1 and 2 recorded the distribution of commodities and the third denoted the contents of a jar ("wheat").

Beersheba (Bīr es-Seba')

Biblical Beersheba is probably located in Bīr es-Saba', about 4 km southwest of Tel Beersheba.[45] As the Iron Age city is buried under the ruins of the Roman–Byzantine and the debris of the recent city, it was discovered in only

---

42. Yohanan Aharoni (ed.), *Beer-sheba I. Excavations at Tel Beer-Sheba 1969–1971 Seasons*, Publications of the Institute of Archaeology 2 (Tel Aviv University: Institute of Archaeology, 1973); Ze'ev Herzog et al., "The Israelite Fortress at Arad," *BASOR* 254 (1984): 1–34; Ze'ev Herzog, "Tel Beer-sheba," *NEAEHL* 1:167–73.
43. Yohanan Aharoni, "The Hebrew Inscriptions," in Aharoni, *Beer-sheba I*, 71–77; Lemaire, *Inscriptions hébraïques*, 271–73; Renz, *Die althebräischen Inschriften*, 232–40; Dobbs-Allsopp et al., *Hebrew Inscriptions*, 115–23; Wimmer, *Palästinisches Hieratisch*, 59–60.
44. For the label ḥṣy lmlk, see recently Oded Lipschits, et al., "The Enigma of the Biblical Bath and the System of Liquid Volume Measurement during the First Temple Period," *UF* 42 (2010): 453–78, esp. 456–57.
45. Albrecht Alt, "Beiträge zur historischen Geographie und Topographie des Negeb: III. Saruhen, Ziklag, Horma, Gerar," *JPOS* 15 (1935): 318–23; Nadav Na'aman, "The Inheritance of the Sons of Simeon," *ZDPV* 96 (1980): 149–51, with earlier literature; Volkmar Fritz, *Das Buch Josua*, HAT I/7 (Tübingen: Mohr, 1994), 163, 165, 186, 253; Shmuel Aḥituv, *Joshua. Introduction and Commentary*, Mikra Leyisra'el (Tel Aviv: Am Oved and Jerusalem: Magnes, 1995), 256 (Hebrew). For a different opinion, see Nava Panitz-Cohen, "A Salvage Excavation in the New Market in Beer-sheba: New Light on Iron Age IIB Occupation at Beer-sheba," *IEJ* 55 (2005): 143–55.

few places.[46] To date, no inscription dated to the late Iron Age was discovered in the excavations.

Ostraca versus Incised Inscriptions in Ninth- to Early Sixth-Century Judah

Whereas the differences in scope and quality of the inscriptions written in Judah in the eighth century in comparison to those written in the seventh and early sixth century have been observed by many scholars, no discussion has emerged to date regarding differences between cities and fortresses. This is due in part to the fact that the latter requires a detailed comparison of a sufficiently reliable amount of data obtained from the two kinds of sites. Such a comparative analysis can only be undertaken with regard to the Beersheba Valley: the sole district where enough sites of both kinds have been excavated.

As noted earlier, in analyzing the results of the above textual survey, we must keep in mind that scribes usually wrote on papyri, and all such writings are unavailable for research. The ink writing on papyrus gradually accelerated over the course of the ninth through seventh centuries and secondarily applied also to potsherds.[47] Scribes and clerks realized the great advantage of writing with ink and started applying this method to all kinds of cheaper surfaces (plaster, stone and pottery). Thus, in the seventh century, ink writing gradually replaced the incision on sherds. Unfortunately, the available data from the Negev district (and the Shephelah as well) is derived from only two snapshots, those of the years 701 and 587; hence, the pace of shift over the course of the seventh century cannot be reconstructed.

Except for the thirty-five ostraca discovered in the eighth century fortress of Arad, only Tel Beersheba produced three eighth-century ostraca. All other eighth century Negev and Shephelah sites produced only incised inscriptions. Moreover, eighth century Arad is the only site where the number of discovered ostraca (35) is much higher compared to the number of incised inscriptions (12). Clearly, the widespread writing with ink on potsherds did not antedate the seventh century BCE.

---

46. Ram Gophna and Yael Yisraeli, "Soundings at Beer-Sheva (Bir es-Seba')," in Aharoni (ed.), *Beer-sheba I*, 115–8; Panitz-Cohen, "Salvage Excavation," 143–52.

47. For the late ninth–early eighth-century bullae with a print of papyrus on the backside discovered in the rock-cut chamber near the Spring of Gihon in Jerusalem, see Ronny Reich, Eli Shukron, and Omri Lernau, "Recent Discoveries in the City of David, Jerusalem," *IEJ* 47 (2007): 157–60, 163.

In contrast to the eighth century, in most seventh and early sixth century sites, incised inscriptions either disappeared completely or are attested in small numbers and ink-inscribed ostraca took their place. Thus, for example, no incised inscription was discovered at Horvat ʻUza, Horvat Radum, and Tel Masos—the three sites that were abandoned in the ninth through eighth centuries and settled during the seventh century. In Strata VII–VI at Arad, forty-two ostraca but only one incised inscription were discovered. In other sites, most of the incised inscriptions are dated to the eighth century and the ostraca to the seventh and early sixth century. However, the date of some ostraca and incised inscriptions is insecure, and these were assigned to the eighth and seventh centuries. For example, nine ostraca from Tel Malhata have been dated to the seventh and early sixth century, and the date of four others is insecure. Moreover, of the five incised inscriptions unearthed in the site, one dates to the eighth century, one to the seventh and early sixth century, and the date of the other three is insecure. At Tel ʻIra, all four incised inscriptions date to the eighth century, one ostracon dates to the seventh and early sixth century, and the date of the two others is insecure.

In sum, given the influence of writing with ink on papyrus, the practice of writing with ink on potsherds became the dominant mode of writing in the Negev in the seventh century and almost entirely replaced the incision on potsherds. In this light, we may assume that most if not all the ostraca whose date is insecure were written in the seventh and early sixth century; and conversely, most of the incised inscriptions whose date is insecure were written in the eighth century.

The fortress of Arad is exceptional not only in the Negev, but also among all major cities of Judah, in respect to its number of inscriptions and mode of writing. Assuming that Aharoni's attribution of the inscriptions unearthed at Arad to the various strata is correct, ink-inscribed inscriptions were written in the site already in the second half of the ninth century (Stratum XI). A first ninth century incised inscription was recently discovered in the excavations of the City of David,[48] but the earliest ostraca unearthed there are dated to no earlier than the late eighth century BCE (see below). Renz dated the one-word inscriptions (ḥmš) on three jugs from Eshtemoaʻ to the ninth century.[49] However, Kletter and Brand, who discussed in detail the jugs and the inscriptions, dated them to the eighth century.[50] Thus, the six ink-inscribed ostraca

---

48. Eilat Mazar, David Ben-Shlomo, and Shmuel Aḥituv, "An Inscribed Pithos from the Ophel of Jerusalem," *IEJ* 63 (2013): 39–49.

49. Renz, *Die althebräischen Inschriften*, 65–66.

50. Raz Kletter and Etty Brand, "A New Look at the Iron Age Silver Hoard from Eshtemoa," *PEQ* 114 (1998): 139–54.

discovered in Stratum XI at Arad antedate by more than a century all other ostraca discovered to date in the kingdom of Judah.

Arad is also exceptional when comparing the number of eighth century ostraca unearthed there to other contemporaneous Judahite sites. As against its thirty-five eighth century ostraca, no ostracon was found in the large-scale excavations conducted so far in the Shephelah (Lachish, Tell Beit Mirsim, Tel Halif, Beth-shemesh).[51] Four ostraca unearthed in Jerusalem were dated to the late eighth century.[52] However, none of these ostraca were found in a secure locus, and the date rests only on paleographic considerations. Thus, except for Arad and the three ostraca from Tel Beersheba, all other ostraca unearthed to date in the kingdom of Judah are dated no earlier than the late eighth or early seventh century BCE.

How should we explain the relatively wide-scale writing with ink on ostraca at Arad in the ninth–eighth centuries BCE? The answer should be sought in the importance of the fortress to the kings of Judah and the presence of royal scribes in the place since its foundation in the ninth century (Stratum XI). The scribes dispatched to Arad were used to writing with ink on papyrus and applied this tradition to writing on potsherds. Whether other royal scribes also applied ink writing to potsherds remains unknown. If indeed they did, the ostraca they wrote might have been dispersed all over the much larger sites where they officiated and have not been found.

Ink-inscribed writing spread in the kingdom of Judah in the seventh century, and is attested in sites all over the country. Ostraca have been discovered in all seventh through early sixth-century Negevite sites excavated so far (except for Beersheba, whose excavation was more limited). And yet, the number of ostraca discovered in the fortresses of Arad (42) and Horvat

---

51. Scholars dated the recently published nonprovenienced ostraca, allegedly excavated in the Shephelah sites, to the late seventh and early sixth century. See, e.g., Robert Deutsch and Michael Heltzer, *New Epigraphic Evidence from the Biblical Period* (Tel Aviv-Jaffa: Archaeological Center Publication, 1995), 81–102; André Lemaire, "Nouvelles données épigraphiques sur l'époque royale Israélite," *REJ* 156 (1997): 456–61; Reinhard G. Lehmann, "Typologie und Signatur. Studien zu einem Listenostrakon aus der Sammlung Moussaieff," *UF* 30 (1998): 397–459; id., "Quatre nouveaux ostraca paléohébreux," *Semitica* 54 (2012): 33–49; Aḥituv, *Echoes from the Past*, 180–207, with earlier literature; André Lemaire and Ada Yardeni, "New Hebrew Ostraca from the Shephelah," in *Biblical Hebrew in Its Northwest Semitic Setting: Typological and Historical Perspectives*, ed. Steven E. Fassberg and Avi Hurvitz (Jerusalem: Magnes; Winona Lake, IN: Eisenbrauns, 2006), 197–223; Martin Heide, "Ein 27-zeiliges Listenostrakon aus der Sammlung Shlomo Moussaieff," *UF* 39 (2007) 399–412.

52. Nahman Avigad, "Excavations in the Jewish Quarter of the Old City of Jerusalem, 1971 (Third Preliminary Report)," *IEJ* 22 (1972): 195–96; André Lemaire, "Les ostraca paléo-hébreux des fouilles de l'Ophel," *Levant* 10 (1978): 156–61; Renz, *Die althebräischen Inschriften*, 194–98; Dobbs-Allsopp et al., *Hebrew Inscriptions*, 212–18, 240–43.

'Uza (34) considerably outnumbered that of other, much larger Negevite centers. Even the small fortresses of Horvat Radum (4) and Tel Masos (4) produced a similar number of ostraca to that of the much larger towns of Tel 'Aroer (5) and Tel 'Ira (3). Tel Malhata produced thirteen ostraca, nine of which are Edomite, and falls short compared to the number of ostraca unearthed at Arad and Horvat 'Uza. It is thus evident that ink-writing on ostraca in the Negev was mainly confined to fortresses and only secondarily took place in the central cities.

How can we explain the different numbers of ostraca found in fortresses versus cities? The answer must be sought in the dissimilar functions of these two types of sites. Some of the fortresses' inhabitants were officials and soldiers whose maintenance and/or salary was paid by the state. Hence, commodities of various kinds, as well as salary paid in silver/copper, were regularly distributed among the state's employees and registered by the royal administration. Although irregular distribution of commodities and payment to workers also took place in the cities, much fewer such payments took place in urban areas and the inscriptions recording these transactions were probably scattered throughout the cities' areas (which are by far larger than those of the fortresses). To save expenses, the royal scribes in the fortresses used potsherds, the cheapest writing material available. The registration on sherds was probably provisional, and occasionally the total amount was summarized on papyrus and the sherds discarded.[53] This practice explains the provisional nature of the ostraca discovered in the Negevite fortresses.

In addition, we should note the royal temple built in Arad Stratum X and destroyed at the end of Stratum VIII. Various ostraca discovered in Strata X–VIII were discovered in the temple and its vicinity and were probably written as part of the administration of the temple and the maintenance of the priests and other personnel.[54]

The military-administrative role of the fortresses and the practice of provisional writing on potsherds before summarizing the text on papyrus might explain the relatively large number of ostraca discovered there. For functions other than regular payments and distribution of commodities, the royal and temple administration, the local scribes and the elite used papyrus—as indicated by the many bullae recently discovered in Judahite cities, in particular Jerusalem.[55] The more extensive writing on perishable material in cities as

---

53. Lemaire, *Inscriptions hébraïques*, 230–31; Na'aman, "Eliashib's Archive," 88.
54. Aharoni, *Arad Inscriptions*, 148–49; Lemaire, *Inscriptions hébraïques*, 227–28.
55. The growth in number of the bullae recently discovered in archaeological excavations is the result of the careful sifting, including wet sifting, practiced lately at excavations. It is clear now that almost all the small artifacts have been lost in the past, due to the inappropriate technique of sifting used in the excavations. The careful sifting taking

against the provisional writing on potsherds in the fortresses might account for the lesser number of ostraca discovered in the central cities of the Negev in the late monarchic period.

The Extent of Literacy in the Negev in the Late Monarchic Period

As noted in the introduction, we must clearly delineate between a basic knowledge of the alphabet and the ability to read and write short texts on the one hand, and the skill to write and understand long, sophisticated texts and literary works, on the other. Lines 4–13 of Lachish 3, a letter sent by Hosha'yah, a local official who served in the Shephelah, to Ya'ush, Lachish's commander, indicate the difference between these skill levels:[56]

> "And now, open the ear of your servant concerning the letter you sent to your servant last night, because the heart of your servant has been sick ever since you sent (it) to your servant, and because my lord said: 'You did not understand it. Call a scribe!' By the life of YHWH, no one has tried to read a letter to me – ever! Moreover, any letter that comes to me, if I have read it, I can afterwards repeat it to the last detail!"

Hosha'yah mentions a letter that he has just received from Ya'ush, in which the latter rebuked him for not understanding an earlier letter he had sent him and suggests that he should use the service of an expert scribe. In answering the accusation, Hosha'yah swears that he can read fluently and does not need the mediation of a scribe. Moreover, he is able to repeat to the last detail the words of each letter he has read.

The lesson learned from Hosha'yah's letter is that understanding all nuances of a text and being able to repeat them verbally form the watershed between a skilled scribe and a person who might be able to decipher letters and identify words and sentences but does not fully understand their meaning. In light of this example, what might have been the skill level of those who wrote the inscriptions discovered in the Beersheba Valley?

Most of the discovered texts in the fortresses are short and basic, written as part of daily life (that is, lists of personal names, simple administrative texts, short notes, etc.), and fall short of the criterion referred to in the Lach-

---

place in recent years brought about a dramatic rise in the number of bullae discovered in the excavations.

56. For translation, see Dobbs-Allsopp et al., *Hebrew Inscriptions*, 309. For discussion, see Na'aman, "Distribution of Messages," 177–78.

ish letter. Certain ostraca were written in clear cursive handwriting and might have reflected a higher level of literacy compared to others written in a less-skilled handwriting.[57] But it is risky to draw conclusions about scribal education on the basis of handwriting alone.

As suggested above, state officials must have written many of the inscriptions, and in particular the ostraca unearthed in the fortresses. As the Negev was a marginal district and administration of the fortresses required the skill to write administrative texts and letters, the scribes working there might not have been of the first class, but rather clerks, the kind of literate officials and officers that the biblical text calls *šōṭᵉrîm*.[58] However, eighth-century Arad (Strata X–VIII) had a royal temple, which required the office of priests and administrators. Holding these cultic and scribal posts required higher education than that of a clerk and possibly indicates that expert scribes served in the fortress in the ninth–eighth centuries.

In sum, the relatively large number of ostraca discovered in the Negev fortresses indicates that at least some scribes with basic scribal skill worked there. However, as the inscriptions available for research are the secondary products of scribal activity and the major scribal products have perished, the picture drawn from these artefacts might be misleading. In particular in the late seventh through early sixth centuries when alphabetical writing spread throughout all districts of the kingdom, scribes might have obtained a higher level of education. This conclusion might be inferred from the discovery of the sapiential composition at Horvat ʿUza, which was probably composed by a local scribe and reflects a high degree of literacy.[59] The same able scribe probably produced some of the ostraca discovered in the gate area, but it is only this unique composition that indicates his scribal skill. Otherwise, we would assume that a clerk who lacks high scribal education wrote the ostraca.

Finally, what might have been the ability of the middle-class inhabitants of the Negev to read and write short, basic texts? I concur with scholars who suggest that soldiers of low rank and low-class citizens were illiterate and that a higher degree of literacy was common among priests and high royal

---

57. Anat Mendel, "Who Wrote the Aḥiqam Ostracon from Horvat ʿUza?" *IEJ* 61 (2011): 57.

58. The *šōṭēr* was an official whose education included the ability to read and write. See: J. van der Ploeg, "Les *šōṭᵉrim* d'Israel," *OTS* 10 (1954): 185–96; Michael Heltzer, "Some Considerations about Hebrew *šōṭēr* and Punic *mšṭr*," *AuOr* 2 (1984): 225–30; Udo Rütersworden, *Die Beamten der israelitischen Königszeit: Eine Studie zu śr und vergleichbaren Begriffen* (Stuttgart: Kohlhammer, 1985), 109–11; Nili S. Fox, *In the Service of the King. Officialdom in Ancient Israel and Judah*, Monographs of the Hebrew Union College 23 (Cincinnati: Hebrew Union College, 2000), 192–96.

59. Naʾaman, "Sapiential Composition," 221–33.

officials and commanders.⁶⁰ But what about the population between these two extremes? The question might be discussed only in the context of sites in which large numbers of inscriptions have been discovered and the distribution of the inscriptions within the site is known. To date, such a distribution map was published only in the excavation report of Horvat 'Uza. The map shows that many inscriptions were discovered in the domestic part of the fortress.⁶¹ The distribution enables the assumption that at least some of the inscriptions were written by the local inhabitants who lived in the domestic quarter of the fortress. But this is the most we can infer. Many more inscriptions are required in order to arrive at a more detailed understanding of literacy in the Negev in the seventh and early sixth centuries BCE.

References

Aharoni, Yohanan. *Arad Inscriptions*. Judean Desert Studies. Jerusalem: Israel Exploration Society, 1981.

———. *Beer-sheba I. Excavations at Tel Beer-Sheba 1969–1971 Seasons*. Publications of the Institute of Archaeology 2. Tel Aviv University: Institute of Archaeology, 1973.

———. "The Hebrew Inscriptions." Pages 71–77 in *Beer-sheba I. Excavations at Tel Beer-Sheba 1969–1971 Seasons*. Edited by Yohanan Aharoni. Publications of the Institute of Archaeology 2. Tel Aviv University: Institute of Archaeology, 1973.

———. *Investigations at Lachish. The Sanctuary and Residency* (Lachish V). Publications of the Institute of Archaeology 4. Tel Aviv: Gateway, 1975.

Ahituv, Shmuel. *Echoes from the Past: Hebrew and Cognate Inscriptions from the Biblical Period. Selected and Annotated*. Translated by Anson F. Rainey. Jerusalem: Carta, 2008.

———. *Joshua. Introduction and Commentary*. Mikra Leyisra'el. Tel Aviv: Am Oved, and Jerusalem: Magnes, 1995. (Hebrew).

Alt, Albrecht. "Beiträge zur historischen Geographie und Topographie des Negeb: III. Saruhen, Ziklag, Horma, Gerar." *JPOS* 15 (1935): 294–324.

Avigad, Nahman. "Excavations in the Jewish Quarter of the Old City of Jerusalem, 1971. Third Preliminary Report." *IEJ* 22 (1972): 193–200.

———. *Hebrew Bullae from the Time of Jeremiah: Remnants of Burnt Archive*. Translated by Raphael Grafman. Jerusalem: Israel Exploration Society, 1986.

Avigad, Nahman, and Benjamin Sass. "South Arabian Inscriptions." Page 228 in

---

60. Young, "Israelite Literacy," 239–53, 408–22; Carr, *Writing on the Tablet of the Heart*, 111–22, 161–7; Rollston, *Writing and Literacy*, 127–35; see also Ian Young, "Israelite Literacy and Inscriptions: A Response to Richard Hess," *VT* 55 (2005): 565–68; David M. Carr, "Response to W. M. Schniedewind, How the Bible Became a Book: The Textualization of Ancient Israel," *JHS* 5 (2005): article 18; Seth L. Sanders, *The Invention of Hebrew* (Urbana: University of Illinois Press, 2009), 143–47.

61. For the map of ostraca distribution, see Beit-Arieh, "Epigraphic Finds," 180.

Tel 'Aroer: The Iron Age II Caravan Town and the Hellenistic–Early Roman Settlement. The Avraham Biran (1975–1982) and Rudolph Cohen (1975–1976) Excavations. Edited by Yifat Thareani. Jerusalem: Nelson Glueck School of Biblical Archaeology, 2011.
Beit-Arieh, Itzhaq. "Epigraphic Finds." Pages 122–87 in *Horvat 'Uza and Horvat Radum: Two Fortresses in the Biblical Negev*. Edited by Itzhaq Beit-Arieh. Monograph Series of the Institute of Archaeology of Tel Aviv University 25. Tel Aviv: Institute of Archaeology, 2007.
———. "Excavations at Tell Malhata: An Interim Report." Pages 17–32 in *The Fire Signals of Lachish: Studies in the Archaeology and History of Israel in the Late Bronze Age, Iron Age, and Persian Period in Honor of David Ussishkin*. Edited by Israel Finkelstein and Nadav Na'aman. Winona Lake: Eisenbrauns, 2011.
———. "A First Temple Census Document." *PEQ* 115 (1983): 105–8.
———. "Horvat Radum: Epigraphic Finds." Pages 323–26 in *Horvat 'Uza and Horvat Radum: Two Fortresses in the Biblical Negev*. Edited by Itzhaq Beit-Arieh. Monograph Series of the Institute of Archaeology of Tel Aviv University. Tel Aviv: Institute of Archaeology, 2007.
———. "'Ira, Tel." *NEAEHL* 2:642–46.
———. "A Literary Ostracon from Horvat 'Uza." *TA* 20 (1993): 55–63.
———. "Malhata, Tel." *NEAEHL* 5:1917–18.
———. *Tel 'Ira: A Stronghold in the Biblical Negev*. Monograph Series of the Institute of Archaeology of Tel Aviv University 15. Tel Aviv: Institute of Archaeology, 1999.
Beit-Arieh, Itzhaq, and Shmuel Aḥituv. "Half.quarter.*glt* – An Inscription from Tel Malhata." Pages 73–76 in *Amnon Ben-Tor Volume*. Edited by Joseph Aviram et. al. ErIsr 30. Jerusalem: Israel Exploration Society, 2011. (Hebrew).
Beit-Arieh, Itzhaq, and Bruce C. Cresson. "Horvat Radum: Stratigraphy and Architecture." Pages 303–17 in *Horvat 'Uza and Horvat Radum: Two Fortresses in the Biblical Negev*. Edited by Itzhaq Beit-Arieh. Tel Aviv: Institute of Archaeology, 2007.
———. "Stratigraphy and Architecture." Pages 15–29 in *Horvat 'Uza and Horvat Radum: Two Fortresses in the Biblical Negev*. Edited by Itzhaq Beit-Arieh. Tel Aviv: Institute of Archaeology, 2007.
Biran, Avraham. "Aroer (in Judea.)" *NEAEHL* 1:89–92.
Biran, Avraham, and Rudolph Cohen. "Aroer, 1977." *IEJ* 27 (1977): 250–51.
Carr, David M. "Response to W. M. Schniedewind, How the Bible Became a Book: The Textualization of Ancient Israel." *JHS* 5 (2005): article 18.
———. *Writing on the Tablet of the Heart: Origins of Scripture and* Literature. Oxford: Oxford University Press, 2005.
Cross, Frank Moore. "A Suggested Reading of the Horvat 'Uza Ostracon." *TA* 20 (1993): 64–65.
Davies, Graham. "Some Uses of Writing in Ancient Israel in the Light of Recently Published Inscriptions." Pages 155–74 in *Writing and Ancient Near Eastern Society: Papers in Honour of Alan R. Millard*. Edited by Piotr Bienkowski, Christopher Mee, and Elizabeth Slater. Library of Hebrew Bible/Old Testament Studies 426. London: T&T Clark, 2005.

Demsky, Aaron. "The MPQD Ostracon from Tel 'Ira: A New Reading." *BASOR* 345 (2007): 33–38.
Deutsch, Robert, and Michael Heltzer. *New Epigraphic Evidence from the Biblical Period*. Tel Aviv-Jaffa: Archaeological Center Publication, 1995.
Dobbs-Allsopp, Frederick W., Jimmy J. M. Roberts, Choon L. Seow, and Robert E. Whitaker. *Hebrew Inscriptions: Texts from the Biblical Period of the Monarchy with Concordance*. New Haven: Yale University Press, 2005.
Fox, Nili S. *In the Service of the King. Officialdom in Ancient Israel and Judah*. Monographs of the Hebrew Union College 23. Cincinnati: Hebrew Union College, 2000.
Freud, Liora. "Horvat Radum: Pottery and Small Finds." Pages 318–22 in *Horvat 'Uza and Horvat Radum: Two Fortresses in the Biblical Negev*. Edited by Itzhaq Beit-Arieh. Tel Aviv: Institute of Archaeology, 2007.
Fritz, Volkmar. *Das Buch Josua*. HAT I/7. Tübingen: Mohr Siebeck, 1994.
Garfinkel, Yosef. "The Meaning of the Word *MPQD* in the Tel 'Ira Ostracon." *PEQ* 119 (1987): 19–23.
Gophna, Ram, and Yael Yisraeli. "Soundings at Beer-Sheva (Bir es-Seba')." Pages 115–18 in *Beer-sheba I. Excavations at Tel Beer-Sheba 1969–1971 Seasons*. Publications of the Institute of Archaeology 2. Edited by Yohanan Aharoni. Tel Aviv University: Institute of Archaeology, 1973.
Heide, Martin. "Ein 27-zeiliges Listenostrakon aus der Sammlung Shlomo Moussaieff." *UF* 39 (2007): 399–412.
Heltzer, Michael. "Some Considerations about Hebrew *šōṭēr* and Punic *mšṭr*." *AuOr* 2 (1984): 225–30.
Herzog, Ze'ev. "Tel Beer-sheba." *NEAEHL* 1:167–73.
Herzog, Ze'ev, Miriam Aharoni, Anson F. Rainey, and Shmuel Moshkovitz. "The Israelite Fortress at Arad." *BASOR* 254 (1984): 1–34.
Hurowitz, Avigdor. "How Were the Israelites Counted? Numbers 1:2 and the Like in the Light of a New Inscription from Tel 'Ira." *Beer-Sheva* 3 (1988): 53–62. (Hebrew)
Kletter, Raz, and Etty Brand. "'A New Look at the Iron Age Silver Hoard from Eshtemoa,'" *PEQ* 114 (1998): 139–54.
Kochavi, Moshe. "Malhata, Tel." *NEAEHL* 3:934–36.
Lehmann, Reinhard G. "Typologie und Signatur. Studien zu einem Listenostrakon aus der Sammlung Moussaieff." *UF* 30 (1998): 397–459.
Lemaire, André. "Épigraphie palestinienne: Nouveaux documents II – décennie 1985–1995." *Henoch* 17 (1995): 209–42.
———. "Les ostraca paléo-hébreux des fouilles de l'Ophel." *Levant* 10 (1978): 156–61.
———. "Notes d'épigraphie nord-ouest Sémitique." *Semitica* 30 (1980): 17–32.
———. "Nouvelles données épigraphiques sur l'époque royale Israélite." *REJ* 156 (1997): 445–61.
———. "Prophètes et rois dans les inscriptions ouest-sémitiques (ixe–vi[e] siècle av. J.-C." Pages 85–115 in *Prophètes et rois: Bible et Proche-Orient*. Edited by André Lemaire. Paris: Cerf, 2001.
———. "Quatre nouveaux ostraca paléo-hébreux." *Semitica* 54 (2012): 33–49.
Lemaire, André. "Writing and Writing Materials." Pages 999–1008 in *The Anchor*

Bible Dictionary 6. Edited by David Noel Freedman. New York: Doubleday, 1992.

———. *Inscriptions hébraïques*, vol. 1: *Les ostraca*. Paris: Cerf, 1977.

Lemaire, André, and Ada Yardeni. "New Hebrew Ostraca from the Shephelah." Pages 197–223 in *Biblical Hebrew in Its Northwest Semitic Setting: Typological and Historical Perspectives*. Edited by Steven E. Fassberg and Avi Hurvitz. Jerusalem: Magnes; Winona Lake, IN: Eisenbrauns, 2006.

Levine, Baruch A. "'The Lord Your God Accept You' (2 Samuel 24:23): The Altar Erected by David on the Threshing Floor of Araunah." Pages 122–29 in ErIsr 24 (Avraham Malamat Volume). Tel Aviv: Israel Exploration Society, 1993. (Hebrew)

Lipschits, Oded, Ido Koch, Arie Shaus, and Shlomo Guil. "The Enigma of the Biblical Bath and the System of Liquid Volume Measurement during the First Temple Period." *UF* 42 (2010): 453–78.

Mazar, Eilat, David Ben-Shlomo, and Shmuel Aḥituv. "An Inscribed Pithos from the Ophel of Jerusalem." *IEJ* 63 (2013): 39–49.

Mendel, Anat. "Who Wrote the Aḥiqam Ostracon from Horvat 'Uza?" *IEJ* 61 (2011): 54–67.

Na'aman, Nadav. "The Distribution of Messages in the Kingdom of Judah in Light of the Lachish Ostraca." *VT* 53 (2003): 169–80.

———. "The Inheritance of the Sons of Simeon." *ZDPV* 96 (1980): 136–52.

———. "A New Look at the Epigraphic Finds from Horvat 'Uza." *TA* 39 (2012): 212–29.

———. "Ostracon No. 40 from Arad Reconsidered." Pages 199–204 in *Saxa loquentur. Studien zur Archäologie Palästinas/Israels. Festschrift für Volkmar Fritz zum 65. Geburtstag*. Edited by Cornelius G. den Hertog, Ulrich Hübner, and Stefan Münger. AOAT 302. Münster: Ugarit-Verlag, 2003.

———. "A Sapiential Composition from Horvat 'Uza." *Hebrew Bible and Ancient Israel* 2 (2013): 221–33.

———. "Textual and Historical Notes on Eliashib's Archive from Arad." *TA* 38 (2011): 83–93.

Naveh, Joseph. "An Edomite Inscription." Page 227 in *Tel 'Aroer: The Iron Age II Caravan Town and the Hellenistic–Early Roman Settlement. The Avraham Biran (1975–1982) and Rudolph Cohen (1975–1976) Excavations*. Edited by Yifat Thareani. Jerusalem: Nelson Glueck School of Biblical Archaeology, 2011.

Panitz-Cohen, Nava. "A Salvage Excavation in the New Market in Beer-sheba: New Light on Iron Age IIB Occupation at Beer-sheba." *IEJ* 55 (2005): 143–55.

Pardee, Dennis. *Handbook of Ancient Hebrew Letters. A Study Edition*. Chico: Scholars Press, 1982.

Parker, Simon B. "Did the Authors of the Books of Kings Make Use of Royal Inscriptions." *VT* 50 (2000): 357–78.

Ploeg, J. van der. "Les šoṭ^{e}rim d'Israel." *OTS* 10 (1954): 185–96.

Rainey, Anson F. "Three Additional Texts." Pages 122–25 in *Arad Inscriptions*. Edited by Yohanan Aharoni. Judean Desert Studies. Jerusalem: Israel Exploration Society, 1981.

Reich, Ronny, Eli Shukron, and Omri Lernau. "Recent Discoveries in the City of David, Jerusalem." *IEJ* 47 (2007): 153–69.

Renz, Johannes. *Die althebräischen Inschriften*. Part I. *Text und Kommentar*. Edited by Johannes Renz and Wolfgang Röllig. Handbuch der althebräischen Epigraphik 1. Darmstadt: Wissenschaftliche Buchgesellschaft, 1995.

Rollston, Christopher A. *Writing and Literacy in the World of Ancient Israel: Epigraphic Evidence from the Iron Age*. WAW 11. Atlanta: Society of Biblical Literature, 2010.

Rösel, Hartmut N. "Die Architektur." Pages 123–26 in *Ergebnisse der Ausgrabungen auf der Khirbet el-Mšāš (Tel Māśōś) 1972–1975*. Part I: *Textband*. Edited by Volkmar Fritz, and Aharon Kempinski. Wiesbaden: Harrassowitz, 1983.

Rüterswörden, Udo. *Die Beamten der israelitischen Königszeit. Eine Studie zu śr und vergleichbaren Begriffen*. Stuttgart: Kohlhammer, 1985.

Sanders, Seth L. *The Invention of Hebrew*. Urbana: University of Illinois Press, 2009.

Shoham, Yair. "Hebrew Bullae." Pages 29–57 in *Excavations at the City of David 1978–1985 Directed by Yigal Shiloh*, vol. 6: *Inscriptions*. Edited by Donald T. Ariel. Qedem 41. Jerusalem: Hebrew University of Jerusalem, 2000.

Singer-Avitz, Lily. "Arad: The Iron Age Pottery Assemblages." *TA* 29 (2002): 110–214.

―――. "Beersheba–A Gateway Community in Southern Arabian Long-Distance Trade in the Eighth Century B.C.E." *TA* 26 (1999): 3–75.

Thareani, Yifat. "Hebrew Inscriptions." Pages 223–24 in *Tel 'Aroer: The Iron Age II Caravan Town and the Hellenistic–Early Roman Settlement. The Avraham Biran (1975–1982) and Rudolph Cohen (1975–1976) Excavations*. Edited by Yifat Thareani. Jerusalem: Nelson Glueck School of Biblical Archaeology, 2011.

―――. *Tel 'Aroer: The Iron Age II Caravan Town and the Hellenistic–Early Roman Settlement. The Avraham Biran (1975–1982) and Rudolph Cohen (1975–1976) Excavations*. Annual of the Nelson Glueck School of Biblical Archaeology/Hebrew Union College–Jewish Institute of Religion 8. Jerusalem: Nelson Glueck School of Biblical Archaeology, 2011.

Toorn, Karel van der. *Scribal Culture and the Making of the Hebrew Bible*. Cambridge, MA: Harvard University Press, 2007.

Vritz, Volkmar. "Die Ostraka." Pages 133–37 in *Ergebnisse der Ausgrabungen auf der Khirbet el-Mšāš (Tel Māśōś) 1972–1975*. Part I: *Textband*. Edited by Volkmar Fritz and Aharon Kempinski. Abhandlungen des Deutschen Palästinavereins. Wiesbaden: Harrassowitz, 1983.

Wimmer, Stefan. *Palästinisches Hieratisch. Die Zahl- und Sonderzeichen in der althebräischen Schrift*. ÄAT 75. Wiesbaden: Harrassowitz, 2008.

Young, Ian. "Israelite Literacy and Inscriptions: A Response to Richard Hess." *VT* 55 (2005): 565–58.

―――. "Israelite Literacy: Interpreting the Evidence." *VT* 48 (1998): 239–53, 408–22.

Zimhoni, Orna. "The Pottery." Pages 127–29 in *Ergebnisse der Ausgrabungen auf der Khirbet el-Mšāš (Tel Māśōś) 1972–1975*. Part I: *Textband*. Edited by Volkmar Fritz and Aharon Kempinski. Wiesbaden: Harrassowitz, 1983.

Scribal Curriculum during the First Temple Period: Epigraphic Hebrew and Biblical Evidence

Christopher A. Rollston

Scribes on the Scribal Profession: Projections and Perceptions

"Scribal wisdom increases wisdom; whoever is free from toil can become wise" (Sir 38:24).[1] With that declaration, penned during the first quarter of the second century BCE, the Jerusalem scribe known as Ben Sira inaugurates his comparison of the life of a scribe to that of four different occupations. Because agriculture and pastoralism were such common occupations in much of the ancient world, Ben Sira singles them out first: The farmer does not have the luxury of acquiring wisdom because "his talk is about bulls," and "his objective is to complete the fattening (of the cattle)," and "his attention is turned toward the fields" (Sir 38:26).[2] Ben Sira then turns his attention to the "artisans" and "master artisans," contending that they must work for long periods, often in arduous and punishing conditions. Thus, the engraver of seals must "labor night and day" in order to "make a realistic likeness" (Sir 38:27).[3] Even worse, the blacksmith must "contend with the heat of the furnace," "searing his flesh," and "deafening his ears"

---

1. This rendering is based on the Hebrew. Compare the Greek: "Scribal wisdom is dependent on the opportunity of leisure, and whoever is free from toil can become wise." Manuscript B preserves much of 38:24–27a, but the remaining portion of the pericope under consideration is not extant in Hebrew. See Pancratius C. Beentjes, *The Book of Ben Sira in Hebrew: A Text Edition of all Extant Hebrew Manuscripts and a Synopsis of all Parallel Hebrew Ben Sira Texts*, VTSup 68 (Leiden: Brill, 1997), 67 and Joseph Ziegler, *Sapientia Iesu Filii Sirach* (Göttingen: Vandenhoeck & Ruprecht, 1965), 303–7.

2. This is not to suggest that these were always entirely separate occupations. Indeed, from antiquity to the modern period, the same family can often practice both.

3. Ben Sira distinguishes the professional of "seal engraver" from that of the scribe. In part, this is because Ben Sira is discussing the scribe of the Second Temple Period as a public intellectual and a religious savant. However, I suspect that even in the First Temple period the profession of the "scribe" (*sōpēr*) was often distinguished from that of "seal

so that he can "complete the projects" (Sir 38:28). So also, the potter toils endlessly at the potter's wheel, with both "hands and feet," because this is necessary to "complete his work" (Sir 38:29). Naturally, Ben Sira considers these vocations necessary, affirming that "all these are skilled with their hands ... without them a city is not habitable, and wherever they stay, they do not hunger" (Sir 38:31, 32). However, Ben Sira is a scribe and he considers the scribal profession to be absolutely superior.[4] After all, those practicing the four occupations he has singled out as representative "are not sought for the council of the people, are not prominent in the assembly," and they "do not deliberate about judicial regulations or expound on discipline and justice" (Sir 38:32, 33). The scribe, however, can be present and prominent in such social contexts. Furthermore, the scribe "seeks out the wisdom of all the ancients," "is in the midst of the great," "travels in the land of foreign peoples," and "many praise his understanding" (Sir 39:1, 4, 9). In sum, according to Ben Sira, the scribe's life is particularly rich and full, and it is distinguished even from the artisans and master artisans.

To be sure, it should be emphasized that this pericope was essentially scribal apologia, something intended to recruit and to retain students, so hyperbole is certainly present but its presence is calculated and reasonable. After all, becoming a scribe required years of commitment, assiduousness in studies, and a willingness (at least for a time) to pursue education (rather than simply entering a trade and beginning to earn money). But according to Ben Sira, the dividends for those years of study were high, in terms of salaries, prestige, and foreign travel. Naturally, it must also be remembered in this connection that the book of Ben Sira contains an explicit reference to a school, and this book also includes explicit exhortations to pursue the scribal vocation (Sir 51:23–30). That is, my belief that this pericope is 'scribal apologia' is based on the verbiage of the book itself. The main point, though, is this: Ben Sira considered the scribal vocation to be a lofty one, a distinct one, and a true vocation in the strictest sense of the term. And Ben Sira was not alone in holding this view.

Within Mesopotamia, the scribal vocation is described in very laudatory language as well.[5] The Mesopotamian composition referred to as In

---

maker," in light of the fact that the techniques and aptitude for making seals is quite different from that of someone writing on papyrus or on pottery.

4. In this connection, it is worth noting that many biblical scholars have historically suggested that Ben Sira was much more affirming of the trades than were Egyptian texts with similar motifs. I have argued that this position is based on a misunderstanding of the essential nature of the Egyptian texts. See Christopher A. Rollston, "Ben Sira 38:24–39:11 and the Egyptian Satire of the Trades: A Reconsideration," *JBL* 120 (2001): 131–39.

5. See especially Åke W. Sjöberg, "In Praise of Scribal Art (Examination Text D),"

Praise of Scribal Art is representative, and it demonstrates the grandiose language sometimes used: (1) "The scribal art is the mother of orators, the father of masters; (2) the scribal art is delightful, one can never have too much of its charms. (3) The scribal art is not (easily) learned (but) he who has learned it need no longer be anxious about it; (4) Strive to (master) the scribal art, and it will enrich you. (5) Be industrious in the scribal art, and it will provide you with wealth and abundance; (6) Do not be careless concerning the scribal art, do not neglect it; (7). The scribal art is a 'house of richness,' the secret of Amanki. (8) Work ceaselessly with the scribal art and it will reveal its secret to you. (9) If you neglect it, they will make malicious remarks about you. (10) The scribal art is a good lot, richness and abundance. (11) Since you were a child it causes you grief, since you have grown up [it . . .] (12) The scribal art is the 'bond' of all . . . [. . . . .] . . . (13) Work hard for it [and it will. . . . you] its beautiful prosperity, (14). To have superior knowledge in Sumerian, to learn. . . . . , [to learn] Emesal. (15) To write a stele, to draw a field, to settle accounts, [. . . . . .] (16) . . . . . . the palace. . . . . (17) May the scribe be its (the scribal art's) servant, he calls for the corvee basket, [. . . .]."[6] The text is fragmentary in places, but the extant content demonstrates that the scribal profession is lauded as something that, though rigorous to pursue, will bring wealth, abundance, prosperity. The final preserved portions of it refer to some of the scribal activities, inscribing a stele, recording the dimensions of a field, maintaining accounts. Arguably, there is also reference to scribal activities within the palace and to the fact that the scribe has the authority to summon the laborers to work, that is, the scribal vocation is one of tremendous gravity.[7]

JCS 24 (1972): 126–31; Sjöberg, "Der Examenstext A," *ZA* 64 (1975): 137–76; Sjöberg, "Der Vater und sein missratener Sohn," *JCS* 25 (1973): 105–69; Miguel Civil, "Sur les 'livres d'écolier' à l'époque paléo-babylonienne," in *Miscellanea Babylonica: Mélanges offerts à Maurice Birot*, ed. Jean-Marie Durand and Jean-Robert Kupper (Paris: Éditions Recherche sur Civilisations, 1985), 67–78; Herman L. J. Vanstiphout, "School Dialogues," *COS* 1.184–186:588–93; Victor A. Hurowitz, "Literary Observations on 'In Praise of the Scribal Art,'" *JANES* 27 (2000): 49–56.

6. With one exception, the translation provided here is that of Sjöberg, "In Praise of Scribal Art (Examination Text D)." The exception is this: within his original translation, Sjöberg rendered the second half of line two as "it never satiates you." I do not believe that this rendering makes good sense in this context. That is, to suggest that the scribal art "never satiates" is to suggest that it does not satisfy fully. Conversely to suggest that "one is never sated by the charms of the scribal art" is to suggest that "one can never have too much of the charms of the scribal art," or more idiomatically, "one can never feel that one has had too much of it." For this reason, I have modified this component of Sjöberg's translation.

7. As an ancillary note, it should be emphasized that there has also been a substantial amount of scholarly attention devoted to the subject of education in Mesopotamia,

Within Egyptian literature, the scribal vocation is lauded at great length as well. The Egyptian Satire of the Trades is among the most cited of these texts. The Satire of the Trades begins its paean to the scribe by noting the place of prominence to which the scribe rapidly ascends: "Barely grown, still a child, he is greeted, sent on errands, hardly returned he wears a gown."[8] Similarly, Papyrus Lansing extols the scribal profession by affirming that the scribe "makes friends with those greater than he.... You will be advanced by your superiors. You will be sent on a mission!" It exhorts the scribal student to persist so that "you may become one whom the king trusts; to make you gain entrance to treasury and granary.... To make you issue the offerings on feast days." The text continues and states that the scribe will "call for one and a thousand will answer you."[9] Along those same lines, Papyrus Anastasi II proclaims that the scribal profession "saves you from toil and protects you from all manner of work. It spares you bearing hoe and mattock, so that you do not carry a basket. It sunders you from plying oar and spares you torment,

---

with some of the most recent work focusing even on the physical aspects of the tablets themselves and on some scribal exercises. After all, practice tablets have been found, the extant corpus of texts has been studied heavily, and much is known about the curriculum of Mesopotamian scribes, from the target literature and languages to mathematics and record keeping. During recent years, the works of Herman L. J. Vanstiphout, Stephen Tinney, Niek Veldhuis, and Andrew George have been among the most authorative and useful. Thus, see Herman L .J. Vanstiphout, "On the Old Edubba Education," in *Centres of Learning: Learning and Location in Pre-Modern Europe and the Near East*, ed. Jan Willem Drijvers and Alastair A. MacDonald (Leiden: Brill, 1995: 3–16; Stephen Tinney, "Texts, Tablets, and Teaching: Scribal Education at Nippur and Ur," *Expedition* 40 (1998): 40–50; Tinney, "On the Curricular Setting of Sumerian Literature," *Iraq* 61 (1999): 159–72; Niek Velduis, "Elementary Education at Nippur: The Lists of Trees and Wooden Objects" (PhD diss., University of Groningen, 1997); Veldhuis, "Mesopotamian Canons," in *Homer, the Bible and Beyond: Literary and Religious Canons in the Ancient World*, ed. Margalit Finkelberg and Guy G. Strousma (Leiden: Brill, 2003): 9–28; Veldhuis, *Religion, Literature and Scholarship: The Sumerian Composition "Nanše and the Birds,"* CM 22 (Leiden: Brill/Styx, 2004); Andrew George, "In Search of the é.dub.ba.a: The Ancient Mesopotamian School in Literature and Reality," in *An Experienced Scribe Who Neglects Nothing: Ancient Near Eastern Studies in Honor of Jacob Klein*, ed. Yitzchak Sefati et al. (Bethesda, MD: CDL, 2005), 127–37. For a brief summary of the salient aspects of this research, see Christopher A. Rollston, "An Old Hebrew Stone Inscription from the City of David: A Trained Hand and a Remedial Hand on the Same Inscription," in *Puzzling Out the Past: Studies in Northwest Semitic Languages and Literatures in Honor of Bruce Zuckerman*, ed. Steven Fine, Marilyn J. Lundberg, and Wayne T. Pitard (Brill: Leiden, 2012), 189–96, esp. 191.

8. Miriam Lichtheim, *The Old and Middle Kingdoms*. Vol. 1 of *Ancient Egyptian Literature* (Berkeley: University of California Press, 1973–1980), 186.

9. Miriam Lichtheim, *The New Kingdom*. Vol. 2 of *Ancient Egyptian Literature* (Berkeley: University of California Press, 1973–1980), 168, 171.

as you are not under many lords and numerous masters."[10] Obviously, within ancient Egypt, the scribes believed that the scribal profession was a particularly important, lofty, and noble one, worthy of pursuit.[11] In sum, the scribal profession was considered an impressive one in the ancient Near East, a position of power and prominence. Naturally, as has already been noted, the literature from the ancient Near East that lauds the scribal profession was also composed by scribes; therefore, this must be factored into the equation as well. But the fact remains that the scribal profession was touted as a laudable and prestigious vocation.[12]

Scribes as Cabinet-Level Officials, Scribes of the Army, Fiscal Scribes, Scribes as Private Professionals

Within most professions, there are hierarchies of some sort (i.e., sometimes spelled out, sometimes not). It seems rational to contend that this was the case within the realm of the ancient scribes as well. The data are our disposal for Israel and Judah are partial, but there are enough to suggest that

---

10. Ricardo Augusto Caminos, *Late Egyptian Miscellanies*, BEStud 1 (London: Oxford University Press, 1954), 51.

11. For the subject of education in ancient Egypt, the scholarly work of Hellmut Brunner remains foundational, but the work of recent scholars such as R. Janssen and J. J. Janssen, Andrea G. McDowell, and Annie Gasse has augmented and refined much of the previous work, with the scribal activities at Deir El-Medina often being paramount in the discussion. See Hellmut Brunner, *Altägyptische Erziehung* (Wiesbaden: Harrassowitz, 1957); R. Janssen and Jac J. Janssen, *Growing Up in Ancient Egypt* (London: Rubicon, 1990); Andrea G. McDowell, *Village Life in Ancient Egypt: Laundry Lists and Love Songs* (Oxford: Oxford University Press, 1999); McDowell, "Teachers and Students at Deir el-Medina," in *Deir el-Medina in the Third Millennium AD: A Tribute to Jac J. Janssen*, ed. Robert J. Demarée and Arno Egberts (Leiden: Nederlands Instituut voor het Nabije Oosten, 2000): 217–33; McDowell, "Student Exercises from Deir el-Medina: The Dates," in *Studies in Honor of William Kelly Simpson*, ed. Peter Der Manuelian, 2 vols. (Boston: Museum of Fine Arts, 1996), 2:601–8; Annie Gasse, *Catalogue des ostraca litteraires de Deir el-Medina: Tome V* (Cairo: Institut français d'archéologie orientale, 2005). For a synopsis of the discussion, see Rollston, "An Old Hebrew Stone Inscription," 191–92.

12. To be sure, there has been some discussion of scribal education in ancient Anatolia and also in ancient Syria (e.g., Ugarit, Emar). Note especially, Yoram Cohen, *The Scribes and Scholars of the City of Emar in the Late Bronze Age*, HSS 59 (Winona Lake, IN: Eisenbrauns, 2009); John Ellison, "The Ugaritic Alphabetic Script," in *An Eye for Form: Epigraphic Essays in Honor of Frank Moore Cross* (Winona Lake, IN: Eisenbrauns, 2014). The focus, however, of this article is not on those regions. For a good general introduction to writing culture throughout much of the ancient Near East, see *Margins of Writing, Origins of Cultures*, ed. Seth L. Sanders (Chicago: The Oriental Institute of the University of Chicago, 2006).

within Israel and Judah not all scribes were equal. For example, scribes in the First Temple period could rise to the rank of high officials in the governmental bureaucracy. (1) In fact, there are some lists of "cabinet-level positions" (to use modern nomenclature for such things) in the Hebrew Bible and scribes are included in some of these lists.[13] For example, the high officials of King David's court are listed: "Joab the son of Seriah was Over the Army, and Jehoshaphat the son of Ahilud was the Herald, and Zadok the son of Ahituv and Ahimelek the son of Abiathar were the Priests, and Seriah was the Scribe" (2 Sam 8:16–18). Regarding King Solomon's court officials, the following is recounted: "And these are his officials, Azariah the son of Zadok was the Priest, and Elihoreph and Ahijah the sons of Shishai were Scribes and Jehshaphat the son of Ahilud was the Herald, and Benaiah the son of Jehoida was Over the Army, and Azariah the son of Nathan was the Chief Officer, and Zabud the son of Nathan the Priest was the Friend of the King, and Ahishar was Over the House, and Adoniram the son of Abda was Over the Forced Laborers" (1 Kgs 4:2–6). During the reign of Hezekiah (r. 715–687 BCE), several Judean officials are reported to have listened to the harangue of the emissaries of the Neo-Assyrian King Sennacherib (r. 705–681 BCE), namely, Eliakim the son of Hilkiah who was Over the House, and Shebnah the Scribe, and Joah the son of Asaph the Herald" (2 Kgs 18:18). Similarly, within the narratives about the discovery of the "Book of the Law" during the reign of Josiah (r. 640–609 BCE), there is reference a command of Josiah to these officials: "Hilkiah the Priest, and Ahikam the son of Shaphan, and Akbor the son of Mikayah, and Shaphan the Scribe, and Asyah the Servant of the King" (2 Kgs 22:12).[14] The full title of the scribe in the cabinet-level position

---

13. To be sure, someone might question the historicity of these lists of officials within Samuel and Kings. As for me, I consider them to be reasonably credible, particularly those from the books of Kings. But I am also comfortable positing a historical core for segments of the books of Samuel, including its list of officials (2 Sam 8:16–18). After all, historical texts written in linear alphabetic are well attested in the Levant in the tenth and ninth centuries BCE; therefore, the scribal apparatus necessary for keeping records and producing historical (and literary) texts was present. For discussion, see Joseph Naveh, *Early History of the Alphabet: An Introduction to West Semitic Epigraphy and Palaeography*, 2nd ed. (Jerusalem: Magnes, 1987); Christopher A. Rollston, "The Dating of the Early Royal Byblian Phoenician Inscriptions: A Response to Benjamin Sass," *Maarav* 15 (2008): 57–93; Rollston, *Writing and Literacy in the World of Ancient Israel: Epigraphic Evidence from the Iron Age*, ABS 11 (Leiden: Brill, 2010), passim. Moreover, even if one were to posit that these lists in Samuel and Kings are fictive, the fact remains that the authors of Samuel and Kings were scribes themselves and that these scribes believed that some scribes could be classified within officialdom.

14. For a good synthetic discussion of these various officials, see Nili S. Fox, *In the Service of the King: Officialdom in Ancient Israel and Judah* (Cincinnati: Hebrew Union College, 2000), with 96–100 containing the discussion of the scribe. See also, David M.

was arguably "the scribe of the king" (cf. 2 Kgs 12:11; 2 Chr 24:11; cf. Esth 3:12; 8:9), although this term may be broader in scope. Note also that there is also reference to a "scribal chamber" which was located in the palace (Jer 36:12) and "the house of Nathan the scribe" was under royal auspices (Jer 37:15, 20; cf. Baruch son of Neriah's access to high officials, Jer 36:11–20). I would suggest that "the scribe of the king" was arguably the loftiest position available for a scribe in the countries of Israel and Judah. Moreover, I would also suggest that the scribe holding this position had at his disposal quite a number (depending on the period) of scribes, ready to do his scribal bidding.[15] This position was, I believe, the top of the hierarchy for scribes. (2) There is also reference within the Hebrew Bible to "the scribe of the commander of the army" (2 Kgs 25:19; Jer 52:25). I consider this title to be historical, not a literary fabrication. Moreover, regarding military scribes, the evidence from the Old Hebrew epigraphic record is of particular important. First and foremost, there is a reference in an Old Hebrew ostracon from the military fortress of Lachish that refers to a scribe who was accessible to the military command (although the officer did not wish to accept the encouragement of his superior officer to summon a professional scribe). Furthermore, much of the Old Hebrew epigraphic material comes from major and minor military sites, such as Arad, Lachish, Horvat 'Uza, Horvat Radum, and Tel 'Ira. Of course, Yavneh Yam (Meṣad Ḥashavyahu) is a military fortress as well.[16] The caliber of the writing in these inscriptions is normally very high and it seems reasonable to argue that most of these inscriptions are from the hands of "state scribes" engaging in scribal duties within the army. It also seems reasonable to posit (based on Lachish 3, combined with the caliber of the script and orthography of Lachish 3) that some military officers had some formal, standardized scribal training (as it would have been useful in

---

Carr, *Writing on the Tablet of the Heart: Origins of Scripture and Literature* (Oxford: Oxford University Press, 2005), 116–18.

15. The Solomonic list has two people in the position (rather than one), but since they are brothers this is an understandable.

16. For the *editio princeps* of this letter, see H. Tur-Sinai (Torczyner), G. Lankester Harding, A. Lewis, and James L. Starkey, *Lachish I: (Tell ed-Duweir): The Lachish Letters* (London: Oxford University, 1938), Letter #3; For the Arad inscriptions, see Y. Aharoni, *Arad Inscriptions* (Jerusalem: Israel Exploration Society, 1981). For discussion of the dating of these texts, see Christopher A. Rollston, "Scribal Education in Ancient Israel: The Old Hebrew Epigraphic Evidence," *BASOR* 344 (2006): 52–53; Y. Beit-Arieh, *Ḥorvat 'Uza and Ḥorvat Radum: Two Fortresses in the Biblical Negev* (Tel Aviv: Institute of Archaeology, 2007); Y. Beit-Arieh, *Tel Ira: A Stronghold in the Biblical Negev* (Tel Aviv: Institute of Archaeology, 1999); Joseph Naveh, A Hebrew Letter from the Seventh Century B.C.," *IEJ* 10 (1960): Naveh, "More Hebrew Inscriptions from Meṣad Ḥashavyahu," *IEJ* 12 (1962): 27–32.

the pursuit of rank within the military).[17] Moreover, because a fairly high percentage of the Old Hebrew epigraphic corpus hails from sites that were military in nature, it also makes sense to suggest that the trained scribes producing these military documents were functioning under the person bearing the title "the scribe of the army."[18] (3) Functioning within the state apparatus were also the sorts of scribes who produced, for example, the Reisner Samaria Ostraca in (early) eighth-century Israel and the Gibeon Inscribed Jar Handles in Judah of the late eighth or early seventh century, that is, economic records associated with the state.[19] (4) I am certain that there were some scribes who were "private professionals," writing up marriage, divorce, adoption, purchase, and sale contracts for elite members of society.[20] Most of these (like most of the written materials in ancient Israel and Judah) were on papyrus and have not survived the ravages of time. Also, the work of some scribal stonemasons has survived, and some of these, such as Khirbet el-Qom, may have been produced by private professionals, rather than state

---

17. For further discussion of this point, see, Christopher A. Rollston, *Writing and Literacy in the World of Ancient Israel: Epigraphic Evidence from the Iron Age*, ABS 11 (Atlanta: Society of Biblical Literature, 2010), 128–35.

18. Someone might wish to posit that there was simply one scribe, that is, "the scribe of the army" who personally wrote all of the military correspondence. I do not think this is all that likely. Rather, because of the amount of material we have in Old Hebrew, because of the varied sites from which it came and went, and because we have numerous different hands in these written materials, it seems reasonable to posit that "the scribe of the army" was the person in charge and that he had a group of scribes working under him, producing the documents necessary for the varied needs of the military. Of course, in addition to this, we also have (e.g., from Lachish) letters going back and forth between these military fortresses.

19. For Samaria, see George A. Reisner, Clarence Stanley Fisher, and David Gordon Lyon, *Harvard Excavations at Samaria: 1908–1910*. Vol. 1: *Text* (Cambridge: Harvard University Press, 1924); for Gibeon, see James B. Pritchard, *Hebrew Inscriptions and Stamps from Gibeon* (Philadelphia: University Museum, University of Pennsylvania, 1959); Pritchard, "More Inscribed Jar Handles from el-Jib," *BASOR* 160 (1962): 2–6; F. Frick, "Another Inscribed Jar Handle from el-Jib," *BASOR* 213 (1974): 46–48. Of course, there have been caches of bullae discovered in Jerusalem (City of David) and Lachish, with several seals also having been found at Arad. These materials were, of course, associated with papyri documents that were produced for the state. For the bullae from the City of David, see Yoav Shoham, "Hebrew Bullae," in *City of David Excavations: Final Report VI*, ed. D. T. Ariel et al., Qedem 41 (Jerusalem: Hebrew University, 2000), 29–57; for the Lachish Bullae, see Y. Aharoni, *Investigations at Lachish: The Sanctuary and the Residency (Lachish V)*, Publications of the Tel Aviv University Institute of Archaeology 4 (Tel Aviv: Gateway, 1975); for the Arad Seals, see Aharoni, *Arad Inscriptions*.

20. Many nonelite members of ancient Israel and Judah would not have found it necessary to employ a scribe for business transactions and social contracts. Verbal agreements would have been sufficient for many of the needs of nonelites. Moreover, the cost of hiring a scribe would arguably have sometimes been prohibitive for nonelites.

scribes or the state's scribal stonemasons.[21] Of course, some of these, such as the Royal Steward Inscription (Silwan), may very well have been the product of state scribes or scribal stonemasons in the employ of the state, but it is very difficult to know with certainty.[22] But, at the end of the day, it is entirely reasonable to contend that although most scribes were in the employ of the state, there were certainly some who were private professionals, not in the direct employ of the state. Again, to reiterate, I am not saying that there were no scribes who were "private professionals." I have stated that there were such people. But I would also wish to emphasize that most of the Old Hebrew corpus hails from officialdom, with the materials from Lachish, Arad, Ḥorvat 'Uza, Ḥorvat Radum, Tel 'Ira, Yavneh Yam (Meṣad Ḥashavyahu), Samaria, and Gibeon are demonstrative of this.[23] There are exceptions, and someone might contend that Kuntillet Ajrud functions as such an exception, but the fact remains that most of the Old Hebrew epigraphic data hails from Israelite and Judean officialdom and this is not something that is easily contested.[24] Finally, I should emphasize that for the scribes working in officialdom, I suspect that there was mobility, both horizontal and vertical. That is, it makes sense to suggest that a scribe working under "the scribe of the army" might find himself summoned by "the scribe of the king" to work in the palace (or some such place that fell under the purview of "the scribe of the king").

In any case, my main point within this entire discussion is to emphasize certain things. First and foremost, we have references in the Hebrew Bible to scribes functioning in high places within officialdom, with titles in keeping with those high functions. Moreover, it seems rational (in light of the amount of epigraphic evidence that we have) to contend that these scribal officials were not working alone, but had a contingent of scribes working under them. I also believe that it is reasonable to suggest that there were additional scribal offices (i.e., not just "the scribe of the king" and "the scribe of the army") for

---

21. For the *editio princeps*, see William G. Dever, "Iron Age Epigraphic Material from the Area of Khirbet el-Kom," *HUCA* 40–41 (1969–1970): 139–204.

22. Nahman Avigad, "The Epitaph of a Royal Steward," *IEJ* 3 (1953): 137–52.

23. Of course, someone might suggest that this is because of the sites that have been excavated, that is, major and minor political sites. To some degree, I am sure that this is the case, but the fact remains that these are the sorts of sites that are producing the most texts, and the fact also remains that this is entirely logical. After all, political bureaucracies needed correspondence and they needed economic and historical records.

24. For Kuntillet Ajrud, see Shmuel Aḥituv, Esther Eshel, and Zeev Meshel, "The Inscriptions," in *Kuntillet 'Ajrud (Ḥorvat Teman): An Iron Age II Religious Site on the Judah-Sinai Border*, ed. Zeev Meshel (Jerusalem: Israel Exploration Society, 2012), 73–142. I date the Old Hebrew inscriptions from this site to the very early eighth century BCE. For discussion of these inscriptions and their *Sitz im Leben*, see Rollston, *Writing and Literacy*, 131.

whom we do not (yet) know the titles. Naturally, it must have been the case that there were scribes who were, in essence, private professionals, not in the direct employ of the state. But, at the end of the day, it must be conceded by all that the Old Hebrew epigraphic evidence at hand comes primarily from those functioning under the auspices of the state. And it seems rational to take that fact very seriously, in any discussion about the locus for the standardized scribal education and also for assessments about the predominant location for scribal activities within society.[25]

Synopsis of the Debate about "Schools" in Ancient Israel and Judah

During recent decades, there has certainly been substantial discussion about the presence or absence of "schools" in ancient Israel and Judah.[26] Some have argued that there were "schools" in ancient Israel and Judah.[27] However, some have contended that the data (biblical, epigraphic, and comparative ancient Near Eastern) supporting the existence of schools are inconclusive at best.[28] Lemaire has proposed that there was widespread and pervasive education at many sites in ancient Israel and Judah,[29] but schol-

---

25. For the subject of specialized scribal tools, see the discussion in Rollston, *Writing and Literacy*, 112.

26. On the problem of defining the term "school," see Rollston, "Scribal Education," 47–74, esp. 49–50 and the literature cited there.

27. Lorenz Dürr, *Das Erziehungswesen im AT und im antiken Orient* (Leipzig: Hinrichs, 1932); Hans-Jurgen Hermisson, *Studien zur israelitischen Spruchweisheit*, WMANT 28 (Neukirchen-Vluyn: Neukirchener, 1968); André Lemaire, *Les écoles et la formation de la bible dans l'ancient israël*, OBO 39 (Göttingen: Vandenhoeck & Ruprecht, 1981); Emile Puech, "Les écoles dan l'Israël préexilique: Données éepigraphiques," in *Congress Volume: Jerusalem 1986*, ed. John A. Emerton, VTSup 40 (Leiden: Brill, 1988): 189–203; Bernhard Lang, "Schule und Unterricht im alten Israel," in *La sagesse de l'ancient testament*, ed. Maurice Gilbert (Leuven: Peeters, 1990): 186–201; Eric William Heaton, *The School Tradition of the Old Testament* (Oxford: Oxford University Press, 1994); G. I. Davies, "Were there Schools in Ancient Israel?" in *Wisdom in Ancient Israel: Essays in Honour of J. A. Emerton*, ed. John Day, Robert P. Gordon, and H. G. M. Williamson (Cambridge: Cambridge University Press, 1995), 199–211.

28. Friedman W. Golka, "The Israelite Wisdom School or 'The Emperor's New Clothes,'" in *The Leopard's Spots: Biblical and African Wisdom in Proverbs* (Edinburgh: Clark, 1993): 11; Stuart Weeks, *Early Israelite Wisdom* (Oxford: Clarendon, 1994), 156; cf. David W. Jamieson-Drake, *Scribes and Schools in Monarchic Judah: A Socio-Archaeological Approach*, JSOTSup 109 (Sheffield: Sheffield Academic Press, 1991): 156; R. N. Whybray, *The Intellectual Tradition in the Old Testament*, BZAW 135 (Berlin: de Gruyter, 1974), 38.

29. Lemaire, *Les écoles et la formation*; Lemaire, "A Schoolboy's Exercise on an

ars such as Menahem Haran, James L. Crenshaw, Stuart Weeks, and Emile Puech have critiqued Lemaire's proposal, contending that Lemaire's broad and sweeping conclusions are sometimes based on tenuous interpretations of the evidence.[30] Although I believe that the epigraphic evidence demonstrates that Lemaire went too far with his conclusions, the fact remains that he is absolutely correct about the fact that the caliber of the epigraphic evidence requires some sort of "school." In fact, although repudiating most of Lemaire's categories of evidence, Puech has come to the same conclusion as well, arguing that the epigraphic evidence does demonstrate that "schools" must have been part of the equation, or, to use his phrase, "an epigraphic given."[31]

Part of the problem in this entire discussion has been the very term "school," which seems to be a lightning rod for both sides. It seems useful to avoid using that term, as it clouds the discussion of the phenomenon. A number of years ago, I proposed using the term "formal, standardized education," as an attempt to bridge the impasse.[32] Part of the problem has also been that some have assumed that for there to have been a "school" in ancient Israel, there would have been a designated "school building," and such scholars have stated that no such building has been found in Israel or Judah. However, aside from the fact that a cardinal rule in the field of archaeology is that "absence of evidence is not evidence of absence," it should also be emphasized that even within Mesopotamia and Egypt scribal activity was often a small enterprise, with a handful of students, often in a domestic context.[33] Therefore, it stands to reason that in Israel and Judah, it would have been a small-scale enterprise as well, with a handful of students, often in a domestic context. No "school building" should be presupposed to have existed. Part of the problem has also been that some have desired for there to have been widespread literacy in ancient Israel, not just of elites but also of nonelites.[34] I do not believe that the evidence is such that there is any

---

Ostracon at Lachish," *TA* 3 (1976): 109–10.

30. Menahem Haran, "On the Diffusion of Literacy and Schools in Ancient Israel," in *Congress Volume: Jerusalem 1986*, ed. John A. Emerton, VTSup 40 (Leiden: Brill, 1988): 81–95; James L. Crenshaw, "Education in Ancient Israel," *JBL* 104 (1985): 605–7; Crenshaw, *Education in Ancient Israel: Across the Deadening Silence* (New York: Doubleday, 1998, 100–108; Weeks, *Early Israelite Wisdom*, 132–56; Puech, "Les écoles dan l'Israël préexilique."

31. Lemaire, *Les écoles et la formation*; Puech, "Les écoles dan l'Israël préexilique."

32. See Rollston, "Scribal Education," 49–50.

33. For a synopsis of the ancient Near Eastern data regarding the locus of schools, see Rollston, *Writing and Literacy*, 115–16 and the literature cited there.

34. And part of the problem in this connection is the definition of literacy. For discussion of this, see Christopher A. Rollston, "The Phoenician Script of the Tel Zayit

good evidence for the education of nonelite masses, much as I might wish for it to be so. In fact, Young has demonstrated on the basis of the biblical evidence that it is the elites who do the reading and writing (based on explicit references to such activities in the Hebrew Bible itself). I believe that the epigraphic evidence (i.e., the high quality of the writing) dovetails rather nicely with the biblical evidence. In fact, the cumulative evidence from antiquity argues in favor of low percentages of trained writers and readers in antiquity, from Mesopotamia and Egypt to Greece and Rome. Basically, I believe that it would be most difficult to make a case for the formal education in writing and reading of the nonelite masses, though some scholars have tried.[35] In fact, throughout much of world history, farmers and pastoralists would not have found it necessary to read and write at anything approximating a sophisticated level (and thus they would not have produced the high-caliber Old Hebrew inscriptions we have at our disposal). Neither would blacksmiths and potters have found it necessary. To be sure, carpenters might have found it useful to have at least some facility in reading and writing, and some merchants may have also found it useful to have some facility in reading and writing. But most would have been able to have functioned quite well without these things. In short, I believe that the things stated in Ben Sira 38:24–39:11 were true not simply for Second Temple Judah, but for much of the ancient and medieval worlds, including Iron Age Israel and Judah. Within the modern world, we live in a print-saturated culture and we tend to assume that antiquity was much the same. But it certainly was not. In fact, prior to the invention of the printing press, exposure to written materials was confined to certain small sectors of human society.[36] Moreover, within the modern world we have also become accustomed to high rates of literacy and we might often assume that this was always the case. But it was not. In fact, high rates

---

Abecedary and Putative Evidence for Israelite Literacy," in *Literate Culture and Tenth-Century Canaan: The Tel Zayit Abecedary in Context*, ed. Ron E. Tappy and P. Kyle McCarter (Winona Lake, IN: Eisenbrauns, 2008), 61–63. Basing my definition to some degree on a UNESCO statement, I define literacy as "substantial facility in a writing system, that is, the ability to write and read, using and understanding a standard script, a standard orthography, a standard numeric system, conventional formatting and terminology, and with minimal errors (of composition or comprehension). Moreover, I maintain that the capacity to scrawl one's name on a contract, but without the ability to write or read anything else is not literacy, not even some sort of "functional literacy."

35. See, Ian M. Young, "Israelite Literacy: Interpreting the Evidence, Part 1," *VT* 48 (1998): 239–53; Young, "Israelite Literacy: Interpreting the Evidence, Part 2," *VT* 48 (1998): 408–22; Young, "Israelite Literacy and Inscriptions: A Response to Richard Hess," *VT* 54 (2005): 565–67; Christopher A. Rollston, "The Phoenician Script of the Tel Zayit Abecedary, 61–96, esp. 67–72.

36. For the dearth of print saturation in antiquity, see Rollston, *Writing and Literacy*, 122–26.

of literacy are normally the result of government mandated education of the entire population. This sort of thing was certainly not the case in antiquity. There was no government mandated education of the masses in antiquity. In short, the ancient and modern data converge quite nicely to reveal that writing and reading in ancient Israel was an elite enterprise.[37] A final thing to remember is that the quality of the Old Hebrew epigraphic material is high, not low. There are some low quality inscriptions, but when we have these it is painfully obvious.[38] And the reason it is so painfully obvious is that these are the exception rather than the rule. To summarize, therefore, I firmly believe that the epigraphic evidence demonstrates nicely that there was some sort of formal, standardized scribal education in antiquity. In fact, the epigraphic evidence mandates this conclusion. I also believe that some high officials (e.g., military officers) would have had available to them this same formal, standardized education (although perhaps not as much of it).[39] Relevant in this connection are the words of G. I. Davies regarding "schools" (his term): "The evidence, both direct and indirect, is sufficient to justify an affirmative answer … the growing corpus of epigraphic evidence is beginning to place the matter beyond doubt."[40] Indeed.

But the curriculum of scribal schools is something that merits discussion. It seems useful to begin in this connection with a citation from one of the finest recent volumes on the subject of scribalism in ancient Israel and Judah, that of van der Toorn. At one point, he states the following: "our knowledge about the scribal curriculum in Israel is almost nil. Nothing comparable to the Babylonian list of textbooks and reference works for apprentice exorcists has been found for Hebrew scribes … we are thus reduced to guesswork when trying to reconstruct what might have been the curriculum."[41] Van der Toorn is certainly correct that we have no list of textbooks or required reference works, but to suggest that there is "almost nil" is to go too far. Conversely, Lemaire has proposed a broad and deep curriculum, in which he envisioned the Hebrew Bible itself to constitute much of the core curriculum.[42] Although I wish that we might have good epigraphic evidence for this, I do not believe that we do. For this reason, I will confine myself primar-

---

37. Note also that writing and reading are related skills, but with independent variables (i.e., they are not the same skill). See Rollston, "Scribal Education," 48, no. 4.
38. For reference to some of these poor quality inscriptions, see Rollston, "An Old Hebrew Stone Inscription, 193.
39. Rollston, "Scribal Education," 47–74; Rollston, *Writing and Literacy*.
40. Davies, "Were There Schools," 209.
41. Karel van der Toorn, *Scribal Culture and the Making of the Hebrew Bible* (Cambridge: Harvard University Press, 2007), 97.
42. Lemaire, *Les écoles et la formation*, 71–83.

ily to the epigraphic evidence, but with occasional reference to the Hebrew Bible in order to fill out the picture slightly. Suffice it to say that I do not believe that we must resort to "guesswork," but neither do I think that we can posit with any certitude the precise nature of the literary or historical works that constituted the curriculum. I do believe, however, that the epigraphic evidence allows us to understand the broad contours of the curriculum for scribes in ancient Israel and Judah.

Scribal Curriculum: Script, Orthography, Hieratic Numerals, Epistolary Formulae, Foreign Language

The Core Curriculum for Old Hebrew: Script

Learning to use a writing system for the first time (i.e., someone's first writing system) is a laborious process, requiring substantial amounts of time to develop the manual dexterity and the cognitive framework. Along those lines, rather than positing rapid proficiency in alphabetic writing, recent systematic and empirical studies for modern languages have delineated development stages, a gradual process normally requiring years, not days, weeks, or months. Within the history of Northwest Semitic, the time required for proficiency in one's first writing system has often not been factored into the discussion all that well.[43] Furthermore, the fact that the caliber of the script used in the corpus of Old Hebrew inscriptions is high, with impressive levels of synchronic consistency, even in the face of diachronic development, has not been factored into the discussion all that well either.[44] To be precise, within the corpus of Old Hebrew inscriptions of the late ninth and early eighth century, there is enormous continuity, with inscriptions from Israelite and Judean sites being very consistent in terms of the morphology and stance of the letters. Furthermore, the Old Hebrew script of the late eighth century and the early seventh century are very consistent in terms of morphology and stance of the letters. And the Old Hebrew inscriptions from the late seventh and early sixth century are very consistent in terms of the morphology and stance of the letters. That is, regardless of the site from which an inscription comes, if it comes from the late ninth or early eighth century, there are shared features that distinguish it from inscriptions hailing from the late eighth and early seventh centuries. Furthermore, regardless of the site from which an inscription was found, if it comes from the late seventh or early sixth cen-

---

43. For discussion and the secondary literature, see Rollston, "Scribal Education," 48–49.

44. For discussion and secondary references, see ibid., 50–61.

tury, there will be shared features that distinguish it from inscriptions from the late eighth and early seventh centuries and features that distinguish it from inscriptions hailing from the late ninth and early eighth centuries. These statements are particularly true of ostraca, but even for inscriptions chiseled or etched into stone, there are normally diagnostic features that allow assignment of a reasonably precise absolute date. Also of significance, there are dramatic differences between the Old Hebrew script, the Phoenician script, and the Aramaic script. Building on the research of those who have worked before me, I have discussed palaeographic methodology and the diagnostic features of the Old Hebrew, Phoenician, and Aramaic scripts in various publications, often in a rather detailed fashion.[45] In short, a trained palaeographer can read the diagnostic features of a script and assign it reliably to a script series (e.g., Phoenician, Old Hebrew, Aramaic) and provide a very reliable absolute date with a plus or minus range of around thirty to forty years. This is, of course, a very different skill set from simply being able to read the letters. That is, there are many people who are capable of reading the letters, but the numbers of people capable of determining script series and a reliable absolute date are relatively few in number. The same is quite true in the field of pottery typology as well. Some archaeologists are very fine masters of pottery typology and some are not, something that normally has a great deal to do with graduate training and also the focus of one's career. In any case, the reason palaeographers can do this is because scribes were carefully trained and there seems to have been little tolerance among scribal teachers for substantial variation (in contrast to the modern world, where much variation is tolerated). Furthermore, because the numbers of scribal students was always rather small (after all, the masses were not educated in writing), maintaining fairly strict quality controls was manageable. In any case, the main point is that the high caliber and consistency of the script used to write Old Hebrew inscriptions during Iron II cannot be a coincidence. It must be a curricular matter. Writing "correctly" must have been carefully taught and strictly enforced. Nothing else can account for the high quality of the writing

---

45. See Christopher A. Rollston, "The Script of Old Hebew Ostraca of the Iron Age: Eighth–Sixth Centuries BC," PhD diss., Johns Hopkins University, 1999; Rollston, "Non-Provenanced Epigraphs I: Pillaged Antiquities, Northwest Semitic Forgeries, and Protocols for Laboratory Tests," *Maarav* 10 (2003): 135–93; Rollston, "Scribal Education; Rollston, "Northwest Semitic Cursive Scripts of Iron II," in *An Eye for Form: Epigraphic Essays in Honor of Frank Moore Cross*, ed. Jo Ann Hackett and Walter Aufrect (Winona Lake, IN: Eisenbrauns, 2014); Rollston, "The Iron Age Phoenician Script," in Hackett and Aufrect, *An Eye for Form*. Within these publications, I refer to the work of previous scholars to whom I am deeply indebted, particularly Frank Moore Cross, Joseph Naveh, Brian Peckham, and P. Kyle McCarter.

and the consistency of morphology, stance, and (often) ductus.[46] Moreover, nothing else can adequately account for the attention given to letter environment, and the ways in which the position of a letter is often impacted by the letters that precede or follow it.[47] A foundational aspect of a scribal school was the proper production of the script.[48]

As an ancillary note, it is worth mentioning that during excavations in the City of David, a stone with an Old Hebrew inscription on it was found (IAA 1986-394). Particularly important, however, is this fact: the personal name Blṭh is written twice on this inscription and in immediate succession, but in two distinct hands. The first hand is a refined hand, trained in the careful execution of the script and with proper morphology and stance. But the second hand is remedial, with the morphology and the stance both executed poorly. In both cases the personal name is preceded by the *lamed* of possession. I consider this to be a scribal exercise, with the refined hand being that of the teacher and the remedial hand that of the student, much as is often said about inscriptions from Mesopotamia, Egypt, Greece, and Rome when two hands are present and these hands are of vastly different calibers.[49] This is, I believe, a priceless relic of ancient Old Hebrew curriculum.

THE CORE CURRICULUM FOR OLD HEBREW: ORTHOGRAPHY

For the corpus of Old Hebrew inscriptions, the orthography reflects synchronic consistency and diachronic development.[50] The Old Hebrew orthographic system can be synthesized as follows: (1) During the ninth

---

46. Ductus refers to the number of strokes used to form a letter, the order of the strokes, and the direction of the strokes. I will be publishing my data regarding ductus in a future publication. For the time being, notice, for example, that the vertical stroke of *'alep* is consistently the last stroke. Notice that the tick on the bottom horizontal of a *zayin* is normally the last stroke. And notice that the *'ayin* is normally formed with two semicircular down-strokes and that it is consistently closed in Old Hebrew (but consistently open in Aramaic, from the late eighth century onwards).

47. On this, for example, see my discussion of the *samek*-pe: Rollston, "Non-Provenanced Epigraphs I," 160–62; Rollston, "Scribal Education," 58–59.

48. Abecedaries often come up in discussions about education in ancient Israel and Judah. On these, see the discussion and secondary references in Rollston, "Scribal Education," 67.

49. See especially Rollston, "An Old Hebrew Stone Inscription," 189–96.

50. It is telling that Weeks (*Early Israelite Wisdom*, 152) has stated that "the use of *matres lectionis* ... shows considerable development over time" and also that "development [in Old Hebrew orthography] is hardly evidence of a static tradition of orthography." In essence, he is assuming that orthographic development through time (i.e., diachronic orthographic development) is incompatible with the presence of formal, standardized education. However, descriptive and prescriptive grammarians concur that orthographic development

and early eighth centuries, Hebrew orthography employed a system of final *matres lectionis:* final /ī/ was represented by *yod;* final /ū/ was represented by *waw;* final /ā/ was represented by *he;* final /ē/ was represented by *he;* final /ô/ was represented by *he.* There is a general absence of the internal *matres lectionis* throughout the lion's share of the eighth century. (2) During the terminal period of the eighth century and the beginning of the seventh century, final *matres lectionis* continued to be used, with final /ī/ represented by *yod,* final /ū/ represented by *waw,* final /ā/ represented by *he,* final /ē/ represented by *he,* and final /ô/ represented by *he.* In addition, there is Old Hebrew evidence for incipient usage of internal *matres lectionis,* with *waw* serving as a *mater lectionis* for internal /ū/, and *yod* serving as a *mater lectionis* for the internal /ī/. (3) During the second half of the seventh century and the beginning of the sixth century, final *matres lectionsis* continued to be used, with final /ī/ represented by *yod,* final /ū/ represented by *waw,* final /ā/ represented by *he,* final /ē/ represented by *he,* and final /ô/ represented by *he.* In addition, there is growing usage of internal *matres lectionis,* with *waw* serving as a *mater lectionis* for internal /ū/ and *yod* serving as a *mater lectionis* for the internal /ī/. In addition, I would also draw attention to some additional features of Old Hebrew orthography, namely, although *he* could serve as a *mater lectionis* for final /ē/ and final /ō/, it was never used as an internal *mater lectionis* in Old Hebrew for any vowel; moreover, although medial /ī/ and /ū/ could be marked with *yod* and *waw,* medial /ā/ was never marked with a *mater lectionis,* not even with *he.* In short, there is a fairly sophisticated system in place with regard to Hebrew orthography. Furthermore, it should be emphasized that the orthographic system with regard to Phoenician was very different from Old Hebrew. Basically, within Phoenician *matres lectionis* were not used at all in the Iron Age. And in Aramaic, *matres lectionis* were used in a manner that is very much like that of Old Hebrew (but with a phonological system that was quite different from Old Hebrew), but the usage of *matres lectionis* in Old Aramaic differs from Old Hebrew, at least in the sense that internal *matres lectionis* were used in Old Aramaic many decades prior to the usage in Old Hebrew. In short, the orthographic system in Old Hebrew inscriptions reflects synchronic consistency and diachronic development. It is an impressive system and the fact that the data are so consistent is a reflection of the fact that there were standard conventions in place, conventions that are most readily understood as an aspect of the education of scribes.[51]

---

can and does occur in living alphabetic writing systems, even though formal, standardized education is present.

51. For further discussion and for references to the secondary literature on the subject, see Rollston, "Scribal Education," 61–65.

That is, an important aspect of scribal education was instruction in the orthographic system.[52]

THE CORE CURRICULUM FOR OLD HEBREW: HIERATIC NUMERALS

Egyptian hieratic numerals are attested at several different Iron Age Israelite and Judaean sites, spanning from the ninth to early sixth centuries.[53] For example, hieratic numerals and Old Hebrew script are both present on an ostracon from Arad XI (Ad76), a site in Judah. Moreover, the Reisner Samaria Ostraca frequently use hieratic numerals (e.g., Sa22, Sa27, Sa28, Sa34, Sa58, Sa61), and this is a site in Israel. Hieratic numerals are also attested for Arad IX (e.g., Ad60; Ad65) and Arad VIII (e.g., Ad42; cf. Ad46). Several of the Arad VI–VII Hebrew ostraca use hieratic numerals and symbols (e.g., Ad 2; cf. Ad22, Ad31, Ad33), and one ostracon consists solely of hieratic numerals (Ad34). Hieratic numerals were also found at Lachish (e.g., Lachish weights) and also arguably at Yavneh Yam, that is, Meṣad Ḥashavyahu (cf. Mh3, Mh4). The use of hieratic numerals at Kadesh-Barnea is particularly significant, because among the Old Hebrew ostraca were several with hieratic numerals, including one that was an ostracon that originally consisted of hieratic numerical data spanning, in numeric order, from one to ten thousand. This ostracon also contained at least the beginning of another similar listing of the numbers. Based on the epigraphic evidence, it is demonstrable that Israelite scribes during the course of the ninth through sixth centuries, at disparate sites in Israel and Judah, were capable of using a complicated, (originally) foreign numeric system. Because of the complexity of the hieratic system, developing proficiency in its writing would not have been simple. For this reason, I believe that it is convincing to argue that learning hieratic numerals was part of the Old Hebrew scribal curriculum.

Someone might counter that it was Egyptian scribes who were responsible for the Hieratic numerals attested in Israel and Judah in the Iron Age. I do not think that this is convincing, for two reasons: the hieratic numerals are normally part of documents that contain Old Hebrew content, not Egyptian; and the system of hieratic numerals used in Israel and Judah originally

---

52. Of course, demonstration of the fact that the orthographic system for Old Hebrew is fairly complex can be ascertained by the reader of this article, who might be hard-pressed to convey all of these details to someone, after having just read it a time or two here.

53. The definitive treatment of Hieratic Numerals in Old Hebrew inscriptions is now Stefan Wimmer, *Palästinisches Hieratisch: Die Zahl- und Sonderzeichen in der althebräischen Schrift*, ÄAT 75 (Wiesbaden: Harrassowitz, 2008). For reference to some of the earlier studies, see Rollston, "Scribal Education," 66–67.

derived from the system of Egyptian hieratic numerals, but had developed into a distinct numeric system, with striking differences from the Egyptian hieratic numeric system of the ninth through sixth centuries BCE.[54] In sum, the totality of the evidence converges nicely to demonstrate in a convincing matter that this complicated numeric system was part of the Old Hebrew scribal curriculum.

The Core Curriculum for Old Hebrew: Letter Formulary

The corpus of Old Hebrew inscriptions contains a number of letters, and these letters reflect certain standard formulary features.[55] (1) These documents will normally begin with some reference to the recipient and often contain some sort of greeting (e.g., "May Yahweh cause my lord to hear a message of peace and good things"; cf. Lh2; Lh3; Lh4; Lh5; Lh6; Ad16; Ad21; Ad40). Sometimes the name of the sender is also provided (e.g., Lh 3; Ad 16; Ad21; Ad40), but this is not a dominant component of Old Hebrew letters. (2) Normally, Old Hebrew letters reflect a clear transition from the traditional greetings to the body of the letter. The word $w't$ ("and now") is a very common mode of transition, although sometimes different transitional formulae can be used. (3) After the transitional component of the letter, the body of the letter was penned. (4) Closing formula (e.g., signature, list of gods, and witnesses) are not a traditional component of Old Hebrew letters.

Of course, it would not be cogent to argue that learning the basic features of Old Hebrew epistolary formulae is a complex procedure; however, the presence of a certain common structure within the epistolary corpus cannot be dismissed as being of no curricular import. That is, it is reasonable to conclude that an aspect of the scribal curriculum in ancient Israel and Judah was some discussion of the standard means of formulating letters. Naturally, it is also reasonable to suggest that the standard formulae for composing legal texts (purchases, sales, marriages, divorces, adoptions) were also taught, but at this time we do not have those sorts of Old Hebrew texts at our disposal, as arguably most would have been written on perishable materials (such as papyri) and so have not survived the passage of time. Naturally, it is also reasonable to suggest that the composition of royal inscriptions would have been part of the curriculum and inscriptions such as the Mesha Stele (Moabite)

---

54. On this, see especially Wimmer, *Palästinisches Hieratisch*, passim.

55. For a recent collection of these letters, see James M. Lindenberger, *Ancient Aramaic and Hebrew Letters*, 2nd ed., WAW 14 (Atlanta: Society of Biblical Literature, 2003). For discussion of the formal features of these (and additional) letters, see especially Dennis Pardee, *Handbook of Ancient Hebrew Letters: A Study Edition* (Chico, CA: Scholars Press, 1982). The discussion presented here is based very heavily on Pardee's analysis.

and the Tell Siran Bottle (Ammonite) demonstrate that there was a tradition of royal inscriptions in the Iron Age Levant and so it is reasonable to contend that these were produced in ancient Israel and Judah as well. Indeed, we have evidence for the writing of monumental inscriptions in Israel (Samaria) and Judah (Jerusalem).[56] In any case, at the very least it can be said that here are numerous epistolary texts in Old Hebrew and based on these it can be stated that standard letter formulae was arguably a component of the scribal curriculum.

THE CORE CURRICULUM FOR OLD HEBREW: FOREIGN LANGUAGE(S) AND LITERATURE

The siege of the Neo-Assyrian King Sennacherib (r. 705–681 BCE) in 701 BCE is among the most documented historical events in the Iron Age history of Judah. The data available include (1) Sennacherib's Palace Reliefs from Nineveh, which depict in graphic fashion the siege of Judean Lachish; (2) Sennacherib's royal records of the campaign (preserved on the Taylor Prism and the Oriental Institute Prism), replete with reference to Judah's King Hezekiah (r. 715–687 BCE) being "trapped in Jerusalem like a bird in a cage"; (3) Evidence from the excavations at Lachish that document the Neo-Assyrian destruction of Lachish during this chronological horizon; (4) The Old Hebrew Siloam Tunnel Inscription, arguably completed during the reign of Hezekiah in order to conduct water from outside the city walls of Jerusalem to a location inside the city walls, much as certain textual traditions suggest (2 Kgs 20:20; 2 Chr 32:30; Ben Sira 48:17–18), something that is supported by the palaeographic dating of the inscription; (5) The narrative in the Hebrew Bible describing the siege (2 Kings 18–19; Isaiah 36–38).[57] In other words, archaeological, epigraphic, and art-historical evidence converge nicely with the biblical text, demonstrating rather nicely that the biblical text is, at least with regard to the siege itself, quite historical.[58] The reason for the recitation of this evidence is this: within the biblical narrative recount-

---

56. See Rollston, "Northwest Semitic Cursive Scripts." In addition to the inscriptions I mention in this article, I would also include both the Siloam Tunnel Inscription and the Royal Steward Inscription in the category of royal inscriptions, and both of these will be included in my forthcoming WAW volume on Northwest Semitic royal inscriptions (Atlanta: Society of Biblical Literature).

57. I do not believe that the recent attempt of Ronny Reich and Eli Shukron to date the Siloam Tunnel Inscription to the late ninth or early eighth century is convincing. The script of this inscription fits nicely into the Old Hebrew script typology for the late eighth and early seventh centuries BCE, not earlier. See Ronny Reich and Eli Shukron, "The Date of the Siloam Tunnel Reconsidered," *TA* 38 (2011): 147–57.

58. Still very useful for its discussion and the literature cited is, David Ussishkin, *The*

ing Sennacherib's campaign is a pericope in which the Judean officials in Jerusalem are reported to have made the following statement to the Neo-Assyrian Rab-Shaqeh: "Please speak to your servants in Aramaic, because we understand it. Do not speak to us in Judahite, in earshot of the people who are on the wall" (2 Kgs 18:26). Of course, according to the narrative, the Rab-Shaqeh absolutely refuses to speak in Aramaic, stating that he definitely wishes for the common people listening to the conversation to hear the threats that he is making.

Naturally, it should be noted that Aramaic was indeed used quite heavily in the Neo-Assyrian Empire during this period, something accurately presupposed, therefore, in the request of the Judean officials.[59] But it is particularly important to notice that this text also presupposes that the Judean officials are capable of understanding Aramaic, an international language of this time period. I take this reference to be historical. That is, I believe that Judean officials in this time period could understand Aramaic. After all, it was an international language, probably at this time the most important international language in the ancient Near East. Thus, I find myself very much in agreement with van der Toorn who wrote that "around 700, the officials of King Hezekiah were able to conduct a conversation in Aramaic which to the common people, was incomprehensible."[60] Furthermore, foreign languages were often taught in scribal schools in the ancient Near East and the cumulative evidence can be understood as supporting the notion that the *lingua*

Conquest of Lachish by Sennacherib (Tel Aviv: Publications of the Institute of Archaeology, 1983).

59. On the use of Aramaic in the Neo-Assyrian Empire, the bibliography is vast. For some discussion, see especially Hayim Tadmor, "The Aramaization of Assyria: Aspects of Western Impact," in *Mesopotamien und seine Nachbarn: Politische und kulturelle Wechselbeziehungen im Alten Vorderasien vom 4. Vis 1 Jahrtausend v. Chr.*, Teil 2, ed. Hans-Jörg Nissen und Johannes Renger (Berlin: Reimer, 1982), 449–70; Jonas Greenfield, "The Dialects of Early Aramaic," *JNES* 37 (1978): 93–99; John Huehnergard, "What is Aramaic?" *ARAM* 7 (1995): 261–82.

60. Karel van der Toorn, *Scribal Culture*, 100. Note also that the Hebrew Bible contains a fair number of Aramaic words, as demonstrated by Max Wagner, *Die lexikalischen und grammatikalischen Aramaismen im alttestamentlichen Hebäisch*, BZAW 96 (Berlin: Töpelmann, 1966). Of course, the usage of Aramaic continued to increase in Judah during the following decades and centuries, with substantial segments of the biblical books of Daniel and Ezra written in Aramaic. For some discussion of Aramaic during the Second Temple period, see also William Schiedewind, "Aramaic, the Death of Written Hebrew, and Language Shift in the Persian Period," in *Margins of Writing, Origins of Cultures*, ed. Seth L. Sanders, OIS 2 (Chicago: Oriental Institute of the University of Chicago, 2006), 137–47.

franca of the ancient Near East was taught as part of the scribal curriculum in ancient Judah.[61]

As for training in things foreign, I doubt that it stopped with foreign language(s). After all, as Carr has succinctly stated "the Hebrew Bible—a complex collection of texts from widely different periods—testifies to a form of cultural reproduction that is intensely textual."[62] And within this intensely textual corpus of literature that is the Hebrew Bible, we have significant dependence on foreign literature and foreign traditions, from the heavy usage of the Egyptian text Wisdom of Amenemope in the section of Proverbs known as The Words of the Wise (Prov 22:17–24:22), the usage of the Birth Legend of Sargon in the Birth Legends of Moses (Exod 2:1-10), the recrafting of Enuma Elish and Gilgamesh in the Hebrew Bible's narratives about creation and the flood (Gen 1–2, 6–8), and the delightful rendition of the Balaam Story (Num 22–24), shared also with a segment of ancient Ammon. Of course, the connections between the Covenant Code (Exod 20–23) and ancient Near Eastern legal traditions are also part of this phenomenon as well. True, someone might suggest that all of this was oral, not written. I have no doubt that lore traveled far and wide in the oral and aural world of the ancient Near East, but I am also confident that it traveled to the Levant in written form as well, the Late Bronze Age Gilgamesh Tablet from Megiddo being a reflection of this, of course. And, of course, a natural locus for such materials in Israel and Judah would be scribal, that is, within some sort of educational context in which some of the great literature of the ancient Near East would be appreciated and perpetuated. Again, I am primarily arguing that within the formal, standardized education of scribes in Israel and Judah, there would have been some focus on Aramaic, but I am also suggesting that

---

61. In fact, it seems reasonable to suggest that those who produced the inscriptions written in the Phoenician script at Kuntillet Ajrud were Israelite or Judean. For these inscriptions, see Aḥituv, Eshel, and Meshel, "The Inscriptions," 105–19. Because the Old Hebrew script had derived from the Phoenician script and because Phoenician was still a prestige language and script during the ninth and eighth centuries, it may be that the Phoenician language and script were also part of the scribal curriculum at certain times in the history of Israel and Judah. Compare also in this connection, Paul V. Mankowski, *Akkadian Loanwords in Biblical Hebrew*, HSS 47 (Winona Lake, IN: Eisenbrauns, 2000). Of course, for books dating to the Second Temple period, Persian and Greek words are also attested. For reference to some of this material (in the Aramaic of the Hebrew Bible), see Franz Rosenthal, *A Grammar of Biblical Aramaic*, Porta Series (Wiesbaden: Harassowitz, 1983). Naturally, it seems reasonable to contend that Aramaic would have been part of the scribal curriculum in Israel as well, from the time of the Omrides to the time of the fall of Israel to the Neo-Assyrian Kings Shalmaneser V and Sargon II. But for the purposes of this paper, I am just arguing that Aramaic was part of the curriculum in Judah.

62. David M. Carr, *Writing on the Tablet of the Heart*, 112.

the evidence from the Hebrew Bible itself suggests that foreign literature was known among the elites of Israel and Judah as well.

Final Thoughts: The Aegis of Scribal Education

The precise nature of the curriculum for scribal students in ancient Israel and Judah cannot be known with the precision that it is in Mesopotamia and Egypt, not yet at least. The turn of a spade can change all of that in a heartbeat, though. Nevertheless, the high caliber of the Old Hebrew inscriptions at our disposal allows us to make some reasoned and empirical statements about the broad contours of the Old Hebrew scribal curriculum. However, it is reasonable to attempt to discern the locus of this scribal education, the aegis under the auspices of which it takes place. Van der Toorn has made the following statement in that regard: "The formation of scribes who were 'expert and wise' required a program of study provided only in the temple school."[63] I am sympathetic with this statement. After all, I suspect that the high priest was literate and that there were a number of priests functioning within the upper echelons of power who worked under him who were literate as well, capable of both writing and reading well. But it seems to me to be too precise to state that scribes could only be trained in the context of the temple. For my part, I would emphasize the nature of the Old Hebrew epigraphic data that we have and I would wish to base my conclusions most squarely on that. And as I have noted already, the majority of the Old Hebrew epigraphic texts at our disposal hail from the state's military and economic apparatus. That is, Tel Arad, Tel Lachish, Horvat 'Uza, and Tel Ira are major sources of Old Hebrew epigraphic data and all of these are sites associated with the state military. Of course, Yavneh Yam (Meṣad Ḥashavyahu) is a military fortress as well. Moreover, the sites of Samaria and Gibeon are major sources of Old Hebrew epigraphic materials, and these epigraphic materials are economic in nature and consist of state documentation regarding commodities. It would be reasonable, therefore, to posit that the locus of the scribal school that produced the scribes who wrote these documents was the palace. This would be entirely logical. But I suspect that even this would be too precise, although the epigraphic evidence would support this position considerably better than it would support the notion of a scribal school confined just to the temple. In reality, I believe that the separation of the sacred (temple) and the secular (palace) that we might wish to propose is actually anachronistic and atomistic. The best manner of accounting for all of the data (epigraphic and

---

63. Van der Toorn, *Scribal Culture*, 97.

biblical) is to contend that scribal education was simply a matter of the state, without attempting to dissect it more than this.

Finally, with regard to aegis, I am afraid that I do not find compelling the proposal of Sanders that the epicenter for the scribal education and scribal work in Israel, Judah, and Lebanon was within some sort of guild, distinct from the aegis of the government. To be precise, Sanders has written that "the epigraphic evidence points to Hebrew scribes working outside of large institutions, which makes them less like merchants or clerks and more like potters or metalworkers ... this sort of scribalism could easily be brought into the service of the state, but did not require the same massing of people and resources as a chancery."[64] Similarly, with regard to the Phoenician script he has written: "In concrete historical terms, this script has no national or ethnic identity ... we cannot explain the first standardized linear alphabet scripts as flowing purely from autocratic decisions of state chanceries: our nation sounding designation 'Phoenician' is a purely modern convenience, with no basis at all in contemporary Phoenician sources."[65] Or again, with regard to Aramaic, "the contemporary Early Standard Aramaic of the Iron Age was also crafted for uniformity, and also was not the property of any single kingdom."[66]

Perhaps part of the difficulty is the broad language Sanders uses to set up his understanding of the ancient context. For example, he suggests that to believe that positing that writing was something that functioned primarily under the aegis of a state would mean that the standardized alphabet in Phoenician should be framed as *"flowing purely from autocratic decisions of state chanceries"* (emphasis mine), and his assumption that affirming that scribal activity in Old Hebrew was primarily under the aegis of Israel and Judah would require a *"massing of people and resources"* (emphasis mine). Similarly, regarding Aramaic, he states that he believes it possessed "uniformity," but that it was *"not the property of any single kingdom."* That is, I do not know of anyone who believes that the Phoenician script flowed "purely from autocratic decisions." Human society is never so neat and clean as that in terms of desires and outcomes. Nor do I think the best of recent scholarship on scribal activity in Israel and Judah would contend that it required a "massing of people and resources." Indeed, this sort of language conjures up the notion of some sort of 'massive' bureaucracy," which I think most people would find difficult to believe. Nor also do I know of anyone who argues that the Aramaic language or script was the "sole property of any

---

64. Seth L. Sanders, *The Invention of Hebrew* (Urbana: University of Illinois Press, 2009), 131.
65. Ibid., 132.
66. Ibid., 136.

single kingdom." Little in the ancient world is probably the "sole property" of a state (and at least in terms of language, I would suggest that there was a fair amount of diversity in both Old and Imperial Aramaic). Moreover, in this connection it is worth mentioning that a distinct Aramaic national script is first attested in the eighth century BCE, and a recent dissertation at Johns Hopkins University has suggested that the Neo-Assyrian Empire is a reasonable candidate for the rise of this national script.[67] In any case, I think that the choice of such stark terminology by Sanders prejudices the argument. I find his rhetoric and elegant command of English breathtaking, but this proposal difficult to embrace.

Rather, I would suggest that the most useful approach is to look at the Iron Age epigraphic evidence we have, in very concrete terms and allow that to be the foundation for our suppositions about aegis. (1) For Old Hebrew, it is a demonstrable fact that during the course of some two hundred years, the vast majority of the epigraphic material comes from Israelite and Judean officialdom. Not all of it, but the majority of it comes from officialdom (see above). And the caliber of this material in terms of script, orthography, numerics, and formulae is very impressive. (2) Regarding the Phoenician alphabet of the late eleventh and early tenth centuries, I am disinclined to accept the notion that the script "has no national or ethnic identity." Ancient Lebanon was diverse, with various city states, but the script and language is a national script, a distinct, standardized, national script. That is not to say that different nations did not use the Phoenician script. Some did.[68] But the epigraphic evidence at our disposal suggests that the standardization occurred under royal auspices in the cities of the region of Lebanon, cities such as Byblos, Tyre, and Sidon for which we normally use the term Phoenician.[69] Note especially that the inscriptions from Byblos dating to the late eleventh, tenth, and early ninth centuries were those of kings, with the Aḥiram Sarcophagus Inscription referring to "Aḥiram King of Byblos," the Yeḥimilk Dedicatory Inscription having been commissioned by, and containing reference to, "Yeḥimilk King of Byblos," the Abibaʻl Inscription being a royal dedicatory inscription commissioned by, and referring to, "Abibaʻl King of Byblos," the Elibaʻl Inscription being a royal dedicatory inscription commissioned by, and referring to, "Elibaʻl King of Byblos," and the Shipiṭbaʻl Inscription containing reference to "Shipiṭbaʻl King of Byblos, son of Elibaʻl

---

67. H. D. Davis Parker, "The Levant Comes of Age: The Ninth Century BCE through Script Traditions" (PhD diss., The Johns Hopkins University, 2013).

68. For brief discussion, see Rollston, *Writing and Literacy*, 27–44.

69. For discussion of the term "Phoenician," see Christopher A. Rollston, "The Phoenicians" in *The World Around the Old Testament*, ed. Brent A. Strawn and William Arnold (Grand Rapids: Baker, forthcoming).

King of Byblos, son of Yeḥimilk King of Byblos." The Azarbaʻl Inscription from Byblos antedates all of these, but is fragmentary and so we do not know the title of Azarbaʻl, but the script is the standard Phoenician script of the late eleventh century BCE or the very early tenth century BCE (i.e., not the Early Alphabetic of preceding decades and centuries).[70] In short, the earliest Phoenician texts of any length at all hail from officialdom, from the royal court of Byblos, probably the most distinguished of the network of cities using the Phoenician language as their native language.[71]

Sanders objects, though, and states that the Phoenician script "had already been used in the previous century" on arrowheads to refer to "the King of Amurru."[72] At first blush, this might seem to some to be useful, even decisive, evidence. Alas, though, one must always probe evidence to discern potential importance, and this is a case in point. (1) There are two arrowheads with the name "Zakarbaʻl King of Amurru." The first was published by Starcky in 1982.[73] The second was published by Deutsch and Heltzer in 1994.[74] (2) Cross and Milik had published the el-Khadr arrowheads decades prior to the "discovery" of these arrowheads published by Starcky, Deutsch, and Heltzer.[75] (3) Neither of these arrowheads with the words "Zakarbaʻl King of Amurru" comes from a stratified context. (4) In fact, both of them are from the antiquities market. The site from which they ostensibly came, therefore, shall never be known. (5) Indeed, I am not even confident about the authenticity of either of these. Deutsch and Heltzer make the following statement about theirs: "the deep corrosion of some places of the arrowhead, especially in places where letters are incised gives us definitive proof that the inscription is genuine." Of course, corrosion on metal surfaces is certainly not something that requires millennia. Indeed, exposure to the elements for a few months or years corrodes various metals rather nicely. As for Starcky's arrowhead, he simply notes that it was "acquired" by the Lebanese Museum. (6) It is also worthy of mention that of all of the inscribed arrowheads known at this time, only the first one, discovered in a tomb in Ruweiseh (Lebanon)

---

70. For discussion of the dates for these inscriptions, see Rollston, "Early Royal Byblian Phoenician Inscriptions," 57–93 passim; Rollston, *Writing and Literacy*, 20–27.

71. Sanders knows the corpora for Old Hebrew and Phoenician, to be sure, but I am reiterating the basic data here, as I think that the concrete specifics of the data must drive the argument, hence, the emphasis here.

72. Sanders, *The Invention of Hebrew*, 132.

73. James L Starckey, "La fleche de Zakarbaʻal, roi d'Amurru," in *Archeologie au Levant: recueil à la memoire de Roger Saidah* (Lyon: Maison de l'Orient, 1982), 179–86.

74. Robert Deutsch and Michael Heltzer, *Forty New Ancient West Semitic Inscriptions* (Tel Aviv: Archaeological Center Publications, 1994), 12–13.

75. Frank Moore Cross and J. T. Milik, "A Typological Study of the El-Khadr Javelin and Arrowheads," *ADAJ* 3 (1956): 15–23.

was found in a secure archaeological context, in the year 1925.[76] (7) In short, I would not wish to saddle these arrowheads from the antiquities market with too much weight, for any discussion about the site from which they come is absolute speculation, and without some sort of stratified context and associated objects, reliance must be entirely on the palaeographic date, and at best, this date would have a plus or minus range of several decades. And, finally, the authenticity of these pieces is not something that can be considered certain.

In sum, the preponderance of the evidence demonstrates, I believe, that there was formal, standardized scribal education in ancient Israel and Judah.[77] I believe that some (nonscribal) elites were able to access this education at times as well. I have argued that we can discern some specific aspects of the curriculum of these scribal schools, based on the nature of the epigraphic evidence itself. And as for the aegis of scribal education, I think that the evidence at hand demonstrates nicely that the most plausible aegis was the government bureaucracies, probably fairly small in this time period, but capable of educating in a sophisticated and standardized manner, an impressive accomplishment indeed.

References

Aharoni, Yohanan. *Investigations at Lachish: The Sanctuary and the Residency (Lachish V)*. Publications of the Tel Aviv University Institute of Archaeology 4. Tel Aviv: Gateway, 1975.

———. *Arad Inscriptions*. Jerusalem: Israel Exploration Society, 1981.

Ahituv, Shmuel, Esther Eshel, and Zeev Meshel. "The Inscriptions." Pages 73–142 in *Kuntillet Ajrud 'Ajrud (Horvat Teman): An Iron Age II Religious Site on the Judah-Sinai Border*. Edited by Zeev Meshel. Jerusalem: Israel Exploration Society, 2012.

Avigad, Nahman. "The Epitaph of a Royal Steward." *IEJ* 3 (1953): 137–52.

Beentjes, Pancratius C. *The Book of Ben Sira in Hebrew: A Text Edition of all Extant Hebrew Manuscripts and a Synopsis of all Parallel Hebrew Ben Sira Texts*. VTSup 68. Leiden: Brill, 1997.

Beit-Arieh, Yitzhaq. *Horvat 'Uza and Horvat Radum: Two Fortresses in the Biblical Negev*. Tel Aviv: Institute of Archaeology, 2007.

———. *Tel 'Ira: A Stronghold in the Biblical Negev*. Nadler Institute of Archaeology: Monograph Series 15. Tel Aviv: Yass Publications in Archaeology, 1999.

---

76. For the publication, see Marc Antoine Guigues, "Pointe de Heche en bronze a inscription Phenicienne," *MUSJ* 11 (1926): 325–28.

77. And, of course, based on the epigraphic evidence, I would contend that there was also formal, standardized scribal education in Lebanon, Syria, Moab, Ammon, Edom, and Philistia.

Brunner, Hellmut. *Altägyptische Erziehung*. Wiesbaden: Harrassowitz, 1957.
Caminos, Ricardo Augusto. *Late Egyptian Miscellanies*. BEStud 1. London: Oxford University Press, 1954.
Carr, David M. *Writing on the Tablet of the Heart: Origins of Scripture and Literature*. Oxford: Oxford University Press, 2005.
Civil, Miguel. "Sur le 'livres d'écolier' à l'époque paléobabylonienne." Pages 67–78 in *Miscellanea Babylonica: Mélanges offerts à Maurice Birot*. Edited by Jean-Marie Durand and Jean-Robert Kupper. Paris: Editions Recherche sur les civilizations, 1985.
Cohen, Yoram. *The Scribes and Scholars of the City of Emar in the Late Bronze Age*, HSS 59. Winona Lake, IN: Eisenbrauns, 2009.
Crenshaw, James L. " Education in Ancient Israel." *JBL* 104 (1985): 601–15.
———. *Education in Ancient Israel: Across the Deadening Silence*. New York: Doubleday, 1998.
Cross, Frank Moore, and J. T. Milik. "A Typological Study of the El-Khadr Javelin and Arrowheads." *ADAJ 3* (1956): 15–23.
Davies, Graham I. "Were there Schools in Ancient Israel?" Pages 199–211 in *Wisdom in Ancient Israel: Essays in Honour of J. A. Emerton*. Edited by Jonathan Day, Robert P. Gordon, and Hugh G. M. Williamson. Cambridge: Cambridge University Press, 1995.
Dever, William. G. "Iron Age Epigraphic Material from the Area of Khirbet el-Kom." *HUCA* 40–41 (1969–1970): 139–204.
Deutsch, Robert, and Heltzer, Michael. *Forty New Ancient West Semitic Inscriptions*. Tel Aviv: Archaeological Center, 1994.
Dürr, Lorenz. *Das Erziehungswesen im AT und im antiken Orient*. Leipzig: Hinrichs, 1932.
Ellison, John. "The Ugaritic Alphabetic Script" Pages 56–71 in *An Eye for Form: Epigraphic Essays in Honor of Frank Moore Cross*. Winona Lake, IN: Eisenbrauns, 2014.
Fox, Nili. S. *In the Service of the King: Officialdom in Ancient Israel and Judah*. Cincinnati: Hebrew Union College, 2000.
Frick, Frank. " Another Inscribed Jar Handle from el-Jib." *BASOR* 213 (1974): 46–48.
Gasse, Annie. *Catalogue des ostraca litteraires de Deir el-Medina*. Tome V. Cairo: Institut français d'archéologie orientale, 2005.
George, Andrew. "In Search of the é.dub.ba.a: The Ancient Mesopotamian School in Literatureand Reality." Pages 127–37 in *An Experienced Scribe Who Neglects Nothing: Ancient Near Eastern Studies in Honor of Jacob Klein*. Edited by Yitzchak Sefati, Pinhas Artzi, Chaim Cohen, Barry L. Eichler, and Victor A. Hurowitz. Bethesda, MD: CDL, 2005.
Golka, Friedman W. "The Israelite Wisdom School or 'The Emperor's New Clothes.'" Pages 4–15 in *The Leopard's Spots: Biblical and African Wisdom in Proverbs*. Edinburgh: T&T Clark, 1993.
Greenfield, Jonas. "The Dialects of Early Aramaic." *JNES 37* (1978): 93–99.
Guigues, Marc-Antoine. "Pointe de Heche en bronze a inscription Phenicienne." *MUSJ 11* (1926): 325–28.
Hallo, William W. and K. Lawson Younger. *The Context of Scripture: Canonical Compositions from the Biblical World*. 3 volumes. Leiden: Brill, 1997–2002.

Haran, Menahem. "On the Diffusion of Literacy and Schools in Ancient Israel." Pages 81–95 in *Congress Volume, Jerusalem 1986.* Edited by John A. Emerton. VTSup 40. Leiden: Brill, 1988.
Heaton, E. W. *The School Tradition of the Old Testament.* Oxford: Oxford University Press, 1994.
Hermisson, Hans-Jurgen. *Studien zur israelitischen Spruchweisheit. Wissenschaftliche Monographien zum Alten und Neuen Testament 28.* Neukirchen-Vluyn: Neukirchener, 1968.
Huehnergard, John. "What is Aramaic?" *ARAM* 7 (1995): 261–82.
Hurowitz, Victor A. "Literary Observations on 'In Praise of the Scribal Art.'" *JANES* 27 (2000): 49–56.
Jamieson-Drake, D. W. *Scribes and Schools in Monarchic Judah: A Socio-Archaeological Approach.* JSOTSup 109. Sheffield: Sheffield Academic, 1991.
Janssen, Rosalind, and Jac J. Janssen, *Growing Up in Ancient Egypt.* London: Rubicon, 1990.
Lang, Bernhard. "Schule und Unterricht im alten Israel." Pages 186–201 in *La sagesse de l'ancient testament.* Edited by Maurice Gilbert. Leuven: Peeters, 1990.
Lemaire, André. *Les écoles et la formation de la bible dans l'ancien Israël.* OBO 39. Göttingen: Vandenhoeck & Ruprecht, 1981.
———. "A Schoolboy's Exercise on an Ostracon at Lachish." *TA* 3 (1976): 109–10.
Lichtheim, Miriam. *The Old and Middle Kingdoms.* Vol. 1 of *Ancient Egyptian Literature.* Berkeley: University of California Press, 1973.
———. *The New Kingdom.* Vol. 2 of *Ancient Egyptian Literature.* Berkeley: University of California Press, 1976.
Lindenberger, James M. *Ancient Aramaic and Hebrew Letters.* 2nd ed. WAW 14. Atlanta: Society of Biblical Literature, 2003.
Mankowski, Paul. *Akkadian Loanwords in Biblical Hebrew.* HSS 47. Winona Lake, IN: Eisenbrauns, 2000.
McDowell, Andrea G. *Village Life in Ancient Egypt: Laundry Lists and Love Songs.* Oxford: Oxford University, 1999.
———. "Teachers and Students at Deir el-Medina." Pages 217–33 in *Deir el-Medina in the Third Millennium AD: A Tribute to Jac J. Janssen.* Edited by Robert J. Demarée and Arno Egberts. Leiden: Nederlands Instituut voor het Nabije Oosten, 2000.
———. "Student Exercises from Deir el-Medina: The Dates" Pages 601–8 in *Studies in Honor of William Kelly Simpson.* Edited by Peter Der Manuelian. 2 volumes. Boston: Museum of Fine Arts, 1996.
Naveh, Joseph. *Early History of the Alphabet: An Introduction to West Semitic Epigraphy and Palaeography.* 2nd ed. Jerusalem: Magnes, 1987.
———. "A Hebrew Letter from the Seventh Century B.C." *IEJ* 10 (1960): 129–39.
———. "More Hebrew Inscriptions from Meṣad Ḥashavyahu." *IEJ* 12 (1962): 27–32.
Pardee, Dennis. *Handbook of Ancient Hebrew Letters: A Study Edition.* Chico, CA: Scholars Press, 1982.
Parker, Heather Dana Davis. "The Levant Comes of Age: The Ninth Century BCE through Script Traditions." PhD diss., The Johns Hopkins University. Baltimore, MD, 2013.
Pritchard, James B. *Hebrew Inscriptions and Stamps from Gibeon.* Philadelphia: Uni-

versity Musuem, University of Pennsylvania, 1959.

———. "More Inscribed Jar Handles from El-Jîb." *BASOR* 160 (1960): 2–6.

Puech, Emile. "Les écoles dans l'Israël préexilique: Données épigraphiques." Pages 189–203 in *Congress Volume: Jerusalem 1986*. Edited by John A. Emerton. VTSup 40. Leiden: Brill, 1988.

Reich, Ronny and Shukron, Eli. "The Date of the Siloam Tunnel Reconsidered." *TA* 38 (2011): 147–57.

Reisner, George Andrew, Clarence Stanley Fisher, and David Gordon Lyon. *Harvard Excavations at Samaria: 1908–1910*. Vol. 1: *Text*. Cambridge: Harvard University Press, 1924.

Rollston, Christopher A. "Ben Sira 38:24–39:11 and the Egyptian Satire of the Trades: A Reconsideration." *JBL* 120 (2001): 131–39.

———. "The Dating of the Early Royal Byblian Phoenician Inscriptions: A Response to Benjamin Sass." *Maarav* 15 (2008): 57–93.

———. "The Iron Age Phoenician Script." Pages 72–99 in *An Eye for Form: Epigraphic Essays in Honor of Frank Moore Cross*. Edited by Jo Ann Hackett and Walter Aufrect. Winona Lake, IN: Eisenbrauns, 2014.

———. "Non-Provenanced Epigraphs I: Pillaged Antiquities, Northwest Semitic Forgeries and Protocols for Laboratory Tests." *Maarav* 10 (2003): 135–93.

———. "An Old Hebrew Stone Inscription from the City of David: A Trained Hand and a Remedial Hand on the Same Inscription." Pages 189–96 in *Puzzling Out the Past: Studies in Northwest Semitic Languages and Literatures in Honor of Bruce Zuckerman*. Edited by Steven Fine, Marilyn Lundberg, and Wayne Pitard. Leiden: Brill, 2012.

———. "Northwest Semitic Cursive Scripts of Iron II." Pages 202–34 in *An Eye for Form: Epigraphic Essays in Honor of Frank Moore Cross*. Edited by Jo Ann Hackett and Walter Aufrect. Winona Lake, IN: Eisenbrauns, 2014.

———. "The Pheonician Script of the Tel Zayit Abecedary and Putative Evidence for Israelite Literacy." Pages 61–96 in *Literature Culture and Tenth-Century Canaan: The Tel Zayit Abecedary in Context*. Edited by Ron E. Tappy and P. Kyle McCarter. Winona Lake, IN: Eisenbrauns, 2008.

———. "The Phoenicians." In *The World Around the Old Testament*. Edited by Brent A. Strawn and William Arnold. Grand Rapids: Baker, forthcoming.

———. "Scribal Education in Ancient Israel: The Old Hebrew Epigraphic Evidence." *BASOR* 344 (2006): 47–74.

———. "The Script of Hebrew Ostraca of the Iron Age: Eighth–Sixth Centuries BCE." PhD diss., The Johns Hopkins University. Baltimore, MD, 1999.

———. *Writing and Literacy in the World of Ancient Israel: Epigraphic Evidence from the Iron Age*. Leiden: Brill, 2010.

Rosenthal, Franz. *A Grammar of Biblical Aramaic*, Porta Series. Wiesbaden: Harassowitz, 1983.

Sanders, Seth L., ed. *Margins of Writing, Origins of Cultures*. Chicago: The Oriental Institute of the University of Chicago, 2006.

———. *The Invention of Hebrew*. Urbana: University of Illinois Press, 2009.

Schniedewind, William M. "Aramaic, the Death of Written Hebrew, and Language Shift in the Persian Period." Pages 137–47 in *Margins of Writing, Origins of Cultures*. OIS 2. Chicago: The Oriental Institute of the University of Chicago, 2006.

Shoham, Yoav. "Hebrew Bullae." Pages 29–57 in *City of David Excavations: Final Report VI*. Qedem 41. Edited by D. T. Ariel et al., Jerusalem: Hebrew University, 2000.
Sjöberg, Åke W. "Der Examenstext A." *ZA* 64 (1975): 137–76.
———. "In Praise of the Scribal Art (Examination Text D)." *JCS* 24 (1972): 126–31.
———. "Der Vater und sein missratener Sohn." *JCS* 25 (1973): 105–69.
Starcky, Jean. "La fleche de Zakarba'al, roi d'Amurru." Pages 179–86 in *Archeologie au Levant: recueil á la memoire de Roger Saidah*. Lyon: Maison de l'Orient, 1982.
Tadmor, Hayim. "The Aramaization of Assyria: Aspects of Western Impact." Pages 449–70 in *Mesopotamien und seine Nachbarn: Politische und kulturelle Wechselbeziehungen im Alten Vorderasien vom 4. Vis 1 Jahrtausend v. Chr.*, Teil 2. Edited by Hans-Jörg Nissen und Johannes Renger. Berlin: Reimer, 1982.
Tinney, Stephen J. "On the Curricular Setting of Sumerian Literature." *Iraq* 61 (1999): 159–72.
———. "Texts, Tablets, and Teaching: Scribal Education at Nippur and Ur."*Expedition* 40/2 (1998): 40–50.
Tur-Sinai, Naftali Herz, G. Lankester Harding, A. Lewis, and James L. Starkey. *Lachish I (Tell ed-Duweir): The Lachish Letters*. London: Oxford University, 1938.
Ussishkin, David. *The Conquest of Lachish by Sennacherib*. Tel Aviv: Publications of the Institute of Archaeology, 1983.
van der Toorn, Karel. *Scribal Culture and the Making of the Hebrew Bible*. Cambridge: Harvard University Press, 2007.
Vanstiphout, Herman L. J. "On the Old Edubba Education." Pages 3–16 in *Centres of Learning: Learning and Location in Pre-Modern Europe and the Near East*. Edited by Jan Willem Drijvers and Alastair A. MacDonald. Leiden: Brill, 1995.
Veldhuis, Niek. "Elementary Education at Nippur: The Lists of Trees and Wooden Objects." PhD diss., University of Gronigen, 1997.
———. "Mesopotamian Canons." Pages 9–28 in *Homer, the Bible and Beyond: Literary and Religious Canons in the Ancient World*. Edited by Margalit Finkelberg and Guy G. Stroumsa. Leiden: Brill, 2003.
———. *Religion, Literature and Scholarship: the Sumerian Composition "Nanše and the Birds."* CM 22. Leiden: Brill/Styx, 2004.
Wagner, Max. *Die lexikalischen und grammatikalischen Aramaismen im alttestamentlichen Hebäisch*, BZAW 96. Berlin: Töpelmann, 1966.
Weeks, Stuart. *Early Israelite Wisdom*. Oxford: Clarendon, 1994.
Whybray, R. N. *The Intellectual Tradition in the Old Testament*. BZAW 135. Berlin: de Gruyter, 1974.
Wimmer, Stefan. *Palästinisches Hieratisch: Die Zahl- und Sonderzeichnen in der Althebräischen Schrift*, ÄAT 75. Wiesbaden: Harrassowitz, 2008.
Young, Ian M. "Israelite Literacy: Interpreting the Evidence Part I." *VT* 48 (1998): 239–53.
———. "Israelite Literacy: Interpreting the Evidence, Part II." *VT* 48 (1998): 408–22.
———. "Israelite Literacy and Inscriptions: A Response to Richard Hess." *VT* 54 (2005): 565–67.
Zeigler, Joseph. *Sapientia Iesu Filii Sirach*. Göttingen: Vandenhoeck & Ruprecht, 1965.

MEMORIALIZING CONFLICT: TOWARD AN IRON AGE "SHADOW" HISTORY OF ISRAEL'S EARLIEST LITERATURE

Brian B. SCHMIDT

IN THE QUEST TO ARTICULATE A HISTORY OF THE ACTUAL, MATERIAL composition of those written works that we now refer to as the books of the Hebrew Bible, epigraphic investigators in search of comparable literary texts of length may surprisingly find themselves, and rather ironically I might add, in an advantageous position. This stands in spite of the overall relative dearth often lamented in the secondary literature commenting on Hebrew and West Semitic inscriptions from the Iron Age southern Levant.[1] Yet, as the veritable clock ticks on, researchers, in their pursuit to articulate that history and the various societal factors at play, will most likely gain ever greater recourse to a steadily growing material cultural and epigraphic database. Nonetheless, lurking beneath the anticipated riches of data lies the daunting prospect of reconstructing a nuanced, compelling history of that Iron Age phenomenon. The present iteration is much more modest. It aims to identify and assess the earliest evidence we have for the production of lengthy literary texts in Iron

---

I wish to thank Ian Young, Billie Jean Collins, and James Bos for their helpful comments on earlier drafts of this essay.

1. This is not meant to dismiss the *relative* paucity of epigraphic data when compared to those, say, of Mesopotamia or Egypt that is widely acknowledged. Yet, the general database is ever and gradually growing. As examples, note the excavation-based discovery of several early brief inscriptions and other epigraphic data over the past few years (the Zayit, Qeiyafa, Rehov, Safi, and Ophel inscriptions to name just a few); the recent recovery of new Iron Age bullae from Jerusalem, many with papyrus traces on their undersides (see Ronny Reich and Eli Shukron, "Recent Discoveries in the City of David, Jerusalem." *IEJ* 57 [2007]: 156–57); and the newly published, full corpus of bullae from Iron Age levels at Tell Jemmeh (see David Ben-Shlomo and Othmar Keel, "Clay Sealings and Seal Impressions," in *The Smithsonian Institution Excavation at Tell Jemmeh, Israel, 1970–1990*, edited by David Ben-Shlomo and Gus W. Van Beek, Smithsonian Contributions to Anthropology 50 [Washington D.C.: Smithsonian Institution Scholarly Press, 2014], 857–75).

Age Israel and Judah with the goal of advancing the collective effort to prognosticate that larger history.[2]

Searching for lengthy literary texts in pre-exilic Israelite society begs many crucial questions, but only three will be addressed here. First, what are we looking for? Maximally, what is in view are texts that approximate the individual biblical books as we now have them in terms of literary quality and length. Minimally, what is in view are texts approximating the length of the final-stage written sources or the forerunners widely recognized as having made up major portions of the biblical books. These may approximate in length and quality for example, a coherent Yahwistic, Deuteronomistic, or Priestly document as articulated in more recent documentary criticism.[3] Such lengthy literary texts in the epigraphic corpus should also be distinguished from much shorter literary texts like the early eighth century, partially preserved, six-line text (a hymn?) from Kuntillet Ajrud or the later nonliterary, eleven-line epigraphic production, Arad ostracon 31, a palimpsest list of grain allocations. The first is very brief and fragmentary, though literary, while the second is twice as long, but nonliterary in character.[4]

Second, what do we have? We have no lengthy literary texts written on papyrus or parchment from earlier Iron Age Israel and clearly none that approximate the lengthy texts of the biblical books or even their shorter forerunners. What we do have are a handful of lengthy texts composed in the late ninth century BCE on stone, or, in one case, on a plastered wall. This prompts a third question: what significance, if any, can one infer then from the production of lengthy monumental inscriptions vis-à-vis the creation of literary texts written on perishable papyrus or parchment? Three possible scenarios present themselves: one might envision a scribal apparatus capable of producing monumental inscriptions of length that was either (1) carrying

---

2. For recent contributions on this front, see Christopher Rollston, *Writing and Literacy in the World of Ancient Israel: Epigraphic Evidence from the Iron Age*, ABS 11 (Atlanta: Society of Biblical Literature, 2010); André Lemaire, "West Semitic Epigraphy and the History of the Levant During the 12th–10th Centuries BCE," in *The Ancient Near East in the 12th–10th Centuries BCE*, edited by Gerson Galil, Ayelet Gilboa, Aren M. Maeir, and Dan'el Kahn (Münster: Ugarit-Verlag, 2012), 291–307, and now Israel Finkelstein and Benjamin Sass, "The West Semitic Alphabetic Inscriptions, Late Bronze II to Iron IIA: Archaeological Context, Distribution and Chronology," *Hebrew Bible/Ancient Israel* 2 (2013): 149–210, each of which in varying ways, invokes a number of different social factors, processes, institutions, and phenomena in order to account for some of the when's, how's and why's of literacy's emergence in ancient Israel and Judah, and see further the several articles in this volume.

3. See here, e.g., David M. Carr, *The Formation of the Hebrew Bible: A New Reconstruction* (Oxford: Oxford University Press 2011), 124–49.

4. On the possible significances of its several hieratic numeric signs, see Rollston, *Writing and Literacy*, 110, 113.

forward a *preexisting* scribal tradition of producing lengthy literary texts on perishable and nonperishable media or (2) composing for the first time both monumental and *contemporaneous* nonmonumental inscriptions of length on nondurable surfaces or (3) producing monumental inscriptions as the first of such lengthy literary texts with nondurable texts of length produced only thereafter. These are our best methodological recourse in light of the significant chronological gap spanning the initial second millennium attestations of alphabetic writing in the southern Levant and the widely acknowledged, much later production of lengthy literature in alphabetic scripts. A noticeable, but narrower time gap also stands between the first indications of Hebrew alphabetic writing and the attested production of lengthy literary texts in Hebrew script and language.

We shall seek to "mind the gaps" here as the conventional arguments based on the perishable nature of writing media (papyrus, parchment or wood), the pre- or nonliterate character of early Israelite society, short-life archives, or inadequate site excavations that have been proffered to fill this gap cannot adequately account for the ostensible enigma that persists between the alphabet's beginnings and the emergence of lengthy literature. All else being equal, the lengthy monumental texts treated here (and of long duration of a sort) may serve as a "sounding" from which one might infer the production of analogous lengthy literary writings on nondurable surfaces. But can we decide which of the above three scenarios is the most likely?

The Earliest Monumental Texts: Proximate Analogies?

The earliest group of texts that calls for assessment is a cadre of epigraphs on which most, if not all, agree as to their cultural and geographic proximity to Israel, their early date, and their sizeable length.[5] These include the Mesha stone stele from Dibhon with its thirty-four or so lines, the ink-on-wall plaster Balaam text from Deir Alla with its thirty-five or more lines (depending on how one reconstructs the badly damaged lines of its second half or installment), the Tel Dan stone stele inscription with its thirteen surviving lines that

---

5. The eight-line Gezer tablet or calendar from the end of the tenth century BCE discovered in 1908 has been widely recognized as the earliest Hebrew inscription. Yet, Pardee recently reassessed the tablet and identified its script and language as Phoenician. Dennis Pardee, "A Brief Case for Phoenician as the Language of the 'Gezer Calendar,'" in *Linguistic Studies in Phoenician in Memory of J. Brian Peckham* (Winona Lake, IN: Eisenbrauns, 2013), 226–46. Its literary quality and length hardly compare with those treated here, let alone with the biblical texts. Its genre and medium, a brief listing of annualized farm duties, reveal its practical character, although its precise function remains elusive (a school boy's practice text or a mnemonic device for a folk song?).

may point to as many as thirty-five lines on the original,[6] and the Amman Citadel stone inscription with its eight lines.[7]

While three are monumental inscriptions etched on stone as commemorative display inscriptions of one sort or another, the Deir Alla ink-on-plaster text likewise served as an elite sponsored display inscription mounted in the context of a cultic room (see further below). Although none of these inscriptions were composed on papyrus scrolls (or animal skins), it has been suggested that the Deir Alla inscription was copied from a pre-existing (papyrus?) original or *Vorlage*. The evidence is gleaned from the opening phrase of line 1, "...the *sepher* of Balaam...": for some, "... the scroll or book of Balaam ...," for others, "...the sayings of Balaam..."; still others view the "book" or "sayings" as referring to the content of the inscription itself and not to a *Vorlage*.[8]

---

6. For an analysis of the fragments that outline the prospective dimensions of the original stele, see George Athas, *The Tel Dan Inscription: A Reappraisal and a New Interpretation* (London: T&T Clark, 2003), 30–35 where he lists 35 × 110 cm as the proposed measurements. These roughly approximate the size of the original Mesha stele (though narrower in width).

7. See Shmuel Aḥituv, *Echoes from the Past: Hebrew and Cognate Inscriptions from the Biblical Period* (Jerusalem: Carta, 2008), 357–63 and see André Lemaire, "West Semitic Inscriptions and Ninth-Century BCE Ancient Israel," in *Understanding the History of Ancient Israel*, edited by H. G. M. Williamson (Oxford: Oxford University Press, 2007), 281 for a proposed date of composition later in the early eighth century for the Citadel inscription. On the later six-line Siloam Tunnel stone inscription from Jerusalem, see André Lemaire, "West Semitic Epigraphy and the History of the Levant During the 12th–10th Centuries BCE," in *The Ancient Near East in the 12th–10th Centuries BCE*, edited by G. Galil, A.Gilboa, A. Maeir, and D. Kahn (Münster: Ugarit-Verlag, 2012), 305–6 and Finkelstein and Sass, "West Semitic Alphabetic Inscriptions," 193–203. It may well be an eighth-century or later nonroyal Hebrew inscription. There are also two fragments of what may constitute monumental inscriptions found in excavations at Jerusalem as well as another small fragment from the Samaria excavations all of which date from the late eighth century or following. For the larger fragment from the City of David, see Y. Shiloh, "City of David Excavation 1978," *BA* 42 (1979): 170; Frank Moore Cross, "A Fragment of a Monumental Inscription from the City of David," *IEJ* 51 (2001): 44–47; Frederick W. Dobbs-Allsopp, Jimmy J. M. Roberts, Choon L. Seow, and Robert E. Whitaker, *Hebrew Inscriptions: Texts from the Biblical Period of the Monarchy with Concordance* (New Haven: Yale University, 2005), 227–29. For the smaller Jerusalem fragment, see Joseph Naveh, "A Fragment of an Ancient Hebrew Inscription from the Ophel," *IEJ* 32 (1982): 195–98; Dobbs-Allsopp et al., *Hebrew Inscriptions*, 226–27. For the Samaria stele fragment, see E. L. Sukenik, "Note on a Fragment of an Israelite Stele Found at Samaria," *PEFQS* (1936): 156; Dobbs-Allsopp et al., *Hebrew Inscriptions*, 496–97; Aḥituv, *Echoes from the Past*, 257.

8. Alan Millard ("Authors, Books, and Readers in the Ancient World," *Oxford Handbook of Biblical Studies*, ed. Judith M. Lieu and J. Roberson [Oxford: Oxford University Press, 2006], 554, doi: 10.1093/oxfordhb/978019923777.003.0031) claims that the Balaam

Based on the monumental inscriptions treated here, a conventional reconstruction concerning the production of lengthy literary texts would conclude that there were earlier-ninth-century Hebrew monumental inscriptions. For example, it is often asserted that Omri had produced such inscriptions (though no longer visible to us) that also served as a model for the one Mesha, his subjugated neighbor, later erected upon his liberation, suggesting as well that various other Hebrew genres circulated during this and earlier periods. While this reconstruction is plausible, the approach here will reassess the surviving epigraphic data along with their known wider sociohistorical contexts as a benchmark for what one should expect to find on the ground in the early Iron II period of the southern Levant. This will be addressed in greater detail on the other side of the following analysis of the inscriptions.

From what can be reconstructed regarding major contemporaneous political events in the wider region of Syria-Palestine, the Tel Dan and the Mesha stelae as well as the Deir Alla text (also the Amman Citadel Inscription) provide a crucial cohort of relative historical benchmarks. Even if their precise dates of composition remain debatable, the earliest can nevertheless, estimate on the basis of content and contexts, their relative proximity in location and date: all three were fashioned, engraved or painted, and clearly set up during the last third or so of ninth century (the 840s and following) within the Israel-Gilead-Ammon-north Moab corridor.[9]

---

text is, "the oldest example of a *book* in a West Semitic language written with the alphabet, and the oldest piece of Aramaic literature" (emphasis mine).

9. Eveline J. Van der Steen, "Nelson Glueck's 'String of Fortresses' Revisited," in *Studies on Iron Age Moab and Neighboring Areas in Honour of Michele Daviau*, ed. Piotr Bienkowski (Leuven: Peeters, 2009), 117–18 locates Moab's heartland in the ninth century north of the Wadi Mujib. The material-cultural data, the ceramics from Deir Alla and Tell Mazar, and Ammonite inscriptions and seals from Tell Mazar, indicate that the central Jordan Valley fell within the orbit of the kingdom of Ammon, though the borders between Ammon and Gilead were flexible in the Iron II period; see Michèle Daviau and Paul Dion, "Independent and Well-Connected: The Ammonite Territorial Kingdom in the Iron II," in *Crossing Jordan: North American Contributions to the Archaeology of Jordan*, ed. Thomas E. Levy et al. (London: Equinox, 2007), 301–7. Lucas Petit, *Settlement Dynamics in the Middle Jordan Valley during the Iron Age II*, BAR 2033 (Archaeopress: Oxford, 2009), 224. Ammon's mention in the campaign accounts of Shalmaneser III (858–824) shows that it was already a discrete polity (a tribal kingdom?) in the mid-ninth century and a coalition partner alongside several kingdoms to the north; Aleppo, Damascus, Hamath, Arvad, and Israel (Ahab). The question of whether Gilead was early on a toponym or an Assyrian province (Galada/i) remains a point of continued deliberation; see Meindert Dijkstra and Karel Vriesen, "The Assyrian Province of Gilead and the 'Myth of the Empty Land,'" in *Exploring the Narrative: Jerusalem and Jordan in the Bronze and Iron Ages*, ed. Eveline van der Steen, Jeannette Boertien, and Noor Mulder-Hymans (London: Bloomsbury, 2014), 1–26.

MIND THE GAP! THE EARLY IRON AGE BREACH

The prior historical context indicates that the Iron 1 and early Iron 2 periods, like the preceding LBA 3 period and LBA–EIA transitional period, generally evince a scarcity of alphabetic writing with no evidence for lengthy literary production in the southern Levant. As urban societies were reemerging in the late Iron 1–early Iron 2 period, state-sponsored scribal apparatuses were still in embryonic development and revitalization, networked economies and political stability were being reestablished, ancient oral traditions were continually being retold and reshaped alongside newer ones, and existing writing technologies were once again in revision so as to align with emerging local standardizing and elitist aspirations. At the same time, conventional alphabetic systems were pressed into service for purposes of marking ownership, apotropaism as well as for administration.[10] Yet the epigraphic data produced were minimal and literary production was, by all appearances, nil.

By virtue of the Iron 1–early Iron 2 gap, researchers have had to turn to the Iron 2 in search of prospective changes in the relative production levels and application of writing both in general and of literature in particular. It is here that two relevant developments take shape. Those diagnostic traces in isolated letterforms of the regional alphabetic scripts that would eventually be adopted and adapted to the inventory of the first emergent national script first appear in what is conventionally referred to as the Old Hebrew (but see n. 33). It is also specifically in the late ninth century, that our four non-Hebrew monumental inscriptions were mounted on the landscape of the southern Levant. These four initiate an abrupt surge in a specific type of lengthy literary writing followed by its rather brusque decrease and tapering off. While there is no direct evidence for other lengthy literary compositions besides these monumental inscriptions, indirect data in the form of bullae with papyrus fiber impressions on their undersides may likewise date to the late ninth century.[11] While often viewed as possibly sealing letters, or inventories, such bullae have been invoked on occasion as evidence for the contemporaneous

---

10. See further, Ryan Byrne, "The Refuge of Scribalism in Iron I Palestine," *BASOR* 345 (2007): 1–31 and Seth L. Sanders, *The Invention of Hebrew* (Urbana: University of Illinois Press, 2009), 106–13.

11. For the recent recovery of bullae from Jerusalem, many with papyrus traces on their undersides, see Reich and Shukron, "Recent Discoveries in the City of David," 156–57. For the newly published, full corpus of some previously known, but only partially assessed bullae from Iron 2 levels at Tell Jemmeh, see Ben-Shlomo and Keel, "Clay Sealings and Seal Impressions," 857–75. On the wet sieving of debris and bullae recovery from excavations, see now Finkelstein and Sass, "West Semitic Alphabetic Inscriptions," 199 who note that pre-late ninth-century levels from Megiddo revealed no bullae with papyrus imprints using the wet sieving method.

production of lengthy literature on nondurable surfaces and if so, they would represent another innovation to the state's administrative uses of writing.

Just to be clear then, we are not seeking the origins of Israelite literature *per se* since it was *orally* dominant in its earlier stages, but the origins of *written literary works of length.* Besides, Levantine scribalism of the Iron 2 period is not an unprecedented phenomenon. Scribalism on a different scale had survived the whole of the preceding Iron 1 to early Iron 2 post crisis transition under the aegis of elite patronage. Though the evidence is sparse, scribes had engaged in small-scale, abbreviated text production marking elite ownership and apotropaism. In other words, what is not at stake here are scribal skill (*could* they write lengthy literary texts?), scribal impetus (*would* they write lengthy literary texts?), or scribal acumen (*should* they write lengthy literary texts?). This treatment is not concerned with the questions of whether Israelite scribes could, would or should compose lengthy literary texts (to which we would respond with a resounding threefold "yes"), but rather, under what circumstances could, would, and should Israelite scribes have first composed lengthy literary texts. The absence of evidence for the production of lengthy literary texts in Iron 1 and the early Iron 2 period Israel does not constitute *a priori* evidence for the lack of technical skill or desire or aesthetic impulse on the part of Israelite scribes or Israelite society at large.

Thus, the apparent epigraphic void may serve as a "shadow" history of more complex circumstances underlying Israelite literary production. One might envision for instance, a "worst case" scenario in which experienced scribes of the post-transitional Iron 1–2 were faced with the prospects of (1) remedial training in the application of new script inventories, of (2) managing emergent infrastructural, material and workforce demands of producing sizeable literary texts above and beyond everyday administrative tasks and of (3) laboring initially under the turbulent conditions of embryonic state formation only to be exasperated further by (4) the traumatic conditions of an ever intensifying half-century of conflict.[12] Together, these factors

---

12. Only the first of these four points may have a parallel at LBA Ugarit in terms of the alphabetic script's technological development (here cuneiform) over the course of a generation or two once it was institutionalized at Ugarit in the mid-thirteenth century. Its rather experimental origins are evident in the variability that characterizes the text corpus of the alphabetic scribe Tab'ilu in terms of find spot, tablet format and layout, paleography and even language (Akkadian, Ugaritic, or Hurrian) as opposed to the regularity and standardization of the alphabet apparent a generation or two later in the corpus of the scribe 'Ilimilku at the end of the thirteenth century/beginning of the twelfth century; see Carole Roche-Hawley and Robert Hawley, "An Essay on Scribal Families, Tradition, and Innovation," *Beyond Hatti: Essays in Honor of Gary Beckman*, edited by Billie Jean Collins and Piotr Michalowski (Atlanta: Lockwood, 2013), 260–62. The authors also refer to the

would have contributed to writing's attenuation, if not postponement, beyond essential administrative tasks, as far as lengthy literary production goes and despite actual scribal capabilities. This "shadow" history of early Israelite literary production will be explored at greater length as it relates to the intra- and interregional conflicts of the mid- and late ninth centuries that engulfed the whole of Syria-Palestine. After all, the two premier emergent states, Aram and Israel, first had repeatedly to confront a new imposing stimulus in the form of Shalmaneser III's mid-ninth century imperialism and invading armies. They then immediately faced off against each other on "home turf" in the late ninth century. The resultant production of the first "conflict" inscriptions by the victors and lengthy writing's otherwise prolonged attenuation for the victors and its postponement for the vanquished were the culmination of almost fifty years of war.

PROTRACTED CONFLICT: ATTENUATION > SUSPENSION > EMULATION

"…And that's when all hell broke loose…." Just as alphabetic writing's technological and infrastructural modifications were on the verge of advancing, the process was blindsided by prolonged, repeated conflicts that consumed the southern Levant. Spanning the mid-ninth century to the close of the ninth century, the conflicts began with Shalmeneser III's numerous, but oft-thwarted attempts to intervene in Syria and Palestine. While the resistance put forward by the malleable coalition of Levantine armies led by Aram-Damascus, Hamath, and Israel and joined by Ammon was apparently successful early on, victory came at significant cost. Given the repetition of engagements, and the length and scale of fifteen years of war, the coalition undoubtedly exhausted significant resources and personnel in stalemating Assyria's repeated advances. Yet, conflict only continued to plague the region, and even intensified, as Aram-Damascus debuted its encore of interventions after Jehu and possibly Hazael had submitted to Assyria, only to have Assyria promptly withdraw from the region owing to more urgent concerns elsewhere in the empire. These new conflicts, immediately following those of Assyria, led to Aram's resounding success where Assyria had all but failed save its final campaign. Hazael and his son Ben Hadad dominated all of Syria-Palestine for some thirty-plus years until Adad-nirari III campaigned in the region at the end of the ninth century eventually resulting in a return to regional stability.[13]

---

decision at Ugarit to write in the local language using a locally developed alphabetic script as a rupture with scribal tradition; an expression of independence.

13. For a thorough treatment of Shalmaneser III's campaigns in the west see Shigeo Yamada, *The Construction of the Assyrian Empire*, CHANE 3 (Leiden: Brill, 2000).

From the outset, an almost lightning fast series of conflicts ensued with six campaigns in fifteen years alone initiated by Shalmaneser III beginning in the mid-ninth century. When the conflicts between Aram and Israel are added, at least twelve total major regional conflicts took place in forty-five-plus years and that is without calculating in the additional war reports in several biblical texts. In some cases, an inscription composed on a display stele commemorating a victory that had just concluded, also makes mention of prior conflicts. For example, in the Tel Dan inscription, an anterior conflict between Hazael's predecessor, "his father" (Hadadezer?) and an unnamed Israelite king (Omri or Ahab?) is recorded and in the Mesha inscription Omri's earlier defeat of Mesha's father Chemosh[yat] is mentioned.[14] Over such a prolonged period, the succession of battle after battle would have created protracted social disruption, destruction, and exploitation that required enormous reallocation of resources, the transport of colossal numbers of men and volumes of raw materials and equipment, intense production levels of hardware, huge amounts of energy expenditure and, if we are to believe the numbers listed in the relevant texts, tens of thousands of humans who participated in the whole of a half-century of conflict.

It is becoming ever more clear that Aram-Damascus' invasion and prolonged occupation of territories to its south minimally spanned the the second half of the eighth century resulting in transformative impact on the southern Levant in various ways and certainly on literate production of length.[15] Three, perhaps all four of the monumental inscriptions we have singled out are intimately tied to that Aramean intervention and impact on the region and were produced in direct or indirect response to it.[16]

---

14. See Andrew Knapp, "The Dispute over the Land of Qedem at the Onset of the Aram-Israel Conflict: A Reanalysis of lines 3–4 of the Tel Dan Inscription," *JNES* 73 (2014): 105–16 for the alternative view that the conflict in lines 3–4 is one between Hazael and Israel at the onset of their conflicts and not a more ancient one involving Hazael's father and his Israelite contemporary.

15. As Mario Liverani (*Israel's History and The History of Israel* [London: Equinox, 2005], 114–15) has pointed out, the Aramean domination of the region may be reflected in the architectural remains at Dan, Megiddo (IV), Hazor (VI), Jezreel, and the reoccupation of Deir Alla after a century of abandonment (phase IX). He estimates Aramean domination as lasting sixty years from 845 to 785 BCE. In *The History of the Ancient Near East* (London: Routledge 2014), 437–41 and esp. p. 439, Liverani comments: "In the south, under the leadership of Hadad-ezer and especially Haza-El, Damascus reached a visible supremacy with Israel, Judah and even the Philistine states recognizing its authority while northern Jordan was directly annexed." Edward Lipiński, *The Arameans: Their Ancient History, Cultures, Religion*, OLA 100 (Leuven: Peeters, 2000), 376–93 suggests a forty-year Aramean domination from 843 to 803 BCE.

16. While we have other inscriptions from the southern Levantine region of the late ninth century, they are brief and nonliterary, but of local origins. For a survey of

The Tel Dan inscription testifies to the subjugation of the Omride and Davidic dynasties by the Aramean kingdom of Damascus in the late ninth century BCE as king Hazael invaded Israel and killed the kings of Israel (J[eh]oram) and of the House of David or Judah (Amaziah). The Mesha stele likewise constitutes an unmitigated witness to Omride Israel's further loss of recently acquired Transjordanian territory to the king of Moab in the late ninth century. As proposed in what follows, the Balaam text was composed by an Aramean enclave that was assigned to oversee the region's burgeoning commercial textile industry and supervise local Ammonite and Israelite workers at the central production site of Deir Alla, located as it was, near major trading routes and political borders intersecting the region. While there is near unanimous agreement on the unmitigated relevance of the Tel Dan and Mesha inscriptions to these historical events, the site of Deir Alla and its now famous Balaam text have resisted a straightforward identification of the site's function and "ethnic" community makeup as well as the language, function and audience of the text.[17]

---

these and others covering the entire ninth century and the larger Syro-Palestinian orbit, see A. Lemaire, "West Semitic Inscriptions and Ninth-Century BCE Ancient Israel," in *Understanding The History of Ancient Israel*, ed. H. G. M. Williamson (Oxford: Oxford University Press, 2007), 279–303, and add Shmuel Ahituv and Amihai Mazar, "The Inscriptions from Tel Reḥov and Their Contribution to the Study of Script and Writing during Iron Age IIA," in *"See, I will bring a scroll recounting what befell me" (Ps 40:8): Epigraphy and Daily Life from the Bible to the Talmud Dedicated to the Memory of Professor Hanan Eshel*, ed. Esther Eshel and Yigal Levin (Vandenhoeck & Ruprecht: Göttingen, 2014), 39–68 and Aren M. Maeir and Esther Eshel, "Four Short Alphabetic Inscriptions from Late Iron Age IIa Tell es-Safi/Gath and Their Implications for the Development of Literacy in Iron Age Philistia and Environs," in *"See, I will bring a scroll recounting what befell me" (Ps 40:8): Epigraphy and Daily Life from the Bible to the Talmud Dedicated to the Memory of Professor Hanan Eshel*, ed. Esther Eshel and Yigal Levin, JAJSup (Göttingen: Vandenhoeck & Ruprecht, 2014), 69–88 for recent finds from Rehov and Safi, and see further below.

17. For representative recent treatments, see Emile Puech, "Balaam and Deir Alla," in *The Prestige of the Pagan Prophet Balaam in Judaism, Christianity and Islam*, ed. George H. van Kooten and Jacques van Ruiten (Leiden: Brill, 2008), 25–48. Erhard Blum ("Die Kombination I der Wandinschrift vom Tell Deir 'Alla. Vorschläge zur Rekonstruktion mit historisch-kritischen Anmerkungen," *Berührungspunkte. Studien zur Sozial- und Religionsgeschichte Israels und seiner Umwelt. Festschrift für Rainer Albertz*, ed. I. Kottsieper, R. Schmitt, J. Wöhrle, AOAT 350 [Münster: Ugarit-Verlag, 2008], 573–601) proposes that line 7 of Combination I, begins a description of a *mundus inversus* or a chaotic reversal of human and animal social structures (lines 7–17) that is not seamlessly congruent with its preceding context. This points to a text made up of disparate parts, some of which were copied from a Vorlage. This in turn suggests that the Balaam text is a kind of *Traditionsliteratur*. Though Blum's thesis may have far reaching implications concerning lengthy literary production, the claim of disparity here seems rather premature as a form critical evaluation given the severely damaged state of the text and our limited knowledge of the

Reassessing Deir Alla: *Un mélange énigmatique*

The archaeological data from phase IX of Deir Alla represent the Iron 2 levels at the site (850–800 BCE) related to the discovery of the Balaam text. This level was relatively well preserved owing to the destruction of the site by earthquake and fire that ended the period's occupation.[18]

Artifact and Text: Aramean Influence or Presence?

Material cultural data like the 675 warped loom weights, various stone implements, selected pottery, and the handful of Aramaic inscriptions in addition to the Balaam inscription with its unique Aramaic dialect, all indicate Aramean influence.[19] The number of warped loom weights is three times as many as any other Iron Age Levantine site both within the region and at greater distance indicating a major textile-production center. That industry took on domestic, religious, as well as regionally commercial applications which Aram would have found attractive.[20] These data converge quite well with what we know of Damascus' wider expansionist policies at the time; that Hazael had penetrated deep into the south including Israel, Judah and Gath as well as in the north.

Artifact and Text: The Religious Dimension

The lay out of Deir Alla is not that of a typical regional village. It does not preserve a regular pattern of houses. Other data such as the bench room where the Balaam text was displayed (EE 335), the nature of the Balaam text along with items suggestive of a ritual assemblage recovered from the asso-

---

context, style, form and conventions of *late ninth century* West Semitic prophetic writings.

18. See now Jeannette Hannah Boertien, *Unraveling the Fabric: Textile Production in the Iron Age Transjordan* (Groningen: Rijksuniversiteit, 2013), 119–20, 295.

19. See Boertien, *Unraveling the Fabric*, 21–22 for the material cultural data, and Peuch, "Balaam and Deir Alla," 25–48 for the Aramaic (or proto- or localized Aramaic) identity of the Balaam text's language. The other very brief Aramaic inscriptions were etched on small objects; a jar, bowl rim, and a stone. The stone (rm. 205) and jar (rm. 418) preserve the words, "the stone of Shera" and the name "Shera" respectively. The bowl fragment preserves six letters in an experienced hand. It might have included an entire abecedary that had an apotropaic function. For the prestige impact of the Aramaic of Aram-Damascus on the Tel Dan and Deir Alla inscriptions as well as the resultant regional Aramaic-Canaanite multilingualism, see now Holger Gzella, *A Cultural History of Aramaic: From the Beginnings to the Advent of Islam*, HO 1.111 (Leiden: Brill, 2014), 78–90, 93–101.

20. Boertien, *Unraveling the Fabric*, 119–20, 146–47, 301.

ciated room complex nearby (rooms 205, 303, 418, 308), and the unique use of hemp cloth lend support to a religious function for the bench room. The textile industry there may have had connections with local religious practices that are reflected both in the site's room that housed the Balaam text and in other religious indicators present at the site.[21] The ritual evidence from the nearby cluster of rooms includes exotic and luxury items: libation goblets, numerous human figurines, both naked males and adorned naked females holding objects some of which have been interpreted as fetishes (note the red stain in the pubic area of one) or identified as "vestal virgins." There are also figurines that functioned as votive offerings, a figure of a female monkey and lap child, a serpentine carved spoon, miniature bowls, bone inlay fragments, a decorated bone pendant, a stone inscribed with "the stone of Shera" etched on it, a jar with the name "Shera" etched on it after firing, a bowl fragment with a partial abecedary etched in it before firing (all three in Aramaic), and an outsized loom weight possessing only a symbolic (ritual?) function.[22] Lastly, there may have been intentional continuity of design and positioning between the bench room and a previous sanctuary from the LBA at Deir Alla.

Boertien points out that the site meets many of the criteria outlined by Renfrew for the identification and presence of ritual in the archaeological database. The bench room with its plastered wall text differs from any other room in the group and the benches therein provide special features and functions unlike any of the other rooms, while the bench room is also widely attested as a form of sanctuary or cult site in the Iron Age Mediterranean. All of these serve to *focus attention* on the room in a way not shared by any of the other rooms or structures. That the room served as a *boundary zone* between this world and the next is clearly delineated by the genre and medium of the plastered wall text clearly displayed within the confines of the room. The mention of the intermediary figure of a prophet clearly sets off the room from all others as does the mention of a number of gods in the text including the main protagonist, El but also the deities Shagar, Ishtar, the Shadayin, the Elohanu, along with an undifferentiated council of the gods. To be added to these indicators is the image of a winged sphinx-like figure, one among a handful of poorly preserved images on the plaster. It was painted above the upper edge of the text. Given the above-mentioned factors indicative of the bench room's religious function, the sphinx-like figure also served to demarcate the room as a boundary zone between the divine and human worlds.

---

21. Ibid., 146–47, 296–97 and see H. J. Franken, "Deir Alla and Its Religion," in *Sacred and Sweet: Studies on the Material Culture of Tell Deir 'Alla and Tell Abu Sarbut*, ed. Margreet Steiner and Eveline J. van der Steen (Leuven: Peeters, 2008), 25–52.

22. Boertien, *Unraveling the Fabric*, 299–300 and see here Kuntillet Ajrud.

A HISTORY OF ISRAEL'S EARLIEST LITERATURE   115

As already mentioned, the benches, like those at other sites, served as locations where votive offerings could be placed. Some of the human figurines functioned as votive offerings or fetishes. Together, these factors are indicative of *ritual participation*. Finally, the text mounted on the plastered wall itself reflects a *significant investment* of time, effort, technical skill and wealth for a professional to apply the text. Viewed collectively, these convergent factors convincingly point to the religious function of the room. In the absence of compelling indicators for alternative uses of the bench room, it appears difficult to avoid the conclusion that the sector of the site that encompassed the bench room and associated chambers was designed to serve a ritual function.[23]

Artifact and Text: Textiles and Religion

Workshops, textile production and storage were commonly associated with various sanctuaries in the ancient world as part of the economic activities of the temples. The use of special fabrics could also be incorporated into the cult to clothe the priests and statues of deities or as materials for various decorations and curtains.

The evidence recovered at Deir Alla indicative of surplus textile production alongside religious practice at a single site has its parallel at the site of Kuntillet Ajrud in the northern Sinai: both are located on or near a junction of trading routes at some distance from urban centers and removed from other large structures, both preserve religious implements in the material culture, both evince abecedaries revealing an experienced writing hand and indicating that they were not beginners' exercises. Rather, given their immediate ritualized contexts, they possessed apotropaic functions and qualities. Both present special textiles of high quality produced on site. At both, weaving activities were concentrated near a bench room that included religious texts and motifs painted on its plastered walls. Both employed special fabrics (hemp at Deir Alla, interwoven linen and wool at Kuntillet Ajrud), and both

---

23. Colin Renfrow, *Archaeology: Theories, Methods and Practice* (London: Thames & Hudson, 1991), 358–63. The terms, "cult" and "cultic" rather than "religious" or "ritual" have intentionally been avoided since they have been employed variously to refer to deity worship and its supposedly distinct paraphernalia or to a much wider range of human inclinations regarding the divine and their material manifestations. For more on cult in Israelite religion, see Ziony Zevit, *The Religions of Ancient Israel* (London: Continuum, 2001), 81–121; Rainer Albertz and Rüdiger Schmitt, *Family and Household Religion in Ancient Israel and the Levant* (Winona Lake, IN: Eisenbrauns, 2012), 11–16, 57–74, 220–41, 474–95; Ruediger Schmitt, "A Typology of Iron Age Cult Places," 265–86; Rainer Albertz, Beth Alpert Nakhai, Saul M. Olyan, and Ruediger Schmitt, *Family and Household Religion* (Winona Lake, IN: Eisenbrauns, 2014).

connected textile production to rituals dedicated to a localized god and goddess, El and Shagar at Deir Alla, Yahweh and Asherah at Kuntillet Ajrud.[24]

Artifact and Text: A Multipurpose Site

In sum, there is ample evidence suggesting Deir Alla's major role in the local and regional textile industry and the religious nature of both the bench room and the related room cluster. It remains to be seen whether or not the site might have also functioned as a regional scribal training site for the recently established Aramean administration of the area. After all, a thriving regional textile industry managed by a central authority such as Damascus based at Deir Alla might have necessitated some form of administrative scribal apparatus. This would dovetail with the multipurpose functionality of the site.

Summary: An Aramean-Controlled Multiethnic Textile-Production Site Dedicated to El and the Goddess Shagar

The southern Levant was transformed into a brave new world dominated by the Aramean state of Damascus following the decades-long abatement of Assyrian pressure during the second half of the ninth century.[25] As Hazael, king of Aram-Damascus initiated his wide ranging expansionist policies, he penetrated deep into the south sustaining for an extended period Aram's

---

24. Boertien, *Unraveling the Fabric*, 308–9 and on Kuntillet Ajrud's multipurpose functionality, see Brian Schmidt, "The Iron Age Pithoi Drawings from Horvat Teman or Kuntillet 'Ajrud: Some New Proposals," *JANER* 2 (2002): 91–125.

25. For the most recent treatment of the details from this period, see K. Lawson Younger, "Aram-Damascus," *OEBA* 1:42–49 and *The Political History of the Arameans: From Their Origins to the End of Their Polities* (Atlanta: The Society of Biblical Literature, 2015). Also see Maria Giulia Amadasi Guzzo, "Un fragment de stèle arame'enne de Tell Afis," *Or* 70 (2009): 336–47; "Tell Afis in the Iron Age: The Aramaic Inscriptions," *NEA* 77 (2014): 54–57 on the possible mention of Hazael in the Tell Afis stele inscription from the end of the ninth century. For other recent treatments of Iron II Aramean history, see Stephania Mazzoni, "The Aramean States during the Iron Age II–III Periods," in *Oxford Handbook of the Archaeology of the Levant (c. 8000–322 BCE)*, ed. Ann E. Killebrew and Margreet L. Steiner (Oxford: Oxford University Press, 2014). doi: 10.1093/oxfordhb/9780199212972.013.045.; Herbert Niehr, "Koenig Hazael von Damaskus im Licht neurer Funde und Interpetationen," in *"Ich Werde Meinen Bund mit Euch Niemals Brechen!" (Ri 2,1): Festschrift fuer Walter Gross zum 70*, ed. Erasmus Gass und Hans J. Stipp (Freiburg: Herder, 2011), 339–56; Niehr, ed., *The Arameans in Ancient Syria* (Leiden: Brill), 2014; Helene Sader, "The Arameans of Syria," in *The Books of Kings: Sources, Composition, Historiography and Reception*, ed. Andre Lemaire and Baruch Halpern (Leiden: Brill, 2010), 273–300.

domination over Israel and Judah (Tel Dan), Ammon-Gilead (Deir Alla) and the Shephelah where he conquered Philistine Gath.[26] His successes led to the Omrides' dramatic loss of power throughout the region and to the Moabite takeover/reclamation of Transjordanian territories from the Omrides. The latter was perhaps made possible by combined allied efforts of Moab and Aram (and note also the similar Hazael-Jehu cooperation suggested by biblical texts). Likewise, his son Ben Hadad attempted a similar expansion a few years later in the north where he pursued Zakkur king of Hamath.

With Aram-Damascus' prolonged rule over most, if not all, of Syria-Palestine, it is a reasonable inference that the thriving textile industry at Deir Alla came to serve as an Aramean controlled commercial enterprise (whether as a startup or as a hostile takeover). Assuming the Balaam text was written in a local Aramaic dialect, it might well have been composed by an Aramean scribe at the end of the ninth century as an expression of Aram's recently acquired role as overlord of Ammon-Gilead and comptroller of Deir Alla's lucrative production site. When originally commissioned, the content of the Balaam text approximated a conventional, state sponsored, prophetic (divinatory) prognostication directed at El concerning an impending Aramean instigated conflict. But when mounted on the wall at Deir Alla, it constituted a religious text now in a local Aramean dialect suited for a new, mixed audience of Aramean bureaucrats and supervisors as well as Ammonite and Israelite (Gileadite?) workers. The recontextualized first several lines were transformed into a doom oracle announcing the defeat of the locals as divine punishment by the localized version of the deity El. The remainder is all but impossible to sort out owing to the damaged state of the fragments. Yet, the initial message would be clear to all. It conveyed a doom oracle of

---

26. See Lipiński, *The Arameans*, 387 and Liverani, *Israel's History*, 114, and on Hazael's taking of Gath see 2 Kgs 12:18 and the late ninth-century siege system and destruction layers at Tell el-Safi, and see Aren M. Maier, ed., *Tell es-Safi/Gath I: Report on the 1996–2005 Seasons*, AAT 69 (Wiesbaden: Harrassowitz, 2012). Hazael may have extended his control into Edom where the copper industry was flourishing, for which see now Thomas E. Levy, Mohammad Najjar, and Erez Ben-Yosef, "Conclusions," in *New Insights into the Iron Age Archaeology of Edom, Southern Jordan*, vol. 1 (Los Angeles: Cotsen Institute of Archeology Press, 2014), esp. 983–85, 989–94. These three editor-authors note that following Sheshonq I's disruption of Edom's copper production in 925 BCE and the new pyrotechnology introduced thereafter by Egyptian agents, opportunities opened up for local polities in peer-polity interaction to take control of the industry. Given the subsequent emergence of the distinct Edomite script as an indicator of Edomite "ethnogensis" and its very close association with the prestige Aramaic script as outlined by Christopher Rollston, "The Iron Age Edomite Script and Language," in Levy, Najjar, and Ben-Yosef, *New Insights*, 961–75, coupled with the historical expansion of Aram-Damascus into the south led by Hazael, a dominant Aramean component in Edom during the last third of the ninth century when copper production had peeked, should not be discounted.

the high god El mediated by the legendary Aramean prophet Balaam: The oracle's envisioned calamitous result signified Aram's domination over Ammon-Gilead as a divinely ordained event. No one in the audience would miss the message regardless of which side of the "victor-vanquished" divide one might find oneself. From the Aramean point of view, Aram had thereby acquired divine right to rule Deir Alla and to reap its riches; from the view of the locals there, the Aramaeans were El's instrument he used to chastise his local people for past inequities so they must accept the punishment and work for their overlords "industriously."

The king of Damascus, as was convention prior to campaigning, undoubtedly had solicited a prognostication from an Aramean seer (was that *hazeh* [Hebrew *hozeh*] an associate of a seers' guild dedicated to Balaam?) directed against Ammon-Gilead whom Aram had planned to invade. It might well have been orally delivered as Aram was on the march.[27] Its original function and form approximated an oracle against the nations (OAN) as we find in later biblical traditions: in this case an oracle pronounced by the Aramean version of the god El against the *foreign* peoples of Ammon-Gilead. Yet, its written version at Deir Alla was composed in a "peculiar" (the local?) Aramean dialect for its mixed audience of Aramaeans, Ammonites, Israelites, (Gileadites?), and who-knows-who-else. When it was put into writing (perhaps in draft), then copied in the local Aramaic dialect and mounted on the wall at Deir Alla in the dispossessed region of the vanquished by the Aramaeans and "placed in the mouth of" the internationally renown Aramean seer, Balaam, it took on new resonances. To be sure, it maintained its function for the Aramaeans at Deir Alla as an oracle of the old *Aramean* god El against a foreign people among whom they now resided. For the locals, however who heard (and/or read?) it, Balaam's vision was performatively transformed into a doom oracle of their god El. Thus, as a factor of its new localization and audience, the oracle could simultaneously be understood by the locals as that of the *Ammonite-Israelite* god El directed against his *own* people. As various epigraphic sources indicate, El continued an active first millennium role throughout the wider southern Levantine region including Aram, Israel (Gilead?) and Ammon.[28]

---

27. Note the somewhat later monumental inscription of Zakkur, the king of Aram-Hamath, in which Baal of the Heavens reveals Zakkur's deliverance from Ben Hadad's coalition through his own Aramean seers (< sing. *hazeh*) and diviners. For similar Mesopotamian scenarios, see Martti Nissinen, "The Prophet and the Augur at Tushan, 611," in *Literature as Politics and Politics as Literature: Essays on the Ancient Near East in Honor of Peter Machinist* (Winona Lake, IN: Eisenbrauns, 2013), 329–38.

28. In addition to the Deir Alla texts, El is documented in contemporary Aramean inscriptions, the Panamuwa I (or Hadad) and Panamuwa II inscriptions, Israelite inscrip-

What obtains then at Deir Alla constitutes a variation on a religious phenomenon also attested at Kuntillet Ajrud vis-à-vis the worship of localized manifestations of the divine. There, two such local manifestations of YHWH are explicitly delineated, YHWH of Samaria and YHWH of Teman, of which the latter apparently possessed a dedicated larger ritual space. Yet, prospective worshippers who might prefer to direct devotion to the former localization of YHWH were not denied the proclivity to do so, but could encounter the divine "interstitially."[29] It was the widely embraced fluidity of such fragmented local manifestations of YHWH that made such possible, in essence attesting to an "ecumenism" at Kuntillet Ajrud. A similar ecumenical spirit was evident at Deir Alla, only in this iteration it involved multiple local manifestations of the El worship, at least two of which we can account for based on the historical and material cultural data reviewed above. One was an imported, possibly imposed, Aramean (Damascene) manifestation. The other was that of the indigenous Ammonites and Israelites who were working there under Aramean supervision in the commercial textile industry, a component of which was also dedicated to the cult at the site. The imported/imposed Aramean El worship, rather than suppressing the local Ammonite-Israelite version of El worship, accommodated or absorbed it.

This may explain the Aramean scribe's selection of a local (or archaizing?) dialect of Aramaic in composing the wall inscription that Aramaeans, Ammonites and Israelites all could share at Deir Alla. As such, it also reinforced the more ancient El traditions common to both religious traditions and their diverse worshippers.[30] In the manifestation of El in Deir Alla's Balaam text, the two fragmented, localized manifestations of El, the Aramean and

---

tions such as those from Kuntillet Ajrud, as well as in Ammonite onomastica.

29. See Jeremy M. Hutton, "Local Manifestations of Yahweh and Worship in the Interstices: A Note on Kuntillet Ajrud," *JANER* 10 (2010): 204.

30. For a review of previous research pertaining to the problematic, but clearly mixed, "ethnic" representation at Deir Alla and its ramifications for ascertaining both population mix and linguistic dialectology (notwithstanding the problematics of the pots and people equation), see Jeremy M. Hutton, "Southern, Northern and Transjordanian Perspectives," in *Reconsidering Diversity in Ancient Israel and Judah*, ed. Francesca Stavrakopoulou and John Barton (London: T&T Clark, 2010), 161–68. For the evidence indicative of the diverse communities represented in the material culture at Deir Alla and Kuntillet Ajrud, see the syntheses in Boertien, *Unraveling the Fabric*, 119–90, 294–315. That El rather than Hadad is mentioned in the plaster cast text merely reflects the Aramean scribe's attempt to incorporate the local population of workers and their god El alongside their Aramean overseers and their god El as his intended audience. After all, the text is not a celebration of a foreign national god's (Hadad's) victory over the local population, but rather a visionary depiction of a localized version of an archaic deity shared by victor and vanquished, El, who foretells of his decision to punish his own people, the rhetoric of which approximates that of the Rab-Shakeh in 2 Kgs 18:25.

the Ammonite-Israelite would have been converged, theologically speaking, by the mixed audience, Similar to the situation at Kuntillet Ajrud, one of the two religious traditions might have received a larger dedicated ritual space, most likely the dominant Aramean, while the other was present on an ad hoc, downgraded, or "unofficial" basis. The Aramean control of the site, Aram's long standing domination of the region as well as the major protagonist in the publicly displayed text, the Aramean seer, Balaam (rather than a more local prophet from Ammon, Israel or Gilead) when viewed together, favor a dominant Aramean cult dedicated to El and Shagar at Deir Alla. In placing in the "mouth" of the renown Aramean prophet Balaam, the local (or an archaic?) Aramaic dialect in what constituted a recontextualized doom oracle, the Aramean scribe conveyed to the vanquished the divine origin of Aram's dominance over the local peoples, namely, their own god El.

What all this entails is that two of our earliest lengthy monumental texts from the region comprise foreign texts and in both cases, Aramaic imposed imports, Tel Dan and Deir Alla, and as such, they and their analogues, provided the stimulus for the production of similar texts like the Mesha stele. Mesha best exemplifies the local elite emulation of an expansionist precedent set by a larger regional entity, Aram-Damascus. This makes better sense of the data than the conjecture that in producing his stele, Mesha emulated Omride Israel, who was none other than his father's former long-time oppressor and arch enemy and for which there is no supporting hard data.[31]

The Mesha Stele: A Local *tour de force*

It becomes readily obvious that besides emulating a royal practice of producing and displaying inscribed monumental stelae similar to the Tel Dan stele, the Mesha inscription also shares some content elements with the Tel Dan inscription. Both are aniconic and celebrate their respective victories over Israel. Nonetheless, the Mesha stele includes other subject matter as well though one need keep in mind that the Tel Dan inscription is missing more than half of its original surface so it is impossible to reconstruct what details filled those lost lines. In any case, Hazael's stele was imposed on Israel, while Mesha's was erected in what most experts consider his own land or territory he had just repossessed. One could infer, however, that as such

---

31. The same may apply in the case of the Amman Citadel inscription. As a dedication inscription of a building (a temple?), it may have been conceptually inspired by similar building dedication inscriptions from Syria as knowledge of them made its way west. The bilingual Fekheriye inscription from Gozan, itself inspired by Assyrian prototypes, is just such an Aramean forerunner, a building inscription dedicated to the god Hadad.

it was also imposed on the Israelite populations that were forced or chose to remain there. More to the point however, its placement in Moab may actually signal Mesha's acquisition of land not formerly his father's (yet, perhaps that of his ancestors?). That is, he had erected it as part of his own expansionist initiative to consolidate the Transjordan. If this is indeed the case, then its similarities in function (and content?) with the Tel Dan stele may be closer than initially surmised.[32]

THE MESHA STELE: ITS SOURCE OF INSPIRATION

The notion that Mesha in producing his stele was inspired by similar monumental inscriptions produced by the Omrides his overlords, though delayed while Mesha was under their rule presents intriguing possibilities. Was Mesha indebted to them for both the script technology employed in the Mesha inscription ("Old Hebrew") and the form and medium he invoked in producing his royal inscribed commemorative stele? There are several problems with this scenario beginning with the most obvious: we have no royal inscribed stelae or monumental inscriptions from Omri, Ahab, or any of their later descendants or from their neighboring Aramean contemporaries.[33] In fact, we have only brief, nonstate epigraphs from the early to mid-ninth

---

32. See Bruce Routledge, *Moab in the Iron Age* (Philadelphia: University of Pennsylvania Press, 2003), 133–61, 213–21. On the new material evidence for contemporary Iron 2 Moabite settlements and their cult sites such as at Wadi ath-Thamad, Khirbet 'Ataruz, Khirbet al-Mudayna, Dhiban, and Balu'a, see now Anlee Dolan, "Defining Sacred Space in Ancient Moab," in *Studies on Iron Age Moab and Neighboring Areas in Honor of Michele Daviau*, ed. Piotr Bienkowski (Leuven: Peeters, 2009), 129–44; Chang-Ho Ji, "The Iron Age II Temple at Hirbet 'Ataruz and Its Architecture and Selected Cult Objects," *Temple Building and Temple Cult: Architecture and Cultic Paraphernalia of Temples in the Levant*, ed. Jens Kamlah (Wiesbaden: Harrassowitz, 2012), 203–21; and Michele Daviau, "Anomalies in the Archaeological Record: Evidence for Domestic and Industrial Cults in Central Jordan," in Albertz et al., *Family and Household Religion*, 103–28.

33. Since Mesha was the first actually to compose epigraphs using the so-called Old Hebrew script, including possibly the al-Karak text and the (two?) new brief Ataruz pedestal inscriptions (see now Christopher Rollston at www.rollstonepigraphy.com), would it not be more fitting to label the script Old Moabite? In our view, Moab had developed either a native script (an "original" Old Moabite script) well before its liberation from Israel which Israel later adopted from Moab, or Moab and Israel had both adopted at differing times, a more ancient common ancestral script of the earlier ninth century, attested, but still under development, at the territorially marginal sites of Rehov and Safi. The ethnic and political makeup of these two sites remains to be clarified, and so too an appropriate label for their scripts. Were the earliest Arad ostraca also written in the Old Moabite script? In any case, Moab subsequently revised its script to distinguish it from the Old Moabite script that Israel and Judah continued to employ. Such a revised script (a "Neo" Moabite script) can be seen in the later altar inscription from Mudayna.

century, and no written materials from the royal court of the Omrides or from the nearest contemporaneous Aramean states.[34] The absence of such writings from the Omride court and from their adjoining Aramean contemporaries has been variously explained: perishable media did not last, royal archives were short lived, they were preliterate, or sites in the north have not been adequately excavated. Yet, it is curious that we have no concurrent spill over from perishable to nonperishable literary writing, from papyrus to stone or ostraca in either Israel or Aram-Damascus at any time before the late ninth century.[35] In any case, the point made previously, preempts this possibility. Prior to the mid-ninth century, neither Israel nor Aram, nor any of the Syro-Palestinian cohort of emergent states, had yet to sufficiently develop the requisite alphabetic inventories and scribal infrastructures to produce lengthy literary texts of any kind.[36] This was followed immediately by a half century of conflicts. One might provisionally entertain the notion that they were "preliterate," if by preliterate one has in view the state's nonproduction of lengthy literary texts, while allowing for other forms of writings such as marking ownership and apotropaism by patron sponsored scribes (are the Rehov and Safi inscriptions relevant here?) and various administrative writings by the state (that are at present, invisible to us).

In any case, there is a much more likely candidate, time period, and situation for modeling a literary prototype for Mesha to emulate as events turned a different course for Moab, than for Israel, Aram's arch enemy. Moab viewed Aram, its new overlord as its liberator from prolonged Israelite oppression. The kings of Damascus ruled over what would become in a post-Omride world, the largest, most powerful territorial kingdom to date encompassing all of Syria-Palestine, beginning with Hadadezer, reaching its zenith under Hazael and continuing with Ben Hadad. In emulation of Aram, Mesha produced his own inscribed monumental stele in celebration of his victory over Israel. On this score, he emulated his overlord and ally Hazael who had erected his stele at Tel Dan in celebration of his defeat of Israel and Judah.[37]

---

34. See Ahituv and Mazar, "Inscriptions from Tel Reḥov" and Maeir and Eshel, "Four Short Alphabetic Inscriptions" for the brief fragmentary Rehov and Safi nonroyal inscriptions from the tenth to ninth centuries. The Rehov stratum IV inscriptions evince the diagnostic elements shared with what is often conventionally referred to as the Old Hebrew script.

35. See here Finkelstein and Sass, "West Semitic Alphabetic Inscriptions," 190–91.

36. On the problematic dating of the earliest Phoenician inscriptions from Byblos, see Finkelstein and Sass, "West Semitic Alphabetic Inscriptions," 180–83 who date them to the second half of the ninth century instead of 1000 BCE in part as a response to Christopher Rollston, "The Dating of the Early Royal Byblian Phoenician Inscriptions: A Response to Benjamin Sass," *MAARAV* 15 (2008): 57–93.

37. See Lipiński, *The Arameans*, 386 and Liverani, *Israel's History*, 113–16 on Aram

Mesha also celebrated his territorial attainments and recounted his other civic achievements for public display.[38]

MESHA'S STELE: ITS FORM AND MEDIUM

Now Hazael had himself earlier mimicked Assyrian royal practice, form and medium in erecting his victory stele at Tel Dan. The Aramean states had experienced ever increasing and sustained exposure to and engagement with Assyrian propagandistic literary models for the duration of the ninth century and especially in the mid-ninth century as Assyria repeatedly invaded Syria. The geographic proximity, long-term trade and exchange, and the peak provided by repeated Assyrian interventions in Syria in the mid-ninth century all contributed to Aram's growing imperial aspirations. This combined with Aram-Damascus' real and immediate rise to power in the late ninth century closely following on Assyria's mostly thwarted campaigns, led to it being the first among western polities to emulate Assyria's expansionist policies and statecraft and to produce and set up monumental inscriptions emulating Assyrian models.[39]

The knowledge of Assyrian forms and media had coursed the length of Syria by the late ninth century, from the northeast (e.g., the Fekheriye inscription), to the southwest arriving at Damascus and Hamath (cf. the Zakkur inscription), and erected by Hazael farther south in Israel (Tel Dan) and, as we have proposed, set up as a plaster wall inscription in Ammon-Gilead (Deir Alla). The Fekheriye bilingual temple dedication inscription was composed ca. 830 BCE on the model of Assyrian dedication inscriptions while Gozan

---

as possible ally to Moab and Aram's wider expansion as a catalyst for Mesha to expel Israel from the Transjordan. Lemaire has noted that the Tel Dan and Mesha inscriptions also share an aniconic format, engraved cursive letters and they contain royal historiographic propaganda with the main themes of war and victory.

38. On the ritual aspects of royal victory inscriptions and their destruction, see now N. Levtow, "Monumental Inscriptions and the Ritual Presentation of War," in *Warfare, Ritual and Symbol in Biblical and Modern Contexts*, ed. Brad Kelle, Frank Ritchel Ames, and Jacob L. Wright (Atlanta: Society of Biblical Literature, 2014), 25–46.

39. See Yamada, *Construction of the Assyrian Empire*, 273–99 for a helpful summary of the Assyrian practice of fashioning, engraving with ad hoc or annalistic contents, and setting up of monuments while on campaign. The monuments included three-dimensional statues, stelae and two-dimensional reliefs. They were located in conquered cities and on open-air landscapes of "quasi-divine" significance; mountains, seashores, lakefronts, or riverbanks. He briefly mentions similar monuments set up while not on campaign in areas such as Assyrian capitals (p. 288 and n. 43). Polities that emulated Assyria in this domain creatively imbued their own versions with culturally distinct creative variants. On the Aramean emulaton of Assyrian royal inscriptions, see Nadav Naaman, "Royal Inscriptions and the Histories of Joash and Ahaz, Kings of Judah," *VT* 48 (1998): 333–49, esp. 334.

served as vassal of Assyria. A few years later Damascus erected Hazael's victory stele at Tel Dan, Zakkur erected his memorial stele in Hamath and an unknown king of Ammon mounted a dedication inscription on a local temple or building. These are not identically inscribed monumental genres by any means. Yet, they can be cited to illustrate the knowledge that the late ninth century Aramean states possessed and to which their neighbors to the south would soon be exposed regarding the variety of contemporary Assyrian monumental forms in circulation.

In sum, Mesha in inscribing and erecting his royal stele was inspired by Aram's example and his audiences were much like those of his mentor; mixed audiences of victors and vanquished, elites and nonelites, literate and nonliterate, natives and nonnatives. All the primary data that we have: the four monumental inscriptions, the bullae with papyrus fiber impressions dating from no earlier than the late ninth century, and the lack of evidence otherwise for lengthy literary writing in the region, when taken together indicate that prior to the late ninth century while scribes *could, would,* and *should* compose lengthy literary texts, circumstances beyond their control of chisel and stone, reed and papyrus, dictated otherwise. Wars and rumors of war had all but postponed lengthy written literature's production in the southern Levant throughout the ninth century. Yet, to the victors went the spoils. In its initial iteration, written literature of length was the privilege of wartime, dominating Syrian-Levantine power and prestige. And so, the West Semitic monumental inscription was born, first to Aram, then to Transjordan, and lastly to Cisjordan.

Conclusions

Three general phases can be delineated in the early history of lengthy literary production in the southern Levant:

(1) Phase one comprises the *state-scribal development* phase. It began with the end of the LBA–EIA transition and lasted through the entire first half of the ninth century. Literature of length in this phase was exclusively oral. Yet, in the hope of eventually emulating Assyria, some emergent polities of Syria-Palestine at some unknown point prior to the mid-ninth century *initiated* the technological adaptation of their conventional alphabetic writing systems in order to create a fully articulated script inventory (are the scripts and inscriptions from the ninth century levels of peripheral sites of Rehov and Safi relevant here?). These polities also began to enhance their literate infrastructures in order to develop a scribal apparatus capable of implementing what would become their new and improved writing systems. All this is

invisible to us and yet it is soundly based on later developments, the precursors of which would have been initiated at the latter end of this phase.

While the above developments were in process, these states began applying their conventional writing systems to various administrative applications within the emergent institutional settings. Scribes of patronage and nonstate scribes continued producing small-scale, brief expressions of ownership and apotropaism for elite clientele as they had in times past (are Rehov's and Safi's inscriptions relevant here?).

(2) Phase two, the *conflict affective* phase, spans most of the second half of the ninth century during which several changes ensued. The processes initiated in the previous phase continued initially into this period, both the technological adaptation of conventional alphabetic writing systems and the enhancement of scribal infrastructures. Sometime in this period, a state or two may have reached the *threshold* of fully implementing their production of lengthy literature. Yet, ever intensifying, protracted and repeated conflicts blindsided developments severely disrupting technological advances and profoundly restricting implementation. Conventional writing systems continued to be used for administrative and small-scale production. Neither Aram nor Israel produced lengthy literary texts for most of this period. This phase developed in two stages:

A. The first stage comprised six intraregional conflicts with Assyria lasting fifteen years. They began at the mid-point of the century and extended into the latter third of the ninth century. The costs of redirection and exhaustion of human and material resources required for the coalition's successful and repeated resistance against Assyria were very high.

B. The second stage involved at least six more devastating interregional conflicts between Aram and its allies and Israel and Judah from the late ninth century down to its end. There may have been several more conflicts with Aram as suggested by a number of biblical passages not included here. These conflicts exasperated the drain and exhaustion of the previous redirected human and material resources. Because these conflicts took place on home soil, they resulted in even greater resource redirection and depletion, localized disruption and instability.

Any prospects for the production of lengthy literature suffered attenuation and postponement during these two stages.

(3) Phase three is the *royal prerogative phase*. It encapsulates the sudden emergence of lengthy monumental writing of the late ninth century produced by Aram and its allies. This phase inserted itself into the second stage of the *conflict affective phase* and the two stages continued in tandem down to

the end of the ninth century. A handful of states as *victors*, Aram, Moab and Ammon, fashioned a context specific form of lengthy literary production, while the *vanquished,* Israel and Judah could not. These victors were also the *first* to realize their aspiration to emulate the literary traditions of imperial Assyria. How else can the precipitous appearance of the four monumental texts, two from Aram, and one each from its allies, Moab and Ammon, be accounted for, having so abruptly arisen from what otherwise comprised a protracted epigraphic paucity and decades of conflict-obstructed literary production? Writing for administrative and small-scale production continued as needed.[40]

(4) Late Bronze Age Ugarit's contrast with the southern Levant of the Iron 2 period is telling. With similar designs on emulating foreign prestige (here, that of Mesopotamia), the Ugaritians produced an indigenous literary repertoire using their own alphabetic writing system. They did so, however, from an advantageous position of a politically stable and sociohistorically conducive scribal environment. As such, Ugarit inversely serves to underscore just how profoundly long lasting political stability (or persistent conflict-affected instability) could impact the production (or nonproduction) of lengthy literary texts in the ancient Levantine theatre.[41]

While the overall epigraphic database will undoubtedly increase, it is very cautiously "predicted" here that lengthy literary texts other than those of the monumental type will not be found prior to the late ninth century but

---

[40]. This in turn suggests that the anepigraphic bullae with papyrus fiber impressions from late ninth-century Israelite and Judean sites were not indicative of other forms of indigenous lengthy literature. Rather they sealed brief administrative writings or perhaps brief letters. The bullae may point to the age-old practice of correspondence attested among the cities and towns of Syria, and to a far lesser extent in Palestine (e.g., Aphek) from the second half of the Late Bronze Age. Regional centers wrote primarily for the purpose of corresponding with their regional overlords (e.g., Egypt, Hatti, Mitanni). Smaller towns even employed what van Soldt labels an "external administration" to correspond by letter with their overlords and otherwise did not write; see Wilfred H. van Soldt, "The Extent of Literacy in Syria and Palestine during the Second Millennium B.C.E.," in *Time and History in the Ancient Near East: Proceedings of the 56th Rencontre Assyriologique Internationale at Barcelona 26–30 July 2010*, ed. Luis Feliu et al. (Winona Lake, IN: Eisenbrauns, 2013), 19–32; van Soldt, "Why Did They Write? On Empires and Vassals in Syria and Palestine in the Late Bronze Age," in *Theory And Practice Of Knowledge Transfer: Studies In School Education In The Ancient Near East And Beyond. Papers Read at a Symposium In Leiden, 17–19 December 2008*, ed. W. S. Van Egmond and Wilfred H. Van Soldt (Leiden: Nederlands Instituut Voor Het Nabije Oosten. 2012), 103–13.

[41]. See Dennis Pardee, *The Ugaritic Texts and the Origins of West-Semitic Literary Compositions* (Oxford: The British Academy, 2012). Pardee highlights the fact that, among writing's various other functions at Ugarit, it was specifically placed into service to set down West Semitic literary works (p. 33).

only thereafter, in the eighth century or later.[42] Once again, we have not sought the *origins* of Israelite "literature" *per se*, which with one exception, the conflict inscription, was exclusively preserved and transmitted in oral form both prior to and throughout the ninth century. Such oral literature possessed ancient origins. Oral poets and, "remembrancers" whose predecessors had carried the old traditions across the LBA–EIA divide kept them alive and current throughout the Iron Age. The search initiated here sought instead to identify evidence for and examples of the production of written literature of length. Although ninth century scribes of the southern Levant were capable of producing written literature of length, persistent conflict postponed any realization of that aspiration. Notwithstanding the possibility that, prior to the end of the ninth century, the regional impulse to transfer ancient, orally composed literature of length to written form might not have arisen in the absence of the emulative stimulus generated by Assyria's power, prestige, and presence, the redirection and exhaustion of material and human resources to meet the demands of prolonged conflict at home and abroad delayed its actualization. The production of lengthy literature would have to await subsequent centuries following the return of stability, stimulus, and production to the region. With Assyria's renewed Levantine interventions beginning with those of Adad-nirari III at the close of the ninth century, the scribes of south Levantine polities were presented with new opportunities to produce written literature of length.[43]

---

42. The ink-on-plastered wall inscription of six or more(?) lines from Kuntillet Ajrud may be relevant here (text 4.2). If 800 BCE is an acceptable approximate date for the production of the inscriptions there, then the texts were possibly composed in a period of relative stability concurrent with Adad-narari III's arrival in the wider region. Moreover, if the site was under northern control at the time, then this theophanic hymn in particular represents Samaria's earliest-attested attempt at producing its own literary texts. Here Deir Alla may be instructive. We proposed that Deir Alla comprised an Aramean controlled site and the Balaam text, also an ink-on-plastered wall inscription, constituted prophecy in the service of state propaganda and economic interests. By way of analogy then, Kuntillet Ajrud might be viewed as an Israelite-controlled site and the hymn a state-sponsored, but locally compatible, expression of divine power (El, Yahweh, Baal, the Holy One, and the Elim or "gods" are mentioned), similarly designed for a diverse audience, namely, Judeans, Phoenicians, and Samarians, as well as a diverse population of travelers visiting the site. As such, the text represents the kind of ecumenism we might come to expect of a regionally controlled, multiethnic, territorially marginal production site of the Iron 2 period.

43. Luis Robert Siddall, *The Reign of Adad-nirari III: Historical and Ideological Analysis of an Assyrian King and His Times* (Leiden: Brill), 2013.

References

Ahituv, Shmuel. *Echoes from the Past: Hebrew and Cognate Inscriptions from the Biblical Period.* Jerusalem: Carta, 2008.

Ahituv, Shmuel, and Amihai Mazar. "The Inscriptions from Tel Reḥov and Their Contribution to the Study of Script and Writing during Iron Age IIA." Pages 39–68 in *"See, I will bring a scroll recounting what befell me" (Ps 40:8). Epigraphy and Daily Life from the Bible to the Talmud Dedicated to the Memory of Professor Hanan Eshel.* Edited by Esther Eshel and Yigal Levin. Göttingen: Vandenhoeck & Ruprecht, 2014.

Albertz, Rainer, and Rüdiger Schmitt. *Family and Household Religion in Ancient Israel and the Levant.* Winona Lake, IN: Eisenbrauns, 2012.

Amadasi Guzzo, Maria Giulia. "Un fragment de stèle araméenne de Tell Afis." *Or* 70 (2009): 336–47.

———. Tell Afis in the Iron Age: The Aramaic Inscriptions." *NEA* 77 (2014): 54–57.

Athas, George. *The Tel Dan Inscription: A Reappraisal and a New Interpretation.* London: T&T Clark, 2003.

Ben-Shlomo, David and Othmar Keel. "Clay Sealings and Seal Impressions." Pages 857–75 in *The Smithsonian Institution Excavation at Tell Jemmeh, Israel, 1970–1990.* Edited by David Ben-Shlomo and Gus W. Van Beek. Smithsonian Contributions to Anthropology 50. Washington D.C.: Smithsonian Institution Scholarly Press, 2014.

Blum, Erhard. "Israels Prophetie im altorientalischen Kontext." Pages 81–114 in *"From Ebla to Stellenbosch": Syro-Palestinian Religions and the Hebrew Bible.* Edited by I. Cornelius and L. Jonker. ADPV 37. Wiesbaden: Harrassowitz, 2008.

———. "Die Kombination I der Wandinschrift vom Tell Deir 'Alla. Vorschläge zur Rekonstruction mit historisch-kritischen Anmerkungen," Pages 573–601 in *Berührungspunkte. Studien zur Sozial- und Religionsgeschichte Israels und seiner Umwelt. Festschrift für Rainer Albertz.* Edited by I. Kottsieper, R. Schmitt, J. Wöhrle. AOAT 350. Münster: Ugarit-Verlag, 2008.

Boertien, Jeannette Hannah. *Unraveling the Fabric: Textile Production in the Iron Age Transjordan.* Groningen: Rijksuniversiteit, 2013.

Byrne, Ryan. "The Refuge of Scribalism in Iron I Palestine." *BASOR* 345 (2007): 1–31.

Carr, David M. *The Formation of the Hebrew Bible*, Oxford: Oxford University Press, 2011.

Cross, Frank Moore, "A Fragment of a Monumental Inscription from the City of David," *IEJ* 51 (2001): 44–47.

Daviau, P. M. Michele. "Anomalies in the Archaeological Record: Evidence for Domestic and Industrial Cults in Central Jordan." Pages 103–28 in *Family and Household Religion: Towards a Synthesis of Old Testament Studies, Archaeology, Epigraphy, and Cultural Studies.* Edited by Rainer Albertz, Beth Alpert Nakhai. Saul Olyan, and Rüdiger Schmitt. Winona Lake, IN: Eisenbrauns, 2014.

Daviau, P. M. Michele, and Paul Dion. "Independent and Well-Connected: The Ammonite Territorial Kingdom in the Iron II." Pages 121–28 in *Crossing Jordan: North American Contributions to the Archaeology of Jordan.* Edited by Thomas E. Levy et al. London: Equinox, 2007.

Dijkstra, Meindert, and Karel Vriesen. "The Assyrian Province of Gilead and the 'Myth of the Empty Land.'" Pages 1–26 in *Exploring the Narrative: Jerusalem and Jordan in the Bronze and Iron Ages*. Edited by Noor Mulder. London: Bloomsbury, 2014.

Dobbs-Allsopp, Frederick W., Jimmy J. M. Roberts, Choon L. Seow, and Robert E. Whitaker. *Hebrew Inscriptions: Texts from the Biblical Period of the Monarchy with Concordance*. New Haven: Yale University, 2005.

Dolan, Annlee. "Defining Sacred Space in Ancient Moab." Pages 129–44 in *Studies on Iron Age Moab and Neighboring Areas in Honor of Michèle Daviau*. Edited by Piotr Bienkowski. Leuven: Peeters, 2009.

Finkelstein, Israel, and Benjamin Sass. "The West Semitic Alphabetic Inscriptions, Late Bronze II to Iron IIA: Archaeological Context, Distribution and Chronology," *Hebrew Bible/Ancient Israel* 2 (2013): 149–210.

Franken, H. J. "Deir Alla and Its Religion." Pages 25–52 in *Sacred and Sweet: Studies on the Material Culture of Tell Deir 'Alla and Tell Abu Sarbut*. Edited by Margreet Steiner and Eveline J. van der Steen. Leuven: Peeters, 2008.

Gass, Erasmus. *Die Moabiter: Geschichte und Kultur eines ostjordanischen Volkes im 1. Jahrtausend v. Chr.* ADPV 38. Wiesbaden: Harrassowitz, 2009.

Gzella, Holger. *A Cultural History of Aramaic: From the Beginnings to the Advent of Islam*. HO 1.111. Leiden: Brill, 2014.

Hagelia, Hallvard. *The Dan Debate: The Tel Dan Inscription in Recent Research*. Sheffield: Sheffield Phoenix, 2009.

———. *The Tel Dan Inscription: A Critical Investigation of Recent Research on Its Palaeography and Philology*. Acta Universitatis Upsaliensis 22. Uppsala: Uppsala Universitet, 2006.

———. "What Is the Problem with the Tel Dan Inscription?" *KUSATU* 15 (2013): 109–23.

Hasegawa, Shuichi. *Aram and Israel during the Jehuite Dynasty*. BZAW 434. Berlin: de Gruyter, 2012.

Hoftijzer Jean, and Gerrit Van der Kooij. *Aramaic Texts from Deir 'Alla*. DMOA 19. Leiden: Brill, 1976.

Hutton, Jeremy M. "Local Manifestations of Yahweh and Worship in the Interstices: A Note on Kuntillet Ajrud," *JANER* 10 (2010): 177–210.

———. "Southern, Northern and Transjordanian Perspectives." Pages 149–74 in *Religious Diversity in Ancient Israel and Judah*. Edited by Francesca Stavrakopoulou and John Barton. London: T&T Clark, 2010.

Ji, Chang-Ho. "The Iron Age II Temple at Hirbet 'Atarus and Its Architecture and Selected Cult Objects." Pages 203–21 in *Temple Building and Temple Cult: Architecture and Cultic Paraphernalia of Temples in the Levant (2.–1. mill. B.C.E.): Proceedings of a Conference on the Occasion of the 50th Anniversary of the Institute of Biblical Archaeology at the University of Tübingen (28–30 May 2010)*. Edited by Jens Kamlah. Wiesbaden: Harrassowitz, 2012.

Knapp, Andrew. "The Dispute over the Land of Qedem at the Onset of the Aram-Israel Conflict: A Reanalysis of lines 3–4 of the Tel Dan Inscription." *JNES* 73 (2014): 105–16.

Lemaire, André. "The Mesha Stele and the Omri Dynasty." Pages 135–44 in *Ahab Agonistes: The Rise and Fall of the Omri Dynasty*. Edited by Lester L. Grabbe. LHBOTS 421. London: T&T Clark, 2007.

———. "West Semitic Epigraphy and the History of the Levant During the 12th–10th Centuries BCE." Pages 291–307 in *The Ancient Near East in the 12th–10th Centuries BCE*. Edited by Gershon Galil, Ayelet Gilboa, Aren M. Maeir, and Dan'el Kahn. Münster: Ugarit-Verlag, 2012.

———. "West Semitic Inscriptions and Ninth-Century BCE Ancient Israel." Pages 279–303 in *Understanding the History of Ancient Israel: Culture and History: Proceedings of the International Conference, Held at the University of Haifa, 25 May, 2010*. Edited by Hugh G. M. Williamson Oxford: Oxford University Press, 2007.

Levtow, Nathan. "Monumental Inscriptions and the Ritual Presentation of War." Pages 25–46 in *Warfare, Ritual and Symbol in Biblical and Modern Contexts*. Edited by Brad E. Kelle, Frank Ritchel Ames, and Jacob L. Wright. AIL 18. Atlanta: Society of Biblical Literature, 2014.

Levy, Thomas E., Mohammad Najjar, and Erez Ben-Yosef. "Conclusions." Pages 977–1001 in *New Insights into the Iron Age Archaeology of Edom, Southern Jordan*, vol. 1. Los Angeles: Cotsen Institute of Archeology Press, 2014.

Lipiński, Edward. *The Arameans: Their Ancient History, Culture, Religion*. OLA 100. Leuven: Peeters, 2000.

Liverani, Mario. *Israel's History and the History of Israel*. London: Equinox. 2005.

Maier, Aren M., ed. *Tell es-Safi/Gath I: Report on the 1996–2005 Seasons*. AAT 69. Wiesbaden: Harrassowitz, 2012.

Maeir, Aren M., and Esther Eshel. "Four Short Alphabetic Inscriptions from Late Iron Age IIa Tell es-Safi/Gath and Their Implications for the Development of Literacy in Iron Age Philistia and Environs." Pages 69–88 in *"See, I will bring a scroll recounting what befell me" (Ps 40:8): Epigraphy and Daily Life from the Bible to the Talmud Dedicated to the Memory of Professor Hanan Eshel*. Edited by Esther Eshel and Yigal Levin. JAJSup 12. Göttingen: Vandenhoeck & Ruprecht, 2014.

Mazzoni, Stephania. "The Aramean States during the Iron Age II–III Periods." *Oxford Handbook of the Archaeology of the Levant (c. 8000–322 BCE)*. Edited by Ann E. Killebrew and Margreet L. Steiner. Oxford: Oxford University Press, 2014. doi: 10.1093/oxfordhb/9780199212972.013.045.

Millard, Alan. "Authors, Books, and Readers in the Ancient World." Pages 545–65 in *Oxford Handbook of Biblical Studies*. Edited by Judith M. Lieu and J. Roberson. Oxdford: Oxford University Press, 2006. doi: 10.1093/oxfordhb/9780199237777.003.0031.

Na'aman, Nadav. "Royal Inscriptions versus Prophetic Story. Mesha's Rebellion according to Biblical and Moabite Historiography." Pages 145–83 in *Ahab Agonistes: The Rise and Fall of the Omri Dynasty*. Edited by Lester L. Grabbe. LHBOTS 421. London: T&T Clark, 2007.

Naveh, Joseph, "A Fragment of an Ancient Hebrew Inscription from the Ophel." *IEJ* 32 (1982): 195–98.

Niehr, Herbert. *The Arameans in Ancient Syria*. Leiden: Brill, 2014.

———. "Koenig Hazael von Damaskus im Licht neurer Funde und Interpretationen." Pages 339–56 in *"Ich Werde Meinen Bund mit Euch Niemals Brechen!" (Ri 2,1): Festschrift fuer Walter Gross zum 70. Geburtstag*. Edited by Erasmus Gass und Hans J. Stipp. Freiburg: Herder, 2011.

Nissinen, Martti. "The Prophet and the Augur at Tushan, 611." Pages 329–38 in *Literature as Politics and Politics as Literature. Essays on the Ancient Near East in*

Honor of Peter Machinist. Edited by David S. Vanderhooft and Abraham Winitzer. Winona Lake, IN: Eisenbrauns, 2013.

Pardee, Dennis. *The Ugaritic Texts and the Origins of West Semitic Literary Compositions*. Oxford: The British Academy, 2012.

———. "A Brief Case for Phoenician as the Language of the 'Gezer Calendar.'" Pages 226–46 in *Linguistic Studies in Phoenician in Memory of J. Brian Peckham*. Winona Lake, IN: Eisenbrauns, 2013.

Petit, Lucas Pieter. *Settlement Dynamics in the Middle Jordan Valley during the Iron Age II*. BAR 2033. Oxford: Archaeopress, 2009.

Puech, Emile. "Bala'am and Deir 'Alla." Pages 25–47 in *The Prestige of the Pagan Prophet Balaam in Judaism, Early Christianity and Islam*. Edited by George H. van Kooten and Jacques van Ruiten. Leiden: Brill, 2008.

Reich, Ronny and Eli Shukron. "Recent Discoveries in the City of David, Jerusalem." *IEJ* 57 (2007): 153–69.

Renfrew Colin. *Archaeology: Theories, Methods and Practice*. London: Thames & Hudson, 1991.

Rollston, Christopher A. "The Dating of the Early Royal Byblian Phoenician Inscriptions: A Response to Benjamin Sass." *Maarav* 15 (2008): 57–93.

———. "The Iron Age Edomite Script and Language." Pages 961–75 in *New Insights into the Iron Age Archaeology of Edom, Southern Jordan*, vol. 1. Edited by Thomas E. Levy, Mohammad Najjar, and Erez Ben-Yosef. Los Angeles: Cotsen Institute of Archeology, 2014.

———. "The Phoenician Script of the Tel Zayit Abecedary and Putative Evidence for Israelite Literacy." Pages 61–96 in *Literate Culture and Tenth-Century Canaan: The Tel Zayit Abecedary in Context*. Edited by Ron E. Tappy and P. Kyle McCarter. Winona Lake, IN: Eisenbrauns, 2008.

———. "What's the Oldest Hebrew Inscription?" *BAR* 38.3 (2012): 32–40, 66, 68.

———. *Writing and Literacy in the World of Ancient Israel*. SBLABS 11. Atlanta: Society of Biblical Literature, 2010.

Roche-Hawley, Carole, and Robert Hawley. "An Essay on Scribal Families, Tradition, and Innovation." Pages 241–64 in *Beyond Hatti: Essays in Honor of Gary Beckman*. Edited by Billie Jean Collins and Piotr Michalowski. Atlanta: Lockwood, 2013.

Routledge, Bruce. *Moab in the Iron Age*. Philadelphia: University of Pennsylvania Press, 2003.

Sader, Helene. "The Arameans of Syria." Pages 273–300 in *The Books of Kings: Sources, Composition, Historiography and Reception*. Edited by Andre Lemaire and Baruch Halpern. Leiden: Brill, 2010.

Sass, Benjamin. The *Alphabet at the Turn of the Millennium: The West Semitic Alphabet ca. 1150–850 BCE. The Antiquity of the Arabian, Greek and Phrygian Alphabets*. Occasional Publication 4. Tel-Aviv: Emery and Claire Yass Publications, 2005.

Schmidt, Brian B. "The Iron Age Pithoi Drawings from Horvat Teman or Kuntillet 'Ajrud: Some New Proposals," *JANER* 2 (2002): 91–125.

Schmitt, Rüdiger. "A Typology of Iron Age Cult Places." Pages 265–86 in *Family and Household Religion*. Edited by Rainer Albertz, Beth Alpert Nakhai, Saul M. Olyan, and Rüdiger Schmitt. Winona Lake, IN: Eisenbrauns, 2014.

Sanders, Seth L. *The Invention of Hebrew*. Urbana: University of Illinois Press, 2009.
Shiloh, Yigal. "City of David Excavation 1978," *BA* 42 (1979): 170.
Siddall, Luis Robert. *The Reign of Adad-nirari III: Historical and Ideological Analysis of an Assyrian King and His Times*. Leiden: Brill, 2013.
Soldt, Wilfred H. van. "The Extent of Literacy in Syria and Palestine during the Second Millennium B.C.E." Pages 19–32 in *Time and History in the Ancient Near East: Proceedings of the 56th Rencontre Assyriologique Internationale at Barcelona 26–30 July 2010*. Edited by Luis Feliu et al. Winona Lake, IN: Eisenbrauns, 2013.
———. "Why Did They Write? On Empires and Vassals in Syria and Palestine in the Late Bronze Age." Pages 103–13 in *Theory and Practice of Knowledge Transfer: Studies in School Education in the Ancient Near East and Beyond. Papers Read at a Symposium In Leiden, 17–19 December 2008*. Edited by W. S. Van Egmond and Wilfred H. Van Soldt. Leiden: Nederlands Instituut Voor Het Nabije Oosten, 2012.
Sukenik, Eleazor L. "Note on a Fragment of an Israelite Stele Found at Samaria," *PEFQS* (1936): 156.
Van der Steen, Eveline J. "Nelson Glueck's 'String of Fortresses' Revisited." Pages 117–28 in *Studies on Iron Age Moab and Neighboring Areas in Honour of Michele Daviau*. Edited by P. Bienkowski. Leuven: Peeters, 2009.
Weeks, Stuart. "Literacy, Orality, and Literature in Israel." Pages 465–78 in *On Stone and Scroll: Essays in Honour of Graham Ivor Davies*. Edited by James K. Aitken, Katharine J. Dell, and Brian A. Mastin. BZAW 420. Berlin: de Gruyter, 2011.
Yamada, Shigeo. *The Construction of the Assyrian Empire*. CHANE 3. Leiden: Brill, 2000.
Younger, K. Lawson. "Aram-Damascus." *OEBA* 1:42–49.
———. *The Political History of the Arameans: From Their Origins to the End of Their Polities*. ABS 13. Atlanta: Society of Biblical Literature, 2015.
Zevit, Ziony. *The Religions of Ancient Israel*. London: Continuum, 2001.

LET THE STONES SPEAK! DOCUMENT PRODUCTION BY IRON AGE WEST SEMITIC SCRIBAL INSTITUTIONS AND THE QUESTION OF BIBLICAL SOURCES

JESSICA WHISENANT

THIS STUDY EXAMINES THE EPIGRAPHIC EVIDENCE FOR THE VARYING LEVELS of writing and literacy in Iron Age Judah (ca. 1200–586 BCE), seeking to analyze this data in light of Judah's historical and geographical context as one of a constellation of small states that emerged in the Levant during the late Iron Age. The findings of this project have direct ramifications for the question of *if* and *when* the earliest versions of several texts now preserved in the Hebrew bible (HB) were composed in Iron Age Judah. At stake here is the common assumption, found in the work of many prominent scholars writing on the connection between Judah's epigraphic record and its development as a state, that a complex, lengthy historiographic text like the Deuteronomistic History (Deuteronomy through 2 Kings; DtrH) was composed in the Iron Age. This study will carefully review the data from epigraphic sources to determine whether such an assumption is warranted, and if not, whether any conclusions regarding the formation of biblical source documents dating to this period can be drawn. In other words, conclusions about *if* and *when* should be derived inductively from an investigation of the epigraphic data, rather than the epigraphic data being interpreted within the presumed framework of a preexilic context that necessarily underlies the composition of the HB in terms of first-generation, full-length scrolls of entire biblical works.

Certainly the vagaries of time and the elements, as well as the destructive effects of numerous conflicts in the region over the millennia, have severely impacted both the quantity and the quality of inscriptions on stone and clay, and frustratingly have left us with but a minute sampling of what was almost certainly a large corpus of writings on papyrus.[1] Nevertheless, this study contends that the epigraphic data from earlier and contemporary

---

1. It should be noted, however, that while we have very few surviving papyrus writings, we *do* have a fairly extensive number of the seal impressions (bullae) that were used

West Semitic cultures in the region (particularly that of Ugarit of the Late Bronze Age and Early Iron Age Phoenicia) can tell us a great deal about the genres and literary traditions that survived the Late Bronze/Iron I transition to impact the scribal institutions of the Iron II polities. Furthermore, the inscriptional evidence from Iron II Israel and Judah gives us a good idea of the categories of texts that were being produced by these same groups of scribes. We shall see that texts such as the tenth-century inscription detailing agricultural activities on limestone from Gezer and the seventh-century priestly blessings inscribed on silver scrolls from Ketef Hinnom in a localized West Semitic script give us a fascinating glimpse at something unique that was taking place in the Levant: the scribal use of the alphabet to express a written vernacular and through that vernacular to represent local political, cultural, and religious concepts.[2] This new development prepared the way for the eventual production of individual scrolls that originally circulated independently but were later gathered together to become that amazing body of work that is the HB, comprising a multitude of genres and perspectives yet presupposing and helping to create a single ethnic group united by a common history.[3]

In light of the above, the primary questions that this study will seek to address center on how scribal attempts to express the written vernacular over and against the dominant *lingua franca* of the age, the Babylonian of the Assyrian and later Babylonian Empires, came to be allied to the emergent political identities in Israel–Judah during the Iron Age. Can the stones (as well as pottery sherds, bullae, seals, etc.) speak to a likely scenario for the development of the scribal institutions in Israel and Judah, and their connection to and appropriation by the state apparatus for its hegemonizing purposes, including the invocation of local forms of ethnicity and identity? And specifically regarding Judah, how might the proliferation of scribes and the elite appropriation of the products of writing have been connected to the creation, reproduction, and transmission of texts that would in turn be consulted, used, cited, quoted, or alluded to by the authors of biblical texts and source texts? And finally, does the epigraphic data for text production in Judah attest the

---

to seal papyrus documents (as well as many of the seals that were used for this purpose. See my treatment later in this paper for details.

2. See Seth L. Sanders, "Writing and Early Iron Age Israel: Before National Scripts, Beyond Nations and States," in *Literate Culture and Tenth-Century Canaan: The Tel Zayit Abecedary in Context*, ed. Ron E. Tappy and P. Kyle McCarter (Winona Lake, IN: Eisenbrauns, 2008), 97–112, and idem, "What Was the Alphabet For? The Rise of Written Vernaculars and the Making of Israelite National Literature," *Maarav* 11 (2004): 25–56.

3. This observation is based on the insightful study by Seth L. Sanders, "What Was the Alphabet For?," 25–56.

presence of lengthy, complex literary works such as the Deuteronomistic History, the Psalms, or the prophetic texts that are preserved in the HB?

Writing and Literacies in the Levant:
The Late Bronze and Early Iron Ages

It is highly informative to examine the epigraphic evidence from the Levantine region from earlier periods before narrowing the focus to Iron II Judah, firstly to establish what we can know about the socio-historical context of writing and literacies, and secondly, so that links between the uses of writing, the identities of those performing writing, and their intended audiences can be identified. This will serve to demonstrate that the developments in the use of writing that took place in Judah were historically rooted in a West Semitic scribal heritage that first emerged at Ugarit in the thirteenth century and that were restored later in the Iron II period despite the relative lack of institutional support and infrastructure during the Late Bronze/Early Iron Age disruptions.

The territory of Late Bronze Canaan, falling as it did within the compass of the Egyptian Empire, was comprised of small centers of power jostling for preeminence. The technology of writing was dominated by a small, elite cast of scribes, who helped their employers (i.e., the rulers of each city-state) legitimize their position within and without the region by means of written correspondence, as attested by the letters that passed between these rulers and the Egyptian court at Amarna (ancient Akhetaten).[4] A close examination of the Amarna Letters as well as of the contemporary epigraphic witnesses to the production of writing found in Canaan reveals that the scripts developed and uses conceived for writing in Canaan evidence a curious amalgam of Mesopotamian forms of literacy and a nascent local tradition of writing and literacy.[5]

This tendency to express a local identity through writing is also in evidence at sites just north of Canaan, in what is now Syria. There, in contrast with the relatively young and immature scribal institutions of Canaan, more advanced and erudite scribal institutions had long been active in places like Ugarit and Ebla. The best-documented scribal culture of the Late Bronze period existed at Ugarit, a relatively cosmopolitan city on the northern

---

4. See Alexander Joffe, "The Rise of Secondary States in Iron Age Levant," *JESHO* 45 (2002): 425–67.

5. See Wayne Horowitz, Oshima Takayoshi, and Seth L. Sanders, *Cuneiform Sources from the Land of Israel in Ancient Times* (Jerusalem: Israel Exploration Society, 2006), 16, 18; Eva von Dassow, "Canaanite in Cuneiform," *JAOS* 124 (2004): 641–74.

Levantine coast, where a cadre of highly trained scribes facilitated extensive trade and other international contacts. Like the scribes in the Canaanite city-states, the scribal cadre at Ugarit was well versed in the Babylonian language (as well as other languages) and employed this prevailing *lingua franca* for certain categories of texts. The excavated texts from Ugarit dating to the thirteenth century reveal, however, that the Ugaritic scribes had generated a standardized written form of their own regional vernacular, and that they deliberately sought to produce a particular literature in a local language and writing system.[6] The Ugaritic literary texts represent the setting down in writing of oral traditions and poetic imagery that went back centuries (if not millennia), and that would survive to find expression again in the poetry of various biblical scrolls.[7]

Although the disruption experienced by the Levant during the thirteenth and twelfth centuries was significant, the data gleaned from archaeological excavations and surveys demonstrate that this process of decline was uneven throughout the region, and that there were significant elements of continuity, especially in material culture, between the beginning of the Iron Age in Canaan and the end of the Late Bronze Age.[8] Despite the collapse of "the international system and its interdependent network of city-states," the period of time from ca. 1300 to 900 BCE saw a continuation of many Old Canaanite forms, including the partial reestablishment of the palatial society during the tenth century.[9] The area of Phoenicia on the coast appears to have successfully navigated the transition from the Late Bronze to Iron I period with only a short period of disruption.[10] (By contrast, the southern Palestinian coast and its immediate hinterland experienced a marked change with the occupation and rebuilding of five towns by the Philistines—the Philistine pentapolis—and the founding of Philistine kingdoms centered on royal palaces.)[11]

---

6. Sanders, "What Was the Alphabet For?," 26.

7. See Dennis Pardee, *The Ugaritic Texts and the Origins of West-Semitic Literary Composition* (Oxford: Oxford University Press, 2012), 72–73, and 92–106.

8. Mario Liverani, *Israel's History and the History of Israel*, trans. Chiara Peri and Philip R. Davies (London: Equinox, 2005), 32–33.

9. Joffe, "The Rise of Secondary States," 431. Cf. Israel Finkelstein, "City-States to States: Polity Dynamics in the 10th–9th Centuries B.C.E.," in *Symbiosis, Symbolism, and the Power of the Past*, ed. William G. Dever and Seymour Gitin (Winona Lake, IN: Eisenbrauns, 2003), 75–83.

10. The area of the Phoenician centers to the north of the Philistine pentapolis quickly recovered from a series of destructions at the beginning of the twelfth century to establish a culture marked by continuity with the Late Bronze Age as well as by the advent of "proto-Phoenician" elements (see Liverani, *Israel's History*, 71).

11. Ibid., 34–37.

Along with the revival of Late Bronze-type urban centers in the northern valleys of Canaan and the flourishing of the Phoenician settlements, the political use of the alphabet resurfaced along the Levantine coast in the eleventh century, where writing was used to inscribe arrowheads with the names of kings, high-ranking people, and warriors.[12] Such items were emblematic of military might and status, and were recovered from mortuary contexts clearly belonging to the elite sphere.[13] Likewise, the limited epigraphic record from the Cisjordan and dating from the end of the Late Bronze through the early Iron I periods (mid-thirteenth century to ca. 1000 BCE) demonstrates the occasional use of the linear alphabet for the inscribing of prestige objects. Some of the most noteworthy exemplars in the Old Canaanite linear script include an ewer inscribed with a dedicatory inscription to a goddess from Tel Lachish (late thirteenth century), a gold ring from Megiddo (ca. 1250–1150 BCE) incised with the name of its owner along with the patronymic, and a seal carved from limestone found at Kibbutz Revadim and inscribed with *l'b'*, "Belonging to Abba" (late twelfth century BCE). These objects are prestige items and two of the three were found in elite contexts.[14] As far as the Iron I period is concerned, however, the meager number of inscriptions (in any script) and the brevity of their contents points to a very limited role for writing in the Iron I period. Moreover, the fact that the linear alphabet was neither standardized nor consistently intelligible during this Iron I period demonstrates that it subsisted largely on "elite wherewithal rather than political or economic exigency."[15] The survival and reproduction of the "trade" of

---

12. Around fifty unprovenanced arrowheads have emerged on the antiquities market bearing the name of the object ("arrow") incised in the bronze along with typical Northwest Semitic possessive formulae consisting of the owner's name, patronym, title, or affiliation. Given the fact that these arrowheads are unprovenanced (with one exception, see n. 13), some of them are probably forgeries.

13. The only arrowhead found in a controlled excavation, the Ruweise arrowhead, was discovered in a tomb in the Biq'a Valley of Lebanon. Contemporary arrowheads with cuneiform inscriptions from western Iran were likewise found in tombs; see Benjamin Sass, *The Genesis of the Alphabet and Its Development in the Second Millennium B.C.* [Wiesbaden: Harrassowitz, 1988], 74.

14. The Lachish ewer was discovered in the Fosse temple; David Diringer, "Inscriptions," in *Lachish IV: The Bronze Age*, ed. O. Tufnell (Oxford: Oxford University Press, 1958), 130. The Megiddo ring was found in an elite tomb that also contained other luxury items. See Emile Puech, "Un anneau inscrit du Bronze Récent à Megiddo," in *Ki Baruch Hu. Ancient Near Eastern, Biblical, and Judaic Studies in Honor of Baruch A. Levine*, ed. Robert Chazan et al. (Winona Lake, IN: Eisenbrauns, 1999), 51–61. For the Revadim seal, see Frank Moore Cross, *Leaves from an Epigrapher's Notebook: Collected Papers in Hebrew and West Semitic Palaeography and Epigraphy* (Winona Lake, IN: Eisenbrauns, 2003), 299–302.

15. Ryan Byrne, "The Refuge of Scribalism in Iron I Palestine," *BASOR* 345 (2007): 23.

scribalism during this period must be connected therefore to elite patronage: these elites commissioned alphabetic writing on prestige objects, in order to render these objects even more prestigious in a socio-economic environment of scribal scarcity.[16]

It was the writing tradition developed in the Phoenician city-states during the Iron I period and centered on the use of the linear alphabet that became the bridge between the older scribal heritage of Ugarit and the later writing traditions of the Iron II states. The lamentably small corpus of extant inscriptions from Phoenicia (and primarily the site of Byblos) dating from the late eleventh through the early ninth centuries is nevertheless sufficient to demonstrate that the technology of linear alphabetic writing was used to articulate the hegemony of the ruling elite in these coastal city-states.[17] This writing system was conscripted for use in monumental inscriptions that laid emphasis on the power, piety and building activities of the ruler by dedicating walls or statues to deities, or by invoking heavy curses against those who disturbed their coffins.[18] Through these royal inscriptions, the Byblian rulers legitimized their position as important potentates and as faithful representatives of the deity in the local language and in the local tradition of West Semitic alphabetic writing, rather than in the language and script of the neighboring superpowers (Egypt and Mesopotamia). For the first time in the Levantine region, therefore, local rulers sought to convey their power and identity in monumental form and in a local language. This touched off a process in the coastal cities as well as later in the emerging states of inland Canaan and the Transjordan in which local dialects of the West Semitic language became one of the markers that distinguished them from each other and from the larger players in the Mediterranean region (i.e., Assyria, Egypt) in the following Iron II period.

The epigraphic record from the coastal region, comprised as it is of monumental and cultic inscriptions on stone and on other nonperishable media, very likely does not reflect the entire scope of the writing activities that took place in Phoenicia. The vigorous commercial activities of the Phoenician

---

16. Ibid., 12–17.

17. Aram's role as a carrier/preserver of an old West Semitic scribal heritage also merits attention (see below).

18. These inscriptions have been described in detail in previous studies; the bibliography is too extensive to be cited here. The standard dating of these inscriptions has been the subject of some debate in recent years; see especially Benjamin Sass, *The Alphabet at the Turn of the Millennium: The West Semitic Alphabet ca. 1150–850 BCE* (Tel Aviv: Yass Publications in Archaeology, 2005). But Rollston has made good case for adhering to the standard chronology, contra Sass, who argues for a late ninth- and eighth-century date for these inscriptions. See Christopher A. Rollston, *Writing and Literacy in the World of Ancient Israel: Epigraphic Evidence from the Iron Age*, ABS 11 (Altanta: Society of Biblical Literature, 2010), 24–27.

centers must have necessitated the use of writing for administrative and economic texts (as it probably did in the previous LB Age as well). Indeed, the needs of commerce are a potent force in the development of communication techniques. Presumably, the normal writing medium of the Phoenicians for documenting such activities was papyrus, and papyrus needs especially dry conditions if it is to be preserved for any length of time. Because such conditions did not exist along the humid coast of Phoenicia, not a scrap of papyrus testifying to this use of writing has survived (although we do have some Phoenician bullae and seals attesting to the practice of sealing papyrus documents).[19]

It seems likely that the Phoenician administrative and economic texts on perishable materials were grouped into archival collections. Archival methods could conceivably have been passed down from Ugarit (before its destruction in the early twelfth century) to Byblos and the other coastal centers of the Levant, or perhaps transmitted to these coastal centers in the Late Bronze/early Iron I periods from Ugarit via sites in Canaan like Taanach and Aphek (where small "mini-archives" of cuneiform letters and administrative tablets in Akkadian have been found dating to the Late Bronze Age).[20] This is not a far-fetched scenario, as the contacts between Ugarit and several coastal cities of the southern Levant (Byblos, Beirut, 'Akko, Sidon, and Tyre) documented in Ugarit's archives reveal that these trading centers had already developed a scribal tradition in the earlier Late Bronze period.[21] Such a tradition (including the adoption of archival methods from Ugarit?) could have informed the renewed and reenergized scribal tradition of these same coastal centers during the Iron I and early Iron II periods. The role of Aram in the late tenth through eighth centuries in the preservation, development, and transmission of a West Semitic writing tradition is less clear but may prove to have been nearly as significant as that of Phoenicia (see the discussion of the Deir Alla and Tel Dan inscriptions below).

---

19. It is quite difficult to get an exact count of the number of Phoenician seals, as most of those seals published thus far have not come to us via regular excavations but have been purchased in the antiquities market and are in private collections. According to the calculation of Eric Gubel, there are around five hundred published examples of ascertained origin coming from the Phoenician east (Tyre, Sidon, Byblos, Arwad, and 'Amrit [Tartous]). These range in date from the second half of the ninth century till the early third century BCE; Eric Gubel, "The Iconography of Inscribed Phoenician Glyptic," in *Studies in the Iconography of Northwest Semitic Inscribed Seals*, ed. Benjamin Sass and Christoph Uehlinger (Fribourg: University Press, 1993), 106.

20. For these "mini-archives," see Horowitz, Oshima, and Sanders, *Cuneiform Sources*, 15–19, 127–51.

21. See Itamar Singer, "A Political History of Ugarit," in the *Handbook of Ugaritic Studies*, ed. Wilfred G. E. Watson and Nicolas Wyatt (Leiden: Brill, 1999), 603–733.

It is indisputable, however, that it was the Phoenician script (and even language, at times) that became "an international, transregional script" during the tenth, ninth, and eighth centuries, not only in the Levant but in Cyprus, Syria, and as far away as Karatepe in Asia Minor.[22] The number of inscriptions from tenth- and early ninth-century Canaan are only marginally more numerous than those from the earlier Iron period; nevertheless, their script clearly demonstrates the profound influence of the Phoenician scribal centers on the Hebrew scribes even during this early Iron II period. The bronze bowl (tenth century) found in an elite burial cave at Kefar Veradim (upper Galilee), and bearing its owner's name and patronymic in Phoenician is a strong testimony to the fact that by this early Iron II period Phoenician had become "the international prestige script of the Levant."[23]

Particularly intriguing is the enigmatic limestone "tablet" discovered at Gezer and dated to the late tenth or early ninth century BCE, whose script likewise appears to be closer to Phoenician than to Hebrew.[24] Because its contents describe seasonal agricultural activities (sowing, harvesting, pruning, etc.), it is usually considered to be some sort of agricultural calendar. While the exact use of the inscription will probably always be a mystery, its contents do seem expressive of "an old, pan-Canaanite vocabulary of time-keeping."[25] Far from representing a school exercise for bureaucrats as commonly has been assumed, the Gezer calendar can be seen as evidence for the phenomenon of 'literization,' that is, in the words of S. Sanders, "the setting down in writing—of local culture."[26] Like the Gezer calendar, the Tel Zayit abecedary, dated by its excavator to no later than the mid-tenth century,[27] appears to be unconnected to a formal scribal-education system (and indeed, given the decentralized nature of the Iron I political economy, it would be difficult to imagine that such a system existed). At most it reflects the presence of a lone Judean scribe somewhat familiar with the prestige Phoenician script tradition, who scratched out the letters of the alphabet on a boulder, perhaps for apotropaic purposes.[28]

---

22. Christopher A. Rollston, "The Tel Zayit Abecedary and Evidence for Israelite Literacy," in Tappy and McCarter, *Literate Culture and Tenth-Century Canaan*, 8.

23. Ibid., 72. For the Kefar Veradim inscription, see the report of the excavator, Yardenna Alexandre, "Phoenician Inscription from Kefar Veradim," in *Eretz Zafon. Studies in Galilean Archaeology*, ed. Zvi Gal (Jerusalem: Israel Antiquities Authority, 2002), 65*–74.*

24. Christopher A. Rollston, *Writing and Literacy*, 31.

25. Sanders, "Writing and Early Iron Age Israel," 101.

26. Ibid.

27. Ron E. Tappy, "Tel Zayit and the Tel Zayit Abecedary in Their Regional Context," in Tappy and McCarter, *Literate Culture and Tenth-Century Canaan*, 1–44.

28. Based on an extensive analysis of the Iron Age Phoenician script of the early Byblian inscriptions (tenth century), Rollston (*Writing and Literacy*, 19–46) has made a

In the highlands of Canaan in general, the role that writing had, if any, is unclear. Most of the hundreds of small highland settlements that were established during the Iron I period were abandoned or destroyed in the tenth century (new settlements, the vast majority of which were not located on Iron I sites, were not established until the ninth through seventh centuries). In the interim between the end of the Iron I and the later Iron II periods, several regional urban centers arose in the highlands and lowlands, including at Hazor, Megiddo, Tell el-Far'ah (N), Beth-Shemesh, Beersheba, and Jerusalem, among others.[29] It was not until later in the Iron II period, however, that writing was enlisted to aid in the development of larger, more centralized polities. Until then, writing (generally in the Phonician script) was used only infrequently in inland Canaan during the tenth through early ninth centuries for the inscription of prestige items (Kefar Veradim bowl), for graffiti (Tel Zayit abecedary), and for objects whose use will always be obscure (Gezer calendar).

Writing and Literacies in Israel/Samaria and the Transjordan in the Iron Age II

It was not long after the destruction of the city-states in the northern valleys of Canaan, probably at the hands of the Egyptians during Pharaoh Sheshonq I's campaign in the late tenth century, that the rulers of the northern hill country extended their power into the lowlands to found a large multi-ethnic state. The small scribal community of this new polity would have been very receptive to the transmission of elite concepts related to the linear alphabetic writing technology that had been developed in the coastal cities. That they readily employed this writing system for administrative and economic purposes is attested indirectly by the prominence achieved by Israel in the Levantine region by the early-to-mid ninth century BCE.[30] It is difficult to imagine that Israel could have effectively managed its resources and administer its conquered territories without the active participation of a scribal community engaged in writing letters and military dispatches, and ensuring that the flow

---

good case for the identity of the script on both the Gezer calendar and the Tel Zayit abecedary as being Phoenician rather than Old Hebrew.

29. Avraham Faust, *Israel's Ethnogenesis: Settlement, Interaction, Expansion and Resistance* (London: Equinox, 2006), 111–34.

30. Israel's appearance as a polity in the historical record is first attested during the mid-ninth century in the inscription on a black obelisk of Shalmaneser III, in which Israel appears as a major regional power (along with Phoenicia and Aram-Damascus) in the coalition that confronted said king at the battle of Qarqar in 853 BCE (*COS* 2.113F:269–70).

of goods from the peripheral regions to the state's center moved smoothly. A possible reflection of the latter scribal activity is to be found in the approximately one hundred ostraca in old Hebrew script (early eighth century) from the Israelite capital city of Samaria, which attest to the implementation of a system of taxation, or of some kind of royal supply system.[31] The elite concepts transmitted from Phoenicia would also have included knowledge about archival techniques—the existence of state archives consisting primarily of perishable materials such as papyrus is intimated by the discovery in Samaria of around fifteen bullae dating to the eighth century and bearing papyrus fiber marks on their reverse sides.[32] The extant epigraphic record from Samaria tellingly hints at what was doubtless the very active role played by Israel's scribal specialists in the administering of the state. Moreover, by engaging in a series of writing practices that were predicated on the existence of Israel as a totality, Israel's scribes in turn helped generate state hegemony.

The way in which a local dynasty in Israel made visible and public its nationalistic claims can be deduced from an examination of the contemporary Levantine monumental inscriptions that have survived. The Tel Dan stele (ninth century) is the quintessential victory stele, set up on lands in northern Israel vanquished by the Aramean victor (probably Hazael) in order to relate his glorious achievements and to send a powerful signal to the Israelites that resisting Aramean hegemony would be futile.[33] The mid-ninth century Mesha Inscription (MI), by contrast, was set up in Mesha's own lands to celebrate the Moabite king's victories over Israel, and to memorialize the "public works" projects enacted by Mesha for the benefit of his people.[34] Furthermore, its contents reveal how new social identities as well as new ethnic categories and boundaries could be articulated through the medium of public display.[35] Through the claims made by Mesha regarding his legitimacy as ruler (and particularly his boasts regarding his patrimony, that is, his father "ruled over Moab"; MI 2), it can be seen how the existence on a basic

---

31. Analysis of the Samaria ostraca and translations of their contents can be found in Frederick W. Dobbs-Allsopp et al., *Hebrew Inscriptions. Texts from the Biblical Period of the Monarchy with Concordance* (New Haven: Yale University Press, 2005), 423–97.

32. These fifteen bullae originally belonged to a larger group, as indicated by the fragments of perhaps as many as fifty bullae found along with the fifteen intact ones. The preserved bullae bore no inscriptions, only common Egypto-Phoenician motifs; John W. Crowfoot and Grace M. Crowfoot, *Early Ivories from Samaria* (London, 1938), 2, 88; pl. 15:29–30.

33. Rollston, *Writing and Literacy*, 51, 53.

34. Ibid., 52–55.

35. See Joffe, "The Rise of Secondary States," 454. Cf. Bruce Routledge, *Moab in the Iron Age. Hegemony, Polity, Archaeology* (Philadelphia: University of Pennsylvania Press, 2004), 133–53.

social level of kinship ties, presumably in the form of lineages, underlay the formation in the elite sphere of dynasties and dynastic traditions. Mesha's reference to his patrimony reflected the primary concern of Iron Age Levantine royalty, that is, sustaining dynastic legitimacy.

The contents of the MI therefore help demonstrate how the development of ethnicity in the southern Levant was aided by the creation of dynastic traditions (such as the "House of Omri") by the Iron Age elites; this stele and the reference to Milkom in the royal inscription from the Amman Citadel (*CAI* 59)[36] likewise demonstrate how these dynasties were closely connected to religious traditions with which the state as a whole came to be identified. Furthermore, the dedication of a high place to Kemosh in Qarhō (probably a citadel in Dibon; MI 3), which constitutes the *raison d'être* behind the inscription's erection, points to the close association of the state hegemonic project with the establishment of large sanctuaries associated with the national cult, and the likely formation of an attendant cultic personnel engaged in performing the requisite rituals. Along with these priestly elite was a coterie of scribes to serve the needs of the temple and smaller, local sanctuaries. The cultivation of writing to aid in the service of the cult and in the expression of local religious traditions is reflected in the numerous dedicatory inscriptions dating to the Iron II period (ca. 900–550 BCE) and found throughout the southern Levant, from Phoenicia, to Philistia, Israel, the Transjordan, and Judah.

It is the spatial context of some of this cultic writing that suggests another way, besides the setting up of royal stelae, that the public and state-controlled dissemination of these new ideologies centering on a national dynasty and cult may have transpired in Israel (and elsewhere). This way is hinted at by the discovery of the early eighth century cultic graffiti at Kuntillet Ajrud, the wayside station situated on an important trading route in northern Sinai which is nonetheless linked to Israel in the north.[37] Inscribed on large pithoi and on the plastered surfaces of the walls of a small sanctuary (building A)

---

36. Walter Aufrecht, *A Corpus of Ammonite Inscriptions* (Lewiston, NY: Edwin Mellen, 1989), 154–63.

37. See Zeev Meshel, *Kuntillet 'Ajrud: A Religious Centre from the Time of the Judean Monarchy on the Border of Sinai* (Jerusalem: Israel Museum, 1978). The influence of the northern kingdom on Kuntillet 'Ajrud (Horvat Teman) is indisputable, as is the strong connection between Israel and Phoenicia evident from the finds at the site. The location has yielded a great quantity of "Samaria Ware" pottery, artifacts with drawings characterized by a marked Syro-Phoenician influence, and several inscriptions in Phoenician. Moreover, the cultic graffiti features linguistic elements that occur frequently in inscriptions from Israel, as well as the phrase "Yahweh of Samaria"; see Anna Soumeka, "The Significance of Kuntillet 'Ajrud for the Study of Early Judahite History and Religion," *Deltion biblikon meleton* 20 (2002): 94.

within the larger complex of the site are formulaic blessings (and even part of a theophany) written in the names of Yahweh, Asherah, and other deities that may have originally emanated from the ritualistic practices of Israel's priests and cultic functionaries in Samaria. The public display of these graffiti as well as their association with a range of related symbols (i.e., drawings connected with the cult and probably the royal dynasty of Israel) would have ensured that the message(s) would have been conveyed to even the most illiterate onlooker.[38] The more general context of the site, i.e., located on one of the desert trade routes that was very likely controlled by Israel during this period, likewise suggests that the inscriptions and wall paintings were officially commissioned by that state.

A similar phenomenon may have been taking place at the site of Deir Alla, given the context of its ca. 800 BCE plaster inscription—written in ink on the wall plaster of a small chamber within a building that was part of a manufacturing and distribution center—and the location of this site in the eastern Jordan Valley, which was crisscrossed by trade routes.[39] Combination I of the Deir Alla plaster text recounts a narrative about the (Aramean?) seer Balaam son of Beor, a figure also known from biblical tradition (Num 22–24). The account details a night vision that came to Balaam regarding the gods' decision to bring about disaster, after which Balaam fasts and mourns. This vision is interwoven with a description of a series of reversals of the traditional social structures of the world. Er Blum has argued that Combination I consists of different texts, and that some of the composition probably was copied from a *Vorlage*.[40] Combination II is only partially readable and has been interpreted in a variety of ways, but Blum's reading of this section as a "sapiental instruction speech or dialogue," with its "questions and addresses in the second person singular," is persuasive.[41]

Blum places the Deir Alla plaster text within the same linguistic idiom (Old Aramaic of the Kingdom of Damascus) and chronological timeframe as the Tel Dan stele, and identifies the site of Deir Alla as a regional outpost for the training of scribes and administrators during a time when Aram had expanded into northern Israel and the Israelite east Jordan. How can we understand the presence of a literary text in a nonurban location? Perhaps the Aramean rulers wished to form and acculturate a local Israelite elite for the service of Damascus. The display of this text on the walls of the chamber

---

38. See Brian B. Schmidt, "The Iron Age Pithoi Drawings from Horvat Teman or Kuntillet 'Ajrud: Some New Proposals," *JANER* 2 (2002): 98.

39. Monique Vilders, "The Stratigraphy and the Pottery of Phase M at Deir 'Alla and the Date of the Plaster Texts," *Levant* 24 (1992): 187–200.

40. Erhard Blum, "Deir 'Alla," *EBR* 6:1–3.

41. Ibid., 2.

suggests a further political dimension to this acculturation process. Sections of the prophetic visions of the seer Balaam, although couched as social critique,[42] could have functioned as political propaganda aimed at another state—perhaps Israel or even Moab or Ammon.

The Deir Alla plaster text reveals two additional facets of Levantine writing activity during the Iron II period. The crafting of this inscription in conformity with the conventions of ancient Canaanite prosody (as exemplified in the Ugaritic poetry) underscores the sophistication of scribal knowledge and activity in the Levant during the Iron II period.[43] The text arguably bears witness to the production of literary traditions, apparently Aramean, upon which later preexilic Judean scribes and prophets drew. Indeed, the Balaam narrative represents an early witness to a type of prophecy familiar to us from the classical prophets of the HB: the prophecy of doom, addressed to a community, rather than a king, and attributing a catastrophic event to divine wrath.[44]

In addition to signaling the development of a relatively sophisticated scribal culture at a remote site, the plaster inscription also attests to the writing down (or composing) of the prophetic oracles of an individual around whom traditions of prophetic sayings had accrued. The recording and perhaps even the collecting of prophetic oracles as a facet of Levantine scribal activity is hinted at in the Amman Citadel Inscription (late ninth or early eighth century), which is written in the style of a prophetic oracle granting the deity Milkom's authorization for the king's building project and assuring the Ammonite king of victory and prosperity. This inscription suggests the involvement of royal scribes in the gathering and recording of oracles (particularly or exclusively those favorable to the king). It can be inferred that these scribes would have selected and reused extracts from these collections of prophetic oracles in the redaction of royal inscriptions. In this example (as at Kuntillet Ajrud and perhaps at Deir Alla), the religious and cultic use of writing was clearly appropriated for state use, in this case by the ruling elite of Ammon.

Writing and Literacies in Iron II Judah

Judah's Scribes, the State Hegemonic Process, and the Private Sphere

Numerous studies have shown that the primary expressions of state hegemony that characterize Judah in the historical and archaeological record for

---

42. Cf. Baruch Margalit, "Studies in NW Semitic Inscriptions," *UF* 26 (1994): 282.
43. Ibid., 282.
44. Blum, "Deir 'Alla," 3.

the late Iron II period—state administrative expansion, agricultural intensification, increased production for trade, and the creation of "detached" elite identities involved in the hegemonic process—should be dated to a period in the late Iron II period (late eighth–early sixth century BCE). What will be investigated here is the increasing participation of the scribal elite in this hegemonic process: that is, how, through their written products, did they both assert state hegemony and engage in practices that were predicated on the existence of the Judean state as a totality? Of particular interest is the effect that this increasing activity of scribes in the public sphere (i.e., in the royal administration) had on the extension of writing practices to the private (but still elite) sphere. It will also be demonstrated how, in turn, the shape and numbers of this scribal class were profoundly affected by their involvement in the state hegemonic process, particularly as this process related to the conditions of Assyrian imperialism (Assyria being the dominant imperial power during much of Judah's existence).

In the use of writing to articulate Judah's hegemony as a state, Jerusalem's scribal community was greatly influenced by Israel's scribal establishment, which in turn had been shaped by other Levantine scribal establishments primarily through a process of elite emulation (in the case of Phoenicia), but perhaps also through a process of domination and acculturation (i.e., during the period of Aram's hegemony). Israel's domination of Judah during the ninth and early to mid-eighth centuries ensured a steady flow of scribal skills from the north to the south,[45] but even more direct transmission of scribal expertise likely took place when waves of refugees from Israel (particularly the Samarian region) arrived in Jerusalem following the dissolution of Israel as a state.[46] This influx would not only have swelled the ranks of Jerusalem's scribal and priestly community, but it would have introduced, through these

---

45. The recent discovery of uninscribed bullae and seals in Jerusalem featuring Phoenician/Samarian iconographic motifs and dating to the late ninth or early eight century BCE suggests the transmission of basic methods of archiving from Samaria to the Jerusalemite scribal community. See Ronny Reich, Eli Shukron, and Omri Lernau, "Recent Discoveries in the City of David, Jerusalem," *IEJ* 57 (2007): 153–69.

46. Israel Finkelstein, *The Forgotten Kingdom: The Archaeology and History of Northern Israel*, ANEM 5 (Atlanta: Society of Biblical Literature, 2013), 154–55; Israel Finkelstein and Neil Silberman, "Temple and Dynasty: Hezekiah, the Remaking of Judah and the Rise of the Pan-Israelite Ideology," *JSOT* 30 (2006): 259–85; Magen Broshi and Israel Finkelstein, "The Population of Palestine in Iron Age II," *BASOR* 287 (1992): 51–52. Moreover, no major settlement crisis afflicted the northern valleys of Canaan during the Late Bronze-Iron I transition: "The number of settlements held steady in the western Jezreel Valley, the Beth-Shean Valley to the east, and the northern Jordan Valley;" see Finkelstein, *The Forgotten Kingdom*, 28).

experts, the most sophisticated scribal conventions and textual types available in the Levant during that time.

One important area of scribal activity in Jerusalem likely affected by the infusion of scribes and priests (or their corresponding skills) from Israel as well as from Phoenicia and perhaps even Aram was the writing down of ritual formulations and/or incantations for use in the cult. The presence of early eighth century inscriptions from the Samarian-controlled and/or –influenced site of Kuntillet Ajrud suggests that Israel's temple scribes had at least by this date begun fixing in writing short (two- or three-line) incantations as well as brief theophanic hymns to render more efficacious their invocation of blessings from the divine world. The discovery of late seventh/early sixth century silver amuletic texts from Jerusalem's Ketef Hinnom,[47] which contain priestly incantations whose phraseology is similar to that found in the earlier Kuntillet Ajrud graffiti on pithoi, may constitute indirect evidence for this process of transmission. The texts on these plaques are particularly intriguing because they contain passages that are strongly reminiscent of the "priestly blessing" found in Num 6:24–26, and of other passages in the biblical texts (particularly Deut 7:9–10). The phenomenon of two different amulets, possibly written by two different hands yet with a similar text, suggests that this particular incantatory blessing had become crystallized at that time as a regular part of ritual tradition.[48] While Jerusalem's priests may not have had a direct hand in writing down and copying such incantations (leaving that to the temple scribes), they would have directed this process by determining the content of this written cultic tradition, and they would have legitimized it by employing these incantations in the official cult.

The influx of scribal expertise from the north probably also enhanced the skills of those responsible for monumentalizing the achievements of Judah's kings. Although it is possible that Judah's ruling elite had commissioned the writing and erecting of royal inscriptions back in earlier periods, when Judah was still an emergent highland polity under Israel's domination and/or influence, the infusion of scribal knowledge in the late eighth century would have all but guaranteed that such inscriptions were composed and set up on behalf of Judah's king.[49] Knowledge of archival methods, if not already transmitted

---

47. See Gabriel Barkay et al., "The Amulets from Ketef Hinnom: A New Edition and Evaluation," *BASOR* 334 (2004): 41–71.

48. The contents of the plaques, comprising the earliest examples of confessional statements concerning Yahweh, do *not* prove that the biblical context in which the "priestly blessing" appears in the HB had already been consolidated, nor that the blessing was already incorporated into a written Pentateuch by the late seventh/early sixth century BCE.

49. Fragments of two monumental inscriptions dating to a period between the late eighth century and ca. 700 BCE have been found in Jerusalem. In all likelihood, these

to Jerusalem's scribes during the Iron IIA period (late tenth–ninthy centuries BCE), would have passed to Judah's scribal community at this time. The continuous saga of destruction and rebuilding in Jerusalem over the millennia has rendered unlikely the survival of such archival materials, particularly since many of the documents would have been written on papyrus. The discovery of archives consisting of ostraca in major sites like Lachish and Arad demonstrates that archives were a real phenomenon in Jerusalem and Judah.[50] That archives of perishable materials such as papyrus were also a feature of Judean literate activity is suggested by the unearthing in a private house in Jerusalem of fifty or so bullae, dating to the late seventh century, with the impressions of papyrus fibers on their backs.[51] Another cache of bullae (seventeen in number) that were apparently used to seal papyrus documents was retrieved from a juglet found at Tel Lachish and dated to the seventh/early sixth centuries.[52]

The increasing number of administrative and economic inscriptions as well as bullae, seals, and inscribed weights dating to the late Iron II period and found throughout Judah points to the increasing exploitation of writing by the state's agents in the palace and the temple, many of whom received a formal, standardized education that was most likely offered under the aegis of the state.[53] This trend likewise implies an expansion in the number of scribes employed by the state, not just in Jerusalem, but also in Judah's sec-

---

fragments come from the royal inscriptions of Judean kings (see Jerusalem 23 and Jerusalem 24 in Dobbs-Allsopp et al., *Hebrew Inscriptions*, 226–27 and 227–29).

50. Around thirty-four Hebrew inscriptions, not counting various seals, seal impressions, and weights, were uncovered at Lachish (Tel ed-Duweir): apart from the letters, the rest are lists, jar labels, and various scribal texts (Dobbs-Allsopp et al., *Hebrew Inscriptions*, 299–347). Most of these inscriptions date to the seventh and sixth centuries, and were recovered from the debris of Lachish Level II, which was destroyed by the Babylonians in 586 BCE. Arad has yielded around twenty-three letters dating to the late seventh and early sixth centuries BCE, as well as five Hebrew seals and over a hundred other Hebrew inscriptions on ostraca and bowls, including various lists and jar labels (ibid., 5–108).

51. See Yigal Shiloh and David Tarler, "Bullae from the City of David: A Hoard of Seal Impressions from the Israelite Period," *BA* 49 (1986): 196–209.

52. Yohanan Aharoni, *Investigations at Lachish: The Sanctuary and the Residency (Lachish V)* (Tel Aviv, 1974), 19–22, pls. 20–21. Apart from these two main groups found at Jerusalem and Lachish, very few Judean bullae have been uncovered in recorded excavations (see notes 61 and 62 below). Two bullae were retrieved from Lachish and another from Beth-Zur, but the contexts of their discovery are not clear. Three additional bullae were discovered out of their original context at Tell el-Hesi, the City of David, and in debris from the Temple Mount (Eran Arie, Yuval Goren, and Inbal Samet, "Indelible Impression: Petrographic Analysis of Judahite Bullae," in *The Fire Signals of Lachish* [ed. Israel Finkelstein and Nadav Na'aman; Winona Lake, IN: Eisenbrauns, 2011], 1–18.)

53. Cf. Rollston, *Writing and Literacy*, 91–113.

ondary cities and even in more remote sites like Arad in the Negev. Not all of these scribes could have been trained in Jerusalem, and not all of them would have needed to acquire much more than the rudimentary skills associated with keeping accounts, etc. As the demand grew for scribes, they would have been trained at sites around Judah, and even in remote areas. In sum, the educational process was increasingly being decentralized over time as demand for writing forced skilled scribes to train others in the rudiments of writing.

The literary text on an ostracon from the Judean fortress of Horvat 'Uza in the Negev, dating to the late seventh century, may be something of an anomaly in terms of the level of scribal sophistication it represents;[54] conversely, its discovery may signal that the scribal skills being taught in even the more remote locations of Judah were becoming more sophisticated as time passed. From the half of the ostracon that is legible, the text appears to forecast judgments against some unnamed adversary. The contents of this ostracon may be of particular significance given the context of its discovery, i.e., at a site (Horvat 'Uza) in a border area that likely was contested between Judah and Edom. Indeed, Victor Sasson has gone so far as to identify the ostracon as an Edomite wisdom text on the basis of a passage in Job (27:10, 12–16), which he views as a parallel text.[55] Nevertheless, Bradley Crowell has noted that Sasson is operating under the mistaken assumption that Edom was the context for a flourishing wisdom school; the Judean scribal circles sponsored by the palace were a more likely setting for the production of wisdom literature.[56] While the literary inscription is probably Judean therefore, Sasson's reading of it as a wisdom text is intriguing, particularly in light of the Deir Alla plaster inscriptions, also discovered at a remote nonurban location. As previously noted, E. Blum has indentified the Deir Alla plaster text as a sapiental lesson that may have been designed for the acculturation of Israelite scribes by their Aramean overlords.[57] Do we have a similar phenomenon here at Horvat 'Uza, i.e., the acculturation of scribes under Judean auspices in a politically contested region, and/or the production of state-sponsored propaganda aimed at another state (i.e., against Edom)?

One of the major trends in the uses of writing that has been traced in the preceding pages of this study is the rapid appropriation of writing by the Judean elite for use in the private domain. Although the written productions

---

54. For a translation of and commentary on this fragmentary text, which is thirteen lines long, see Dobbs-Allsopp et al., *Hebrew Inscriptions*, 521–27.
55. Victor Sasson, "An Edomite Joban Text With a Biblical Joban Parallel," *ZAW* 117 (2005): 611.
56. See Bradley Crowell, "A Reevaulation of the Edomite Wisdom Hypothesis," *ZAW* 120 (2008): 404–16.
57. Blum, "Deir 'Alla," 2.

for which the Judean elite demanded the services of scribes were not directly connected to official state activities, through the commissioning of such productions the elite nonetheless contributed to the assertion of Judah as a state. In other words, through the inscriptions commissioned by these elite was projected a notion of social identity that revolved around the employment of a distinct dialect and the belief in the particular efficaciousness of a national deity or set of deities (e.g., Yahweh and Asherah).

How and why did it happen that members of the Judean elite came to appropriate the products of writing for their own private uses? It has already been argued above that the expanding number of elites in Judah is to be correlated with the state's growing need for them to participate in the state hegemonic process (as landowners, administrators, military officers, merchants, priests, etc.). It is further maintained here that the increased exposure of these elites to written products occasioned by this participation led them to appropriate writing for their personal uses. For example, the increasing prevalence of economic inscriptions dating to the late Iron II period at sites throughout Judah and the find-spots of inscribed weights (often in private residences[58]) suggests that a growing merchant class involved in the southern trade began to employ their own accountants and bookkeepers who had specialized, albeit rudimentary writing skills. Texts deriving primarily from Lachish and Arad demonstrate that military officers employed the services of scribes in the writing of military dispatches and communiqués; not all of the letters written for these officers pertained to official, military business, however. Arad No. 16, from a brother to a person not identified by epithet, appears to deal with a money matter.[59] Exposure to writing was common enough at some sites in Judah by at least the second half of the seventh century that a Judean farm laborer hired a scribe to fix his appeal for justice in writing.[60]

Nowhere is the appropriation of writing by the elite more evident than in the dramatic increase in the quantity of inscribed seals and seal impressions (bullae) over the course of the eighth through early sixth centuries BCE, the majority of which are aniconic (i.e., featuring only written names and perhaps titles, but no iconography).[61] This trend towards aniconism arguably

---

58. For a thorough analysis of these inscribed weights, including a discussion of the largely domestic contexts in which they have been found, see Raz Kletter, "Pots and Polities: Material Remains of Late Iron Age Judah in Relation to its Political Borders," *BASOR* 314 (1999): 32–34.

59. See Pardee, *Handbook of Ancient Hebrew Letters*, 154.

60. Ibid., 154–56. The ostracon containing this written appeal was unearthed at the small military fortress of Mesad Hashavyahu on the border of ancient Judah facing the Philistine city of Ashdod.

61. Well over a one thousand Hebrew bullae dating to this period have been published to date. Unfortunately, the vast majority of these inscribed bullae and seals originate

reflected a growing desire on the part of the Judean elite to signal their social status through a display of script only.[62] Although some of these seal owners may indeed have possessed literate skills (e.g., the king and some upper level royal officials), most were probably not functionally literate. It really did not matter if they were not able to do much more than recognize their own names on their seals; it was the display of (supposed) literacy that was sufficient to indicate the power and authority of the seal's owner in a society in which the vast majority of people were nonliterate. While the proliferation of aniconic seals can tell us very little about the percentage of people who were functionally literate therefore, it does underscore the ideological use made of writing—that is, its importance as a symbol of power and prestige.

Indeed, the fact that all extant monumental inscriptions (those that are more than fragments) derive from the Judean elite suggests the high demand for scribes who could replicate the scribal conventions pertaining to the composition of royal inscriptions, and who could adapt them so as to publicly commemorate the lives and deeds of nonroyal individuals. Take, for example, the commemoration of a major feat of engineering in the late eighth century Siloam Tunnel inscription, as well as the Silwan Tomb Inscriptions (also late eighth century). The latter echo earlier Phoenician royal inscriptions in identifying and commemorating the dead, addressing prayers to the deity (in this case, Yahweh), and cursing any who deface or in some way interfere with the grave and its inscriptions.[63]

The clusters of graffiti found in burial chambers at Khirbet el-Qôm (late eighth century) and Khirbet Beit Lei (seventh–early sixth centuries) in Judah[64] likewise reveal the efforts of the elite to employ (albeit in a more

---

from illicit excavations or so-called chance finds and not from controlled excavations. The possibility exists that some or even many of the items in these collections are forgeries, as there is no foolproof method for determining for certain that an isolated seal or bullae is authentic. Since the vast majority of the seals and bullae published to date are of unknown provenance, the conclusions regarding the dramatic increase in aniconic seals and bullae must remain somewhat provisional. It is worth noting, however, that the two main groups that have been found during controlled excavations at Jerusalem and Lachish (dating to the seventh/early sixth centuries) primarily consist of inscribed bullae with little or no iconography.

62. For example, of the 255 (unprovenanced) bullae published by Nahman Avigad (*Hebrew Bullae from the Time of Jeremiah: Remnants of a Burnt Archive* [Jerusalem: Israel Exploration Society, 1986], 118), only 13 display iconography. Of the 401 (unprovenanced) bullae published by Robert Deutsch (*Messages from the Past. Hebrew Bullae from the Time of Isaiah Through the Destruction of the First Temple* [Tel Aviv: Archaeological Center Publications, 1999], 50), iconographic Hebrew bullae comprise only 4.5 percent.

63. See David Ussishkin, *The Village of Silwan: The Necropolis from the Period of the Judean Kingdom* (Jerusalem: Israel Exploration Society, 1993), 247–54.

64. See Dobbs-Allsopp et al., *Hebrew Inscriptions*, 125–32.

rudimentary fashion that at Silwan) in their tombs and elsewhere a technology whose display conveyed status and whose use in this largely oral culture possessed the numinous power to alter spaces, rendering them sacred. The cultic content and incantatory character of much of these graffiti, together with the context in which it is found (i.e., burial tombs) suggests the deliberate manipulation of letters and words for apotropaic and ritualistic purposes. The symbolic and apotropaic character of these graffiti points to the demand for scribes and/or literate stonecutters who could replicate, although with perhaps less skill given the brief and fragmentary nature of these inscriptions, the types of written incantations together with the repertoire of images that they saw used in the state cult in Jerusalem (and perhaps in the smaller temples in Judah's secondary cities).

Judean Scribal Activity and the Production of Biblical Source Texts: Some Suggestions

We return then to the question that initiated this study: does the epigraphic data support the assumption that first versions of several biblical texts, most notably the Deuteronomistic History (DtrH: Deuteronomy through 2 Kings), were composed during the preexilic period in Judah? For the majority of the Iron Age (i.e., twelfth through the ninth centuries), the answer is clearly "no." This period has provided us with only a limited quantity of inscriptions, and also with very little in the way of evidence for the emergence of a Judean polity that might have supported a scribal class experienced and sophisticated enough to compose lengthy literary texts on scrolls. Even the longest texts from the southern Levant that we do possess—the mid-ninth-century Mesha Stele, the mid-ninth-century Tel Dan inscription, and the early eighth-century Deir Alla plaster texts—hardly justify the notion that reams of scrolls were composed prior to the eighth and seventh centuries. The fact that the majority of provenanced inscriptions, including the two groups of Hebrew bullae from controlled excavations, bear dates in the late eighth through early sixth century range suggest this late Iron II period as the likeliest candidate for the production of scrolls of any great length.

It is the further contention of this study that the epigraphic data surveyed in previous pages cannot be pushed any farther than to posit the creation of various kinds of documents that served as *sources* for the HB. The scenario for the creation of such "source documents" proposed here is connected with the enlistment of writing by the state's bureaucratic and cultic sectors, as well as with the diffusion of writing practices into the private sector, as demonstrated by the increasing number of inscriptions apparently commissioned by the Judean elite for its own business, commemorative, and ritualistic needs.

This development contributed to the growing demand for scribes, a demand that had already been sparked by the needs of the increasingly centralized Judean state.

How might the proliferation of scribes and scribal activity at this time have been connected with the creation, reproduction, and transmission of texts and what would those texts have looked like in terms of length, complexity, and genre? The increasing prevalence of scribes and their written products over the course of the eighth through sixth centuries instigated a process whereby the compiling of texts such as incantations and prophecies was gradually decentralized. The gathering together of a variety of incantatory formulae, brief hymns, and theophanies on the tomb wall of Khirbet Beit Lei in particular and, to a lesser extant, at Khirbet el-Qôm, suggests that a process of collecting specifically Yahwistic texts had begun to transpire in the ever-expanding scribal circles of Judah. The discovery of inscribed plaques in a private tomb at Ketef Hinnom, both of which carry similar incantatory blessings addressed to Yahweh, likewise signifies that parts of ritual tradition were being crystallized in written form by the late seventh/early sixth century for the private use of individuals. This fixing in writing of elements of ritual practice may have echoed an ongoing project among Jerusalem's temple scribes, whereby brief hymns, prayers, incantations, etc. that had been circulating independently in Judah (and earlier in Israel) as part of a living ritual tradition—we would conjecture—were being brought together into scrolls.[65] The fact that initially these efforts may have centered primarily or even exclusively on the collection of texts addressed to Yahweh and Asherah, the divine patrons of Jerusalem's royal dynasty, suggests a state-directed initiative. As an initiative designed to establish the primacy of the ruler's patron deities and their cult, this strategy would in turn help unite the region around a single royal dynasty, urban center, and cultic tradition.

Another potential writing practice of Jerusalem's royal and temple scribes that could have been taken up by Judah's growing scribal community as writing practices were decentralized was the reporting and perhaps even collecting of prophecies. On analogy with the Neo-Assyrian collections of oracles found in the palace archives of Esarhaddon and Assurbanipal, many of these prophecies may have even been associated with specific

---

65. Our evidence for this is conjecture is indirect, namely, the gathering together of incantations, hymns, and/or literary traditions in remote areas within Judah (e.g., Kh. Beit Lei) or outside of Judah (the early eighth century cultic inscriptions on pithoi and other media at Kuntillet 'Ajrud, and the ca. 800 BCE collection of literary traditions at Deir 'Alla). The contents of exilic and postexilic biblical texts such as the Psalms and the prophetic works also indirectly suggest that such collections probably took place in earlier periods and were used in the later composition of those same biblical texts.

prophets, although these collections could have been easily expanded later with additional prophecies that did not originate with the prophet.[66] While the epigraphic data for the practice of collecting oracles outside of the royal sphere is inconclusive, both the contents of royal inscriptions from the Levant (including the Amman Citadel inscription, the Zakkur stele, and perhaps even the Deir Alla plaster inscription) and the collections of oracles from Nineveh clearly demonstrate that the copying and compiling of oracles in palace archives by royal scribes for the service of the king and for later consultation was a preoccupation of king and court in the ancient Near Eastern world.[67] Although no royal inscriptions from Judah have survived, the practice of recontextualizing prophecies to serve as propaganda in monumental inscriptions (as perhaps took place at Deir Alla) would very likely have been an eventual feature of royal scribal activity in Jerusalem as well.

Moreover, the Judean state may have encouraged the writing down and displaying of oracles and prophecies which had the character of political critiques at more remote locations, in order to serve as propaganda in its assertion of hegemony vis-à-vis another state (e.g., against Edom in the context of Judah's Negev fortresses and outposts). Such state-directed scribal activity could account for the Hebrew literary ostracon (late seventh century BCE) from the Negevite site of Horvat 'Uza, which predicts some unnamed deity's judgments and imminent destruction against some unnamed adversary.[68] It is suggested here that such short texts served as possible sources for later, longer prophecies as we have in the prophetic works that later made up the HB.

At the very least then, the epigraphic record points to the probability that royal inscriptions providing information about military campaigns and/or building activity, as well as lists and collections of brief texts (of incantations and possibly prophetic oracles), represented the corpus of written tradition to emerge in Judah during the Iron II period and to inform the com-

---

66. See John Van Seters, "The Role of the Scribe in the Making of the Hebrew Bible," *JANER* 8 (2008): 108.

67. Martti Nissinen, *References to Prophecy in Neo-Assyrian Sources*, SAAS 7 (Helsinki: Neo-Assyrian Text Corpus Project, 1998), 4, and see also 170. Cf. Van Seters, "The Role of the Scribe," 123.

68. The presence of a state-directed production of texts at a site in a potentially contested border area may reflect a phenomenon similar to that of Deir 'Alla. At this site in the eastern Jordan Valley, a region that likely switched hands several times over the course of the Iron II period, a small scribal community produced, copied, and set up for display a text the first part of which has as its main theme an "oracle of doom." As has been argued earlier in this treatment, this small site may have played an important role in the formulation of (Aramean?) state-sponsored propaganda aimed at another state (perhaps Israel, or even Moab or Ammon).

position in later periods of more complex literary texts such as are found in the HB. Could a similar scenario be proposed for the formulation of state-sponsored historical written traditions: ones that were created to support the state hegemonic project, and which would have emerged within the context of Jerusalem's scribal community? In view here as an example is the historiographic tradition pertaining to the account of the monarchies of Israel and Judah, as ultimately preserved in the biblical books of Samuel through 2 Kings. Clearly the epigraphic record from Judah, as it has been surveyed above, cannot sustain the assumption of many scholars that the Iron period in Judah witnessed the composition of the kind of sweeping portrait of the past that integrates a variety of forms in order to present in a narrative of the entire foundation of Israelite history, such as is found in the DtrH. The DtrH is a complex genre that has no equivalent in the extant ancient Near Eastern corpus from the Iron Age and represents the work of an exilic/postexilic author/redactor.

If we widen the scope of our study for a moment, we see that there is evidence from the ancient Near Eastern world for the existence of several historical and chronological genres that potentially could have served as source texts for later works of lengthier historiographic scope, including the royal inscription, king list, annal, and chronicle. Of these genres, the royal inscription is the most attested in the Levantine world, and certainly was employed in Judah as well as a way to monumentalize the great achievements of its rulers. Moreover, as Nadav Na'aman and others have suggested, the erection of monuments with inscriptions represents the first steps towards history writing.[69] For the first time, in their own scripts, kings made public their account of the formation of the state (buildings erected, peoples slaughtered or "set free"). The state enlisted writing to assert publicly that it existed; in other words, through the public erection of stelae, a king such as Mesha of Moab attempted to persuade the people, used to thinking of their identities in tribal terms, that they were part of a larger, more all-encompassing political entity. As Seth Sanders has observed, these monuments were in effect calling a people as a self-conscious group into being.[70]

The king list and the annals are two other historical genres whose presence is attested in the ancient Near East during the Iron II period (and earlier). The king list typically supplied the length of reign, filiation, and

---

69. Nadav Na'aman, "Three Notes on the Aramaic Inscription from Tel Dan" in *Ancient Israel's History and Historiography: The First Temple Period* (Winona Lake, IN: Eisenbrauns, 2006), 173–86. Cf. Bruce Routledge, "The Politics of Mesha: Segmented Identities and State Formation in Iron Age Moab," *JESHO* 43 (2000): 221–56 and Seth L. Sanders, "Writing and Early Iron Age Israel," 107–9.

70. Sanders, "Writing and Early Iron Age Israel," 107.

perhaps short notices or changes in dynastic succession and usurpation of power through assassinations, while the annals portrayed political events according to a precise chronology.[71] A case could be made that scribes in both Israel and Judah may have compiled king lists, as such texts were well known in both Mesopotamia and Egypt during the Bronze and Iron Ages. A king list in alphabetic script from Ugarit (*KTU* 1.113) represents a Levantine example; despite its lacunae, there appear to be entries for about thirty names of kings whose reigns date from ca. 1850 to 1180 BCE.[72] During the course of their domination by Assyria, Judean scribes quite possibly became familiar with the Assyrian annals (or *limmu* lists), a method of chronological reckoning devised by the Assyrians for keeping a record of their kings, treaties, and important events on a year-by-year basis.[73]

The chronicle, as developed by the Babylonians later in the Persian period, represents a more-complex historical genre, in that it gives a continuous history in an exact chronological sequence of the important political events that fell during the reigns of the Neo-Babylonian kings.[74] The best argument that can be made for the composition of a chronicle within the earlier Judean context is primarily circumstantial; that is, that Judah's long domination by Israel, when combined with the need to integrate a large number of refugees, including elites, from Israel might have provided the impetus for a more ambitious scribal project—one that sourced king lists from both states, supplemented with records from monumental inscriptions and collections of oracles, to create a synchronized chronicle of the important political events in both Israel and Judah, with precise dates in strict chronological sequence from one monarch to another. The scribe(s) may also have provided this chronicle with a mythical prologue asserting a common history in the distant past—one that consisted of a golden age of unity, a "United Monarchy" based not in Samaria, but in Jerusalem.[75]

The creation of this written tradition would have had the effect of strengthening Jerusalem's primacy, uniting the region around a single royal

---

71. John Van Seters, *In Search of History: Historiography in the Ancient World and the Origins of Biblical History* (Winona Lake, IN: Eisenbrauns, 1997), 292–302.

72. Manfred Dietrich, Oswald Loretz, and Joaquín Sanmartín, *Die keilalphabetischen Texte aus Ugarit*. Pt. 1: *Transcription* [Neukirchen-Vluyn: Neukirchener Verlag, 1976]: 119, text 1.113, verso.

73. Cf. J. Maxwell Miller and John Hayes, *A History of Ancient Israel and Judah*, 2nd ed. (Louisville, KY: Westminster John Knox, 2006), 246–47.

74. Van Seters, *In Search of History*, 294.

75. A similar argument has been made recently by Finkelstein and Silberman ("Temple and Dynasty," 259–85), although they believe that this work was an early version of the biblical narrative concerning the early days of the Davidic dynasty and the establishment of the United Monarchy of Israel, as found in 1 Samuel through 1 Kings 2.

dynasty and a single cultic tradition. Admittedly, such a scribal creation would have been somewhat of an anomaly in the ancient Near Eastern world during the Iron Age. The closest contemporary analogy to such a chronographic work would have to be the Assyrian Synchronistic History, but this work does not provide a continuous history of the Assyrian and Babylonian regions, nor does it synchronize the chronologies.[76] Seth Sanders suggests an additional element that quite possibly distinguished a Judean historical account from the contemporary king lists, annals, and chronicles found in the ancient Near Eastern world: a dual emphasis on *the people* as an underlying political and religious concept, as well as on kings and dynasties. As argued by Sanders, this difference in the way of "doing history" and expressing a culture has its roots in Ugarit, where the scribes there were the first to give a written form to the old Amorite idea of *the people* as a political unit (see *KTU* 1.40).[77] But this hypothetical historical document would have been different from the Ugaritic material in that it was more interested in representing the people group to itself, that is, in addressing that group as its audience and in keeping that group as its subject matter. The scribes responsible for this account facilitated a distinctly local process of political and religious unification by grounding their account in an old and familiar political unit and by appealing to that presupposed people group as their audience.

Thus, the adaptation of writing to express local forms of culture, a process that was initiated at Ugarit, hinted at in early Iron Age inscriptions such as the tenth-century Gezer calendar, and attested in numerous texts (such as the Deir Alla plaster inscription) from Iron II Levant,[78] would eventually pave the way for a unique manner of crafting history unparalleled in ancient times—where the people as well as the king would become the main protagonists of events. Expressive of a heritage of ancient West Semitic tribal and political concepts, this account would provide the inspiration for later extensive historiographic works like the Deuteronomistic History.

---

76. Van Seters, *In Search of History*, 295.

77. Sanders, "What Was the Alphabet For?," 51. For this text, entitled a "Ritual for National Unity" by its editor, see Dennis Pardee, *Ritual and Cult at Ugarit*, WAW 10 (Atlanta: Society for Biblical Literature, 2002), 77.

78. Note especially the Balaam narrative of the Deir 'Alla plaster text, which implies a community (not the king) as the audience for the prophecy of doom (see Blum, "Deir 'Alla," 3).

References

Aharoni, Yohanan. *Investigations at Lachish: The Sanctuary and the Residency (Lachish V)*. Tel Aviv: Gateway, 1974.

Alexandre, Yardenna. "Phoenician Inscription from Kefar Veradim." Pages 65*–74* in *Eretz Zafon: Studies in Galilean Archaeology*. Edited by Zvi Gal. Jerusalem: Israel Antiquities Authority, 2002.

Arie, Eran, Yuval Goren, and Inbal Samet. "Indelible Impression: Petrographic Analysis of Judahite Bullae." Pages 1–18 in *The Fire Signals of Lachish*. Edited by Israel Finkelstein and Nadav Na'aman. Winona Lake, IN: Eisenbrauns, 2011.

Aufrecht, Walter. *A Corpus of Ammonite Inscriptions*. Lewiston, NY: Edwin Mellen, 1989.

Avigad, Nahman. *Hebrew Bullae from the Time of Jeremiah: Remnants of a Burnt Archive*. Jerusalem: Israel Exploration Society, 1986.

Barkay, Gabriel, Andrew G. Vaughn, Marilyn J. Lundberg, and Bruce Zuckerman. "The Amulets from Ketef Hinnom: A New Edition and Evaluation." *BASOR* 334 (2004): 41–71.

Blum, Erhard. "Deir 'Alla." *EBR* 6:1–3.

Broshi, Magen and Israel Finkelstein. "The Population of Palestine in Iron Age II." *BASOR* 287 (1992): 47–60.

Byrn, Ryan. "The Refuge of Scribalism in Iron I Palestine." *BASOR* 345 (2007): 1–31.

Cross, Frank Moore. *Leaves from the Epigrapher's Notebook: Collected Papers in Hebrew and West Semitic Palaeography and Epigraphy*. Winona Lake, IN: Eisenbrauns, 2003.

Crowell, Bradley. "A Reevaulation of the Edomite Wisdom Hypothesis." *ZAW* 120 (2008): 404–16.

Crowfoot, John W., and Grace M. Crowfoot. *Early Ivories from Samaria*. London: Palestine Exploration Fund, 1938.

Davies, Graham. *Ancient Hebrew Inscriptions: Corpus and Concordance*. Cambridge: Cambridge University Press, 1991.

———. "Hebrew Inscriptions." Pages 270–86 in *The Biblical World*. Edited by John Barton. New York: Routledge, 2002.

Deutsch, Robert. *Messages from the Past. Hebrew Bullae from the Time of Isaiah Through the Destruction of the First Temple*. Tel Aviv: Archaeological Center Publications, 1999.

Dietrich, Manfred, Oswald Loretz, and Joaquín Sanmartín. *Die keilalphabetischen Texte aus Ugarit*. Pt. 1: *Transcription*. Neukirchen-Vluyn: Neukirchener Verlag, 1976.

Diringer, David. "Inscriptions," in *Lachish IV: The Bronze Age*. Edited by O. Tufnell. Oxford: Oxford University Press, 1958.

Dobbs-Allsopp, Frederick W., Jimmy J. M. Roberts, Choon L. Seow, and Robert E. Whitaker. *Hebrew Inscriptions: Texts from the Biblical Period of the Monarchy with Concordance*. New Haven: Yale University, 2005.

Faust, Avraham. *Israel's Ethnogenesis: Settlement, Interaction, Expansion and Resistance*. London: Equinox, 2006.

Finkelstein, Israel. "City-States to States: Polity Dynamics in the 10th–9th Centuries B.C.E." Pages 75–83 in *Symbiosis, Symbolism, and the Power of the Past*.

Canaan, Ancient Israel, and Their Neighbors from the Late Bronze Age through Roman Palaestina. Edited by William G. Dever and Seymour Gitin. Winona Lake, IN: Eisenbrauns, 2003.

———. *The Forgotten Kingdom: The Archaeology and History of Northern Israel.* ANEM 5. Atlanta: Society of Biblical Literature, 2013.

Finkelstein, Israel, and Neil Silberman. "Temple and Dynasty: Hezekiah, the Remaking of Judah and the Rise of the Pan-Israelite Ideology." *JSOT* 30 (2006): 259–85.

Gubel, Eric. "The Iconography of Inscribed Phoenician Glyptic." Pages 101–28 in *Studies in the Iconography of Northwest Semitic Inscribed Seals.* Edited by Benjamin Sass and Christoph Uehlinger. Freiburg: University Press, 1993.

Hallo, William W., and K. Lawson Younger, eds. *Monumental Inscriptions from the Biblical World.* Vol. 2 of *The Context of Scripture.* Leiden: Brill, 2000.

Horowitz, Wayne, Takayoshi Oshima, and Seth L. Sanders. *Cuneiform Sources from the Land of Israel in Ancient Times.* Jerusalem: Israel Exploration Society, 2006.

Joffe, Alexander H. "The Rise of Secondary States in the Iron Age Levant." *JESHO* 45 (2002): 425–67.

Kletter, Raz. "Pots and Polities: Material Remains of Late Iron Age Judah in Relation to its Political Borders." *BASOR* 314 (1999): 19–54.

Lemaire, André. *Les Écoles et la formation de la Bible dans l'ancien Israël.* Fribourg, Switzerland: Éditions Universitaires, 1981.

Liverani, Mario. *Israel's History and the History of Israel.* Translated by Chiara Peri and Philip R. Davies. London: Equinox, 2005.

Margalit, Baruch. "Studies in NW Semitic Inscriptions." *UF* 26 (1994): 271–315.

Meshel, Ze'ev. *Kuntillet 'Ajrud: A religious centre from the time of the Judean monarchy on the border of Sinai.* Jerusalem: Israel Museum, 1978.

Miller, John Maxwell, and Joseph Hayes. *A History of Ancient Israel and Judah.* 2nd ed. Louisville, KY: Westminster John Knox, 2006.

Na'aman, Nadav. "Three Notes on the Aramaic Inscription from Tel Dan." *IEJ* 50 (2000): 92–104.

Nissinen, Martti. *References to Prophecy in Neo-Assyrian Sources.* SAAS VII. Helsinki: Neo-Assyrian Text Corpus Project, 1998.

Pardee, Dennis. *Ritual and Cult at Ugarit.* Atlanta: Society for Biblical Literature, 2002.

———. *The Ugaritic Texts and the Origins of West-Semitic Literary Composition.* Oxford: Oxford University Press, 2012.

Pardee, Dennis and S. David Sperling, eds. *Handbook of Ancient Hebrew Letters: A Study Edition.* Chico, CA: Scholars Press, 1982.

Puech, Emile. "Un anneau inscrit du Bronze Récent à Megiddo." Pages 51–61 in *Ki Baruch Hu. Ancient Near Eastern, Biblical, and Judaic Studies in Honor of Baruch A. Levine.* Edited by Robert Chazan, William W. Hallo, and Lawrence H. Schiffman. Winona Lake, IN: Eisenbrauns, 1999.

Reich, Ronny, Eli Shukron, and Omri Lernau. "Recent Discoveries in the City of David, Jerusalem." *IEJ* 57 (2007): 153–69.

Rollston, Christopher A. "The Tel Zayit Abecedary and Evidence for Israelite Literacy." Pages 61–98 in *Literate Culture and Tenth-Century Canaan: The Tel Zayit Abecedary in Context.* Edited by Ron E. Tappy and P. Kyle McCarter. Winona Lake, IN: Eisenbrauns, 2008.

———. *Writing and Literacy in the World of Ancient Israel: Epigraphic Evidence from the Iron Age*. Altanta: Society of Biblical Literature, 2010.
Routledge, Bruce. *Moab in the Iron Age. Hegemony, Polity, Archaeology*. Philadelphia: University of Pennsylvania Press, 2004.
———. "The Politics of Mesha: Segmented Identities and State Formation in Iron Age Moab." *JESHO* 43 (2000): 221–56.
Sanders, Seth L. 2008. "Writing and Early Iron Age Israel: Before National Scripts, Beyond Nations and States." Pages 97–112 in *Literate Culture and Tenth-Century Canaan: The Tel Zayit Abecedary in Context*. Edited by Ron E. Tappy and P. Kyle McCarter. Winona Lake, IN: Eisenbrauns.
———. "What Was the Alphabet For? The Rise of Written Vernaculars and the Making of Israelite National Literature." *Maarav* 11 (2004): 25–56.
Sass, Benjamin. *The Alphabet at the Turn of the Millennium*. Tel Aviv: Emery and Claire Yass Publications in Archaeology, 2005.
———. *The Genesis of the Alphabet and Its Development in the Second Millennium B.C.* Wiesbaden: Harrassowitz, 1988.
Sasson, Victor. 2005. "An Edomite Joban Text. With a Biblical Joban Parallel." *ZAW* 117: 601–15.
Schmidt, Brian B. "The Iron Age Pithoi Drawings from Horvat Teman or Kuntillet 'Ajrud: Some New Proposals." *JANER* 2 (2002): 91–125.
Shiloh, Yigal, and David Tarler. "Bullae from the City of David: A Hoard of Seal Impressions from the Israelite Period." *BA* 49 (1986): 196–209.
Singer, Itamar. "A Political History of Ugarit." Pages 603–733 in *Handbook of Ugaritic Studies*. Edited by Wilfred G. E. Watson and Nicolas Wyatt. Leiden: Brill, 1999.
Soumeka, Anna. "The Significance of Kuntillet 'Ajrud for the Study of Early Judahite History and Religion." *Deltion biblikon meleton* 20 (2002): 80–98.
Tappy, Ron E. "Tel Zayit and the Tel Zayit Abecedary in Their Regional Context." Pages 1–44 in *Literate Culture and Tenth-Century Canaan: The Tel Zayit Abecedary in Context*. Edited by Ron E. Tappy and P. Kyle McCarter. Winona Lake, IN: Eisenbrauns, 2008.
Ussishkin, David. *The Village of Silwan: The Necropolis from the Period of the Judean Kingdom*. Jerusalem: Israel Exploration Society, 1993.
Van Seters, John. "The Role of the Scribe in the Making of the Hebrew Bible." *JANER* 8 (2008): 99–129.
———. *In Search of History. Historiography in the Ancient World and the Origins of Biblical History*. Winona Lake, IN: Eisenbrauns, 1997.
Vilders, Monique. "The Stratigraphy and the Pottery of Phase M at Deir 'Alla and the Date of the Plaster Texts." *Levant* 24 (1992): 187–200.
Von Dassow, Eva. "Canaanite in Cuneiform." *JAOS* 124 (2004): 641–74.

ORALITY, TEXTUALITY, *AND* MEMORY: THE STATE OF BIBLICAL STUDIES

DAVID M. CARR

Dedicated to Susan Niditch

ABOUT TWENTY ONE YEARS AGO, IN NOVEMBER OF 1991, THE UNIVERSITY of Michigan hosted a conference in Ann Arbor on "Palimpsest: Editorial Theory in the Humanities."[1] The bulk of the papers focused on issues surrounding contemporary editing, and the paper on Hebrew Bible, by David Noel Freedman, discussed a series of text-critical problems in biblical texts. Nevertheless, one of the papers, a contribution on "Reconstructing the Classics" by James E. G. Zetzel (of Columbia University) touched on themes of text and memory that are the focus my discussion here. In this essay, Zetzel noted the varied aims and assumptions of tradents of ancient Greek and Latin texts, none of whom shared the particular objectives and assumptions of contemporary editors. Depending on their aims in reproducing manuscripts, they introduced different sorts of changes. For example, with texts incorporating practical learning, such as cookbooks or lawbooks, scribes often quite freely

---

1. This essay is dedicated to Susan Niditch in celebration of her contributions to my own work and scholarship at large. Susan has been foremost in introducing considerations of orality, including the work of Milman Parry, Gregory Nagy and other classicists into biblical studies, along with many other creative and original contributions to the field. I am grateful for the stimulation she has provided to my research and the specific support and advice she has offered to me personally over the years. This essay emulates her use of work from classics to enrich biblical studies.

This piece is based on my contribution to a panel at the outset of the 2012 conference on Orality and Literacy expertly organized and hosted by Brian Schmidt at the University of Michigan. In accordance with the aims of that opening evening panel (to expose a broader audience to work on orality and literacy), this essay synthesizes and builds on work published earlier, particularly in my book *The Formation of the Hebrew Bible: A New Reconstruction* (New York: Oxford University Press, 2011). In that book I apply insights on orality and memory learned from Niditch and others to the problem of the formation of the Hebrew Bible.

altered their exemplar. In contrast, scribes often were more careful to preserve works in the school curriculum. But even when they were at their most careful, ancient scribes did not systematically compare manuscripts and were not compelled to depend on a manuscript reading to introduce a change. As a result, Zetzel concluded, "Every ancient text is a palimpsest: it embodies within itself, in ways which we can scarcely now discern, the history of the changes of taste and purpose through which it passed, and the preoccupations of the readers who used it."[2]

This quote bears unpacking. In what ways have biblical scholars come to see biblical texts as palimpsests? What preoccupations do biblical texts reveal in their transmission? What "changes of taste and purpose"? Zetzel believed that such changes were minimal in the most holy texts of ancient Greece, but I maintain that even religious texts like those of the Bible show variation comparable to that seen in early Homeric manuscripts. And as in the case of early Homeric manuscripts, there are some different ways to understand what these variations reveal about the mode of transmission of biblical texts and the purposes of their tradents.

Before moving to the Bible, I should note how this line of questioning was originally opened by Milman Parry's critique of standard text-critical treatments of the early manuscript tradition for Homer. Where the standard treatments tried to reconstruct the earliest written text of Homer through developing stemmatic trees and eliminating errors, Parry asked, "How have they explained the unique number of *good* variant readings in our text of Homer, and the need for laborious editions of Aristarchus and of the other grammarians, and the extra lines, which grow in number as new papyri are found?"[3] Here, *in nuce*, was Parry's intuition that the *written* tradition of Homer bore in itself clues to nonwritten elements of performance and memory. Where text-critics were focused on the sorts of errors produced by mistaken visual copying, early Homeric manuscripts varied in ways atypical of visual copying. In these manuscripts whole lines were added or subtracted, scenes included, synonyms exchanged, etc. Such wholesale changes are not

---

2. James E. G. Zetzel, "Religion, Rhetoric, and Editorial Technique: Reconstructing the Classics," in *Palimpsest: Editorial Theory in the Humanities*, ed. George Bornstein and Ralph G. Williams (Ann Arbor: University of Michigan, 1993), 112–13.

3. Emphasis is in Parry's original: Milman Parry, "Studies in the Epic Technique of Oral Verse-Making. II. The Homeric Language as the Language of An Oral Poetry," *HSCP* 43 (1932): 75–76; reprinted on p. 268 of Milman Parry and Adam Parry, *The Making of Homeric Verse: The Collected Papers of Milman Parry* (Oxford: Clarendon, 1971). See also his discussion of some such variants on pp. 112–14 (297–98 of the reprint) of the essay and his comments on pp. 46–47 of his Parry, "Studies II," 46–47 (p. 361 of the collected papers).

typical of transmission processes focused exclusively on visual copying. They reflect something else.

Biblical scholars have likewise noticed these sorts of larger-scale variations in textual traditions, though often not informed by parallel discussions of such changes in classics and cognate disciplines. In 1949, about sixteen years after Parry's observations noted above, Helmer Ringgren studied parallel versions of several biblical psalms and prophetic poems. In the process he classified the different variants in these parallel texts by whether they were graphic errors typical of visual copying, evidence of aural slippage from dictation, conscious alterations or other errors.[4] Years later, in 1992, Ed Greenstein noted a number of examples of "misquotation of scripture" at Qumran that seemed to show the kinds of shift typical of errors in memory: replacement of one synonym for another, seemingly random rearrangement of the order of poetic lines, exchange of semantically equivalent grammatical expressions. Furthermore, Greenstein placed this phenomenon of misquotation of scripture in the Dead Sea Scrolls within the broader context of such misquotation of scripture from memory in early Judaism and Christianity.[5] Similar work was done by Raymond Person as well in his 1998 article on the Israelite scribe as performer, where he argued that several variants found in the parallel Isaiah-Hezekiah narratives and in the ancient 1QIsa^a scroll from Qumran were best explained by the "oral mindset" of the scribes that produced these narratives, and he has expanded significantly on this work in publishing his 2010 book on *The Deuteronomic History and the Book of Chronicles: Scribal Works in an Oral World*.[6]

There have been several additional publications during the same period in New Testament studies on textuality, orality, and memory, from Gerhardsson's classic 1961 study of oral tradition and written transmission in Judaism and Christianity to more recent treatments of gospel source criticism and memory by Taylor (1959), Abel (1971), and McIver and Carroll (2002).[7] Many of these latter studies were based on methods and/or findings

---

4. Helmer Ringgren, "Oral and Written Transmission in the Old Testament: Some Observations," *Studia Theologica* 3 (1949): 34–59.

5. Edward L. Greenstein, "Misquotation of Scripture in the Dead Sea Scrolls," in *The Frank Talmage Memorial Volume*, ed. Barry Walfish (Haifa: Haifa University Press, 1993), 71–83.

6. Raymond F. Person, "The Ancient Israelite Scribe as Performer," *JBL* 117 (1998): 601–9 and idem., *The Deuteronomistic History and the Book of Chronicles: Scribal Works in an Oral World*, AIL 6 (Leiden: Brill, 2010).

7. Birger Gerhardsson, *Memory and Manuscript: Oral Tradition and Written Transmission in Rabbinic Judaism and Early Christianity* (trans. Eric Sharpe; Uppsala: Almqvist & Wiksells, 1961); W. S. Taylor, "Memory and the Gospel Tradition," *ThTo* (1959): 470–79; Ernest L. Abel, "The Psychology of Memory and Rumor Transmission and Their

regarding textual memorization best known from Bartlett's studies of memorization done in the early part of the twentieth century (published in 1932).[8] Among various particulars, Bartlett chronicled the way subjects memorizing a text manifested an "effort after meaning" where they produced a version of the memorized text that "made sense" to them. They would adapt the memorized text into familiar frames of meaning, and elements of the text that were not understood quickly disappeared. New Testament scholars using Bartlett's research or similar experiments have argued that the New Testament gospels show too much variation between themselves to have been produced through the writing, copying, and combination of sources.

At this point it would be helpful to note that most discussions of these issues are dominated by binary oppositions between textuality on the one hand and orality on the other, or scribalism on the one hand and an "oral mindset" on the other. Thus, biblical scholars are quite familiar on the one hand with textual treatments that are exclusively focused on the dynamics of writing, and the standard textbooks for biblical text criticism focus almost exclusively on the sorts of errors produced by visual copying: confusion of similar looking letters with each other, the eye skipping from one line to another that begins in a similar way, repetition of similar elements, etc. At the same time, thanks to Parry, Lord and many others in recent scholarship, biblical scholars are also conscious of the *oral* dimension of ancient traditions, that is the extent to which traditions of the Bible and elsewhere were shaped in a context where the oral performance and reception of traditions were crucial. Thus we have literacy on the one hand, and orality on the other. The 2012 University of Michigan conference for which this essay was originally written was labeled "Orality and Literacy," and this title reflects the binary way biblical scholars typically think about these issues.

I think it important, however, to thematize more explicitly a third pole to these two elements of writing and orality, and that is *memory*. Memory is often implicitly meant when people talk about "orality" or an "oral mindset." When doing so, they often mean that people in oral contexts carry traditions in their mind rather than in written form. But we should distinguish the dimension of "memory" and "memorization" from "orality" for several reasons. I illustrate by discussing three different sorts of textual variants that we often find in ancient texts, each one of which can be correlated with one

---

Bearing on Theories of Oral Transmission in Early Christianity," *JR* 51 (1971): 270–81; Robert K. McIver and Marie Carroll, "Experiments to Develop Criteria for Determining the Existence of Written Sources, and Their Potential Implications for the Synoptic Problem," *JBL* 121 (2002): 667–87.

8. Frederic C. Bartlett, *Remembering: A Study in Experimental and Social Psychology* (Cambridge: Cambridge University Press, 1932; repr. 1995).

of these three poles: literacy, orality and memory. I've already mentioned the sorts of variants typical of visual copying of written texts: confused letters, skipped lines, phrases skipped as the eye moves from one phrase to a similar one further on, etc. These sorts of *graphic* variants are most closely connected with the written dimension of ancient traditions, and as I have stated, they have pride of place in most text-critical handbooks. Some random examples from parallel passages in the Bible could include the letter exchange that explains the variation between whether Hiram's ships brought Solomon Almug wood (1 Kgs 9:11) or Algum wood (2 Chr 9:11) or whether the high priest Jehoidah brought out the officers (ויוצא 2 Chr 23:14) or commanded the officers (ויצו 2 Kgs 11:15).

Then there are some variants that truly are particular to *oral* performance of ancient traditions, indeed they are *aural* variants that arise when a text is misheard in the midst of oral performance. This would be the case, say, when a given copy of a text has a similar *sounding* word to its parallel, such that the variation came in hearing a word or phrase differently. Let me give two examples from the story of Hezekiah and Isaiah in the face of Assyrian attack, as it is found in numerous parallel Old Testament traditions, including 2 Kings, 2 Chronicles, and the book of Isaiah, each of which is variably preserved in different textual traditions (and studied in detail, I should mention, by Raymond Person). Thus, at one point, Hezekiah in his prayer to God says either "and now"—Hebrew *ve'atah* in the Hebrew versions of both 2 Kings and Isaiah or "but you"—equivalent to *ve'atah* ועתה as ואתה in the Old Greek tradition for Isa 37:20. For complex reasons these graphically distinct expressions sounded similar or the same, and so it would have been easy for a scribe to hear one when the other was meant. Similarly, just a few verses later, Isaiah is quoted as giving God's response, including a quote of the Assyrian king's boast that he has entered Lebanon's "furthest recesses" (מְלוֹן קִצֹּה 2 Kgs 19:23) or "its farthest height (מְרוֹם קִצּוֹ Isa 37:24). The two sound similar. The medium for variation, likely, is at least partly a purely *aural* confusion of the two phrases in some kind of oral performance.

So far, both graphic mistakes and aural/oral variants are prone to produce confusion in the textual tradition. They are, in an important sense, errors. They are places where a tradent imperfectly sees or hears her or (more often) his text, and the result is often identifiable by the fact that it reads less well than the original. In many such cases, whether with a graphic or a specifically aural variant, the text-critic is aided in determining a relatively earlier reading by the fact that one of the variants is *bad*. In other words, neither graphic nor oral/aural variants fit the criteria described by Parry in my original quote, where I noted the frequent presence in early Homeric manuscripts of multiple *good* variants.

Such *good* variants are typically produced by a third type of variation; the sorts of slips and textual transformations that occur when a textual tradition is carried *in the mind*, memorized, and then reproduced. They are what I would term "memory variants:" the exchange of one word for a synonym with the same meaning, the rearrangement of poetic lines or lists at points where the meaning is not altered by such rearrangement, the insertion or excision of minor particles that are not semantically or grammatically necessary. For example, the Hebrew direct-object particle, את can, but need not, mark a direct object. It would not be any harder for a copyist to copy this word than others, nor for someone hearing dictation to hear it, but this particle shows an unusual propensity to appear or disappear in parallel biblical passages and ancient Hebrew manuscripts. So also, the divine designations Yahweh and Elohim are quite graphically distinct and would not be confused for one another in spoken performance, but a number of ancient manuscripts exchange the two, seemingly indicating that ancient scribes who reproduced them considered these divine designations to be, in a sense, "the same" and exchanged the one for the other. This often happens with other synonyms, such as, for example, the different Hebrew words for "maidservant" שפחה and אמה that are exchanged in manuscript traditions not because some copyist did not see the word right or someone heard it wrong, but because a tradent remembered that a "maidservant" was mentioned in a given context, but forgot which word was used for maidservant.

Sometimes a scribe may even exchange phrases that seem quite distinct to us, as when one version of a proverb says that the "teaching of the wise" is a "well of life" and another asserts that "the fear of Yahweh" is a "well of life." If these proverbs are related, perhaps one scribe or another considered "the teaching of the wise" to be identical to "the fear of Yahweh" and exchanged the two, whether consciously or unconsciously. For him, "the teaching of the wise" *was* "the fear of Yahweh" in a profound sense. There was no difference for him between "the teaching of the wise" and "the fear of Yahweh." He did not give it a second thought. Where *for us* there might seem to be a distinction between "teaching of the wise" and "fear of Yahweh," there was *none* for the ancient scribe. *We* might call it a variant. *He* may well have not, and that precisely explains the shift. In either case, it is clear that whatever happened, this was not a problem of someone miscopying the proverb or mishearing it. It is a shift that occurs *in the mind* of the tradent as that tradent processes and reproduces the semantic content of the text. And it is the ancient equivalence that is operative in memory and other sorts of cognitive variation.

In any case, these are all examples where both variants are good, fit ancient diction, are grammatically permissible, and conform to the cognitive and ideological rules of ancient biblical literature. In sum, these ancient memory variants reflect the "effort after meaning" that Bartlett found in all reproductions of texts from memory. In cases like these, the text critic cannot easily choose between one variant that is an error and another that is the original. Such memory variants, precisely because they all "make sense" are notoriously difficult to sort into earlier text and later deviation.

The main point at this juncture does not concern the text-critic's difficulties, but with how these three types of variants, all of them variants in ancient *writing,* point to three different, and highly interrelated dimensions of ancient textual transmission. Some variants are characteristic of the written medium itself—graphic variants that come from imperfect copying. In addition, since ancient texts were created in oral-primary cultures and often were integrated into oral performance contexts, especially literary texts, we see some variants that would come from imperfect oral reception of a given text, truly *oral/ aural* variants. Then there is a third type of variant. Some would call them "oral" variants, but, as mentioned, the term "memory variant" better catches their distinctive character. These are the types of substitutions, reorderings, minor insertions or deletions, etc. that ancient tradents would exercise on their tradition as they reproduced it from memory. The results, even when they diverged from the precursor tradition, "made sense." They were, as Parry says, "good variants," because they were the result of the "effort after meaning" seen in all faithful attempts to reproduce ancient tradition from memory.

To be sure, these three types of variation are not always distinct. Sometimes, for example, it may be that a given variant of similar sounding words also yields the same sense, so that a given variant could be an aural/oral variant, a memory variant, or some combination of the two. Indeed, part of what makes someone "hear" a given text a particular way is that they can make sense of that text in that way too. The same is somewhat true for graphic variation that yields texts that sound and/or mean a similar thing. People can "see" a word or phrase a certain way partly because they can understand it that way too. Categories like aural, graphic and memory variants are only proximately distinct in the real world of ancient textual transmission.

Furthermore, multiple forms of variation are often present *in the same text.* Take the Qumran Temple Scroll, for example. The concluding part of this scroll revises and recapitulates large portions of the law of Deuteronomy, now representing this law as direct divine speech at Sinai rather than Moses's review of divine law at Moab, as it is presented in the biblical book of Deuteronomy. In addition, this Temple Scroll version of the Deuteronomic law often includes excerpts from other laws found elsewhere in Leviticus and Numbers that pertain in some way to topics discussed in Deuteronomy. When the Temple scroll is reproducing large swathes of Deuteronomy, it follows other known texts of Deuteronomy quite closely, deviating from its parallels only to present those sections as divine speech. Yet when the scroll diverted to quote excerpts of laws on similar topics from Leviticus, Numbers, or other parts of Deuteronomy, the proportion of memory variants increases. This can be observed particularly in cases where a certain text in Deuteronomy is reproduced at one point in the Temple Scroll [something missing?] where it is part of the virtually continuous reproduction of parts of Deuteronomy and also inserted at another point (into that base text reproduction of parts of Deuteronomy) because its topic relates to another law being reproduced there. For example, the law about killing a mother with her young in Deut 22:6 is virtually identical with the MT (with the exception of an added תא) when it is reproduced as part of the base text in 11QT LXV, 4, but 11QT varies significantly from the MT when it adds this same law to the end of a set of laws on sacrifice in 11QT LII, 6–7: ולא תכה אם על הבנים 1QT versus ולא תקח האם על בנים proto-MT of Deut 22:6 (varying in verb and use of definite article for the object).[9] Similarly, the Temple Scroll follows its base text much more closely than the material it conflates with that text in 11QT II, 1–15 (conflating Deut 7:25 in 2:7–11); LII, 7–21 (conflating Deut 17:5 in 55:21), and 11QT LXVI, 8–16 (adding material from Lev 20:21, 17; 18:12–13). It seems that the scribe who produced the Temple Scroll relied on visual access to a scroll of Deuteronomy when producing the latter portion of the scroll, but quoted laws by memory from other books when they related to topics covered in Deuteronomy.

In this respect it is important to bear in mind how cumbersome scroll technology was in the ancient world, particularly for accessing brief quotes from literary theological works. Rarely, certainly not in the case of the Temple Scroll, but also in other cases, did ancient authors go to the trouble of finding and unrolling a large scroll to make sure that their quote was accurate. Instead, the presence of memory variants in the Temple Scroll and other early Jewish texts, as well as systematic "misquotation" of scripture in many early rabbinic and Christian works, is good evidence that ancient authors accessed and quoted many works by way of their memory. It was mainly when they were performing the continuous tradition (e.g., in Jewish liturgy) or copying an entire scroll that they would access and work through a scroll from beginning to end.

In sum, these different forms of variation point to *three* not *two* major poles in ancient textual transmission: the written text, the oral performance/

---

9. Yigael Yadin, *The Temple Scroll: Text and Commentary* (Jerusalem: Israel Exploration Society, 1983), 233.

reception dimension, *and the medium of memory*. Furthermore, in many contexts these three poles are integrally interrelated. In my book *Writing on the Tablet of the Heart*, I argued that the writing of ancient literary texts was largely in service of a process of memorizing them in school and other contexts.[10] At least up through the Second Temple period of Jewish scribalism, writing was not *opposed* to memory, but served it. It is much like the example of music, in this case like music performed in the European classical tradition, where one initially learns many classical pieces from a musical score. The goal often is to be able to play the music without the score. But it helps, of course, to have a musical score to start with, especially as a beginner. And in music there is also the performance, the specifically aural/oral aspect. With time, many master musicians often gain the ability to pick up a piece purely from hearing it played. And, I will fully acknowledge, there are many, many musical cultures where music is never written down and is transmitted purely by performance and hearing.[11] But biblical literature, qua written literature, was written in a context where the memorization and performance of ancient tradition was *writing-supported*, so that one internalized and/or performed biblical traditions through the help of written manuscripts.

It is out of this context, then, that we see graphic, aural/oral *and* memory variants bound together in the palimpsests that are ancient biblical manuscripts. Especially in parallel biblical texts and in our most ancient textual witnesses there are constant textual pointers to the fact that these texts were not just copied, though they were indeed often copied, nor were they just heard, though we have evidence for that too, but they were also memorized. Indeed, based on my own survey of the most ancient textual witnesses and parallel textual traditions, I suggest that "memory variants" far outnumber graphic and aural/oral variants. This points to how the writing of long-duration, literary-theological texts was integrally interwoven in ancient Israel, as in other parts of the ancient world, with ongoing oral performance and mental internalization. The three parts of the triad were deeply interconnected: Orality, Literacy, *and* Memory. They were not opposites. Indeed, to forget—so to speak—"memory" is to lose one of the crucial connectors between literacy and oral performance.

This is not because all ancient texts were memorized. Many ancient cultures had a substantial scribal component that produced receipts and other documentary texts that were not performed orally or memorized. But if we

---

10. David M. Carr, *Writing on the Tablet of the Heart: Origins of Scripture and Literature* (New York: Oxford University Press, 2005).

11. A superb study comparing different levels of use of writing in music and comparing it to written textuality is Ruth Finnegan, *The Hidden Musicians: Music-Making in an English Town* (Cambridge: Cambridge University Press, 1989).

are focused on "long-duration" texts preserved for us in writing—usually literary-theological texts that encapsulated a given culture's most cherished collective memories—they were written down as part of a process of aiding in more precise internalization and performance than would be possible without the use of written aids. Thus the writing of the tradition testifies to some level of anxiety about standardized transmission and reflects an attempt to stabilize textual transmission across space and time.

This takes me to my final topic, which is the various ways in which ancient biblical authors, and modern scholars, conceive of textual innovation at different stages. In an evocative section of *Poetry as Performance*, Gregory Nagy nicely observes that participants inside a given tradition can only evaluate change as positive if it is not really change after all. "In other words, positive change must be a 'movement' that leads back to something that is known ... In fact, it will be an improvement precisely because such positive 'movement' aims at the traditional, even the archetypal."[12] Thus, what to the outsider looks like "change" to the insider looks like restoration.

This idea that changes might be believed to be restorations seems quite alien to many biblical scholars. Nevertheless, it should be remembered that many commentaries on biblical books are full of text-critical suggestions of readings for biblical passages, *readings unattested in any extant biblical manuscript*, that correct supposed errors in biblical passages. Such conjectural textual emendations by biblical scholars are complete innovations in the textual traditions for biblical books, yet the scholars proposing these emendations believe them to reflect a yet earlier and more true form of the biblical books than can be accessed by any manuscript. These modern scholars have revised the biblical tradition, but with the view toward restoring it to an earlier state. From the scholarly perspective, such scholars have not changed the text, but restored it. For example, the contemporary Oxford Hebrew Bible edited by Ron Hendel and published by Oxford University Press is based on the idea that it is possible to reconstruct an earlier form of the biblical text than is preserved in any existing manuscript. The project will produce complete new editions of biblical books which its editors believe reflect likely earlier stages of those books. An alternative perspective could maintain that, at least in some cases, these Oxford editions of biblical books will advance modern corruptions of biblical books, in this case corruptions justified as conjectural emendations.[13]

Turning to the earliest manuscripts of the Bible, we see a remarkable level of fluidity both in terms of smaller-scale memory variants and—in

---

12. Gregory Nagy, *Poetry as Performance: Homer and Beyond* (Cambridge: Cambridge University Press, 1971), 22.

13. James A. Sanders has been particularly outspoken on this point.

some instances—harmonization and coordination of different parts of the Torah with each other. For example, the Samaritan Pentateuch and a number of more ancient textual witnesses found at Qumran feature expansions that coordinate Exodus and Numbers with the review of events there in the book of Deuteronomy, as well as a few that coordinate Deuteronomy with the preceding material that it reviews. Again, from the outside, such expansionistic harmonizations and coordinations appear to be significant changes, *innovations*. Yet the tradents believed themselves to be making the Torah yet truer to itself than it was before. In other words, these harmonizations and coordinations were a form of "hyper-memorization." They were expansionist variations, but believed to be truer to the tradition than were earlier copies.

In considering these sorts of variation in early Homeric papyri, Nagy suggests that they reflect an ongoing, living oral performance culture. Paralleling Parry's early observation about "good variants," Nagy and more recently Graeme Bird, highlight the way many substantial variants in early Homeric papyri manifest "relative archaism,"[14] "conformity with traditional oral epic diction,"[15] or (for Graeme Bird) "heightened emotional tone."[16] For Nagy and Bird, these elements show early Homeric papyri to be reflective of a multiform, ongoing tradition of oral performance of Homeric epic. These manuscripts are not dead "scriptures," but instead "transcripts" of performances or (later in history) "scripts" to aid such performances.

Such memory variants and coordinating expansions in biblical texts are marks of the vital ongoing role of memory and mental processing in early transmission of biblical manuscripts. Early biblical manuscripts, though fluid, betray a level of widespread verbatim agreement atypical of transcripts of purely oral performance traditions. Meanwhile, such early manuscripts feature a relatively small proportion of specifically aural/oral variants. Thus, there is insufficient evidence, in my view, to see early biblical manuscripts as originating in a tradition of exclusively-oral performance. Our earliest manuscripts already stand at the end of a process of scribal authoring and transmission. At the same time, early biblical manuscripts do feature a remarkable number of small-scale memory variants and—in some instances—harmonization and coordination of different parts of the Torah, harmonizations that are analogous to so-called concordance interpolations in Homeric manuscripts. These biblical variants generally make "good sense," feature "authentic oral diction," and otherwise would stand as "authentic

---

14. Nagy, *Poetry as Performance*, 148.
15. Ibid., 153.
16. Graeme Bird, *Multitextuality in the Homeric Iliad: The Witness of the Ptolemaic Papyri*, Hellenic Studies 43 (Washington, D.C.: Center for Hellenic Studies, 2010), 100.

variants" in Nagy's terminology, but again, they do not stand as good evidence that biblical manuscripts are transcripts of oral performance.

Then, starting toward the very end of the Second Temple period, around the turn of the millennium, a graphically precise textual tradition for the Hebrew Bible—the proto-Masoretic text—begins to emerge. This tradition manifests very little memory variation. In this time and tradition, biblical manuscripts are increasingly prepared through careful graphic copying, and the forms of variation are almost exclusively those typical of visual errors. Notably, as pointed out by Greenstein and others, we *still* see evidence of memorization in variants that now appear in early rabbinic and Christian quotations of scripture, here reflecting the fact that such scholars again accessed scripture by way of memory rather than consulting cumbersome, expensive and often unavailable scrolls or codices.[17] These memory variants in citations testify to the ongoing role of memory in the performance of biblical traditions that have been fixed through use of text. Nevertheless, the memory variants seen in such citations should not be taken as evidence that the manuscript tradition for the biblical texts themselves was still subject to the influence of memory or the dynamics of oral performance. Any production of biblical manuscripts by dictation was long past by the time of the rabbis and early Christian theologians, Instead, at least in the Hebrew Bible, these variants in rabbinic and early Christian quotes show the way memory continued to play a role in the use of scriptural tradition long after the scriptures themselves (in manuscript form) were being reproduced through careful, graphic copying.

In sum, where Nagy and Bird see "orality" and more specifically "oral performance" as indicated by the multiform early Homeric textual tradition along with some quotes of Homer in classical authors, I see evidence more specifically of the crucial operations of "memory" in a similarly multiform early manuscript (in the Second Temple period) and quotation tradition (Second Temple period into the Roman period and beyond) for the Hebrew Bible. This derives from my increasing appreciation for the ways that written biblical texts served as supports somewhat like Nagy's "scripts," for broader processes of memorization and performance. In light of this reality in the ancient world, I would urge that we add "memory" as a *distinct,* yet related dimension to the poles of "orality" and "literacy," a component not to be conflated with orality nor separated from literacy, but integrally intertwined with both. This may help overcome ongoing tendencies, even now, to see orality and literacy as opposites, and enable scholars to properly integrate ancient

---

17. Greenstein, "Misquotation of Scripture."

written texts into a broader cultural fabric that included textual internalization and oral performance.

Bibliography

Abel, Ernest L. "The Psychology of Memory and Rumor Transmission and Their Bearing on Theories of Oral Transmission in Early Christianity." *JR* 51 (1971): 270–81.
Bartlett, Frederic C. *Remembering: A Study in Experimental and Social Psychology*. Cambridge; New York: Cambridge University Press, 1932; repr. 1995.
Bird, Graeme D. *Multitextuality in the Homeric Iliad: The Witness of the Ptolemaic Papyri*. Hellenic Studies 43. Washington, D.C.: Center for Hellenic Studies, 2010.
Carr, David M. *The Formation of the Hebrew Bible: A New Reconstruction*. New York: Oxford University Press, 2011.
———. *Writing on the Tablet of the Heart: Origins of Scripture and Literature*. New York: Oxford University Press, 2005.
Finnegan, Ruth. *The Hidden Musicians: Music-Making in an English Town*. Cambridge: Cambridge University Press, 1989.
Gerhardsson, Birger. *Memory and Manuscript: Oral Tradition and Written Transmission in Rabbinic Judaism and Early Christianity*. Translated by Eric Sharpe. Uppsala: Almqvist & Wiksells, 1961.
Greenstein, Edward L. "Misquotation of Scripture in the Dead Sea Scrolls." Pages 71–83 in *The Frank Talmage Memorial Volume*. Edited by Barry Walfish. Haifa: Haifa University Press, 1993.
McIver, Robert K., and Marie Carroll. "Experiments to Develop Criteria for Determining the Existence of Written Sources, and Their Potential Implications for the Synoptic Problem." *JBL* 121 (2002): 667–87.
Nagy, Gregory. *Poetry as Performance: Homer and Beyond*. Cambridge: Cambridge University Press, 1971.
Parry, Milman. "Studies in the Epic Technique of Oral Verse-Making. II. The Homeric Language as the Language of an Oral Poetry." *HSCP* 43 (1932): 1–50.
Parry, Milman, and Adam Parry. *The Making of Homeric Verse: The Collected Papers of Milman Parry*. Oxford: Clarendon, 1971.
Person, Raymond F. "The Ancient Israelite Scribe as Performer." *JBL* 117 (1998): 601–9.
———. *The Deuteronomistic History and the Book of Chronicles: Scribal Works in an Oral World*. AIL 6. Leiden: Brill, 2010.
Ringgren, Helmer. "Oral and Written Transmission in the Old Testament: Some Observations." *ST* 3 (1949): 34–59.
Taylor, W. S. "Memory and the Gospel Tradition." *ThTo* (1959), 470–79.
Yadin, Yigael. *The Temple Scroll: Text and Commentary*. Jerusalem: Israel Exploration Society, 1983.
Zetzel, James E. G. "Religion, Rhetoric, and Editorial Technique: Reconstructing the Classics." Pages 99–120 in *Palimpsest: Editorial Theory in the Humanities*. Edited by George Bornstein and Ralph G. Williams. Ann Arbor: University of Michigan, 1993.

The Performance of Oral Tradition in Ancient Israel

Robert D. MILLER II

For the past half-century, much of the time that biblical scholars have worked with scholarship on oral tradition and folklore, they have drawn on the "Oral-formulaic Theory" or "Parry-Lord School" associated with the work of Milman Parry and his student Albert Lord.[1]

In the 1930s, Milman Parry sought to understand Homeric Greek poetry by studying modern South Slavic oral tradition. Parry's key conclusion about this poetry, a conclusion that he then applied to the Homeric epics, was that its authors were illiterate, without knowledge of writing, and that they composed in a special, "formulaic" language.

Albert Lord further elaborated on this theory in his classical work of 1960, *The Singer of Tales*, which was his 1949 Harvard dissertation begun under Parry. Lord argued that a percentage of formulaic language could be calculated for a given *written* text and then used as an unmistakable indicator that such a text had been composed, and no doubt circulated, orally.[2] Lord set up his South Slavic model as the paradigmatic case of orality and felt free to define any nonliterate composition that did not fit the mold "written composition without writing."[3]

Parry and Lord furthermore understood that oral bards compose during their performances.[4] Each iteration of an oral piece of literature was original

---

1. E.g., Albert B. Lord, *The Singer of Tales*, Harvard Studies in Comparative Literature 24 (Cambridge, MA: Harvard University Press, 1960).
2. Albert B. Lord, "Homer as Oral Poet," *HSCP* 71 (1968): 1–46.
3. Albert B. Lord, "The Traditional Song," in *Oral Literature and the Formula*, ed. Benjamin A. Stolz and Richard S. Shannon III (Ann Arbor: Center for the Coordination of Ancient and Modern Studies, 1976), 175–76.
4. Lord, *Singer of Tales*, 100; idem, *Epic Singers and Oral Tradition* (Ithaca: Cornell University Press, 1991), 46.

in detail, in spite of its formulaic and thematic consistency.[5] The same tale was different each time it was performed.[6]

Most scholars were convinced of Parry and Lord's applicability to Homeric poetry, but the impact of Parry and Lord was widespread beyond classics. "Many researchers, mostly from English-speaking countries, in fact, wasted no time in setting forth the equation: oral style = formulaic style."[7] The work of Parry and Lord had, in fact, more impact on the study of written texts than on the study of oral tradition. The more a text had formulas, the more likely its oral origin.

In spite of Lord's own warnings that "Application of the formulaic test for orality requires special adaption if it is to work at all ... in biblical poetry,"[8] important works from the 1960s to 1980s, especially by Harvard University doctoral graduates, applied Parry and Lord to the Hebrew Bible.[9] Even in the twenty-first century, biblical scholars referring to Lord as "current research on mnemonic techniques of modern oral societies,"[10] still regularly use Lord's work to define, for example, redaction processes.[11] Although David

---

5. Lord, *Singer of Tales*, 102–23. I am here and throughout embracing the awkward term "oral literature." Alan Dundes (*Holy Writ as Oral Lit* [Lanham, MD: Rowman & Littlefield, 1999], 11) rejects it as a "term used by elitist literary scholars who are uncomfortable with the term 'folklore' and who are trying to upgrade the material by calling it 'literature.'" For Ruth Finnegan's explanation of the benefits of the expression, see *Oral Traditions and the Verbal Arts,* Association of Social Anthropologists Research Methods 4 (New York: Routledge, 1992), 9–10. My use of the term "oral *literature*" requires severing the lexical links between "literature" and "literate"/"literacy."

6. Lord, *Singer of Tales*, 101; idem, *Epic Singers*, 47.

7. Paul Zumthor, *Oral Poetry,* Theory and History of Literature 70 (Minneapolis: University of Minnesota Press, 1990), 97. This began with such seminal works as F. P. Magoun Jr., "The Oral-Formulaic Character of Anglo-Saxon Narrative Poetry," *Speculum* 28 (1953): 446–67.

8. Lord, "Formula and Non-Narrative Theme in South Slavic Oral Epic and the Old Testament," *Semeia* 5 (1976): 96. Nevertheless, Lord dismissed those who hesitated in making the attempt (e.g., Robert Coote) as "a bit too pessimistic" (p. 99).

9. See Robert C. Culley, "Exploring New Directions." In *The Hebrew Bible and Its Modern Interpreters*, ed. D. A. Knight (Chico, CA: Scholars Press, 1985), 181–83; Culley, *Oral Formulaic Language in the Biblical Psalms* (Toronto: University of Toronto Press, 1967); idem, "Oral Traditions and the OT," *Semeia* 5 (1976): 1–33; idem, *Studies in the Structure of Hebrew Narrative* (Minneapolis: Fortress Press, 1976); and David M. Gunn, "The 'Battle Report': Oral or Scribal Convention," *JBL* 93 (1974): 513–18; idem, "Narrative Patterns and Oral Tradition in Judges and Samuel," *VT* 24 (1974): 286–317. Gunn ("'Threading the Labyrinth': A Response to Albert B. Lord," *Text and Tradition*, ed. Susan B. Niditch, SemSt [Atlanta: Scholars Press, 1990], 19) writes, "I read it [*Singer of Tales*], and it changed my life." Ronald Hendel, *The Epic of the Patriarch,* HSM 42 (Atlanta: Scholars Press, 1987), esp. 35, 37, 137.

10. Kofoed, "Remember the Days of Old (Deut 32, 7)," *SEE-J Hiphil* 1 (2004): 8.

11. Jean-Louis Ska, "A Plea on Behalf of the Biblical Redactors," *ST* 59 (2005): 11.

Carr, Karel van der Toorn, and others are exceptions, it is not uncommon to read statements like, "Compositions exhibiting signs of oral-formulaic composition provide us with our best glimpse into Israel's prebiblical narrative traditions."[12]

In his *Formation of the Hebrew Bible,* David Carr laments,

> Though scholars decades ago deconstructed the idea that there was a 'great divide' between orality and literacy, a remarkable number of high quality publications still work with a strong distinction between the two, or at least a 'continuum' with orality at one end and literacy at the other.[13]

This orality/literacy dichotomy is another legacy of Parry and Lord. For them, oral poets were always illiterate. This means there is a clear dichotomy between orality and literacy. The literate do not compose oral poetry, and written text is either orally derived or literary. The implications of this were developed by Walter Ong and Jack Goody. According to this school—in what Piotr Michalowski called the "interminable number of studies that keep coming out on orality *vs.* literacy in various disciplines in the humanities as well as in the social sciences"[14]—there is both a qualitative difference between oral and written language and a particular mindset. The particular features that the Parry-Lord School believed revealed oral composition also revealed corresponding thought patterns. Oral composition, therefore, was tied to social organization. Oral societies were, said Ong, "highly traditionalist or conservative."[15] Literacy brought "quicker and more radical innovation."[16]

Scholars held that "the acquisition of literacy, [was] the most profound of all revolutions in technology, it marks a 'Great Divide' in human history, and the changes it brings are qualitative, placing oral societies on the one side

---

12. Robert Kawashima, "From Song to Story," *Prooftexts* 27 (2007): 152; idem, "Comparative Literature and Biblical Studies," *Prooftexts* 27 (2007): 331. He applies the Parry-Lord formulaic test to the Song of Deborah ("From Song to Story, " 155). Kawashima emphasizes "the landmark comparative studies of Milman Parry and Albert Lord" ("Comparative Literature," 334), but also uses the 1960s theoretical work of Walter Benjamin and Victor Shklovsky (ibid., 332).

13. David M. Carr, *The Formation of the Hebrew Bible: A New Reconstruction* (New York: Oxford University Press, 2011), 5.

14. Piotr Michalowski, "Orality and Literacy and Early Mesopotamian Literature," in *Mesopotamian Epic Literature,* ed. Marianna E. Vogelzang and Herman L. J. Vanstiphout (Lewiston, NY: Edwin Mellen, 1992), 231.

15. Walter J. Ong, *Orality and Literacy* (New York: Methuen, 1982), 41.

16. W. J. Henderson, "Tradition and Originality in Early Greek Lyric," in *Oral Tradition and Innovation: New Wine in Old Bottles?*, ed. E. R. Sienaert, A. N. Bell, and M. Lewis (Durban: University of Natal Oral Documentation and Research Centre, 1991), 249.

and literate ones on the other." Even those who held that "this shift is certainly not to be described as an event, a drastic change, but instead as a slow process," agreed that "the shift from an oral society to a writing society ... has decisive implications for a culture, to such an extent that it becomes the fundamental basis for an intellectual revolution." Since literacy "provides a substitute for memory, ... [it] restructures consciousness, enabling the development of analytical skill and logical, sequential reasoning."[17]

Biblical scholars were quick to embrace this and are still repeating it. One scholar's linguistic criteria for tracing the development of Hebrew syntax depend on Goody's pronouncements about the stylistic differences between oral and scribal texts. It is only on the authority of Goody that he can say, "The specific features by which the three main [phases of narrative language] differ from one another are connected to the characterization of written language as against oral discourse."[18] Another relies on the Goody-Ong notion of an "oral mindset" for his understanding of ancient authorship,[19] while a third considers written literature and oral tradition "autonomous categories."[20] A recent work on the origins of the Bible builds explicitly on the "new approaches" of Goody and Ong: "Writing is a technology that transforms culture," it claims.[21] So "determining the degree of literacy in Judah is critical for placing the Hebrew Bible on the orality-literacy continuum."[22] Since Goody and Ong propose that literacy devalues the art of memory, the author is able to imagine conflict in ancient Israel between "literary elites whose authority was threatened by the oral tradition ... [and] a critique of the written word by those with a vested interest in the authority of ... the oral tradition."[23] In short, biblical scholars, though not all of them to be sure, seem to have drunk deeply of this literacy hypothesis.

Although one or two contemporary folklorists continue to work in the Parry-Lord school of thought,[24] by the late 1980s its "unnuanced determin-

---

17. See critique in Jacques Le Goff, *History and Memory*, European Perspectives 8 (New York: Columbia University Press, 1992), 54.

18. Frank H. Polak, "The Oral and the Written," *JANES* 26 (1988): 101

19. Raymond Person, "A Rolling Corpus and Oral Tradition," in *Troubling Jeremiah*, JSOTSup, 260 (Sheffield: Sheffield Academic Press, 1999), 263–71.

20. Kawashima, "Comparative Literature," 325.

21. William Schniedewind, *How the Bible Became a Book* (Cambridge: University Press, 2004), 35.

22. William Schniedewind, "Orality and Literacy in Ancient Israel," *RelSRev* 26 (2000): 331.

23. Schneidewind, *How the Bible Became a Book*, 91, 108, 219 n. 1.

24. E.g., Gísli Sigurðsson, *The Medieval Icelandic Saga and Oral Tradition*, Publications of the Milman Parry Collection of Oral Literature 2 (Cambridge, MA: Harvard University Press, 2004), 38–41.

istic view"[25] had been called into question by classicists, anthropologists, and ethnomusicologists alike.[26] Mark Amodio wrote in 1998, "Today there are few, if any, oralists who would classify themselves as oral-formulaicists."[27] While the South Slavic epic poet "provided an excellent analogue for Homeric epic in many ways, ... the model that was generalized outward to hundreds of other traditions and forms was too narrow to be widely applicable."[28] For example, Old Norse-Icelandic oral skaldic poetry does not use formulas.[29] In India, "the tendency towards greater frequency of formulaic *pādas* in the later parts of the *Ramayana*, as of the *Mahabharata*, seems in fact to be a symptom of the breakdown of the true oral tradition."[30] "No one these days believes that there is any one touchstone for the oral style," writes John Niles.[31]

Field studies of Rosalind Thomas, Ruth Finnegan, and others challenged further the compositional theories of Parry and Lord.[32] Lord had underrated the role of memorization.[33] But oral poems are regularly orally composed and memorized in advance of performance in Tonga, Kiribati, and among the

---

25. Paul Griffiths, *Religious Reading* (New York: Oxford University Press, 1999), 34.

26. Ruth Finnegan, *Literacy & Orality* (Oxford: Basil Blackwell, 1988), 13.

27. Mark C. Amodio, "Contemporary Critical Approaches and Studies in Oral Tradition," in *Teaching Oral Traditions*, ed. John Miles Foley, Modern Language Association Options for Teaching 13 (New York: Modern Language Association, 1998), 96.

28. John Miles Foley, "The Challenge of Translating Traditional Oral Epic," in *Dynamics of Tradition*, ed. Lotte Tarkka (Helsinki: Finnish Literature Society, 2003), 260; Dagmar Burkhart, "Märchen nach dem Märchen," *Fabula* 49 (2008): 49; Ruth Finnegan, "Problems in the Processing of 'Oral Texts,'" in Sienaert, Bell, and Lewis, *Oral Tradition and Innovation*, 2.

29. Jesse L. Byock, "Saga Form, Oral Prehistory, and the Icelandic Social Context," *New Literary History* 16 (1984): 156.

30. John Brockington, "The Textualization of the Sanskrit Epics," in *Textualization of Oral Epics*, Trends in Linguistics Studies and Monographs 128 (Berlin: de Gruyter, 2000), 201.

31. John D. Niles, "The Myth of the Anglo-Saxon Oral Poet," *Western Folklore* 62 (2003): 10.

32. Rosalind Thomas, *Literacy and Orality in Ancient Greece*, KTAH 2 (Cambridge: University Press, 1992), 17–19, 33.

33. Thomas, *Literacy and Orality*, 34–36; Ruth Finnegan, "How Oral Is Oral Literature," *BSOAS* 37 (1974): 60; Michael Chesnutt, "Orality in a Norse-Icelandic Perspective," *Oral Tradition* 18 (2003): 197; Dorothy Noyes, "The Social Base of Folklore," in *A Companion to Folklore*, ed. R. F. Bendix and G. Hasan-Rokem, Blackwell Companions to Anthropology 15 (New York: Wiley-Blackwell, 2011), 25. Raymond Person and Stuart Weeks continue to emphasize the "afresh each time" originality of biblical oral-written literature; Person, "The Role of Memory in the Tradition Represented by the Deuteronomic History and the Book of Chronicles," *Oral Tradition* 26 (2011): 543, 547–48; Stuart Weeks, "Literacy, Orality, and Literature in Israel," in *On Stone and Scroll*, ed. J. K. Aitken, K. J. Dell, and B. A. Mastin, BZAW 420 (Berlin: de Gruyter, 2011), 478.

Netsilik Inuit.[34] Lord considered these bards no longer oral poets because he believed they ceased innovating in performance.[35] Yet literacy in Indonesia "does not seem to inhibit a performer's improvisational skills, nor does it affect his ability to compose written poetry in an oral style."[36] Icelandic skalds had very limited opportunities for improvisation on poems composed generations before.[37] On the other hand, there *are* clearly cases where oral narratives are "changing every time they are performed," as in Indian-performed *Ramayana*.[38] "In some cultures the ethnopoetic canon requires close adherence to traditional literary rules; in other cultures, the canon encourages variation and change within the limits of certain general rules."[39]

The main latter-day representative of the Parry-Lord school was the late John Miles Foley. Foley, however, moved Oral Formulaic thought beyond Lord while incorporating most of the criticisms of Finnegan, Thomas, and others. He wrote, "We may, and we should, continue to evolve newer and better methods for such studies, and inevitably such progress will lead to revision or perhaps outright dismissal of earlier theories and practices. That is the nature of a healthy field of intellectual inquiry ... The formulaic test *as it has generally been carried out* cannot prove oral provenance."[40] Foley chastised those who imported the model without taking into consideration differences in prosody, phraseology, and poetics between cultures, leaving Lord's method "a useless index."[41]

Recent field studies in oral tradition and folklore have also shown that many societies produced oral and written literature simultaneously. Not only should oral tradition and written literature not be considered unrelated phenomena, but writing often supports oral tradition and vice versa. "The Parry-Lord paradigm," as Joseph Harris writes, "overlooks both oral perfor-

---

34. Finnegan, "How Oral Is Oral Literature?" 61. Albert B. Lord, "What Is Oral Literature Anyway?" in *Oral Literature and the Formula*, ed. Benjamin A. Stolz and Richard S. Shannon III (Ann Arbor: Center for the Coordination of Ancient and Modern Studies, 1976), 175.

35. Lord, "What Is Oral Literature?" 175.

36. Thérèse De Vet, "Context and the Emerging Story," *Oral Tradition* 23 (2008): 165.

37. Russell Poole, "Skaldic Verse and Anglo-Saxon History," *Speculum* 62 (1987): 265.

38. C. M. Bandhu, "Common Languages and Common Narratives," *Folklore and Folkloristics* 1 (2008): 24–25.

39. Heda Jason, *Ethnopoetry*, Forum Theologiae Linguisticae 11 (Bonn: Linguistica Biblica, 1977), 59.

40. John Miles Foley, *Traditional Oral Epic* (Berkeley: University of California Press, 1990), 4.

41. Ibid., 4

mance as a *goal* of writing or writing down and also modes of composition that do not employ writing (i.e., are oral) but are not improvisatory."[42]

Ancient Egypt, for example, displays various interdependent modes of written and oral literature. Works composed in writing were intended for performance. "In several of the royal burial suites where Pyramid Texts are inscribed, each column begins with 'to be spoken,' marking the whole as being for recitation; what is written is an ideal oral form."[43] Even in later Egyptian wisdom texts, the fictional audiences described in the "texts are very often groups of people, suggesting that the poems were intended for audiences rather than single readers."[44]

In Mesopotamia, too, oral tradition existed alongside written literature. Even long after literature was committed to writing, it was written *ana zamāri*, for singing.[45] *Atrahasis* (seventeenth century BCE) is not a tale, but a *zamāru*, a ballad (8.16–19). A thousand years later, the *Song of Erra* (eighth century BCE) still refers to its bards (5.49.53–54). In the cases of significant examples, and probably for particular genres, written texts developed as improvisations based on oral registers of storylines, plot elements, and narrative excerpts.[46]

In fact, predominantly oral societies are *not* the most common settings for oral literature, nor literate societies the normal home of written texts. "The largest majority of the examples of oral literature which we possess and analyze have not been collected from pure [oral] cultures."[47] Some of this literature has been collected from societies that have recently become literate but preserve much orality, but there are also many societies that have been literate from antiquity and yet oral literature has continued to flourish. The oral and the written "have interacted and overlapped for centuries in vast areas of our planet."[48] And in Israel both before and after the Exile,

---

42. Joseph Harris and Karl Reichl, "Performance and Performers," in *Medieval Oral Literature,* ed. Karl Reichl (Berlin: de Gruyter, 2012), 161.

43. John Baines, *Visual and Written Culture in Ancient Egypt* (Oxford: Oxford University Press, 2007), 150–51.

44. Richard B. Parkinson, "Individual and Society in Middle Kingdom Literature," in *Ancient Egyptian Literature*, ed. Antonio Loprieno, PÄ 10 (Leiden: Brill, 1996), 143.

45. Anne Kilmer, "Fugal Features of Atrahasis," in *Mesopotamian Poetic Language*, ed. Marianna E. Vogelzang and Herman L. J. Vanstiphout, CM 6 (Groningen: Styx, 1996), 133.

46. Joan Westenholz, "Historical Events and the Process of Their Transformation in Akkadian Heroic Traditions," in *Epic and History,* ed. David Konstan and Kurt A. Raaflaub, The Ancient World: Comparative Histories 4 (Chichester, UK: Wiley-Blackwell, 2010), 30.

47. Finnegan, "How Oral Is Oral Literature?" 53; italics original.

48. Finnegan, *Oral and Beyond*, 103.

as in Egypt and Mesopotamia, ancient literate audiences "still preferred and even expected to experience their literature *orally*."[49] Even a text as late as Rev 1:1–4 refers to one reader and multiple hearers.[50]

Older models viewed the literary process as linear for ancient Israel. First, there were oral stories that circulated among early Israelite bards or storytellers. Eventually, these were written down. Great debate has mounted over just when this writing down took place. How much literary production was there in preexilic Israel and Judah? How much literary production could have taken place under the constraints of the Babylonian Exile? And these questions are of course primarily about the biblical texts. When (and where) ought we place the *writing down* of the Hebrew Bible?

My argument is that these questions all presuppose a faulty model. There is no simple progression from oral lore to written biblical text. The process is not nearly so linear and many scholars have now replaced it with a vision of a more "mixed economy," as Stuart Weeks calls it.[51] If Christopher Rollston is correct about literacy and David Carr is correct about educational systems, a literary text circulating by text only was virtually unknown in ancient Israel, just as a tale circulating orally only was equally rare, at least in the postexilic period.[52] Weeks perhaps oversimplifies this duality by stating: "What we actually have is literature, and the fact of that literature's emergence in a primarily oral culture."[53] We are concerned here with more than the literature's emergence, but with its performance in a culture that was not merely "primarily oral" but oral-and-written. Written texts circulated in spoken form by recitation long after they were committed to writing. And those recited forms begat oral forms that were not in writing, or were not put in writing for some time afterwards. Oral texts that circulated from bard to audience or bard to bard could be recorded in writing, could be consulted by writers, and could be consulted by bards of other stories.[54]

---

49. Elizabeth W. Barber and Paul T. Barber *When They Severed Earth from Sky* (Princeton: Princeton University Press, 2005), 151; italics original; Ruth Scodel, "Social Memory in Aeschylus' *Oresteia*," *Orality, Literacy, Memory in the Ancient Greek and Roman World,* Mnemosyne Supplement 298 (Leiden: Brill, 2008), 118. As evidence, see Plato, *Phaedrus*, 275C, D; 276D.

50. Cf. also Galen's explanation that owning texts requires hiring professional *lectors* to read them out loud; *De Propriorum Animi Cuiuslibet Affectuum Dignotione et Curatione* 5.48.

51. Weeks, "Literacy, Orality, and Literature," 465.

52. See the contributions by David Carr and Chris Rollston in this volume.

53. Weeks, "Literacy, Orality, and Literature," 474.

54. Francisco Vaz de Silva, "Tradition without End," in *A Companion to Folklore,* ed. R. F. Bendix and G. Hasan-Rokem, Blackwell Companions to Anthropology 15 (New York: Wiley-Blackwell, 2011), 43. I do not deny that there may have been a time in Israel's

In this case, although we should rightly call Israel and Judah from the seventh century BCE on literate societies, the "literature" of both was predominantly oral,[55] then when we study examples of this literature—such as supposed orally derived passages from the Hebrew Bible—we need a distinct set of performance-critical tools.[56] We would not imagine a musicologist who only studied scores or a classicist who studied Greek dramas but never saw a modern theatrical performance of one (or tried, with the help of ethnography, to understand ancient performance).

"Performance criticism" looks for aural, kinetic, and visual aspects of performance—that is, for matters of voice and instrumentation, gesture, and setting and performer identity (gender, status, kinship, adornment).[57] Performance criticism looks at these elements to understand implicit audiences and performer identity and the way they weave together to constitute a performative scheme,[58] itself determined by social and cultural conventions familiar to the original performer and audience.[59] And at the same time, oral performance serves as the verbal expression of that identity and social convention, inviting the audience into the closed community of the social group.[60] Oral literature "rejects any analysis that would dissociate it from within its social function and from its socially accorded place—more than a written text would."[61] Governing conditions of performance shape the kinds of performative schemes a society—not the individual innovating bard—will generate.[62]

---

past, before the eighth century, where stories and ballads circulated *only* orally. But that question has monopolized our scholarly attention and is not my focus here.

55. E.g., Carr, *Formation of the Hebrew Bible*, 19.

56. Terry Giles and William Doan, "Performance Criticism of the Hebrew Bible," *Religion Compass* 2 (2008): 273.

57. Jason, *Ethnopoetry*, 68–69, 251.

58. Peter Seitel, "Three Aspects of Oral Textuality," in *A Companion to Folklore*, ed. R. F. Bendix and G. Hasan-Rokem (Blackwell Companions to Anthropology 15; New York: Wiley-Blackwell, 2011), 77.

59. Giles and Doan, "Performance Criticism," 273; Edward L. Schieffelin, "Problematizing the Performance," in *Ritual, Performance, Media*, ed. Felicia Hughes-Freeland, ASA Monographs 35 (New York: Routledge, 1998), 196; Richard Bauman, "Verbal Art as Performance," in *Performance*, ed. Philip Auslander (New York: Routledge, 2003), 3:39–40; Jason, *Ethnopoetry*, 7.

60. Ulrich Marzolph, "Presidential Address at the Opening of the ISFNR Interim Conference," *International Society for Folk Narrative Research Newsletter* 6 (February 2012): 5.

61. Zumthor, *Oral Poetry*, 1990; Giles and Doan, "Performance Criticism," 276; Seitel, "Three Aspects of Oral Textuality," 80, 83.

62. Noyes, "Social Base of Folklore," 25; Giles and Doan, "Performance Criticism," 279–80.

This is not to eliminate the creative work of the individual bard. Although Parry and Lord underestimated memorization, their insight of composition-in-performance largely holds true.[63] Every performance "belongs to" a particular bard and their particular audience in a unique way.[64] But examining individual performances and performers "also reveals the structure of a community and a tradition ... The communality acts through particularity."[65] Performances are "shaped by the interplay between individually-generated variations and community-enacted selection mechanisms."[66]

We can begin to reconstruct these performance contexts for Israelite oral prose and narrative poetry. Ancient Near Eastern evidence helps a great deal here. But for the ancient past, ethnography will be an important means to reconstruct performance practices where we "have texts but no directly experienceable contexts."[67] As Joseph Harris and Karl Reichl have written, "reconstruction is possible: philological analysis can extract clues about performance from texts [and] comparative studies of living oral traditions and oral performance provide" additional evidence.[68]

In ancient Egypt, it is first necessary to remove "audience-less" performances, the large number of attested performances that were put on only for the gods.[69] Alongside these, there are performances of personal memoires, humorous morality tales, and encomia to the king that involve "reciting" (šdỉ),[70] often with vertical harps.[71] A court setting is commonly depicted,

---

63. Mark Griffith, "'Telling the Tale': A Performing Tradition from Homer to Pantomime," in *The Cambridge Companion to Greek and Roman Theatre*, ed. M. McDonald and J. M. Walton (Cambridge: Cambridge University Press, 2007), 18–19; Jason, *Ethnopoetry*, 6–7, 12–13.

64. James Loxley, *Performativity* (New York: Routledge, 2007), 92.

65. Giedrė Šmitienė, "Life-Tradition: Contribution to the Concept of Life-World," *International Society for Folk Narrative Research Newsletter* 6 (February 2012): 28.

66. Vaz da Silva, "Tradition without End," 41; Seitel, "Three Aspects of Oral Textuality," 91

67. Harris and Reichl, "Performance and Performers," 143.

68. Ibid., 145.

69. Ronald J. Leprohon, "Ritual Drama in Ancient Egypt," in *The Origins of Theatre in Ancient Greece and Beyond*, ed. E. Csapo and M. C. Miller (Cambridge: Cambridge University Press, 2007), 286. I am grateful to my student Kelly Wilson for bringing this to my attention.

70. Donald Redford, "Scribe and Speaker," in *Writing and Speech in Israelite and Ancient Near Eastern Prophecies,* ed. E. Ben Zvi and M. H. Floyd, SymS10 (Atlanta: Society of Biblical Literature, 2000), 160–61, 169, 183. For example, lines 2–14 of the Song to Merneptah from Hermopolis presented by Günthe Roeder, "Zei Hieroglyphische Inschriften aus Hermopolis," *Annales du Service des Antiquités d'Egypt* 52 (1954): 328–40.

71. Bo Lawergren and O. R. Gurney, "Sound Holes and Geometrical Figures," *Iraq* 49 (1987): 37.

bards are depicted in stylized "rapt" poses,[72] and bard-audience interaction is important for composition.[73] The fullest presentation of a performance context is in the Middle Kingdom text King Cheops and the Magicians of Papyrus Westcar.[74] The story relates how in the court of King Khufu (Cheops), "The king's son Khafra arose [to speak, and he said: I should like to relate to your majesty] another marvel, one which happened in the time of [your] father, Nebka" (1.16–20). He then tells a sort of "marvel tale." This is followed by, "Bauefre arose to speak, and he said: Let me have [your] majesty hear a marvel which took place in the time of your father King Snefru" (4.18–20). There are two more such tales.[75] Each is accompanied by a favorable response from Khufu, which encourages and molds the performance of the next one. Although we cannot assume this is an accurate record of real court practices,[76] here we see a depiction of a court setting and an interplay of audience and poet in a sort of a feedback loop.

Within various Mesopotamian texts, there are numerous prologues like "I will sing ..." and epilogues such as "This is a ballad in praise of..." or "Whoever recites this text...."[77] *Atrahasis*, as we have seen, is written "for singing," and Anne Kilmer has extensively explored how this would have been done.[78] Harps (*sammû*) are abundantly attested in iconography, especially from the Assyrian period.[79] Lyres occur as early

---

72. Adelheid Schlott, "Eine Beobachtungen zu Mimik und Gestik von Singenden," *Göttinger Miszellen* 152 (1996): 55, 57, 59–63, 69, figs. 3 (Fifth Dynasty grave of En-cheftka), 6 (grave of Amanamhet [Thutmosis III]), and 15 (Twelfth Dynasty grave of Uchotep).

73. Redford, "Scribe and Speaker," 187, citing the role of Sehtepibre-onkh in the court of Amenemhet II.

74. English translation by William Kelly Simpson in *The Literature of Ancient Egypt*, ed. William Kelly Simpson (New Haven: Yale University Press, 1973), 15–30; Ángel Sánchez Rodriguez, *El Papiro Westcar* (Seville: ASADE, 2003), 1. Hans Goedicke ("Thoughts about the Papyrus Westcar," *ZÄS* 120 [1993]: 23–24, 35) has challenged such an early date.

75. Originally, there were at least five tales; only the last words of the first are preserved, the second and fifth have lacunae, and the third and fourth are complete; Berggren, '*Ipwt*, 2.

76. H. M. Hays, "The Historicity of Papyrus Westcar," *ZÄS* 129 (2002): 20–30.

77. Marianna E. Vogelzang, "Some Aspects of Oral and Written Tradition in Akkadian," in *Mesopotamian Epic Literature*, ed. Marianna E. Vogelzang and Herman L. J. Vanstiphout (Lewiston, NY: Mellen, 1992), 266.

78. Kilmer, "Fugal Features of Atrahasis," 133 and passim.

79. Richard J. Dumbrill, *The Archaeomusicology of the Ancient Near East* (Victoria, BC: Trafford, 2005), 182, 218; Lawergren and Gurney, "Sound Holes and Geometrical Figures," 40. A lyre, unlike a harp, is characterized by a yoke. They lyre is the *kinnārum*; Theo J. H. Krispijn, "Music in the Syrian City of Ebla in the Late Third Millennium B.C.," in *Proceedings of the International Conference of Near Eastern Archaeomusicology*, ed. R. Dumbrill (Piscataway, NJ: Gorgias, 2010), 57; Yelena Kolyada, *A Compendium of Musical*

as third-millennium Ebla, but seem to have decreased in popularity in the second millennium.[80]

Some Hittite texts are labeled "ballads" (*išḫamai*),[81] and one work (although not such a ballad), the Song of Illuyanka (*CTH* 321), is thought to be performed in the Hittite Purulli festival.[82] The Song of the Ullikummi is, in Hurrian, "sung" (*šir-ad-ilu*), before an audience (lines 1–7), probably accompanied by music.[83]

For Syria-Palestine, we have much less information. The author of the Egyptian Story of Wen-Amun thought it plausible to depict an Egyptian female bard singing in the court at Byblos (2.68–69). From Ugarit, there are a number of texts that refer to harp playing and singing within the narrative.[84] A performance scene similar to Papyrus Westcar's is found in the Baal Cycle (Anat 1 = 4AB (KTU/CAT 1.3.i = CTA 3.1), at a feast in Baal's court:

> He stood, chanted [*yabuddu*] and sang [*yašîru*],
> Frame drums [*maṣillatâmi*] in the virtuoso's hands
> Sweet of voice the hero sang,
> About Baal on the summit of Zaphon (lines 18–22)[85]

Instruments and Instrumental Terminology in the Bible, BibleWorld 18 (London: Equinox, 2009), 44.

80. Krispijn, "Music in the Syrian City of Ebla," 57, 59

81. Gary Beckman, "Hittite and Hurrian Epic," in *A Companion to Ancient Epic*, ed. John Miles Foley (Chichester, UK: Wiley-Blackwell, 2005), 256.

82. Gary Beckman, "The Anatolian Myth of Illuyanka," *JANES* 14 (1982): 18; Beckman, "The Religion of the Hittites," *BA* 52 (1989): 104.

83. Alfonso Archi, "Transmission of Recitative Literature by the Hittites," *AoF* 34 (2007): 198–99. The Hurrian system of musical notation was used at Ugarit, and if interpreted according to Babylonian tuning texts, produces a sort of Lydian Mode of fourths and fifths; Koitabashi Matahisa, "The Musical Score from Ugarit," *Bulletin of the Society for Near Eastern Studies in Japan* 39.2 (1996): 16–32. An attempt at recreating the music of the "scored" Hurrian hymns found at Ugarit can be heard at http://youtu.be/4izrFUISZw4.

84. Nicolas Wyatt, *Word of Tree and Whisper of Stone, and Other Papers on Ugaritian Thought*, Gorgias Ugaritic Studies 1 (Piscataway, NJ: Gorgias, 2007), 136.

85. English translation of Mark S. Smith, *Poetic Heroes: The Literary Commemoration of Warriors and Warrior Culture in the Early Biblical World* (forthcoming), 321–22; nearly identical to that in Simon B. Parker, *Ugaritic Narrative Poetry*, WAW 9 (Atlanta: Scholars Press, 1997), 106. Smith (p. 325) notes the absence of women in such a public feast, in contrast to those in the private feast of *ANEP* #157; *Poetic Heroes*. The drums here are not unimportant, as most of the musical instruments of antiquity seem to have been percussion instruments; see Mireai López-Bertran and Agnès Garcia-Ventura, "Materializing Music and Sound in Some Phoenician and Punic Contexts," *SAGVNTVM* 40 (2008): 33.

A word should be added regarding masks. Masks are found throughout Syria, Mesopotamia, and Iran. There are Humbaba masks from Old Babylonian Kish, with the means to attach them to one's face.[86] Masks have been found in Iron I Palestine in Philistine Temple 200 at Tel Qasile, dated to the eleventh century, and from eleventh/tenth-century Ashdod (Strata X–IX) and tenth-century Tel Ser'a.[87] There are countless examples from the Iron II period (from Shufat, Jerusalem, Beersheba, and Akhziv, among others).[88] The function of these masks remains unclear. Those from Hazor, Kition, Enkomi, Korioun, and Sarepta were all found in or near sacred areas.[89] Lucian reports that ritual masks were used in the Attis cult at Syrian Hierapolis (*Dea Syr.* 15).

But we cannot exclude more "dramatic" uses of masks. A block from a twenty-fourth-century BCE tomb from Giza depicts a procession of young dancers, scourged by a youth or a dwarf in a Bes mask,[90] similar to nineteenth-century BCE painted-canvas Bes masks found in a house at Kahun.[91] Numerous masks have been found in sixth-century BCE tombs in Carthage together with cymbals and fragments of lyres.[92] Still, we cannot tell if these belong to performances more akin to concerts than to epic balladry.

I have argued elsewhere at length that the best ethnographic analogies to ancient Israelite balladry are Icelandic Skaldic and some Eddic poetry, although these, too, are ancient and there are thus no ethnographic accounts

---

86. Jane B. Carter, "Masks of Ortheia," *AJA* 91 (1987): 362. The image of Humbaba, although not on masks, is found as early as the First Dynasty of Babylon (1895–1595 BCE); ibid., 361. Similar masks come from later Cyprus; ibid., 363. On possible connections to the Akhziv mask, see ibid., 364.

87. Raz Kletter, "To Cast an Image," in *Up to the Gates of Ekron: Essays on the Archaeology and History of the Eastern Mediterranean in Honor of Seymour Gitin*, ed. Sidnie White Crawford et al. (Jerusalem: Albright Institute for Archaeological Research, 2007), 189.

88. Ibid., 190, 195. There were mask fragment found in the cultic area of Tel Dan from the so-called Bamah A, which Biran connected with Jeroboam I. Christoph Uehlinger ("Eine Anthropomorphe Kulstatue des Gottes von Dan?" *BN* 72 [1994]: 85–100) argued that these fragments were from a statue, but Dalia Pakman has shown that the mask was originally fixed to an incense stand found nearby. The mask in question, however, has no eye holes and was not intended to be worn. See Dalia Pakman, "'Mask-like' Face Reliefs on a Painted Stand from the Sacred Precinct at Tel Dan," *ErIsr* 27 (2003): 196–203.

89. Rainer Albertz and Rüdiger Schmitt, *Family and Household Religion in Ancient Israel and the Levant* (Winona Lake, IN: Eisenbrauns, 2012), 105–6, 226, 471; Carter, "Masks of Ortheia," 370.

90. Geraldine Pinch, *Magic in Ancient Egypt* (Austin: University of Texas Press, 1995), 84, 121–22, fig. 63.

91. Ibid., 122, 132, fig. 71.

92. López-Bertran and Garcia-Ventura, "Materializing Music," 29.

of their performance.[93] There are accounts of performances found in some Icelandic sagas, but these must be used cautiously as they reveal only the authors' perceptions of performance. Nevertheless, what is evident in such saga descriptions is similar to the ancient Near Eastern evidence.[94] Ethnographic evidence supports a similar portrait of performance contexts for oral literature, including audience-speaker interaction, variety of genres, court setting, and even the harp (but not masks).[95]

Icelandic Eddic poetry in the *Fornyðislag* meter was probably sung or chanted in the court, accompanied by harp or lyre.[96] Such court setting, with reward from the patron for good performance, is also the performance context for *all* Icelandic Skaldic poetry.[97] The verb used for the performance of Skaldic poetry is usually translated "chant," but its precise meaning is unclear.[98] Benjamin Bagby finds for Eddic poetry that, "all aspects of the singer's art are called into use, including the wide and flexible spectrum of vocal utterance: plain speech, heightened speech, sung speech, spoken song, simple syllabic song, melismatic song, as well as the more radical elements of human vocal sound."[99]

With caution we can examine the Bible's own picture of oral performance. As Foley wrote of Homer, "We may be able to revivify the ... extruded texts to some extent by interviewing the poet about his specialized language, by enrolling in a brief tutorial on the traditional poetic idiom."[100] Here it is necessary first to eliminate musical song, hymns and the like, in order to limit ourselves to narrative balladry and oral prose.

Narrative recitation seems to have been accompanied in particular by the *kinnôr*—likely a lyre, not a harp or lute, although the term seems in some places to have been used as a generic term for all stringed instruments.[101] The lyre was performed at the feasts envisioned by Isa 5:12, and the scene

---

93. Robert D. Miller II, *Oral Tradition in Ancient Israel*, Biblical Performance Criticism 4 (Eugene, OR: Cascade, 2011).

94. Harris and Reichl, "Performance and Performers," 148.

95. Jason, *Ethnopoetry*, 61.

96. Harris and Reichl, "Performance and Performers," 155, 164.

97. Ibid., 151; Terry Gunnell, *Origins of Drama in Scandinavia* (Cambridge: Brewer, 1995), 330.

98. E. O. G. Turville-Petre, *Scaldic Poetry* (Oxford: Clarendon, 1976), lxxvi.

99. Benjamin Bagby, "*Beowulf*, the *Edda*, and the Performance of Medieval Epic," in *Performing Medieval Narrative*, ed. Evelyn B. Vitz, Nancy F. Regalado, and Marilyn Lawrence (Woodbridge, Suffolk: Boydell & Brewer, 2005), 186. Bagby's performance of *Beowulf* in this style can be found at http://mednar.org/2012/02/13/beowulf/.

100. Foley, "Fieldwork on Homer," in *New Directions in Oral Theory*, ed. Mark C. Amodio, Medieval and Renaissance Texts and Studies 287 (Tempe: Arizona Center for Medieval and Renaissance Studies, 2005), 18.

101. Kolyada, *Compendium of Musical Instruments*, 32.

might resemble that in Iceland or Papyrus Westcar.[102] There are also passages that envision performance settings for oral historical narrative. As with Icelandic Saga and Papyrus Westcar, we are dealing with the author's own perceptions of performance, yet commonly, "the narrative's described performance is often closely and deliberately connected to the immediate performance space in which the story *itself* was told."[103] Post-battle celebrations typically include commemoration in ballad, as with Baal's feast in the Ugaritic material. Examples include the "Song of the Sea" and the "Song of Deborah." There also seems to be a particular dance, the *māḥôl,* associated with such post-battle celebratory songs (Exod 15:20; Judg 11:34; 1 Sam 18:6–7; 21:12; 29:5).[104] Post-battle laments are also attested (2 Sam 2:19–25a; Zeph 2:14–18).[105]

Ancient Israel had performance settings that were standard for its quasi-secular oral prose and narrative poetry. These performance contexts probably conform to the Icelandic portrait that applies also for Papyrus Westcar and other texts. We should envision a court setting with royal audiences. The purpose of much of this material—some of it performed serially—would have been to praise or otherwise support the ruler.[106] Audience-performer interaction would have been of great importance in determining the form of the performed material. Finally, music, especially harp and lyre, would have accompanied recitation, chanting, or singing.[107]

One final note for future study. Some early scholars of oral tradition in the Hebrew Bible used orality to "rescue" the text from higher criticism. When Wellhausen and others had denigrated the historical veracity of the Hebrew Bible, an appeal to oral tradition both salvaged the antiquity of the traditions in "late texts" and provided a basis for historicity in the supposed unfailing power of oral tradition to preserve accurate memories over many generations.

But the historical value of oral tradition depends greatly on genre. The extent of propagandistic elements in praise poetry masks genuine illuminating historical data.[108] Formalized historical accounts are useful

---

102. Ibid., 39.
103. Terry Gunnell, "Narratives, Space and Drama," *Folklore* 33 (2006): 13.
104. Mayer I. Gruber, "Ten Dance-Derived Expressions in the Hebrew Bible," *Biblica* 62 (1981): 341–42.
105. Smith, *Poetic Heroes,* 325.
106. Cf. Jason, *Ethnopoetry,* 250.
107. Carr, *Formation of the Hebrew Bible,* 25.
108. Ruth Finnegan, "A Note on Oral Tradition and Historical Evidence," *History and Theory* 9 (1970): 196.

when treated with caution,[109] but their chronologies should be particularly suspect.[110]

Yet increasingly in many parts of the world, historians and anthropologists are finding legitimate oral tradition to be "a fund of additional evidence and explanation" that can enhance critical historiography.[111] Often it may be the most minor elements of an oral tradition that yield the best fruit for the interpretation of archaeological remains.[112] For all their innovation, oral traditions like ceremonial performances that reference a specific site, for instance, "contain a great deal of consistently reported information, with strong internal standards of verifiability."[113]

And here is where oral tradition studies dovetail with research into the role of cultural practices in constituting collective memory.[114] "Collective memory" is Maurice Halbwachs's term (1925); "cultural memory" is Jan Assmann's (1992).[115] The determined anti-individualism of both versions will probably require reevaluation.[116] And theorists have been all too prone to conceptualizing collective memory exclusively in terms of individual remembering: collectives are said to remember, forget, or repress a past, "without any awareness that such language is at best metaphorical and at worst misleading."[117] Nevertheless, the interface of orality study with the scholarship of collective memory is surely the next avenue of research that lies before us.

---

109. Finnegan, "A Note on Oral Tradition," 197.

110. J. K. Davies, "The Reliability the Oral Tradition," in *The Trojan War*, ed. L. Foxhall and J. K. Davies (Bristol: Bristol Classical Press, 1984), 91.

111. Peter M. Whiteley, "Archaeology and Oral Tradition," *American Antiquity* 67 (2002): 406.

112. Ibid., 410.

113. Ibid., 411–12. I omit here the sticky issue of "canonization," a process not restricted to "sacred texts," but a process that occurs in some cultures—and certainly did in Israel, though at what period remains unclear—whereby the texts are fixed and innovation ceases; Weeks, "Literacy, Orality, and Literature," 477.

114. Chris Weedon and Glenn Jordan, "Collective Memory," *Social Semiotics* 22 (2012): 144. On cultural memory in biblical studies, see Ronald Hendel, "Cultural Memory and the Hebrew Bible," *Bible and Interpretation* 2011, www.bibleinterp.com/opeds/hen358016.shtml.

115. Halbwachs, *Les Cadres sociaux de la mémoire* (Paris: Alcan, 1925); Assmann, *Das kulturelle Gedächnis* (Munich: Beck, 1992).

116. Wulf Kansteiner, "Finding Meaning in Memory," *History and Theory* 41 (2002): 181.

117. Ibid., 185–86; Frank H. Polak, "Afterword: Perspectives in Retrospect," in *Performing Memory in Biblical Narrative and Beyond*, ed. Athalya Brenner and Frank H. Polak (Sheffield: Sheffield Phoenix Press, 2009), 297–98.

Bibliography

Albertz, Rainer, and Rüdiger Schmitt. *Family and Household Religion in Ancient Israel and the Levant.* Winona Lake, IN: Eisenbrauns, 2012.
Amodio, Mark C. "Contemporary Critical Approaches and Studies in Oral Tradition." Pages 95–105 in *Teaching Oral Traditions.* Edited by John Miles Foley. Modern Language Association Options for Teaching 13. New York: Modern Language Association, 1998.
Archi, Alfonso. "Transmission of Recitative Literature by the Hittites." *AoF* 34 (2007): 185–203.
Assmann, Jan. *Das kulturelle Gedächnis.* Munich: Beck, 1992.
Bagby, Benjamin. "*Beowulf*, the *Edda*, and the Performance of Medieval Epic." Pages 181–92 in *Performing Medieval Narrative.* Edited by Evelyn B. Vitz, Nancy F. Regalado, and Marilyn Lawrence. Woodbridge, Suffolk: Boydell & Brewer, 2005.
Baines, John. *Visual and Written Culture in Ancient Egypt.* Oxford: Oxford University Press, 2007.
Bandhu, C. M. "Common Languages and Common Narratives." *Folklore and Folkloristics* 1 (2008): 20–27.
Barber, Elizabeth W., and Paul T. Barber. *When they Severed Earth from Sky.* Princeton: Princeton University Press, 2005.
Bauman, Richard. "Verbal Art as Performance." Pages 32–60 in *Performance*, vol. 3. Edited by Philip Auslander. New York: Routledge, 2003.
Beckman, Gary. "Hittite and Hurrian Epic." Pages 255–63 in *A Companion to Ancient Epic.* Edited by John Miles Foley. Chichester, UK: Wiley-Blackwell, 2005.
———. "The Anatolian Myth of Illuyanka." *JANES* 14 (1982): 11–25.
Berggren, Jenny. *The 'Ipwt in Papyrus Westcar. 7, 5–8. 9,1–5.* PhD diss., Uppsala University, 2006.
Brockington, John. "The Textualization of the Sanskrit Epics." Pages 193–215 in *Textualization of Oral Epics.* Edited by Lauri Honko. Trends in Linguistics Studies and Monographs 128. Berlin: de Gruyter, 2000.
Burkhart, Dagmar. "Märchen nach dem Märchen." *Fabula* 49 (2008): 47–69.
Byock, Jesse L. "Saga Form, Oral Prehistory, and the Icelandic Social Context." *New Literary History* 16 (1984): 153–73.
Carr, David M. *The Formation of the Hebrew Bible.* Oxford: Oxford University Press, 2011.
Carter, Jane B. "Masks of Ortheia." *AJA* 91 (1987): 355–83.
Chesnutt, Michael. "Orality in a Norse-Icelandic Perspective." *Oral Tradition* 18 (2003): 197–99.
Culley, Robert C. "Exploring New Directions." Pages 181–83 in *The Hebrew Bible and Its Modern Interpreters.* Edited by D. A. Knight. Chico, CA: Scholars Press, 1985.
———. *Oral Formulaic Language in the Biblical Psalms.* Toronto: University of Toronto Press, 1967.
———. "Oral Traditions and the OT." *Semeia* 5 (1976): 1–33.
———. *Studies in the Structure of Hebrew Narrative.* Minneapolis: Fortress, 1976.

Davies, J. K.. "The Reliability of the Oral Tradition." Pages 87–110 in *The Trojan War*. Edited by Lin Foxhall and John K. Davies. Bristol: Bristol Classical Press, 1981.
Dumbrill, Richard J. *The Archaeomusicology of the Ancient Near East*. Victoria, BC: Trafford, 2005.
Dundes, Alan. *Holy Writ as Oral Lit*. Lanham, MD: Rowman & Littlefield, 1999.
Finnegan, Ruth. "How Oral Is Oral Literature?" *BSOAS* 37 (1974): 52–64.
———. *Literacy & Orality*. Oxford: Blackwell, 1988.
———. "A Note on Oral Tradition and Historical Evidence." *History and Theory* 9 (1970): 195–201.
———. *The Oral and Beyond*. Chicago: University of Chicago Press, 2007.
———. *Oral Traditions and the Verbal Arts*. Association of Social Anthropologists Research Methods 4. New York: Routledge, 1992.
———. "Problems in the Processing of 'Oral Texts.'" Pages 1–23 in *Oral Tradition and Innovation*. Edited by E. R. Sienaert, A. N. Bell, and M. Lewis. Durban: University of Natal Oral Documentation and Research Centre, 1991.
Foley, John Miles. "The Challenge of Translating Traditional Oral Epic." Pages 248–65 in *Dynamics of Tradition*. Edited by Lotte Tarkka. Helsinki: Finnish Literature Society, 2003.
———. "Fieldwork on Homer." Pages 15–42 in *New Directions in Oral Theory*. Edited by Mark C. Amodio. Medieval and Renaissance Texts and Studies 287. Tempe: Arizona Center for Medieval and Renaissance Studies, 2005.
———. *Traditional Oral Epic*. Berkeley: University of California Press, 1990.
Giles, Terry, and William Doan. "Performance Criticism of the Hebrew Bible." *Religion Compass* 2 (2008): 273–86.
Gísli Sigurðsson. *Medieval Icelandic Saga and Oral Tradition*. Publications of the Milman Parry Collection of Oral Literature 2. Cambridge: Harvard University Press, 2004.
Goedicke, Hans. "Thoughts about the Papyrus Westcar." *ZÄS* 120 (1993): 23–26.
Griffith, Mark. "'Telling the Tale': A Performing Tradition from Homer to Pantomime." Pages 13–34 in *The Cambridge Companion to Greek and Roman Theatre*. Edited by M. McDonald and J. M. Walton. Cambridge: Cambridge University Press, 2007.
Griffiths, Paul J. *Religious Reading*. Oxford: University, 1999.
Gruber, Mayer I. "Ten Dance-Derived Expressions in the Hebrew Bible." *Biblica* 62 (1981): 328–46.
Gunn, David M. "The 'Battle Report': Oral or Scribal Convention." *JBL* 93 (1974): 513–18.
———. "Narrative Patterns and Oral Tradition in Judges and Samuel." *VT* 24 (1974): 286–317.
———. "'Threading the Labyrinth': A Response to Albert B. Lord." Pages 19–24 in *Text and Tradition*. Edited by Susan B. Niditch. SemSt. Atlanta: Scholars Press, 1990.
Gunnell, Terry. "Narratives, Space and Drama." *Folklore* 33 (2006): 7–26.
———. *Origins of Drama in Scandinavia*. Cambridge: Brewer, 1995.
Halbwachs, Maurice. *Les Cadres sociaux de la mémoire*. Paris: Alcan, 1925.
Harris, Joseph, and Karl Reichl. "Performance and Performers." Pages 141–202 in

Medieval Oral Literature. Edited by Karl Reichl. Berlin: de Gruyter, 2012.
Hays, H. M. "The Historicity of Papyrus Westcar." *ZÄS* 129 (2002): 20–30.
Hendel, Ronald. "Cultural Memory and the Hebrew Bible." *Bible and Interpretation* (2011). http://www.bibleinterp.com/opeds/hen358016.shtml.
———. *The Epic of the Patriarch*. HSM 42. Atlanta: Scholars Press, 1987.
Henderson, W. J. "Tradition and Originality in Early Greek Lyric." Pages 249–56 in *Oral Tradition and Innovation*. Edited by E. R. Sienaert, A. N. Bell, and M. Lewis. Durban: University of Natal Oral Documentation and Research Centre, 1991.
Jason, Heda. *Ethnopoetry*. Forum Theologiae Linguisticae 11. Bonn: Linguistica Biblica, 1977.
Kansteiner, Wulf. "Finding Meaning in Memory." *History and Theory* 41 (2002): 179–97.
Kawashima, Robert S. "Comparative Literature and Biblical Studies." *Prooftexts* 21 (2001): 324–44.
———. "From Song to Story: The Genesis of Narrative in Judges 4 and 5." *Prooftexts* 21 (2001): 151–78.
Kilmer, Anne. "Fugal Features of Atrahasis." Pages 127–39 in *Mesopotamian Poetic Language: Sumerian and Akkadian*. Edited by Marianna E. Vogelzang and Herman L. J. Vanstiphout. CM 6. Groningen: Styx, 1996.
Kletter, Raz. "To Cast an Image." Pages 189–208 in *Up to the Gates of Ekron: Essays on the Archaeology and History of the Eastern Mediterranean in Honor of Seymour Gitin*. Edited by S. W. Crawford et al. Jerusalem: Albright Institute for Archaeological Research, 2007.
Kofoed, Jens B. "Remember the Days of Old. Deut 32, 7: Oral and Written Transmission in the Hebrew Bible." *SEE-J Hiphil* 1. http://www.see-j.net/hiphil.2004.
Kolyada, Yelena. *A Compendium of Musical Instruments and Instrumental Terminology in the Bible*. London: Equinox, 2009.
Krispin, T. J. H. "Music in the Syrian City of Ebla in the Late Third Millennium B.C." Pages 55–61 in *Proceedings of the International Conference of Near Eastern Archaeomusicology*. Edited by R. Dumbrill. Piscataway, NJ: Gorgias, 2010.
Lawergren, Bo, and O. R. Gurney. "Sound Holes and Geometrical Figures." *Iraq* 49 (1987): 37–52.
Le Goff, Jacques. *History and Memory*. European Perspectives 8. New York: Columbia University Press, 1992.
Leprohon, Ronald J. "Ritual Drama in Ancient Egypt." Pages 259–92 in *The Origins of Theatre in Ancient Greece and Beyond*. Edited by E. Csapo and M. C. Miller. Cambridge: Cambridge University Press, 2007.
López-Bertran, Mireai, and Agnès Garcia-Ventura. "Materializing Music and Sound in Some Phoenician and Punic Contexts." *SAGVNTVM* 40 (2008): 27–35.
Lord, Albert B. *Epic Singers and Oral Tradition*. Ithaca: Cornell University Press, 1991.
———. "Formula and Non-Narrative Theme in South Slavic Oral Epic and the OT." *Semeia* 5 (1976): 93–105.
———. "Homer as Oral Poet." *Harvard Studies in Classical Philology* 72 (1967): 1–46.
———. *The Singer of Tales*. Cambridge, MA: Harvard University Press, 1960.

———. "The Traditional Song." Pages 1–15 in *Oral Literature and the Formula*. Edited by Benjamin A. Stolz and Richard S. Shannon III. Ann Arbor: Center for the Coordination of Ancient and Modern Studies, 1976.

———. "What Is Oral Literature Anyway?" Pages 175–76 in *Oral Literature and the Formula*. Edited by Benjamin A. Stolz and Richard S. Shannon III. Ann Arbor: Center for the Coordination of Ancient and Modern Studies, 1976.

Loxley, James. *Performativity*. New York: Routledge, 2007.

Magoun, F. P., Jr. "The Oral-Formulaic Character of Anglo-Saxon Narrative Poetry." *Speculum* 28 (1953): 446–67.

Marzolph, Ulrich. "Presidential Address at the Opening of the ISFNR Interim Conference." *International Society for Folk Narrative Research Newsletter* 6 (February 2012): 4–11.

Matahisa, Koitabashi. "The Musical Score from Ugarit." *Bulletin of the Society for Near Eastern Studies in Japan* 39.2 (1996): 16–32

Michalowski, Piotr. "Orality and Literacy and Early Mesopotamian Literature." Pages 227–46 in *Mesopotamian Epic Literature*. Edited by Marianna E. Vogelzang and Herman L. J. Vanstiphout. Lewiston, NY: Mellen, 1992.

Miller, Robert D., II. *Oral Tradition in Ancient Israel*. Biblical Performance Criticism 4. Eugene, OR: Cascade, 2011.

Niles, John D. "The Myth of the Anglo-Saxon Oral Poet." *Western Folklore* 62 (2003): 7–61.

Noyes, Dorothy. "The Social Base of Folklore." Pages 13–39 in *A Companion to Folklore*. Edited by R. F. Bendix and G. Hasan-Rokem. Blackwell Companions to Anthropology 15. New York: Wiley-Blackwell, 2011.

Ong, Walter J. *Orality and Literacy: The Technologizing of the Word*. London: Methuen, 1982.

Pakman, Dalia. "'Mask-like' Face Reliefs on a Painted Stand from the Sacred Precinct at Tel Dan." *ErIsr* 27 (2003): 196–203.

Parker, Simon B., ed. *Ugaritic Narrative Poetry*. WAW 9. Atlanta: Scholars Press, 1997.

Parkinson, Richard B. "Individual and Society in Middle Kingdom Literature." Pages 137–56 in *Ancient Egyptian Literature*. Edited by Antonio Loprieno. Probleme der Ägytpologie 10. Leiden: Brill, 1996.

Person, Raymond R., Jr. "The Role of Memory in the Tradition Represented by the Deuteronomic History and the Book of Chronicles." *Oral Tradition* 26 (2011): 537–50.

———. "A Rolling Corpus and Oral Tradition." Pages 263–71 in *Troubling Jeremiah*. JSOTSup 260. Sheffield: Sheffield Academic Press, 1999.

Pinch, Geraldine. *Magic in Ancient Egypt*. Austin: University of Texas Press, 1995.

Polak, Frank H. "Afterword: Perspectives in Retrospect." Pages 296–99 in *Performing Memory in Biblical Narrative and Beyond*. Edited by Athalya Brenner and Frank H. Polak. Sheffield: Sheffield Academic Press, 2009.

———. "The Oral and the Written." *JANES* 26 (1988): 59–105.

Poole, Russell, "Skaldic Verse and Anglo-Saxon History." *Speculum* 62 (1987): 265–98.

Redford, Donald B., "Scribe and Speaker." Pages 145–218 in *Writings and Speech in Israelite and Ancient Near Eastern Prophecies*. Edited by Ehud Ben Zvi and Michael H. Floyd. SymS 10. Atlanta: Society of Biblical Literature, 2000.

Roeder, Günthe. "Zei Hieroglyphische Inschriften aus Hermopolis." *Annales du Service des Antiquités d'Egypt* 52 (1954): 315–442.
Sánchez Rodríguez, Ángel. *El Papiro Westcar*. Seville: ASADE, 2003.
Schieffelin, Edward L. "Problematizing the Performance." Pages 194–207 in *Ritual, Performance, Media*. Edited by Felicia Hughes-Freeland. ASA Monographs 35. New York: Routledge, 1998.
Schlott, Adelheid. "Eine Beobachtungen zu Mimik und Gestik von Singenden." *Göttinger Miszellen* 152 (1996): 55–70.
Schniedewind, William M. *How the Bible Became a Book*. Cambridge: University Press, 2004.
———. "Orality and Literacy in Ancient Israel." *RelSRev* 26 (2000): 327–31.
Scodel, Ruth. "Social Memory in Aeschylus' *Orestia*." Pages 115–42 in *Orality, Literacy, Memory in the Ancient Greek and Roman Worlds*. Edited by E. Anne Mackay. Mnemosyne Supplement 298. Orality and Literacy in Ancient Greece 7. Leiden: Brill, 2008.
Seitel, Peter. "Three Aspects of Oral Textuality." Pages 75–93 in *A Companion to Folklore*. Edited by R. F. Bendix and G. Hasan-Rokem. Blackwell Companions to Anthropology 15. New York: Wiley-Blackwell, 2011.
Simpson, William Kelly, trans. "King Cheops and the Magicians." Pages 15–30 in *The Literature of Ancient Egypt*. New Haven: Yale University Press, 1973.
Ska, Jean-Louis. "A Plea on Behalf of the Biblical Redactors." *Studia Theologica* 59 (2005): 4–18.
Smith, Mark S. *Poetic Heroes: The Literary Commemoration of Warriors and Warrior Culture in the Early Biblical World*. forthcoming.
Šmitienė, Giedrė. "Life-Tradition: Contribution to the Concept of Life-World." *International Society for Folk Narrative Research Newsletter* 6 (February 2012): 27–35.
Thomas, Rosalind. *Literacy and Orality in Ancient Greece*. KTAH 2. Cambridge: University, 1992.
Turville-Petre, E. O. G. *Scaldic Poetry*. Oxford: Clarendon, 1976.
Uehlinger, Christoph. "Eine Anthropomorphe Kulstatue des Gottes von Dan?" *BN* 72 (1994): 85–100.
Vaz de Silva, Francisco. "Tradition without End." Pages 40–54 in *A Companion to Folklore*. Edited by R. F. Bendix and G. Hasan-Rokem. Blackwell Companions to Anthropology 15. New York: Wiley-Blackwell, 2011.
Vet, Thérèse de. "Context and the Emerging Story." *Oral Tradition* 23 (2008): 159–79.
Vogelzang, Marianna E. "Some Aspects of Oral and Written Tradition in Akkadian." Pages 265–80 in *Mesopotamian Epic Literature*. Edited by Marianna E. Vogelzang and Herman L. J. Vanstiphout. Lewiston, NY: Mellen, 1992.
Weedon, Chris, and Glenn Jordan. "Collective Memory." *Social Semiotics* 22 (2012): 143–53.
Weeks, Stuart. "Literacy, Orality, and Literature in Israel." Pages 465–78 in *On Stone and Scroll*. Edited by J. K. Aitken, K. J. Dell, and B. A. Mastin. BZAW 420. Berlin: de Gruyter, 2011.
Westenholz, Joan G. "Oral Traditions and Written Texts in the Cycle of Akkade." Pages 123–54 in *Mesopotamian Epic Literature*. Edited by Marianna E. Vogelzang and Herman L. J. Vanstiphout. Lewiston, NY: Mellen, 1992.
Whiteley, David S. "Archaeological Evidence for Conceptual Metaphors as Enduring

Knowledge Structures." *Time and Mind* 1 (2008): 7–29.

Wyatt, Nick. *Word of Tree and Whisper of Stone, and Other Papers on Ugaritian Thought*. Gorgias Ugaritic Studies 1. Piscataway, NJ: Gorgias, 2007.

Zumthor, Paul. *Oral Poetry*. Theory and History of Literature 70. Minneapolis: University of Minnesota Press, 1990.

TEXT CRITICISM AS A LENS FOR UNDERSTANDING THE TRANSMISSION OF ANCIENT TEXTS IN THEIR ORAL ENVIRONMENTS

RAYMOND F. PERSON JR.

IN *THE DEUTERONOMIC HISTORY AND THE BOOK OF CHRONICLES: SCRIBAL WORKS in an Oral World*, I combine the insights of the Parry-Lord approach to oral traditions with the text criticism of Samuel–Kings, in order to argue that the Deuteronomic History and the Book of Chronicles are both faithful representations of the same broader tradition, despite what from our modern perspectives appear to be significant theological differences. For this purpose, the most important insight of the Parry-Lord approach is multiformity as a characteristic of oral traditions—that is, oral bards think of their songs as "a flexible plan of themes, some of which are essential and some of which are not," rather than an "ideal" or "original" text; therefore, every performance exists within "an ever-changing phenomenon" so that no two performances are exactly alike.[1] The most important insight from text criticism is the observation that the biblical text existed in a multiplicity of text-types, so that in ancient Israel textual plurality was the norm rather than the existence of a single, standardized, authoritative text. When these insights are combined we can conclude that the ancient Israelite scribes were performers of their tradition in ways analogous to oral bards. Thus, as texts in a primarily oral society like ancient Israel, each manuscript represents the broader tradition as an imperfect instantiation of the broader tradition that existed, on the one hand, in the interplay of coexisting parallel written texts, none of which alone can possibly represent the fullness of the tradition, and, on the other hand, in the mental text in the collective memory of the people.[2] When this observation

---

1. Albert B. Lord, *The Singer of Tales* (Cambridge: Harvard University Press, 1960), 99–100. For my fuller discussion of multiformity as a characteristic of oral traditions, see Raymond F. Person, Jr., *The Deuteronomic History and the Book of Chronicles: Scribal Works in an Oral World*, AIL 6 (Atlanta: Society of Biblical Literature, 2010), ch. 3.

2. See also Raymond F. Person, Jr., "The Role of Memory in the Tradition Rep-

is extended further, we can conclude that both the Deuteronomic History and the Book of Chronicles faithfully preserve and represent a broader tradition.

In order to provide further support for this contention that every individual text is necessarily an incomplete representation of this fuller tradition, I explore similar arguments concerning text-critical studies of other ancient and medieval literature, specifically Homeric epic, Old English literature, and the Thousand and One Nights, as well as text-critical observations from the study of the Dead Sea Scrolls, thereby providing additional text-critical evidence from a comparative perspective. I then analyze a synoptic passage in Samuel//Chronicles, in order to provide another illustration of the thesis that both the Deuteronomic History and the Book of Chronicles are faithful representations of the same broader tradition.

TEXT CRITICISM OF SELECTED ANCIENT AND MEDIEVAL LITERATURE

In this section I briefly review arguments that the text-critical "variants" found in selected ancient and medieval literature demonstrate that these texts were transmitted in ways that require an understanding of the role of the scribes in these traditions to compose/perform the texts in the transmission process in ways analogous to oral bards. That is, in their act of copying a text, these scribes were not mere copyists and the "variants" suggest that each manuscript produced by a scribe is an imperfect representation of the tradition as preserved in the collective memory of the community. Furthermore, these "variants" are "organic" to the tradition, in that they reflect what Lord called the "special grammar" of the traditions. Other scholars have made similar arguments for a variety of literary texts with roots in oral traditions, including Homeric epic, Old English poetry, and medieval Arabic prose tales.

In *Multitextuality in the Homeric Iliad*, Graeme Bird examined the text-critical evidence of the Ptolemaic papyri of the *Iliad* as they relate to the Parry-Lord approach to oral traditions. He noted that in those classical works that clearly descend from one individual writer (for example, Virgil's *Aeneid*) the earliest manuscripts tend to be the most reliable in establishing the original text with the later manuscripts containing scribal corruptions. In contrast, the earliest manuscripts of Homer, including especially the Ptolemaic papyri,

---

resented by the Deuteronomic History and the Book of Chronicles," *Oral Tradition* 26 (2011): 537–50. In this article, I am more explicit about the role of memory in oral traditions as discussed by Albert Lord and John Miles Foley and how their insights apply to Samuel–Kings//Chronicles.

contain the most divergent readings, while the later manuscripts "converge toward the 'received text'" of Homer.³ Thus, Bird concluded as follows.⁴

> The variation in our surviving manuscripts of Homer ... is inconsistent with a single archetype, but rather points back to a multiplicity of archetypes, a situation which arises from the oral nature of the transmission of Homeric epic.

When he analyzed the variants in the Ptolemaic papyri, Bird noted that they do not betray differing origins.⁵

> The nature of the variation is "organic"—lines have not been "dropped" into place arbitrarily; rather, they give the appearance of having "grown" in their current locations, in the process modifying their surroundings and resulting in a coherent "version" of an episode that is no less "Homeric."

In other words, the Ptolemaic pluses preserve the poetic structures of Homeric epic—that is, the hexameter poetic line and related formulaic system—and they are incorporated into the thematic structures in ways that are consistent with the Homeric tradition.

The study of medieval manuscripts has led to a rejection of our modern notion of a literary text as applied to medieval literature. Joyce Tally Lionarons wrote:⁶

> The familiar concept of the literary text, defined as an autonomous arrangement of words shaped by an individual writer and reflecting that writer's authorship, is taken for granted in most contemporary scholarship. In recent years, however, the applicability of the idea of the text to medieval literary works has been challenged by scholars studying the manuscript culture of the Middle Ages. Medievalists have argued convincingly that it was only "the development of printing with moveable type" that created the conditions that allowed the literary texts as such to come into existence in the first place. ... Nevertheless, the language [that] scholars have traditionally used to describe manuscripts and their contexts carries with it an assumption of textuality born in a print culture—we speak of textual "archetypes" and "variants;" we identify scribal "corruption" and "errors," just as if a

---

3. Graeme D. Bird, *Multitextuality in Homeric Iliad: The Witness of the Ptolemaic Papyri* (Washington: Center for Hellenic Studies, 2010), 32.
4. Ibid., 28.
5. Ibid., viii.
6. Joyce Tall Lionarons, "Textual Appropriation and Scribal (Re)Performance in a Composite Homily: The Case for a New Edition of Wulfstan's *De Temporibus Anticristi*," in *Old English Literature in Its Manuscript Context*, ed. Joyce Tally Lionarons (Morgantown: West Virginia University Press, 2004), 67–68.

separate, uncorrupted master text did in fact exist outside of and prior to the manuscript work.

Lionarons then made the case for a new edition of Wulfstan's *De Temporibus Anticristi* that would not make the same mistaken assumptions.

Lionarons' assertion was influenced by the work of Kathleen O'Brien O'Keeffe and A. N. Doane (among others). In *Visible Song: Transitional Literacy in Old English Verse*, O'Brien O'Keeffe noted that visual differences between Latin manuscripts and Old English manuscripts strongly suggest that the Anglo-Saxon scribes approached the reading and writing of these manuscripts differently. For the Latin manuscripts the scribes used a complex standardized system of lineation, capitalization, and punctuation, which is virtually lacking in the vernacular Old English manuscripts. She assumed that "the more sophisticated the cues, the more 'literate' the reading community, that is, the more they rely on conventional visual phenomena (rather than memory) for constructing or reconstructing meaning."[7] Therefore, the reading of the Latin texts required more visual aids, since they were further removed from the contemporary culture. On the other hand, "[b]ecause its manuscripts were low both in orthographic redundancy and in graphic cues, Old English verse must have required a good deal of predictive knowledge from its readers."[8]

Similarly, in "Scribal Textuality and a Exeter Riddle," A. N. Doane analyzed two instances of the same riddle that are clearly recorded by the same scribe in the Exeter Book, a tenth century anthology of Old English poetry. He concluded that the textuality of this scribe differed remarkably from our modern notions of textuality. He noted that these two riddles are, "in terms of *writing*, virtually identical in their layout, spacing, and letter forms," even though the variety in the words of the two riddles demonstrates that the scribe "was capable of freely substituting elements that made as good metrical, rhetorical or semantic sense."[9] Thus, on the one hand, the scribe's choice of words in the riddles themselves suggests a more "speaker-based" textuality rather than a "reader-based" textuality, in that the words can vary as long as they fit within the aesthetic presentation of the basic meaning of the riddles.[10] On the other hand, the fact that the scribe more carefully recon-

---

7. Katherine O'Brien O'Keeffe, *Visible Song: Transitional Literacy in Old English Verse* (Cambridge: Cambridge University Press, 1990), x.

8. O'Brien O'Keeffe, *Visible Song*, 190.

9. A. N. Doane, "Scribal Textuality and an Exeter Riddle," in *New Approaches to Editing Old English Verse*, ed. Sarah Larrant Keefer and Katherine O'Brien O'Keeffe (Woodbridge: Brewer, 1998), 60, 63.

10. Doane, "Scribal Textuality and an Exeter Riddle," 49–50.

structed the same visual layout of the riddles suggests that his understanding of textuality was more spatial than phonemic—that is, the graphic layout of the words was more important than the particular sounds of the words themselves. Therefore, the scribe could vary the phonemic string more easily than the spatial layout of the words.[11]

Both O'Brien O'Keeffe and Doane have demonstrated how a close study of the actual manuscripts of medieval texts rather than published critical editions can open up new insights that correct earlier interpretations of medieval texts based on our modern notions of textuality. That is, the literary texts published in our critical editions are abstracted from their manuscript environment in ways that often leads to misinterpretations. Lionarons summarized well the materiality of the manuscript as follows.[12]

> Before the appearance of print technology, each occurrence of a written work was unique, the product of a specific, historically conditioned intersection between one or more authors, one or more scribes, and the material conditions of a particular manuscript's creation, which might include the state of the exemplar; the skill of the scribe or scribes in terms of calligraphy, illumination, and graphic design; and the proposed or *de facto* literary context, that is, which works were chosen or simply available to be copied and bound together to form a manuscript book.

Both O'Brien O'Keeffe and Doane also discussed how these so-called variants that are plentiful when we compare manuscripts are, in Bird's language, "organic" to the native poetic structures. O'Brien O'Keeffe wrote that, "in the cases where variants are metrically, semantically and syntactically appropriate, the scribe has read 'formulaically' and has become a participant in and a determiner of the text."[13] Doane wrote that "the Exeter scribe was willing to compose by ear as he copied by eye and was capable of freely substituting elements that made as good metrical, rhetorical or semantic sense one way as the other."[14] Doane characterized what from our modern perspectives appear to be either different texts or corrupted texts as "recomposed performances"—that is, the scribes were not merely copyists but, much like oral bards, they were performers of the text.[15] O'Brien O'Keeffe similarly discussed what she called "residual orality" in relationship to the work of Anglo-Saxon scribes. Thus, O'Brien O'Keeffe and Doane understood the

---

11. Doane, "Scribal Textuality and an Exeter Riddle," 64.
12. Lionarons, "Textual Appropriation and Scribal (Re)Performance," 67.
13. O'Brien O'Keeffe, *Visible Song*, 191.
14. Doane, "Scribal Textuality and an Exeter Riddle," 63.
15. Ibid., 64. See also A. N. Doane, "The Ethnography of Scribal Writing and Anglo-Saxon Poetry: Scribe as Performer," *Oral Tradition* 9 (1994): 420–39.

Anglo-Saxon scribes as performing the texts in ways that are somewhat analogous with how oral bards compose/perform oral traditions.[16]

In his study of the Thousand and One Nights, David Pinault stated that "throughout the medieval and early modern eras ... *Alf laylah* was never a static or fixed collection, ... it continued to grow until the late eighteenth and early nineteenth centuries."[17] He noted that the manuscript evidence clearly shows that some of the tales were once independent of the Thousand and One Nights and then were later incorporated into it. Even after being incorporated into the Thousand and One Nights, some of these tales continued to be copied in the independent manuscript tradition as well. He specifically discussed the following four tales as examples of this phenomenon: The Fisherman and the Genie, The Enchanted Prince, The False Caliph, and The City of Brass.[18] Furthermore, he concluded that often the versions of these tales found in the Thousand and One Nights and in the independent manuscript tradition differ substantially in terms of both wording and narrative structure.[19] However, despite such differences, all of the versions share "a stock of conventional actions and gestures" and "a stock of conventional patterned phrases" or "prose-formulae," influences from their origins in oral storytelling. Thus, Pinault asserted that these Arabian tales provide an example of a prose analogue to Lord's "special grammar" for orally composed poetry—that is, this is another example of the "variants" being "organic" to the tradition.[20] Pinault concluded as follows, "The storyteller—whether writer or reciter—prefers not to improvise ex nihilo."[21]

What all of these studies strongly suggest is that the text-critical "variants" we find in the manuscript traditions of many ancient and medieval texts reflect a general cultural acceptance of the time for the type of multiformity found in living oral traditions and that this cultural acceptance not only influenced the oral bards behind these literary traditions (in those traditions in which they existed), but also significantly influenced the numerous scribes who transmitted the texts (even those texts that may have had only a loose connection to an oral tradition). Thus, the scribes themselves can be understood as performers of the texts in ways analogous to the oral bards, so that no one performance or text can be understood to represent fully the tradition. This analogy, however, does not require us to assume that multiformity

---

16. See also Lionarons, "Textual Appropriation and Scribal (Re)Performance," 69.
17. David Pinault, *Story-Telling Techniques in the Arabian Nights* (Leiden: Brill, 1992), 6.
18. Ibid., chs. 3–5.
19. Ibid., 11.
20. Ibid., 113.
21. Ibid., 114.

worked exactly the same for both oral bards and textual scribes, because there does appear to be what David Carr has labeled a "trend towards expansion" in the process of written textualization.[22] For example, Bird noted that over time the written text of Homer expands as it preserves more of the tradition.[23] Similarly, Pinault showed how the Thousand and One Nights continued to expand into the early nineteenth century as it incorporated additional tales from the independent manuscript traditions. However, even this trend provides us with evidence of how the tradition can expand "organically," to use Bird's terminology, in ways that are analogous to oral traditions.

Text Criticism and the Dead Sea Scrolls

Above we saw how the study of specific manuscripts of other ancient and medieval literature has brought about serious questions concerning our modern notions of "text" based on critical editions and how the language we tend to use in relationship to such "texts" is profoundly anachronistic. The study of the Dead Sea Scrolls—that is, the ancient manuscripts themselves of Second Temple literature rather than scholarly reconstructions in the form of eclectic critical editions based on multiple manuscripts—has raised strikingly similar questions such as the following: What is a biblical text and what is a nonbiblical text? And where do we draw the line between different versions of the same literary text and those new literary texts that use an earlier text as its primary source—that is, reworked or rewritten texts? As we will see below, although such distinctions might continue to have some heuristic value, they are often difficult to maintain in light of the multiplicity of extant texts.

Before the discovery of the Dead Sea Scrolls, a debate occurred concerning the priority of the Masoretic Text over and against the other versions, especially the Septuagint and Samaritan Pentateuch. The general consensus was that the Masoretic Text generally preserved the *Urtext* of the Hebrew Bible and that the other "versions" were "sectarian" or "vulgar" texts that diverged significantly from the *Urtext*. Although this model continues to have significant influence, especially among those scholars who are not text critics, the evidence of the Dead Sea Scrolls significantly undercuts this position, not because similar evidence did not exist earlier in the other so-called "sectarian" (for example, the Samaritan Pentateuch) or "vulgar" (for example, the Septuagint) versions, but because the antiquity of the Dead Sea

---

22. David M. Carr, *The Formation of the Hebrew Bible: A New Reconstruction* (Oxford: Oxford University Press, 2011), 65–72.

23. Bird, *Multitextuality in Homeric Iliad*, 49.

Scrolls, including the "biblical" manuscripts, made the categorization of any of the versions as "sectarian" or "vulgar" much more difficult in comparison to the much later medieval manuscripts of the Masoretic Text. That is, the textual plurality exhibited by the "sectarian" or "vulgar" versions had been too quickly dismissed until the discovery of the Dead Sea Scrolls proved the antiquity of some of their readings and how textual plurality was a characteristic of the Qumran library itself. Thus, the new paradigm for first-century CE Judaism can be illustrated well by this quote from Sidnie Crawford:[24]

> Most groups within the broad parameters of Judaism at this time did not insist upon a single textual tradition, but were willing to accept a certain amount of textual flux, even to the point of accepting two parallel literary editions of the same text as valid Scripture.

Thus, we will see that it is difficult to maintain a sharp distinction between a biblical and a nonbiblical text as well as the distinction between a source text and another text that used the source text as its primary source, what has often been called a "reworked" or "rewritten" text.

When the Psalms Scroll of Cave 11 (11QPs[a]) was first published by James Sanders, many scholars argued that it should not be understood as a biblical text, because it varied too much from MT-Psalms in the order of the psalms and in the inclusion of noncanonical psalms (some known from LXX and the Syriac), but rather it should be understood as a secondary liturgical text. Today it is widely understood as one of the various versions of the Book of Psalms that circulated throughout Second Temple Judaism—that is, it is not some "sectarian" version that can be easily dismissed as an anomaly. This discussion clearly illustrates how the consensus concerning the priority of the Masoretic Text as best preserving the *Urtext* of the Hebrew Bible influenced and still influences many discussions concerning the textual history of the Hebrew Bible.[25]

As the study of the scrolls has continued, other works that were originally classified as "nonbiblical" are increasingly being understood as "biblical" or "scriptural." For example, the so-called Reworked Pentateuch (4QRP = 4Q364–67) has been classified as "nonbiblical," but there are good arguments for including it in the same category as other pentateuchal texts. For example, Eugene Ulrich has argued that the variation we see in the Reworked Penta-

---

24. Sidnie White Crawford, *Rewriting Scripture in Second Temple Times* (Grand Rapids: Eerdmans, 2008), 37.

25. See Sarianna Metso, "When the Evidence Does Not Fit: Method, Theory, and the Dead Sea Scrolls," in *Rediscovering the Dead Sea Scrolls: An Assessment of Old and New Approaches and Methods*, ed. Maxine L. Grossman (Grand Rapids: Eerdemans, 2010), 12–13.

teuch consists of additions, omissions, substitutions, and different sequences that are typical of the variations between Exodus and Deuteronomy as well as between the Masoretic Text and the Samaritan Pentateuch. Thus, from the perspective of the Qumran community, if not more broadly in Second Temple Judaism, the Reworked Pentateuch may "constitute simply a variant literary edition of the Torah, alongside the MT and SP."[26] In fact, Ulrich described the composition/transmission process that produced the Hebrew Bible in language very similar to what we saw above for the other ancient and medieval literature.[27]

> The process of the composition of the Scriptures was organic, developmental, with successive layers of tradition, revised to meet the needs of the historically and religiously changing community.

This process continued, according to Ulrich, until after the two Jewish revolts—that is, until the late second century CE.[28]

As we have just seen, the Reworked Pentateuch raises the question of the relationship between a source text that by its very nature is understood as authoritative and a "rewritten" or "reworked" text that as suggested by the label itself is derived from the earlier source text. Is this distinction itself anachronistic? In some ways I suspect not—that is, such a distinction may very well have been made in Second Temple Judaism. However, we must ask the question of whether or not we can reconstruct this distinction *as made by the ancients themselves* rather than as based on our anachronistic notions of such distinctions. In order to explore this question, I find George Brooke's

---

26. Eugene Ulrich, "The Text of the Hebrew Scriptures at the Time of Hillel and Jesus," in *Congress Volume Basel 2001*, ed. André Lemaire, VTS 92 (Leiden: Brill, 2002), 102. See also Crawford, *Rewriting Scripture in Second Temple Times*, 56–57 and Metso, "When the Evidence Does Not Fit," 6.

27. Eugene Ulrich, "The Evolutionary Production and Transmission of the Scriptural Books," in *The Dead Sea Scrolls: Transmission of Traditions and Production of Texts*, ed. Sarianna Metso, Hindy Najman, and Eileen Schuller (Leiden: Brill, 2010), 218. See also Ulrich, "The Text of the Hebrew Scriptures," 86 and Eugene Ulrich, "Methodological Reflections on Determining Scriptural Status in First Century Judaism," in Grossman, *Rediscovering the Dead Sea Scrolls*, 147. See also Hans Debel, "Rewritten Bible, Variant Literary Editions and Original Text(s): Exploring the Implications of a Pluriform Outlook on the Scriptural Tradition," in *Changes in Scripture: Rewriting and Interpreting Authoritative Traditions in the Second Temple Period*, ed. Hanne von Weissenberg, Juha Pakkala, and Marko Marttila (Berlin: de Gruyter, 2011), esp. 67–71, 75–76. Debel asserts, correctly in my opinion, that text critics such as Tov and Ulrich have held on too much to an *Urtext* theory and, therefore, do not follow their own arguments to their logical conclusion.

28. Ulrich, "Methodological Reflections," 147. See also idem, "The Text of the Hebrew Scriptures," 100 and "Evolutionary Production and Transmission," 211.

definition helpful: "A rewritten scriptural text is essentially a composition which shows clear dependence on a scriptural text."[29] He expanded upon this definition by noting four characteristics: (1) "the source text is thoroughly embedded ... not as explicit citation but as a running text," (2) "the order of the source is followed extensively," (3) "the content of the source is followed relatively closely without very many major insertions or omissions," and (4) "the original genre or genres stay(s) much the same."[30] Nevertheless, variations occur between the two texts. "This running text may resemble word for word that which may be deemed to be its source, or it may be more free in its handling of the supposed source—paraphrasing, abbreviating, omitting, glossing, and expanding as may be deemed appropriate by its composer."[31] After he has acknowledged that such rewritten scripture can be found in the Law, Prophets, and Psalms, Brooke concluded as follows: "In one sense every copy of an authoritative scriptural book made in the late Second Temple period is a rewritten scriptural manuscript."[32] Thus, even though Brooke's definition is helpful, he also concluded that in one sense this distinction does not apply well to any authoritative scriptural book in Second Temple Judaism.

In sum, we have seen that the study of the Dead Sea Scrolls has blurred significantly what were once mutually exclusive distinctions between "biblical" and "nonbiblical" as well as scripture as source text and "reworked"/"rewritten" text, thereby explaining, on the one hand, the multiplicity in the extant manuscript evidence of what appears to be the same literary text and, on the other, what appears to be completely different literary texts that nevertheless are closely related to each other. Even though these distinctions continue to have some heuristic value and even though the ancients may have made somewhat similar distinctions in some cases, the nature of the evidence, especially given the textual plurality of the extant texts, makes it extremely difficult for us to make such distinctions for many of the ancient texts we study without first anachronistically imposing our modern notions of "text" and "canon" on the ancient texts. Therefore, given the textual plurality of the texts and the apparent general acceptance of mul-

---

29. George J. Brooke, "The Rewritten Law, Prophets and Psalms: Issues for Understanding the Text of the Bible," in *The Bible as Book: The Hebrew Bible and the Judean Desert Discoveries*, ed. Edward D. Herbert and Emanuel Tov (London: The British Library and Oak Knoll Press, 2002), 31–32.

30. Brooke, "The Rewritten Law, Prophets and Psalms," 32–33. See also Crawford, *Rewriting Scripture*, 9-15 and Debel, "Rewritten Bible," 82. Crawford and Debel craft their definitions of "Rewritten Scripture" closely following Brooke.

31. Brooke, "The Rewritten Law, Prophets and Psalms," 32.

32. Ibid., 34–35.

tiformity by the ancients as well as our lack of clear methodological criteria by which to make such distinctions, I choose to err on the side of accepting a high degree of multiformity, thereby minimizing the type of distinctions made too often by modern scholars of ancient and medieval texts.

THE RELATIONSHIP BETWEEN SAMUEL–KINGS AND CHRONICLES

Above we have seen how different manuscripts containing different readings can nevertheless be understood as representing the same literary text (preserved in the collective memory of the people and its written representations) within the same tradition. We have also explored how the distinctions often made between "biblical" and "nonbiblical" and between source text and "rewritten" or "reworked" text is often difficult to maintain in light of the various textual traditions. Now we bring these insights to bear on our study of Samuel–Kings and Chronicles in our examination of 2 Sam 12:26–31//1 Chr 20:1b–3. In *The Deuteronomic School and the Book of Chronicles*, I drew substantially from the work of Julio Trebolle in my analysis of 1 Sam 1:1–1 Kgs 2:12//1 Chr 10:1–29:30 in its entirety and argued for a shorter common source behind these two passages with a close discussion of both synoptic (2 Sam 6:12–19a//1 Chr 15:25–16:3; 2 Sam 23:8–39//1 Chr 11:10–47) and nonsynoptic passages (2 Sam 1–4; 1 Chr 12; 2 Sam 6:20b–23; 1 Chr 27).[33] I argued with Trebolle that both passages, 2 Sam 12:26–31 and 1 Chr 20:1b–3, were likely later additions to the written tradition initially based on this shorter common source, since this synoptic passage occurs after the end of the non-*kaige* recension of Samuel LXX (that is, after 2 Sam 11:1a) that probably represents a different ancient division of the book.[34] However, due to limitations of space, I did not elaborate on this specific synoptic passage there, so I will do so here. Note that due to limitations of space here I am only providing my English translation of the Masoretic Text of these two passages. The inclusion of other versions (such as 2 Sam 12:26–31 LXX) would have demonstrated even more variations.[35]

---

33. Person, *The Deuteronomic History*, 89–105, 131–38, 144–52. Julio C. Trebolle, "Samuel/Kings and Chronicles: Book Division and Textual Composition," in *Studies in the Hebrew Bible, Qumran, and the Septuagint Presented to Eugene Ulrich*, ed. Peter W. Flint, Emanuel Tov, and James C. Vanderkam, VTS 101 (Leiden: Brill, 2006). Trebolle and I are both influenced significantly by the work of Graeme Auld concerning a common source behind Samuel-Kings//Chronicles, even though we differ somewhat from his perspective: A. Graeme Auld, *Kings without Privilege: David and Moses in the Story of the Bible's Kings* (Edinburgh: T&T Clark, 1994).

34. Person, *The Deuteronomic History*, 89–94.

35. For a more detailed analysis of the relationship between MT-Samuel–Kings and

2 Sam 12:26–31 MT	1 Chr 20:1b–3 MT
²⁶Joab fought against Rabbah of the Ammonites and he captured the royal city.	¹ᵇJoab attacked Rabbah and he destroyed it.
²⁷Then Joab sent messengers to David and said, "I have fought against Rabbah. Moreover, I have captured the city's water supply. ²⁸Now gather the rest of the people and encamp against the city and capture it, lest I myself capture the city and my name be proclaimed over it."	
²⁹So, David gathered all of the people and went to Rabbah and he fought against it and captured it.	
³⁰He took the crown of their king from his head; its weight was a talent of gold and [upon it was] a precious stone; and it was placed on David's head. And the spoil of the city he brought out, a vast amount.	²David took the crown of their king from his head; he found that its weight was a talent of gold and upon it was a precious stone; and it was placed on David's head. And the spoil of the city he brought out, a vast amount.
³¹The people who were in it he brought out and he set [them to work] with saws, iron picks, and iron axes or sent them to the brickworks. Thus he did to all the cities of the Ammonites. Then David and all the people returned to Jerusalem.	³The people who were in it he brought out and he cut up [the city] with saws, iron picks, and axes. Thus David did to all the cities of the Ammonites. Then David and all the people returned to Jerusalem.

The consensus model asserts that Chronicles is a late rewriting of portions of Samuel–Kings, so that a comparison of Chronicles to Samuel–Kings provides an empirical control on how the Chronicler used his sources for his own peculiar theological agenda.[36] Thus, in this specific case the Samuel

---

LXX-Samuel–Kings in relationship to Chronicles for other passages, see Person, *The Deuteronomic History*, chs. 4–5.

36. However, there is disagreement about how useful the label "Rewritten Bible" is

account of the capture of Rabbah (2 Sam 12:26–31) is generally understood to have a preexilic royal annal as its source[37] and the Chronicles account (1 Chr 20:1b–3) is secondary, further removed from these preexilic sources by the postexilic interpretation of the earlier Samuel account. For example, Knoppers concluded that the Chronicler "excluded an enormous amount of material in 2 Samuel relating to David's reign" in order to obscure "David's private, familial, and state struggles" and thereby idealize David by emphasizing the theme of his victory over his enemies.[38] Knoppers' interpretation is representative of others who assume the consensus model, including Ralph Klein and Sara Japhet; however, Klein and Japhet are more forthcoming in their understanding of how imperfect the Chronicler was in his interpretation of Samuel. For example, Klein insisted that the "omission" of 2 Sam 12:27–29, which includes Joab's summons of David and David's coming to Rabbah, creates a problem—that is, in Chronicles David is still in Jerusalem and therefore is unable to take "the crown of their king from his head" (1 Chr 20:2; Klein's translation: "the crown of Milcom from his head"). Thus, Klein and others conclude that the Chronicler knew the longer text of Samuel and in many cases assumed that his readers would also know the longer text.[39] In fact, Klein argued that the harmonistic addition in some of the minor Septuagint manuscripts of Chronicles—that is, "and Joab sent messengers to David, saying, 'Go, seize Rabbah lest I capture it and my name be called over it.' David gathered the troops and went to Rabbah and captured it"—is an attempt to overcome "this awkwardness" by restoring the omitted material.[40]

According to the consensus model, this is just one case of this type of "awkwardness" created by the Chronicler's "imperfect" or "problematic"

---

for Chronicles. Gary N. Knoppers (and most others) have insisted that the label is too restrictive for Chronicles, since it is more creative than he seems to allow for this genre (*1 Chronicles 1-9* [Anchor Bible; New York: Doubleday, 2003], 131). In contrast, George J. Brooke found the label helpful in understanding the formation of Chronicles ("The Books of Chronicles and the Scrolls from Qumran," in *Reflection and Refractions: Studies in Biblical Historiography in Honour of A. Graeme Auld*, ed., Robert Rezetko, Timothy H. Lim, and W. Brian Aucker [Leiden: Brill, 2007], 40–43, 47). Brooke explicitly criticized Knoppers for having too narrow of a definition of "Rewritten Bible" that would in his opinion exclude some of the obvious examples of rewritten scripture in the Dead Sea Scrolls.

37. For example, P. Kyle McCarter, Jr., *II Samuel*, AB (New York: Doubleday, 1980), 313.

38. Knoppers, *I Chronicles 10–29*, 737, 739–40. For my discussion of another passage (1 Chr 12) in which Knoppers sees a more idealized version of David in Chronicles, see Person, *The Deuteronomic School*, 145–50.

39. Ralph W. Klein, *1 Chronicles*, Hermeneia)Minneapolis: Fortress, 2006), 407.

40. Klein, *1 Chronicles*, 407. The translation of the LXX plus is Klein's (*1 Chronicles*, 400 n. 32). See also Steven L. McKenzie, *The Chronicler's Use of the Deuteornomistic History*, HSM 33 (Atlanta: Scholars Press, 1985), 66.

manipulation of his source text in Samuel. For example, Japhet noted that 1 Chr 20:3—"Then David and all the people returned to Jerusalem"—is "completely inexplicable" in Chronicles, because of the omission of 2 Sam 12:27–29. Such so-called problems in this one passage have been multiplied in their discussion of other passages.[41]

These so-called problems have been handled within the consensus model in one of two ways. Japhet described these two options well. Her description of the first is as follows:[42]

> The exegete may assume that, in spite of the contradictory elements in the editing process, the author succeeded in producing a fully coherent story, and that the present text is therefore a result of corruption and does not faithfully represent the Chronicler's original composition.

She illustrated this option by pointing to the work of W. Rudolph, who often emended the text of Chronicles before he interpreted his reconstructed "original" composition. Japhet's description of the second option is as follows:[43]

> The exegete may also adopt a less interventive mood, and accept the present text as authentic, observing that its adaptation did not reach perfection because of the natural mutual interference of the two tendencies: literary adherence and theological adaptation.

Japhet's own reading follows this second option, as do most others in the consensus model.

If we examine these two options closely, we see that they both make the same assumptions concerning what a good literary text necessarily is—that is, they imagine that a creative individual author necessarily produced an "original" text that is more or less perfect according to our modern notions of consistency as an element of good writing and the necessity to provide all of the relevant information. However, the work of these imagined individuals (for example, Dtr[1] or Dtr[2] for Samuel and the Chronicler for Chronicles) can only be understood if we can adequately reconstruct their "original" texts behind the textual plurality of the extant texts. Since such a reconstruction is even being abandoned by many text critics,[44] it seems to me that we must

---

41. For my summary of and critique of similar arguments concerning other passages in Chronicles, see Person, *The Deuteronomic History*, 101–3, 111, 114–15, 134–38.

42. Sara Japhet, *I & II Chronicles*, OTL (Louisville: Westminster John Knox, 1993), 362.

43. Japhet, *I & II Chronicles*, 363.

44. For example, Emanuel Tov has softened his stance about reconstructing the original text. Compare the first and third editions of his influential book, *Textual Criticism of*

take seriously a third option, one that is consistent with the above text-critical studies of Homer, Old English, the Thousand and One Nights, and the Dead Sea Scrolls. That is, rather than assuming that the literary history began with one authoritative text that was either corrupted by errors or deliberately changed for theological reasons, we should assume that the history of these texts began with a multiplicity of texts, all of which were imperfect instantiations of the broader traditions in that they were necessarily selective in what to represent but at the same time they were all (or at least most of them) accepted as faithful representations of the tradition. The strong preference for one text as *the* faithful representation over all others was thus a much later development in the tradition that eventually led to the standardization of the received canonical text, but even then both Samuel–Kings and Chronicles were preserved. Thus, extending this line of argument further, both Samuel–Kings and Chronicles can be understood as faithful representations of the broader tradition without necessarily judging one as superior and one as inferior, even though in specific instances one text may preserve more of the details of the tradition than the other. Let me illustrate how this third option may illuminate the literary history differently by returning to our example of 2 Sam 12:26–31//1 Chr 20:1b–3.[45]

Most adherents of the consensus model assume a common source for Samuel MT and Chronicles MT—that is, an "original" text closer to Samuel LXX that was expanded into Samuel MT and revised significantly into Chronicles MT. In contrast, I assert that, given the textual plurality of the extant manuscripts, especially of Samuel, and the relationship between Samuel–Kings and Chronicles, the common source should not be imagined as a single text but as a mental text preserved in the collective memory of the community that was also recorded in a multiplicity of written texts that (at least from our modern view) differed widely one from the other because they selectively represented various elements of the tradition and did so in ways that were more or less elaborate, analogous to how oral bards perform oral traditions.[46] Therefore, although in this passage Samuel preserves a longer text that more fully represents the broader tradition, one does not have to conclude that the Chronicler abbreviated an earlier authoritative text of Samuel for theological reasons, while at the same time assuming that

---

the Hebrew Bible (Minneapolis: Fortress, 1992, 2011), especially his discussion of the history of the biblical text in ch. 3.

45. See Person, *The Deuteronomic History*, for discussions of other passages, illustrating this third option.

46. See also Raymond F. Person, Jr., "The Ancient Israelite Scribe as Performer," *JBL* 117 (1998): 601–9, which builds significantly upon Doane, "The Ethnography of Scribal Writing."

his readers will know the text of Samuel well enough to have a successful reading. Rather, one can conclude that both of these texts assume that their readers/hearers will know the broader tradition better than either text reproduces, even though Samuel generally reproduces more of the tradition. Therefore, for example, the "omission" in Chronicles of Joab summoning David and David's arrival in Rabbah (as preserved in 2 Sam 12:27–29) is not, in Japhet's words, "completely inexplicable," when one accepts that both texts made certain assumptions about how much the readers/hearers know about the tradition in their collective memory so that neither text necessarily preserved the full tradition in written form. Therefore, this so-called omission in Chronicles does not necessarily require our understanding Samuel as the earlier, more "original" text. In fact, I think we should explore the possibility that the material that is unique in Samuel is actually an "addition" to the Samuel *Vorlage(n)* of Chronicles in terms of being added to the written record of the tradition.

What I have just argued concerning the common source does not require us to prefer one text over the other as the earlier, more "original" text; however, what David Carr has called the "trend towards expansion" would seem to give preference to Chronicles in this instance as the shorter text.[47] At least we can see a similar expansion in other ancient and medieval texts, including Homeric epic and the Thousand and One Nights. That is, although Samuel preserves the tradition here more so in its fullness, Chronicles may nevertheless be closer to the earliest written forms of the tradition with the extant versions of Samuel representing later expansions as the process of textualization continued to record more and more of the tradition that had been located primarily in the collective memory of the community. . ([In other instances Chronicles preserves more of the tradition, so that Samuel may be closer to the earlier written forms of the tradition.[48])] But, again, whether this material is an "omission" in Chronicles or an "addition" in Samuel in some ways is beside the point, especially since in a real sense both texts faithfully preserved the tradition for the Second Temple community, even though neither text represented the fullness of that tradition.

---

47. Carr's understanding of Samuel-Kings//Chronicles has changed. In his 2006 essay ("'Empirische' Perspektiven auf das Deuteronomistischen Geschichtswerk," in *Die deuteronomistischen Geschichswerke Redaktions- und religionsgeschichtliche Perspektiven zur "Deuteronomismus"-Diskussion in Tora und Vorderen Propheten*, ed. Markus Witte et al., BZAW 365 (Berlin: de Gruyter, 2006], 1–17), Carr supported Auld's thesis of a common source, concluding that this was consistent with the trend towards expansion. However, in his 2011 monograph he returned to the consensus model and concluded that Chronicles is an exception to this trend (Carr, *The Formation of the Hebrew Bible*, 73–78).

48. For my discussion of unique material in Chronicles, see Person, *The Deuteronomic History*, 144–59.

It may be helpful to close with a summary of my reconstruction of the historical social settings that produced the Deuteronomic History and the Book of Chronicles.[49] The Deuteronomic school formed in the Babylonian exile from the scribal elites whose roots were in the monarchic administration and they combined various preexilic sources with their own redactional material to produce the first editions of the Deuteronomic History. This scribal guild then experienced a split when some of the scribes returned to Jerusalem under Zerubbabel to provide scribal support for the rebuilding of the temple and some remained in Babylon. Those that returned to Jerusalem continued their redactional work on the Deuteronomic History (the postexilic Deuteronomic school) and those that remained in Babylon continued their redactional work on what was an early form of Samuel–Kings, a common source, that led to the Book of Chronicles (the Chronistic school). Thus, the Deuteronomic History and the Book of Chronicles were competing contemporary historiographies of the postexilic period that had an exilic common source. The two scribal groups came into contact again, when Ezra and his scribes (the Chronistic school) returned to Jerusalem, displacing the Deuteronomic school, thereby leading to its institutional demise. Despite the linguistic differences between Samuel–Kings and Chronicles and the institutional conflict that occurred between the Deuteronomic school and the Chronistic school under Ezra, the broader community nevertheless understood the literatures of both of these groups as faithfully representing the broader tradition, therefore the community maintained the broader tradition by preserving both works. Thus, we as scholars of this ancient literature should strive to discern how this literature that from our modern perspective appears to contain numerous "additions," "omissions," and "substitutions" was nevertheless understood by the ancients as faithful representations of this broader tradition by our drawing from the insight of multiformity in the comparative study of oral traditions and the insight of textual plurality from text criticism.

References

Auld, A. Graeme. *Kings without Privilege: David and Moses in the Story of the Bible's Kings*. Edinburgh: T&T Clark, 1994.

Bird, Graeme D. *Multitextuality in the Homeric Iliad: The Witness of the Ptolemaic Papyri*. Hellenic Studies 43. Washington, D.C.: Center for Hellenic Studies, 2010.

Brooke, George J. "The Books of Chronicles and the Scrolls from Qumran." Pages 35–48 in *Reflection and Refractions: Studies in Biblical Historiography in Honour*

---

49. See further, Person, *The Deuteronomic History*.

of A. Graeme Auld. Edited by Robert Rezetko, Timothy H. Lim, and W. Brian Aucker. Leiden: Brill, 2007.

———. "The Rewritten Law, Prophets and Psalms: Issues for Understanding the Text of the Bible." Pages 31–40 in *The Bible as Book: The Hebrew Bible and the Judean Desert Discoveries*. Edited by Edward D. Herbert and Emanuel Tov. London: The British Library and Oak Knoll Press, 2002.

Carr, David M. "'Empirische' Perspektiven auf das Deuteronomistischen Geschichtswerk." Pages 1–17 in *Die deuteronomistischen Geschichswerke Redaktions- und religionsgeschichtliche Perspektiven zur "Deuteronomismus"-Diskussion in Tora und Vorderen Propheten*. Edited by Markus Witte et al. BZAW 365. Berlin: de Gruyter, 2006.

———. *The Formation of the Hebrew Bible: A New Reconstruction*. Oxford: Oxford University Press, 2011.

Crawford, Sidnie White. *Rewriting Scripture in Second Temple Times*. Studies in the Dead Sea Scrolls and Related Literature. Grand Rapids: Eerdmans, 2008.

Debel, Hans. "Rewritten Bible, Variant Literary Editions and Original Text(s): Exploring the Implications of a Pluriform Outlook on the Scriptural Tradition." Pages 65–91 in *Changes in Scripture: Rewriting and Interpreting Authoritative Traditions in the Second Temple Period*. Edited by Hanne von Weissenberg, Juha Pakkala, and Marko Marttila. Berlin: de Gruyter, 2011.

Doane, A. N. "The Ethnography of Scribal Writing and Anglo-Saxon Poetry: Scribe as Performer." *Oral Tradition* 9 (1994): 420–39.

———. "Scribal Textuality and an Exeter Riddle," Pages 45–65 in *New Approaches to Editing Old English Verse*. Edited by Sarah Larrant Keefer and Katherine O'Brien O'Keeffe. Woodbridge: Brewer, 1998.

Japhet, Sara. *I & II Chronicles*. OTL. Louisville: Westminster John Knox, 1993.

Klein, Ralph W. *1 Chronicles*. Hermeneia. Minneapolis: Fortress, 2006.

Knoppers, Gary N. *1 Chronicles 1–9*. Anchor Bible. New York: Doubleday, 2003.

Lionarons, Joyce Tall. "Textual Appropriation and Scribal (Re)Performance in a Composite Homily: The Case for a New Edition of Wulfstan's *De Temporibus Anticristi*." Page 67–93 in *Old English Literature in Its Manuscript Context*. Edited by Joyce Tally Lionarons. Morgantown: West Virginia University Press, 2004.

Lord, Albert B. *The Singer of Tales*. Cambridge: Harvard University Press, 1960.

McCarter, P. Kyle, Jr. *II Samuel*. Anchor Bible. New York: Doubleday, 1980.

McKenzie, Steven L. *The Chronicler's Use of the Deuteronomistic History*. HSM 33. Atlanta: Scholars Press, 1985.

Metso, Sarianna. "When the Evidence Does Not Fit: Method, Theory, and the Dead Sea Scrolls." Pages 11–25 in *Rediscovering the Dead Sea Scrolls: An Assessment of Old and New Approaches and Methods*. Edited by Maxine L. Grossman. Grand Rapids: Eerdemans, 2010.

O'Brien O'Keeffe, Katherine. *Visible Song: Transitional Literacy in Old English Verse*. Cambridge: Cambridge University Press, 1990.

Person, Raymond F., Jr., "The Ancient Israelite Scribe as Performer." *JBL* 117 (1998): 601–9.

———. *The Deuteronomic History and the Book of Chronicles: Scribal Works in an Oral World*. AIL 6. Atlanta: Society of Biblical Literature, 2010.

———. "The Role of Memory in the Tradition Represented by the Deuteronomic History and the Book of Chronicles." *Oral Tradition* 26 (2011): 537–50.
Pinault, David. *Story-telling Techniques in the Arabian Nights*. Studies in Arabic Literature 15. Leiden: Brill, 1992.
Tov, Emanuel. *Textual Criticism of the Hebrew Bible*. Minneapolis: Fortress, 1992. Repr. 2011.
Trebolle, Julio C. "Samuel/Kings and Chronicles: Book Division and Textual Composition." Page 96–108 in *Studies in the Hebrew Bible, Qumran, and the Septuagint Presented to Eugene Ulrich*. Edited by Peter W. Flint, Emanuel Tov, and James C. Vanderkam. VTS 101. Leiden: Brill, 2006.
Ulrich, Eugene. "The Evolutionary Production and Transmission of the Scriptural Books." Pages 209–25 in *The Dead Sea Scrolls: Transmission of Traditions and Production of Texts*. Edited by Sarianna Metso, Hindy Najman, and Eileen Schuller. Leiden: Brill, 2010.
———. "Methodological Reflections on Determining Scriptural Status in First Century Judaism." Pages 145–61 in *Rediscovering the Dead Sea Scrolls: An Assessment of Old and New Approaches and Methods*. Edited by Maxine L. Grossman. Grand Rapids: Eerdemans, 2010.
———. "The Text of the Hebrew Scriptures at the Time of Hillel and Jesus." Pages 85–108 in *Congress Volume Basel 2001*. Edited by André Lemaire. VTS 92. Leiden: Brill, 2002.

Oral Substratum, Language Usage, and Thematic Flow in the Abraham-Jacob Narrative

Frank H. POLAK

In biblical scholarship the relationship between the written text and the oral tradition has always been highly problematic. But the modern study of such subjects as narrative structure, oral literature, and language usage opens up new perspectives. In this study I want to defend the view that the tales of the patriarchs preserve an underlying oral-epic substratum that formed the base structure for the narrative in its present, written form. This vista allows us to overcome the tension between historical growth and narrative unity. What is traditional, and ultimately based on oral narrative/poetry, is the underlying unity of the overarching narrative,[1] whereas the problems of repetition and contradiction originate with the activity of various different narrators, whether oral or writing, within this tradition.

Orality is more than merely oral transmission by traditionists. What is at stake is the live performance in front of an audience by singers or narrators. The artistry of those performers, fed by their knowledge of the tales of their mentors and predecessors, and of other narrators/singers, includes voice, gesture, and interaction with the audience.[2] These aspects are lost in writing, but some features may be preserved, and demand our utmost attention.

The narratives of Abraham and Jacob in Genesis 12–35 require analysis along these lines, since these narratives contain a number of features that suggest an oral substratum. A number of literary stock phrases reveal close connections to the epic-formulaic repertoire of Ugaritic (and Akkadian) poetry. The language usage of these tales is in many respects similar

---

1. The position of the overarching narrative is noted, as a later stage in the redaction-transmission process (proto-Genesis) by David M. Carr, *Reading the Fractures of Genesis: Historical and Literary Approaches* (Louisville: Westminster John Knox, 1996), 201–3.

2. Linda Dégh, *Folktales and Society: Story-Telling in a Hungarian Peasant Community* (Bloomington, IN: Indiana University Press, 1989), 165–285; John D. Niles, *Homo Narrans: The Poetics and Anthropology of Oral Literature* (Philadelphia: University of Pennsylvania Press, 1999), 173–203.

to spontaneous spoken discourse, and thus to oral narrative. Language usage of this kind is an important pointer, for the means of expression imply societal habitus and thereby sociocultural and sociohistorical background. In addition, these tales are permeated with recurrent thematic patterns that are well-known from Ugaritic texts, suggesting a traditional milieu.[3] Plot structure, then, is the first subject that demands our attention.

1. An Epic Plot Sequence

1.1 Plot Structure, Macrotext, and Microtext

Any discussion of narrative tradition has to address three distinct but interconnected levels:

1. The *fabula*, the large-scale narrative content, which can be reproduced in different paraphrases, in translation, and in different media, such as the plastic arts. One notes the retelling of biblical antiquities by Flavius Josephus, or the way in which Shakespeare used the medieval English chronicles and other narratives.
2. The plot (or *syuzhet*), the narrative in the given ordering of motifs and time sequence, causality, contrast, parallelism, and character shaping.[4]
3. The wording by which the plot is shaped in the various episodes, the various small-scale patterns and the game of focalization and point of view.

The *fabula* remains unchanged in paraphrase, in different media, and of course, in translation, whereas the *syuzhet* is subject to change by paraphrase and transfer to other media, but not by translation. Translation, however, necessarily affects the *wording*.

Within an oral milieu the fabula largely remains stable even when presented by different narrators, whereas the details of the plot construction are variable.[5] In such contexts, the wording is to a large extent variable (although

---

3. See Mark S. Smith, "Biblical Narrative between Ugaritic and Akkadian Literature. Part I: Ugarit and the Hebrew Bible: Consideration of Comparative Research," *RB* 114 (2007), 8–13, 22–27.

4. Viktor Shklovsky, *Theory of Prose,* trans. B. Sher (Elmswood Park, IL: Dalkey Archive, 1991), 52–64, 170; Quintilian would have spoken of *invention, disposition,* and *elocution* (*Inst.* 6.4.1; 6.5.1; 7.10.11–13; 8 proeemium 6, 13; 8.1.1).

5. See, e.g., Gottfried Henssen, *Überlieferung und Persönlichkeit: Die Erzählungen*

fixed themes may be verbalized by a given series of traditional phrases), but the characteristic oral diction with its traditional, formulaic repertoire is basically maintained. On the other hand, exact memorization is attested as well, sometimes by means of particular techniques.[6]

1.2 THE STRUCTURE OF THE ABRAHAM-JACOB NARRATIVE

Careful observation of the literary and stylistic features of the Abraham-Jacob narrative in Genesis indicates a substratum of an overarching oral epic with a traditional plot sequence. The narratives of the two patriarchs form a diptych that consists of two panels, bound together by a series of parallels and contrasts and hinging on the tales of Isaac and Rebecca, which serve to bridge the tales of the first and the third generation. The main parallel relates to the movement between Canaan and Upper Mesopotamia (Aram Naharaim). Abraham moves with his family from Haran to Canaan, but in the end he initiates a countermovement when he sends his servant to his family in Haran in order to fetch a bride for his son. The Jacob narrative mirrors this sequence. Abraham's grandson has to flee to Haran, to his mother's brother, in order to escape Esau's fury.[7] There he builds his family, in the end returning to Canaan, to be reconciled with his brother. These sequences are linked by the contrasting roles of Isaac and Rebecca. As son to Abraham and father to Jacob, Isaac blesses his son, destined for this status by his mother, Rebecca, who was wedded to Isaac by Abraham's initiative and divine destination.[8]

The parallel-contrast is underlined by two thematic similarities. The divine promise to Abraham and Sarah that they will be blessed with a son is given after the *meal* under the terebinth at Mamre (Gen 18), a theme that reappears in Isaac's blessing of Jacob and Esau (25:19–25, 27:1–4, 18–40), and the agreement with Laban (31:54). A second theme is the *separation* from the sibling: Abraham's separation from Lot is final, like Ishmael's separation from Isaac,[9] whereas Jacob in the end is reconciled with Esau.

---

und Lieder des Egbert Gerrits (Münster, Westfalen: Aschendorff, 1951), 28–35.

6. Ruth Finnegan, *Oral Poetry: Its Nature, Significance and Social Context* (Cambridge: Cambridge University Press, 1977), 156; see also 73–86, 135–42; on the role of memory see also Niles, *Homo Narrans*, 180–90.

7. The parallels are noted by Carr, *Reading the Fractures of Genesis*, 177–79, 195–96, 203. On the role of parallelism in plot construction see n. 10.

8. Gen 24:15–16, 27, 50; see Ina Willi-Plein, "Genesis 27 als Rebekkageschichte," *TZ* 45 (1989): 315–44; Lieve M. Teugels, *Bible and Midrash: The Story of 'The Wooing of Rebekah'* (Leuven: Peeters, 2004), 119–29; Jub. 19:15–31, 22:10–23:2.

9. But the brothers cooperate in Abraham's burial (Gen 25:8–10; Jub. 22:1, 23:6–7).

This intricate complex of parallel and contrast suggests significant links between the two narratives.[10] In Gunkel's analysis, any structuration along these lines is necessarily secondary, since he separates the Jacob-Esau tales from the Laban narratives. However, the reasoning behind this argument is extremely weak, for Gunkel essentially argues that Jacob would not be able to escape Esau. [11] This argument from literary plausibility is misleading: According to the narrative, it was Jacob who drew his brother's attention, when he conveyed him a message in order to appease him (Gen 32:4–6). On the contrary, the opposition of the basic structures of the narratives of Abraham and Jacob indicates a fundamental coherence that now demands our attention.

1.3 THE ABRAHAM NARRATIVE: COUNTERPOINT AND CORNERSTONES

The Abraham narrative is characterized by the contrast between opening and closure. The double opening includes the note on the fate of Sarai, who remained childless (11:30),[12] and the divine call "Go-you-forth from your land, from your kindred, from your father's house, to the land that I-will-let-you-see," (Gen 12:1), followed by the promise "I will make a great nation of you" (v. 2). The counterpoint of this promise and Sarai's childlessness is the overarching principle of the Abraham cycle.[13] Thus Abram sets out with "Sarai his wife and Lot his brother's son, all their property that they had gained, and the persons whom they-had-made-their-own in Haran" (v. 5).[14] The last step before the closure is the dispatch of his servant to his Haran family in order to fetch a worthy wife for his son. The counterbalance of these steps is accentuated by the wording, in particular in the indication of Abraham's blessing: "Abraham, now, was old, advanced in years, and YHWH had *blessed* Abraham in everything" (24:1). This statement, the opening

---

10. The role of parallel and contrast, for instance in Tolstoi's novels, is discussed by Shklovsky, *Theory of Prose*, 54, 61–65, 192–93.

11. Hermann Gunkel, *Genesis*, 3rd edition, HKAT I.1 (Göttingen: Vandenhoeck & Ruprecht, 1910), 292; idem, "Jacob," in Hermann Gunkel, *What Remains of the Old Testament,* trans. A. K. Dallas (London: Allen & Unwin, 1928), 168–71.

12. One notes the poetic balance: ילד? parallels עקרה: וַתְּהִי שָׂרַי עֲקָרָה / אֵין לָהּ וָלָד. Judg 13:2–3, 1 Sam 2:5, Isa 54:1, Job 24:1.

13. See in particular David J. A. Clines, *The Theme of the Pentateuch*, JSOTSup 10 (Sheffield: Sheffield Academic Press, 1978), 45; Claus Westermann, *The Promises to the Fathers,* trans. David E. Green (Philadelphia: Fortress, 1980), 132–34; Naomi Steinberg, *Kinship and Marriage in Genesis: A Household Economics Perspective* (Minneapolis; Fortress, 1993), 36, 45–48; Carr, *Reading the Fractures of Genesis*, 184–85.

14. The renderings follow Everett Fox, *The Five Books of Moses* (New York: Schocken, 1995), sometimes with slight variation.

motto for the mission of Abraham's servant, matches the divine blessings by which the Abraham narrative is opened: "I will give you *blessing* and will make your name great. Be a *blessing!*" (12:2). By the same token Abraham's instruction to his representative balances the divine order to leave Aram Naharaim: "Rather, you are to go to my land and to my kindred and take a wife for my son, for Isaac" (24:4). Nouns and verbs used in this exchange are similar to those employed in the divine orders to Abraham and the description of his departure from his country of birth. The continuation of this tale clarifies that the blessing is embodied by his riches, "all the bounty of his master" (24:10): "YHWH has greatly blessed my master, and he has become rich: He has given him sheep and cattle, silver and gold, male and female slaves, camels and asses" (v. 35). These assets are mentioned next to Abraham's son: "And Sarah, my master's wife, has born my master a son in her old age, and he has assigned to him everything he owns" (v. 36). The macrostructural contrast between opening and final development, together with the microstructural links on the level of wording, indicates a connection between the two stages of the narrative. These stages constitute a coherent structure, shaped as *inclusio* and underlined by wording and thematic links.

Apart from the correspondence in wording we note repeated elements: the family, the wife, and the slave who is allowed to play a central role (12:5). In chapters 12 and 22 one notes the counterpoint of father and son ("Take your son, your favored one, Isaac, whom you love, and go to the land of Moriah," 22:2, matching 12:2: "Go forth from your native land and from your father's house").[15] In the tale of the servant's mission, the equilibrium is reached when Isaac brings Rebecca into his mother's tent (24:67), and thus finally finds comfort over his mother's death. This note represents the counterpoise to the expositional statement that Sarai remained childless (11:29–30): now her tent is used by her son's wife.

So let us now consider the way in which these elements develop. When Abraham leaves his kindred (Gen 12:1–5), he is accompanied by his *wife*, his *nephew* (representing the promised posterity),[16] and his *property*, while the goal of his migration is "the *land* that I-will-let-you-see," v. 1).[17] These elements form the cornerstones of the narrative, for they define the "house" as a socioeconomic unit and a constitutive element of the symbolic universe

---

15. The father–son counterpoint is discussed by Devora Steinmetz, *Kinship, Conflict and Continuity in Genesis* (Louisville: Westminster John Knox, 1991), 24–42.

16. See ibid., 68–70.

17. The intricate connection between the promises of land, the future inheritance, and posterity (the heirs) is discussed by Carr, *Reading the Fractures of Genesis*, 185. Additional recurrent elements are the slave/servant and the gracious/ungracious foreign potentate (Pharaoh, Abimelech, and, in a sense, Laban and Esau).

of this tale, and thus as a *symbolic household*.[18] The role of "property" was established by Polzin, who also points to the wife's role as ancestress.[19] The importance of posterity and land has always been clear, but these matters were tied to the promise theme as an independent, theological issue, and were not sufficiently considered in their connection with the narrative flow.[20] The integration of promise and narrative, advocated by David Clines, opens new perspectives, in particular thanks to his crucial recognition that the promise is never realized in full, and is still awaited with Moses' death.[21]

Thus the cornerstones of the symbolic household are constitutive for the flow of patriarchal narrative in its entirety. With Abraham's arrival in the land, these cornerstones start to move. The tale of Sarai in Pharaoh's palace involves three cornerstones: land, wife, and property, and an ungracious but repentant foreign ruler (12:10–20). Abraham has to abandon the land and temporarily loses his wife, but receives compensation in property (12:16). When the family returns to the land (13:1), the symbolic household is complete, since Abraham is a wealthy man now. But at this juncture his nephew Lot, who represents the coming generations, abandons him (13:11). This setback is counterbalanced by a renewed promise of the inheritance of the land (13:15) and posterity. Thus loss in one corner is offset by gain in another corner, but there is no completion: when all cornerstones are present, the narrative continues with a loss or an impending loss. This series of setbacks, interruptions and uncertainties, reflects a basic feature of all narrative: the build up of expectations and their breakdown, in "canonicity and breach."[22]

The importance of the matter is revealed by the tale of Abraham's challenge of the divine promise "Here, to me you have not given seed, here, my house born slave (בֶּן־בֵּיתִי) will be my heir" (15:3; related to ch. 13 rather than to ch. 14), and even more so in the next narrative: the tale of Hagar, who is to substitute for Sarai and to give Abraham an heir. The promise of a solution leads to a renewed removal of a cornerstone: Hagar's flight from her mistress (16:6–13). The next step in the narrative, the renewed promise to Abraham,

---

18. See Steinberg, *Kinship and Marriage*, 5–7, 10–11, 15–30.

19. See n. 11 above; Robert Polzin, "'The Ancestress of Israel in Danger' in Danger," *Semeia* 3 (1975): 83–85; Paul Vrolijk, *Jacob's Wealth: An Examination into the Nature and Role of Material Possessions in the Jacob-Cycle (Gen 25:19–35:29)*, VTSup 146 (Leiden: Brill, 2011).

20. So, e.g., Rolf Rendtorff, *The Problem of the Process of Transmission in the Pentateuch*, trans. John J. Scullion, JSOTSup 89 (Sheffield: Sheffield Academic Press, 1990), 48–85; the integration of the promise theme and the narrative matter is highlighted by Carr, *Reading the Fractures of Genesis*, 203–4.

21. Clines, *The Theme of the Pentateuch*, 106.

22. Quoting Jerome Bruner, "The Narrative Construction of Reality," *Critical Inquiry* 18 (1991): 11.

in the special revelation (17:1–8, 15–22; with the removal of Ishmael from the status of heir) and at the terebinths of Mamre (18:9–14) is followed by a contrast-parallel, namely, the destruction of Sodom and Gomorrah, and a setback, namely, the departure to Gerar (ch. 20) and the ensuing endangerment of Sarah. On the positive side is the recurrent restoration of property by means of the compensation by the foreign ruler, and the unharmed release of his wife. This well-known doublet of the Pharaoh tale (12:10–20) shows how narrative expansions are in keeping with the basic pattern.[23]

When the goal of the couple is finally achieved with the birth of Isaac, setbacks are encountered again. The expulsion of Hagar and her son Ishmael diminishes the household, even though they too are receivers of a divine promise (21:13–21). An even greater threat is the divine command to sacrifice Isaac as an "offering-up" (22:3), formulated as counterpoint to the initial command to Abraham to leave home and kindred in order to migrate to Canaan (12:1).[24] When this threat is repealed, the next setback is the death of Sarah (23:1–2), which is compensated by a gain in land, the acquisition of the Machpelah cave and the nearby fields (23:7–20). The Abraham narrative is concluded by the expedition of his servant slave to Haran, a reversal of the opening tale, in order to fetch Isaac a wife, who will complete the family.[25] Abraham's death is compensated for by the renewal of the family ties in the common burial by Isaac and Ishmael (25:9).

Thus the themes of wife, land, posterity, and property provide the cornerstones for the tales of Abraham and Sarah. Gain in one domain leads to reversal in another corner in a sustained alternation of achievement and setback within the symbolic household.

1.4 THE JACOB NARRATIVE

The Abraham narrative is followed by the tale of Rebecca's pregnancy and the promise of twins (25:8–10). This tale of achievement opens with a

---

23. This is not the place to explore the possibility that the relationship between the two narratives might be more complicated.

24. See Steinmetz, *Kinship, Conflict and Continuity*, 82–85; Clines, *The Theme of the Pentateuch*, 45.

25. Separatistic tendencies cannot provide the ultimate explanation for Abraham's decision to let Isaac marry a woman from his Haran family. After all, any woman from a region to the North, East, or South of Canaan would have fulfilled the condition of not marrying a woman from Canaan. Thus Abraham's marriage preferences still relate to the *bint 'amm*, the father's brother's daughter (24:48, with בת as granddaughter); see William Robertson Smith, *Kinship and Marriage in Early Arabia*, ed. S. A. Cock, 2nd edition (London: Black, 1903), 99–100, 123, 163–64.

setback, for Rebecca does not conceive until Isaac's prayer is answered (vv. 21-24). This opening, then, posits an initial parallel between Rebecca and Sarah. The birth of the twins poses a new problem, for they are immediately at conflict, when the second son holds the heel of his elder brother. Thus the Jacob narrative opens with achievement and threat intertwined. Jacob's endeavors to obtain the status of the firstborn though initially crowned with success (25:29-34; 27:18-29), are followed by a main setback, since he has to flee from Esau, and to stay with his mother's family at Haran (vv. 42-46). This pennyless flight involves land, property and wife (or in this case, his mother), but is offset by the divine promise at Bethel (28:13-15).

At Haran, however, Jacob's flight is balanced by his gain, as he is accepted by his mother's family, and is given two wives (with their slave girls),[26] who give birth to twelve sons and at least one daughter, Dinah. He also succeeds in amassing property (the herds; 30:32-43). Still, these gains are counterpoised by a setback: the need to leave his family when his material gains arouse their envy (31:1-2).[27] But this reversal is offset by Laban's acknowledgement of their mutual boundaries, a motif that is germane to the land theme. Moreover, the renewed encounter and reconciliation with his brother and the acquisition of fields near Shechem indicate completion (33:1-20).

At this juncture the symbolic household is in perfect balance: land, wives, posterity, and prosperity are all granted to Jacob. But once again the narrative continues with setbacks. Near Shechem his daughter Dinah elopes with or is violated and abducted by the son of the foreign leader, and the brutal interference of his sons who raid the city and kill off all its men, endangers his position over against his neighbors. The divine encouragement to move to Bethel (35:1) leads to a new achievement, the birth of Benjamin, which is, however, accompanied by a major loss with Rachel's death in childbirth (35:17-19).

The disruption of Jacob's family is almost final when his sons kidnap Joseph and sell him off to Egypt: the preferred son turns, albeit temporarily, into a slave. When the family is reunited, it is in Egypt (loss of land), and the

---

26. The sequence of gain and setback is at work again in the story of Jacob's marriages, since his wife turns out to be Leah, and he has to work an additional seven years for Rachel. Moreover, since his marriage to Rachel remains childless the themes of the narrative of Abraham and Sarah are taken up again.

27. I fail to discern "a close resemblance" (Carr, *Reading the Fractures of Genesis*, 213) between Jacob's separation from Laban and the migration theme in the Abraham narrative. The migration theme is presupposed in the Jacob tale, for Jacob's place in Laban's household is dependent on their family relationship. In the Abraham narrative the problem of childlessness relates to his sole wife, whereas in the Jacob tale only Rachel is affected.

final reconciliation between Joseph at his brothers follows only after Jacob's death in that country.

2. Narrative Platform and Oral-Epic Tradition

The Abraham-Jacob tales, then, are characterized by the recurrent alternation of gain and loss, where achievement is offset by reversal, and setback counterbalanced by success; by the mirror imaging of the two narratives; and by the repeated use of a limited repertoire of motifs: the movement between two countries, the childless wife, the competition of rival siblings and wives, the gracious or hostile foreign ruler, the position of servant and slave. This theme is continued by the Joseph tale. The sequence of cornerstones and recurring features entails a narrative coherence that goes far beyond the limitations of the small-scale tale and redactional adaptation, and actually demands the recognition of a large-scale epic platform, cognate to the Ugaritic narrative poems of Kirta and Aqhat.[28] In fact, as pointed out already by Klaus Koch and Claus Westermann, these poems share two themes with patriarchal narrative: the problem of a wife and descendants (Kirta), and the divine promise of posterity (Kirta and Aqhat); additional themes are bereavement (Kirta and Aqhat) and the rivalry of the siblings (Kirta).[29] In the Aqhat tale one also notes the theme of the divine visit (Gen 18).

However, the recognition of a platform of this kind does not imply literary unity, which is precluded by the doublets, internal contradictions (the age of Ishmael; Rachel's death), and undeniable stylistic differentiation.[30] In my view, the Abraham-Jacob narrative formed a narrative platform for various different narrators employing the *fabula* and, in the sphere of the *syuzhet*, certain features of its ordering, its narrative logic and its character presentation (as plot), together with traditional elements of the wording. In this vista, the various tales of Pentateuchal narrative in their present state or states, and the redactional layer, all form variants, continuations, or further developments/

---

28. On the remains of a similar text in Israelite Kuntillet ʿAjrud, see Erhard Blum, "Die Wandinschriften 4.2 und 4.6 sowie die Pithos-Inschrift 3.9 aus Kuntillet ʿAǧrūd," *ZDPV* 129 (2013): 21–54. This text uses the Phoenician script. A certain North Syrian association is suggested by the enigmatic vocable פבנה, best explained as reflecting Hurrian *pabn*, "mountain"; see ibid.," 26–27; P. K. McCarter, "Kuntillet ʿAjrud: Plaster Wall Inscription (2.47D)," *COS* 2.47:173.

29. Klaus Koch, "Die Sohnesverheißung an den Ugaritischen Daniel," *ZA* 58 (1967): 221; Westermann, *Promises to the Fathers*, 132–34, 167–80 (with detailed comparison of the narrative patterns).

30. Hence the status of this platform is not congruent with the G source proposed by David N. Freedman, "Pentateuch," *IDB* 3:714, following Noth.

expansions of the basic elements of the traditional *fabula*. The preservation of small-scale patterning, semantic fields and wording during the tradition process is demonstrated, for example, by the notion of "rest," which persists from the Babylonian deluge narrative until the biblical/postbiblical tradition of Noah, whose name means "rest." Another example is the role of the triad rock/water/wood in the Exodus narrative and the Elisha tales (2 Kgs 2:15–18, 19–22, 23–25).[31]

The basic platform of the Abraham-Jacob narrative was to a large extent defined by the oral performance. This much is implied by some of the characteristic features of language usage in this narrative in its present state.

3. Discourse Profile and Oral Substratum

3.1 Syntactic Features and Discourse Profile

The main argument for the idea of an oral background of patriarchal narrative in its present form is based on language usage to be analyzed by means of three main parameters:[32]

(1.) The number of explicit syntactic constituents (explicit lexicalized constituent, ELC) that are dependent immediately on the predicate: subject, direct/indirect object(s), modifiers (in so far as not implicit in prefix, affix or object/possessive suffix), such as, for example:

וַיָּסֻרוּ (1) אֵלָיו / וַיָּבֹאוּ (1) אֶל־בֵּיתוֹ / וַיַּעַשׂ (1) לָהֶם (2) מִשְׁתֶּה / (1) וּמַצּוֹת אָפָה / וַיֹּאכֵלוּ

So they turned in *to him* and came *into his house*; he made *them a supper* and baked *flat-cakes*, and they-ate (Gen 19:3)

(2.) The number of subordinate clauses: relative clauses, object, time clauses, etc., indicated by a hyphen:

וָאֹמַר אֵלֵכֶם בָּעֵת הַהִוא- לֵאמֹר / לֹא־אוּכַל לְבַדִּי- שְׂאֵת אֶתְכֶם

---

31. Frank H. Polak, "The Restful Waters of Noah: מי נח–מי מנחות," *JANES* 23 (1995): 70–71; idem, "Water, Rock and Wood: Structure and Thought Pattern in the Exodus Narrative," *JANES* 25 (1997): 40–42.

32. This method (very much a project in progress) is developed in detail in my articles "Sociolinguistics, a Key to the Typology and the Social Background of Biblical Hebrew," *Hebrew Studies* 47 (2006): 128–36, 141–51 and "The Book of Samuel and the Deuteronomist: A Syntactic-Stylistic Analysis," in *The Books of Samuel and the Deuteronomists,* ed. C. Schäfer-Lichtenberger, BWANT 188 (Stuttgart: Kohlhammer, 2010), 38–54.

Now I said to you at that time, *saying*: I am not able, I alone, *to carry you* (Deut 1:9)

(3.) The number of noun groups within a given constituent: construct state, noun with adjective attribute or apposition, junctions:

(18:7). שָׂרַי גְּבִרְתִּי, הָגָר שִׁפְחַת שָׂרַי (Gen 16:8), בֶּן־בָּקָר רַךְ וָטוֹב

Systematic analysis of segments including at least thirty clauses makes it possible to count the various categories and to establish their percentage in the text: short clauses (0–1 ELC), long clauses (2+ ELC), subordinate clauses, and mean noun groups (the number of all grouped nouns, divided by 2). In addition I count two particular categories:

(4.) The number of clauses that are either dependent on subordinate clauses, or contain two ELC's apart from the relative or a long noun phrase (indicated by an equal sign), for example,

וָאֲבָרֵךְ אֶת־יְהוָה .... אֲשֶׁר הִנְחַנִי [בְּדֶרֶךְ אֱמֶת] = לָקַחַת [אֶת־בַּת־אֲחִי אֲדֹנִי] לִבְנוֹ
Thus I blessed Yʜᴡʜ, God of my lord Abraham, who led me on the true journey *to take the daughter of my lord's brother for his son* (24:48)

(5.) Clauses containing 3 ELC's or more:

(1) [בְּכֶסֶף מָלֵא] יִתְּנֶנָּה (2) לִי (3) בְּתוֹכְכֶם (4) [לַאֲחֻזַּת־קָבֶר]
for the full silver worth let him give *me* it *in your midst for a burial holding.* (23:9)

The following pages offer a few examples for a stylistic analysis along these lines (partial quotes). For instance, in Gen 33:

1: וַיִּשָּׂא יַעֲקֹב עֵינָיו / וַיַּרְא / וְהִנֵּה עֵשָׂו בָּא / וְעִמּוֹ אַרְבַּע מֵאוֹת אִישׁ
Four clauses: three short / one long, one noun group (3 nouns)

2: וַיַּחַץ אֶת־הַיְלָדִים עַל־לֵאָה וְעַל־רָחֵל וְעַל שְׁתֵּי הַשְּׁפָחוֹת
One long clause, one noun group (4 nouns)

4: וַיָּרָץ עֵשָׂו לִקְרָאתוֹ / וַיְחַבְּקֵהוּ / וַיִּפֹּל עַל־צַוָּארָו / וַיִּשָּׁקֵהוּ / וַיִּבְכּוּ
Five clauses: four short / one long, no noun group

Counting the different clause types we indicate the relative frequency of each clause type within the unit at hand, and thus arrive at a discourse profile. The entire unit (Gen 33:1–17) includes seventy-two clauses, with forty-one short paratactic clauses (predicate only, or predicate with one explicit constituent, 57% of all clauses), and no more than eight subordinate clauses (around a tenth of all clauses, 11%). Noun groups are found in less than a third of all clauses (31%). The classes of complex hypotaxis and long clauses contain both less than ten percent of the text. This type of style may be characterized as the lean, brisk style (LBS).

A similar analysis of a segment in Deuteronomy (Deut 2:26–3:7) yields a very different picture:[33]

26: וָאֶשְׁלַח מַלְאָכִים מִמִּדְבַּר קְדֵמוֹת אֶל־סִיחוֹן מֶלֶךְ חֶשְׁבּוֹן דִּבְרֵי שָׁלוֹם־לֵאמֹר
Two clauses: one long+ , one subordinate, three noun groups (7 nouns)

3a: וַיִּתֵּן יְהוָה אֱלֹהֵינוּ בְּיָדֵנוּ גַּם אֶת־עוֹג מֶלֶךְ־הַבָּשָׁן וְאֶת־כָּל־עַמּוֹ
One clause, long+ , two noun groups (7 nouns)

3b: וַנַּכֵּהוּ עַד־בִּלְתִּי הִשְׁאִיר־לוֹ שָׂרִיד
Two clauses, one short, one in complex hypotaxis, no noun groups

4a: וַנִּלְכֹּד אֶת־כָּל־עָרָיו בָּעֵת הַהִוא
One clause, long, two noun groups (4 nouns)

4b: לֹא הָיְתָה קִרְיָה־אֲשֶׁר לֹא־לָקַחְנוּ מֵאִתָּם
Two clauses, one short, one subordinate, noun group including relative clause

4c: שִׁשִּׁים עִיר כָּל־חֶבֶל אַרְגֹּב מַמְלֶכֶת עוֹג בַּבָּשָׁן
One clause, short, one noun group (8 nouns)

In this tale, the class of short clauses (1–0 ELC) contains a third of all clauses (33–34%), like the class of subordinate clauses (30%). Almost all clauses (93%) contain a noun group. Nearly a quarter of the text consists of clauses in complex subordination (22–23%); the class of long clauses includes more than ten percent of all clauses. This is the intricate, elaborate style (IES). The differences between this style and LBS can be illustrated by the following scheme:

Gen 33:1–17: short clauses – *more than half* of all clauses (56%)
Deut 2:26–3:7: " " – *a third* of the text (34%)
Gen 33:1–17: subordinate clauses – *a tenth* of the text (11%)

---

33. A detailed analysis of a number of Deuteronomistic units is offered in my articles "Samuel and the Deuteronomist," 42–48, 57–63 and "Language Variation, Discourse Typology, and the Socio-Cultural Background of Biblical Narrative," in *Diachrony in Biblical Hebrew,* ed. Cynthia L. Miller-Naudé and Ziony Zevit (Winona Lake, IN: Eisenbrauns, 2012), 301–38 (324–5).

ORAL SUBSTRATUM, LANGUAGE USAGE, AND THEMATIC FLOW 229

Deut 2:26–3:7: " " – *a third* of the text (31%)
Gen 33:1–17: noun groups – *less than a third* of the text (23%)
Deut 2:26–3:7: " " – *almost all* clauses (94%)[34]

3.2 The Discourse Profile of the Abraham-Jacob Narrative

The Abraham narrative reveals a clear inclination to the LBS.[35] In many tales in this cycle, more than half of all clauses belong to the category of short clauses (0–1 ELC): the tale of the terebinths at Mamre (Gen 18:1–15);[36] the Sodom narrative (Gen 19:1–22);[37] Hagar's flight (Gen 16; 21:7–21);[38] large sections of the tale of Abraham's servant (Gen 24:22–67; unlike vv. 1–21, IES);[39] the tale of Isaac's binding (Gen 22:1–19);[40] the narrative of the divine promise to Abraham and Sara (Gen 17:1–8, 15–21; the sections on the circumcision represent IES).[41] This is the Type 1 style (48–60% short clauses). A second class contains the tales in which the class of short clauses contains slightly less than half of the text (Type 2; 39–47%): the tale of Abraham's migration (Gen 12:1–9),[42] the two tales of the endangerment of Sarah (Gen 12:10–20, 20:1–18),[43] and the narrative of the covenant between the pieces (Gen 15:1–12, 17–18).[44]

An unequivocal intricate style characterizes the tales of Abraham's separation from Lot (Gen 13:1–17)[45] and his agreement with Abimelech

---

34. Complex hypotaxis in Gen 33: 5–6%; in Deut 2–3: 23%; long + clauses (3+ ELC): Gen 33: 7%, as against Deut 2–3: 12%.

35. In the Abraham cycle the units in the type 1 style include 1520 content words (nouns, verbs, adjectives, numerals, adverbs), and the type 2 class 431 content words. The IES class includes 1104 content words (268 in Gen 13; 21; this count was performed on Accordance 10.3.3; OakTree Software; www.accordancebible.com, 2013).

36. Gen 18:1–15 (61 clauses): 0–1 ELC 60%; hypotaxis 14%; noun phrases 28%.

37. Gen 19:1–22 (115 clauses): 0–1 ELC 52%; hypotaxis 19%; noun phrases 28%.

38. Gen 16:1–2, 4–12 (48 clauses): 0–1 ELC 56%; hypotaxis 6%; noun phrases 35%; 21:7–21 (68 clauses): 0–1 ELC 51.5%; hypotaxis 12%; noun phrases 38%.

39. Gen 24:22–23, 50–67 (121 clauses): 0–1 ELC 64%; hypotaxis 11–12%; noun phrases 40%; 24:34–49 (72 clauses): 0–1 ELC 51%; hypotaxis 21%; noun phrases 37–38%.

40. Gen 22:1–19 (87 clauses): 0–1 ELC 48%; hypotaxis 10%; noun phrases 39%.

41. Gen 17:1–8, 15–21 (55 clauses): 0–1 ELC 58%; hypotaxis 7%; noun phrases 64%.

42. Gen 12:1–9 (37 clauses): 0–1 ELC 43%; hypotaxis 21.5%; noun phrases 42. This unit would merit further analysis, although it seems too small for more refinement.

43. Gen 12:10–20 (39 clauses): 0–1 ELC 46%; hypotaxis 18%; noun phrases 38–39%; 20:1–18 (75 clauses): 45%; hypotaxis 15%; noun phrases 52%.

44. Gen 15:1–12, 17–18 (52 clauses): 0–1 ELC 46%; hypotaxis 19%; noun phrases 45%.

45. Gen 13:1–17 (54 clauses): 0–1 ELC 37%; hypotaxis 28%; noun phrases 70%; 3+

concerning the wells (Gen 21:22–32),[46] as well as the tale of the Machpelah cave (Genesis 23; "P"),[47] and the opening of the tale of Abraham's servant (Gen 24:1–21; vv. 22–67 represent LBS).[48] The tale of Abraham "the Hebrew" as a warrior (Gen 14:1–24) is characterized by the mixture of LBS features (the frequency of short clauses) and features that fit IES (the high frequency of noun groups and subordinate clauses).[49] It is difficult to decide whether this blend is due to attempts at imitiation of the dominant style in the overall narrative, or to revision of a LBS tale. However, since it seems hardly possible to extract a tale in LBS, the assumption of partial imitation seems preferable. On the other hand, the tale of the mission of Abraham's servant (Genesis 24) reveals clear traces of a revision in IES. The high incidence of noun phrases also stands out in the short section of Abraham's death and burial (Gen 25:1–12).[50]

A similar profile is revealed by the Jacob narratives.[51] One notes a number of tales in the type 1 style: the tales of Isaac's blessing and the encounter with Esau (Gen 25:29–34; 27; 33);[52] the tale of Jacob at the Jabbok (Gen 32:25–32);[53] the encounter with Rachel and Jacob's flight (Genesis 29, 31).[54] Other tales reveal a type 2 style: the dream theophany at Bethel (Genesis 28) and Jacob's prayer (Genesis 32);[55] the agreement with

---

ELC 15%.

46. Gen 21:22–32 (35 clauses): 0–1 ELC 31–32%; hypotaxis 29%; noun phrases 43%; 3+ ELC 14%.

47. Gen 23:1–16, 19–20 (56 clauses): 0–1 ELC 27%; hypotaxis 23%; noun phrases 83%; 3+ ELC 21–22%.

48. Gen 24:1–21 (90 clauses): 0–1 ELC 32%; hypotaxis 30%; noun phrases 44%; 3+ ELC 18%.

49. Gen 14:1–12 (32 clauses): 0–1 ELC 56%; hypotaxis 6%; noun phrases 137.5%; vv. 13–24 (41 clauses): 0–1 ELC 44%; hypotaxis 22%; noun phrases 78%.

50. The section of 25:1–12 (19 clauses) is too short for reliable analysis, and may represent different layers; vv. 5–12 represent the dominant genealogical framework ("P"). The Isaac tales (26:1–33) reveal a mixture of types 1–2; the tales of Judah and Tamar and the kidnapping of Joseph (37:4–21, 22–36; 38:1–11) represent type 1.

51. In the Jacob cycle the type 1 class includes 985, and the type 2 class 707 content words. The IES class comprises 559 content words.

52. Gen 27:18–26, 30–38 (95 clauses): 0–1 ELC 62%; hypotaxis 8.5%; noun phrases 30.5%; 33:1–13 (41 clauses): 0–1 ELC 57%; hypotaxis 11%; noun phrases 31%; Gen 25:29–34 (23 clauses only): 0–1 ELC 52.17%; hypotaxis 4.35%; noun phrases 13.04%.

53. Gen 32:25–32 (37 clauses): 0–1 ELC 57%; hypotaxis 13.5%; noun phrases 30.

54. Gen 29:9–35 (106 clauses): 0–1 ELC 53%; hypotaxis 10%; noun phrases 40%; 31:4–16 (53 clauses): 0–1 ELC 53%; hypotaxis 24.5%; noun phrases 53%.

55. Gen 28:10–22 (58 clauses): 0–1 ELC 46.5%; hypotaxis 26%; noun phrases 41%; complex hypotaxis 15.5%; 32:2–24 (86 clauses): 0–1 ELC 42%; hypotaxis 26%; noun phrases 40%; complex hypotaxis 20%.

Laban (Genesis 31),[56] and the birth tales.[57] By contrast, we encounter IES in the tales of Jacob's blessing before his departure (Gen 28:1–9),[58] Dinah at Shechem (Genesis 34),[59] and the episode of Jacob's magic (Gen 30:32–43).[60]

4. Sociocultural Background and Historical Context

Previous research has resulted in the insight that the IES is largely characteristic of narrative in the Deuteronomic/Deuteronomistic corpus, including the Jeremiah *Vita* (Judean corpus), and the narratives from the Persian era (Persian corpus). Like the patriarchal narrative, the Samuel-Saul-David cycle and the tales of Elijah-Elisha (together forming the Classical corpus) are largely characterized by the LBS.[61]

Analysis in terms of the median yields the following scheme:[62]

Class. Corpus (Type 1; 25 units):	Short Clauses: *more than a half* of the text (56%)
(Type 2, 21 units):	" ": *less than a half* of all clauses (44%)
Judean Corpus (21 units):	" ": *less than a third* of all clauses (30–31%)
Persian Era (17 units):	" ": *less than a third* of all clauses (30–31%)
Class. Corpus (Type 1):	All Hypotaxis: *slightly more than a tenth* (11%)
Class. Corpus (Type 2):	" ": More than a tenth (14–15%)
Judean Corpus:	" ": Almost a third (28–29%)
Persian Era:	" ": Almost a third (29–30%)
Class. Corpus (Type 1)	Noun Groups: *less than a half* of all clauses (42%)
Class. Corpus (Type 2):	" ": less than a half of all clauses (42%)
Judean Corpus	" ": almost all clauses (87%)
Persian Era	" ": almost all clauses (86–87%)

A massive differentiation of this kind demands systematic explanation.[63] Common sense and literary intuition suggest that stylistic variety is a matter

---

56. Gen 31:45–54 (36 clauses): 0–1 ELC 44.5%; hypotaxis 11%; noun phrases 41.5%.
57. Gen 30:1–24 (88 clauses): 0–1 ELC 40%; hypotaxis 9%; noun phrases 27%.
58. Gen 28:1–9 (31 clauses): 0–1 ELC 22.5%; hypotaxis 35.5%; noun phrases 84%.
59. Gen 34:1–17 (67 clauses): 0–1 ELC 34%; hypotaxis 27%; noun phrases 36%; vv. 18–31 (49 clauses): ELC 0–1 34.5%; hypotaxis 22.5%; noun phrases 87%.
60. Gen 30:32–43 (71 clauses): 0–1 ELC 38%; hypotaxis 25.5%; noun phrases 58.5.
61. See Polak, "Language Variation, Discourse Typology," 302–4, 310–12.
62. All figures relate to the median, that is to say, the middle value of the data set: half of the data appears above the median and half below the median. Thus the median of 1, 17, 22, 36, and 45 is 22. In a set that consists of an even number of values, the median is the arithmetic mean of the two middle values. The units counted represent the four thematic groups mentioned in the next paragraph (see notes 65 and 66 below).
63. For complex hypotaxis the figures are: Type 1: 3–4%; Type 2: 6–7%; Judean

of free rhetorical design.[64] This assumption, however, is a hypothesis, to be validated by testing. Thus I have analyzed more than eighty units in four different thematic groups with diverging expressive content and rhetoric stance: Cultic/Festive Meal; Anointment/Public Honor; Battle Account; Prophetic/Religious Discourse.[65] The hypothesis of free literary design entails free variation along the different corpora and rhetorical preferences according to theme. However, the actual picture is quite different:

1. Within the Judean and the Persian corpora all four thematic groups are dominated by IES.
2. All four thematic groups in the Medial corpus are for more than eighty percent characterized by LBS.

Generally speaking, then, the variation between the LBS and IES is largely connected to corpus rather than to theme (apart from minor variation).[66] In view of the differences in expressive content and rhetoric of the four themes discussed, we can only conclude that in the large majority of cases our differentiation is not a matter of free literary design. The wide range of this variation suggests societal rather than individual distinctions.

The proposed LBS/IES distinction fits a cardinal differentiation in language usage: LBS manifests some of the basic features of spontaneous spoken language, whereas IES in its intricacy is representative of written discourse.[67] The IES demands considerable skill in the design of intricate, elaborate sentences and paragraphs, and thus an advanced scribal education, an expert scribal chancery, and consequently a developed bureaucracy, as witnessed in the Lachish and Arad ostraca and the widespread use of aniconic seals in the seventh century.[68] Quite a different sociocultural context

---

Corpus: 15–16%; Persian Era 18–19%; and for long + clauses (3+ ELC): Type 1: 8–9%; Type 2: 7–8%; Judean Corpus: 13–14%; Persian Era: 12–13%.

64. Susan Niditch, "Epic and History in the Hebrew Bible: Definitions, 'Ethnic Genres,' and the Challenges of Cultural Identity in the Biblical Book of Judges," in *Epic and History*, ed. David Konstan and Kurt A. Raaflaub (Oxford: Blackwell, 2010), 91; Ian M. Young, Robert Rezetko, and Martin Ehrensvärd, *Linguistic Dating of Biblical Texts: An Introduction to Approaches and Problems*, 2 volumes (London: Equinox, 2008), 2:83.

65. Polak, "Sociolinguistics, a Key," 134–48; "Samuel and the Deuteronomist," 54–59, 70–73.

66. On the literary-pragmatic aspects of such variation see my remarks in "Samuel and the Deuteronomist," 58–60.

67. The cross-cultural, cross-linguistic work of Wallace Chafe, Michael Halliday, Douglas Biber, Jim Miller, and Regina Weinert (and others) is discussed in my articles, "Sociolinguistics, a Key," 136–40; "Samuel and the Deuteronomist," 61–67.

68. Polak, "Language Variation, Discourse Typology," 323–27; "Sociolinguistics, a Key," 137, with further references.

is presupposed by LBS. In its resemblance to spontaneous spoken discourse, this style reveals a strong proximity to orally performed poetry and narrative. In other words, if the IES narratives represent the scribal chancery, LBS tales adhere to the habitus of the oral performance, by way of "oral-derived literature."[69] The sociocultural aspect of the distinction has led me to the conclusion that the use of LBS mostly represents the period before the full development of the scribal chancery and the royal bureaucracy at the end of the eighth century BCE.[70]

5. From Oral Performance to Scribal Desk

5.1 The Oral/Written Interface in Patriarchal Narrative

If the stylistic differentiation in patriarchal narrative represents crucial differences in cultural and historical background, we have to raise the question how these different styles interrelate within the narrative. Three avenues seem to be of interest: literary design, stylistic profile, and redaction process.

The tale of the terebinths at Mamre (Gen 18:1–15) imposes a dual perspective. The mythic theme of a divine visit to a human king is represented by the Ugaritic tale of Aqhat, whose father receives the god of handicraft, Kothar-waKhasis, at a festive meal, and is given a bow and arrows as present for his son. In the tale of Mamre the gift is the promise of a son (a promise that in the Ugaritic tale was realized by the birth of Aqhat). In both tales the host's wife plays a central role. In Genesis 18, the wording contains a series of epic formulae: וַיִּשָּׂא עֵינָיו וַיַּרְא ("he lifted his eyes and saw"; 18:2a); וַיִּשְׁתַּחוּ אָרְצָה ("he bowed down to the earth"; v. 2b); וַיִּקַּח (בֶּן־בָּקָר רַךְ וָטוֹב) (אֶל־הַנַּעַר) וַיִּתֵּן ("*he took* a calf, tender and choice, and *gave* it to a servant-boy; v. 7); וַיִּקַּח חֶמְאָה וְחָלָב ... וַיִּתֵּן לִפְנֵיהֶם ("*he took curds and milk* ... and *set these before them*"; v. 8a); וַיִּתֵּן לִפְנֵיהֶם ... וַיֹּאכֵלוּ ("he set these before them ... and they ate"; v. 8b). In particular one notes the consecutive repetition of

---

69. Quoting John M. Foley, *The Singer of Tales in Performance* (Bloomington, IN: Indiana University Press, 1995), 137–43.

70. Polak, "Sociolinguistics, a Key," 149–59; "Samuel and the Deuteronomist," 63–70; "Language Variation, Discourse Typology," 315–18, 322–24. As I have argued earlier (ibid., 325–26), the thesis that the LBS texts were composed in the seventh century or later entails strong assumptions concerning the author's sociocultural indentity. According to such hypothesis the author would have positioned himself as an adept of the oral, nonliterate arena. He would have passed up recognition as an expert scribe belonging or closely connected to the prestigious scribal chancery (or the cultic center) and the official administration.

לקח–נתן ("give"–"take/set") in verses 7–8.[71] Moreover, the syntactic-stylistic profile of the entire tale is high on the LBS scale, with 60% short clauses and 28% clauses containing noun groups. This combination of mythic theme, formulaic language, and discourse profile in one single unit demonstrates close links with the oral arena.

But the oral platform is only one aspect of this tale. On the other hand, the mythic character of the hospitality theme is thoroughly dimmed by concealment of the wayfarers' identity. Only during the dialogue does the narrator reveal the identity of the divine speaker, without, however, indicating his location (v. 13), while an actual divine presence is entailed when "Abraham was still standing before YHWH" (v. 22). Here the mythic theme is integrated within a system that recoils from the mythic worldview and thus implies a profoundly hybridic literary culture.[72] In the tale of Isaac's binding, formulaic language appears in almost every verse, while its hybridity is revealed by the complex dialectics of mention/rejection of the idea of human sacrifice.

Such cultural hybridity likewise stands out in other narratives, such as the tales of Hagar's encounter with the divine messenger (Genesis 16, 21), and the tale of Jacob's struggle near the Jabbok (32:25–32). Magic working, crucial for the tale of Jacob's herds (30:32–43), is relativized by his account of his dreams (31:10–12), without however entirely losing its power. Similar notions come to light in the tale of Jacob's blessing by Isaac, which hinges on the presupposition that the blessing is effective in its own right.

Tales of type 2 may basically reflect the activity of writing narrators adhering to the oral habitus without abandoning the scribal world. Among the Jacob tales one notes, for instance, the tale of the revelation at Bethel, and the tales of the birth of his children. Hybridity shows in the episode of Jacob's agreement with Laban, which does not refrain from the mention of Nahor's god near "the god of Abraham" (Gen 31:53). By the same token, the Abraham narrative features the mythic-magic "smoking oven, and a flaming torch that passed between the pieces" (Gen 15:17).

---

71. On Genesis 18 see also Polak, "Sociolinguistics, a Key," 141–42; on formulaic language see my article, "Linguistic and Stylistic Aspects of Epic Formulae in Ancient Semitic Poetry and Biblical Narrative," in *Biblical Hebrew in Its Northwest Semitic Setting,* ed. Steven E. Fassberg and Avi Hurvitz (Jerusalem: Magnes; Winona Lake, IN: Eisenbrauns, 2006), 286, n. 9.

72. Polak, "Language Variation, Discourse Typology," 323–24, with further references. Residues of ancient Israelite hybridity are studied by Mark S. Smith, *The Memoirs of God: History, Memory, and the Experience of the Divine in Ancient Israel* (Minneapolis: Augsburg Fortress, 2004); Ziony Zevit, *The Religions of Ancient Israel: A Synthesis of Parallactic Approaches* (London: Continuum, 2001), 586–609, 646–90.

A few episodes are set in the intricate style, placing them in the Judean corpus (lacking features that would point to the Persian era).[73] This class unsurprisingly includes the tale of Abraham's war with the four kings (Genesis 14) and two texts attributed, by consensus, to "P": the tales of the acquisition of the Machpelah cave (Genesis 23), and of Abraham's burial (Gen 25:5–12). In addition one notes the tale of Abraham's separation from Lot (Genesis 13), which indeed has sometimes been described as a redactional combination of various different narrative features.[74] Thus the present elaboration of this tale represents the Judean framework. Jacob tales belonging to this stratum are found in, for instance, the tale of Dinah and the massacre at Shechem (Genesis 34) with its separatist presuppositions, and the episode of Jacob's blessing before his departure to Haran ("P"; 28:1–9).

Redactional intervention in a LBS narrative seems obvious in the case of the tale of the mission of Abraham's servant.[75] The language of the opening of this tale (24:1–21) is far more complex than the style of its continuation (vv. 22–67). The servant's oath gesture, placing his hands under Abraham's thigh (vv. 2, 9; similarly 47:29), still points, in my view, to a basic cultural hybridity,[76] which was adapted to the later Judean framework. Probably, then, the present state of this tale represents redactional revision of a traditional version.

5.2 THE NEXUS: ORAL PERFORMANCE AND SCRIBAL DESK

Thus the relationship between the written text and the oral arena involves particular intricacies. In view of the crucial distinctions in cultural tradition and social position between this performance and scribal activity the relationship between these activities is to be described as a complex nexus, always subject to the creative input of the singers and narrators in the oral arena and writers of tales in the compositional arena. When the style is extremely close to spoken discourse, one could envision a direct connection, for instance dictation by the singer/narrator.[77] Albert Lord envisions a "transitional text"

---

73. The Aramaic lexemes which Rendsburg found in the Jacob-Laban tales do not represent the administrative register characteristic of the Persian corpus; see Gary Rendsburg, "Linguistic Variation and the "Foreign" Factor in the Hebrew Bible," *IOS* 15 (1995), 182–83; Polak, "Sociolinguistics, a Key," 119–27.

74. Gunkel, *Genesis*, 176–77.

75. On the use of dromedary camels in the last third of the tenth century see now Lidar Sapir-Hen and Erez Ben-Yosef, "The Introduction of Domestic Camels to the Southern Levant: Evidence from the Aravah Valley," *TA* 40 (2013): 277–85.

76. See Meir Malul, "Touching the Sexual Organs as an Oath Ceremony in an Akkadian Letter," *VT* 37 (1987): 491–92.

77. James A. Notopoulos, "Homer and Cretan Heroic Poetry," *AJP* 73 (1952): 229;

composed by the oral narrator himself,[78] or by a writing narrator who was extremely well acquainted with the oral performance of the narrative that he recreated in writing (primary orality/ secondary entextualization).[79]

If the style is less close to orality (in particular in the type 2 style), the connection probably is less direct, for instance when the writing narrator employs the oral style in general, without dependence on a specific performance.[80] But even then we should endeavor not to lose sight of the oral arena at the background. The speaking voice should still be audible and the performer's gesture must remain imaginable if not visible. A significant distance from the oral performance is implied by redactional revision, elaboration or abridgement of narratives reflecting the oral habitus, as demonstrated in, for example, Genesis 13, 24, and 32. No such connection is involved in scribal continuation, elaboration, and reformulation of themes that ultimately originated in the oral world,[81] as found, for example, in the narrative sections of Deuteronomy (primary scribality).

References

Amodio, Mark C. *Writing the Oral Tradition*. Notre Dame, IN: University of Notre Dame Press, 2004.

Blum, Erhard. "Die Wandinschriften 4.2 und 4.6 sowie die Pithos-Inschrift 3.9 aus Kuntillet 'Ağrūd," *ZDPV* 129 (2013): 21–54.

Bruner, Jerome. "The Narrative Construction of Reality," *Critical Inquiry* 18 (1991): 1–21.

Carr, David M. *Reading the Fractures of Genesis: Historical and Literary Approaches*. Louisville: Westminster John Knox, 1996.

Clines, David J. A. *The Theme of the Pentateuch*. JSOTSup 10. Sheffield: Sheffield Academic Press, 1978.

Dégh, Linda. *Folktales & Society: Story-Telling in a Hungarian Peasant Community*. Bloomington, IN: Indiana University Press, 1989.

Finnegan, Ruth. *Oral Poetry: Its Nature, Significance and Social Context*. Cambridge: Cambridge University Press, 1977

Susan Niditch, *Oral World and Written Word: Ancient Israelite Literature* (Louisville: Westminster John Knox, 1996), 117–21.

78. The role of the singer-poet/prince-bishop Pjetar Njegoš (1813–51) is discussed by Albert B. Lord, *The Singer Resumes the Tale*, ed. Mary Louise Lord (Ithaca: Cornell University Press, 1995), 233–35.

79. Niditch, *Oral World and Written Word*, 120–22. On the oral-like historical narrative of Andrija Kačić's history (1756) see Lord, *The Singer Resumes*, 225–33; the Old/Middle English context is discussed by Mark C. Amodio, *Writing the Oral Tradition* (Notre Dame, IN: University of Notre Dame Press, 2004), 27–32.

80. Niditch, *Oral World and Written Word*, 125–27.

81. See in particular Amodio, *Writing the Oral Tradition*, 188–202.

Foley, John M. *The Singer of Tales in Performance*. Bloomington, IN: Indiana University Press, 1995.
Fox, Everett. *The Five Books of Moses*. New York: Schocken, 1995.
Freedman, David N. "Pentateuch." *IDB* 3:711–27.
Grigson, Caroline. "Camels, Copper and Donkeys in the Early Iron Age in the Southern Levant: Timna Revisited," *Levant* 44 (2012): 82–100.
Hallo, William W. and K. Lawson Younger, eds. *The Context of Scripture: Canonical Compositions from the Biblical World*. 3 volumes. Leiden: Brill, 1997–2002.
Hermann Gunkel. *Genesis*. 3rd edition. HKAT I/1. Göttingen: Vandenhoeck & Ruprecht, 1910.
———. "Jacob." Pages 150–86 in *What Remains of the Old Testament*. Trans. A. K. Dallas. London: Allen & Unwin, 1928.
Henssen, Gottfried. *Überlieferung und Persönlichkeit: Die Erzählungen und Lieder des Egbert Gerrits*. Münster, Westfalen: Aschendorff, 1951.
Koch, Klaus. "Die Sohnesverheißung an den Ugaritischen Daniel," *ZA* 58 (1967): 211–21.
Lord, Albert Bates. *The Singer Resumes the Tale*. Edited by Mary Louise Lord. Ithaca: Cornell University Press, 1995.
Malul, Meir. "Touching the Sexual Organs as an Oath Ceremony in an Akkadian Letter," *VT* 37 (1987): 491–92.
Niditch, Susan. *Oral World and Written Word: Ancient Israelite Literature*. Louisville: Westminster John Knox, 1996.
———. "Epic and History in the Hebrew Bible: Definitions, "Ethnic Genres," and the Challenges of Cultural Identity in the Biblical Book of Judges." Pages 86–102 in *Epic and History*. Edited by David Konstan and Kurt A. Raaflaub. Oxford: Blackwell, 2010.
Niles, John D., *Homo Narrans: The Poetics and Anthropology of Oral Literature*. Philadelphia: University of Pennsylvania Press, 1999.
Notopoulos, James A. "Homer and Cretan Heroic Poetry." *AJP* 73 (1952): 225–50.
Okpewho, Isidore, *The Epic in Africa: Toward a Poetics of the Oral Performance*. New York: Columbia University Press, 1975.
Polak, Frank H. "The Book of Samuel and the Deuteronomist: A Syntactic-Stylistic Analysis." Pages 34–73 in *The Books of Samuel and the Deuteronomists*. Edited by Christa Schäfer-Lichtenberger. BWANT 188. Stuttgart: Kohlhammer, 2010.
———. "Language Variation, Discourse Typology, and the Socio-Cultural Background of Biblical Narrative." Pages 301–38 in *Diachrony in Biblical Hebrew*. Edited by Cynthia L. Miller-Naudé and Ziony Zevit. Winona Lake, IN: Eisenbrauns, 2012.
———. "Linguistic and Stylistic Aspects of Epic Formulae in Ancient Semitic Poetry and Biblical Narrative," Pages 285–304 in *Biblical Hebrew in Its Northwest Semitic Setting*. Edited by Steven E. Fassberg and Avi Hurvitz. Jerusalem: Magnes; Winona Lake, IN: Eisenbrauns, 2006.
———. "The Restful Waters of Noah: מי נח–מי מנחות." *JANES* 23 (1995): 69–74.
———. "Sociolinguistics, a Key to the Typology and the Social Background of Biblical Hebrew." *Hebrew Studies* 47 (2006): 115–62.
———. "Water, Rock and Wood: Structure and Thought Pattern in the Exodus Narrative." *JANES* 25 (1997): 19–42.

Polzin, Robert. "The Ancestress of Israel in Danger," *Semeia* 3 (1975): 81–98.
Rendsburg, Gary. "Linguistic Variation and the "Foreign" Factor in the Hebrew Bible," *IOS* 15 (1995): 177–90
Rendtorff, Rolf. *The Problem of the Process of Transmission in the Pentateuch*. Translated by John J. Scullion. JSOTSup 89. Sheffield: Sheffield Academic Press, 1990.
Sapir-Hen, Lidar and Erez Ben-Yosef. "The Introduction of Domestic Camels to the Southern Levant: Evidence from the Aravah Valley," *TA* 40 (2013), 277–85.
Shklovsky, Viktor. *Theory of Prose*. Translated by B. Sher. Elmswood Park, IL: Dalkey Archive, 1991.
Smith, William Robertson. *Kinship and Marriage in Early Arabia*. Edited by S. A. Cook. 2nd edition. London: Black, 1903.
Smith, Mark S. *The Memoirs of God: History, Memory, and the Experience of the Divine in Ancient Israel*. Minneapolis: Augsburg Fortress, 2004.
———. "Biblical Narrative between Ugaritic and Akkadian Literature. Part I: Ugarit and the Hebrew Bible: Consideration of Comparative Research," *RB* 114 (2007): 5–29.
Steinberg, Naomi. *Kinship and Marriage in Genesis: A Household Economics Perspective*. Minneapolis; Fortress, 1993.
Steinmetz, Devora. *Kinship, Conflict and Continuity in Genesis*. Louisville: Westminster John Knox Press, 1991.
Teugels, Lieve M. *Bible and Midrash: The Story of 'The Wooing of Rebekah.'* Leuven: Peeters, 2004.
Vrolijk, Paul. *Jacob's Wealth: An Examination into the Nature and Role of Material Possessions in the Jacob-Cycle (Gen 25:19–35:29)*. VTSup 146. Leiden: Brill, 2011.
Westermann, Claus. *The Promises to the Fathers*. Translated by David E. Green. Philadelphia: Fortress, 1980.
Willi-Plein, Ina. "Genesis 27 als Rebekkageschichte." *ThZ* 45 (1989): 315–44.
Young, Ian M., Robert Rezetko, and Martin Ehrensvärd. *Linguistic Dating of Biblical Texts: An Introduction to Approaches and Problems*. 2 volumes. London: Equinox, 2008.
Zevit, Ziony. *The Religions of Ancient Israel: A Synthesis of Parallactic Approaches*. London: Continuum, 2001.

Royal Letters and Torah Scrolls: The Place of Ezra-Nehemiah in Scholarly Narratives of Scripturalization

Elsie STERN

SINCE THE LATE NINETEENTH CENTURY, IF NOT BEFORE, SCRIPTURALIZATION has been a key theme in scholarly narratives regarding the development of Judaism. Since Wellhausen's *Prolegomena to the History of Ancient Israel*, the emergence of torah as scripture is understood to be one of the defining turning points in the journey from ancient Israelite religion to classical Judaism. While the exact characterizations of scripture vary from scholar to scholar, the following aspects are most relevant to the subject of this volume:[1]

- A shift from a predominantly oral modality to a primarily written one. In prescriptural economies, most culturally significant material is transmitted orally. Once cultures become scriptural, writing becomes the primary mode of transmission for authoritative material.
- A shift in the locus of primary authority from venerated teachers to texts. In prescriptural economies, prophets, priests, elders, and other authorities are the understood to be the transmitters and brokers of culturally authoritative material even when the ultimate source of that material is understood to be God or figures from the mythic past. In a scriptural economy, the text itself is understood to be the primary source of authority.
- A shift in the locus of creativity from composition to interpretation. In prescriptural economies, newly composed material can become

---

1. For representative examples, see William Schniedewind, *How the Bible Became a Book* (Cambridge: Cambridge University Press, 2004), 179–90; Karel van der Toorn, *Scribal Culture and the Making of the Hebrew Bible* (Cambridge, MA: Harvard University Press, 2007), 227–32.

part of the primary cultural patrimony. In scriptural economies, the primary sources are closed and subsequent literary-theological creativity takes the form of interpretation of the preexistent, closed, scripture.

The book of Ezra-Nehemiah in general, and the character of Ezra in particular have played starring roles in these scholarly narratives of scripturalization. Since at least the fifth century CE, the character of Ezra has been identified with Judaism's identity as a scriptural religion. The Babylonian Talmud identifies Ezra as a second Moses who restored torah to Israel after the exile.[2] The identification was reiterated in a far less laudatory key by Wellhausen, who identified Ezra with the transition from prophetic ethical charisma to priestly legalism.[3] The identification persists among scholars who vehemently reject Wellhausen's ideological perspective but continue to identify Ezra with the emergence of Judaism as a scriptural religion. In 1985, Michael Fishbane wrote, that under Ezra's leadership, "the returning 'community of the exile' was formed with Torah and its exegesis at its living centre."[4] More recently, Juha Pakkala wrote:

> The author of Neh 8 may represent an entirely new position in relation to orality and literacy in the divine tradition. He implies that the exact will of God can be found in the physical book, in the written words that have divine authority. God's will would now be bound to the written word more clearly than in the past.[5]

It is not surprising that Ezra-Nehemiah (hereafter, E–N) figures prominently in these narratives. The representation of torah in E–N is markedly different from its portrayal elsewhere in the Hebrew Bible. First, physical texts of torah figure prominently in the book. They are venerated, recited, cited and studied. Second, the contents of these scrolls have the force

---

2. b. Sanh. 21b; b. Suk. 20a.

3. Julius Wellhausen, *Prolegomena to the History of Ancient Israel*, trans. J. S. Black and A. Menzies (Cleveland: World Publishing, 1957), 404–9.

4. Michael Fishbane, *Biblical Interpretation in Ancient Israel* (Oxford: Clarendon, 1985), 114; See also Joseph Blenkinsopp, *Ezra-Nehemiah* (Philadelphia: Westminster, 1988), 139; Lester Grabbe, *Ezra-Nehemiah* (London: Routledge, 1998), 150; James Watts, "Using Ezra's Time as a Methodological Pivot for Understanding the Rhetoric and Functions of the Pentateuch," in *The Pentateuch: International Perspectives on Current Research*, ed. Thomas B. Dozeman, Konrad Schmid and Baruch J. Schwarz (Tübingen: Mohr Siebeck, 2011), 489–506.

5. Juha Pakkala, *Ezra the Scribe: The Development of Ezra 7–10 and Nehemia 8* (Berlin: de Gruyter, 2004), 278–79.

of imperially sanctioned law (Ezra 7:12–26).[6] Third, the protagonists in the book are presented as teachers and cultural transmitters who engage intensely with written scrolls of the law. Finally, as I will discuss at length below, there are notable discrepancies between E–N's laws and those found in extant pentateuchs. These discrepancies have been largely understood as evidence of interpretation—an activity at the heart of classical Judaism. These peculiarities have generated the identification of E–N as a watershed text in the history of scripturalization.

The integration of insights from the fields of orality and textuality into the field of biblical studies invites us to reconsider this identification. As the other essays in this volume attest, this integration has led to significant revisions of regnant narratives regarding the composition and transmission of the Hebrew Bible and the relationship between orality and textuality in these processes.[7] Most notably for my purposes is the change in our understanding of the role of written texts in largely illiterate societies, like that of Judea in the Persian and Hellenistic periods. Before the integration of insights from orality studies, it was assumed that orality and literacy were chronologically sequential modalities and that at some point in the history of literate cultures, writing replaced speaking as the primary mode of cultural production and transmission and reading replaced hearing as the primary mode of reception. According to this model, it was assumed that engagement with written texts of scripture replaced oral engagement and transmission at some point in early Judaism. However, it is now clear that in societies with low rates of literacy (like Judea in the Persian, Hellenistic, and Roman periods), the primary mode of cultural production is not exclusively oral or written but is a hybrid oral-literary mode. Just as the mode of composition is both oral and literary, so too is the mode of literary transmission. In such societies, most communally authoritative material is transmitted through text-supported oral performance. This oral-literary modality differs from a scriptural modality in several ways. In an oral-literary economy,

---

6. For the relationship between torah law and imperial sanction in E–N, see James Watts, ed., *Persia and Torah: The Theory of Imperial Authorization of the Pentateuch* (Atlanta: Society of Biblical Literature, 2001). Josiah's implementation of the scroll of the law found in the Temple in 2 Kings 22–23 is the other narrative example in which torah mandates are implemented as "governmental" law.

7. David Carr, *Writing on the Tablet of the Heart* (Oxford: Oxford University Press, 2005), *The Formation of the Hebrew Bible* (Oxford: Oxford University Press, 2011); Susan Niditch, *Oral World and Written Word: Ancient Israelite Literature* (Louisville: Westminster John Knox, 1996); Raymond Person, *The Deuteronomic History and the Book of Chronicles: Scribal Works in an Oral World* (Atlanta: Society of Biblical Literature), 2010; Schniedewind, *How the Bible*; van der Toorn, *Scribal Culture*.

- Texts function as *aides-memoire* and archives for material that is primarily transmitted orally and preserved in human memory.
- The primary mode for the transmission of culturally significant material is text-supported oral performance by communally recognized text-brokers. These text-brokers are members of a literate, educated elite whose training consists of education and enculturation in the material that is inscribed in texts along with related material, such as explanations, applications or elements of context, that travelled with it orally.
- Performances of culturally authoritative material are audience and context specific. The precise content and nature of any given performance might be determined by a range of contextual factors. Thus, the degree of identity between the material preserved in writing and the material performed by the text-broker would vary from performance to performance. In some contexts, the performance might be a verbatim, or near verbatim performance of the received material. In other cases, it might be an abridgement of the received material or might include other material that was transmitted orally along with the material inscribed in the text.[8]
- Within an oral-literary modality, there is little, if any, self-consciousness about the distinction between material that is transmitted in writing and related material that is transmitted orally.[9]

In what follows, I will argue that the representation of torah in E–N corresponds to an oral-literary economy rather than a scriptural one. By *torah* here, I mean mandates for behavior, which are identified with God or Moses, and are presented and received as authoritative by the community. In such an economy, torah is produced and transmitted through text-supported oral performance. In these performances, texts of torah serve as resources and authorizers for the articulations of torah performed by the text-brokers. However, the mandates that are ultimately transmitted and received as authoritative are not identical to the material contained in the texts, nor are they generated exegetically by them. Rather, they are audience and context specific utterances, authored by their speakers. Within these torah utterances, the distinctions between the preexistent written sources and the torah mandates themselves are elided and unmarked. The texts do not betray any

---

8. Martin Jaffee, *Torah in the Mouth: Writing and Oral Tradition in Palestinian Judaism, 200 BCE–400 CE* (Oxford: Oxford University Press, 2001), 8; Van der Toorn, *Scribal Culture*, 102–3.

9. Jaffee, *Torah in the Mouth*, 10.

anxiety about the relationship between the material in the written texts of torah and the material that is ultimately transmitted as torah. In my conclusion, I will suggest that within the larger ideological program of E–N then, the written texts of torah function to support the authority of Ezra and his compatriots as legitimate sources of authoritative law.

In order to make my case, I will analyze the status and relationship of the oral and written components of torah in key passages in E–N. I will demonstrate that in each of these cases, key markers of scripturalization are absent whereas key markers of the oral-literary mode are robustly present. To make the contrast between the modalities clear however, I will begin by analyzing the representation of another body of texts that figure prominently in E–N: royal writing and, in particular, royal correspondence. As I will demonstrate below, the royal writing in E–N conforms closely to the scriptural mode. Consequently, it can provide a point of comparison—a heuristic control group—for my analysis of the representation of torah in E–N.

Royal Correspondence in E–N:

There is an abundance of royal writing and royal correspondence in E–N and their representation is intensely textual—meaning that their written-ness is emphasized within the narrative.[10] The royal writing is represented explicitly as writing and is distinguished rhetorically and semantically from surrounding discourse. In all but one case, it is represented as a verbatim copy of the original (albeit fictive) royal writing.[11] The representation of the "verbatim" text of the correspondence is one of the most significant markers of the scripturalization paradigm. Rhetorically, the representation of the actual text of a letter asserts that the letter is a discrete and bounded entity that exists independent of any mediation. In the experience of the reader or hearer of E–N, the royal writing literally speaks for itself, unmediated by subjective text-brokers within the narrative. The correspondence in Ezra 4:7–24 demonstrates these features.

> [7]And in the time of Artaxerxes, Bishlam, Mithredath, Tabeel, and the rest of their colleagues wrote to King Artaxerxes of Persia, a letter written in Aramaic and translated. Aramaic:

---

10. These include paraphrases and representations of royal edicts as well as representations of correspondence written by or addressed to the Persian king (Ezra 1:1–5, 4:8–16, 4:17–22, 5:6–17, 6:2–5, 6:6–12, 7:11–26; Neh 2:7–9).

11. Neh 2:7–9 describes the gist of the letters, not their verbatim content.

> [8]Rehum the commissioner and Shimshai the scribe wrote a letter concerning Jerusalem to King Artaxerxes as follows: ([9]Then Rehum the commissioner and Shimshai the scribe, and the rest of their colleagues, the judges, officials, officers, and overseers, the men of Erech, and of Babylon, and of Susa—that is the Elamites—[10]and other peoples whom the great and glorious Osnappar deported and settled in the city of Samaria and the rest of the province Beyond the River [wrote]—and now [11]this is the text of the letter which they sent to him:)—"To King Artaxerxes [from] your servants, men of the province Beyond the River. And now [12]be it known to the king that the Jews who came up from you to us have reached Jerusalem and are rebuilding that rebellious and wicked city; they are completing the walls and repairing the foundation. [13]Now be it known to the king that if this city is rebuilt and the walls completed, they will not pay tribute, poll-tax, or land-tax, and in the end it will harm the kingdom. [14]Now since we eat the salt of the palace, and it is not right that we should see the king dishonored, we have written to advise the king [of this] [15]so that you may search the records of your fathers and find in the records and know that this city is a rebellious city, harmful to kings and states. Sedition has been rife in it from early times; on that account this city was destroyed. [16]We advise the king that if this city is rebuilt and its walls are completed, you will no longer have any portion in the province Beyond the River." [17]The king sent back the following message: "To Rehum the commissioner and Shimshai the scribe, and the rest of their colleagues, who dwell in Samaria and in the rest of the province of Beyond the River, greetings. [18]Now the letter that you wrote me has been read to me in translation. [19]At my order a search has been made, and it has been found that this city has from earliest times risen against kings, and that rebellion and sedition have been rife in it. [20]Powerful kings have ruled over Jerusalem and exercised authority over the whole province of Beyond the River, and tribute, poll-tax, and land-tax were paid to them. [21]Now issue an order to stop these men; this city is not to be rebuilt until I so order. [22]Take care not to be lax in this matter or there will be much damage and harm to the kingdom."[12]

This unit consists of a blow-by-blow representation of the correspondence between Rehum, the commissioner and Shimshai, the scribe and Artaxerxes regarding the past and present disposition of the city of Jerusalem. The unit painstakingly describes the participants in the correspondence, the various steps of commissioning, composition, recitation, response, and enactment that make up the correspondence as a whole. In addition, the text purports to "reproduce" a verbatim copy of the "original" correspondence. While these letters are most probably fictive, the authors of E–N went to great

---

12. Unless otherwise noted, all translations are from Jewish Publication Society *Tanakh* (1985).

lengths to create a rhetoric of epistolary verisimilitude. The letters are in Aramaic, as was typical of correspondence between the Persian king and his regional underlings. In addition, the letters are replete with the conventions of formal correspondence. They begin with formal greetings and are marked by formal rhetoric. Finally, the high degree of correspondence between the language of Artaxerxes' response and the letter from Rehum and Shimshai creates the impression that Artaxerxes heard and responded to the actual letter "reproduced" in the text, not a précis or paraphrase thereof.[13] Throughout the episode, the written words of the letters are distinguished strongly from actions that occur in "real time" in the narrative. As a result, there is a doubled articulation of the central event of the episode. In Ezra 4:21 the king orders the cessation of reconstruction work. Ezra 4:23–24 describes the execution of this command in the "real world" of the narrative. Within this unit, both letters are fully self-interpreting. They are written and recited to their recipients "verbatim" and the recipients act on their plain sense meaning. The meticulous description of composition, text, recitation, and response clearly represents the unmediated nature of the written communication. With the exception of the necessary translation for the king, there is no brokering of these texts. The characters in the narrative receive and respond to the words of the written texts themselves.

In addition to being highly textualized, royal writing in E–N is remarkably authoritative and efficacious. It settles disputes and consistently yields results—as Tamara Eskenazi states, "signaling, like traffic lights, 'stop' and 'go'...."[14] Each time the officials of Beyond the River receive a written order from the king, they do exactly what it says. The account of their obedience is followed by a narratorial comment on the progress (or lack thereof) of the building project. Ezra 4:23–24 states,

> [23]When the text of the letter of King Artaxerxes was read before Rehum and Shimshai, the scribe and their colleagues, they hurried to Jerusalem, to the Jews, and stopped them by main force. [24]At that time, work on the

---

13. The king's response contains eight phrases that either duplicate phrases from Rehum's letter or reuse vocabulary from it. The high degree of correspondence between the two letters contrasts with the degree of correspondence between the Judahites/Benjaminites paraphrase of Cyrus's decree in Ezra 5:13–15 and the text of the decree that Darius finds in Ecbanata (Ezra 6:3–5). In this case, the paraphrase of the Judahites/Benjaminites anticipates the content of the cited decree but does not anticipate its precise wording or emphases.

14. Tamara Eskenazi, *In an Age of Prose: A Literary Approach to Ezra-Nehemiah* (Atlanta; Scholars Press, 1988), 58.

House of God in Jerusalem stopped and remained in abeyance until the second year of the reign of King Darius of Persia.[15]

One might argue that the cessation noted in verse 24 is the natural consequence of the action of the officials in verse 23. However, that is not the case elsewhere in the book. Ezra 5:5 states that when Tattenai, Shetharbozenai, and their colleagues challenged the rebuilding of the temple, "God watched over the elders of the Jews and they were not stopped while a report went to Darius and a letter was sent back in reply to it." Similarly, Neh 2:19–4:16 narrates the success of Nehemiah and his compatriots in rebuilding the walls *despite* the opposition of their opponents. Only in the cases of the written decrees, does the opposition of the local authorities successfully block the reconstruction efforts. In E–N, the textualization of royal writing is deployed to support the authority of the writing as a transparent and verifiable expression of the will of the king.[16] These same strategies of textualization are central to establishing the authority of the text within a scriptural economy. Like scripture, royal writing is a clearly bounded, authoritative discourse, emanating from an authoritative source. Its textuality functions as a sign of its authenticity and immutability and as a marker of the boundaries at which the scriptural text ends and its interpretation begins.

When contrasted with the representation of royal writing, the representation of torah in E–N appears distinctly undertextualized. Rather than conforming to the highly scripturalized paradigm that characterizes the royal writing, the depictions of torah reflect the fluidity of content and the intermingling of oral and written modes that characterize oral-literary production. In addition, in the representations of torah in E–N, the authority of any given torah mandate lies in the fact of its articulation as torah by an authorized text broker, not in its verifiable inclusion in a written text.

---

15. See also, Ezra 6:13–15.

16. The representation of royal writing resonates with historical data. In his essay, "Scribe and Speaker" (in *Writings and Speech in Israelite and Ancient Near Eastern Prophecy*, ed. in Ehud ben Zvi and Micahel Floyd, SymS 10 [Atlanta: Society of Biblical Literature, 2000], 147–52), Donald Redford argues that writing was essential to the Egyptian imperial ideology. If the pharaoh was to assert his unmediated authority over his far-flung subjects, he needed to be able to command them in an unmediated fashion. Despite vast geographical distances, his subjects had to "hear" exactly what he commanded and writing, unlike oral communication through a messenger, was the medium that insured this verbatim transmission.

REPRESENTATIONS OF TORAH IN E–N

There is a high concentration of torah discourse in E–N. Forms of the word *torah* or its Aramaic equivalent *dat,* appear twenty-eight times in the books.[17] Within these attestations, there is wide terminological variation: some attestations refer explicitly to scrolls of torah (e.g., Neh 8:1, 5), others do not specify the torah's medium (e.g., Neh 8:13–14). Some are identified with Moses as their author or authorizing source (e.g., Neh 8:1); others with God (e.g., Neh 9:3). In addition to these attestations of torah language, there are additional references to God's will, commandments, laws and rules (e.g., Neh 10:30). Because my primary interest here is on the relationship between the oral and written in E–N's representation of torah, I will focus on those episodes in which written texts appear in the narrative or are invoked in absentia.

The majority of these are clustered in Neh 8–10, which recount three distinct engagements with scrolls of torah.[18] Nehemiah 8:1–12 describes an oral performance that occurs on the first day of the seventh month and features a "scroll of the torah of Moses." Nehemiah 8:13–19 describes a torah study session which takes place on the second day of the seventh month and the communal observance of Sukkot that results from it. Nehemiah 9–10 describe another public ritual, occurring on the twenty-fourth day of the month. This episode begins with penitential rituals and consists of a performance from a "scroll of the torah of YHWH, their God," followed by prayer and confession. It culminates in the commitment of a group of signatories to a set of behaviors identified as "all the commandments of the Lord our Lord, his rules and laws (Neh 10:30)." Nehemiah 13:1–3 describes an additional performance from a torah scroll.

In addition to these episodes in which performances from torah scrolls are described, the following episodes invoke certain mandates as *torah* or as *written* but do not narrate any engagement with a written torah text: Ezra 3:2, 3:4, 6:18, 10:3; Neh 13:1–3. In these passages, the construction of an altar and the offering of sacrifices upon it (Ezra 3:2), the observance of Sukkot (Ezra 3:4), the establishment of priests and Levites over the sacrificial cult in Jerusalem (Ezra 6:18), and the expulsion of foreign wives (Ezra 3:2; Neh

---

17. Ezra 3:2; 6:18; 7:6, 10, 21; 10:3; Neh 8:1, 2, 3, 7, 8, 13, 14, 15, 18; 9:3, 13, 26, 29, 34; 10:29, 30, 35, 37; 13:1, 3.

18. This unit has been the subject of extensive source critical and redactional analysis. Hypotheses abound regarding its compositional and redactional history and its original location within earlier strata of E–N. For recent examples see Pakkala, *Ezra the Scribe*, 145–77; Jacob Wright, *Rebuilding Identity: The Nehemiah-Memoir and Its Earliest Readers* (Berlin: de Gruyter, 2004), 319–22.

13:1–3), are identified as being *according to/corresponding to torah (katorah)*, or *according to/corresponding to what is written (kakatuv)*.

NEHEMIAH 8: 1–12

¹The entire people assembled as one man in the square before the Water Gate, and they asked Ezra the scribe to bring the scroll of the torah of Moses with which the LORD had charged Israel.[19] ²On the first day of the seventh month, Ezra the priest brought the torah before the congregation, men and women and all who could listen with understanding. ³He read from it, facing the square before the Water Gate, from the first light until midday, to the men and the women and those who could understand; the ears of all the people were given to the scroll of the torah.

⁴Ezra the scribe stood upon a wooden tower made for the purpose, and beside him stood Mattithiah, Shema, Anaiah, Uriah, Hilkiah, and Maaseiah at his right, and at his left Pedaiah, Mishael, Malchijah, Hashum, Hashbaddanah, Zechariah, Meshullam. ⁵Ezra opened the scroll in the sight of all the people, for he was above all the people; as he opened it, all the people stood up. ⁶Ezra blessed the LORD, the great God, and all the people answered, "Amen, Amen," with hands upraised. Then they bowed their heads and prostrated themselves before the LORD with their faces to the ground. ⁷Jeshua, Bani, Sherebiah, Jamin, Akkub, Shabbethai, Hodiah, Maaseiah, Kelita, Azariah, Jozabad, Hanan, Pelaiah, and the Levites explained the torah to the people, while the people stood in their places. They read (*yiqr'u*) from the scroll of the torah of God, translating it and giving the sense (*meforash vesom sekhel*); so they understood the reading (*vayavinu bamiqra*).

⁹Nehemiah the Tirshatha, Ezra the priest and scribe, and the Levites who were explaining to the people said to all the people, "This day is holy to the LORD your God: you must not mourn or weep," for all the people were weeping as they listened to the words of the torah. ¹⁰He further said to them, "Go, eat choice foods and drink sweet drinks and send portions to whoever has nothing prepared, for the day is holy to our Lord. Do not be sad, for your rejoicing in the LORD is the source of your strength." ¹¹The Levites were quieting the people, saying, "Hush, for the day is holy; do not be sad." ¹²Then all the people went to eat and drink and send portions and make great merriment, for they understood the things they were told.[20]

---

19. JPS *Tanakh* translates *torah* as "Torah" throughout E–N. I have restored the term "torah" to all cited passages.

20. There is debate regarding the compositional and redactional history of this passage. Most scholars suggest that the text has undergone at least one layer of redaction resulting in a composite text featuring both Ezra and the Levites as protagonists. See, e.g., Blenkinsopp, *Ezra-Nehemiah*, 286–87; Pakkala, *Ezra the Scribe*, 165–67, 177–79; Wright, *Rebuilding Identity*, 319–30. Tamara Eskenazi (*In an Age of Prose*, 98–99), however, argues

This passage is frequently invoked as a prime piece of evidence for the scripturalization of torah in E–N.[21] First, it identifies the contents of a scroll (*sefer torat moshe*) with that which YHWH had commanded Israel (8:1). Second, it describes a highly ritualized performance of the contents of the scroll. The passage is saturated with attestations to the scroll's holiness. It is performed on a sacred occasion, by a cultic professional on a platform erected precisely for this purpose that is located at a communally significant spot. When it is performed, the people respond to it as they would to a sacred object: they rise, and after Ezra delivers a blessing, they respond "amen, amen" and then prostrate themselves (8:6). Each of these details contributes to what James Watts calls the ritualization of the iconic valence of the scroll. Ritualization of the iconic dimension of a text occurs when the text itself, as a material object, is presented and received as a sacred object that participates in the holiness and, in some cases, the power, of the divine source with which it is associated.[22] This passage, which clearly presents the scroll as a sacred object, imbedded in the network of sacred time, space, and personnel associated with YHWH, is an exemplary case of this ritualization of the iconic dimension of the text.[23] While Watts identifies this iconic ritualization as a key aspect of scripturalization, it is not unique to scriptural economies. The idea that some texts are holy objects is an ancient one that predates E–N by centuries and is often operative within oral-textual paradigms as well as more textual paradigms. In societies where few people can read, writing in general, and writing that is associated with the deity or the cult in particular, are often understood to be sacred objects with numinous power.[24] Thus, the ritualization of the scroll's iconic dimension bears witness to its identity as a sacred object, but not necessarily to its identity as scripture.

While Neh 8:4–6 emphasizes the sacrality of the torah scroll and the role of Ezra, the priest-scribe, as its broker, the next unit emphasizes the perfor-

---

that there is a literary integrity to the final version, regardless of its prior redactional history.

21. Eskenazi, *Age of Prose*, 96–100, 109–11; Fishbane, *Biblical Interpretation in Ancient Israel*, 108–9; Grabbe, *Ezra-Nehemiah*, 145–47; Schniedewind, *How the Bible*, 197; James Watts, "Using Ezra's Time," 489–506; Pakkala, *Ezra the Scribe*, 278–80.

22. James Watts, "The Three Dimensions of Scriptures," *Postscripts* 2:2–3 (2006): 142–43.

23. Wright (*Rebuilding Identity*, 395–96) suggests that the sacralization of the torah scroll here is a polemical alternative to the more traditional sacralization of the temple and altar articulated in earlier redactional strata of E–N. Lisbeth Fried ("The Torah of God as God: The Exaltation of the Written Law Code in Ezra-Nehemiah," forthcoming) has argued that the torah scroll plays a role analogous to the cult statue in Mesopotamian religion.

24. Niditch, *Oral World*, 106; Schniedewind, *How the Bible*, 24–34.

mative dimension of the scroll.[25] It identifies the performers and the mode of performance and underscores the performers' *gravitas* and authority. Nehemiah 8:7–13 focuses on a group of named individuals and unnamed Levites, and their effective articulation of torah.[26] Their activity is described as follows:

> Jeshua, Bani, Sherebiah, Jamin, Akkub, Shabbethai, Hodiah, Maaseiah, Kelita, Azariah, Jozabad, Hanan, Pelaiah, and the Levites taught (*mevinim*) the torah to the people, while the people stood in their places. They read from the scroll of the torah of God, clearly and in a sense-making way (*meforash vesom sekhel*); so they understood what was recited. (translation mine)

The key phrase in this passage is *meforash vesom sekhel*. While it is difficult to find exact English equivalents for these terms, in the aggregate, they emphasize the text-brokers' role in facilitating the people's understanding of the torah.[27] They do this through a clear and sense-making performance of the material in the scroll. In most translations of this passage, the clause *vayiqr'u vasefer betorat ha'elohim meforash vesom sekhel* is translated in such a way as to suggest that the activities of recitation (*vayiqr'u*) clarification or translation (*meforash*) and sense-making (*som sekhel*) are sequential. However, in the Hebrew text, the terms *meforash* and *som sekhel* are adverbial. They describe the manner of the performance, not activities that are subsequent to it. If we take this grammatical distinction seriously, the torah performers are not engaging in the read and paraphrase style of performance that is familiar to many of us from classroom and confessional settings. Rather, the performance itself is the Levites' sense-making version of the content of the scroll. According to the passage, the Levites' text-brokering is effective. Nehemiah 8:8 concludes by stating that the people understood the torah.

Nehemiah 8:9–12 describe the aftermath of the Levites' performance. Their words had caused the people to weep and Nehemiah, Ezra and the Levites instruct them to be joyful instead. As was the case in the preceding

---

25. Watts, "Three Dimensions of Scriptures," 141–42.

26. Scholars disagree over the identity of the named individuals. Williamson (*Ezra and Nehemiah*, 289) argues that they are laypeople and that their lay identity is key to the representation of the torah as a civic document that is not exclusively the provenance of the cultic elite. Based on the levitical nature of the names and the parallel text in 1 Esdras 9:48 which omits the conjunction between the list of names and *the Levites,* Blenkinsopp (*Ezra-Nehemiah*, 284) argues that the named individuals are to be identified as Levites.

27. See Fishbane, *Biblical Interpretation in Ancient Israel*, 108; Blenkinsopp, *Ezra-Nehemiah*, 288, for surveys of the options.

verses, their instruction is effective. The pericope ends by stating: "Then all the people went to eat and drink and send portions and make great merriment, *for they understood the things they were told*" (emphasis mine). Once again, the text has attested to the text-brokers' success in fostering understanding on the part of the people.

While the redacted passage emphasizes both the iconic and performative aspects of the text-supported oral performance, it does not represent the contents of the torah scroll or the Levites' sense-making performance of it at all. The only authoritative discourse whose content is represented in the text is the final mandate, uttered by Nehemiah, Ezra, and the Levites. These characters tell the people to rejoice rather than weep and the people obey.[28] This final mandate, which is the only one reproduced in the text, countermands the people's natural response to the torah they had received previously. That torah made them weep but the text-brokers told them to rejoice instead. It is this mandate that shapes the audience's behavior. This sequence of events asserts the authority of the text-brokers. Their mandate trumps the people's natural response to the content of the recited torah.

A brief comparison to the representation of royal writing makes the distinctiveness of this representation clear. The royal writing was highly textualized. The text itself was "reproduced" verbatim within the text and the authors of E–N went to great lengths to represent it as issuing straight from the king's mouth/pen, unmediated by potentially partisan interpreters. Finally, the plain sense of the king's letters determined the action of the characters. In the case of torah, the contents of the scroll are neither quoted nor paraphrased and the text underscores the role of the text-brokering middle men. Their text-brokering behavior is described in detail (8:8) and we are told twice that they enable the people's comprehension of the text. The text-brokers' mandates, ungrounded in any reference to torah, determine how the audience behaves. Finally, this pericope does not distinguish between the written text and its oral, mediated transmission. Rather, the torah received by the people is the sense-making performance uttered by the Levites and their compatriots.

NEHEMIAH 8:13–17

> On the second day, the heads of the clans of all the people and the priests and Levites gathered to Ezra the scribe to study the words of the torah.

---

28. The mandate to rejoice on the first of Tishrei is not attested to in any extant pentateuchal text. The pentateuchal texts which identify the day as a sacred occasion do not identify it as a day of rejoicing (Lev 23:23–25; Num 29:1–6). The closest pentateuchal analogues are the mandates to rejoice on Shavuot (Deut 16:11) and Sukkot (Deut 16:15).

> [14]They found written in the torah that the LORD had commanded Moses that the Israelites must dwell in booths during the festival of the seventh month, [15]and that they must announce and proclaim throughout all their towns and Jerusalem as follows, "Go out to the mountains and bring leafy branches of olive trees, pine trees, myrtles, palms and [other] leafy trees to make booths, as it is written." [16]So the people went out and brought them, and made themselves booths on their roofs, in their courtyards, in the courtyards of the House of God, in the square of the Water Gate and in the square of the Ephraim Gate. [17]The whole community that returned from the captivity made booths and dwelt in the booths—the Israelites had not done so from the days of Joshua son of Nun to that day—and there was very great rejoicing.

The textual encounter described here largely conforms to the norms of ancient Near Eastern scribal education. In it, an authorized text broker instructs a group of communal elites.[29] In this case, Ezra the scribe is the teacher and the secular and cultic leadership of the community are the students. The object of their study is identified as issues/words of torah (*divrei hatorah*) and engagement with written material is an element of the study process. In this case, the written material deals with the observance of the festival of Sukkot. It prescribes that the Israelites should dwell in booths and mandates a proclamation ordering the collection of leafy branches for the construction of the booths. The pericope ends with notice of the people's compliance with this mandate.

The roles of written and oral transmission here conform to what we would expect from such a scene. The scroll of torah is identified as a source for torah and plays the archival function common to texts in largely oral societies. According to verse 17, the booth-building practice had lain dormant for centuries. The mandate's inscription and storage in the scroll allows for its resuscitation. While the scroll contains vital information, only a limited number of elites encounter this material in the form of the written text. The majority of the population receives the material orally, as articulated by the literate and educated torah-brokers. Even for the literate elites, the torah material is not located in the text alone, it is also transmitted by Ezra, who is well-versed in the torah of God (Ezra 7:5; Neh 8:1).

Like Neh 8:1–12, this episode depicts torah as an oral-textual phenomenon. However, there is a greater emphasis on the textuality of torah in

---

29. For a discussion of the social context of education in the ancient Near East, see Carr, *Writing on the Tablet of the Heart*, 17–30; van der Toorn, *Scribal Culture*, 54–73. This scene differs from the norm in that the "students" are already established as communal leaders. In the documentary evidence from the ancient Near East, the students are usually young men engaged in an ongoing course of study.

this episode. In this short passage, the "writtenness" of the torah is invoked twice (Neh 8:14, 15). In addition, the written text is quoted within the passage itself. The people's compliance conforms exactly to the quoted mandate whose textuality is reinforced by the coda, *as it is written*, in verse 15. Within this narrative, torah is depicted as a textual phenomenon: The contents of the scroll are quoted and the quotation generates compliance on the part of both the elites and the larger community.

However, if we step back from the narrative itself and explore the relationship between this passage and other Sukkot mandates in extant versions of the pentateuch, the situation becomes more complicated. As has been noted repeatedly in the scholarship, the material identified as *found written in the torah* and further identified as *kakatuv* does not correspond precisely to any extant pentateuchal material. Whereas Lev 23:40–42 MT mandate both the collection of boughs and the dwelling in booths, it does not state that the boughs are to be used to build the booths. The identification of the boughs as building material is also absent from the other extant versions of Lev 23:40. This situation has generated ample scholarly attention.[30] To date, the majority of scholars assume that Lev 23:40–42 form the basis for the mandate in Nehemiah 8. A wide range of hypotheses have been suggested to explain the process through which the Sukkot mandate in Nehemiah 8 was generated from the text in Leviticus. Central to these hypotheses are analyses of the meaning and role of the term *kakatuv* in the passage. Some scholars have argued for a restrictive reading of the term, arguing that it applies only to the parts of Neh 8:15 that also occur in the Leviticus text.[31] Others have read the term as a marker of focused exegetical activity that can be reconstructed through a close reading of relevant texts;[32] while others have read it more loosely, as inclusive of implications of the written law that were obvious to the authors of the text.[33] A small number of scholars argues that the authors of E–N were working with a text which included the mandate in Neh

---

30. See Brent Strawn, *"As It Is Written" and Other Citation Formulae in the Old Testament: Their Use, Development, Syntax and Significance* (Berlin: de Gruyter, 2002), 101–4, for a survey and analysis of the literature. See also David Clines, "Neh 10 as an Example of Early Jewish Biblical Exegesis," *JSOT* 21 (1981): 111–17.

31. See, e.g., Williamson, *Ezra and Nehemiah*.

32. See, e.g., Fishbane, *Biblical Interpretation in Ancient Israel*, 109–12.

33. See, e.g., David Clines, *Ezra, Nehemiah, Esther: Based on the Revised Standard Version* (London: Marshall, Morgan & Scott, 1984), 187. See also, Sara Japhet's analysis of the relationship of the exogamy prohibitions in E–N to earlier pentateuchal material ("Law and 'the Law' in Ezra-Nehemiah" in *From the Rivers of Babylon to the Highlands of Judah: Collected Studies on the Restoration Period* (Winona Lake, IN: Eisenbrauns, 2006), 137–51.

8:15, but did not make it into extant versions of the Pentateuch.[34] If this final group of scholars is correct, this pericope serves as an example of the scripturalization of torah in which the written text of torah is cited verbatim and articulates a mandate that is authoritative for the community without any mediation by the text-brokers. However, if the authors of Nehemiah 8 were working with a text similar to extant versions of Lev 23:40–42, then the relationship between the mandate in Neh 8:15 and the mandates in Lev 23:40–42 represent a typical case of torah production within an oral-literary modality. The Sukkot mandate in Neh 8:15 is an audience and context specific oral composition, grounded in, but not identical to the written text. Within this scenario, the citation formula *kakatuv* should be understood as a marker of relationship between the articulated mandate and the written mandate. As the multitude of hypotheses attests, it is impossible to conclusively reconstruct the actual genesis of that relationship from the extant texts themselves. It is important to note however, that the Neh 8:13–17 betrays no interest in, or concern over, the discrepancy between the mandate in the written text and the authoritative performed torah. Whereas the documentation of the relationship of the primary text to its interpretation is often central to the authorization of interpretation in scriptural economies, it is not an object for reflection in oral-literary modalities.[35]

There is a second fluidity worth noting here. In contrast to the representation of royal writing in which the narrative clearly distinguished between quotation of text and description of action, these two modes of discourse are elided here. In the MT of Nehemiah 8, verses 14–15 function as a quotation and paraphrase of the material that was, theoretically, found written in the torah.[36] However, the verse also functions as the communal leaders' own proclamation to the people in the present action of the text. Unlike the descriptions of royal writing, this text does not represent the written mandate to "proclaim" and its execution as separate, distinct entities. Rather verses 14–15 function as both the preexistent mandate found in the text and the text-brokers' own authoritative discourse. Like the fluidity between what the text identifies as *kakatuv* and what is written in extant pentateuchal versions, this elision is further evidence for the lack of self-

---

34. See, e.g, Pakkala, *Ezra the Scribe*, 158–64.

35. Compare this text with, e.g., the Qumran pesharim, rabbinic midrash, or patristic exegesis in which the exegetes begin with a citation of a written text and then deploy a range of technical terms and rhetorical strategies to lead their readers/audiences from the plain sense of the text to its articulated interpretation.

36. The Septuagint more clearly differentiates between the proclamation mandated by the text and the proclamation made by Ezra in the present of the narrative.

conscious differentiation between the elements of torah discourse that are inscribed in the written text and the dicta that are articulated as torah by the book's protagonists.

The features I have noted here characterize other key representations of torah in E–N. Like this pericope, the remaining representations identify mandates that are absent from extant pentateuchal texts as *kakatuv* or *katorah*. They also elide distinctions between the mandates presumably encountered by the text-brokers in written texts and the mandates that they, in turn, articulate. As is the case in the two examples here, the mandates and directives articulated by the text-brokers are received as authoritative torah by the public. Finally, the subsequent texts exhibit no anxiety or self consciousness about these fluid identifications and discourses.

Nehemiah 9–10

These chapters describe a communal gathering occurring on the twenty-fourth of Tishrei of the same year. The account begins:

> [1] On the twenty-fourth day of this month, the Israelites assembled, fasting, in sackcloth, and with earth upon them. [2] Those of the stock of Israel separated themselves from all foreigners, and stood and confessed their sins and the iniquities of their fathers. [3] Standing in their places, they read from the scroll of the torah of the LORD their God for one-fourth of the day, and for another fourth they confessed and prostrated themselves before the LORD their God. (Neh 9:1–3)

The passage continues with a "transcript" of the penitential prayer recited by the Levites: a deuteronomistic, sin-saturated version of Israel's history from the time of creation to the text's present (Neh 9:6–10). This unit contains several of the elements of the representation of *torah* that we have already seen. First, the recitation from a torah scroll is narrated as a ritual event that moves the people to liturgical action—here penitential prayer. As was the case in Neh 8:1–8, the content of the recited text is absent from the narrative. However, the prayer that follows the narrative is heavily saturated with language that resonates with, but does not replicate language found in extant pentateuchal versions.

The episode continues with the "real time" announcement of an oath that is made both orally and in writing and is inscribed in a sealed document. "In view of all this, we make this pledge and put it in writing; and on the sealed copy, our officials, our Levites, and our priests (Neh 10:1)." It continues with the list of signatories (Neh 10:2–28) followed by the assertion that

> ²⁹And the rest of the people, the Levites, the gatekeepers, the singers, the temple servants, and all who separated themselves from the peoples of the land to follow the torah of God, their wives, sons and daughters, all who know enough to understand, ³⁰join with their noble brothers and take an oath with sanctions to follow the torah of God, given through Moses the servant of God, and to observe carefully all the commandments of the Lord our Lord, His rules and laws. (Neh 10:29–30)

This narrative statement is followed by the stipulations themselves, introduced by the particle *va'asher* (namely) in verse 31. As was the case in Neh 8:13–17, the boundaries between the representation of the written text and the action that surrounds it are quite porous and it is difficult to disentangle the representation of written material from the surrounding speech. The entire unit is framed as a speech by an unnamed speaker. Citation or recitation of the written document is enfolded within the speech and supports its larger rhetorical aims.

As was the case in Neh 8:13–17, the mandates identified as torah in this pericope are related, but not identical, to pentateuchal material.[37] As David Clines has noted, they are, for the most part, more elaborate or more intensive versions of related pentateuchal or preexilic prophetic mandates.[38] For example, in verse 32, the signers pledge not to buy merchandise from the people of the land on Sabbaths or festivals. These restrictions exceed other related biblical mandates. The pentateuchal Sabbath laws do not prohibit either buying or selling. While Amos 8:5 assumes a prohibition against selling on the Sabbath, it does not mention buying. Thus, E–N's prohibition of buying on the Sabbath and the extension of the commerce prohibition to festivals are unique to E–N. The prohibition of intermarriage in verse 31 is structurally similar. While pentateuchal mandates prohibit Israelite men (Exod 34:1) or Israelite men and women (Deut 7:1–3) from marrying members of certain ethnicities, the extant pentateuchal texts never articulate a blanket prohibition against exogamy.

The uses of the term *kakatuv* in this pericope also parallel those in Neh 8:15. Nehemiah 10:35–37 states:

> ³⁵We have cast lots among the priests, the Levites, and the people, to bring the wood offering to the House of our God by clans annually at set times in order to provide fuel for the altar of the LORD our God, as is written in the torah. ³⁶ And we undertake to bring to the House of the LORD annually the

---

37. See Blenkinsopp, *Ezra-Nehemiah: A Commentary* (London: SCM, 1988), 313–19 and Clines, "Nehemiah 10 as an Example," 111–17, for detailed analyses of each stipulation and its relationship to pentateuchal material.
38. Ibid.

first fruits of our soil, and of every fruit of every tree; 37 also, the first-born of our sons and our beasts, as is written in the torah; and to bring the firstlings of our cattle and flocks to the House of our God for the priests who minister in the House of our God.

While the extant pentateuch certainly mandates a sacrificial cult that needed wood, it does not mandate a wood offering. Similarly, the extant Pentateuch mandates a cultic tax on some first fruits. The offerings mandated in this passage are not identical to any of them.[39] The first-fruits mandate here is more expansive than its pentateuchal counterparts. Despite these discrepancies, the plain sense of the text describes the articulation, by the text's protagonists, of mandates that are identified and received as torah. In other words, Neh 10:29–40 represents the oral composition of torah. The speakers articulate an audience and context-specific mandate and identify it as torah. The audience within the text subsequently accepts it as such. For both the characters within the story and presumably its authors as well, the mandates identified as torah in Nehemiah 10 are torah, *not* interpretations of it, despite their lack of identity with dicta in extant sources. As was the case in Neh 8:13–17, Neh 10:31–41 does not seem to betray any anxiety about this modality of composition/transmission. With the exception of the two *kakatuv*'s, the text of E–N makes no attempt to ground these in a written text nor does it betray anxiety about the absence of textual grounding. Rather, the text seems unselfconscious about representing in real time the composition of torah in oral performance.

NEHEMIAH 13:1–3; EZRA 9:10–12, 10:3–4

The most notorious invocations of torah in E–N are those that are used to support the various exogamy prohibitions.[40] Variations of this prohibition occur five times in E–N (Ezra 9:1–3, 10–12; 10:1–4, 10–11; Neh 10:31; 13:1–3). Each of the invocations of torah manifests the characteristics discussed above. The material identified as *katorah* or *kakatuv* bears some similarity to material in the extant biblical collection but is nowhere identical to it either in wording or in effect. Most notably, the various pentateuchal prohibitions forbid marriage between Israelites and members of a restricted set of nations. Exodus 34:1 prohibits marriage between Israelite men and the seven Canaan-

---

39. For a detailed analysis of the relationship between Neh 10:36–37 and related pentateuchal material, see Pakkala, *Ezra the Scribe*, 198–202.
40. For analyses of the content of these prohibitions, see Sara Japhet, "Law and 'the Law' in Ezra-Nehemiah," in *From the Rivers of Babylon to the Highlands of Judah: Collected Studies on the Restoration Period* (Winona Lake, IN: Eisenbrauns, 2006), 137–51.

ite nations. Deuteronomy 7:1–3 prohibits marriage between both Israelite men and women and members of these seven nations. The prohibitions in E–N are far more extreme, forbidding marriage between members of the returned exilic community and "people of the land" (Neh 10:31; cf. Neh 13:3). Ezra 10:2–4 not only prohibits marriage with the people of the land, it also mandates the expulsion of "foreign" wives and their children. Despite these significant differences from the pentateuchal laws, the mandates in E–N are identified variously as elements of *the torah of God . . . his rules and laws* (Neh 10:29–30), *the bidding of God*, and *torah* (Ezra 10:3).

Nehemiah 13:1–3 manifests a different kind of slippage. The text reads:

> [1]At that time they read to the people from the Book of Moses, and it was found written that no Ammonite or Moabite might ever enter the congregation of God, [2]since they did not meet Israel with bread and water, and hired Balaam against them to curse them; but our God turned the curse into a blessing. [3]When they heard the torah, they separated all the alien admixture from Israel.

This passage is as close as E–N comes to a quotation of a pentateuchal source. While the E–N text is shorter and phrased in the third person rather than the second, it otherwise parallels Deut 23:4–6.[41] In this case, the representation of torah is not only textualized (13:1), but there is also a high degree of identity between material that is identified as written torah and material in the extant pentateuch. There is, however, a significant gap between the represented text and the actions it effects. While the utterance that is represented as written torah prohibits the entrance of Ammonites and Moabites from entering the congregation of God, the people respond by separating *all the alien admixture from Israel*. In plain-sense terms, this response is clearly something other than compliance with the performed mandate. Compliance would entail measures that kept Ammonites and Moabites out of *the congregation of God*. These might include prohibitions against circumcision and consequent assimilation of members of these groups as well as prohibitions against marriage with them and perhaps even the dissolution of current marriages and expulsion of the products of these unions. In separating *all the admixture*, the returnees take action that exceeds the mandate in the written text and is unsupported by the justification articulated there. According to both Deuteronomy 23 and its version in Neh 13:1–3, the exclusion of the Ammonites and Moabites from the congregation is justified by their hostile

---

41. Shift in grammatical person (in this case from third to first perdon) are also common in the Temple Scroll in units that are otherwise verbatim parallels to texts in Deuteronomy.

behavior to the Israelites in the wilderness period. This "historical" episode does not explain the exclusion of *all the alien admixture* who are innocent of this offense. Unlike Neh 8:13–17 and Neh 10:30–41, in which the disparity between the written text and the articulated torah was not accessible from the E–N text alone, the slippage here is entirely transparent. Both the audience within the text and the audience of the text itself witness the gap between the written torah mandate and the consequent action. Here too though, the text betrays no anxiety about this gap. To the contrary, throughout E–N, the zealous separators are lauded.

Conclusion

The survey of representations of torah in E–N has yielded the following observations. First, scrolls of torah make their appearance for the first time in the Tanakh and their role is significant. As Juha Pakkala has noted, the identification of torah with a single scroll in Neh 8:1 is novel. While Deut 31:9–13 describes Moses' inscription of *this law (hatorah hazot)* and his mandate to read it aloud in the presence of all Israel every seventh year, *this law* presumably identifies the preceding material in Deuteronomy. Ezra's torah scroll seems to be more inclusive than that because it refers to material found outside of Deuteronomy.[42]

Secondly, written scrolls are identified as important components or reference points for torah and reference to written scrolls functions as an authorizing strategy within the text. The various identifications of mandates as *kakatuv* bear witness to this phenomenon as does the invocation of written texts in the assertion of potentially controversial or novel mandates.

Finally, the authors of E–N present the torah scroll as a sacred object. The people respond to it as they would to other, more traditional sancta. These data demonstrate a heightened emphasis on the textuality of torah that is nascent in Deuteronomy, but is absent in its full-fledged form elsewhere in Tanakh texts that are usually dated to or before the composition of E–N. Within the construction of torah then, E–N demonstrates an intensification in the iconic dimension of scripture: the scroll is clearly viewed as an object of sancta. Similarly, there is an intensification in the performative aspect of scripture: the two ritual recitations of scripture in E–N demonstrate that such recitations were seen to be ritually important and also effective: in both cases the recitation of scripture leads to a response on the part of the people.

---

42. Pakkala, *Ezra the Scribe*, 284–90.

At the same time however, on the level of meaning and content, written torah in E–N is not scripturalized: the contents of the text do not determine the authoritative discourse; nor are they understood to be the generating source of the authoritative discourse. Rather, on this semantic level, E–N's torah conforms to the oral-literary mode. Throughout the examples I cited, those dicta that are identified by the narrator as torah, and accepted by the text's characters as such are all utterances of authorized tradents (Ezra, the Levites, etc) that are related to, but not identical to extant pentateuchal texts. Discrepancies between written texts of torah and mandates that are identified as torah and function as torah within the text are either elided or unremarked upon. Throughout the text, the tradents are identified as articulators of torah, not interpreters or even brokers of it. From the perspective of orality studies, these articulations of torah within E–N are compositions of torah—not inventions *de novo*, but rather compositions in the oral-literary mode. They are audience and context specific articulations that are grounded in received material, preserved in text and orally, that has been internalized by the authorized tradents. Within this modality, the references to written torah serve to identify the articulated torah as being grounded in, and in some way generated by, the received tradition that the tradent has internalized.

While I can describe precisely the representation of torah in E–N and relate that representation to scriptural and oral-literary modes of cultural production and reception, it is more difficult to determine the function of this representation within E–N itself. What is innovative about this representation of torah? Is the representation of torah a key component to the ideological messages of the book? Two elements of the ideological program of E–N are: (1) the assertion that the torah of Moses/God is the legitimate "constitution" for Persian Yehud and (2) the assertion that Ezra, Nehemiah, their compatriots and, presumably, their political descendants, are the rightful local communal authorities. While these propositions may have been widely accepted by some point in the history of E–N's transmission, it is likely that they were contested in the actual historical context of Persian Yehud. While earlier texts certainly argue that obedience to God's will is key to Israel/Judah's political success and survival, there is no evidence that any formal corpus, known as the torah was every deployed as the law of the land in the preexilic period. As for the second proposition, E–N itself admits to power struggles between the authorities of the province of Beyond the River and the leaders of the "returnee" community.

The representation of torah is relevant to both these propositions. In E–N, the torah of God/Moses, which is proclaimed as the legitimate law of the land, is not identical to the written text associated with that torah. It is, instead, identified with a traditional, prescripturalized understanding of torah as the distillation of a body of material comprised of oral and written components and transmitted in its fullest, hybrid form from one generation of authorized text-broker to the next. In an environment where some imperial texts may have been increasingly scripturalized, E–N maintains the traditional conviction that texts of torah are not. Unlike royal writing that might have been presented as self-sufficient and fully self-explanatory texts, torah texts are only a part of the expression of torah. Mediation by authorized text-brokers is still necessary.

E–N supports its claim regarding the the protagonists' right to political power by presenting them as the only sources of torah in Persian Yehud. As I note in the analyses above, representations of torah in E–N often omit the content of the written torah but they never omit the identity of the text-brokers. In some cases, they are identified by name (Neh 8:7); in other cases they are identified by status (Neh 8:13). However, they are always identified. In addition, their articulations of torah are always accepted as such by the community. When the protagonists utter a torah proclamation, the secondary heroes of the book (those who have separated themselves from the people of the land) accept the proclamation as authoritative and follow it. This narrative pattern places E–N's representation of torah at the intersection of the book's two central propositions. Ezra, Nehemiah, and their compatriots are the unquestioned and unchallenged sources of torah and the torah that they generate is the only legitimate law of the land. Thus the authors of E–N use the traditional ideology of torah as the product of an oral-literary modality to support what may have been a far-more radical or contested proposition regarding the right of the returnee community to function as local authorities in postexilic Yehud.

References

Blenkinsopp, Joseph. *Ezra-Nehemiah: A Commentary*. London: SCM, 1988.
Carr, David M. *The Formation of the Hebrew Bible: A New Reconstruction*. New York: Oxford University Press, 2011.
———. *Writing on the Tablet of the Heart: Origins of Scripture and Literature*. New York: Oxford University Press, 2005.
Clines, David. *Ezra, Nehemiah, Esther: Based on the Revised Standard Version*. London: Marshall, Morgan & Scott, 1984.
———. "Nehemiah 10 as an Example of Early Jewish Biblical Exegesis," JSOT 21 (1981): 111–17.
Eskenazi, Tamara. *In an Age of Prose: A Literary Approach to Ezra-Nehemiah*. Atlanta, Scholars Press, 1988.
Fishbane, Michael. *Biblical Interpretation in Ancient Israel*. Oxford: Clarendon, 1985.
Jaffee, Martin S. *Torah in the Mouth: Writing and Oral Tradition in Palestinian Juda-*

ism, 200 BCE–400 CE. Oxford: Oxford University Press, 2001.
Grabbe, Lester. *Ezra-Nehemiah*. London: Routledge, 1998.
Japhet, Sara. "Law and 'the Law' in Ezra-Nehemiah." Pages 137–51 in *From the Rivers of Babylon to the Highlands of Judah: Collected Studies on the Restoration Period* Winona Lake, IN: Eisenbrauns, 2006.
Niditch, Susan. *Oral World and Written Word: Ancient Israelite Literature*. Louisville: Westminster John Knox, 1996.
Pakkala, Juha. *Ezra the Scribe: The Development of Ezra 7–10 and Nehemia 8*. Berlin: de Gruyter, 2004.
Person, Raymond. *The Deuteronomic History and the Book of Chronicles: Scribal Works in an Oral World*. AIL 6. Atlanta: Society of Biblical Literature, 2010.
Redford, Donald. "Scribe and Speaker," Pages 145–218 in *Writings and Speech in Israelite and Ancient Near Eastern Prophecy*, ed. Ehud ben Zvi and Micahel Floyd. SymS 10. Atlanta: Society of Biblical Literature, 2000.
Schniedewind, William. *How the Bible Became a Book*. Cambridge: Cambridge University Press, 2004.
Spawn, Kevin L. *"As it is Written" and Other Citation Formulae in the Old Testament: Their Use, Development, Syntax and Significance*. Berlin: de Gruyter, 2002.
Van Der Toorn, Karel. *Scribal Culture and the Making of the Hebrew Bible*. Cambridge, MA: Harvard University Press, 2007.
Watts, James, ed. *Persia and Torah: The Theory of Imperial Authorization of the Pentateuch*. Atlanta: Society of Biblical Literature, 2001.
———. "The Three Dimensions of Scriptures." *Postscripts* 2:2–3 (2006): 135–59.
———. "Using Ezra's Time as a Methodological Pivot for Understanding the Rhetoric and Functions of the Pentateuch," Pages 489–506 in *The Pentateuch: International Perspectives on Current Research*. Edited by Thomas B. Dozeman, Konrad Schmid and Baruch J. Schwarz. Tübingen: Mohr Siebeck, 2011.
Wellhausen, Julius. *Prolegomena to the History of Ancient Israel*. Translated by J. S. Black and A. Menzies. Cleveland: World Publishing, 1957.
Williamson, H. G. M. *Ezra and Nehemiah*. Sheffield: Society for Old Testament Study, 1987.
Wright, Jacob. *Rebuilding Identity: The Nehemiah-Memoir and Its Earliest Readers*. Berlin: de Gruyter, 2004.

THE "LITERARIZATION" OF THE BIBLICAL PROPHECY OF DOOM

JAMES M. BOS

PRIOR TO THE VERY LATE TWENTIETH CENTURY, VERY FEW SCHOLARS researching the composition of the various biblical books took into account the significant factor of literacy in the Iron Age Levant.[1] This was due in part to the rather widespread notion that alphabetic literacy was easily attained, and thus the number of men (and perhaps women) reading and writing in ancient Israel and Judah would have been (or could have been) relatively high, even early in the Iron Age. Scholars like Millard and Lemaire also pointed to the distribution and variety of epigraphic remains in the ancient southern Levant, as well as references to writing (and in the case of Lemaire, instruction more broadly construed) in the Hebrew Bible, as evidence for widespread literacy.[2] Regarding the prophetic books in particular, many scholars simply assumed (and some still do) that the prophets themselves could write, in many cases even designating them the "Writing Prophets." However, such unstated assumptions about the prophets' "literateness" appear to be undermined by recent research on literacy in the Levant, and in Israel and Judah in particular.[3] First, as Sanders[4] and others have

---

1. I want to thank Brian B. Schmidt for reading several drafts of this essay and providing numerous helpful comments.

2. See André Lemaire, *Les écoles et la formation de la Bible dans l'ancien Israël*, OBO 39 (Fribourg: Universitaires; Göttingen: Vandenhoeck & Ruprecht, 1981), and Alan Millard, "The Knowledge of Writing in Iron Age Palestine," *Tyndale Bulletin* 46 (1995): 207–17. Lemaire's position, that schools were widespread in ancient Israel and Judah, has widely been considered an overstatement of the available evidence. See as an example the review of his book by James Crenshaw (*JBL* 103 [1984]: 630–32).

3. Cross-cultural comparisons with the Mari and Neo-Assyrian archives also suggest that individuals whose roles overlap with those of the biblical "prophets" did not themselves write. See Martti Nissenin, "How Prophecy Became Literature," *SJOT* 19 (2005): 157, 163.

4. Seth L. Sanders, *The Invention of Hebrew* (Urbana, IL: University of Illinois Press, 2009), 36–47. See also the brief discussion in Karel van der Toorn, *Scribal Culture and the*

demonstrated, to attain a high level of literacy, even with an alphabetic script, takes a significant amount of time and resources. Its ease was overestimated by modern literate scholars who were unconsciously reflecting upon the relative ease with which they themselves picked up a second or third language written in an alphabetic script. Becoming literate for the first time requires significant time, effort, and resource expenditure (and we need look no further than contemporary public education to recognize that this is so).[5]

This brings us to the second point, which requires that we rethink the composition and transmission of the biblical prophetic books. Rollston's careful analysis of the epigraphic data from Iron Age II Judah and Israel strongly suggests that literacy was largely the product of the state.[6] I will not repeat his arguments in full here, but a brief summary of his main points includes the following: Synchronic consistency in letter shape and formation, as well as the spatial relationship of letters to each other (*samek-pe* sequence being the most important); synchronic consistency in orthography; and the use of complicated Egyptian hieratic numerals all indicate that scribal training in Israel and Judah was standardized, and such widespread standardization is difficult to account for outside the context of the state administration.[7] An earlier study by Ian Young also arrived at a similar conclusion: Literacy in ancient Israel was primarily the prerogative of the elite, specifically those involved in state administration.[8] One can infer from the data evaluated in

---

Making of the Hebrew Bible (Cambridge, MA: Harvard University Press, 2007), 10–11, and his note (p. 269 n. 11) about how ideology influences one's perception of literacy (citing Millard as an example).

5. I had the privilege of teaching more than 250 students in the prior academic year. All had received at least thirteen years of training in alphabetic literacy (and requiring tens of thousands of dollars of investment for each student to reach that level). While most could hammer out several paragraphs or pages of their own composition, no more than two or three of them were highly competent writers.

6. See Christopher A. Rollston, "Scribal Education in Ancient Israel: The Old Hebrew Epigraphic Evidence," *BASOR* 344 (2006): 47–74. Richard Hess has written an essay in support of more-widespread literacy in ancient Israel that in part responds to Rollston's arguments, but he fails to counter any of the substantive epigraphic data that Rollston used to argue his position. Instead Hess resorts to the "Hebrew has so few letters" argument as well as comparative ethnographic evidence, which suggests large numbers of ancient Arabian nomads had rudimentary literacy ("Questions of Reading and Writing in Ancient Israel," *BBR* 19 [2009]: 6–7). However, nomads capable of writing their own name and those of their ancestors is not the same as someone writing a more sophisticated literary text that is transmitted in writing over a long period of time (see below).

7. Rollston, "Scribal Education." I have included a fuller discussion of his argument in James M. Bos, *Reconsidering the Date and Provenance of the Book of Hosea: The Case for Persian-Period Yehud*, LHBOTS 580 (New York: Bloomsbury, 2013), 8–9.

8. Ian M. Young, "Israelite Literacy: Interpreting the Evidence, Part I," *VT* 48 (1998): 239–53; idem, "Israelite Literacy: Interpreting the Evidence, Part II," *VT* 48 (1998): 408–

these two studies that the capacity to write more than a few easily memorized words like one's own name, that is, the capacity to write lengthy or sophisticated literature, was not widespread, nor was it available to just anyone. Random persons unaffiliated with the state bureaucracy were likely not producing any kind of literature (nor did they have need to). This stands even if some such persons did understand the mechanisms of writing and reading, or could even write their own name or had some additional rudimentary literacy skills.[9] Scribes in the ancient Levant were highly trained individuals, and the state administration, the only institution as far as I can determine that had both the need for literate employees as well as the resources to produce them, was the social location for and financier of their training. If this premise be accepted, then it has significant implications for understanding the composition and transmission of the literature that we now term the prophetic books, especially those texts that "predict" the downfall of the state (whether king, temple, cities, or all of the above), in other words, the prophecy of doom.[10]

Prophecies or oracles of doom are quite common in the prophetic books of the Hebrew Bible, but if one takes a broader geographic and chronological view of things, this literary genre is quite unique in the Near East.[11] People predicting with great earnestness the collapse of their own society appears to be a bit of an historical quirk, an abnormality. In the wider Near East, *written*

---

22. One should note that he does not preclude some prophets writing, but suggests that those prophets who could write "came from a background in the literate sections of the community—priests and the upper class" ("Interpreting the Evidence II," 17).

9. There was no doubt a spectrum of writing proficiency in ancient Judah, from those who could write a few letters to those who composed sophisticated literary texts. It is not implausible that a significant number of Judahites might have been found at the bottom of the spectrum, that is, with very rudimentary literacy skills, but these were not the individuals recording, interpreting, archiving, and transmitting prophetic oracles. Only those at the higher end of the spectrum were capable of doing such. One should also note here that the activity of reading required different skills and different training than writing, and for the ancient world, its extent is even more difficult to judge than writing literacy due to the fact that reading leaves no direct evidence. However, the writing of texts presupposes a reading audience (in most cases a human audience), and thus, the question of which group(s) consumed the prophetic literature is relevant to how and when these texts came into being. See Nissinen, "How Prophecy Became Literature," who writes, "The literarization of prophecy presupposes a community that adopts, repeats, interprets and reinterprets prophetic messages for its own purposes" (155).

10. Should it be determined that significant numbers of Judahites not affiliated directly with the state administration were highly literate (i.e., capable of composing literature), my thesis would be significantly weakened.

11. It is not my purpose here to give a detailed description of this rather familiar genre. My discussion will be more general, applicable to any and all passages in the prophetic books of the Hebrew Bible that appear to predict the thorough destruction of Israel or Judah, regardless of the specifics.

texts predicting, even promoting, the destruction of the state (one's own, not a rival's) as we find in the Hebrew Bible appear to be few and far between.[12] Sure, there are several preserved oracles from the Near East that chide or issue minor threats to the reigning king if he does not maintain this or that temple or properly provision the statue of this or that deity,[13] and one or two that promote the downfall of one king in favor of another,[14] but nothing that envisions as thoroughgoing a destruction of the society (including the most significant institutions and political-religious offices) as the biblical prophecies of doom. None that I am aware of calls for a thorough reworking of the political, social, and religious *status quo* in the way that the biblical prophecies of doom do. I do not think the rarity of such texts in the wider Near East is an accident of preservation. Rather, such rarity is easily explainable by the elevated status of the kings in their respective state, their perceived role in creating and maintaining cosmic order, as well as by the fact that literacy was the prerogative of the state. In general, kings would likely not have allowed texts to be produced (and archived, studied, interpreted, disseminated, used in the state curriculum, etc.) that threatened their position or their territory.

---

12. Granted, written prophecy of any kind is somewhat rare in the ancient Near East, with just two significant corpora (the Mari correspondence and the Neo-Assyrian archives) of texts containing prophetic oracles. Prophetic oracles in fact begin as an oral genre and only secondarily become a written genre (and even later, it would seem, a literary genre). See Nissinen, "How Prophecy Became Literature." Joachim Schaper also touches on this issue of prophecy being adapted to a literary context in "Exilic and Post-Exilic Prophecy and the Orality/Literacy Problem," *VT* 55 (2005): 324–42.

13. For a translation of such examples from the Mari correspondence, see numbers 13, 25, 27, and 29 in Martti Nissinen, with contributions by C. L. Seow and Robert K. Ritner, *Prophets and Prophecy in the Ancient Near East*, ed. Peter Machinist, WAW 12 (Leiden: Brill, 2003); and for the Neo-Assyrian oracles, see especially number 88 in the same volume.

14. See the few extant examples in Martti Nissinen, "Prophecy against the King in Neo-Assyrian Sources," in *Lasset uns Brücken bauen: Collected communications to the XVth Congress of the International Organization for the Study of the Old Testament, Cambridge 1995*, ed. Klaus-Dietrich Schunck and Matthias Augusti, BEATJ 42 (Frankfurt: Lang, 1998), 157–70, as well as a detailed discussion of the political circumstances that occasioned one of the oracles uttered on behalf of a rival of Esarhaddon in Karen Radner, "The Trials of Esarhaddon: The Conspiracy of 670 BC," in *Assur und sein Umland*, ed. Peter A. Miglus, Joaquín M. Cordoba, Isimu 6 (Madrid: Universidad Autónoma de Madrid, 2003), 165–84. Notably, the Succession Treaty of Esarhaddon presupposes that oracles would at least be potentially uttered against the king in favor of another. But significantly for this study, such oracles do not undermine the institution of monarchy itself nor the society as a whole, and secondly, both the prophet giving the subversive oracle(s) and the scribe recording the oracle(s) would presumably be subordinate to another claimant to the throne. In other words, even in a situation where the reigning king was opposed by a prophet, the writing down and preservation of his oracles took place in the context of state politics.

Furthermore, virtually everyone who could write would likely have been an employee of the state, so producing texts that envisioned the downfall of said state (whether by military defeat or other means) would have been effectively suicide.[15] Yet, in ancient Judah (and perhaps Israel[16]) such literature was in fact produced, literature predicting (ostensibly at least) chaos and disorder, the overthrow of king and cult. How and when did this happen? Many scholars have assumed that the prophecies of doom so common in the Hebrew Bible can be traced back to an historical prophet.[17]

However, a growing minority tends to view these oracles as *ex eventu* prophecy, largely disassociated from an historical prophet, postdating and responding theologically to the catastrophic events in Judah in the early sixth century BCE.[18] The above discussion on the locus and extent of high-level literacy, in my opinion, strongly favors the latter position. Writing and writers generally served the interest of the elite, and it is only with great difficulty that one can imagine an elite person or group of persons in monarchic Israel and Judah who benefited from the production, archiving, and transmission of the prophetic oracles of doom that called for the downfall of the state and its various elites. Furthermore, those who imagine not simply the recording of

---

15. On the contrary, oracles that were supportive of the reigning king and contemporary society were the norm, and it is not surprising that most of the preserved oracles from Mesopotamia fall into this category. Furthermore, it is highly likely that the earliest literary strands of some of the biblical prophetic books were archived oracles of immediate wellbeing or success (as opposed to some distant, ill-defined salvation or restoration, which are common in more advanced forms of such books), as Matthijs de Jong has demonstrated quite clearly for the Isaiah tradition (*Isaiah among the Ancient Near Eastern Prophets: A Comparative Study of the Earliest Stages of the Isaiah Tradition and the Neo-Assyrian Prophecies*, VTSup 117 [Leiden: Brill, 2007]). But these "positive" oracles are not puzzling or unexpected and are thus not my focus.

16. I have argued at length that the book of Hosea is a Judahite book (Bos, *Date and Provenance of the Book of Hosea*).

17. For a contemporary example, see Jacques Vermeylen, "Des redactions deutéronomistes dans le livre d'Esaïe?" in *Les recueils prophétiques de la Bible: Origines, milieu, et context proche-oriental*, ed. Jean-Daniel Macchi, et al. (Fribourg: Labor et Fides, 2012): 145–87, who specifically rejects the position of de Jong (and Becker, whose works I have not consulted) that the historical Isaiah was largely supportive of king and state, and in contrast, views Isaiah as a prophet of doom (147–49). In earlier periods of biblical scholarship it was not unusual for scholars to point to the absolute uniqueness of Israel's prophets, their moral conscience and elevated spirituality, as an explanation for their opposition to the morally corrupt society in which they lived. This is an overly romantic view of matters and has rightly been largely discarded.

18. In addition to de Jong's monograph on Isaiah, see also his essay, "Biblical Prophecy, a Scribal Enterprise: The Old Testament Prophecy of Unconditional Judgment considered as a Literary Phenomenon," *VT* 61 (2011): 39–70; Karl-Friedrich Pohlmann, "La question de la formation du livre d'Ezéchiel," in Macchi, *Les recueils prophétiques de la Bible*, 309–36; and Bos, *Date and Provenance of the Book of Hosea*.

an individual oracle or two, but rather, lengthier literary elaborations during the monarchic period must also reckon with a cadre of scribes (likely trained by the state, over several generations) who read, copied, interpreted, recopied this literature that was predicting the downfall of their own society. And a series of monarchs who allowed them to engage in such activity (and at least indirectly contributed financially to the composition, preservation, and transmission of such texts). This, to me, would be incredible, and from a comparative perspective, highly implausible. However, there is one literary text from the Iron Age Levant that potentially presents a challenge to my thesis and perhaps provide some support for the notion that literature corresponding closely to biblical prophecies of doom was in fact composed and transmitted in the monarchic period of Israel and Judah, namely the Balaam Inscription from Deir Alla. This inscription, dating (most likely) to the eighth century BCE,[19] shares some similarities with biblical prophecies of doom, and thus may indicate that such prophecies were put in writing in neighboring Israel and Judah prior to 586 BCE.

The most thorough recent study of this inscription as it relates to the writing down and preserving of oracles of doom, potentially as a model for understanding the origin of oracles of doom in the biblical corpus, was carried out by Erhard Blum.[20] His analysis of this inscription's relevance to biblical prophecies of doom can be summarized as follows:[21]

(1) The Balaam Inscription presupposes a prophetic work that has as its opponents/addressees the *community* to which the prophet/seer belongs, *not* the king (emphasis his).

---

19. Jo Ann Hackett (*The Balaam Text from Deir ʿAllā*, [Chico, CA: Scholars Press, 1984], 19) argues from the paleographical data that the early seventh century BCE is a likely date. Baruch Levine ("The Deir ʿAlla Plaster Inscriptions," *COS* 2.27:141), pointing to laboratory tests carried out by the excavators, prefers the very early eighth century.

20. Erhard Blum, "Israels Prophetie im altorientalischen Kontext: Anmerkungen zu neueren religionsgeschichtlichen Thesen," in *"From Ebla to Stellenbosch": Syro-Palestinian Religions and the Hebrew Bible*, ed. I. Cornelius and L. Jonker, ADPV 37 (Wiesbaden: Harrassowitz, 2008), 81–115. For earlier treatments of this inscription and its relation to the Hebrew Bible, one should also see Meindert Dijkstra, "Is Balaam also among the Prophets?" *JBL* 114 (1995): 43–64; and Manfred Weippert, "The Balaam Text from Deir ʿAllā and the Study of the Old Testament," in *The Balaam Text from Deir ʿAlla Reevaluated: Proceeedings of the International Symposium Held at Leiden 21–24 August 1989*, ed. J. Hoftijzer and G. Van der Kooij (Leiden: Brill, 1991), 151–84. Both of these scholars wrote before the "new paradigm" in prophetic studies was significantly underway, and to which Blum is responding, so I have primarily restricted my comments and analysis to Blum's treatment of the inscription.

21. Translated and adapted from Blum, "Israels Prophetie," 95–96.

(2) It narrates an announcement of a comprehensive, almost cosmic, event; it is *not* about daily decisions like those provided by oracle inquiries.
(3) It narrates a comprehensive disaster brought about by the gods, *not* a prophecy of salvation.
(4) It sees this disaster, with some probability, as a divine reaction (anger) to a disturbance of the human and natural order.
(5) It profiles the task of the prophet (who beheld the council of the gods) as that of communicator between the divine and human worlds.
(6) It can be deduced that the author and tradents in the ninth/eighth century (in the near vicinity of ancient Israel) were familiar with the basic model of a judgment prophecy, and they transmitted its paradigmatic elements in this narrative.[22]
(7) The pragmatics of the inscription (including Combination II) was probably wisdom instruction, that is, in a broader sense of "a teaching." The Balaam Inscription thus possessed material from the educational circles that required a corresponding curriculum for either the professional or for those who could afford it, even in a relatively remote place like Tell Deir Alla.

He then proceeds to discuss the plausibility of preexilic prophecies of judgment in Israel and Judah, remarking that one cannot disallow for cultural innovation nor regional differences (i.e., the distinctiveness of such prophecy in Israel and Judah cannot be used incautiously as an argument against its historicity) while also arguing that attempts to place such prophecies in the postmonarchic period have been unsuccessful.[23] This leads him to the essay's two-fold thesis: first, the necessary conceptual presuppositions for a prophecy of judgment were present in the wider ancient Near East, and second, specific constellations in [preexilic] Israel are visible that could give rise to such a phenomenon.[24] These presuppositions, supported with several comparative examples, include the ideas that 1) the gods punish the misconduct of humans, 2) that a national god can hand over his people to the

---

22. As will be seen below, this is the only point on his list with which I am in substantial disagreement.
23. Blum, "Israels Prophetie," 96–99. He notes that collective disasters were not infrequent in the ancient Near East and asks why it would be that only tiny Judah responded to the events of 586 with *ex eventu* prophecy. Such a statement appears to me, however, to undermine his immediately prior statement about allowing for cultural innovation and regional distinctiveness.
24. Ibid., 102.

enemy, and 3) that the gods may communicate a planned disaster through a seer.[25] He concludes the essay by briefly discussing the historical scenario (namely, the expansion of Assyrian hegemony in the Levant and its aftermath) under which the prophecies of judgment found in the books of Amos, Hosea, and Isaiah might have first been put into writing.[26] Significantly, at least for Hosea, he reckons with, in part, "a wide-ranging literary composition by the prophet himself."[27] I find this highly unlikely for the reasons I outlined above.

However, Blum certainly is correct that there are literary and conceptual aspects of the prophecy of doom that existed prior to 586 BCE (and of course, no literary genre is birthed *ex nihilo*). According to the dominant worldview in the ancient Near East, any kind of hardship, whether drought, plague, or military defeat, could be considered the result of one or more gods' disfavor resulting from some "incorrect" behavior. This is certainly an underlying assumption in the biblical prophecy of doom. Significantly, however, in the majority of instances in the wider Near East when the gods' anger is referenced as an explanation for a given calamity, it is an after-the-fact explanation.[28] Should we expect something different from Israel and Judah? Furthermore, and this is getting to the heart of my argument, the written texts in which the divine anger occurs as an explanation for a disaster are seemingly always "state literature," that is, the writing is produced by scribes working for a king whose interests are served by the information in the text being disseminated. To cite two of the examples brought forward by Blum, the text from the period of Esarhaddon's reign that explains the destruction of Babylon by Sennacherib as due to Marduk's anger was a political text. It served to justify Esarhaddon's building activity. The Mesha Inscription, which assigns Moab's subjugation to Israel as due to Kemosh's anger, was also a political text. It served to legitimize Mesha. In many cases it would appear, then, that the motif of the god's anger (and its appeasement) serves to legitimize a transition in leadership or a new phase in the life of a city or state. Thus, rather than suggesting the potential for preexilic prophecies of doom, the concept of divine anger in the wider Near East points instead to them

---

25. Ibid., 102–4.
26. Ibid., 105–8.
27. Ibid., 104. Translation mine.
28. See de Jong, "Biblical Prophecy, a Scribal Enterprise," who writes concerning divine anger, "This kind of reflection or explanation always *followed* the events which it aimed to explain" (42; emphasis his). The exception might be the Balaam inscription, if it does in fact reference the anger of a deity in line 7 (the translation of the verb *thgy* is at issue), and if in fact there was an actual calamity following the prediction. See below for my interpretation of this text.

being a postdisaster literary explanation for Jerusalem's defeat.[29] In postmonarchic Judah such "prophecies" served the interests of the priestly elite, those working in Yahweh's new temple specifically. It helped explain away the apparent weakness of their god and legitimized their new socio-religious community and its attendant worldview. And these temple functionaries were literate, or at least some of them were. They had sufficient reason to produce, archive, copy, and transmit texts that "predicted," by the mouth of Yahweh's legendary prophets, the fall of their state, because it had already happened, and because the figures of the prophets of old were models for the Yahwism they endorsed and promoted.

So this brings me to the third presupposition that Blum considers to be an ingredient in the biblical prophecies of doom, namely, that the gods could communicate a future or planned disaster to a community through a prophet or seer (with the Balaam Inscription being the only example he cites). Another way to phrase this would be that prophecy was one method of divination among many utilized in the ancient Near East.[30] Kings often consulted divinatory specialists, and this would include figures that we designate as "prophets," to receive counsel regarding upcoming military campaigns and a whole host of other issues.[31] Divination by its very nature allowed for the possibility of multiple outcomes, some of which could be classified as "doom" for the king or state. That said, neither the divinatory methods nor the diviners themselves were entirely objective; data and the interpretation of data could be manipulated when necessary. Furthermore, whenever a divinatory method did point to a potential disaster, the ritual specialists had the means to deal with it to avoid the catastrophe.[32] In fact, that was a significant

---

29. This does not mean that divine anger is not a presupposition of the prophecy of doom as Blum states. It is. But it is a matter of when this motif is realized in writing, specifically in the form of a written prediction of doom due to this anger that is at issue.

30. My discussion in this paragraph and the following depends heavily on de Jong, "Biblical Prophecy, a Scribal Enterprise." For discussions of prophecy as a form of divination, see Martti Nissinen, "Prophecy and Omen Divination: Two Sides of the Same Coin," in *Divination and the Interpretation of Signs in the Ancient World*, ed. Amar Annus (Chicago: The Oriental Institute of the University of Chicago, 2010), 341–51; Joann Scurlock, "Prophecy as a Form of Divination; Divination as a Form of Prophecy," in Annus, *Divination and the Interpretation of Signs*, 277–307; Zak Kotzé, "Old Testament Prophecy as Divination: The Case of Isaiah 14:28–32," *Journal for Semitics* 22 (2013): 90–100.

31. Nonelite people could also consult with diviners, but they less frequently left behind a record of their activity. (And I assume that if recorded, it was recorded by a literate person associated with the state.)

32. In this regard see Stefan M. Maul, "How the Babylonians Protected Themselves against Calamities Announced by Omens," in *Mesopotamian Magic: Textual Historical, and Interpretative Perspectives*, ed. T. Abusch and K. Van der Toorn, AMD 1 (Groningen: Styx, 1999), 123–29; the ritual of the substitute king is relevant here as well, for examples of

component of their role. The diviner who foresaw disaster served to protect his state from the foreseen disaster. His role was to maintain cosmic order, including protecting the king. He certainly was not calling for radical social or religious transformation. Moreover, if literate, he was trained in the context of the state administration, and all texts that he consulted, composed, or edited were also produced and preserved to serve the interest of state and king.

It is with this divinatory context of the ancient Near East in view that the Balaam Inscription is best interpreted. If Balaam was an actual historical figure (which is far from certain), then he apparently was a highly regarded diviner whose role overlapped with that of figures we deem "prophets" or "seers" (based primarily on the image of such figures in the Hebrew Bible). In one instance, later to be memorialized in the Deir Alla inscription, he claimed to have received a vision of the divine council (whether induced or not is unclear). By means of the vision he divines the danger facing his community and alerts them of the coming cosmic chaos. Unfortunately, this is where Combination I of the inscription breaks off. The "end of the story" is thus unknown, but it seems plausible that it was a "happy ending" based on the fact that the story was put up for display. Thus, I infer that Balaam (again if we want to assume some historicity to the story in the Deir Alla inscription[33]) subsequently performed the necessary rituals to avert the disaster, which then never arrived, making Balaam a hero whose activity was valued by his community and king, the latter in his gratitude then commissioning the story to be commemorated in the shrine at Deir Alla.[34] The prior sentence contains a great deal of speculation, but if I were to distill the most important points regarding the potential of the Balaam Inscription as a forerunner or near generic parallel to the biblical prophecies of doom, they would be: 1) In contrast to the biblical prophetic figures, Balaam is not presented as a critic of his people or king[35] (even if divine anger is involved in the reason for the

---

which during Esarhaddon's reign, see Radner, "The Trials of Esarhaddon."

33. If the story is entirely fictional, and it may very well be, then the story simply presents a prototypical diviner doing his job. Thus, it would not change my argument significantly.

34. Brian B. Schmidt has informed me (personal communication) that he has an essay in progress in which he proposes that the Deir Alla inscription was originally an oracle given and recorded on behalf of Aram against Ammon-Gilead. In this scenario, the text is an oracle against a foreign nation put up for display in the foreign, conquered territory, being read then as an oracle of doom by the native populace. See below on the oracle of doom as a reversal or inversion of the oracle against a foreign nation.

35. De Jong writes, "[Balaam] is *with* them, not *opposed to* them as are the protagonists in the biblical books," ("Biblical Prophecy, a Scribal Enterprise," 64; emphasis his). For an alternate view, see Dijkstra, "Is Balaam also among the Prophets?" who finds in

"predicted" disaster); and 2) he is presented as desiring to maintain cosmic order, not destroy it; and finally, 3) there is not a single sentence in the text that is in any way threatening to a king or another elite.[36] I believe that Blum is correct in seeing this inscription as the product of *Traditionsliteratur*[37] and potentially as part of the scribal curriculum for one of the Aramaean petty states precisely because it served to promote social stability (unless we have to reckon with a surprise ending). It presented a diviner carrying out his role in exemplary fashion and potentially served as a model for other aspiring diviners (who would also work to protect their community). In other words, it was the kind of text a king could get behind (which from my discussion of

---

Combination II (which he believes was intended to follow directly after Combination I) a disputation between seer and people (55). However, Combination II is badly preserved and not all scholars are convinced that it is directly connected with Combination I, many hesitating to interpret it as such. Even if we assume for the moment that Combination II does continue Combination I, and we also assume that it involves, in part, a dispute between Balaam and his audience, it may simply be that the audience is being presented as initially incredulous about his message rather than that he is opposed to them or they to him.

36. At least in Combination I. There are potentially a few preserved clauses in Combination II that, devoid of a full literary context due to the fragmentary nature of its preservation, can be interpreted as antimonarchical in nature. C. L. Seow translates line 18 as "I have punished the king" (in Nissinen, *Prophets and Prophecy*, 212). If this is the correct reading of this line (most translators have opted not to translate the line due to its illegibility), it may undermine my thesis that the Deir Alla texts are not threatening to a sitting king. However, if this reading is adopted, it is not clear who either of the referents might have been. It is plausible that the "I" is a deity and the king a native, recently deceased king (note that other parts of the Combination appear to reflect an underworld setting). But even in this situation, a discussion about a king of the past could be presented in such a way as to bolster the position of the current king. More significantly, though, this reading is far from secure. I consulted several photographs of this line in the InscriptiFact Digital Image Library (University of Southern California) but unfortunately could not distinguish even a single letter. Furthermore, even if the root *mlk* appears in the line, it does not necessarily refer to a king. This Northwest Semitic root may also be translated as "to counsel." This is the meaning assigned by Blum to the root's occurrence in line 18, but he also notes that it "represents an 'imagined' reading of several possible" ("'Verstehst du dich nicht auf die Schreibkunst...?' Ein weisheitlicher Dialog über Vergänglichkeit und Verantwortung: Kombination II der Wandinschrift vom Tell Deir 'Alla" in *Was ist der Mensch, dass du seiner gedenkst? (Psalm 8,5): Aspekte einer theologischen Anthropologie (Festschrift für Bernd Janowski zum 65. Geburtstag)*, ed. M. Bauks, et al. (Neukirchen-Vluyn: Neukirchener Verlag, 2008), 38. Hackett opts to see Combination II as an example of *mulk* child sacrifice known from neo-Punic inscriptions (80–85). In sum, the occurrence of *mlk* in Combination II may or may not designate a king, but even if it does, the context is not sufficiently clear to determine whether or not the inscription can be classified as "antimonarchic."

37. For this understanding of the Balaam Inscription, see Blum, "Israels Prophetie," 96. It derives in part from the fact that the inscription appears to have been copied from a scroll and the word *spr* is part of the heading (see Weippert, "The Balaam Text," 178).

literacy above is confirmed by the very fact that it was a literary text put up for display; I do not think such display literature was possible in the Near East without royal support). Thus, while Blum is correct that the Balaam inscription presupposes certain aspects of the conceptual worldview also present in the biblical prophecies of doom, it is ultimately not a close generic parallel to these biblical prophecies, for which royal sponsorship seems highly unlikely.[38] Consequently, neither does it suggest that prophecies of doom were likely texualized before 586 BCE in Judah (or Israel). When this textualization (put into writing) and ultimately their literarization (arranged into larger literary works) occurs is still a question, although hinted at above, and in an attempt to try to answer it more fully, I would like to return to the topic of divination.

As mentioned above, virtually all forms of divination allowed for at least two possible outcomes, and sometimes the result could be classified as "negative." But more often than not (because of the subjectivity inherent in the method as well as the diviner's desire for self-preservation, promotion, payment, etc.), the method would yield a result that was favorable for the person regarding whom the oracle was given (whether solicited or not). It was thought that a deity could (and would) ensure the military defeat of another nation, and furthermore, he or she could convey the certainty of this future event to the king via a prophetic intermediary and/or other divinatory method. If the Mari correspondence and Neo-Assyrian oracle collections are in any way representative of prophetic divinatory results in the wider Near East, then such favorable results on matters of national and international policy, including in particular warfare and the overall well-being of the king, were common. At the very least, and this is crucial to my argument, oracles predicting favorable results were sought by (or welcomed by) the king and they were the ones written down and archived. In other words, divinatory practices that predicted the downfall of *rival* nations or kings were frequent and normative and would be the most likely to be written down and preserved. On the other hand, those oracles predicting a defeat of the native king by a foreign opponent (or some other devastating event), when they did occur, even if less frequently than oracles of success, required various rituals to avoid the negative prediction and furthermore were less likely to be preserved (even if initially written down on a tablet or potsherd—not memorialized on a wall).

---

38. To a question posed by James Crenshaw regarding the necessity of institutional sponsorship being required for the survival of prophetic oracles, Nissinen answers emphatically in the affirmative ("How Prophecy Became Literature," 172). It is my contention that the postmonarchic temple context provides a more suitable sponsor than the royal palace (before 586).

Moreover, when an oracle yielded a "positive" result for the king in question, it would be simultaneously, from the perspective of the rival, a prediction of his defeat and thus a "negative" result, or in other words, an oracle of doom for the enemy.[39] In other words, any given oracle could function as both an oracle of success and an oracle of doom, depending on with which side one was aligned. This may provide a helpful way to think about biblical prophecies of doom. It appears to me that, generically speaking, the biblical prophecy of doom (targeting Judah or Israel) is an oracle against a foreign nation or king (which equals an oracle of success for the native nation or king) turned on its head, or turned inward. It is an unexpected reversal of the norm:[40] a positive divinatory outcome for the enemy king or nation (with the prescribed ritual procedures for avoiding the disaster often being a return to proper cultic behavior).[41] Thus, the oracle against a foreign nation is the literary genre from which the biblical prophecy of doom arises—the latter is an adaptation, reapplication, and eventually, a literary expansion of the earlier genre of the oracle against a foreign nation now directed at the native state.[42]

However, this assessment of the birth of the genre of the oracle of doom does not address when the genre first appeared as an adaptation of the earlier oracle against a foreign nation. I see three primary options for when this inversion—the historical circumstances when the norm became *written* oracles overwhelmingly containing "negative" results for the native nation— might have developed in ancient Judah. The first is to consider all biblical oracles of doom as prophecy *ex eventu*. In this scenario, the scribal elite in Judah only first start writing "predictions" of Judah's defeat after Judah had suffered successive military losses in the early sixth century. They reapplied the genre of the oracle against a foreign nation to their own nation and they did so as a means to explain why Judah had been destroyed. Couching the

---

39. It should be noted, however, that not every oracle of success for the "native" king involves a specific rival who will lose. Some refer simply to the generic success for the king in his endeavors. Others include nameless "enemies."

40. At least in terms of the quantity and intensity of the denunciations.

41. And thus significantly less specific than is often the case (cf. the NAM.BÚR.BI ritual discussed in Maul, "How the Babylonians Protected Themselves").

42. Oracles against foreign nations are well attested in the Near East, including the Levant. In addition to the numerous examples from the Mari correspondence and the Neo-Assyrian archives, one can also find a rather typical example in the inscription of Zakkur (ca. 800 BCE), where Baal Shamayn is presented as speaking through the seers of Hamath and informing the king that he will save him from the besieging army. Despite its fragmentary condition the Amman Citadel also appears to be an oracle of success granted by the god Milcom to an Ammonite king (9th century BCE). For translations of these two texts see Walter E. Aufrecht, "The Amman Citadel Inscription," *COS* 1.24:139 and Alan Millard, "The Inscription of Zakkur, King of Hamath," *COS* 1.35:155.

"predictions" in the past, in the mouths of Yahweh's trusted spokespersons, served to justify Yahweh's actions, including his apparent weakness.[43] It allowed them to make sense of Yahweh's inability or unwillingness to protect his people. The defeat of Judah was in fact orchestrated by Yahweh, because he was angry at them, as the prophetic voices in the texts made clear. Thus, the oracle of doom arose after the events of the early sixth century as a means of rationalizing the nation's military defeats and loss of political autonomy.

The second option is related to the first but instead of placing this "flip" from oracle against a foreign nation to oracle against one's own nation after the defeat of Judah, the process began after the defeat of Israel in 721 BCE. In other words, scribes in Judah (or less likely in Israel itself) sought to explain Assyria's defeat of Israel by means of *ex eventu* prophecy.[44] Or, scribes in Judah might have recorded oracles predicting their northern rival's doom, and after Israel's fall, a small collection of such oracles were preserved that formed the basis for later literary expansion and interpretation.[45] However, if this kind of scribal activity occurred in the seventh century in Judah, it is still rather unlikely in my view that full-fledged oracles of doom (in this case, oracles against Judah by Judahites) were textualized. One would still be dealing with oracles that focused on the disaster that befell a close neighbor, and therefore oracles that were not technically aimed at one's own nation. Furthermore, the dominant ideology of the Judahite elite at this time highlighted the eternal nature of David's lineage and the inviolability of Jerusalem. Scribes trained in Judah would have been no doubt exposed to, and likely immersed in, this ideology, and thus, the recording and preserving of oracles that were explicitly and forcefully in opposition to this ideology would seem unlikely. However, once Judah was destroyed in 586, the prior oracles against Israel (written down by Judahite scribes and preserved in Judah) could have served as a conceptual and generic model for explaining the fall of Judah, giving rise to Judahite *ex eventu* prophecies of doom. The adaptation and reapplication of the earlier oracles against Israel (preserved in Judah) into *ex eventu* oracles against Judah would likely have been aided by the postmonarchic Judahite elite increasingly designating themselves as "Israel." They saw in the earlier fall of Israel their own similar downfall.

---

43. Pohlmann in particular stresses that the prophetic books originated as a way to deflect accusations of Yahweh's impotence (see "La question de la formation," 336).

44. De Jong allows for this possibility ("Biblical Prophecy, a Scribal Enterprise," 55–56) but notes that it would be unlikely for Judahites to consider their own doom inevitable once Israel had fallen.

45. Note that in this scenario, it is still not a matter of a prophet predicting the fall of his own nation, but rather the fall of a rival nation, which is not unusual or unexpected as discussed above.

Finally, I would like to propose a third option, namely, that the earliest written oracles of doom (Judahites predicting Judah's defeat) might have arisen during the midst of the inner-Judahite diplomatic squabbles of the early sixth century. Numerous scholars have reconstructed a historical scenario in which there were two main factions in Judah, one promoting loyalty to Babylon, the other disloyalty (with Egypt's aid).[46] Lipschits has demonstrated convincingly, on both literary and archaeological grounds, that the pro-Babylonian faction was probably predominantly located in northern Judah in the area associated with the tribe of Benjamin.[47] If the tension between the two factions was high enough, and it seems it could have been, then it would not be unexpected that one or more prophets associated with the Benjaminite elite could have uttered oracles predicting the fall of Jerusalem and the Davidic dynasty. This would have benefitted the Benjaminite elite who presumably would replace them, and historically, they appear to have done so, at least temporarily, in the person of Gedaliah. Notably, Dutcher-Walls argues that each faction would have had representatives from the "full range of elite social roles" (including professional scribes),[48] so it is not inconceivable that such oracles favorable to the Benjaminite faction (and critical of Jerusalem and the Davidides) could have been put down in writing.[49] If this historical reconstruction, or some scenario not too dissimilar to it, took place (and I recognize there is a good deal of speculation here), then we are dealing with Judahites issuing and recording oracles against Judah, and thus approximating later expressions of the biblical prophecies of doom. Such oracles also make sense in the context of the rivalry between the two factions as well due to the fact that both factions had access to scribes who in turn had the motivation to put such oracles into writing and to preserve them. Needless to say, once Jerusalem was destroyed, such oracles were ripe for further literary expansion and interpretation, spawning even further oracles (these being *ex eventu*). Eventually, in the century that followed, with the rebuilding of Jerusalem and the temple of Yahweh located there, the earlier textualized oracles against Judah grew into a distinct literary genre that also included oracles of restoration intermixed with the oracles of doom. The development of this

---

46. See, e.g., Patricia Dutcher-Walls, "The Social Location of the Deuteronomists: a Sociological Study of Factional Politics in Late Pre-Exilic Judah," *JSOT* 16 (1991): 77–94.

47. Oded Lipschits, *The Fall and Rise of Jerusalem* (Winona Lake, IN: Eisenbrauns, 2005).

48. Dutcher-Walls, "The Social Locations of the Deuteronomists," 91. If we can trust the texts, one of the scribes involved in the conflict was a member of the Shaphanide family (87).

49. Without being too specific, early versions of oracles now appearing in Jeremiah 21–22 are possible examples of such oracles.

genre enabled the Judahite (Jerusalemite) elite to comprehend more fully the prior disaster and promote their ideological vision for the present and future, an ideology dominated by the exclusive worship of Yahweh.

My third option is in some ways a broadening of the first option, allowing for a few early, written oracles that actually predicted Jerusalem's fall (on behalf of a rival party within the Judahite elite) while viewing the majority of the biblical prophecies of doom as later *ex eventu* explanations of the disaster that used the few early oracles as a generic model. Over time these were greatly expanded and adapted. Nor does the third option exclude the second option: it is still possible that Judahite oracles involving Israel's defeat informed and influenced later Judahite oracles involving Judah's defeat. In any case, if my reconstruction of literacy in ancient Israel and Judah is correct, then it would appear to me that the "literarization" of the prophecies of doom occurred sometime in the early sixth century BCE at the earliest, with broadening and wider application of the genre extending well into the fifth century and perhaps beyond.

References

Blum, Erhard. "Israels Prophetie im altorientalischen Kontext: Anmerkungen zu neueren religionsgeschichtlichen Thesen." Pages 81–115 in *"From Ebla to Stellenbosch": Syro-Palestinian Religions and the Hebrew Bible*. Edited by I. Cornelius and L. Jonker. ADPV 37. Wiesbaden: Harrassowitz, 2008.

———. "'Verstehst du dich nicht auf die Schreibkunst...?' Ein weisheitlicher Dialog über Vergänglichkeit und Verantwortung: Kombination II der Wandinschrift vom Tell Deir 'Alla." Pages 33–53 in *Was ist der Mensch, dass du seiner gedenkst? (Psalm 8,5): Aspekte einer theologischen Anthropologie (Festschrift für Bernd Janowski zum 65. Geburtstag)*. Edited by M. Bauks, et al. Neukirchen-Vluyn: Neukirchener Verlag, 2008.

Bos, James M. *Reconsidering the Date and Provenance of the Book of Hosea: The Case for Persian-Period Yehud*. LHBOTS 580. New York: Bloomsbury, 2013.

Crenshaw, James. Review of André Lemaire, *Les écoles et la formation de la Bible dans l'ancien Israël. JBL* 103 (1984): 630–32.

De Jong, Matthijs J. "Biblical Prophecy, a Scribal Enterprise: The Old Testament Prophecy of Unconditional Judgment considered as a Literary Phenomenon." *VT* 61 (2011): 39–70.

———. *Isaiah among the Ancient Near Eastern Prophets: A Comparative Study of the Earliest Stages of the Isaiah Tradition and the Neo-Assyrian Prophecies*. VTSup 117. Leiden: Brill, 2007.

Dijkstra, Meindert. "Is Balaam also among the Prophets?" *JBL* 114 (1995): 43–64.

Dutcher-Walls, Patricia. "The Social Location of the Deuteronomists: A Sociological Study of Factional Politics in Late Pre-Exilic Judah." *JSOT* 16 (1991): 77–94.

Hackett, Jo Ann. *The Balaam Text from Deir 'Allā*. Chico, CA: Scholars Press, 1984.

Hallo, William W., and K. Lawson Younger, eds. *The Context of Scripture*. 3 volumes. Leiden: Brill, 1997–2002.
Hess, Richard. "Questions of Reading and Writing in Ancient Israel." *BBR* 19 (2009): 1–9.
Kotzé, Zak. "Old Testament Prophecy as Divination: The Case of Isaiah 14:28–32." *Journal for Semitics* 22 (2013): 90–100.
Lemaire, André. *Les écoles et la formation de la Bible dans l'ancien Israël*. OBO 39. Fribourg: Editions universitaires; Göttingen: Vandenhoeck & Ruprecht, 1981.
Lipschits, Oded. *The Fall and Rise of Jerusalem*. Winona Lake, IN: Eisenbrauns, 2005.
Maul, Stefan M. "How the Babylonians Protected Themselves against Calamities Announced by Omens." Pages 123–9 in *Mesopotamian Magic: Textual Historical, and Interpretative Perspectives*. Edited by T. Abusch and K. Van der Toorn. AMD 1. Groningen: Styx, 1999.
Millard, Alan. "The Knowledge of Writing in Iron Age Palestine." *Tyndale Bulletin* 46 (1995): 207–217.
Nissenin, Martti. "How Prophecy Became Literature." *SJOT* 19 (2005): 153–72.
———. "Prophecy against the King in Neo-Assyrian Sources." Pages 157–70 in *Lasset uns Brücken bauen: Collected Communications to the XVth Congress of the International Organization for the Study of the Old Testament, Cambridge 1995*. Edited by Klaus-Dietrich Schunck and Matthias Augustin. BEATJ 42. Frankfurt: Lang, 1998.
———. "Prophecy and Omen Divination: Two Sides of the Same Coin." Pages 341–51 in *Divination and the Interpretation of Signs in the Ancient World*. Edited by Amar Annus. Chicago: The Oriental Institute of the University of Chicago, 2010.
———, with contributions by C. L. Seow and Robert K. Ritner. *Prophets and Prophecy in the Ancient Near East*. Edited by Peter Machinist. WAW 12. Leiden: Brill, 2003.
Pohlmann, Karl-Friedrich. "La question de la formation du livre d'Ezéchiel." Pages 309–36 in *Les recueils prophétiques de la Bible: Origines, milieu, et context proche-oriental*. Edited by Jean-Daniel Macchi, et al. Fribourg: Labor et Fides, 2012.
Radner, Karen. "The Trials of Esarhaddon: The Conspiracy of 670 BC." Pages 165–84 in *Assur und sein Umland: Im Andenken an die ersten Ausgräber von Assur*. Edited by Peter A. Miglus and Joaquín M. Cordoba. Isimu: Revista sobre Oriente Proximo y Egipto en la antiguedad 6. Madrid: Universidad Autónoma de Madrid, 2003.
Rollston, Christopher A. "Scribal Education in Ancient Israel: The Old Hebrew Epigraphic Evidence." *BASOR* 344 (2006): 47–74.
Sanders, Seth L. *The Invention of Hebrew*. Urbana, IL: University of Illinois Press, 2009.
Schaper, Joachim. "Exilic and Post-Exilic Prophecy and the Orality/Literacy Problem." *VT* 55 (2005): 324–42.
Scurlock, JoAnn. "Prophecy as a Form of Divination; Divination as a Form of Prophecy." Pages 277–307 in *Divination and the Interpretation of Signs in the Ancient World*. Edited by Amar Annus. Chicago: The Oriental Institute of the University of Chicago, 2010.

Van der Toorn, Karel. *Scribal Culture and the Making of the Hebrew Bible.* Cambridge, MA: Harvard University Press, 2007.
Vermeylen, Jacques. "Des redactions deutéronomistes dans le livre d'Esaïe?" Pages 145–87 in *Les recueils prophétiques de la Bible: Origines, milieu, et context proche-oriental.* Edited by Jean-Daniel Macchi, et al. Fribourg: Labor et Fides, 2012.
Young, Ian M. "Israelite Literacy: Interpreting the Evidence, Part I." *VT* 48 (1998): 239–53.
———. "Israelite Literacy: Interpreting the Evidence, Part II." *VT* 48 (1998): 408–22.

WHAT IF THERE AREN'T ANY EMPIRICAL MODELS FOR PENTATEUCHAL CRITICISM?

SETH L. SANDERS

CAN EMPIRICAL MODELS EXPLAIN WHAT IS DIFFERENT ABOUT THE PENTATEUCH?

THIS PAPER QUESTIONS A KEY ASSUMPTION OF BIBLICAL CRITICISM BY ASKING whether empirical models can actually explain what is different about the Pentateuch. That is, are there known pre-Hellenistic Near Eastern examples of the Pentateuch's most prominent formal literary feature, the interweaving of parallel variants of narratives? If not—and I will argue that there are not—was the Pentateuch's creation a radical break from both Israelite and Near Eastern text-building? Using ancient Near Eastern literary evidence historically, I will argue from the case of the Primeval History that the Pentateuch's lack of parallels actually gives us a crucial clue for placing its composition in history.

By showing that the most distinctive literary values of the Primeval History depart not only from attested contemporary Near Eastern narrative but also those of the Primeval History's own sources, it becomes clear that Hebrew writers must have experienced a shift in their literary values, from a shared value of coherence to a new value of comprehensiveness.[1] But as is widely recognized, the Pentateuch's distinctive preference for comprehensiveness over coherence was itself strange to its early Jewish inheritors, who set about the monumental task of harmonizing and reconciling its richly polysemous contradictions—in the process creating a new set of literary values. A historically anchored comparison of the literary values implicit in

---

1. This raises two important questions, naturally impossible to treat in a short, focused paper. First, the absolute dating of the shifts and second, the relationship with textual interweaving in the rest of the Hebrew Bible. I am currently treating both in a research project supported by the Guggenheim Foundation and the National Endowment for the Humanities, planned as a book for Oxford entitled *Why We Can't Read the Torah: The Form of the Pentateuch and the History of Ancient Hebrew Literature*.

the Primeval History's distinctive form shows that this literary form has historical implications. The sharp difference between the predominant literary values of the Pentateuch and its contemporaries and successors entails an historical stratification. The result is a relative chronology of ancient Hebrew literature based not on conjecture but literary form attested in history.

I will address the oldest and most influential major work on this, Jeffrey Tigay's *Empirical Models for Biblical Criticism*,[2] and his work on a particularly clear and widely agreed-upon example, the Primeval History (Genesis 1–11, with emphasis on 1–9) in comparison with one of the best-documented cases of Mesopotamian literary text building, that of the Gilgamesh epic's flood tablet. But the conclusions also bear on broader issues such as conflation and memory-based textual variation emphasized by David Carr in his recent work.[3] The problem, I will argue, with Tigay's pre-Hellenistic "empirical models" argument is that the Pentateuch actually does not resemble Mesopotamian literature in its most problematic and important feature, namely, the interweaving of parallel variants of the same event. The biblical Flood shares a plot with the Mesopotamian Flood but does not read like it. Each key event of the plot happens once in the Gilgamesh flood tablet, but twice in a row in Genesis, resulting in a biblical text that is radically incoherent, yet still strangely readable.

In fact, what the editorial picture of the Gilgamesh epic resembles is not the form of the Pentateuch itself but that of its sources. While Tigay does not emphasize the most obviously distinctive aspect of the Pentateuch—its

---

2. Jeffrey Tigay, *Empirical Models for Biblical Criticism* (Philadelphia: University of Pennsylvania Press, 1985). A promising recent approach, parallel to the one adopted here, is taken by Joel Baden in a 2014 paper at the Hebrew University Institute for Advanced Studies, "Continuity between the Gaps: The Pentateuch and the Kirta Epic."

3. In particular, David M. Carr (*The Formation of the Hebrew Bible: A New Reconstruction* [New York: Oxford University Press, 2011], 37–48) uses as one of his key "empirical" cases the comparison of early second-millennium Old Babylonian versions of literary texts (ca. 1800–1600 BCE) to first-millennium Neo-Assyrian counterparts (ca. 800–600 BCE), a time gap of some thousand years, during which Babylonian education and text production appear to have shifted from a more memory-based model in the second millennium to a more visually based model in the first. Perhaps the clearest example of this shift is the systematic acknowledgement of first-millennium scribes of breaks (adj. *hepû* "broken, split;" *ḫīpu*, "break"; *CAD* H s.v.) in the *gabarû* "exemplar" from which they are copying, an interest exceedingly rare and inconsistent in second-millennium scribal work. This stands in contrast with the much shorter transmission period and closer cultural context of the biblical and early Jewish materials to which he applies the model. A collective study is needed by experts in ancient Near Eastern literatures of how text-creation and transmission changed in each. The results of a 2015 American Oriental Society session I organized to address this need are forthcoming in an issue of the *Journal of Ancient Near Eastern Religions*.

narrative incoherence, what he does focus on reveals a crucial historical point. This is that the Gilgamesh epic, with its coherent literary integration of a self-contained flood narrative, strongly resembles the coherent literary integration of the flood in the Priestly (P) and Yahwistic (J or non-P) elements accepted among all major schools of bible critics. The aspect of the Pentateuch for which there is the best-attested ancient Near Eastern scribal precedent is not its present form but its most widely agreed-on continuous layers, namely, the P and non-P Primeval History. It is the fact that the Pentateuch itself departs from attested empirical models, while the elements it contains resemble them, that provides the most powerful tool for placing it in the history of ancient Near Eastern literary culture.

Is the Pentateuch ancient Near Eastern, Jewish, or Neither? Competing Models of Text-Making

When Solomon Schechter referred to Christian biblical criticism as "the higher anti-Semitism,"[4] he had in mind its severing of Judaism's historical and literary connection to the Bible. Wellhausen's poetic but harsh line was that what ancient Israel's prophets and poets drank from "living springs" their Jewish inheritors, the epigones, "stored up in cisterns."[5] With the rise of early Judaism a rupture had occurred, and the conditions for creating the incomparable literature of ancient Israel had been lost. New and inferior modes of text-making had taken over, marked above all by Midrash, the endless harmonization, reinterpretation, and application of a fixed canon. In arguing that the Jews were not authentic heirs of ancient Israel, and the tradition had actually been killed by its tradents, he resembled nothing so much as the academic stereotype of Paul.

The old Protestant accusation was of a rupture between the living creative culture of ancient Israel and the dead interpretive culture of Judaism, with the establishment of the written law as the breaking point. Once the Torah was created as a fixed object, an unalterable sacred text demanding endless reapplication, a new but derivative and disconnected culture is created. Midrash, seen as irrational and secondary, is the natural response to the ossification of Torah.

Remarkably, an analogous early Jewish consciousness of this break with ancient Israelite text-making actually existed.[6] A striking example is

---

4. From his 1903 address, Solomon Schechter, "Higher Criticism—Higher Anti-Semitism," *Seminary Addresses & Other Papers* (New York: Burning Bush, 1960), 35–39.

5. Wellhausen, Julius, *Prolegomena to the History of Israel*, trans. J. Black and A. Menzies. (Edinburgh: A&C Black, 1885).

6. Jay Michael Harris, *How Do We Know This? Midrash and the Fragmentation of*

the concern that much of *halakha* is not really founded in the Torah. So the famous statement in the Mishnah that the laws of the Sabbath "are like mountains hanging by a hair, for Scripture on them is scanty and the rules many" (m. Hagigah 1:8) In contrast to Harold Bloom's famous term "the anxiety of influence," we could call this "the anxiety of outside influence," "the anxiety of invention"—or perhaps just separation anxiety.

To this anxiety about rupture with the past, ancient Near Eastern studies added a new dimension: a lack of uniqueness. Assyriologists and biblical scholars pointed out that the famous "flood tablet" of the Gilgamesh epic shared the key plot elements of Noah's flood but was originally a thousand years older. During the same period, scholars of early Judaism were pointing out that early Jewish interpretive techniques shared key points with Hellenistic Greek exegesis.[7] Was Midrash, no less than Torah, merely borrowed from neighbors at the predictable times when the Hebrews came into contact with them?

If the accusation was that the creation of the Torah represents a radical break between Judaism and ancient Israel, this claim had historically unsavory associations, and elicited powerful responses, ones that explored new forms of continuity instead. Perhaps the most compelling is typified in Simon Rawidowicz's brilliant and defiant definition of the continuity between Judaism and earlier Hebrew literary culture.[8] From its earliest times Judaism was based on the principle "interpret or perish," and this goes back to the origins of Torah, the very thing being interpreted! In answer to the question of where Midrash ends and the primary source being interpreted, Torah, begins, Rawidowicz argued it was Midrash all the way down.

In biblical studies, the notion of inner-biblical exegesis formalized Rawidowicz's position: the idea that rather than phenomena like Midrash being new developments of the Hellenistic or at the earliest the Persian period, Jewish reinterpretation of canon was a primal phenomenon that went back to the Bible's roots in ancient Israel. By the beginning of the twenty-first century it became a common view that the process of creation of scripture may have been continuous with its interpretation: Torah and Midrash were

---

Modern Judaism, SUNY Series in Judaica (Albany: State University of New York Press, 1995) is an insightful history of early modern Jewish scholarship on this problem, which also provides a useful introduction to the ancient sources for it.

7. The first phase of this program reached an English-language apogee in the work of Saul Lieberman (1950), but the cultural patterns it addresses continue to be real and of crucial important (Maren R. Niehoff, "Commentary Culture in the Land of Israel from an Alexandrian Perspective," *Dead Sea Discoveries* 19 [2012]: 442–63).

8. Simon Rawidowicz, "On Interpretation." *Proceedings of the American Academy for Jewish Research* 26 (1957): 83–126.

born together. Thus, inner-biblical exegesis is both a decisive step forward in scholarship and has sometimes served an apologetic function.

A parallel movement existed in Pentateuchal criticism, begun by both Jewish and Protestant scholars.[9] Here the study of exegesis intertwined with the study of the composition of the Torah itself. Fishbane hinted at this in implying that the creation of the Torah was already a midrashic process, but Protestant scholars like Rolf Rendtorff had already gone much further. Bringing together powerful intellectual currents from German Romantic predecessors like Gunkel as well as Midrashically oriented scholars like Sandmel, he argued that the Torah itself could be seen now as many layers of interpretation.[10]

This non-Documentary approach allows a view of profound continuity, in which the Torah is created through reinterpretation—there is a limited, discontinuous set of original core texts, which have been built up by succeeding layers of interpretation. Text-building and exegesis merged, so that in the work of scholars like Reinhard Kratz and Andrew Teeter it is explicitly stated that text-building and exegesis within the bible and outside of it are seamless, that there is no essential differentiation.[11] At these points, the scholarly stream of inner-biblical exegesis merges with the non-Documentary tradition of seeing Pentateuchal composition itself as reinterpretation. The two together allow a view of Torah and Midrash as born together—if Pentateuchal composition was always already interpretation, it's "Midrash all the way down."

Other scholars see a break: recent work in the neo-Documentary school sees Pentateuchal composition as a process in which major texts do respond to others, but not seamlessly. Rather than continuity, we find radical revisions, with the goal of replacement.[12] This is especially clear in law, where

---

9. Samuel Sandmel, "The Haggada within Scripture." *JBL* 80 (1961): 105–22; Géza Vermès, *Post-Biblical Jewish Studies*, SJLA 8 (Leiden: Brill, 1975); Rolf Rendtorff, *Das Überlieferungsgeschichtliche Problem Des Pentateuch*, 1. Aufl., BZAW 147 (Berlin: de Gruyter, 1977).

10. One could see this school's appeal to both German and Israeli scholars after the holocaust. If assertions of the Torah's incommensurability had worked as a threat—disinheriting the Jews by cutting them off from their most ancient patrimony, then it was an act of responsibility and solidarity to explore continuity instead.

11. Reinhard G. Kratz, "'Abraham, Mein Freund': Das Verhältnis von inner- und ausserbiblischer Schriftauslegung," in *Die Erzväter in der biblischen Tradition*, ed. Anselm C. Hagedorn and Henrik Pfeiffer (Berlin: de Gruyter, 2009), 115–36. D. Andrew Teeter, "On 'Exegetical Function' in Rewritten Scripture: Inner-Biblical Exegesis and the Abram/ Ravens Narrative in Jubilees," *HTR* 106 (2013): 373–402.

12. Bernard M. Levinson *"The Right Chorale": Studies in Biblical Law and Interpretation* (Tübingen: Mohr Siebeck, 2008); Jeffrey Stackert, "The Holiness Legislation and Its Pentateuchal Sources: Revision, Supplementation, and Replacement," in *The Strata of the*

the Hebrew slave laws of Deuteronomy make major revisions to the Covenant Code, and the slave laws of the Holiness code in Leviticus simply eliminate the practice. By contrast, this school sees the main narratives of the Tetrateuch not as interpretations of prior texts but as independent sources.[13] Remarkably, these sources were then interwoven without attention to these attempts at replacement, leaving the question of what you do with your Hebrew slave to be rather open.

On the neo-Documentary reading, the legal layers of the Torah are literally made of successive failed attempts to erase their predecessors. The great embarrassment of Deuteronomy was that it was brought together with the Covenant Code, and the great embarrassment of the Holiness Code is that it was brought together with Deuteronomy. At a key moment, these independent sources were interwoven to create a remarkable new document that then requires extremely active interpretation to even be read.

Gershom Scholem had already argued forcefully against the idea of an endless Jewish continuity:[14] The techniques and ideology of Midrash are an original historical formation, and it is this originality and historicity, their anchoring in historical change, from which their significance as a religious formation derives. But if interpretation is a truly eternal Jewish essence, and so all reuse of religious texts in Judah from the beginning has already been Midrash, then it becomes difficult to understand its distinctiveness, since all human culture reuses and contests a preexisting body of texts and utterances. Have Jews always had Scripture, with their survival always based on "interpret or perish!" the exegesis of an exclusive treasury of fixed texts?

I will argue here that discontinuity need not be a source of anxiety: first because the evidence shows that profound discontinuity existed, and second because within a creative human culture, discontinuity is never just that. Instead, the Torah's sharp formal divergence from both contemporary ancient Near Eastern and later Jewish literature are precisely what allow us to place it in history as part of a dialogue in which new literary values arise. The Torah's formal literary uniqueness, its ruptures with Near Eastern and Jewish texts alike, is a fundamental datum that actually connects the vital productivity of biblical literature to history as a process of change.

Priestly Writings: Contemporary Debate and Future Directions, ed. Sarah Shectman and Joel S. Baden, ATANT 95 (Zürich: Theologischer Verlag, 2009), 187–204.

13. Menahem Haran, *The Biblical Collection. Hebrew*, 3 volumes (Jerusalem: Bialik/Magnes, 1996); Joel S. Baden, *J, E, and the Redaction of the Pentateuch* (Tübingen: Mohr Siebeck, 2009).

14. Gershom Scholem, *The Messianic Idea in Judaism and Other Essays on Jewish Spirituality* (New York: Schocken, 1971).

Why the Pentateuch Is Formally Unique among Ancient Near Eastern Narratives: Editing in the Biblical Flood vs. Editing in Gilgamesh

The thesis of essential continuity in Hebrew literature has one major problem: the Torah itself. The Pentateuch stands out from every other pre-Hellenistic text from the ancient Near East in its narrative incoherence. Scholars from Moshe Greenberg to Robert Alter have argued that this does not matter if we focus on its final edited form: it is in this form that it had its great influence on Judaism, Christianity, Islam, and beyond. But this requires that we concede the argument to Wellhausen and St. Paul (or some version of him) and separate the Jews from their deep past, cutting them off sharply around the time of Jesus Christ. Otherwise it may be no use at all, because it fails to address what people in ancient Israel and Judah wrote and read, and indeed experienced and thought, before the Hellenistic period.

Can empirical models explain what is different about the Torah? In what is still the most influential published attempt to show that the Pentateuch is typical of a known ancient Near Eastern type of editing, Jeffrey Tigay argued that the evolution of the Gilgamesh epic is a good model for "biblical literature."[15] This phrase is already problematically vague; what he seems to mean is biblical literature's most influential problem, namely, Pentateuchal narrative. Tigay showed that the famous tablet XI of the Gilgamesh epic, the flood story, did show editorial seams, but of a very common sort. It was an originally independent story that was joined to the end of the Gilgamesh epic. Gilgamesh's editors simply added a frame in which the flood hero is telling his old story to Gilgamesh.

In Tigay's pioneering work on the Evolution of the Gilgamesh epic,[16] he identifies three basic phases of the Epic's existence:

I. Preexisting, independent Sumerian poems about Gilgamesh were freely renarrated by an Old Babylonian poet or poets in an integrated new work, ca. 1800 BCE.

---

15. Tigay vacillates between describing the problem he is addressing as one based in the Pentateuch (e.g, *Empirical Models for Biblical Criticism,* 22) and describing it as one of biblical literature overall (cf. the title "Empirical Models for Biblical Criticism" and pp. 21, 51, 52).

16. Jeffrey Tigay, *The Evolution of the Gilgamesh Epic* (Philadelphia: University of Pennsylvania Press, 1982). A sign of its thoroughness and merit is that it is still drawn on extensively by Andrew George in his definitive recent edition of the epic, though for a critique of its Assyriological limitations see the review by Wilfred G. Lambert in *JBL* 104 (1985): 115, who points out that it draws only on transliterated and edited sources.

II. After transmission through various channels and in various versions, the originally Old Babylonian narrative was gradually edited into a Standard Babylonian epic of some eleven tablets ca. 1200–900 BCE. This text shows editorial seams from integrating a further episode at the end, the Babylonian flood story of tablet XI. These seams include vacillation in the name of flood hero, idioms such as the phrase for introducing speech, "he spoke," and the term for woman/wife. Yet since meeting the flood hero and understanding his fate had been a theme of the earliest narratives about Gilgamesh, the flood story now forms a tightly integrated organic whole with the epic.

III. Finally, this integrated eleven-tablet epic had a second conclusion added in tablet XII, a more loosely integrated, relatively literal translation of part of an old Sumerian poem called Enkidu and the Netherworld. This further ending served to shift the emphasis of the poem from tablet XI's immortal deeds to the poem's emphasis on mortuary rituals to feed the dead and may have been added on the occasion of the death of Sargon II.[17]

Tigay demonstrated that Mesopotamian narrative, like biblical narrative, used preexisting narrative sources. But he never explained why this set it apart from other literature, found from ancient India to early modern Britain, which did the same thing. The problem is that the way the Pentateuch used sources is different from Gilgamesh, the Mahabharata, or Shakespeare. The process of Pentateuchal composition is more distinctive, and stranger, than merely integrating a story into the plot.

The distinctive strangeness of Pentateuchal composition becomes apparent if we compare the flood story of Genesis 6–9 with the Gilgamesh Epic. The biblical flood shares a plot with the flood story of tablet XI but reads nothing like it because key events happen once in Gilgamesh flood tablet, but twice in a row in Genesis, as the following chart of the key events of the floor narrative shared between Gilgamesh tablet XI, the P and the non-P/J accounts makes clear.[18]

---

17. Eckart Frahm, "Nabû-Zuqup-Kenu, das Gilgamesch-Epos und der Tod Sargons II," *JCS* 51 (1999): 73–90.

18. Below the P source is in italics. Biblical translation is NRSV; Gilgamesh translation is after Andrew R. George, *The Babylonian Gilgamesh Epic: Introduction, Critical Edition and Cuneiform Texts*, 2 volumes (New York: Oxford University Press, 2003). While the key plot elements can be divided up slightly differently, as does for example Claus Westermann (*Genesis 1–11: A Commentary* [Minneapolis: Augsburg, 1984], 395–96), five out of the six categories are the same. Furthermore, comparison with Westermann's division serves to strengthen the parallels between the Mesopotamian and biblical versions, since each of Westermann's divisions of the biblical narrative also corresponds to an ele-

Obvious Doublets in the Biblical Flood Story (Gen 6–9)

1. Defect in world and divine decision to destroy it.

Gen 7:1 Then the LORD said to Noah, "Go into the ark, with all your household, for you alone have I found righteous before Me in this generation. Of every clean animal you shall take seven pairs, males and their mates, and of every animal that is not clean, two, a male and its mate; of the birds of the sky also, seven pairs, male and female, to keep seed alive upon all the earth. For in seven days I will make it rain upon the earth, forty days and forty nights, and I will blot out from the earth all existence that I created."	Gilg XI 23–27 Man of Shuruppak, son of Ubartutu, Destroy this house, build a ship, Forsake possessions, seek life, Build an ark and save life. Take aboard ship seed of all living things.[19]
Gen 6:17 [*God said*] *"For My part, I am about to bring the Flood—waters upon the earth—to destroy all flesh under the sky in which there is breath of life; everything on earth shall perish. But I will establish My covenant with you, and you shall enter the ark, with your sons, your wife, and your sons' wives. And of all that lives, of all flesh, you shall take two of each into the ark to keep alive with you; they shall be male and female. From birds of every kind, cattle of every kind, every kind of creeping thing on earth, two of each shall come to you to stay alive. For your part, take of everything that is eaten and store it away, to serve as food for you and for them." Noah did so; just as God commanded him, so he did.*	

---

ment of tablet XI. I have chosen the below division instead because it preserves the key themes of the narrative somewhat more fully than Westermann's, which is made at the cost of removing significant elements. His "Response to the preservation: sacrifice" does not include a category for the J/non-P promise not to flood the earth, and his "God's decision to preserve humanity" does not include a category for the Priestly prohibition on shedding blood in 9:4-6, since it fits with neither his "blessing" of Noah, which only covers 9:1–3, or the covenant with Noah, which begins in 9:8.

19. In new tablet published by Finkel, "animals two by two."

2. A divinely favored hero is chosen to survive the destruction.

Gen 6:8 But Noah found favor with the LORD.

Gilgamesh XI [*Gilgamesh already knows Uta-Napishti was favored by the gods, leading him to ask:*]

Gen 6:9 *This is the line of Noah.—Noah was a righteous man; he was blameless in his age; Noah walked with God.*

7 How was it you (Uta-Napishti) stood with the gods in assembly?

How was it you gained eternal life?

3. Announcement of flood to hero, how he must escape, and instruction to take a set of animals on board

Gen 6:5 The LORD saw how great was man's wickedness on earth, and how every plan devised by his mind was nothing but evil all the time. 6 And the LORD regretted that He had made man on earth, and His heart was saddened. 7 The LORD said, "I will blot out from the earth the men whom I created—men together with beasts, creeping things, and birds of the sky; for I regret that I made them."

Gilgamesh XI [Assumed background: *gods cannot sleep because of the terrible disturbance humans create*]

14 The great gods resolved to send the delug

Gen 6:11 *The earth became corrupt before God; the earth was filled with lawlessness.* 12 *When God saw how corrupt the earth was, for all flesh had corrupted its ways on earth,* 13 *God said to Noah, "I have decided to put an end to all flesh, for the earth is filled with lawlessness because of them: I am about to destroy them with the earth.*

4. Flooding of world for a set number of days (7, 40, or 150).

Gen 7:17 The Flood was forty days on the earth, and the waters increased and raised the ark so that it rose above the earth. 18 The waters swelled and increased greatly upon the earth, and the ark drifted upon the waters.

Gilg XI 128–131...134–135...137–138
For six days and [seven] nights, there blew the wind, the downpour, the gale, the Deluge—it flattened the land.

Gen 7:24 *The waters swelled on the earth one hundred and fifty days 8:1, then God remembered Noah and all the beasts and all the cattle that were with him in the ark, and God caused a wind to blow across the earth, and the waters subsided. 2 The fountains of the deep and the floodgates of the sky were stopped up, and the rain from the sky was held back...*

But when the seventh day came,
The gale relented, the Deluge ended...
I looked at the weather, it was quiet and still, but all the people had turned to clay...
Down I sat, I knelt and I wept,
down my cheeks the tears were coursing.

5. Discovery that the flood has ended.

Gen 8:6 At the end of forty days, Noah opened the window of the ark that he had made ... 8 Then he sent out the dove to see whether the waters had decreased from the surface of the ground. 9 But the dove could not find a resting place for its foot, and returned to him to the ark, for there was water over all the earth. So putting out his hand, he took it into the ark with him. 10 He waited another seven days, and again sent out the dove from the ark. 11 The dove came back to him toward evening, and there in its bill was a plucked-off olive leaf! Then Noah knew that the waters had decreased on the earth. 12 He waited still another seven days and sent the dove forth; and it did not return to him any more.

Gen 8:7 *Then [Noah] sent out a raven; it went to and fro until the waters had dried up from the earth.* ...13 *In the six hundred and first year, in the first month, on the first of the month, the waters were drying from the earth; and when Noah removed the covering of the ark, he saw that the surface of the ground was drying up.* 14 *And in the second month, on the twenty-seventh day of the month, the earth was completely dry.* God spoke to Noah, saying, 16 "Come out of the ark, together with your wife, your sons, and your sons' wives. 17 Bring out with you every living thing of all flesh that is with you: birds, animals, and everything that creeps on earth; and let them swarm on the earth and be fertile and increase on earth...*

Gilg XI 147ff
When the seventh day arrived, I released a dove to go free. The dove went and returned. No landing place came to view, so it turned back.

I released a swallow to go free. The swallow went and returned, No landing place came to view, so it turned back. I sent a raven to go free. The raven went forth, saw the waters receding, finding food...it did not come back to me.

6. Killing of animals and divine decision never to flood again.

Gen 8:20 Then Noah built an altar to the LORD and, taking of every clean animal and of every clean bird, he offered burnt offerings on the altar. 21 The LORD smelled the pleasing odor, and the LORD said to Himself: "Never again will I doom the earth because of man, since the devisings of man's mind are evil from his youth; nor will I ever again destroy every living being, as I have done. ...

Gen 9:1 God blessed Noah and his sons, and said to them, "Be fertile and increase, and fill the earth. ... Every creature that lives shall be yours to eat; as with the green grasses, I give you all these. 4 You must not, however, eat flesh with its life-blood in it. 5 But for your own life-blood I will require a reckoning...Whoever sheds the blood of man, By man shall his blood be shed; For in His image Did God make man. Be fertile, then, and increase; abound on the earth and increase on it."

Gen 9:8 And God said to Noah and to his sons with him, 9 "I now establish My covenant with you and your offspring to come, 10 and with every living thing that is with you ...1 I will maintain My covenant with you: never again shall all flesh be cut off by the waters of a flood... "This is the sign that I set for the covenant between Me and you, and every living creature with you, for all ages to come. I have set My bow in the clouds, and it shall serve as a sign of the covenant between Me and the earth. 14 When I bring clouds over the earth, and the bow appears in the clouds, 15 I will remember My covenant between Me and you and every living creature among all flesh, so that the waters shall never again become a flood to destroy all flesh. ...
Gilg XI 157–167

I set up an offering stand on the top of the mountain.... The gods smelled the savor, The gods smelled the sweet savor. The gods crowded around the sacrificer like flies.

As soon as Belet-ili arrived, She held up the great fly-ornaments that Anu had made her in his infatuation. 'O these gods here, as surely as I shall not forget his lapis on my neck, I shall be mindful of these days, and not forget, forever!

Comparison of the Genesis flood with the Gilgamesh tablet XI flood shows that the biblical version is aggressively and thoroughgoingly interwoven. This simple but still slightly jarring comparison shows that critical scholars are not being really "anachronistic" by "imposing their values" on the biblical text—because the interweaving of two parallel variant plots was not a shared ancient Near Eastern literary value. Indeed, one looks in vain for this pattern in other contemporary Mesopotamian narratives such as the myth of Erra and Ishum, Nergal and Erishkegal, or Adapa. While scantily preserved, the Aramaic narratives of Ahiqar, Sheikh Fadl, and Papyrus Amherst 63 show no such interweaving, and the earlier West Semitic narratives from Ugarit yield no meaningful parallels. Indeed, the process seems alien to the whole of ancient Near Eastern narrative art, and one cannot find interwoven texts in Hurrian, Luwian, Hittite, Sumerian, Phoenician, Moabite, Egyptian, or Elamite.

Why the Pentateuch Is Formally Unique among Ancient Near Eastern Narratives II: Editing in the Gilgamesh Series vs. Editing in the Pentateuch

The most basic way scholars built extended texts in Mesopotamia was by adding different elements in sequence.[20] Textual traditions were created by connecting new materials one after the other in a series of clay tablets. Thus the section of the Gilgamesh Epic containing the flood story is known as "tablet XI," because it always appeared on the eleventh tablet in a series of twelve. By contrast, tablet XII always contains Enkidu's melancholy report on the netherworld.

The pattern appears in every major Mesopotamian scholarly work but is especially clear in the most popular texts such as the astronomical-astrological series Enūma Anu Enlil, the incantation series Utukkū Lemnūtu, and the temple description text Tintir. Whether logically organized by topic or location (as Enūma Anu Enlil or Tintir) or simply collected in sequence (as in Utukkū Lemnūtu), the texts are always built additively. Every scholarly library of the first millennium BCE attests significant quantities of serialized texts, and most are predominated by them. This agglutinative organizing concept, adding different elements in series, was an inextricable part of a distinctively Mesopotamian scholarly culture. It was organized around the

---

20. For serialization as a Mesopotamian analogue of canonization, see Francesca Rochberg-Halton, "Canonicity in Cuneiform Texts," *JCS* 36 (1984): 127–44. The comparative typology here was first offered in my paper, "Placing Scribal Culture in History: Deuteronomy and Late Iron-Age Text Production" (paper presented at the Annual Meeting of the Society of Biblical Literature. Baltimore, MD, 2013).

iconic shape of a clay tablet, making it symbolic of cuneiform culture and the physical techniques and media that transmitted it.

What we never find in Mesopotamian scholarly text-making is what virtually defines the Pentateuch: the interweaving of variant versions of parallel events. Whether following each other in blocks, such as the two creations of Genesis 1 and 2–3, or tightly interdigitated as in the two interwoven flood stories of Genesis 6–9, this way of combining parallel variants is the clearest and most distinctive editorial feature of the Pentateuch.[21] This is a process with no significant role in Mesopotamia.

The development of Gilgamesh during the first millennium exemplifies the difference between the standard modes of text-building in first-millennium Sumero-Akkadian culture versus the literary culture that produced the Pentateuch. The literary work known as the Gilgamesh Epic is a perfectly integrated and quite musically symmetrical eleven tablets. As its most recent editor and most thorough analyst, Andrew George, shows, it represents an extended and highly coherent narrative that already included the flood as its climax. This was a natural process since the earliest Old Babylonian narrative traditions and poetic allusions to Gilgamesh already mention his relation to the flood hero. In the Death of Bilgames and the Ballad of Early Kings, Gilgamesh is the great hero who sought life but failed, while Zisudra is the one who uniquely succeeded.

By contrast with the eleven-tablet epic proper, a highly integrated narrative, the Gilgamesh series (*iškuru*) is twelve tablets long, because it has an addition that is thematically resonant but narratively incoherent at its very end: a prose translation of the second half of the old Sumerian "Gilgamesh and the Netherworld" poem. Tablet XII disrupts the plot because it is narrated by Enkidu, whose irreversible death in tablet VII motivates the actions of VIII–XI, with no mention of how he might have returned from his permanent end. It would be difficult to find a clearer case of text-building by serialization.

The Primeval history of Genesis is a particularly strong area for a comparison because it not only contains the flood story, closely parallel content with the Gilgamesh series, but also is an area of solid, long-term consensus among competing schools of Bible criticism. Both neo-Documentarian[22] and

---

21. As we shall see, in the case of the Primeval history it represents the second of three universally agreed-on stages of text-building.

22. Baruch Schwartz, "The Flood-Narratives in the Torah and the Question of Where History Begins," in *Shai Le-Sara Japhet: Studies in the Bible, Its Exegesis and Its Language*, ed. by Bar-Asher et al. (Jerusalem: Bialik Institute, 2007), 139–54; Joel S. Baden, *The Composition of the Pentateuch: Renewing the Documentary Hypothesis*, The Anchor Yale Bible Reference Library (New Haven: Yale University Press, 2012).

the wide spectrum of non-Documentarian scholars[23] agree that the primeval history of Genesis 1–11 represents the interweaving of two previously integrated literary sources. The first source is universally agreed to be Priestly, part of a work that extends through the book of Numbers. While this source drew on earlier material,[24] it has reworked them into a remarkably coherent extended piece of literature. The second source, whether termed J or more noncommittally "non-P," is similarly widely agreed to be an equally coherent, preexisting literary work.

This agreement on the interweaving of two preexisting coherent sources allows us an unusual opportunity to compare undisputed literary evidence, not only of existing texts, but also of a basic sort of textual development between Mesopotamian and Judahite scribal cultures.

The Gilgamesh Epic is a particularly revealing artifact since it intersects with three distinct phases and modes of Babylonian text creation. Each different mode of text creation can be clearly seen around the single example of this durable icon.

We can observe distinct Old Babylonian, Middle Babylonian, and first-millennium modes of text building. The difference between the Old Babylonian re-narration of the individual Sumerian poems, on the one hand,

---

23. For a judicious survey see Jan Christian Gertz, "The Formation of the Primeval History," in *The Book of Genesis: Composition, Reception, and Interpretation*, ed. Craig A. Evans, Joel N. Lohr, and David L. Petersen, VTSup 152 (Leiden: Brill, 2012), 107–35. This classical position (held, e.g., by Martin Noth, *A History of Pentateuchal Traditions* [Englewood Cliffs, NJ: Prentice-Hall, 1972], 238 and Gerhard von Rad, *The Problem of the Hexateuch: And Other Essays* [Edinburgh: Oliver & Boyd, 1966], 1–78) is still accepted as foundational by Frank Crüsemann, "Die Eigenständigkeit der Urgeschichte," in *Die Botschaft und die Boten: Festschrift Hans Walter Wolff*, ed. Jörg Jeremias and Lothar Perlitt (Neukirchen-Vluyn: Neukirchener, 1981), 11–29; Markus Witte, *Die biblische Urgeschichte: Redaktions- und Theologiegeschichtliche Beobachtungen Zu Genesis 1, 1–11, 26*, BZAW 265 (Berlin: de Gruyter, 1998); and John Van Seters, *Prologue to History: The Yahwist as Historian in Genesis*, 1st edition (Louisville, KY: Westminster John Knox, 1992); as well as the range of scholars contributing to Thomas B. Dozeman and Konrad Schmid, eds., *A Farewell to the Yahwist? The Composition of the Pentateuch in Recent European Interpretation*, SymS 34 (Atlanta: Society of Biblical Literature, 2006), including Erhard Blum, "The Literary Connection between the Books of Genesis and Exodus and the End of the Book of Joshua," 106; Christoph Levin, "The Yahwist and the Redactional Link between Genesis and Exodus," 132, 141; and Konrad Schmid, "The So-Called Yahwist and the Literary Gap between Genesis and Exodus," 29.

24. An important possible example of an inherited "western" flood story element not found in Mesopotamian versions is P's calendrical framework, in which each event is given a relative date. Guy Darshan ('The Calendrical Framework of the Priestly Flood Story in Light of a New Akkadian Text from Ugarit (RS 94.2953)," *JAOS* [forthcoming]) has recently demonstrated that this tradition is probably already attested in an Akkadian version of the flood story from Ugarit.

and the powerful and logical integration of the flood narrative to create a climax in the Standard Babylonian version. but then a last stage of text building with Gilgamesh is especially fascinating: after this artful re-narration of the flood as a tale-within-a-tale in the eleven-tablet epic a disconnected work appears.[25] The narratively disconnected tablet XII shatters the logical flow of narrative: it presents the first inconsistency in plot along with the first break in style. Not coincidentally, it also represents a completely different way of building texts—the integrated epic is eleven tablets long, the series is twelve tablets long.

While it presents a clear break in narrative flow, this picture of the power of mortuary ritual is far from irrelevant to the epic's concerns. Indeed, Frahm has argued that its addition was a historical response to the circumstances of Sargon II's death, and George concurs that the most plausible context for its serialization for mortuary ritual purposes, a reassertion of Gilgamesh's earliest religious role.[26]

---

25. As Ryan Winters emphasizes to me (personal communication), the story of Gilgamesh having traveled to meet the flood hero is certainly very old: in addition to references to this deed in the Death of Bilgames, line 11 of the Ballad of Former Kings (edited in Bendt Alster, *Wisdom of Ancient Sumer* [Bethesda, MD: CDL, 2005]) asks "where is Bilgames, who like Zisudra sought (eternal) life?" then follows with allusions to the slaying of Huwawa and the death of Enkidu. Yet in the individual Sumerian poems except Death of Bilgames, these are not mentioned together. But clearly there was a widespread awareness that Gilgamesh had done a set of things attested not only in Death of Bilgames but also the Ballad. Furthermore the larger integrating theme of Gilgamesh's anxiety about death and resulting quest for fame is already prominent in Gilgamesh and Huwawa.

This is an issue for Pentateuchal composition because scholars of non-Documentarian orientation often argue that in an early literary phase, some scribes might have only narrated stories about Abraham, others only about Jacob, each independently of stories about the Exodus (for the most developed form of this argument with extensive bibliography see Konrad Schmid, *Genesis and the Moses Story: Israel's Dual Origins in the Hebrew Bible* (Winona Lake, IN: Eisenbrauns, 2010). For a critique of these arguments see my review of Schmid, *The Old Testament: A Literary History*, trans. Linda M. Maloney (Minneapolis: Fortress, 2012) in *NEA* 77 (2014): 317–19.

26. Eckart Frahm, "Nabû-zuqup-kenu, Gilgamesh XII, and the Rites of Du'uzu," *NABU* 2005, no. 5. Evidence for the literary purpose of the addition lies in its deviation from its Sumerian *Vorlage*, which is generally follows. But a key line has been moved from the middle and placed at the very end of the Akkadian version to create a new concluding line. It warns of the bleak fate of those who leave no descendants, creating a grim contrast with the last lines of XI: "Did you see the spirit of he-who-has-no-provider-of-funerary-offerings? I saw it!" (*ša eṭemmāšu pāqida la išû tamur? atamar!*) "He eats the pot-scrapings and bread-crusts thrown in the street!" (XI 152–153). The *pāqidu* is already prominent in the Genealogy of the Hammurapi dynasty (J. J. Finkelstein, "The Genealogy of the Hammurapi Dynasty," *JCS* 20 [1966]: 95–118) and coercing the inheritor or even the reader into this role becomes the main concern of Iron Age mortuary inscriptions; see Jonas C. Greenfield, "Un rite religieux arameen et ses parallèles," *RB* 80 (1973): 46–52 and Seth

THE EMPIRICAL MODELS DO FIT WIDELY ACCEPTED PREVIOUS LAYERS OF
JUDAHITE LITERATURE: THE P AND J/NON-P PRIMEVAL HISTORY

There is a second crucial insight about the nature of the two variant versions of the flood story found in Genesis. This is that they are both part of larger literary wholes. This is purely a matter of plot, as well as other storytelling techniques like the interrelation of theme and word choice, and does not depend on assumptions about the history of the text's editing. Indeed, the most powerful demonstrations come precisely from holistic literary readings of the canonical text, done without source-critical assumptions.

Fishbane singles out powerful coherence in the non-P/J elements when he describes Noah's origin story, as a comfort (root *nḥm*, alliteratively punning on *nōᵃḥ*) from the painful toil (*'iṣṣabôn*) on the earth (*'ǎdāmâ*) which the Lord has cursed (*'ērᵉrāh*) in Gen 5:29.[27] He notes that this was clearly "intended to balance the curse to the first man in Gen 3:17 where God says the earth (*'ǎdāmâ*) is cursed (*'ǎrûrâ*) because of you; you will only eat of it through painful toil (*'iṣṣabôn*). When the Lord decides to put an end to the earth, then (3:5), he regrets (*wayyinnāḥem*) making it and is troubled (*wayyit'āṣṣev*) in his hear ... at the end of the flood he vows never to curse it again.

Similarly, without Fishbane taking any interest in identifying Priestly elements, he notices coherence between another part of the flood story and the first creation account of Gen 1: The world begins with a divine wind (*ruᵃḥ 'elōhîm*) over the deep (*tᵉhôm*). But when Elohim (not Yahweh) decides to end the flood, he causes a *ruᵃḥ* to blow and stops up the gates of the *tᵉhôm* (8:1), causing a re-creation.

The stylistic coherence of each flood story in Genesis 6–9 with elements in Genesis 1–3 shows that each was part of its own integrated narrative edifice. The combination of narrative and literary coherence shows that each must have been part of a cycle or collection that existed before the two were interwoven to create the Pentateuch's primeval history. The result is that Genesis is radically incoherent, yet still strangely readable because of the way it was interwoven.

Tigay does not focus on what distinguishes the Pentateuch—its *narrative* incoherence. But his "Empirical Models" actually are very helpful for placing Pentateuchal composition in history—perhaps more so than has

---

L. Sanders "The Appetites of the Dead: West Semitic Linguistic and Ritual Aspects of the Katumuwa Stele," *BASOR* 369 (2013): 35–55. The addition shifts the concluding tone from the value of immortal acts to the need for kin to feed one's spirit after death.

27. Michael A. Fishbane, *Text and Texture: Close Readings of Selected Biblical Texts* (New York: Schocken, 1979).

been realized. This is not because the Pentateuch as we have it looks like Gilgamesh; as we have seen, for the Pentateuch itself there are no direct pre-Hellenistic analogues from the ancient Near East, but because if you separate sources by event and plotline, they show exactly the kind of re-narration we see in Old Babylonian Gilgamesh.

In fact it is not the Pentateuch as we have it but the pre-Pentateuchal layers that look like Gilgamesh: separate incidents or cycles that have been framed in a larger coherent context. We have seen that this applies narrowly, to the P and non-P/J threads of the Primeval History, but the argument may be extended. In the neo-Documentarian view, P, D, and the further non-P elements responsible for the Covenant Code, E, even joined together diverse genres of text at their disposal, adding a new frame so that the scholastic collection of the covenant code was revealed at Sinai or the story of Joseph segued into Exodus' story of Egyptian enslavement.

Conclusion: How the Lack of Empirical Models for the Pentateuch helps us Place it in Near Eastern Literary History

A more precise identification of the empirical models for Pentateuchal criticism allows us to pose the problem of its composition more precisely and in a freshly historical way. For there to be highly coherent strands evident in the Pentateuch that have been interwoven, there needs to be one set of values that created the coherent strand, but a different later set of values that created the incoherent interwoven source.

But the new literary values attested in the Pentateuch did not persist. Early Jewish responses to precisely the points at which the Pentateuch's form diverges from the common coherent form of the flood tablet and its P and non-P sources demonstrate the rise of a third set of values responsible for the harmonizing additions and conflations we find in Second Temple Judaism. While these values as applied to the Pentateuch have been compellingly summarized by James Kugel as assumptions that the text was cryptic, relevant, harmonious, and divine,[28] actual early Jewish responses to the text are less tidy and more heterogeneous.

Yet when we examine how key elements of the Primeval history are treated in Jubilees and Philo, we nevertheless see a clear-cut shift in literary values. In Jubilees, the two creations of Genesis 1 vs. 2–3 are retold without substantial harmonizing; by contrast, Philo's *On the Creation of the World* and

---

28. James L. Kugel, *Traditions of the Bible: A Guide to the Bible as It Was at the Start of the Common Era* (Cambridge, MA: Harvard University Press, 1998), 15–19.

Questions and Answers on Genesis and Exodus subjects their inconsistencies to extended harmonizing exegesis. When we reach the flood, its inconsistent dates are lightly harmonized in Jubilees but again subject to extended harmonizing in Philo. The glaringly inconsistent command to include both a pair of each animal and a pair plus seven is simply ignored in Jubilees while once again being subject to detailed interpretation and harmonization in Philo. Finally, the jarring sequence of birds is once again ignored by Jubilees and richly interpreted in Philo.

While incipient harmonizing additions and rewritings appear earlier in the Pentateuch, in legal collections like Exodus 34 and new narratives like Chronicles, all of our secure examples of extended explicit harmonization arise in the Hellenistic period. A beautiful example of this full-blown harmonizing is the Temple Scroll, which interweaves and conflates ritual law from across the Pentateuch into what Bernie Levinson (2013) calls "a more perfect Torah."

This external evidence attests three different sets of values that dominated three stages of Hebrew literature. These values can be ordered in a relative chronology. Their absolute chronology, the specific dating of the shifts, is a separate question, one with which this study does not deal.

Stage one was a process of integrating literary collection, like creation of the Standard Gilgamesh epic—multiple traditions, most probably at different sites under the impetus of court literatures and scribal networking, collected different versions of narratives like creation, the flood, patriarchal narratives, and the exodus. Each tradition at this first stage asserted the unity of a single "Israel's story" while exemplifying the literary value of coherence. This is confirmed by contemporary literary evidence found in epigraphic form: people created local literatures in the alphabet, deliberately transforming their own traditions, into written form. Local craftsmen working for local rulers created parallel competing royal inscriptions as assertions of local language and tradition.

Stage two attests a set of literary values apparently unique to Judea: the interweaving of existing literary collections. This process is not attested in other ancient Near Eastern texts but is clearly evident in the literary form of the primeval history.[29] A sort of metaliterary collection, interweaving two or

---

29. Interestingly this general principle does have parallels in Mesopotamian scholarship, but ones that were never applied to narrative in this culture. This is the phenomenon of the scholarly collection: elements of divination such as astronomical or historical observations, sign shapes, or medical diagnoses. Yet in Mesopotamia these were never applied to narrative, only to scholarly knowledge: the result was the distinctive forms of each literature: Mesopotamian scholarly collections were organized by topic, while Judean literary collections were organized by plot.

more different stories according to plot, in chronological order, which makes it still readable.[30] This second stage reasserts the unity of a single "Israel's story" but in a new way, with a new dominant literary value: now comprehensiveness trumps coherence.

In stage three, the distinctive new values that guided the creation of the Pentateuch faded. In this post-Pentateuchal stage, various emphases on the perfection, relevance, and divine nature of text led to heterogeneous sorts of harmonization and conflation, as seen in Chronicles, late additions like Exodus 34, the Samaritan Pentateuch, and the Temple Scroll. Retellings like Jubilees and exegesis like that of Philo let us look systematically back on how the new values transformed the results of the older ones. In fresh and diverse ways we see the unity of a single "Israel's story" asserted precisely through the old value of coherence, forced onto the text through the work of harmonization and conflation, with the new values of perfection and relevance added.

To conceptualize this history of changing literary values we can draw on a concept from the Prague school of linguistics articulated by Roman Jakobson: the dominant.[31] This is a shifting criterion that "makes literature literature." Jakobson points out that at one point, Czech poetry all has to have syllable meter, a few centuries later it required stress meter. The value of the dominant lies precisely in its ideological nature: it is not that each dominant value erased others, but that each new one served as an organizing principle. Thus we see the values of coherence in the first and third stages, but in the latter it has been joined by relevance and divine origin.

What we may be seeing here are the traces of a shift in the ancient Hebrew literary dominant. At the knowable beginnings of Hebrew literature, which created the extended narratives attested in the primeval history, the value coherence drove the integration of separate preexisting stories into larger arcs. At the later stage of interweaving we find a literary culture that valued comprehensiveness above all. And in Second Temple literature we see not a rupture but a dialectical response, with different literary values.

This historically anchored comparison of the literary values implicit in the primeval history's distinctive form teaches us a lesson. This is that it is at the points of greatest assertion of continuity that we find the most radical

---

30. While "compilation" has become a favored term in the Neo-Documentary school, it is not as specific as "interweaving" because it does not emphasize what is distinctive about the Pentateuchal collection vis-a-vis Near Eastern literature; compare Mesopotamian collections like udug.hul or the Assyrian and Babylonian chronicles that are typically termed "compilations" by scholars.

31. Roman Jakobson, Krystyna Pomorska, and Stephen Rudy, *Language in Literature* (Cambridge, MA: Belknap, 1987).

reinvention. New text-making techniques and literary values arose together in response to the now-problematic older ones. Scholem argued that rabbinic Judaism's late invention of the oral Torah, imagined already at Sinai, its most aggressive assertion of continuity, was also a point of profound rupture—a fiction and a total anachronism. What this philological and historical evidence we have surveyed shows is that these moments of rupture that create and invoke new forms of continuity go much farther back than he would have imagined, to the genesis of Hebrew literature itself.

REFERENCES

Alster, Bendt. *Wisdom of Ancient Sumer*. Bethesda, MD: CDL, 2005.
Baden, Joel S. *The Composition of the Pentateuch: Renewing the Documentary Hypothesis*. The Anchor Yale Bible Reference Library. New Haven: Yale University Press, 2012.
———. *J, E, and the Redaction of the Pentateuch*. Tübingen: Mohr Siebeck, 2009.
Baumgart, Norbert C. *Die Umkehr des Schöpfergottes: Zu Komposition und religionsgeschichtlichem Hintergrund von Gen 5–9*. Herders Biblische Studien 22. Freiburg: Herder, 1999.
Blum, Erhard. "The Literary Connection between the Books of Genesis and Exodus and the End of the Book of Joshua." Pages 89–105 in Dozeman and Schmid, *A Farewell to the Yahwist?*
Carr, David M. *Reading the Fractures of Genesis: Historical and Literary Approaches*. Louisville: Westminster John Knox, 1996.
———. *The Formation of the Hebrew Bible: A New Reconstruction*. New York: Oxford University Press, 2011.
Crüsemann, Frank. "Die Eigenständigkeit der Urgeschichte." Pages 11–29 in *Die Botschaft und die Boten: Festschrift Hans Walter Wolff*. Edited by Jörg Jeremias and Lother Perlitt. Neukirchen-Vluyn: Neukirchener, 1981.
Darshan, Guy. 'The Calendrical Framework of the Priestly Flood Story in Light of a New Akkadian Text from Ugarit (RS 94.2953)." *JAOS* (forthcoming).
Dozeman, Thomas B., and Konrad Schmid. *A Farewell to the Yahwist? The Composition of the Pentateuch in Recent European Interpretation*. SymS 34. Atlanta: Society of Biblical Literature, 2006.
Finkelstein, J. J. "The Genealogy of the Hammurapi Dynasty." *JCS* 20 (1966): 95–118.
Fishbane, Michael A. *Text and Texture: Close Readings of Selected Biblical Texts*. New York: Schocken, 1979.
Frahm, Eckart. "Nabû-Zuqup-Kenu, das Gilgamesch-Epos und der Tod Sargons II." *JCS* 51 (1999): 73–90.
George, Andrew R. *The Babylonian Gilgamesh Epic: Introduction, Critical Edition and Cuneiform Texts*. 2 volumes. New York: Oxford University Press, 2003.
Gertz, Jan Christian. "The Formation of the Primeval History." Pages 107–35 in *The Book of Genesis: Composition, Reception, and Interpretation*. Edited by Craig A.

Evans, Joel N. Lohr, and David L. Petersen. VTSup 152. Leiden: Brill, 2012.
Greenfield, Jonas C. "Un rite religieux arameen et ses paralleles." *RB* 80 (1973): 46–52.
Haran, Menahem. *The Biblical Collection. Hebrew.* 3 volumes. Jerusalem: Bialik/ Magnes, 1996.
Harris, Jay Michael. *How Do We Know This? Midrash and the Fragmentation of Modern Judaism.* SUNY Series in Judaica. Albany: State University of New York Press, 1995.
Jakobson, Roman, Krystyna Pomorska, and Stephen Rudy. *Language in Literature.* Cambridge, MA: Belknap, 1987.
Kratz, Reinhard G. "'Abraham, Mein Freund': Das Verhältnis von inner- und ausserbiblischer Schriftauslegung." Pages 115–36 in *Die Erzväter in der biblischen Tradition.* Edited by Anselm C. Hagedorn and Henrik Pfeiffer. Berlin: de Gruyter, 2009.
Kugel, James L. *Traditions of the Bible: A Guide to the Bible as It Was at the Start of the Common Era.* Cambridge, MA: Harvard University Press, 1998.
Lambert, Wilfred G. Review of Jeffrey H. Tigay. *The Evolution of the Gilgamesh Epic. JBL* 104 (1985): 115.
Levin, Christoph. "The Yahwist and the Redactional Link between Genesis and Exodus," Pages 131–41 in *A Farewell to the Yahwist? The Composition of the Pentateuch in Recent European Interpretation.* Edited by Thomas B. Dozeman and Konrad Schmid. SymS 34. Atlanta: Society of Biblical Literature, 2006.
Levinson, Bernard M. *A More Perfect Torah: At the Intersection of Philology and Hermeneutics in Deuteronomy and the Temple Scroll.* Vol. 1. CSHB 1. Winona Lake, IN: Eisenbrauns, 2013.
———. *"The Right Chorale": Studies in Biblical Law and Interpretation.* Tübingen: Mohr Siebeck, 2008.
Lieberman, Saul. *Hellenism in Jewish Palestine: Studies in the Literary Transmission, Beliefs and Manners of Palestine in the 1st Century B. C. E.–IV Century C.E.* Texts and Studies of the Jewish Theological Seminary of America 18. New York: Jewish Theological Seminary of America, 1950.
Niehoff, Maren R. "Commentary Culture in the Land of Israel from an Alexandrian Perspective." *Dead Sea Discoveries* 19 (2012): 442–63.
Noth, Martin. *A History of Pentateuchal Traditions.* Englewood Cliffs, NJ: Prentice-Hall, 1972.
Rad, Gerhard von. *The Problem of the Hexateuch: And Other Essays.* Edinburgh: Oliver & Boyd, 1966.
Rawidowicz, Simon. "On Interpretation." *Proceedings of the American Academy for Jewish Research* 26 (1957): 83–126.
Rendtorff, Rolf. *Das Überlieferungsgeschichtliche Problem Des Pentateuch.* 1. Aufl. BZAW 147. Berlin: de Gruyter, 1977.
Rochberg-Halton, Francesca. "Canonicity in Cuneiform Texts." *JCS* 36 (1984): 127–44.
Sanders, Seth L. "The Appetites of the Dead: West Semitic Linguistic and Ritual Aspects of the Katumuwa Stele." *BASOR* 369 (2013): 35–55.
———. "Placing Scribal Culture in History: Deuteronomy and Late Iron-Age Text Production." Paper presented at the Annual Meeting of the Society of Biblical Literature. Baltimore, MD, 2013.

———. Review of Kondrad Schmid, *The Old Testament: A Literary History*. *NEA* (forthcoming).
Sandmel, Samuel. "The Haggada within Scripture." *JBL* 80 (1961): 105–22.
Schechter, Solomon. "Higher Criticism—Higher Anti-Semitism." Pages 35–40 in *Seminary Addresses & Other Papers*. New York: Burning Bush, 1960.
Schmid, Konrad. *The Old Testament: A Literary History*. Translated by Linda M. Maloney. Minneapolis: Fortress, 2012.
———. "The So-Called Yahwist and the Literary Gap between Genesis and Exodus." Pages 29–49 in Dozeman and Schmid, *A Farewell to the Yahwist?*
Scholem, Gershom. *The Messianic Idea in Judaism and Other Essays on Jewish Spirituality*. New York: Schocken, 1971.
Schwartz, Baruch. 'The Flood-Narratives in the Torah and the Question of Where History Begins." Pages 139–54 in *Shai Le-Sara Japhet: Studies in the Bible, Its Exegesis and Its Language*. Edited by Mosheh Bar-Asher et al. Jerusalem: Bialik Institute, 2007.
Stackert, Jeffrey. "The Holiness Legislation and Its Pentateuchal Sources: Revision, Supplementation, and Replacement." Pages 187–204 in *The Strata of the Priestly Writings: Contemporary Debate and Future Directions*. Edited by Sarah Shectman and Joel S. Baden. ATANT 95. Zürich: Theologischer Verlag, 2009.
Teeter, D. Andrew. "On 'Exegetical Function' in Rewritten Scripture: Inner-Biblical Exegesis and the Abram/Ravens Narrative in Jubilees." *HTR* 106 (2013): 373–402.
Tigay, Jeffrey. *Empirical Models for Biblical Criticism*. Philadelphia: University of Pennsylvania Press, 1985.
———. *The Evolution of the Gilgamesh Epic*. Philadelphia: University of Pennsylvania Press, 1982.
Van Seters, John. *Prologue to History: The Yahwist as Historian in Genesis*, 1st edition. Louisville, KY: Westminster John Knox, 1992.
Vermès, Géza. *Post-Biblical Jewish Studies*. SJLA 8. Leiden: Brill, 1975.
Wellhausen, Julius. *Prolegomena to the History of Israel*. Translated by J. Black and A. Menzies. Edinburgh: A&C Black, 1885.
Westermann, Claus. *Genesis 1–11: A Commentary*. Minneapolis: Augsburg, 1984.
Witte, Markus. *Die biblische Urgeschichte: Redaktions- und Theologiegeschichtliche Beobachtungen Zu Genesis 1, 1–11, 26*. BZAW 265. Berlin: de Gruyter, 1998.

SCRIPTURALIZATION IN ANCIENT JUDAH

WILLIAM M. SCHNIEDEWIND

How did ancient scrolls become scripture? It is not obvious that ancient Israel should have produced a large corpus of literary traditions that would be collected into a book, but it is even less obvious that these texts should ever come to be regarded as having religious authority for the masses, that is, that they should become scripture. For example, the Epic of Gilgamesh never became scripture in Mesopotamia, the Ba'al Epic was not scripture for the Canaanites, the Odyssey never became scripture for the Greeks. Given this, it is even more curious that a Judean literary corpus would gain authoritative religious status. In this paper, I will illustrate how this process begins in the Neo-Assyrian context. There are three aspects of ancient Near Eastern writing that could have helped foster nascent scripturalization: the notion of divine writing, the so-called revelation paradigm, and the ritual use of writing.

The first issue must be how to define "scripturalization." The topic of scripturalization is relatively new in the academy.[1] Some have focused on the citation of texts as religious authority. Only when a text is understood as sacred scripture, can it be cited as a religious authority. This idea was especially advanced in the 1999 book by Judith Newman entitled, *Praying by the Book: The Scripturalization of Prayer in Second Temple Judaism*. Newman defines scripturalization as "the reuse of biblical texts or interpretive traditions to shape the composition of new literature."[2] She distinguishes scripturalization from "inner-biblical interpretation" because "the reuse of scripture does not necessarily entail the conscious interpreta-

---

1. This paper particularly profited from a 2010 SBL session dedicated to the topic of "Scripturization." The session was organized by David M. Carr for the "Orality, Textuality, and the Formation of the Hebrew Bible" Group. My thanks to the other participants—James W. Watts, Charlotte Hempel, and Kurt Noll—for their insights that helped sharpen my own thinking.

2. Judith Newman, *Praying by the Book: The Scripturalization of Prayer in Second Temple Judaism*, EJL 14 (Atlanta: Scholars Press, 1999), 12–13.

tion of scripture."³ Kurt Noll has criticized Newman's definition suggesting that she "is content to identify scripturalization with scribal re-use."⁴ While Newman's definition of scripturalization seems more nuanced that Noll has acknowledged, he is nevertheless correct in pointing out that mere scribal reuse and even interpretation of texts should not necessarily be understood as scripturalization. For example, Noll points to David Carr's work, *Writing on the Tablet of the Heart*, to illustrate how scribes routinely made creative reuse of earlier texts.⁵ Thus, the reuse of texts is not the defining characteristic of scripturalization. I would suggest that scripturalization implies the sacred and authoritative quality of a text, not necessarily its reuse by other texts. To be sure, sacred texts are cited and reused, but this is not what makes them scripture.

The role of ritual reading seems particularly important for underscoring the religious authority of texts and has been highlighted in James Watts' research. Indeed, Watts even argues, "The textual authority of Western scriptures had ritual origins."⁶ The ritualized reading in Nehemiah 8 is a critical example for illustrating this understanding of scripturalization. Watts also notes a variety of other ancient examples of the ritual use of texts in Hittite, Egyptian, and Greco-Roman contexts. This use of texts is certainly part of the story, but I would broaden the analysis, particularly focusing on the use of writing in ritual magic. On the other hand, Kurt Noll's discussion seems to downplay the role of ritual in scripturalization, but he emphasizes a few of other issues that I would consider peripheral. For example, Noll argues that scripturalization is dependent upon "a reader's idea and not a scribe's activity."⁷ Related to this is Noll's belief that widespread literacy is required for scripturalization, and his misleading assertion that there was "perhaps only a handful" of scribes in Judah's sparsely populated, illiterate agrarian society.⁸ The distinction between Noll's scribes and readers is problematic

---

3. Ibid., 13.

4. Kurt L. Noll, "Did 'Scripturalization' Take Place in Second Temple Judaism?" *SJOT* 25 (2011): 204.

5. Ibid., 204; citing Carr, *Writing on the Tablet of the Heart: Origins of Scripture and Literature* (Oxford: Oxford University Press, 2005), 38–39.

6. James Watts, "Ritual Legitimacy and Scriptural Authority," *JBL* 124 (2005), 402. Watts has written extensively on aspects of scripturalization; see further "Ten Commandments Monuments and the Rivalry of Iconic Texts," *Journal of Religion & Society* 6 (2004); "The Three Dimensions of Scriptures," *Postscripts* 2 (2006), 135–59; "Scripturalization and the Aaronide Dynasties," in *JHS* 13 (2013), doi:10.5508/jhs.2013.v13.a6.

7. Noll, "Did 'Scripturalization' Take Place," 205.

8. There was certainly more than a handful of scribes in the late Iron Age. The number was much more restricted in the Persian period but rebounds in the Hellenistic period. For a survey of the spread of writing during the late Iron Age through Hellenistic

on a couple levels. We only know of "the reader's ideas" through the pen of scribes. The scribes are the first readers, and they were responsible for shaping the meaning of texts in an ancient society. Indeed, this distinction seems like an anachronistic application of reader response theory or audience criticism to an ancient society. Moreover, the number of scribes and extent of literacy varied in different periods (e.g., late Iron Age, Neo-Babylonian period, early Persian, late Persian, Hellenistic, Roman) and among various communities (e.g., priests, farmers, merchants, Qumran sectarians, early rabbis). It is unclear why mass literacy should be essential for scripturalization. Mass literacy is a modern phenomenon. Most importantly, texts can be sacred and authoritative even to those who cannot read them. Indeed, the very nature of the use of writing for ancient magic often assumed that most people could not read the writing, yet it nevertheless had ritual power.

Just as scripturalization is not dependent on literacy, it must also be distinguished from the problem of canonization.[9] These are two separate issues. The editing and limits of the corpus of sacred and authoritative literature can linger long after the process of scripturalization has begun. Texts can be used ritually even though the exact canon of texts may be evolving, and the texts themselves may even evolve and make new claims as religious authorities. Conflating canonization with scripturalization places its beginnings in a much later context that obscures some of the factors that influenced scripturalization. Indeed, nascent scripturalization begins long before canonization. The question of when the scripturalization process begins is particularly useful because it allows us to contextualize the social and cultural influences that encouraged the emergence of scripture. In this article, nascent scripturalization will be traced to a Neo-Assyrian context, that is, to the eighth and seventh centuries BCE.

There are two examples that are sometimes thought to be relevant to scripturalization in the First Temple period inscriptions. These are the Yavneh-Yam inscription and the Ketef Hinnom amulets. The Yavneh-Yam inscription is a late seventh century BCE worker's petition and complaint that reads as follows:

---

period, see Schniedewind, *How the Bible Became a Book: the Textualization of Ancient Israel* (Cambridge: Cambridge University Press, 2004), 64–194.

9. See Steven Weitzman, Song and Story in Biblical Narrative: The History of a Literary Convention in Ancient Israel (Bloomington, IN: Indiana University Press, 1997), 59–92; Shalom Paul, "Heavenly Tablets and the Book of Life," *JANES* 5 (1973), 345–53; William W. Hallo, "The Concept of Canonicity in Cuneiform and Biblical Literature: A Comparative Appraisal," in *The Biblical Canon in Comparative Perspective*, ed. K. Lawson Younger, William W. Hallo, and Bernard F. Batto (Lewiston, NY: Mellon, 1991), 1–19. Weitzman points out that most discussions of "canonization" address the stabilization and standardization of the text, not its endowment with scriptural authority.

> Your servant did his reaping, finished, and stored (the grain) a few days ago before the Sabbath. When your servant had finished reaping and had stored it a few days ago, Hoshayahu ben Shabay came and took your servant's garment.... All ... my companions will vouch for me (that) truly I am guiltless of any in[fraction]. [(So) please return] my garment. If the official does not consider it an obligation to return [your servant's garment, then have] pity upon him [and return] your servant's [garment] from that motivation. You must not remain silent [when your servant is without his garment].

Aside from the pathos of the petitioner's plea, the striking aspect of this inscription is the apparent allusion to the biblical requirement for the return of a confiscated garment known from Exod 22:25–26 and Deut 24:12–15. In Deuteronomy, we read, "If the person is poor, you shall not sleep in the garment given you as the pledge. You shall give the pledge back by sunset, so that your neighbor may sleep in the cloak." Is it possible that the petitioner was aware of the biblical requirement for the return of a confiscated garment? How would a worker at a remote outpost have known of such a textual tradition? Could a local scribe have helped the worker with his plea and introduced an indirect citation of deuteronomic law? Unfortunately, these are difficult questions to answer. The complaint certainly does not have an explicitly textual basis; rather, it was a loose appeal to legal tradition that could have been known orally.

In contrast to the Yavneh-Yam inscription, the Ketef Hinnom silver amulets come from the upper classes of society. Since scripturalization likely began among the elite classes of society, they are worth including in our discussion. The amulets date to the late seventh century and were excavated in upper-class tombs just outside of Jerusalem.[10] They seem to reuse biblical texts—in particular Num 6:24–26 and Deut 7:9—to shape the composition of new literature; however, scholars have noted that the form of these texts do not follow the canonical form of the biblical text. Indeed, Jeremy Smoak has also pointed to connections with other biblical texts such as Prov 3:1–4, Psalm 88, and Psalm 103.[11] So, are the amulets citing known textual traditions or are they ritually textualizing oral tradition? The physical form of

---

[10]. See Gabriel Barkay et al., "The Amulets from Ketef Hinnom: A New Edition and Evaluation," *BASOR* 334 (2004), 41–71.

[11]. I am particularly indebted to Jeremy Smoak for his insights into the Ketef Hinnom amulets; see Jeremy Smoak, "May YHWH Bless You and Guard You from Evil: The Rhetorical Argument of Ketef Hinnom Amulet I and the Form of the Prayers for Deliverance in the Psalms," *JANER* 12 (2012), 202–36; Smoak, "Yahweh's Shining Face and the Ritual Logic of the Judahite Amulets from Ketef Hinnom," *ARelG*, forthcoming; and Smoak, *May Yahweh Bless You and Keep You: The Early History and Ritual Background of the Priestly Blessing* (Oxford: Oxford University Press, forthcoming).

these texts is particularly critical for addressing this question. Namely, they are amulets—that is, magical charms. The power of the charm is partly in the writing itself. Although we may think of texts like the so-called Priestly Blessing as oral, an amulet draws some of its power from the numinous power of writing in magic rituals. The physical production of amulets in the near east is associated with priests and the use of writing in ritual magic.[12] It is this numinous power of writing that appears to be one of the more significant underpinnings to scripturalization (see further below the discussion of the *Sotah* ritual). In addition, Smoak highlights the unique aniconic aspect of the amulets. In Near Eastern amulets, the phrase "bless you and keep you" is often accompanied by iconography on amulets and other inscriptions, but the Ketef Hinnom amulets have references to the favor of YHWH instead. This appears to be associated more broadly with the aniconic nature of Judean seals and inscriptions. This connection has been also recognized by Othmar Keel and Christoph Uehlinger. With regard to the Ketef Hinnom amulets they write, "it is worth noting that there are no terracottas of doves, goddesses, or riders in the graves of Ketef Hinnom. Not Asherah, and not an 'angel of Yahweh,' but Yahweh himself—mediated by the presence of a text!—accompanies the deceased with his blessing and protection, into the cold darkness of the grave."[13] In fact, the aniconic nature of late Judean inscriptions and seals probably reflects the iconization of writing itself in Judean society. This could certainly have contributed to the sacred and religious authority of texts in Judah. In this respect, the Ketef Hinnom amulets seem to have more to contribute to the discussion of scripturalization than the Yavneh-Yam inscription.

To my mind, the religious authority of texts is more of a defining characteristic of scripturalization than literary reuse, allusion, or intertextuality. This observation also generates the main question of scripturalization, namely, from where do biblical texts derive their authority? One possible answer is simply that biblical literature contains many school texts. That is, biblical literature compares to texts like the Epic of Gilgamesh or the Enuma Elish that were studied and copied by students for practice and training. While this may

---

12. Also see Theodore J. Lewis's critique of Y. Kaufman's old arguments dismissing the prevalence of amulets and incantations in ancient Israelite religion: "Job 19 in Light of the Ketef Hinnom Inscriptions and Amulets," in *Puzzling Out the Past: Studies in Northwest Semitic Languages and Literatures in Honor of Bruce Zuckerman*, ed. Marilyn J. Lundberg, Steven Fine, and Wayne Pitard (Leiden: Brill, 2012), 97–111. On the magical nature of the Ketef Hinnom amulets, see recently Brian B. Schmidt, "The Social Matrix of Early Judean Magic and Divination: From 'Top Down' or 'Bottom Up'?" in *Beyond Hatti: A Tribute to Gary Beckman*, ed. Billie Jean Collins and Piotr Michalowski (Atlanta: Lockwood, 2013), 279–93.

13. Keel and Uehlinger, *Gods, Goddesses, and Images of God in Ancient Israel* (Minneapolis: Fortress, 1998), 367.

account for the origins, transmission, and citation for some biblical literature, this cannot be offered as an explanation for the sacred authority of biblical literature. This explanation would not be sufficient to explain the development of the authoritative and sacred aspect of biblical literature. More than this, it is difficult to prove that any biblical literature served as school texts even though we may suspect that some literature served in this capacity (note, for example, Proverbs 1–9).

A recent book by Karel van der Toorn provides some striking examples relevant to scripturalization from Neo-Assyrian sources.[14] However, we must begin with a couple observations about van der Toorn's approach before discussing how his work can help move the discussion forward. I think that van der Toorn has been trapped in a paradigm that envisions the formation of the Bible among temple scribes during the Persian and Hellenistic periods, which is chronologically incongruous with the most striking Neo-Assyrian evidence that he adduces. To be sure, during the Second Temple period, Jewish scribes were located in the temple, and these priestly scribes were the primary caretakers of the scriptures during the Persian and Hellenistic periods. This explains why van der Toorn feels the need to associate the scribal profession with the temple; however, the exclusive basis a temple and priestly locus for scribes is less persuasive in the Iron Age. This can be illustrated by a general survey of the locations of archives and libraries in the Near East. Temples are not the main locus of either archives or school texts in the ancient Near East. For example, Olof Pedersén notes that only 36 of 127 archives in "official buildings" were found in structures designated as temples, while 91 were in palaces or similar buildings.[15] Nearly twice as many archives, 253, were associated with private houses. The overwhelming majority of texts are administrative, most commonly associated with the royal bureaucracy or private enterprise. Closer inspections of individual archives also yield even more problematic results than do the archives that allegedly come from temples. For instance, in Yoram Cohen's exhaustive study of the scribes at Emar, he uncovers no evidence of a temple scribal workshop even though the archive was originally alleged to have come from a temple. On closer examination, Cohen notes, "it was a private dwelling, large enough to accommodate a family along with some fellow students if they made the house their home."[16] The archive was labeled as coming from a temple

---

14. Karel van der Toorn, *Scribal Culture and the Making of the Hebrew Bible* (Cambridge, MA: Harvard University Press, 2007).

15. Olaf Pedersén, *Archives and Libraries in the Ancient Near East 1500–300 B.C.* (Bethesda: CDL, 1998), 260–70.

16. Yoram Cohen, *Scribes and Scholars of the City of Emar in the Late Bronze Age* (Winona Lake, IN: Eisenbrauns, 2009), 55–56.

because the home mentioned the craftsman and scribal gods Ea and Nabu as its patron, but it also had a bureaucratic official or *aklu* as a supervisor. The role of the temple in the scribal profession was not significant, and the mislabeling of buildings as temples leads to overstating the role of the temple in state administration in the pre-Persian periods.

Scribes were often palace employees that had a bureaucratic function. In Neo-Assyrian times, for example, the *aklu* was a royal bureaucrat sent to teach conquered peoples as part of the imperial administration; such imperial officials might provide a mechanism for the communication of Mesopotamian scribal traditions to the provinces (e.g., treaties or law codes). Unfortunately, the royal scribes of Assurbanipal's famous library in Nineveh are not investigated by van der Toorn; rather, he cites the important colophon of the Ugaritic scribe Ilimilku, a self-described student of the diviner Urtenu, to bolster his case. Even this evidence is equivocal. The preponderance of archives excavated in Ugarit were outside the temple. Moreover, as W. H. van Soldt pointed out, one of the titles of Ilimilku should be translated as "royal secretary" or "secretary-of-state."[17] Thus, even though this colophon of Ilimilku appears in a religious text found in a temple, the colophon itself refers to the king as the patron of the scribe. Additional examples from ancient Hebrew epigraphy would include ostraca of Hebrew administrative texts excavated at Lachish and Arad, which were located in the gate areas and not in temples. Although this review does not exhaust the epigraphic evidence, it should become apparent that the temple is not the primary locus of the scribal profession in the Near East during the Iron Age. The palace played a much more prominent role in the scribal profession during the Neo-Assyrian period. In other words, we cannot rely on the temple alone in order to explain the authority of the written word in ancient Judah.

A critical piece in van der Toorn's argument are the "Levitical Scribes," an institution reconstructed from sources like Chronicles, Jubilees, and the Dead Sea Scrolls. The evidence in these postexilic sources supports his hypothesis that "the Levites were involved in activities that required high literacy."[18] Van der Toorn's "telltale" piece of evidence for temple scribes is based on a common mistranslation of Deut 17:18–19; quoting van der Toorn, "when [the king] accedes to the royal throne, he shall have a copy of this Torah *written for him* on a scroll before the Levitical priests"[19] [emphasis mine]. Deuteronomy, however, uses the active verb. The king does not have the Torah written for him, but rather the king "shall write for himself a copy of this instruction." The common mistranslation is highlighted by the slight

---

17. Van Soldt, "The Title TʿY," *UF* 20 (1988), 321.
18. Van der Toorn, *Scribal Culture*, 90.
19. Ibid., 95–96.

changes in the Temple Scroll from Qumran that rewrites Deuteronomy as follows, "They [that is, "the priests"] shall write for him [that is, "the king"] this law before the priests" (11Q19 LVI, 20–21).[20] The Temple Scroll thus makes the change that reflects the role of the temple scribes in the Hellenistic period, and thereby rewrites the Book of Deuteronomy that originally portrayed the king as scribe. With regard to Deuteronomy's description of the king as scribe, this should recall the Neo-Assyrian king Assurbanipal who was purportedly trained as a scribe.[21] As strange as it would seem to later translators, it was the king in Deuteronomy who functioned as the scribe, and the priests served as witnesses.

One particularly useful contribution to the topic of scripturalization is the Neo-Assyrian "revelation paradigm." Van der Toorn cites several examples, but one example is particularly striking, namely, the Neo-Assyrian Catalogue of Texts and Authors, which may be dated between 750–700 BCE. This catalogue describes texts that are dictated by the god Ea and written down by scribes, other texts in the catalogue are ascribed directly from "the mouth of Ea." The text makes revelation a scribal construct. Van der Toorn explains "the emergence of the revelation paradigm as a consequence of the shift in the tradition from the oral to the written."[22] This becomes an occasion for van der Toorn to reflect on the role of the written scroll in the Josianic Reforms as well as the formation of Deuteronomy. It is also worthwhile to reflect on Exodus 24—the other text (besides 2 Kgs 23:2) that mentions the "scroll of the covenant" (v. 7) as well as depicting Moses as writer (v. 4) and the divine tablets that are "written by the finger of God" (v. 12; 31:18). This depiction in Exodus has a parallel with the Myth of Enmeduranki, where the gods Shamash and Adad introduce the king to the art of divination and provide him with the tablet of the gods. These parallels provide evidence for revelation as a scribal construct well back into the Neo-Assyrian period beginning at least in the eighth century BCE. The revelation paradigm is critical to making writing sacred and authoritative, which is key to the process of scripturalization. There were three avenues in which this process might have been productive for scripturalization in ancient Judah: first, the use of divine writing; second, the adoption of the messenger formula for God; and, third, the use of magic and ritual texts.

---

20. See Serge Fraade, "The Torah of the King (Deut 17:14–20) in the Temple Scroll and Early Rabbinic Law," in *The Dead Sea Scrolls as Background to Postbiblical Judaism and Early Christianity: Papers from an International Conference at St. Andrews in 2001*, ed. James R. Davila (Leiden: Brill. 2003), 25–60.

21. See, for example, the colophon to *Erra and Ishum* (Stephanie Dalley, *COS* 1.113:416).

22. Van der Toorn, *Scribal Culture*, 217.

Critical to the scripturalization of texts is the advancement of divine writing or magical writing. One well-known example of divine writing is the "book of life," where God writes or erases names according to their fate. Another example is the giving of the two tablets in Exod 24:12. This verse begins a literary unit that concludes in Exod 31:18. The closure of this literary unit is marked by an *inclusio*—that is, by a literary repetition that recalls the opening of the literary unit and intentionally brings the literary unit to a close. Thus, the narrative that begins in Exod 24:12 is closed off by recalling this verse in 31:18:

> [24:12] YHWH said to Moses, "Come up to me on the mountain, and wait there; and I will give you the tablets of stone, with the law and the commandment, which I have written for their instruction."
> ... [plans for the tabernacle and the Sabbath commandment] ...
> [31:18] When God finished speaking with Moses on Mount Sinai, he gave him the two tablets of the covenant, tablets of stone, written with the finger of God.

The narrative is closed by one of the most powerful and inspiring anthropomorphic images of Scripture. According to Exod 31:18, God literally wrote the tablets with his own finger. This actually looks to be an anthropomorphic interpretation of 24:12 where God speaks in first person—"I have written." It seems unlikely that such radical anthropomorphizing was late (that is, postexilic) as it goes in the opposite direction of later tendencies. Moreover, later tradition makes Moses the author of the Torah rather than the finger of God. The content of the tablets also points to an early date. What was written by the finger of God on these tablets? The literary framing is for Exodus 25–31, that is, for the plans for building the tabernacle (and by extension the Temple).[23] Thus, the biblical narrative here simply frames and justifies an ancient religious building in a way that is reminiscent of a Near Eastern foundation text. According to this reading of the text, it was not the legal code of ancient Israel nor the Decalogue written on the famous two stone tablets; rather, God had revealed the plans for his own house, its facilities, as well as the Sabbath commandment for worship at the tabernacle. The best ancient

---

23. Archaeological and comparative research indicates that the plan and conception of the tabernacle is quite ancient. On the antiquity of the Tabernacle, see Frank Moore Cross, "The Tabernacle," *BA* 10 (1947): 45–68. This may be supplemented by more recent articles by idem, "The Early Priestly Tabernacle in Light of Recent Research," in *Temples and High Places in Biblical Times*, ed. Avraham Biran (Jerusalem: Magnes, 1981), 169–80; Kenneth A. Kitchen, "The Tabernacle: A Bronze Age Artifact," *ErIsr* 24 (1993): 119*–29*.

analogy for such a claim would be the Mesopotamian Tablets of Destiny.[24] The Tablets of Destiny are a divine writing produced at the very creation of the world and are accompanied by the foundation of Marduk's temple in Babylon. In this context, the inclusion of the Sabbath commandment as part of the tabernacle building instructions introduces an important conceptual connection between the tablets of Exod 24:12–31:18 and the biblical creation narrative. This can also be compared to Mesopotamian foundation texts, which are often found in the foundations of Mesopotamian temples such as the temple at Larsa.

The revelation paradigm should also recall for us the textual background of the writing prophets. Here, it is important to highlight that the messenger formula is the form-critical backbone to the writing prophets. In a classic essay on "Assyrian Statecraft and the Prophets of Israel," John Holladay argued that two categories of Assyrian statecraft had a particular influence on the rise of the writing prophets: first, international treaties; and second, royal letters.[25] Of course, the treaty genre is quintessentially a royal document prepared by royal scribes. And, as the Sefire Inscriptions illustrate, the treaty genre was not limited to the cuneiform world but spread also to Aramaic scribes (through which it presumably could also have been passed on to Hebrew scribes). The royal messenger was also a figure and a form that transcended boundaries. Holladay speaks about "the spectacular rise to prominence of the royal herald as an essential instrument of imperial government,"[26] and many scholars have noted how the classical prophets adopt the messenger formula (that is, a formula that was prominent from the Late Bronze Age through the Neo-Assyrian period) as a model for their mediation of the divine word to the people. This model originally endowed the written text with royal authority and then—through its adaptation to the writing prophets—with divine authority. By replacing the human sender with a divine sender, the messenger—that is, the prophet—carries a divine text. A significant aspect of the messenger formula in the ancient Near East is the obligation of the messenger to transmit carefully the message, which is encoded in writing, to the audience. In one Mesopotamian tradition, writing was invented in order for a messenger to transmit the precise words of the sender.[27] The adoption of the messenger formula for divine speech high-

---

24. Andrew R. George, "Sennacherib and the Tablet of Destinies," *Iraq* (1986), 133–46.

25. John S. Holladay Jr., "Assyrian Statecraft and the Prophets of Israel," in *Prophecy in Israel: Search for an Identity*, ed. David L. Petersen (Philadephia: Fortress; London: SPCK, 1987), 122–43.

26. Ibid., 130.

27. Thorkild Jacobsen, "Enmerkar and the Lord of Aratta," in *COS* 1.170:548.

lights a key aspect of the process of scripturalization, namely, the endowment of divine authority to writing.

Mesopotamia tradition preserves two different accounts of the origins of writing. The more well known accounts parallel ancient Egypt in making writing a gift of the gods. A lesser known account is told in the story of Enmerkar and the Lord of Aratta.[28] Enmerkar ruled in Uruk as "priest-king," and he forced the submission of the ancient city of Aratta, which then supplied raw materials for building the temple in Uruk. In his correspondence with Enmerkar, the lord of Aratta posed a series of seemingly insurmountable problems. However, Enmerkar returned a messenger with the solution to each of the problems. Finally, in one particular instance, when Enmerkar's message became too long for his messenger's memory, Enmerkar invented the written letter for his messenger to take with him to Aratta. In this account, the messenger formula and the letter genre has a special origin in remote antiquity indicating its special ability to transmit speech accurately.

Where else is the written word endowed with special authority in the ancient Near East? There are two other social contexts for the textualization and authority of the written word in the ancient world: treaties and magic. Magical texts are another genre (like messenger formulas) where the exact representation of speech is critical. Holladay also noted the importance of treaties along with the messenger formula for the rise of the writing prophets. The other realm where ancient writing had inherent authority and power was ritual magic. Indeed, other types of written texts derive their power from the inherent connection between writing and magic or divination. This is obviously true of the treaty. Treaties use "blessings and curses"—that is, forms of ritual magic—to seal the covenant relationship between the parties in the treaty relationship. Indeed, as striking as the similarities are between the Treaty of Esarhaddon and the Curses of Deuteronomy,[29] even more striking parallels can be cited from texts like Maqlû and Šurpu.[30]

A central concern of the Neo-Assyrian magical rituals Maqlû and Shurpu as well as Neo-Assyrian Vassal Treaties is the binding oath, recited and then written down and enforced by divine power. Deuteronomy 27–29,

---

28. *COS* 1.170:548. The text also has interesting parallels to Genesis 11 and the idea of "one language." See Thorkild Jacobsen, *The Harps That Once: Sumerian Poetry in Translation* (New Haven: Yale University Press, 1987), 275–319.

29. See the classic study by Rintje Frankena, "The Vassal-Treaties of Esarhaddon and the Dating of Deuteronomy," *OTS* 14 (1965): 122–54.

30. This was first pointed out to me by a seminar paper of Melissa Ramos, "Ritual Oath and Ritual Curse: The Influence of *Maqlû* and *Šurpu* upon Deuteronomy 27:11–28:68," which is the basis for her doctoral dissertation, "You Shall Write on the Stones: Deuteronomy 27 and the Inscribing of Ritual Curses" (University of California, Los Angeles, 2015).

Maqlû, and Shurpu employ parallel terminology as well as parallel themes and linguistic structures within the list of punishments or curses. At their core, the ritual performances in Deuteronomy 27–29, Maqlû, Shurpu, and the Neo-Assyrian Vassal Treaty genre are dependent upon ritual magic rather than political ideas for their efficacy. As is well known, a central part of the treaty ritual was the writing down of the stipulations of the treaty. This is also critical to the conclusion of the ritual in Deuteronomy. In Deuteronomy chapter 27, the ritual recitation of the blessings and curses begins with writing. In v. 3 we read, "inscribe upon them all the words of this teaching [Hebrew *tôrâ*]." And, of course, v. 8, which says, "And on those stones you shall inscribe every word of this teaching most clearly." Here it is essential to recognize that the author is not important. The religious authority is not in authorship, as would be the case in later redactions. Moses does not write down the Torah in Deuteronomy 27, rather Moses commands "the elders and all the people" to write down his teaching as in text on specially plastered stones after Israel crosses the Jordan into the promised land.

A similar ritual can be found in Joshua 8. Again, an altar is built on a sacred mountain. Joshua concludes the treaty between God and Israel with writing. In v. 32 we read, "Joshua wrote on the stones a copy of the teaching/torah of Moses, which he had written before the Israelites." More generally, it must be noted that writing was a central part of many magical rituals. For example, the magical power of written texts is evident in Egyptian evidence and could be illustrated by many examples such as the Execration Texts. Probably the most interesting example of writing as a magical ingredient in a biblical tradition is the Sotah ritual in Num 5:16–30. There, a priest brings a woman accused of adultery before YHWH and then concocts a potion in which the key ingredient is writing:

> Then the priest shall put these curses in writing, and wash them off into the water of bitterness. He shall make the woman drink the water of bitterness that brings the curse, and the water that brings the curse shall enter her and cause bitter pain.

The critical moment in this ritual of the jealous husband is when the priest writes the curse down, probably on a broken potsherd, and then washes the writing off into the water of bitterness. The writing, now washed into the water, gives the water a magical property. The magic water now can discern whether the jealous husband is right in his accusation. The ritual testifies to the power and magic of written words. What remains is to transfer this power from a ritual text to the Mosaic Torah more generally.

By way of conclusion, we may point out a few examples of the citation and use of texts as scripture in the Deuteronomistic History. The first example is the citation of the altar law in Josh 8:31: "just as Moses the servant of the LORD had commanded the Israelites, as it is written in the scroll of the teaching/torah of Moses, 'an altar of unhewn stones, on which no iron tool has been used'." The language here—particularly, the expression "an altar of unhewn stones"—seems to be an allusion to Exod 20:25, which is usually understood as among the earliest texts in the Bible. Exodus reads, "if you make for me an altar of stone, do not build it of hewn stones; for if you use a chisel upon it you profane it." While the language of Joshua reminds us of Exod 20:25, not surprisingly, it shows even more striking similarities with Deut 27:5–6: "And you shall build an altar there to the LORD your God, an altar of stones on which you have not used an iron tool. You must build the altar of the LORD your God of unhewn stones." Joshua 8:31 and Deut 27:5–6 are products of the deuteronomistic school. They mention both the "altar of unhewn stones" and the injunction that it should not be worked with an iron tool. These ideas are first presented in Exod 20:25, but the exact language is different. For example, Exodus uses the more generic language stating that the altar stones should not be worked with a "chisel." The writer of Joshua cites Deuteronomy as a sacred and binding scripture.

The second example of an explicit citation is in 2 Kgs 14:6, when Amaziah punishes the conspirators who murdered his father, Joash, as we read in vv. 5–6:

> As soon as the royal power was firmly in his hand he killed his servants who had murdered his father the king. But he [Amaziah] did not put to death the children of the murderers; according to what is written in the scroll of the *teaching* of Moses, where the LORD commanded, "The parents shall not be put to death for the children, or the children be put to death for the parents; but all shall be put to death for their own sins."

The citation refers to Deut 24:16, which states, "Parents shall not be put to death for their children, nor shall children be put to death for their parents; only for their own crimes may persons be put to death." This actually countermands the tradition of generational punishment known from the Ten Commandments, namely, that God is "a jealous God, punishing children for the iniquity of parents, to the third and the fourth generation" (Exod 20:5). It is worth pointing out the expression, "as it is written in the scroll of the teaching of Moses, where the LORD commanded." In this scroll is written what God commands and by virtue of that, the written word is sacred and authoritative.

More generally, the formation of the book of Deuteronomy might be read as a case of scripturalization.[31] To return to Judith Newman's definition, what is Deuteronomy if it is not "the reuse of biblical texts or interpretive traditions to shape the composition of new literature." Moreover, Deuteronomy also utilizes the form of a Neo-Assyrian treaty to scripturalize the law. It is ultimately the treaty form and its accompanying ritual reciting the blessings and curses that make the law sacred and authoritative. Deuteronomy culminates with a treaty ceremony with the ritual writing of the law. In 27:2–3a, "On the day that you cross over the Jordan into the land that the LORD your God is giving you, you shall set up large stones and cover them with plaster. You shall write on them all the words of this teaching/torah." Then the written treaty curses are ritually recited. As we know from other ritual contexts, the writing down of the curses imbues the writing with special power. Indeed, the writing now has magical power. Writing itself could have ritual power in certain contexts. The treaty formula borrows this ritual to give the written text sacred authority.

The transfer of sacred authority to written texts is not an easy transition. It requires the transfer of authority from the oral to the written, which necessarily required shifting social loci of authority. Scripturalization implies a transformative moment in human society, and as such it would have met with resistance. With this in mind, perhaps the strongest proof for nascent scripturalization is in the rejection of the text. The book of Jeremiah includes several examples of the resistance to the textualization of tradition, though the most striking one is Jer 8:8, which describes "the false pen of the scribes that have turned the torah of Yahweh into a lie." Jeremiah seems to play on the semantic shift in the word torah itself, where the pen of the scribes have made the oral teaching into a text.[32] Texts like this highlight the fact that the scripturalization process is only *nascent* in the Neo-Assyrian period.

In conclusion, a key aspect of the process of scripturalization is the endowment of sacred authority to the written word. The written word must have authority, particularly religious authority, in order for it to become

---

31. The date of the final redaction of Deuteronomy is debated, but the beginnings of its composition must date back at least into the Neo-Assyrian period. Indeed, the scribal techniques that have been documented by scholars like Bernard Levinson and Eckart Otto have their clear parallels in the Neo-Assyrian period. See, e.g., Bernard Levinson, ed., *Theory and Method in Biblical and Cuneiform Law: Revision, Interpolation and Development* (Sheffield: Sheffield Academic Press, 1994); Eckart Otto, *Das Deuteronomium: Politische Theologie und Rechtsreform in Juda und Assyrien* (Berlin: de Gruyter, 1999).

32. See further Schniedewind, "The Textualization of Torah in Jeremiah 8:8," in *Was ist ein Text? Alttestamentliche, ägyptologische und altorientalistische Perspektiven*, ed. Ludwig Morenz and Stefan Storch, BZAW 162 (Berlin: de Gruyter, 2007), 93–107.

sacred. There are at least three social contexts for the textualization and authority of the written word in the Neo-Assyrian period: first, divine writing (especially as in the foundation of temples); second, messenger formulas; and, third, ritual magic especially as used in treaty curses.

I have intentionally avoided discussing the story of the textually based Josianic reforms in this paper, but it is worth some reflection in light of this discussion. According to the account of the book of Kings, the Josianic reforms were inspired by the discovery and reading of a text—indeed, the reading of a sacred scroll. Although the account of the reading of the text is not nearly as elaborate as in Nehemiah 8, nevertheless the centrality of the text is striking in the reforms. But what made this written text was authoritative? The story of the Josianic reforms explicitly utilizes two of the contexts discussed above, namely, the appeal to a treaty genre and the solicitation of a prophet who utilizes a messenger formula; and, it may allude to my third category: divine writing. In the story, the prophetic message formula is employed a way of textualizing divine speech. The prophecy of Huldah in 2 Kgs 22:15–16 is quite striking in this respect: "She declared to them, 'Thus says the LORD, the God of Israel: Tell the man who sent you to me, Thus says the LORD, I will indeed bring disaster on this place and on its inhabitants—all the words of the scroll that the king of Judah has read." The form of Huldah's speech utilizes a messenger formula in its traditional messenger *Sitz im Leben*. That is, the "word of the Lord" comes to Josiah in the form of a letter carried by a messenger, and the letter then invokes the written curses of the treaty written on the scroll. As we have noted above, such treaty curses invoked in Huldah's prophecy are derived from ritual magic. Through these typical forms of authoritative Neo-Assyrian writing, the Josianic Reform narrative scripturalizes the scroll. Moreover, the finding of the scroll itself points back to the divine writing on Mount Sinai. In 2 Kgs 23:2, it says that the king "read to them the entire text of the *sepher habberith* (that is, the scroll or record of covenant) that had been found in the House of the LORD." The word *berîth* is usually translated "covenant," but it is the word for "treaty." The expression *sēper habbᵉrît* occurs in only two places in the entire Hebrew Bible. The other is Exod 24:7 when Moses ascends the mountain and returns and receives the terms of the treaty and then ritually recites it; "he took the *sēper habbᵉrît* and read it aloud to the people, and the people responded, 'All that the LORD has spoken we will faithfully do.'" It seems quite intentional that the term from Exodus 24, *sēper habbᵉrît*, is used in the account of the Josianic story about the finding of a sacred text. It is an account of the ritual reading of a treaty. As such, this story may embody some of the earliest illustrations of the scripturalization process.

References

Barkay, Gabriel, Marilyn Lundberg, Andrew Vaughn, and Bruce Zuckerman. "The Amulets from Ketef Hinnom: A New Edition and Evaluation." *BASOR* 334 (2004): 41–71.

Carr, David M. *Writing on the Tablet of the Heart: Origins of Scripture and Literature.* Oxford: Oxford University Press, 2005.

Cohen, Yoram. *Scribes and Scholars of the City of Emar in the Late Bronze Age.* Winona Lake, IN: Eisenbrauns, 2009.

Cross, Frank M. "The Early Priestly Tabernacle in Light of Recent Research." Pages 169–80 in *Temples and High Places in Biblical Times*. Edited by Avraham Biran. Jerusalem: Magnes, 1981.

———. "The Tabernacle." *BA* 10 (1947): 45–68.

Fraade, Serge. "The Torah of the King (Deut 17:14–20) in the Temple Scroll and Early Rabbinic Law." Pages 25–60 in *The Dead Sea Scrolls as Background to Postbiblical Judaism and Early Christianity. Papers from an International Conference at St. Andrews in 2001*. Edited by James R. Davila. Leiden: Brill. 2003.

Frankena, Rintje. "The Vassal-Treaties of Esarhaddon and the Dating of Deuteronomy." *OTS* 14 (1965): 122–54.

George, Andrew R. "Sennacherib and the Tablet of Destinies." *Iraq* (1986): 133–46.

Hallo, William W. "The Concept of Canonicity in Cuneiform and Biblical Literature: A Comparative Appraisal." Pages 1–19 in *The Biblical Canon in Comparative Perspective*. Edited by K. Lawson Younger, William W. Hallo, and Bernard F. Batto. Lewiston, NY: Mellon, 1991.

Hallo, William W., and K. Lawson Younger, eds. *The Context of Scripture*. 3 volumes. Leiden: Brill, 1997–2002.

Holladay Jr., John S. "Assyrian Statecraft and the Prophets of Israel." Pages 122–43 in *Prophecy in Israel: Search for an Identity*. Edited by David L. Petersen. Philadephia: Fortress; London: SPCK, 1987.

Jacobsen, Thorkild. *The Harps That Once: Sumerian Poetry in Translation*. New Haven: Yale University Press, 1987.

Keel, Othmar, and Christoph Uehlinger. *Gods, Goddesses and Images of God in Ancient Israel*. Translated by Thomas H. Trapp. Philadelphia: Fortress, 1998.

Kitchen, Kenneth A. "The Tabernacle: A Bronze Age Artifact." *ErIsr* 24 (1993): 119*–129*.

Levinson, Bernard, ed. *Theory and Method in Biblical and Cuneiform Law: Revision, Interpolation and Development*. Sheffield: Sheffield Academic Press, 1994.

Lewis, Theodore. "Job 19 in Light of the Ketef Hinnom Inscriptions and Amulets." Pages 97–111 in *Puzzling Out the Past: Studies in Northwest Semitic Languages and Literatures in Honor of Bruce Zuckerman*. Edited by Marilyn J. Lundberg, Steven Fine, and Wayne Pitard. Leiden: Brill, 2012.

Newman, Judith. *Praying by the Book: The Scripturalization of Prayer in Second Temple Judaism*. EJL 14. Atlanta: Scholars Press, 1999.

Noll, Kurt L. "Did 'Scripturalization' Take Place in Second Temple Judaism?" *SJOT* 25 (2011): 201–16.

Otto, Eckart. *Das Deuteronomium: politische Theologie und Rechtsreform in Juda und Assyrien*. Berlin: de Gruyter, 1999.

Paul, Shalom. "Heavenly Tablets and the Book of Life." *JANES* 5 (1973): 345–53.
Pedersén, Olaf. *Archives and Libraries in the Ancient Near East 1500–300 B.C.* Bethesda: CDL, 1998.
Schmidt, Brian B. "The Social Matrix of Early Judean Magic and Divination: From 'Top Down' or 'Bottom Up'?" Pages 279–94 in *Beyond Hatti: A Tribute to Gary Beckman*. Edited by Billie Jean Collins and Piotr Michalowski. Atlanta: Lockwood, 2013.
Schniedewind, William M. *How the Bible Became a Book: the Textualization of Ancient Israel*. Cambridge: Cambridge University Press, 2004.
———. "The Textualization of Torah in Jeremiah 8:8." Pages 93–107 in *Was ist ein Text? Alttestamentliche, ägyptologische und altorientalistische Perspektiven*. Edited by Ludwig Morenz and Stefan Storch. BZAW 162. Berlin: de Gruyter, 2007.
Smoak, Jeremy. "May YHWH Bless You and Guard You from Evil: The Rhetorical Argument of Ketef Hinnom Amulet I and the Form of the Prayers for Deliverance in the Psalms." *JANER* 12 (2012): 202–36.
———. *May Yahweh Bless You and Keep You: The Early History and Ritual Background of the Priestly Blessing*. Oxford: Oxford University Press, forthcoming.
———. "Yahweh's Shining Face and the Ritual Logic of the Judahite Amulets from Ketef Hinnom." *ARelG* (forthcoming).
Van der Toorn, K. *Scribal Culture and the Making of the Hebrew Bible*. Cambridge, MA: Harvard University Press, 2007.
Van Soldt, Wilfred. "The Title *T'Y*." *UF* 20 (1988): 313–21.
Watts, James. "Ritual Legitimacy and Scriptural Authority." *JBL* 124 (2005): 401–17.
———. "Scripturalization and the Aaronide Dynasties." *JHS* 13 (2013). doi:10.5508/jhs.2013.v13.a6.
———. "Ten Commandments Monuments and the Rivalry of Iconic Texts." *Journal of Religion & Society* 6 (2004).
———. "The Three Dimensions of Scriptures." *Postscripts* 2 (2006): 135–59.
Weitzman, Steven. *Song and Story in Biblical Narrative: The History of a Literary Convention in Ancient Israel*. Bloomington, IN: Indiana University Press, 1997.

Hebrew Culture at the "Interface between the Written and the Oral"

Joachim SCHAPER

IT IS IMPOSSIBLE TO TRACE THE PREHISTORY OF THE CULTURES OF ISRAEL AND Judah[1] back to the point when they first made contact with the technology of writing.[2] While it is possible to trace palaeo-Hebrew writing back to its predecessor scripts and to establish a genealogy of Northwest Semitic writing systems,[3] there are no sources that might help us to reconstruct the history of the earliest times of Israelite (prestatehood) society and culture.[4]

---

1. It is difficult to determine whether they really developed independently of each other, as has now been claimed by Israel Finkelstein, *The Forgotten Kingdom: The Archaeology and History of Northern Israel*, ANEM 5 (Atlanta: Society of Biblical Literature, 2013). In any case, both cultures did develop separately, while using the same (though regionally different) language, worshipping the same god, and giving rise to similar social, political, and legal institutions. On regional variations of the Hebrew language, see W. Randall Garr, *Dialect Geography of Syria-Palestine, 1000–586 B.C.E.* (Philadelphia: University of Pennsylvania Press, 1985). A good example of the difference between the northern (Israelite) and southern (Judahite) varieties of Hebrew is provided by the word for "year" (שת in Israelite and שנת in Judahite dialect).

2. For a discussion of writing as a "technology," see Walter J. Ong, *Orality and Literacy: The Technologizing of the Word* (London: Methuen, 1982; repr. London: Routledge, 2002), 80–82.

3. For an overview of the history of the Phoenician and palaeo-Hebrew alphabetic scripts from the tenth to the sixth centuries BCE, see Johannes Renz, *Die althebräischen Inschriften*, Teil 2: *Zusammenfassende Erörterungen, Paläographie und Glossar*, HAHE 2.1 (Darmstadt: Wissenschaftliche Buchgesellschaft, 1995), 95–208. For palaeographic tables depicting the stages of the development of the palaeo-Hebrew script, see Johannes Renz, *Texte und Tafeln*, HAHE 3 (Darmstadt: Wissenschaftliche Buchgesellschaft, 1995), 37–75. For an overview of the origins and development of Semitic alphabetic writing see Wolfgang Röllig, "Das Alphabet und sein Weg zu den Griechen," in *Die Geschichte der hellenischen Sprache und Schrift: Vom 2. zum 1. Jahrtausend vor Chr.: Kontinuität oder Bruch? 03.–06. Oktober 1996, Ohlstadt/Oberbayern-Deutschland* (Altenburg: Verlag für Kultur und Wissenschaft, 1998), 359–86.

4. For want of a better term, I use the biblical adjective "Israelite" to refer to that which Israel and Judah have in common, and in this case to the earliest form of that society

Only from the late tenth century BCE onwards does the veil start to lift a little. The tenth century witnessed the beginnings of the Davidic "monarchy," a political entity that was by no means as complex as the structurally advanced entities in the neighborhood, some of which do deserve to be called "states," and has been described as a "patrimonial kingdom."[5] The division of labor characterizing a "kingdom" such as that of the early Hebrews was not complex enough to require an elaborate bureaucratic machine. The few extant texts from the century that saw the very beginnings of Israelite statehood, that is, the tenth century, are still quite clearly of a Phoenician type, building on the earlier developments of a proto-Canaanite writing system, and were written in a world in which Phoenician, Hebrew, and Aramaic were still intertwined and developing together.[6] Just a few very early West Semitic inscriptions known today point to literary production—in the widest sense—in Palestine before the ninth century BCE, but they are not necessarily witnesses to palaeo-Hebrew script. They are the Gezer calendar (tenth century); some of the Arad ostraca (tenth century?); inscriptions from Tel Batash and Beth Shemesh; the Tel Zayit abecedary; and the Khirbet Qeiyafa ostracon (tenth century).[7] Older still is the Izbet Sartah ostracon, which probably dates from the eleventh century BCE.

Only in the ninth century, the century that also produced the first inscriptions that indicate the existence of a Davidic monarchy, was a script devised that was used for the notation of texts in the three languages of Hebrew, Moabite, and Ammonite, a development that was followed by the emergence of a clearly distinct Hebrew script towards the end of the ninth century.[8] The link between the devising of a "national" script and a more elaborate form of statehood is significant and needs to be discussed, which I shall do in due course.[9]

It is therefore only two of the "three aspects of the interface between the oral and the written which are often confused" that the present essay

---

and culture from which both Israel and Judah sprang.

5. Philip J. King and Lawrence E. Stager, *Life in Biblical Israel*, LAI (Louisville: Westminster John Knox, 2001), 201–58.

6. Cf. Johannes Renz, "Die vor- und außerliterarische Texttradition: Ein Beitrag der palästinischen Epigraphik zur Vorgeschichte des Kanons," in *Die Textualisierung der Religion*, ed. Joachim Schaper, FAT 62 (Tübingen: Mohr Siebeck, 2009), 66.

7. Cf. Haggai Misgav, Yosef Garfinkel, and Saar Ganor, "The Khirbet Qeiyafa Ostracon," in *New Studies in the Archaeology of Jerusalem and Its Region*, ed. David Amit, Guy D. Stiebel, Orit Peleg-Barkat (Jerusalem: Israel Antiquities Authority and the Institute of Archaeology, the Hebrew University of Jerusalem, 2009), 111–23 (in Hebrew).

8. Cf. Renz, "Die vor- und außerliterarische Texttradition," 66.

9. See below, ch. 2.

addresses:[10] while I am not concerned with "the meeting of cultures with and without writing,"[11] I will discuss "societies that employ writing to varying degrees in various contexts" as well as "the interface between the use of writing and speech in the linguistic life of any individual"[12] in those societies.

When we speak of "Hebrew culture," we think that culture

> may be defined as the totality of the mental and physical reactions and activities that characterize the behavior of individuals composing a social group collectively and individually in relations to their natural environment, to other groups, to members of the group itself and of each individual to himself.[13]

Furthermore, we think that

> [i]t also includes the products of these activities and their role in the life of the groups. The mere enumerations of these various aspects of life, however, does not constitute culture. It is more, for its elements are not independent, they have a structure.[14]

For the purposes of the present paper, I am interested in the functions and effects of orality and literacy, of oral and written discourse amongst the Israelites and Judahites as elements of "the totality of the mental and physical reactions and activities that characterize the behavior of individuals composing a social group collectively and individually."[15] I will concentrate on that period of the history of Israel and Judah in which writing increasingly gained prominence and importance among administrators, religious functionaries, and other key groups in society, viz. the eighth, seventh, and sixth centuries BCE. I will thus remain within the boundaries of the palaeo-Hebrew textual tradition, which began in the ninth century and ended in the sixth.[16] This was

---

10. Jack Goody, *The Interface between the Written and the Oral*, Studies in Literacy, Family, Culture and the State (Cambridge: Cambridge University Press, 1987), ix.
11. Ibid.
12. Ibid.
13. Franz Boas, *The Mind of Primitive Man* (New York: Macmillan, 1911), 149. Unfortunately, there is no room here to discuss the fascinating and complex history of the concept of "culture." Suffice it to say that Boas's pragmatic definition gave rise to a distinguished tradition of "cultural anthropology" and is still useful as a starting point of reflection on a notoriously vague, yet indispensable concept at the heart of the exploration of human social being.
14. Ibid.
15. Ibid.
16. Cf. Christopher A. Rollston, *Writing and Literacy in the World of Ancient Israel: Epigraphic Evidence from the Iron Age*, ABS 11 (Atlanta: Society of Biblical Literature, 2010), 42: "There is sufficient data to state that the Old Hebrew script became a distinct

the period in the beginnings of which the groundwork for the later, remarkable literary productivity was laid and which then brought forth the first great examples of Hebrew poetic and narrative literature. In terms of the historical development of the Hebrew language, we are thus dealing with "Archaic Hebrew" as well as (classical) Biblical Hebrew, but not with late Biblical Hebrew.[17]

The topographical and temporal distribution of epigraphic finds and the information yielded by biblical texts lead to the conclusion that, while writing had always been important, its practice increased significantly from the eighth century onwards. It is indicative of this development that it was in the late eighth and early seventh centuries that the palaeo-Hebrew script displayed "the greatest variation of forms for most letters."[18] Only from the late ninth century onwards had there been a significant increase in the production of written texts in Palestine. As in many other ancient cultures, including the very first culture ever to use writing, the production of texts among the Hebrews started in economic and administrative contexts. The earliest *religious* texts we know of can be dated to the late ninth or early eighth century (Kuntillet Ajrud).[19] The monumental inscriptions found at Khirbet Beit Lei display formulaic religious language. They probably date to the end of the eighth or the beginning of the seventh century. Although they can probably

---

national script during the ninth century BCE. The earliest evidence for the Old Hebrew script hails from the region of Moab. This region had been under Israelite hegemony during the ninth century and it can reasonably be postulated that Moabite scribes began to use the fledgling Old Hebrew script during this period of Israelite hegemony.... During succeeding chronological horizons, the Old Hebrew script and the Phoenician script continue to develop along different trajectories."

17. Cf. Angel Sáenz-Badillos, *A History of the Hebrew Language*, trans. John Elwolde (Cambridge: Cambridge University Press, 1993), 52: "The Hebrew of the poetic sections of the Bible, some of which are very old despite possible post-exilic revision, as well as the oldest epigraphic material in inscriptions dating from the tenth to sixth centuries BCE, we call Archaic Hebrew, although we realize that there is no general agreement among scholars regarding this term. The language used in the prose sections of the Pentateuch and in the Prophets and the Writings before the exile, we call Classical Biblical Hebrew, or BH proper. Late Biblical Hebrew (LBH) refers to the language of the books of the Bible written after the exile." While this suffices as a general, rough outline of the development of Hebrew, one may of course wonder, with E. Ullendorff ("Is Biblical Hebrew a Language?," *BSOAS* 34 [1971]: 241–55), what we can really claim to know about the Hebrew of the Bible and the way in which it relates to the actual Hebrew spoken in the streets of Jerusalem and in the circles of the literati (see Sáenz-Badillos, *History of the Hebrew Language*, 53, for a pithy historical comment on the central point made by Ullendorff).

18. Renz, *Die althebräischen Inschriften*, 102: "Alle genannten Entwicklungen führen dazu, daß das ausgehende 8. und beginnende 7. Jhdt. bei den meisten Buchstaben die größte Formenvielfalt aufweist."

19. Cf. Renz, "Die vor- und außerliterarische Texttradition," 71–72.

be categorized as "preliterary" texts, they do betray a degree of stylistic accomplishment and are reminiscent of Exod 34:6–7.[20]

Other well-known inscriptions include the later Arad ostraca (late seventh or early sixth century). It is significant that a certain number of texts from the Hebrew Bible mirror the type of Hebrew found in the ancient Hebrew inscriptions that can be dated to the period ranging from the late eighth to the early sixth century.[21]

Karel van der Toorn has rightly drawn attention to the importance of the *material* culture of Israel and Judah and the way in which it determined the development of the work of the scribes who produced the Israelite and Judaean literature known to us through the Hebrew Bible.[22] It is important to understand the relations of production, the productive forces, and especially the means of production that gave rise to and shaped the work of the scribes. I will address them in the following section and follow this with a discussion of the effects of writing on the individual.

Spoken Language, the Increasing Division of Labor, and the Rising Prominence of Writing

The rising prominence of writing is a direct result of the increasing division of labor in the Israelite and Judahite societies of the ninth and eighth centuries. The development of the division of labor and the increase in the practice of writing went hand in hand; they were interdependent. "Changes in the means of communication, changes that are external to the actor (...), alter the range of possibilities open to man, internal as well as external, increasing not his abilities but his capacities and the skills needed to take advantage of these."[23] The development of a distinctively *Hebrew* notation system, the so-called palaeo-Hebrew script, in the context of the emerging Israelite state, is a

---

20. Ibid., 74–75.
21. Cf. ibid., 65, with references to secondary literature.
22. See Karel van der Toorn, *Scribal Culture and the Making of the Hebrew Bible* (Cambridge: Harvard University Press, 2007).
23. Goody, *Interface between the Written*, 272. Cf. also the immediate context, ibid., 271–72: "So while the mind is in no sense a *tabula rasa*, its basic processes of treating information can and must be influenced by the many changes in the means and modes of communication. An acceptance of this proposition affects the social, psychological and linguistic levels of analysis. Neither the spoken nor the written language are simply manifestations of some abstract linguistic ability that lies forever hidden in the depths, unchanging, sempiternal. We accept a broadly 'functional' view of cognitive processes (if in that characterization we can include dysfunctional elements)."

key feature of the configuration of orality and literacy in the Hebrew culture of the ninth century BCE.

It has long been a matter of speculation just how deep-reaching the consequences of the invention of the alphabet were. It is certainly true that "the invention of the alphabet, and to some extent the syllabary, led to a considerable reduction in the number of signs, and to a writing system that was potentially unrestricted both in its capacity to transcribe speech and in its availability to the general population,"[24] in marked contrast to, say, cuneiform writing. Indeed, Jack Goody has stressed the connection between the development of the Northwest Semitic alphabets, the growth of literacy in Syria-Palestine, and ancient Hebrew literature by pointing out that "the uses of writing seem to have expanded in the religious and the historical-literary domains relative to the political and economic; of this expansion the Old Testament of the Hebrews may be considered one of the major products."[25]

While it is clear that the expansion "in the religious and the historical-literary domains relative to the political and economic" that Goody mentions is indeed a fascinating fact of ancient Israelite cultural history, Christopher Rollston has postulated that the palaeo-Hebrew script that emerged in the ninth century BCE was the result of a conscious effort on behalf of the nascent Israelite state; he contends "that the fledgling Israelite kingdom(s) [sic] made a conscious decision to create a national Hebrew script during this time period, thereby formally breaking with the Phoenician *Mutterschrift* that had been used prior to this in Israel. The creation of the Old Hebrew script was, I believe, a nationalistic statement, not merely an evolutionary development."[26] Apart from the fact that "nationalism," if and when applied to an ancient society, is an anachronistic category, there is no indication that the features that distinguish the palaeo-Hebrew from the Phoenician script are the results of conscious efforts. It is more likely that they developed as the expression of a move towards a uniform style employed by Israelite scribes once they became a distinct category of functionaries. This development in turn was ultimately dependent on the economic factors that gave rise to the need for the use of writing for bureaucratic and administrative purpose in the emergent Hebrew state when it made the transition from charismatic to traditional authority, of which more later.

---

24. Ibid., 55.
25. Ibid.
26. Rollston, *Writing and Literacy*, 44.

The Individual at the Interface between the Oral and the Written

Let us now explore the differences between spoken and written language and the respective effects of both on the individual, especially on the literate individual. But what is literacy? Defining it is a notoriously difficult task that has generated fierce debates among scholars, educators, and politicians working towards the improvement of literacy levels in our own time. Defining it with regard to ancient societies is no easier. It seems justified not to entertain the notion of "functional literacy" and thus to class minimal skills, like signing one's name to a document, as "literacy."[27] Rather, it makes sense to postulate,

> for the southern Levant during antiquity, ... as a working description of literacy the possession of substantial facility in a writing system, that is, the ability to write and read, using and understanding a standard script, a standard orthography, a standard numeric system, conventional formatting and terminology, and with minimal errors of composition or comprehension.[28]

It is of crucial importance to understand the difference between spoken and written language and the respective effects they have on human beings. The better we understand those effects, the better we shall be able to understand what "happens" at the interface between the oral and the written, especially in cultures that are not characterised by high literacy rates. The work done by philosophers in the phenomenological tradition, especially the writings of Merleau-Ponty and Derrida, will help us to understand the nature and effects of both speech and writing, and of the ways in which both "collide" with and complement each other. Speech is a medium that, in the act of speaking, immediately and efficiently effaces itself. We need to understand such self-effacement, not least in order to comprehend better in which sense precisely writing is different from speaking.

Speaking calls forth, in the individual speaker, the notion—or rather, the *illusion*—of *immediacy*. Speech produces that notion because it generates the illusion of immediate comprehension of and contact with the object signified, since "the word [*mot*] is lived as the elementary and undecomposable unity

---

27. See ibid., 127: "I would affirm that the capacity to scrawl one's name on a contract, but without the ability to write or read anything else is not literacy, not even some sort of 'functional literacy.' Rather, those with this level of eptitude [*sic*] should be classed as illiterate. However, I would also argue that there were some in ancient Israel who should be classed as semi-literates. That is, there were ostensibly those who were capable of reading the most remedial of texts with at least some modest level of comprehension and often the ability to pen some of the most common and simplest of words."

28. Ibid., 127.

of the signified and the voice."[29] The effacement of the signifier suggests both to the speaker and to the listener that they are experiencing the signified directly and immediately. Spoken language "propels us toward the things it signifies."[30]

There are many biblical texts that reflect the notion of immediacy generated by spoken language and especially by conversation. Certain passages in the Hebrew Bible betray that the sensation of being in contact with the signified could be experienced as being immediate and direct and was consequently projected onto the perceived communication between the deity and human beings, for example, when Moses is described as communicating with YHWH "face to face, as a man speaketh unto his friend" (Exod 33:11 KJV). It is clear that the narrative of the conversation between Moses and Yahweh is the result of the fascination experienced by humans in the interaction taking place in face-to-face conversations with each other. Human beings perceive such conversational interaction as an act of immediacy, as something that can be experienced as a (temporary) "union" between the self and the other: "There can be speech (and in the end personality) only for an 'I' which contains the germ of a depersonalization."[31] That "depersonalization" lets the conversational "union" between friends happen; Moses is, indeed, temporarily on par with YHWH.

Let us now turn to writing. It is often seen simply as a means of "conserving" and "reviving" speech; this view has a long tradition and has Ferdinand de Saussure as one of its best-known supporters.[32] Saussure's view has, however, not gone uncontested. In fact, it was contested—and rightly so—by other linguists quite early on. Vachek, a representative of the "Prague School," made the suggestion to differentiate between the "written" and the "spoken norm" of language.

> The spoken norm of language is a system of phonically manifestable language elements whose function is to react to a given stimulus (which, as a rule, is an urgent one) in a dynamic way, i.e. in a ready and immediate manner, duly expressing not only the purely communicative but also the emotional aspect of the approach of the reacting language user.
>
> The written norm of language is a system of graphically manifestable language elements whose function is to react to a given stimulus (which, as a rule, is not an urgent one) in a static way, i.e. in a preservable and easily

---

29. Jacques Derrida, *Of Grammatology*, trans. Gayatri Chakravorty Spivak (Baltimore: Johns Hopkins University Press, 1974), 20.
30. Maurice Merleau-Ponty, *The Prose of the World* (London: Heinemann, 1974), 10.
31. Ibid., 19.
32. Ferdinand de Saussure, *Cours de linguistique générale*, ed. Charles Bally and Albert Sechehaye, with the collaboration of Albert Riedlinger (Lausanne: Payot, 1916).

surveyable manner, concentrating particularly on the purely communicative aspect of the approach of the reacting language user.[33]

Vachek's views were discussed and accepted by Jack Goody, who, in doing so, also effectively retracted some of his own older views on the interplay between orality and literacy. As becomes obvious from Vachek's highly perceptive observations, writing introduces a new quality to human communication. Vachek's research makes it abundantly clear that it would be naive to regard writing simply as a storage medium. It is that, but it is also much more, since it does not just conserve the orally/aurally delivered but also "shifts language from the aural to the visual domain, and makes possible a different kind of inspection, the re-ordering and refining not only of sentences, but of individual words" which can be understood "as a process of de-contextualization, even though the word involves some conceptual difficulties."[34]

Generally speaking, in the words of Walter J. Ong, "writing is a technology,"[35] and it "restructures consciousness."[36] Indeed, "writing is a solipsistic operation."[37] As has rightly been pointed out, all writers produce their texts for *fictionalized* audiences because authors do not, and cannot, fully know their future audiences. "The ways in which readers are fictionalized is the underside of literary history, of which the topside is the history of genres and the handling of character and plot."[38] And it is difficult for a reader to find a place for herself "in" the text, to "fictionalize" himself in such a way as to benefit most from the text. It is indeed the case that ancient authors made more of an effort to help the reader than modern ones: "Early writing provides the reader with conspicuous help for situating himself imaginatively. It presents philosophical material in dialogues, such as those of Plato's Socrates, which the reader can imagine himself overhearing."[39] In Hebrew literature, other devices were employed; among them, a particularly intriguing one is that chosen in Deuteronomy, where the rhetorical strategy aims at drawing the readers "into" the text, in the sense that they are being addressed, so to speak, *together with* the audience in the world of the text,

---

33. Josef Vachek, *Written Language: General Problems and Problems of English*, Janua Linguarum. Series Critica 14 (The Hague: Mouton, 1973), 15–16.
34. Jack Goody, *The Domestication of the Savage Mind,* Themes in the Social Sciences (Cambridge: Cambridge University Press, 1977), 78.
35. Ong, *Orality and Literacy*, 80 (cf. 80–82).
36. Ibid., 77.
37. Ibid., 100.
38. Ibid., 101.
39. Ibid., 101.

so that the readers and the Israelites addressed by Moses in the world of the text are amalgamated into *one* group of listeners. This strategy betrays that, unsurprisingly in antiquity, Hebrew culture at the time of the growth of the book of Deuteronomy continued to be dominated by orality; the dynamics of literacy, or rather of textuality,[40] were operative, but they operated within a predominantly oral culture.

Vachek rightly points out that one of the effects of the introduction of written language (and thus the production of written utterances) in a given society is its autonomy vis-à-vis spoken language: written utterances establish written language as a primary (!) sign system, in the sense that written texts no longer signify *signs*, but *things*.[41] The autonomy of the "written norm," in Vachek's terminology, leads to a new kind of perceived immediacy between words and things; that between *written* words and things. The "written norm" is no longer secondary; it is now primary. What this leads to, one might say, is a fetishization of the written word, indeed, a fetishization of writing and writing systems generally. The Bible provides us with fascinating examples of that development. Deuteronomy probably contains the most salient ones: the fact that God is depicted as a scribe writing down the commandments he has previously uttered orally and the self-reflexivity of the "book within the book,"[42] which is such a fascinating feature of Deu-

---

40. Ong (*Orality and Literacy*, 100) was probably the first scholar to use the term "dynamics of textuality."

41. Cf. Josef Vachek, "Zum Problem der geschriebenen Sprache," in *A Prague School Reader in Linguistics*, ed. Josef Vachek, Indiana University Studies in the History and Theory of Linguistics (Bloomington: Indiana University Press, 1964), 450, on the historical ("diachronisch") analysis of the relation between spoken and written language: "Da kann man nun sicher nicht leugnen, daß die ersten Schriftäußerungen einer Sprachgemeinschaft von den Sprechäußerungen ausgehen und daß die Schriftnorm eine bloße Transposition der Sprechnorm darstellen will. Dies wurde übrigens schon von Artymovyč anerkannt. Wir möchten zugeben, daß in einer solchen Phase die Schriftnorm als sekundäres Zeichensystem betrachtet werden muß, da jeder von den Bestandteilen dieses Systems ein Zeichen für ein Zeichen darstellt—mit anderen Worten, das ganze sekundäre Zeichensystem spiegelt nicht das System der Dinge wider, sondern nur das primäre Zeichensystem (in diesem Falle die Sprechnorm), und erst von diesem gibt es einen geraden Weg zum System der Dinge. Aber die spezifische Form der Schriftäußerungen erzwingt sich in jeder Sprachgemeinschaft sehr bald jene Autonomie der Schriftnorm, die zuerst von Artymovyč nachdrücklich betont wurde. Und sobald dies geschehen ist, nimmt die Schriftnorm im System der sprachlichen Werte eine neue Stellung ein: aus einem sekundären wird ein primäres Zeichensystem, das heißt von nun an stellen Bestandteile der Schriftnorm nicht Zeichen von Zeichen, sondern Zeichen von Dingen dar. Somit wird die Schriftnorm der Sprechnorm koordiniert. Diese zwei Normen sind natürlich allen Gliedern der Sprachgemeinschaft nicht gleich geläufig."

42. Jean-Pierre Sonnet, *The Book within the Book: Writing in Deuteronomy*, BibInt 14 (Leiden: Brill, 1997).

teronomy, indicate how far such fetishization could go. Other ancient Near Eastern cultures and Egyptian culture, of course, provide us with other, equally characteristic features of the fetishization of writing. In that sense, writing is a deeply ambiguous—or indeed dialectical—medium; while it creates distance, it can also "produce" immanence.

But then, the "tenaciousness of orality"[43] is a force to be reckoned with. Even in the most literate societies of the contemporary world, orality has not been completely marginalized. And throughout antiquity, it remained a powerful component of discourse.[44] Hebrew culture was no different in this respect. We might even say that, just like in any other ancient culture, literacy—or rather, precisely speaking, textuality—forever remained auxiliary to orality. In order to understand the significance of written texts, the significance of orality needs to be taken into consideration.[45] Since the production of written texts of high quality was inordinately expensive in antiquity, with Israel and Judah being no exceptions, few written texts were available. In fact, most members of society came into contact with written texts only when they were *read out* to them. Even reasonably literate Israelites probably did not fully comprehend written texts that had been produced by professional scribes; those texts being unvocalized was part of the problem. It is no overstatement to say that written texts served an *auxiliary* purpose; they provided the basis on which literate Israelites "performed" texts on significant occasions. The recitation of the "law" in Nehemiah 8 provides us with a particularly interesting example of such a "performance."[46]

MAKING SENSE OF WRITING (AND OF SPEAKING) IN WRITING

The Hebrew Bible contains significant witnesses to the (subconscious) desire of Israelite and Judahite *literati* to understand the nature of speech (acts), and of spoken language generally, as well as of written texts, and of writing generally. Famously, it is a key fact of the theology of the Priestly Document that it describes creation as a sequence of creative speech acts. Equally, the account of Adam naming the animals betrays just how important the spoken word was in Hebrew culture. As Ong points out, "explanations of Adam's naming of the animals in Gen 2:20 usually call condescending attention to this presumably quaint archaic belief. Such a belief is in fact far less quaint

---

43. Cf. the subsection thus entitled in Ong, *Orality and Literacy*, 113–14.
44. Ibid., 113 (cf. 113–14).
45. Renz, "Die vor- und außerliterarische Texttradition," 77.
46. On texts and performance, cf. James W. Watts, "Ritual Rhetoric in Ancient Near Eastern Texts," in *Ancient Non-Greek Rhetorics*, ed. Carol Lipson and Roberta Binckley (West Lafayette, IN: Parlor, 2009), 39–66.

than it seems to unreflective chirographic and typographic folks."[47] As Ong rightly says, "oral folk have no sense of a name as a tag, for they have no idea of a name as something that can be seen. Written or printed representations of words can be labels; real, spoken words cannot be." They are much more than a tag could ever be.

This is confirmed by the remarkable attention which the *divine voice* receives in the Bible and in Jewish tradition. We shall have to concentrate here on some characteristic components of the biblical evidence, since we have no space to discuss later Jewish (mystical) writings.[48] To name just a few biblical texts that make much of the voice of YHWH and the function ascribed to it in key acts of revelation: Exodus 19 and 32–34, Deuteronomy 4, and 1 Kings 19. The "still, small voice" of 1 Kings 19 provides a counterpoint to the overwhelming voices of Exodus and Deuteronomy.[49]

Knohl has observed that, compared to the importance of the divine voice to many biblical writers, the human voice plays much less of a role in the Hebrew Bible.[50] Be that as it may, what is important for the purposes of this essay is that the attention that the divine voice receives is a direct result of the everyday experience of the human voice, projected onto the deity.

However, it is equally interesting that, with regard to writing and contrary to Ong's remark, one encounters in Hebrew culture the sense of a powerful link between the *written* signifier and the (material or immaterial) signified, between the written word and the *thing*. We saw earlier that, in written language, the perceived link between the (written) word and the signified becomes very strong once written language has fully established itself. It is well known that primary oral societies invest the spoken word with magical qualities. It is perhaps less well known that writing is also often invested with such qualities. This may well be a direct result of the "written norm" establishing its autonomy: once the perceived direct link between written words and things has been established, it is easy to conclude that the manipulation of the former effects the manipulation of the latter.

---

47. Cf. Ong, *Orality and Literacy*, 33.

48. On the divine voice in the Sefer Yetzirah and elsewhere, cf. Moshe Idel, "Die laut gelesene Tora: Stimmengemeinschaft in der jüdischen Mystik," in *Zwischen Rauschen und Offenbarung: Zur Kultur- und Mediengeschichte der Stimme*, ed. Friedrich Kittler, Thomas Macho, and Sigrid Weigel (Berlin: Akademie, 2002), *passim*.

49. Idel, "Die laut gelesene Tora," 20–21.

50. See Israel Knohl, *The Sanctuary of Silence: The Priestly Torah and the Holiness School* (Minneapolis: Fortress, 1995), 128–49.

Writing, the Economy, and the State

According to Jack Goody, "the actual or potential effects of changes in the modes of communication on patterns of government"[51] are among the neglected factors in the exploration of the formation of premodern states. Even a superficial consideration of the differences between a social unit that governs itself without the help of writing and one that can avail itself of that technology will give an impression of the huge difference writing makes.

History provides examples of states, indeed of fairly complex states, that were built and maintained without writing. "Writing was not essential to the development of the state but of a certain type of state, the *bureaucratic* one."[52] A perfect example of an early state that nevertheless is a perfect example of a "bureaucratic state" is the Neo-Sumerian empire in the Ur III period towards the end of the third millennium BCE: it was characterized by an amazingly intricate and efficient use of planning resources.

In Weberian terminology, the transition from the prestatehood period of Israelite history to that of the early monarchy was an instance of the transition from charismatic to traditional authority.[53] It is not surprising that it went hand in hand with a growth in the importance of writing. While a transition from charismatic to bureaucratic rule would have been inconceivable (given the scarce resources and the concurrent, relatively slow pace of administrative development), the charismatic rule of the earliest Israelite kings turned into the "traditional authority" of established monarchies.

The Oral, the Written, and Literature: Consequences for the Development of Israelite Religion, with Special Regard to Prophecy

In the reconstruction of the history of any "national" literature of antiquity (and that includes, of course, the history of Israelite and Judahite literatures), it is important to distinguish between the literary and the nonliterary uses of writing.[54]

---

51. Jack Goody, *The Logic of Writing and the Organization of Society*, Studies in Literacy, Family, Culture and the State (Cambridge: Cambridge University Press, 1986), 90.

52. Goody, *Logic of Writing*, 92. The ideal type of "bureaucratic authority"—as opposed to other ideal types of authority, like the traditional and the bureaucratic ones postulated by Weber—was developed by Max Weber in his *Wirtschaft und Gesellschaft*, Grundriß der Sozialökonomik Abt. 3 (Tübingen: Mohr Siebeck, 1922); see sp. p. 140.

53. See the previous footnote.

54. On the definition of "literature," see Renz, "Die vor- und außerliterarische Texttradition," 74.

Israel's literature had a long literary "prehistory" of non- and preliterary writing. The roots of Israelite and Judahite literature (in the wider sense, i.e., with the term "literature" denoting written texts) can be found in the economic, social, political, and cultic life of the political entities that preceded Israelite statehood. We need not go into detail here. Instead, we need to understand how the transition from the oral to the written, from "oral literature" (for want of a better term) to actual literature (in the sense of written texts) came about. It is fruitless to engage in speculation about the preliterary, oral stage of the development of biblical texts, but it will be helpful to address the problem of the transition from oral delivery to written "storage," and to do so with special attention to preexilic prophecy. The exploration of Israelite oral "literature"[55] was a key element of biblical research in the previous two centuries and often led to mistaken reconstructions of the history of the literary corpora that constitute the Hebrew Bible.[56] Some of the narratives handed down as part of the Deuteronomistic History, to name just one example, may well derive from an "oral literature" stage. Yet it cannot be the objective of this essay to discuss putative "oral texts"[57] that were used in the formation of biblical narratives and poetry. While the possibility of the existence of oral texts can reasonably be assumed, scholarship will have to focus on the extant written texts and use them as a key to the interplay between the oral and the written in Hebrew culture.

The rising importance of writing in Hebrew culture led to a momentous change in the recording, perception, and transmission of, amongst many other things, prophetic oracles. The book of Jeremiah, especially Jeremiah 36, is interesting in this respect.[58] Karel van der Toorn has surmised that the story that describes Jeremiah as dictating his oracles to a scribe "is historically suspect because it is obviously designed to prove that the collection had the authority of the prophet.... Prophets ... were not in the habit of writ-

---

55. On oral "literature," see Jack Goody, *Myth, Ritual and the Oral* (Cambridge: Cambridge University Press, 2010), 41–57.

56. This was the case especially in Pentateuch research.

57. For a discussion of the (seemingly) paradoxical notion of "oral texts," cf. Konrad Ehlich, 'Textualität und Schriftlichkeit," in *Was ist ein Text? Alttestamentliche, ägyptologische und altorientalistische Perspektiven*, ed. Ludwig Morenz and Stefan Schorch, BZAW 362 (Berlin: de Gruyter, 2007), 3–17.

58. Cf. Joachim Schaper, "On Writing and Reciting in Jeremiah 36," in *Prophecy in the Book of Jeremiah*, ed. Hans M. Barstad and Reinhard G. Kratz, BZAW 388 (Berlin: de Gruyter, 2009), 137–47. Also see idem, "Exilic and Post-Exilic Prophecy and the Orality/Literacy Problem," *VT* 55 (2005), 324–42 and idem, "The Death of the Prophet: The Transition from the Spoken to the Written Word of God in the Book of Ezekiel," in *Prophets, Prophecy, and Prophetic Texts in Second Temple Judaism*, ed. Michael H. Floyd and Robert L. Haak, LHBOTS 427 (New York: T&T Clark, 2006), 63–79.

ing their messages; nor were they accustomed to dictating them to others."[59] Yet the practice of dictating prophetic texts was by no means unknown in the ancient Near East, as is clearly evident from Mari texts.[60] It is therefore not acceptable to exclude the possibility that prophets actually dictated their oracles to professional scribes.

This is just one observation that relativizes previous thinking about the relation between the oral and the written in Hebrew culture. It throws light on the beginnings of the history of the prophetic books of the Bible. Equally significant, it tells us how the "written norm" eventually achieved autonomy: as a result of that autonomy, prophecy turned into a religious activity that became more and more text-centered, so much so that after a few hundred years prophecy ceased to be an oral/aural activity and turned into *Schriftprophetie* in the strictest sense (i.e., prophecy that was *composed* in writing), as witnessed, amongst others, by the collection of texts referred to as "Trito-Isaiah."

Conclusion

I have stressed the function of writing as a "means of communication" in the development of an increasingly complex division of labor, and I have explored its effects on individuals. It remains to be stressed that the means of communication are more than just that—they are, ultimately, means of production. Goody treats them as if they belonged to two different categories. He intends, as he says himself, "to shift part of the emphasis put on the means and modes of production in explaining human history to the means and modes of communication."[61] He thus postulates a false dichotomy between the two.

Raymond Williams states that "means of communication ... are not only forms but means of production, since communication and its material means are intrinsic to all distinctively human forms of labor and social organization, thus constituting indispensable elements both of the productive forces and of the social relations of production."[62] Once one discerns just how writing, *qua* means of communication, effected the increase in efficiency of Israel's and Judah's administrative systems and of their military operations (cf. the Lachish ostraca!), it becomes apparent that writing functioned, *qua* means of

---

59. Van der Toorn, *Scribal Culture*, 186.
60. Cf. No 414 (= A.431+A.4883) in the *Archives Royales de Mari* critical edition.
61. Goody, *Logic of Writing*, xi.
62. Raymond Williams, "Means of Communication as Means of Production," in Raymond Williams, *Culture and Materialism: Selected Essays* (London: Verso, 2005), 50–63.

communication, as a means of production and that it was an important factor in the overall fabric of the social relations of production.

What Williams has to say about "all modern and ... all foreseeable societies" is also true of ancient societies, including those of Israel and Judah: "physical speech and physical non-verbal communication ... remain as the central and decisive communicative means;" thus "it is ... possible to distinguish types of use or transformation of non-human material, for communicative purposes, in relation to this persistent direct centrality."[63]

While the autonomy of the "written norm" established itself in Israel and Judah, the dialectic between the oral and the written persisted. The result was an ever-increasing veneration of the written word, resulting in phenomena like the rise of *Schriftauslegung*[64] and of *schriftgelehrte Prophetie*, in the overall contexts of predominantly oral societies.

References

Boas, Franz. *The Mind of Primitive Man*. New York: Macmillan, 1911.
Derrida, Jacques. *Of Grammatology*. Translated by Gayatri Chakravorty Spivak. Baltimore: The Johns Hopkins University Press, 1974.
Ehlich, Konrad. "Textualität und Schriftlichkeit." Pages 3–17 in *Was ist ein Text? Alttestamentliche, ägyptologische und altorientalistische Perspektiven*. Edited by Ludwig Morenz and Stefan Schorch. BZAW 362. Berlin: de Gruyter, 2007.
Finkelstein, Israel. *The Forgotten Kingdom: The Archaeology and History of Northern Israel*. ANEM 5. Atlanta: Society of Biblical Literature, 2013.
Garr, W. Randall. *Dialect Geography of Syria-Palestine, 1000–586 B.C.E.* Philadelphia: University of Pennsylvania Press, 1985.
Goody, Jack. *The Domestication of the Savage Mind*. Themes in the Social Sciences. Cambridge: Cambridge University Press, 1977.
——. *The Interface between the Written and the Oral*. Studies in Literacy, Family, Culture and the State. Cambridge: Cambridge University Press, 1987.
——. *The Logic of Writing and the Organization of Society*. Studies in Literacy, Family, Culture and the State. Cambridge: Cambridge University Press, 1986.
——. *Myth, Ritual and the Oral*. Cambridge: Cambridge University Press, 2010.
Hengel, Martin. "'Schriftauslegung' und 'Schriftwerdung' in der Zeit des Zweiten Tempels." Pages 1–71 in *Schriftauslegung im antiken Judentum und im Urchristentum*. Edited by Martin Hengel and Hermut Löhr. WUNT 74. Tübingen: Mohr Siebeck, 1994.
Idel, Moshe. "Die laut gelesene Tora: Stimmengemeinschaft in der jüdischen Mystik,"

---

63. Williams, "Means of Communication," 55.
64. Cf. Martin Hengel, "'Schriftauslegung' und 'Schriftwerdung' in der Zeit des Zweiten Tempels," *Schriftauslegung im antiken Judentum und im Urchristentum*, ed. Martin Hengel and Hermut Löhr, WUNT 74 (Tübingen: Mohr Siebeck, 1994), *passim*.

Pages 19–53 in *Zwischen Rauschen und Offenbarung: Zur Kultur- und Mediengeschichte der Stimme*. Edited by Friedrich Kittler, Thomas Macho, and Sigrid Weigel. Berlin: Akademie, 2002.

King, Philip J., and Lawrence E. Stager. *Life in Biblical Israel*. LAI. Louisville: Westminster John Knox, 2001.

Knohl, Israel. *The Sanctuary of Silence: The Priestly Torah and the Holiness School*. Minneapolis: Fortress, 1995.

Merleau-Ponty, Maurice. *The Prose of the World*. London: Heinemann, 1974.

Misgav, Haggai, Yosef Garfinkel, and Saar Ganor. "The Khirbet Qeiyafa Ostracon," Pages 111–23 in *New Studies in the Archaeology of Jerusalem and Its Region*. Edited by David Amit, Guy D. Stiebel, and Orit Peleg-Barkat. Jerusalem: Israel Antiquities Authority and the Institute of Archaeology, the Hebrew University of Jerusalem, 2009 (in Hebrew).

Ong, Walter J. *Orality and Literacy: The Technologizing of the Word*. London: Methuen, 1982; repr. London: Routledge, 2002.

Renz, Johannes. *Die althebräischen Inschriften*, Teil 2: *Zusammenfassende Erörterungen, Paläographie und Glossar*. HAHE 2.1. Darmstadt: Wissenschaftliche Buchgesellschaft, 1995.

———. *Texte und Tafeln*. HAHE 3. Darmstadt: Wissenschaftliche Buchgesellschaft, 1995.

———. "Die vor- und außerliterarische Texttradition: Ein Beitrag der palästinischen Epigraphik zur Vorgeschichte des Kanons." Pages 53–81 in *Die Textualisierung der Religion*. Edited by Joachim Schaper. FAT 62. Tübingen: Mohr Siebeck, 2009.

Röllig, Wolfgang. "Das Alphabet und sein Weg zu den Griechen." Pages 359–84 in *Die Geschichte der hellenischen Sprache und Schrift: Vom 2. zum 1. Jahrtausend vor Chr.: Kontinuität oder Bruch? 03.–06. Oktober 1996, Ohlstadt/Oberbayern-Deutschland*. Altenburg: Verlag für Kultur und Wissenschaft, 1998.

Rollston, Christopher A. *Writing and Literacy in the World of Ancient Israel: Epigraphic Evidence from the Iron Age*. ABS 11. Atlanta: Society of Biblical Literature, 2010.

Sáenz-Badillos, Angel. *A History of the Hebrew Language*. Translated by John Elwolde. Cambridge: Cambridge University Press, 1993.

Saussure, Ferdinand de. *Cours de linguistique générale*. Edited by Charles Bally and Albert Sechehaye, with the collaboration of Albert Riedlinger. Lausanne: Payot, 1916.

Schaper, Joachim. "The Death of the Prophet: The Transition from the Spoken to the Written Word of God in the Book of Ezekiel." Pages 63–79 in *Prophets, Prophecy, and Prophetic Texts in Second Temple Judaism*. Edited by Michael H. Floyd and Robert L. Haak. LHBOTS 427. New York: T&T Clark, 2006.

———. "Exilic and Post-Exilic Prophecy and the Orality/Literacy Problem." *VT* 55 (2005): 324–42.

———. "On Writing and Reciting in Jeremiah 36." Pages 137–47 in *Prophecy in the Book of Jeremiah*. Edited by Hans M. Barstad and Reinhard G. Kratz. BZAW 388. Berlin: de Gruyter, 2009.

Sonnet, Jean-Pierre. *The Book Within the Book: Writing in Deuteronomy*. BibInt 14. Leiden: Brill, 1997.

Ullendorff, Edward. "Is Biblical Hebrew a Language?" *BSOAS* 34 (1971): 241–55.
Vachek, Josef. "Zum Problem der geschriebenen Sprache." Pages 441–60 in *A Prague School Reader in Linguistics*. Edited by Josef Vachek. Indiana University Studies in the History and Theory of Linguistics. Bloomington: Indiana University Press, 1964.

———. *Written Language: General Problems and Problems of English*. Janua Linguarum. Series Critica 14. The Hague: Mouton, 1973.

van der Toorn, Karel. *Scribal Culture and the Making of the Hebrew Bible*. Cambridge, MA: Harvard University Press, 2007.

Watts, James W. "Ritual Rhetoric in Ancient Near Eastern Texts." Pages 39–66 in *Ancient Non-Greek Rhetorics*. Edited by Carol Lipson and Roberta Binckley. West Lafayette, IN: Parlor, 2009.

Weber, Max. *Wirtschaft und Gesellschaft*. Grundriß der Sozialökonomik Abt. 3. Tübingen: Mohr Siebeck, 1922.

Williams, Raymond. "Means of Communication as Means of Production." Pages 50–63 in Raymond Williams, *Culture and Materialism: Selected Essays*. London: Verso, 2005.

Subject Index

abecedaries, 16, 140, 324
Abel, Ernest L., 163
Abibaal, 12
Abibaal (Abibaʻl) Inscription, 13, 95
Abraham-Jacob narrative, 217–37. See also patriarchal narrative
  alternation of gain and loss in, 225
  contradiction in, 217, 225
  cornerstones in, 223, 225
  discourse profile of, 226–31
  doublets in, 225
  explicitly syntactic constituents (explicitly lexicalized constituent, ELC) in, 226–28
  fabula in, 225–26
  hybridity in, 234
  language usage in, 217–18, 226–31
  as narrative platform, 225–26
  noun groups in, 226–28
  oral performance and, 226
  oral substratum of, 226–31
  pattern in, 225–26
  plot in, 225–26
  structure of, 219–20
  stylistic differentiation in, 225
  subordinate clauses in, 226–27
  syuzhet in, 225–26
  wording of, 225–26
Abraham narrative, 217–37
  contrast between opening and closure, 220–21
  counterpoint and cornerstones, 220–23
  discourse profile of, 229–30
  intricate, elaborate style (IES) in, 228–30
  lean, brisk style (LBS) in, 228–30
  property in, 222
  repeated elements in, 221
  structure of, 219–20
  symbolic household in, 222
  themes in, 219, 223
accountants, 150
acculturation, 146
Adad, 312
Adad-nirari III, 110, 127, 127n42
administrative writing, 47–48, 65, 75–80, 76n13, 108–9, 126n40, 139, 213
  alphabetic systems and, 108
  at Deir Alla, 144
  in fortresses, 63
  in Judah, 47
  literacy and, 264–65
  in Malhata, 56
  scribal education and, 264–65
  of temples, 63
Afis, 25, 30
Ahab, 20, 121
Aharoni, Yohanan, 49–50, 61
Ahiram Sarcophagus Inscription, 95
Ahirom, 12
aklu, 311
al-Karak text, 121n33
alphabetic writing
  for administrative purposes, 108, 141
  basic knowledge of, 47–48, 64
  during the early Iron Age breach, 108–11
  for economic purposes, 141
  elites and, 138, 141
  for indicating ownership of vessels, 23
  invention of, 328
  in the Levant, 11–34

alphabetic writing, *continued*
  linear, 137, 138
  in monumental inscriptions, 138
  ownership and, 108
  political use of, 137
  scribal use to express a written vernacular, 134–35
  West Semitic, 138
Alter, Robert, 287
'Amal/Nir David, 22
Amarna Letters, 135
Amman Citadel, 106, 143
Amman Citadel Inscription, 30, 107, 120n31, 145, 275n42
Ammon, 118, 124, 126, 145
Ammon-Gilead, 117, 118, 123, 272n34
Ammonites, 112, 117, 118
Ammonite script, 324
Amodio, Mark, 179
Amos, 270
amulets, 147, 307, 308–9
Amurru, 96
aniconism, 150–51, 232, 309
annals, 155–56, 157
Aphek, 139
apotropaism, 108, 115, 152
Aqhat, poem of, 225
Arad, 28, 148, 150
  Arad 88, 51–52
  Arad No. 16, 150
  epigraphic evidence in, 77, 79, 93
  exceptionality of, 61–62
  importance of, 62
  inscriptions in, 49–52, 148n50, 327
  letters in, 50–52
  military scribes in, 77, 79
  mode of writing in, 61–62
  number of inscriptions in, 61–62
  ostraca in, 49–51, 60–63, 121n33, 232, 311, 324, 327
  potsherds in, 50
  scribes in, 149
  temple in, 65
Aram, 111n15, 112–13, 122–23, 122–23n37, 139, 272n34
  Aram-Damascus, 110–12, 111n15, 116–18, 120, 123, 144–45

Aram-Hamath, 118n27
  domination by, 116–18, 117n26
  emulation of Assyrian models by, 126
  literary production in, 125–26
  monumental inscriptions in, 124
Aramaeans, 23–26, 29, 33, 112, 113–20, 122, 149
  emulation of Assyrian models by, 123–24
  influence on inscriptions, 110–11, 111n15
Aramaic scribes, 314
Aramaic script, 31–32, 85, 87, 91, 92, 94–95, 324
Aratta, 315
archival methods, 139, 147–48, 267n15
archives, 242, 311
Aristarchus, 162
'Aroer (Khirbet 'Ar'ara), 56–57, 56–57n31, 58
arrowheads, 13–14, 96–97, 137, 137n12, 137n13
Arslan Tash, 23, 29
Asherah, 116, 153
Asia Minor, Phoenician script in, 140
Assmann, Jan, 190
Assurbanipal, 153–54, 311–12
Assyrians, 48, 55, 110, 120n31, 134, 146
  Assyrian dedication inscriptions, 123–24
  Assyrian models, 126
  Assyrian statecraft, 314
  Assyrian Synchronistic History, 157
  defeat of Israel by, 276
  forms and media of inscriptions, 123–24, 123n39
  Levantine interventions by, 127
  literary traditions of, 126
"Assyrian Statecraft and the Prophets of Israel" (Holladay), 314, 315
Astarte temple, 27
Ataruz pedestal inscriptions, 121n33
authority
  of biblical texts, 309–10
  scripturalization and, 239, 318–19
  of source texts, 205–6, 211
  of text-brokers, 251, 254–55, 260–61

SUBJECT INDEX 343

texts and, 239, 242–43, 246, 306, 309–10, 314–15, 318–19
transfer from the oral to the written, 318
transition from charismatic to traditional, 335
writing and, 242–43, 246, 254–55, 312, 314–15, 318–19
Azarbaʻl Inscription, 96

Baal Cycle, 186–87
Baal of the Heavens, 118n27
Babylon, 52, 134, 213
  destruction by Sennacherib, 270
  Judah and, 277
  Middle Babylonian Traditions, 296–97
Babylonian exile, 213
Babylonian Kish, 187
Babylonian language, 134
Babylonians, 48, 52, 156
Babylonian Talmud, 240
Bagby, Benjamin, 188
Balaam, 118, 120, 144, 145
Balaam Inscription, 32, 34, 105–6, 112–20, 127n42
  divination and, 272–73
  as product of *Traditionsliteratur*, 273
  prophecy and, 145, 268–73, 268n23, 270n28, 272–73n35, 272n34, 273n36, 274
bards, scribes as analogous to, 197, 198–203
Bartlett, Frederic C., 164, 167
Batash/Timnah, 18, 324
Beersheba, 59–60, 62, 141
Beersheba Valley, 48–60. See also Negev
Beit-Arieh, Itzhaq, 52, 55
Beit-Gush (Arpad), 25
Beit Mirsim, 62
Ben Hadad, 110, 117, 118n27, 122
Benjamin, tribe of, 277
Ben Sira, 71–72, 71–72n3, 72n4, 82
Beor, 144
Berachiah, 58
Bes masks, 187
Beth-Shean Valley, 20
Beth-Shemesh, 17, 18, 62, 141, 324

Beyond the River, 260
the Bible. See Hebrew Bible
biblical criticism, Christian, 283
biblical evidence, epigraphic Hebrew and, 71–101
biblical Flood narrative, 282–83, 288–94
  calendrical framework of, 296n24
  compared to Gilgamesh Flood narrative, 289–302
  comprehensiveness of, 294
  editing in, 287–94
  incoherence of, 294
  interweaving of parallel variants of narrative in, 294
  obvious doublets in, 289–94
  variants of, 295–302
biblical source texts, 133–58
  historical events and, 90–91
  production of, 152–57
biblical studies, 161–73
  orality and, 241–42
  orality studies and, 241
  state of, 161–73
  textuality and, 241–42
biblical texts
  authority of, 309–10
  dating of, 11
  definitions of, 203–5
  multiformity of, 197
  vs. nonbiblical texts, 203–7
  religious authority of, 306, 309–10
  school texts and, 309–10
Biqʻa Valley, 137n13
Bird, Graeme, 171, 172, 201, 203
  Multitextuality in the Homeric Iliad, 198–99
blessings, 144, 147, 318
Bloom, Harold, 284
Blum, Erhard, 144, 149, 268–73, 268n23, 271n29, 273n36, 274
Boertien, Jeannette, 114, 119n30
bookkeepers, 150
"book of life," 313
bowls, 27, 54, 141
Brand, Etty, 61
bronze, 22
Bronze Age, 135–41. See also Late Bronze Age

Brooke, George, 205–6, 208–9n36
bullae, 50–51, 108, 126n40, 133–34n1, 139, 141, 148, 150, 152
    clay, 30–31n118
    excavations of, 63–64n55
    in Jerusalem, 63, 146n45, 150–51n61
    in Judah, 148n52
    in Lachish, 148n52, 150–51n61
Bunimovitz, Shlomo, 17
burial chambers, 151–52
Byblos, 14, 22, 27, 95–96, 138–39, 186
    inscriptions in, 33
    kings of, 12, 13
    rulers of, 138

Canaan, 139
    Canaanite inscriptions, 11
    Canaanite prosody, 145
    continuation of Old Canaanite forms, 136
    destruction of city-states in northern valleys of, 141
    Iron I, 141
    Iron II, 141
    Late Bronze Age, 135
    material cultural in, 136
    palatial society of, 136
    scribes in, 135–36
    urban centers in, 137
    vernacular in, 138
    writing in, 135–36, 141
canon
    modern notions applied anachronistically, 211
    reinterpretation and, 284–85
    scripturalization and, 307
Carr, David, 92, 176–77, 182, 203, 212, 212n47, 217n1, 282, 282n3
    Formation of the Hebrew Bible, 177
    Writing on the Tablet of the Heart, 169, 306
Carroll, Marie, 163
Carthage, 187
Chemosh[yat], 111
chronicle genre, 155–57
Chronicles, 197–98, 207–13, 207n33, 208–9n36, 211–12, 300, 301

chronological genres, 155–56, 157
Cisjordan, 19–23, 33, 124, 137
cities, 60, 63
City of David, 61, 86
clay, 47
clerks, as scribes, 65
Clines, David, 222
coastal region, epigraphic record in, 138–39
Cohen, Yoram, 310–11
coherence, literary value of, 281–82, 301
collective memory, 190, 197–203, 207
commerce, writing and, 139
composition, 239–40. See also specific texts
    improvisatory, 180–81
    oral-literary mode of, 241–42
    representation in real time through oral performance, 257
comprehensiveness, literary value of, 281–82, 294, 301
conflation, 282, 299–300
conflict
    literary production and, 110–13, 124
    memorializing, 103–31
    protracted, 108–12
consistency, modern conceptions of, 210–11
contradiction, 217
copying
    graphic, 172
    visual, 161–63, 164, 165, 172
Covenant Code, 286, 299
Crawford, Sidnie, 204
Crenshaw, James L., 81, 274n38
critical editions, as abstractions of texts from their manuscript environment, 201–2, 203
critical historiography, oral tradition and, 189–90
Cross, Frank Moore, 26n86, 96
Crowell, Bradley, 149
cultic writing, 145, 147, 152–53, 157, 305. See also ritual
    cultic graffiti, 143
    cultic inscriptions, 138–39
    spatial context of, 143–44

cultural memory, 190
cultural tradition, social position and, 235
curses, 316, 318, 319
Curses of Deuteronomy, 315
Cyprus, 15, 27, 140
Czech poetry, 301

Damascus, 23–24, 29, 32, 110–13,
  111n15, 116–18, 120, 122–24, 144–45.
  See also Aramaeans; Aram-Damascus
Dan, 120
  Aram's domination of, 117
  architectural remains at, 111n15
  inscriptions at, 29, 111–12
  stele from, 24–25, 105–6, 107, 120–21,
    122–23n37, 123–24, 142, 144, 152
Darshan, Guy, 296n24
Davidic dynasty, 112, 276, 277, 324, 335
Davies, G. I., 83
Dead Sea Scrolls, 163, 198, 203–7, 208–9n36, 211
decrees, royal, 47
Deir ʿAllā, 31, 33, 34, 112, 116, 119,
  127n42, 154n68, 268–74, 268n23,
  272n34
  administration at, 144
  Aramean presence and influence in,
    113, 117–20
  artifact and text in, 113–16
  benches and bench rooms in, 114–15
  "ethnic" representation of, 119–20,
    119n30
  evidence of ritual at, 114
  inscriptions at, 105–7, 144–45, 149
  lay out of, 113–14
  material cultural data at, 105–7, 113–16, 113n19, 119n30, 144–45, 149
  as a multipurpose site, 116
  reassessing, 113–16
  as regional outpost for training of
    scribes, 144
  religious dimensions of material
    culture in, 113–15
  ritual space in, 120
  scribal culture at, 144–45
  scribal education at, 116, 144
  textile industry in, 114–19

deities. See the divine; gods
de Jong, Matthijs, 267n15, 267n17,
  270n28, 271n30, 276n44
Derrida, Jacques, 329
De Temporibus Anticristi (Wulfstan), 200
*The Deuteronomic History and the Book
  of Chronicles: Scribal Works in an Oral
  World* (Person), 163, 197, 207, 207n33
Deuteronomic school, 213
Deuteronomistic History, 135, 155, 157,
  197–98, 336
  citation and use of texts as scripture
    in, 316–18
  composition of, 133, 152
  historical social settings that
    produced, 213
  as one of competing contemporary
    historiographies of postexilic period,
    213
Deuteronomy, 205, 236, 311–12. See also
  Deuteronomistic History
  discourse profile of, 231–32
  intricate, elaborate style (IES) in, 231
  language usage in, 228–29, 231–32
  ritual in, 316
  scripturalization in, 318
  slave laws of, 286
Deutsch, Robert, 96
Dhibân, 28
Dibhon, 105–6
divination, 273–74
  Balaam Inscription and, 272–73
  prophecy as a form of, 271–72,
    271n30
  writing and, 315
the divine, localized manifestations of,
  119–20 (see also gods)
divine anger, 270–71, 270n28, 271n29,
  276, 276n43
divine voice, 334
divine writing, 305, 312–14, 319
division of labor, 327–28, 337
Doane, A. N., 200–202
  Scribal Textuality and a Exeter
    Riddle, 200
Dobbs-Allsopp, Frederick W., 50
document production, 133–58. See also
  writing; specific texts

ductus, 86n46
Dutcher-Walls, Patricia, 277
dynasties, 142–43. See also specific dynasties
　religious traditions and, 143
　writing and, 142–43, 157

Ea, 312
Early Iron Age. See Iron I
Ebla, 135–36, 185
economics, writing and, 335
Edom, 117n26, 149
Edomites, 48, 52, 53
Edomite script, 52–53, 55–56, 57
education. See also literacy; scribal education, handwriting as an indication of, 65
effort after meaning, 164, 167
Egypt, 13, 52, 74–75, 135, 141, 181, 184–86, 246n16
El, 114, 116–20, 118–19n28, 119n30
Elat Mazar, Ophel excavations of, 19
el-Farʻah, Tell (N), 41
el-Farʻah, Tell (S), 16
el-Hamme, 20
Eliashib, 50
Elibaal, 12, 13
Elibaʻl Inscription, 95
Elijah-Elisha, 231
Elisha, 22
elites, 138
　alphabetic writing and, 138, 141, 142
　appropriation of writing by, 149–53
　Benjaminite, 277
　educated, 242
　emulation of, 146
　Judean, 149–53
　priestly, 143
　prophecies of doom and, 276
　scribalism and, 137–38
　as text-brokers, 242
　writing and, 135, 137–38, 142–43, 267
El-Kerak, 28
el-Khadr arrowheads, 96–97
El-Milh, 55–56
　inscriptions in, 55–56
Elohanu, 114

el ʻOrēme/ Kinneret, 15
empirical models, 281–304
Empirical Models for Biblical Criticism (Tigay), 282–83
Enkomi, 187
Enmerkar, 315
Enūma Anu Enlil, 294
epic plot sequence, 218, 219–25
epigraphic evidence, 47, 103–4, 103n1
　in coastal region, 138–39
　composition of Hebrew Bible and, 152–53
　for document production, 133–58
　excavations and, 103n1
　future increase in, 126–27
　Levantine, 29–34
　literacy and, 264–65, 264n6
　literary texts and, 103–16
　military and administrative nature of, 93–94, 95–96
　Moabite, 28
　from Samaria, 142
　West Semitic, 29–34
　writing and, 326–27
epigraphs, 105–6. See also monumental inscriptions
epistolary formulary. See letter formulary
errors
　modern conceptions of, 199–202
　produced by visual copying, 162–63, 164, 165, 172
　textual innovation and, 170
Esarhaddon, 153–54, 270
Eskenazi, Tamara, 245
eṣ-Ṣafi/Gath, 15, 121n33
es-Sarem, 22
Es-Sebaʻ. See Beersheba
Es-Semuʻ/Eshtemoaʻ, 19, 61
ethnicity, public display and, 142–43
The Evolution of the Gilgamesh Epic (Tigay), 287–94, 287n15, 287n16
ewers, 137n14
Execration Texts, 316
exegesis, 254n35, 284–85, 299–300, 301
　See also interpretation
Exeter Book, 200, 201
Exodus, 205, 300, 301, 313–14

SUBJECT INDEX 347

explicitly syntactic constituents (explicitly lexicalized constituent, ELC), 226–28
Ezra, 213, 240, 257–59. See also Ezra-Nehemiah
Ezra-Nehemiah, 239–62
  compared to royal writing, 251–52
  elision of quoted text and described action in, 254–55
  ideological program of, 243
  law in, 241
  mandates in, 252–59, 260
  oral-literary economy of representing torah in, 239–43, 246–61
  oral-literary modes of transmission in, 243
  representations of Torah in, 239–41, 247–59
  royal correspondence in, 243–46
  Sukkot mandates in, 252–54
  Torah and, 239–41

fabula, 218–19, 225–26
Fekheriye inscription, 120n31, 123–24
Finkelstein, Israel, 11, 16, 17
Finnegan, Ruth, 179, 180
First Temple period, 48, 54, 71–101, 76, 307–9
Fishbane, Michael, 240, 285, 298
Foley, John Miles, 180, 188, 198–99n2
folklore, field studies in, 180–81
folklorists, 178–79
foreign language(s) and literature, 90–93
Formation of the Hebrew Bible (Carr), 177
formulaic language, 175–77
fortresses, administrative texts in, 63–65
Fosse temple, 137n14
Frahm, Eckhart, 297, 297–98n26
Freedman, David Noel, 161
Freund, Liora, 55

Gedaliah, 277
Genesis, 217–37. See also patriarchal narrative; specific narratives
  interweaving of parallel variants of narrative in, 295–97
  Primeval History of, 295–97
  variants of flood narrative in, 295–302
genres, 155–56, 157, 189–90. See also specific genres
George, Andrew, 287n16, 295, 297
Gerhardsson, Birger, 163
Gezer, 134
  Gezer calendar/tablet, 17, 105n5, 140–41, 157, 324
  inscriptions in, 134
Gibeon
  epigraphic evidence in, 79, 93
  military scribes in, 79
Gilgamesh epic, 297n25
  coherence of, 295
  development of, 295
  editing in, 287–94
  editorial picture of, 282–83
  evolution of, 287–94, 287n15, 287n16, 296–97, 300
  flood narrative of, 288–94, 295
  flood tablet, 282, 284, 287–94
  as model for biblical literature, 287
  narrative coherence of, 283
  text-building of, 296–97, 297–98n26, 299, 300
  three phases of existence, 287–88, 296–97
Gilgamesh flood narrative, compared to biblical Flood narrative, 289–302
Gilgamesh series (iskuru), editing in, 294–97
Giza, 187
gods, 114, 116. See also specific gods
Goody, Jack, 177, 178, 328, 331, 335, 337
government. See administrative writing
Gozan/Guzana (Beit Bahian), 26, 120n31, 123–24
graffiti, 25, 141, 143, 147, 151–52
Greek texts, 161–62
Greenberg, Moshe, 287
Greenstein, Ed, 163, 172
Gubel, Eric, 139n19
guilds, 94
Gunkel, Hermann, 220, 285

Hadad, 32, 119n30, 120n31

Hadadezer, 122
Hadadyis'i, statue of, 26
Halaf, 26
halakha, 284
Halbwachs, Maurice, 190
Halif, 62
Hamath, 24–25, 110, 117, 123–24
handwriting, 65
Haran, Menahem, 81
Harris, Joseph, 184
Hazael, 11n2, 15, 23–25, 29, 32, 110–13, 111n15, 116–18, 117n26, 120–24, 142
Hazor, 15, 141, 187
Hebrew, 52–53, 324. See also Hebrew script
   Archaic Hebrew, 326, 326n17
   biblical evidence and, 71–101
   classical Biblical Hebrew, 326, 326n17
   Hebrew script, 55–56, 94, 324
   Late Biblical Hebrew, 326, 326n17
   Old Hebrew script, 84–90, 86n46, 95, 108, 121n33, 142, 325–26n16, 328 (see also palaeo-Hebrew)
   palaeo-Hebrew, 323, 324–28
Hebrew Bible, 283. See also biblical texts; Pentateuch; Torah; specific books and narratives
   application of Parry–Lord theory to, 176–77
   composition of, 103–4, 133–34, 152, 155, 241
   epigraphic data and, 152–53
   expansion of, 212
   foreign language(s) and literature and, 92–93
   history of its composition, 336
   hybrid oral-literary mode of composition and transmission, 241–42
   manuscripts of, 170–71
   Masoretic Text, 203–4
   memory variants in, 170–71, 172
   orality and, 189–90, 241
   proto-Masoretic text, 172
   sapiential literature in, 54
   sources of, 152–53
   textual history of, 172, 203–5
   textuality and, 172, 203–5, 241
   transmission of, 241
   versions of, 203–4
Hebrew culture, 323–39
   literary, 284
   orality and literacy in, 325–38
   rising prominence of writing in, 336–37
   tenaciousness of orality in, 333
Hebrew literature, 326
   chronology of, 282
   continuity in, 283–86, 287
   the dominant in, 301–2
   harmonization and conflation stage, 301
   Hebrew narrative, 326
   Hebrew poetry, 326
   integrating literary collection stage of, 300
   interweaving of parallel variants of narrative in, 300–301
   literary values of, 300–301
   post-Pentateuchal stage, 301
   shift in literary values of, 299–300
   three stages of, 300–301
Hebrew script, 31, 55–56, 94, 324. See also Old Hebrew script; palaeo-Hebrew; specific inscriptions
Hebrew writers. See also scribes, shift in literary values of, 281–82, 281n1
Hellenistic period, 241, 300
Heltzer, Michael, 96
Hess, Richard, 264n6
Hezekiah, 90, 91
Hierapolis, 187
hieratic numerals, 88–89, 264
historical events, biblical source texts and, 90–91
historical genres, 155–56, 157
historiographic tradition, state-sponsored, 155
Hittite texts, 185
Holiness Code, 286
Holladay, John, "Assyrian Statecraft and the Prophets of Israel," 314, 315
Homeric textual tradition, 172, 175–76, 179, 188, 198–99

expansion of, 203, 212
Homeric manuscripts, 162–63, 165–67, 171, 198–99
text-critical treatments, 211
Horvat Radum (Khirbet Umm Redim), 54–55, 61, 63, 77, 79
Horvat 'Uza (Khirbet Ghazzeh), 52–54, 61, 62–63, 65, 66, 77, 79, 93, 149, 154
Hosea, 270
Hosha'yah, 64–65
Huldah, prophecy of, 319
Humbaba mask, 187
Hurrian, 185
Hutton, Jeremy M., 119n30
hymns, 153

iconic ritualization, scripturalization and, 249–51
the Iliad, Ptolemaic papyri of, 198–99
illiterate societies, orality and writing in, 241–42
Ilmilku, 311
incantations, 147, 152, 153
India, 179
the individual, at the interface between the oral and the written, 329–33, 337
Indonesia, 180
ink writing, 34, 53
  on leather, 32, 34
  on ostraca, 62–63
  on papyrus, 32, 34
  on pottery, 30
  spread of, 62–63
inner-biblical interpretation, vs. scripturalization, 305–6
In Praise of Scribal Art, 72–73
inscriptions, 33. See also specific sites; specific types of inscriptions
  administrative, 148
  altar, 26
  aniconic, 309
  Aramaean, 29, 120
  Aramaic, 23, 113, 119–20, 119n30
  on arrowheads, 137
  Assyrian models of, 123–24, 123n39
  on bowls, 54
  Canaanite, 15–16

cultic, 138–39
dating of, 12–13, 22, 29
dedicatory, 143
discovery of, 22–23
economic, 148, 150
in the first half of the eighth century BCE, 29–34
in fortresses, 64–65
funerary, 15
incised, 60–64
in ink, 30, 53, 55–56, 60, 127n42 (see also ink writing)
ivory, 23–24
on jars, 53
level of literacy indicated by, 47
in limestone, 134
in local language, 138
monarchical period inscriptions unearthed in the Negev, 48–60
monumental, 23, 26–30, 33, 104–5, 105–16, 118n27, 124, 126, 138–39, 147–48, 151, 155, 326–27
nationalistic claims and, 150
Neo-Hittite, 24
on nonperishable material, 47
on perishable materials, 65
on plaster, 30, 31–32, 34, 104–5, 144–45, 149
prestige use of, 137, 138
royal, 33, 138, 147–48, 151, 154–55
on seals, 29, 30
on silver scrolls, 134
social identities and, 150, 155
in the vernacular, 138
West Semitic, 23–34
interpretation, 239–40, 241, 283–86. See also exegesis
intrabiblical references, limited value of, 47
intricate, elaborate style (IES), 228–30, 231–33, 235
'Ira, Tel (Khirbet Gharra), 57–58, 61, 77, 79, 93
Iran, masks in, 187
Iron Age, 124. See also Iron I; Iron II
  breach in, 108–10
  document production in, 133–58

Iron Age, *continued*
  history of early literature in, 103–31
  in Judah, 133–58
  literacy in, 263
  material cultural in, 136
  writing in the Levant during, 135–41
Iron I, 124, 127, 137
  Canaan in, 141
  document production in, 133–58
  inscriptions from, 137
  in Levant, 135–41
  limited role for writing in, 137
  Phoenician city-states during, 138
  writing in, 135–41
Iron II
  Canaan in, 141
  document production in, 133–58
  epigraphic data from, 264
  Israel during, 141–45
  Judah during, 145–57
  literacy in, 141–57
  masks from, 187
  Phoenician city-states during, 138
  Samaria during, 141–45
  writing in, 138, 141–57
Isaiah, 270
Isaiah–Hezekiah narratives, variants in, 163
Ishtar, 114
Israel, 110, 112, 117, 118, 143n37
  Aram's domination of, 116–18, 142
  Assyria's defeat of, 276
  ca. 850–800 BCE, 27–28
  Davidic dynasty, 112
  debate about schools in, 80–84
  defeat in 721 BCE, 276
  domination of Judah, 156
  expulsion from Transjordan, 122–23n37
  first appearance as polity in historical record, 141n30
  inscriptions in, 19–23
  invasion by Hazaël, 112
  during Iron Age II, 141–45
  literacy in, 19–23, 141–45, 182–83, 263–64, 325–38
  literary production in, 125–26, 182
  living creative culture of, 283
  Omride dynasty, 112
  orality in, 325–38
  oral tradition in, 181–82
  political identities in, 134
  prominence achieved by, 141–42
  prophecy in, 335–37
  scribal community in, 75–76, 141–42, 146
  statehood and, 327–28
  technology of, 323–41, 323n1
  uses of writing in, 335–36
  writing in, 141–45, 181–82, 325–38
Ittobaal, 12
'Izbet Ṣarṭah, 17, 324

Jacob narrative, 223–25
  discourse profile of, 230–31
  Jacob-Esau tales, 220
  structure of, 219–20
  symbolic household in, 224
Jahath the Levite, 58
Jakobson, Roman, 301
Japhet, Sara, 209–10
jars, 20, 27, 53, 59
Jehu, 22, 110, 117
Jeremiah, 318, 336–37
Jeremiah Vita (Judean corpus), 231, 232, 235
Jeroboam II, 30
Jerusalem, 19, 141, 153, 213
  archival methods in, 148
  bullae in, 63, 150–51n61
  fall of, 277–78
  ostraca in, 62
  rebuilding of, 277
  royal scribes in, 153, 154
  scribal community of, 146–48, 153–54
  seals in, 150–51n61
  strengthened by written tradition, 156–57
  temple scribes in, 153
Jewish continuity, between Torah and Midrash, 283–86, 287
Joash, 30
Job, 149
Jordan Valley, 20, 31

SUBJECT INDEX

Joseph tale, 225
Joshua, 316, 317
Josianic Reforms, 312, 319
Jubilees, 299–300, 301
Judah, 11, 30, 49
  administration in, 47
  Aram's domination of, 116–18
  archival methods in, 148
  Babylon and, 277
  bullae in, 148n52
  ca. 850–800 BCE, 27–28
  catastrophic events in early sixth century BCE, 267–68
  debate about schools in, 80–84
  defeat of, 275–76
  destruction of, 276
  document production in, 133–58
  increase in scribal skills in, 149
  inner diplomatic struggles of the early sixth century, 277
  inscriptions in, 19–23
  Iron Age, 133–58
  Iron II, 145–57
  Israel's domination of, 146, 156
  kings of, 147–48
  literacy in, 19–23, 47, 133–58, 182–83, 263–66, 265n10, 325–38
  literary production in, 126, 133–58
  monumental inscriptions in, 147–48
  ninth- to early sixth-century, 60–64
  orality in, 325–38
  ostraca vs. incised inscriptions in, 60–64
  political identities in, 134
  production of biblical source texts in, 152–57
  rebellion against Babylonia, 52
  royal inscriptions in, 147–48
  scribal community of, 75–76, 147–50, 152–57
  scripturalization in, 305–21
  technology of, 323–41, 323n1
  uses of writing and, 335–36
  writing in, 133–58, 325–38
  writing proficiency in, 265
Judaism
  the Bible and, 283
  continuity with earlier Hebrew literary culture, 284
  dead interpretative culture of, 283
  first-century CE, 204
  identity as scriptural religion, 240
  rupture in early, 283
  Second Temple period, 204–5, 212
  textual traditions and, 204
Judea, 241
Judean literary corpus, scripturalization of, 305–21
Judean Shephelah, 15–18
juridical texts, 47–48

Kahun, 187
Kazel, Tell, 14
Karatepe, Phoenician script in, 140
Keel, Othmar, 309
Kefar Veradim bowl, 141
Kemosh, 143, 270
Ketef Hinnom, 134, 147, 153
Ketef Hinnom amulets, 307, 308–9
Khirbet 'Ar'ara, 56–57
Khirbet Beit Lei, 153
  burial chambers at, 151–52
  graffiti at, 151–52
  monumental inscriptions in, 326–27
Khirbet El-Mshash, 57
  inscriptions in, 57
Khirbet el-Mudeyine, 28
Khirbet el Qôm, 30, 151–52, 153
Khirbet Gharra, 57–58
Khirbet Ghazzeh, 52–54
Khirbet Qeiyafa, 17, 18, 20, 324
Khirbet Raddana, 20
Khirbet Tannin, 20
Khirbet Umm Redim, 54–55
Kibbutz Revadim, 137
Kilmer, Anne, 185
King Cheops and the Magicians of Papyrus Westcar, 185
king lists, 155–56, 157
Kings, book of, 155, 207n33, 317, 319
  Chronicles and, 207–13
  Parry–Lord approach to, 197
  text criticism of, 197
kings, elevated status of, 266–67

SUBJECT INDEX

Kiribati, 179
Kirta, poem of, 225
Kition, 27, 187
Klein, Ralph, 209
Kletter, Raz, 61
Knohl, Israel, 334
Knoppers, Gary N., 208–9n36, 209
Koch, Klaus, 225
Korioun, 187
Kratz, Reinhard, 285
Kugel, James, 299
Kulamuwa inscription, 12, 26
Kuntillet Ajrud (Ḥorvat Teman), 30–31, 34, 79, 92n61, 115–16, 118–19n28, 119–20, 119n30, 127n42, 143, 143n37, 145, 147, 326

Laban narratives, 220
labor, division of, 327–28
Lachish, 51–52, 62, 64–65, 137, 148, 150
  bullae in, 148n52
  epigraphic evidence in, 77, 79, 93
  ewer in, 137n14
  inscriptions in, 148n50
  Neo-Assyrian destruction of, 90
  ostraca in, 232, 311
  ostracon from, 77
  seals in, 150–51n61
  siege of, 90
language usage, 217
  in Abraham-Jacob narrative, 217–18, 226–31
  in Deuteronomy, 228–29, 231–32
  oral substratum and, 217–37
  in patriarchal narrative, 226–31, 235
  scribal education and, 232–33
  thematic flow and, 217–37
Late Bronze Age, 17, 124–25, 127
  Canaan in, 135
  document production in, 133–58
  in Levant, 135–41
  material culture in, 136
  scribal culture of, 135–41
  writing in, 135–41
Latin texts, ancient Latin texts, 161–62
law, 285–86. See also mandates
  in Ezra-Nehemiah, 241

  rewritten scripture in, 206
  ritual, 300
leadership transitions, motif of god's anger as serving to legitimize, 270–71
lean, brisk style (LBS), 228–32, 233n70, 234
leather, ink on, 32, 34
Lebanon, 13–14, 95, 137n13
Lederman, Zvi, 17
Lemaire, André, 80–81, 80–81n29, 122–23n37, 263
letter formation, synchronic consistency of, 264
letter formulary, 89–90
letters, 135
  in Arad, 50–52
  from Hoshaʿyah to Yaʾush, 64–65
  letter formulary, 89–90
  royal, 47, 50–52, 243–46
the Levant
  in the alphabetic script, 11–34
  coastal cities in, 138–39
  disruption in during thirteenth and twelfth centuries, 136
  Early Iron Age, 135–41
  Late Bronze Age, 135–41
  Levantine armies, 110
  literacy in, 11–23, 29–34, 135–41, 146, 263
  literary production in, 103–16
  in the monumental inscriptions, 108–9
  Phoenician script in, 140
  protracted conflict in, 110–11
  scribal establishment and, 146
  scribalism in, 109
  writing in, 135–41
Levinson, Bernie, 300
Levites, 250–51, 250n26, 311–12
Levitical Scribes, 311–12
Leviticus, 286
limestone, 134, 140
limmu lists, 155
Lionarons, Joyce Tally, 199–200, 201
Lipschits, Oded, 277
literacy
  acquisition of, 177–78
  administration and, 264–65

SUBJECT INDEX 353

alphabetic, 263–64
attainment of, 263–64
definitions of, 81–82n34, 329
display of, 150–51
epigraphic data and, 11, 264–65, 264n6
in Hebrew culture, 325–38
individual, 329
Iron Age, 141–57, 263
in Israel, 141–45, 182–83, 263–64, 325–38
in Judah, 47, 133–58, 182–83, 263–66, 265n10, 325–38
late monarchical period, 64–66
in the Levant, 11–45, 29–34, 135–41, 146, 263
local traditions of, 135
low levels of in ancient Near East, 82–83
memory and, 178
Mesopotamian forms of, 135
of middle class, 65–66
in the Negev, 47–70
orality and, 164, 241
as prerogative of the elite, 264–65
of priests, 65–66
problem of, 11
as a product of the state, 264–65
of prophets, 263–64
of royal administration, 65–66
in Samaria, 141–45
scripturalization and, 306–7
of soldiers, 65
spectrum of, 47–48, 64, 265, 265n9
in Transjordan, 141–45
writing ability and, 47–48
literary design, 232–33
literary production, 47–48. See also writing; specific texts
in Aram, 125–26
conflict affective phase, 125–26
conflict and, 110–13, 124
early history of, 103–31
historical phases of, 124–27
in Israel, 125–26, 182
in Judah, 126, 133–58
in the Levant, 103–16

in the Levant, 103–16
oral stages of, 109, 127
political stability and, 126
royal prerogative phase, 125–26
shadow history of, 103–16
state-scribal development phase, 124–25
in Ugarit, 126
literary texts, 152
epigraphic evidence and, 103–16
monumental inscriptions and, 104–5
origins of, 109
production of (see literary production; writing)
Ugaritic, 136
written in the service of memorization, 169–70
written on perishable papyrus or parchment, 104–5
literary traditions
advantages and disadvantages of, 34
Aramaean, 145
Aramaic, 32, 34
Assyrians, 126
beginnings of, 34
expansion of, 202
Phoenician, 32, 34
special grammar of, 198, 202
textual plurality and, 211
trend toward expansion in process of, 212
literary values, 302
of coherence, 281–82, 301
of comprehensiveness, 281–82, 294, 301
of the Pentateuch, 299
in Primeval History, 301–2
Second Temple period, 301
shift in, 281–82, 281n1, 286, 299–300
loom weights, 113
Lord, Albert, 164, 175–77, 179–80, 184, 197, 198, 198–99n2, 202, 235–37. See also Parry–Lord School
The Singer of Tales, 175
Lucian, 187
lyres, 188–89

macrotext, 218–19
magic
    magic texts, 312–14
    ritual, 308–9, 319
    treaty genre and, 315–16
    writing and, 315, 318
Malhata (Tell El-Milh), 55–56, 61
mandates, 252–60. See also law
manuscripts. See also Homeric
    manuscripts; specific works
    critical editions and, 202, 203
    environment of, 201–2
    multiformity of, 206–7
    representing the same literary texts, 198–207
    standardized, 200
    vernacular, 200
    visual differences between Latin and Old English, 200
Maqlû, 315–16
Marduk, 270, 314
Mari correspondence, 274, 275n42
Mari texts, 10, 337
masks, 187, 187n88
Masoretic Text, 203–4, 205, 207
Masos (Khirbet El-Mshash), 57, 61, 63
material culture
    continuity in, 136
    writing and, 327–37
matres lectionis, 86–87n50, 87–88
Mazar, Amihai, 20
McIver, Robert K., 163
medieval literature
    expansion of, 212
    text-critical variants of, 198–203
Megiddo, 141
    ring from, 137
memorization, 164–65, 172. See also memory
    oral performance and, 179–80, 184
    performance and, 172–73
    role of, 179–80
    textual, 163–64
memory, 161–73
    collective memory, 190
    cultural memory, 190
    literacy and, 178

orality and, 161–73
performance and, 168–69
texts and, 242, 282, 282n3
textuality and, 161–73
writing and, 168–70
memory variants, 166, 167, 169–72
merchant class, 150
Merleau-Ponty, Maurice, 329
Mesha, 28, 111, 120–23, 121n33, 122–23n37, 142–43, 155, 270
Mesha Inscription (MI). See Mesha stele
Mesha stele, 28–29, 33, 105–7, 111–12, 120–24, 122–23n37, 142–43, 152, 155, 270
    Aramean influence and, 120
    as emulation of Dan stele, 120–22, 124
    form and medium, 123–24
    inspired by Aram's example, 124
    source of inscription, 121–22
Mesopotamia, 23–24, 25
    divine writing in, 314–15
    masks in, 187
    oracles from, 267n15
    oral performance in, 185–86
    oral tradition in, 181
    scribes in, 72–73, 73–74n7
    writing in, 181
Mesopotamian literature, 282, 287–88, 314
    agglutinative organizing concept in, 294–95
    Mesopotamian Flood narrative, 282–83, 288–94, 296–97
    narrative sources of, 287–88
messenger formula, 312, 314–15, 319
Michalowski, Piotr, 177
microtext, 218–19
middle class, literacy of, 65–66
Midrash, Torah and, 283–85, 286
Milik, 96
military scribes, 77–79, 78n18, 93, 150
Milkom, 143, 145, 275
Millard, Alan, 12–13, 263
Milqart stele, 25
Mishnah, 284
Moab, 33, 112, 117, 121–23, 121n33,

SUBJECT INDEX

122–23n37, 142, 145, 325–26n16
  ca. 850–800 BCE, 28–29
  literary production in, 126
  subjugation to Israel, 270
Moabite script, 29, 121n33, 324
monumental inscriptions, 104–16, 126, 138–39, 151, 155. See also public display; specific inscriptions
  in Aram, 124
  Aramean intervention and, 110–11, 111n15
  in Cisjordan, 124
  in Deir Alla, 105–6
  emulating Assyrian models, 123
  in Judah, 147–48
  in Khirbet Beit Lei, 326–27
  in the Levant, 108–9
  literary texts and, 104–5
  nationalistic claims and, 142
  power and, 138
  in Transjordan, 124
  in Zakkur, 118n27
Mudayna, 121n33
multiformity, 213
  acceptance of, 202–3, 206–7
  as a characteristic of oral traditions, 197, 213
  of manuscripts, 206–7
  text criticism and, 213
  textual plurality and, 213
Multitextuality in the Homeric Iliad (Bird), 198–99
Myth of Enmeduranki, 312

Na'aman, Nadav, 155
Nagy, Gregory, 161n1, 171, 172
  Poetry as Performance, 170
Nahal Beersheba (Wadi Seba'), 59
Nahal Hebron (Wadi Khalîl), 59
narrative
  oral-epic tradition and, 225–26
  overarching, 217, 217n1
  structure of, 217
narrative poetry, 184, 187–89,
narrative recitation, accompaniment for, 188–89
nationalistic claims
  inscriptions and, 150
  local languages and, 150
  monumental inscriptions and, 142
  writing and, 142–44, 155–56
Naveh, Jospeh, 26n86
Near Eastern narrative, interweaving of parallel variants of narrative in, 281–82
Near Eastern studies, 284
Negev
  destruction by the Assyrians, 48
  destructions by the Babylonians and Edomites, 48
  dominance of writing with ink on potsherds in, 61
  dry climate of, 48
  late monarchical period, 47–70
  middle-class inhabitants of, 65–66
  monarchical period inscriptions in, 48–60
Negev-Aravah route, 53, 56
Nehemiah, 248–59. See also Ezra-Nehemiah
Neo-Assyrian archives, 275n42
Neo-Assyrian Catalogue of Texts and Authors, 312
Neo-Assyrian oracle collections, 274
Neo-Assyrian period, 90–91, 95, 305–21
  revelation paradigm and, 312
  scribes in, 310–11
  scripturalization in, 305–21
Neo-Assyrian Vassal Treaties, 315–16
neo-Documentary school, 285–86, 295–96, 299, 301n30
Neo-Sumerian empire, 335
Netsilik Inuit, 179
Newman, Judith, 318
  Praying by the Book: The Scripturalization of Prayer in Second Temple Judaism, 305–6
New Testament gospels, variations in, 164
New Testament studies, 163–64
Niditch, Susan, 161n1
Niles, John, 179
Nimrud, 23, 24
Nineveh, 154, 311
  Palace Reliefs from, 90

Nissinen, Martti, 274n38
Noll, Kurt L., 306–7
nonbiblical texts
  vs. biblical texts, 206–7
  definitions of, 203–5
non-Documentary approach, 285, 295–96, 297n25
Nora stele, 27
Numbers, 296
numerals, hieratic, 88–89, 264

oaths, 315–16
Obadiah the Levite, 58
O'Brien O'Keeffe, Kathleen, 200–202
  Visible Song: Transitional Literacy in Old English Verse, 200
Ödekburnu stele, 26
Old Babylonian narrative traditions, 287–94, 295, 296–97
Old Canaanite forms, 136, 137
Old English literature, 198, 211
Old Hebrew script, 86n46, 95, 108, 121n33, 328. See also palaeo-Hebrew
  diachronic development of, 86–88
  high caliber of during Iron II, 84–85
  letter formulary, 89–90
  matres lectionis and, 87–88
  origins of, 325–26n16
  orthographic system of, 86–87
  ostraca in, 142
  synchronic consistency of, 86–88
Old Moabite, 121n33
Old Norse-Icelandic oral skaldic poetry, 179
omissions, 213
Omri, 107, 111, 121
Omride dynasty, 112, 117, 120–22, 143
Ong, Walter J., 177, 178, 331, 333–34
On the Creation of the World (Philo), 299–300
Ophel excavations, 19
oracles, 153–54, 264–68, 274n38. See also prophecies
  archived, 267n15
  of doom, 118, 272n34, 275–76
  against foreign nations, 118, 275–76, 275n42
  from Mesopotamia, 267n15
  Neo-Assyrian collections of, 153–54, 274
  politics and, 273–75, 274n38
  of restoration, 277–78
  scribes and, 145
  state politics and, 264–68, 267n15
  written, 275–76
oral composition, 175–77
oral-epic substratum, 217–37
Oral Formulaic thought, 175–79, 180
orality, 161–73, 161n1
  biblical studies and, 241–42
  in Hebrew culture, 325–38
  importance of, 34
  in Israel, 325–38
  in Judah, 325–38
  literacy and, 164, 241
  literature and, 335–37
  memory and, 161–73
  residual, 201–2
  style and, 235–36
  tenaciousness of, 333
  textuality and, 161–73, 241–42
  writing and, 323–39
Orality and Literacy conference, 161n1, 164
orality/literacy dichotomy, 177–78, 180–82
orality studies, 241
oral-literary modality, 241–42
oral literature, 176n5, 217, 336
oral mindset, 164–65, 178
oral performance, 172, 217. See also performance
  Abraham-Jacob narrative and, 226
  composition during, 175–77
  context specificity of, 242
  in Egypt, 184–86
  as a goal of writing, 180–82
  Icelandic Eddic, 188
  Icelandic Skaldic, 188
  memorization and, 179–80, 184
  in Mesopotamia, 185–86
  narrative poetry and, 187–89
  oral performance culture, 171
  performance criticism, 183

SUBJECT INDEX

royal audiences and, 189
scribes and, 233–36
in Syria-Palestine, 186
text-supported, 241–42, 249–51
Ugaritic, 186–87
variations in, 242
writing and, 233–36
oral platform, patriarchal narrative and, 233–34
oral prose, Israelite, 184
oral substratum
  discourse profile and, 226–31
  language usage and, 217–37
  thematic flow and, 217–37
oral tradition
  critical historiography and, 189–90
  in Egypt, 181
  field studies in, 180–81
  genre and, 189–90
  Hebrew Bible and, 189–90
  Indian, 179–80
  in Israel, 181–82
  in Mesopotamia, 181
  multiformity and, 197, 213
  narrative platform and, 225–26
  Old Norse-Icelandic oral skaldic poetry, 179–80
  oral tradition studies, 190
  Parry–Lord approach to, 198–99
  performance of, 175–95
  simultaneous with writing, 181–82
  South Slavic, 175, 179
  special grammar of, 202
  written text and, 163, 217–37
  written transmission and, 163
oral transmission, 11, 108
oral/written interface, in patriarchal narrative, 233–35
ornaments, bronze, 23–24
orthography, 86–87n50, 86–88, 264
ostraca, 30, 62–63, 148. See also specific sites
  in cities, 63
  Edomite, 53
  in fortresses, 63
  handwriting on, 65
  Hebrew, 28, 30

vs. incised inscriptions, 60–64
ink-writing on, 62–63
in Old Hebrew Script, 142
in Samaria, 142
ownership, alphabetic systems and, 108

Pakkala, Juha, 240, 259
Pakman, Dalia, 187n88
Palace Reliefs, from Nineveh, 90
palaces, scribes in, 311
palaeo-Hebrew, 323, 324–28
Palestine, 27–28, 32–33, 110–11, 136, 186, 187, 324
palimpsests, 161–62, 167
Panamuwa I (Hadad) inscriptions, 118–19n28
Panamuwa II inscriptions, 118–19n28
papyrus, 62, 139, 141
  archives of, 148
  extensive writing on, 63–64
  influence of writing with ink on, 61
  ink on, 32, 34
  perishability of, 47–48, 60, 65, 78, 133, 133–34n1, 139
  summarizing of text on, 63–64
Papyrus Anastasi II, 74–75
Papyrus Lansing, 74
Papyrus Westcar, 186, 189
parchment, perishability of, 47, 65
Pardee, Dennis, 105n5
Parry, Milman, 161n1, 162–65, 167, 171, 175–77, 184. See also Parry–Lord School
Parry–Lord School, 175–81, 184, 197, 198–99
patriarchal narrative, 217–37
  discourse profile of, 226–31
  explicitly syntactic constituents (explicitly lexicalized constituent, ELC) in, 226–28
  hybridity in, 234
  language usage in, 226–31, 235
  literary design and, 232–33
  noun groups in, 226–28
  oral platform and, 233–34
  oral substratum of, 226–31
  oral/written interface in, 233–35

patriarchal narrative, *continued*
  redaction process and, 233, 235
  stylistic differentiation in, 228–36
  stylistic profile and, 228–35
  subordinate clauses in, 226–27
patronage, scribalism and, 137–38
Paul, 283, 287
Pedersén, Olof, 310
The Pentateuch. See also Hebrew Bible; Torah; specific books
  competing models of text-making and, 283–86
  composition of, 281–304
  editing in, 294–97
  flood narrative of, 288–94
  formal uniqueness of, 287–97
  harmonizing additions and conflations in, 299–300
  incoherence of, 298–99
  interweaving of parallel variants of narrative in, 282, 295–97, 301, 301n30
  as Jewish, 283–86
  laws in, 241
  literary values of, 281–82, 299
  mandates in, 252–59, 260
  narrative incoherence of, 282–83
  as Near Eastern, 283–86
  Pentateuchal composition, 285, 285–86, 288–94, 297n25, 298–302
  Pentateuchal criticism, 281–304
  place in Near Eastern literary history, 299–302
  polysemous contradictions in, 281–82
  preference for comprehensiveness over coherence, 281–82
  as radical break from Israelite and Near Eastern text-building, 281
  shift in literary values of, 299–300
  sources of, 282–83
  Sukkot mandates in, 253–54
  text-making techniques in, 281–304
  uniqueness among ancient Near Eastern narratives, 287–99
  what is different about, 281
Pentateuchal composition, 297n25
  history of, 298–302

  as process in which major texts respond to others, 285–86
  as reinterpretation, 285
  uniqueness of, 288–94
Pentateuchal criticism, empirical models for, 281–304
performance, 172–73. See also oral performance
  memorization and, 172–73
  memory and, 168–69
  performance criticism, 183
  scribal activity and, 217–37
  torah and, 250–51
  writing and, 168–69
Persian corpus, 231, 232, 235
Persian period, 241
Persian Yesud, 260–61
Person, Raymond F., Jr.
  The Deuteronomic History and the Book of Chronicles: Scribal Works in an Oral World, 163, 197, 207, 207n33
pharaoh statues, 13
Philistia, 15–18, 27–28, 33
Philistines, 136, 136n10
Philistine Temple 200, 187
Philo, 301
  On the Creation of the World, 299–300
  Questions and Answers on Genesis and Exodus, 299–300
Phoenicia, 143n37
  ca. 850–800 BCE, 27–28
  elite concepts transmitted from, 141
  inscriptions in, 12–15
  during Iron I, 138
  during Iron II, 138
  literacy in, 12–15
  settlements in, 137
  transition from Late Bronze to Iron I period, 136, 136n10
  writing tradition in, 138–39
Phoenician script, 85, 92n61, 94–96, 138–39, 324, 328
  in Asia minor, 140
  in Cyprus, 140
  as international, transregional script, 140

in Karatepe, 140
in the Levant, 140
matres lectionis and, 87
in Syria, 140
Pinault, David, 202, 203
pithos, 19
plaques, inscribed, 153
plaster, inscriptions on, 30, 31–32, 34, 104–5
plot, 218, 225–26
Poetry as Performance (Nagy), 170
Pohlmann, 276n43
politics
  divine anger and, 270–71, 270n28
  oracles and, 273–75, 274n38
  political identities, 134
  prophecies and, 264–71, 266n14, 267n15, 273–75
  prophets and, 264–68
Polzin, 222
potsherds, 14, 15, 19, 20–22, 50, 55–56, 58, 59, 61–64
pottery, 30, 59, 85, 113, 143n37. See also ostraca; potsherds; sherds
power. See also politics, writing and, 137–38, 142–43, 150–51
Prague School, 330–31
Praying by the Book: The Scripturalization of Prayer in Second Temple Judaism (Newman), 305–6
prestige, writing and, 137, 138, 141, 150–51
prestige objects, 137, 138, 141, 150–51
Priestly Document, 333
priests
  literacy of, 65–66
  as scribes, 65
Primeval History, 281–82, 283, 295–97, 299, 301–2
print technology, 199–201
Prolegomena to the History of Ancient Israel (Wellhausen), 239
propaganda
  prophecies as, 154, 154n68
  royal, 29, 33
  writing as, 155
prophecies, 153–54, 153n65, 263–79, 266n12, 335–37
  composition of, 145, 264–65
  of doom, 145, 154n68, 263–79
  as a form of divination, 271–72, 271n30
  politics and, 154, 264–71, 266n14, 267n15, 273–75
  as propaganda, 154, 154n68
  transmission of, 264–65
  written, 135, 264–67, 266n12, 336–37
Prophets, rewritten scripture in, 206
prophets, 154
  Assyrian statecraft and, 314
  literacy of, 263–64
  politics and, 264–68
prose-formulae, 202
Protestant scholars, 283, 285
Psalms, 135, 153n65, 204
  rewritten scripture in, 206
psalms, noncanonical, 204
Psalms Scroll of Cave II (11QPS$^{a)}$), 204
public display
  ethnic categories and, 142–43
  social identities and, 142–43
  state hegemonic process and, 155
public sphere, scribes and, 145–52
Puech, E., 32
Puech, Emile, 81

Qarhō, 143
Qarqar, battle of, 141n30
Qasile, 187
Que (Cilicia), 26
Questions and Answers on Genesis and Exodus (Philo), 299–300
Qumran, 163, 204, 205, 311–12

Rab-Shaqeh, 91
Radner, Karen, 266n14
Ramayana, 179–80
Rawidowicz, Simon, 284
readers, vs. scribes, 306–7
reading, ritual, 306–7
"Reconstructing the Classics" (Zetzel), 161
redaction process, 233, 235
Redford, Donald, 246n16

Reḥov, Tell, 28, 121n33
Reichl, Karl, 184
religion. See also cultic writing; Judaism
    dynasties and, 143
    religious instructions, 47
    religious texts, 47–48
    textiles and, 115–16 (see also ritual)
    writing and, 143
religious authority, of biblical texts, 306
Rendtorff, Rolf, 285
Renfrew, Colin, 114
Renz, 61
Renz, Johannes, 56–57n31
repetition, 217
research, sources available for, 47
residual orality, 201–2
revelation paradigm, 305, 312, 314
Reworked Pentateuch, 204–5
Ringgren, Helmer, 163
ritual, 152
    magic, 315–16
    mortuary, 297
    Neo-Assyrian, 315–16
    to prevent negative predictions from coming true, 274
    ritual magic, 308–9, 319
    ritual reading, 306–7
    ritual space, 120
    ritual texts, 312–14
    scripturalization and, 305–7
    writing and, 153, 305, 315–16, 318 (see also cultic writing)
    writing down of ritual formulations, 147
Rollston, Christopher A., 16, 182, 264, 264n6, 328
royal administration, 30, 34, 47, 63–66. See also administrative writing
royal audiences, 189
royal correspondence, 243–46. See also letters
royal scribes, 153–54, 314. See also administrative writing; royal writing
royal writing, 143, 153–55, 243–46, 246n16, 314. See also administrative writing
    compared to Ezra-Nehemiah, 251–52
    distinction between quoted text and described action in, 254
    in Egypt, 246n16
    emulation of, 151
    in Judah, 147–48
    Phoenician, 151
    scriptural mode and, 243
    textualization of, 246, 251–52
Rudolph, W., 210
rupture
    anxiety about, 284, 286, 287
    continuity created through, 302
Ruweise arrowhead, 137n13
Ruweiseh, Lebanon, 96–97

Sam'al, 26, 29
Samaria, 147
    epigraphic evidence from, 79, 93, 142
    excavations of, 30
    iconographic motifs from, 146n45
    Iron II, 141–45
    literacy in, 141–45
    military scribes in, 79
    ostraca in, 142
    Samaria Ware pottery, 143n37
    scribal tradition in, 31
    writing in, 141–45
Samaritan Pentateuch, 203–4, 205, 301
Samuel, 155, 198, 207n33, 211–12
    Chronicles and, 207–13
    Parry–Lord approach to, 197
    text criticism of, 197
Samuel-Saul-David cycle, 231
Sanders, James, 204
Sanders, Seth L., 94–95, 96, 140–41, 155, 157, 263–64
Sandmel, Samuel, 285
sapiential literature, 54, 65, 149
Sardinia, 27
Sarepta, 14, 187
Sargon II, 297
Sass, Benjamin, 12, 16, 17
Sasson, Victor, 149
Satire of the Trades, 74–75
Saussure, Ferdinand de, 330
Schechter, Solomon, 283
Schmidt, Brian, 161n1, 272n34

SUBJECT INDEX 361

Scholem, Gershom, 286, 302
schools, debate about, 80–84
school texts, biblical texts and, 309–10
scribal activity, 11
  in Jerusalem, 147
  in Judah, 152–57
  performance and, 217–37
  proliferation of, 153
scribal community, 146
  of Israel, 141–42, 146–48
  of Judah, 147–50, 153
scribal corruption, modern conceptions of, 199–202
scribal culture, 135–41, 144–45, 164. See also scribal education
  in Ebla, 135–36
  elites and, 137–38
  Levantine, 109
  patronage and, 137–38
  scribal tradition, 30–31, 34
  survival and reproduction as a trade, 137–38
  of Ugarit, 138
  West Semitic, 135
scribal curriculum, 83–86. See also scribal education
  during the first temple period, 71–101
  foreign language(s) and literature, 90–93
  Hebrew Bible as core curriculum of, 83–84
  hieratic numerals, 88–89
  letter formulary, 89–90
  orthography, 86–88
  script, 84–86
scribal education, 309–10
  administration and, 264–65
  aegis of, 93–97
  debate about schools in Israel and Judah, 80–84
  at Deir Alla, 116, 144
  evidence for, 80–84
  in foreign language(s) and literature, 91–93
  Hebrew Bible as core curriculum of, 83–84
  language usage and, 232–33

orthographic development and, 86–87, 86–87n50
scribal curriculum, 84–93
standardization of, 148–49, 264
text-brokers and, 252
scribal elites, 213
  state hegemonic process and, 145–52
scribal guild, split after Babylonian exile, 213
scribal institutions
  in Ebla, 135–36
  in Ugarit, 146
  West Semitic, 133–58
scribal knowledge/skills
  increase in, 149
  sophistication of, 145
scribal re-use, 305–6
"Scribal Textuality and a Exeter Riddle" (Doane), 200
scribes, 63
  administrative function of, 65, 75–80, 311 (see also administrative writing)
  alterations by, 161–63
  Anglo-Saxon, 200, 201–2
  in Arad, 149
  Aramaean, 117
  as cabinet-level officials, 75–80
  in Canaan, 135–36
  clerks as, 65
  compared to other occupations, 71–72, 71–72n3, 74–75
  demand for, 153
  education of, 34
  Egyptian, 88–89
  in Egyptian literature, 74–75
  employed by the state, 148–49
  explaining historical events, 275–76
  as first readers, 306–7
  in the First Temple period, 76
  fiscal, 75–80
  in government, 75–80, 76n13
  hierarchies among, 75–76, 79–80
  in Israel, 75–76
  in Judah, 75–76, 145–57
  Levitical Scribes, 311–12
  loftiness of scribal vocation, 72–75
  in Mesopotamia, 72–73, 73–74n7

military, 75–80, 78n18, 93, 150
mobility within government posts, 79
in Neo-Assyrian period, 310–11
numbers of, 306–7, 306–7n8
offices of, 79–80
oracles and, 145
oral performance and, 233–36
in palaces, 311
as performers analogous to bards, 197, 198–203
priests as, 65
professional, 47–48, 64, 75–80
proliferation of, 134, 153
prophecies of doom and, 268
public sphere and, 145–52
vs. readers, 306–7
royal, 145, 153, 314
on the scribal profession, 71–75
scribal stonemasons, 78–79
skill levels of, 47–48, 64–65 (see also scribal education)
temple, 147, 153, 310–11
use of vernacular to represent concepts, 134–35
script, 84–86. See also writing; specific languages
scriptural economy, authority of written texts in a, 242–43, 246
scripturalization
in ancient Judah, 305–21
canonization and, 307
definitions of, 305–6, 309–10, 318
in Deuteronomistic History, 316–18
endowment of written word with sacred authority, 318–19
in First Temple period inscriptions, 307–9
iconic ritualization and, 249–51
iconization of writing and, 309
implying the sacred and authoritative qualities of a text, 306
vs. inner-biblical interpretation, 305–6
literacy required for, 306–7
in Neo-Assyrian context, 307–21
role of ritual in, 306–7
scholarly narratives of, 239–62
shift from oral to written modality, 239
shift in locus of creativity from composition to interpretation, 239–40
shift of authority from teachers to texts, 239
as transformative moment, 318
scriptural modality
vs. oral-literary modality, 241–42
royal writing and, 243
scriptural texts
definitions of, 205–6
rewritten, 205–6
scripture
anthropomorphic images of, 313–14
authoritative qualities of, 306
characterizations of, 239–40
creation of as continuous with interpretation, 284–85
iconic dimension of, 249–51, 259
misquotation of, 163
performative dimensions of, 259
sacred qualities of, 306
scrolls, 134, 153, 153n65
blessings inscribed on, 134
iconic ritualization and, 249–51
performative dimensions of, 249–51
references to written, 249–51, 259
as sacred objects, 249–51
scripturalization of, 305–21
scroll technology, 168
seals, 137, 148, 150–51n61
aniconic, 232, 309
Aramaic, 30
dating of, 29
inscribed, 29, 30, 150
in Jerusalem, 146n45, 150–51n61
in Lachish, 150–51n61
Moabite, 29, 30
Phoenician, 139, 139n19
as prestige objects, 150–51
seal impressions (see bullae)
Sebastieh, excavations of, 30
Second Temple period, 169, 172, 204–5, 212, 301, 310–11
Sefire (Sfiré) Inscriptions, 29, 314
Sennacherib, 90–91, 270

SUBJECT INDEX

Septuagint, 203–4, 254n36
Ser'a, 187
Shadayin, 114
Shagar, 114, 116, 120
Shalmeneser III, 110–11
   black obelisk of, 141n30
Shamash, 312
Sheikh Shible, 20
Shephelah, 33, 60, 62, 64–65, 117
sherds. See potsherds
Sheshonq I, 141
Shipitbaal, 12
Shipitba'l Inscription, 95–96
Shurpu, 315–16
Sidon, 95
Siloam Tunnel Inscription, 90, 90n56, 90n57, 151
Silwan Tomb Inscriptions, 151, 152
Singer-Avitz, Lily, 16
The Singer of Tales (Lord), 175
Smoak, Jeremy, 308–9
social identities
   cultural tradition and, 235
   inscriptions and, 150, 155
   public display and, 142–43
soldiers, literacy of, 65
Song of the Ullikummi, 185
Sotah ritual, 316
source texts, 152–53
   anachronistic notions of, 205–6, 211
   authority of, 205–6, 211
   definitions of, 205–6
South Slavic oral tradition, 175, 179
speech, 327–37. See also orality
   illusion of immediacy and, 329–30
   uses of, 325
   writing and, 329–34
speech acts, 333–34. See also performance
standardization, 211
Starcky, Jean, 96
the state. See also politics; statehood, writing and
   prophecies of doom and, 264–68
   state administration, 47
   state hegemonic process, 145–52
statehood, writing and, 324, 327–28, 335

stelae, 155. See also specific stelae
   basalt, 25
   funerary, 15, 27, 30, 33
   Milqart, 25
   Phoenician, 30
   victory, 142
stone implements, 113
Story of Wen-Amun, 186
style, in patriarchal narrative, 228–36
Succession Treaty of Esarhaddon, 266n14
Sukkot mandates, 252–54
Sumerian poems, 287–88, 296–97, 297–98n26, 297n25
Syria, 110–11, 123–24, 135–36, 140, 186, 187
syuzhet, 218, 225–26

Taanach, 139
Tablets of Destiny, 314
tale of Aqhat, 233–34
tale of terebinths at Mamre, 233–34
Tanakh, 259. See also Hebrew Bible; Pentateuch; specific books
Taylor, W. S., 163
Teeter, Andrew, 285
temples. See also temple scribes
   administration of, 63
   in Arad, 65
   buildings mislabeled as, 310–11
   role in scribal profession, 310–11
   temple administration, 63–64
   textiles and, 115–16
temple scribes, 147, 153, 310–11
Temple Scroll, 300, 301, 311–12
Tetrateuch, 286
Text/Book of Balaam son of Beor, the seer of the gods, 32, 34
text-brokers, 242, 250–51
   authority of, 251, 254–55, 260–61
   scribal education and, 252
text-building, 296–97, 297–98n26, 299, 300
text criticism, 162
   Dead Sea Scrolls and, 203–7
   multiformity and, 213
   Parry–Lord approach, 197

text criticism, *continued*
  of Samuel–Kings, 197
  of selected ancient and medieval literature, 198–203
  transmission of texts and, 197–215
textiles
  in Deir Alla, 115–19
  religion and, 115–16
  temples and, 115–16
text-making
  competing models of, 283–86
  in first-millenium Sumero-Akkadian culture, 295
  Mesopotamian, 294–95
  in Pentateuch, 281–304
texts, 161
  as aides-memoire, 242
  as archives, 242
  authority and, 242–43, 246
  authority of, 239, 306, 309–10, 314–15, 318–19
  broader traditions of, 197–203
  in collective memory, 197–203
  creation of, 153
  divine, 314–15
  educational, 162
  iconic ritualization and, 249–51
  as incomplete representations of fuller traditions, 197–203, 210–11
  incorporating practical learning, 161–62
  magic, 312–15
  memory and, 242, 282, 282n3
  modern notions applied anachronistically, 199–201, 206–7, 211
  monumental, 105–16
  oral dimension of, 164
  in oral environments, 197–215
  oral tradition and, 217–37
  as palimpsests, 161–62
  reconstruction of, 210–11, 210–11n44
  reproduction of, 153
  ritual, 312–14
  text-critical variants of, 198–203
  text criticism of, 198–203
  text production (see literary production)
  textual innovation, 170
  tradents of, 161–62
  transitional texts, 235–36
  transmission of, 153, 161–63, 197–215, 242–43
textual internalization, 172–73. See also memorization
textuality, 161–73
  biblical studies and, 241–42
  memory and, 161–73
  modern conceptions of, 199–203
  orality and, 161–73, 241–42
  print technology's affect on conceptions of, 199–201
  spatial vs. phonemic understanding of, 200–201
  of torah, 252–53, 259
textualization
  resistance to, 318
  trend toward expansion in process of, 203, 212
textual plurality, 197–98, 203–4, 206–7, 210–11, 210–11n44, 213. See also multiformity
textual traditions. See also specific traditions
  expansion of, 212
  variations in (see variants)
textual transmission
  dimensions of, 164, 168–69
  oral tradition and, 163
textual variants. See variants
theophanies, 153
Thomas, Rosalind, 179, 180
Thousand and One Nights, 198, 202, 203, 211, 212
Tigay, Jeffrey, 298–99
  Empirical Models for Biblical Criticism, 282–83
  The Evolution of the Gilgamesh Epic, 287–94, 287n15, 287n16
Tonga, 179
Torah. See also Hebrew Bible; Pentateuch; Tanakh
  composition of, 285
  created through reinterpretation, 285

SUBJECT INDEX

creation of as midrashic process, 285
creation of as radical break between Judaism and Israel, 283–84
emergence as scripture, 239–62
exegesis and, 285
Ezra-Nehemiah and, 239–41, 247–59
as a fixed object, 283
formal uniqueness of, 287–97
legal layers of, 285–86
as many layers of interpretation, 285
Midrash and, 283–85, 286
non-Documentary approach, 285
ossification of, 283
physical texts of, 240
torah. See also Torah
articulation of, 250–51
oral and written components of, 239–41, 243, 246–59, 302
oral-literary economy of representation in Ezra-Nehemiah, 239–41, 246, 252–53, 260–61
performance and, 242, 250–51
produced and transmitted through text-supported oral performance, 242
scrolls of, 249–51, 259
textuality of, 252–53, 259
torah utterances, 242–43
Tov, Emanuel, 210–11n44
tradents, 161–62, 171, 260, 283
trade routes, 53, 56, 144
Traditionsliteratur, 273
Transjordan, 112, 117, 122–23n37
literacy in, 141–45
monumental inscriptions in, 124
vernacular in, 138
writing in, 141–45
transmission, 161–63
dimensions of textual, 164, 168–69
oral, 11
oral-literary mode of, 241–42
through text-supported oral performance, 241–42
of written text, 242–43
treaty genre, 314, 318–19
curses and, 319
magic and, 315–16
Treaty of Esarhaddon, 315

Trebolle, Julio, 207, 207n33
Tyre, 31, 95
Tyre al-Bass, cemetery of, 15, 27, 30, 33

Uehlinger, Christoph, 309
Ugarit, 109–10n12, 135, 139, 157, 186
archives in, 311
literary production in, 126
scribal heritage of, 138
scribal institutions in, 135–36
Ugaritic narrative poems, 225
Ugaritic poetry, 145, 217–18
Ugaritic tales, 233–34
Ulrich, Eugene, 204–5
University of Michigan, 161, 161n1, 164
Urhilina, 24
Ur III, 335
Urtenu, 311
Uruk, 315
Utukkū Lemnūtu, 294

Vachek, Josef, 330–33
Van der Toorn, Karel, 83–84, 91, 93, 177, 310–12, 327, 336–37
Van Soldt, W. H., 311
variants, 161–65
of ancient literature, 198–203
authentic, 171–72
good, 165–67, 171
graphic, 165, 167, 169
of medieval literature, 198–203
memory, 166, 167, 169–72, 282, 282n3
multiple present in the same text, 167–68
Old Hebrew script, 203–4
oral/aural, 165, 167, 169, 171
as organic to native poetic structures, 201–3
as reflecting acceptance of multiformity, 202–3
text-critical, 198
three forms of, 165–69
vernacular, 134, 138, 150
Visible Song: Transitional Literacy in Old English Verse (O'Brien O'Keeffe), 200

Watts, James, 249, 306

Weeks, Stuart, 81, 86–87n50, 182
weights, inscribed, 148, 150
Weippert, Manfred, 32
Wellhausen, Julius, 189, 240, 283, 287
    Prolegomena to the History of Ancient Israel, 239
Westermann, Claus, 225
West Semitic cultures, 23–34, 133–58. See also specific cultures
Williams, Raymond, 337–38
Williamson, H. G. M., 250n26
Winters, Ryan, 297n25
writers. See scribes
writing
    adapted to express local forms of culture, 157
    administrative, 108–9, 139, 326–28, 335, 337–38
    alphabetical, 47
    for apotropaic purposes, 152
    authority of, 312, 314–15, 318–19
    autonomy of, 332–33, 336–38
    in Canaan, 135–36, 141
    commerce and, 139
    cultic, 143–44, 145, 147, 152, 153, 157
    decentralization of, 153
    diffusion of use of, 33–34
    divination and, 315
    divine, 305, 312–15, 319
    division of labor and, 327–28, 337
    dynasties and, 142–43, 157
    during early Iron Ages, 135–41
    economic, 150, 326–27, 328, 335
    in Egypt, 181
    elites and, 134, 135, 137–38, 142–43, 149–53, 267
    epigraphic evidence and, 326–27
    expression of local identity through, 135–36
    as a gift of the gods, 315
    iconization of, 309
    ink, 30, 34, 62–63
    introduction of, 332–33
    Iron I, 137, 138
    Iron II, 138, 141–57
    in Israel, 141–45, 181–82, 325–38
    in Judah, 133–58, 325–38
    Late Bronze Age, 135–41
    in the Levant, 135–41
    literary vs. nonliterary uses, 335–36
    literature and, 335–37
    local traditions of, 135
    magic and, 315, 318
    material culture and, 327–37
    as a means of communication, 337–38
    as a means of production, 337–38
    memory and, 168–70
    in Mesopotamia, 181
    in Moab, 29
    national cult and, 143–44
    nationalistic claims and, 142–43, 155–56
    orality and, 181–82, 233–36, 323–39
    origins of, 315, 326–27
    performance and, 168–69, 233–36
    in Phoenician city-states, 138–39
    political use of, 142–45
    power and, 137–38, 142–43, 150–51
    prestige use of, 33, 138, 150–51
    production of, 327–37
    as propaganda, 155
    prophetic oracles and, 336–37
    religious, 143, 145, 326–27
    rising prominence of, 327–37
    ritual use of, 152, 153, 305, 307, 315–16, 318 (see also cultic writing)
    royal, 243–46, 246n16
    sacred, 312, 318–19
    in Samaria, 141–45
    secondary productions of, 48
    as secondary to speech, 330–31
    speech and, 329–34
    state hegemonic process and, 142–43
    statehood and, 324, 327–28, 335
    in Syria, 135–36
    technology of, 108, 135, 177–78, 323–41
    textualization of, 315, 318–19
    in Transjordan, 141–45
    uses of, 325
    West Semitic, 34
Writing on the Tablet of the Heart (Carr), 169, 306
writing proficiency, 47–48, 265, 265n9

writing prophets, 263, 314
Wulfstan, *De Temporibus Anticristi*, 200

Yahweh, 116, 153, 271, 276, 276n43
Yahwism, 271
Ya'ush, 64–65
Ya'ush archive, 51
Yavneh Yam (Meṣad Ḥashavyahu), 77, 79, 93, 307–9
Yavneh-Yam inscription, 307–8, 309
Yeḥimilk, 12, 95–96
Young, Ian, 82, 264

Zakkur, 118n27, 124, 275n42
Zayit, Rosh, 14
Zayit, Tell, 16, 140, 324
Zerubbabel, 213
Zetzel, James E. G., 162
    "Reconstructing the Classics," 161
Zincirli, excavations of, 26

Ancient Sources Index

Hebrew Bible

Genesis

1	298	12:5	220–21
1–2	92	12:10–20	223, 229, 229n43
1–21	229	13	229n35, 235
2:20	333	13:1–17	229, 229n45
3:5	298	13–24	230n49
3:17	298	14	235
5:29	298	14:1–12	230n49
6–8	92	14:1–24	230
6–9	289	15:17	234
6:5	290	15:1–12	229, 229n44
6:8	290	15:17–18	229, 229n44
6:9	290	16	229, 234
6:11	290	16:1–2	229n38
6:17	289	16:4–12	229n38
7:1	289	16:8	227
7:17	291	17:1–8	223, 229, 229n41
7:24	291	17:15–21	229, 229n41
8a	233	17:15–22	223
8b	233	17:1–18	223, 229n41
8:6	292	18	219, 225, 233, 233n71
8:7	292	18–40	219
8:20	293	18:1–15	229, 229n36, 233
9:1	293	18:2a	233
9:8	293	18:7	227
11:30	220	18:9–14	223
12–35	6	19:1–22	229, 229n37
12:1	220	19:3	226
12:1–5	221	20:1–18	229
12:1–9	229, 229n42	21	229n35, 234
12:2	220–21	21:7–21	229
		21:13–21	223

ANCIENT SOURCES INDEX

21:22–32	230	29:9–35	230n54
21:22–32	230n46	30:1–24	231n57
22:1–19	229, 229n40	30:32–43	224, 231,
22:2	221		231n60
22:3	223	31	230, 231
23	230, 235	31:1–2	224
23:1–2	223	31:4–16	230n54
23:1–16	230n47	31:10–12	234
23:7–20		31:45–54	231n56
23:19–20	230n47	31:53	234
24	230, 236	31:54	219
24:1	220	32	230, 236
24:1–21	229,	32:2–24	230n55
	230n48, 235	32:4–6	220
24:2	235	32:25–32	230, 230n53
24:4	221	33	229n34, 230
24:9	235	33:1–13	230n52
24:10	221	33:1–17	227, 229
24:15–16, 27, 50	219n8	33:1–20	224
24:22–23	229n39	34	231, 235
24:22–67	229–30, 235	34:1–17	231n59
24:34–49	229n39	34:18–31	231n59
24:35	221	35:1	224
24:50–67	229n39	35:17–19	224
24:67	221	37:4–21	230n50
25:1–12	92, 230,	37:22–36	230n50
	230n50	38:1–11	230n50
25:5–12	235	47:29	235
25:8–10	219n9, 223		
25:9	223	Exodus	
25:19–25	219		
25:27	230	2:1–10	92
25:29–34	224, 230,	15:20	189
	230n52	19	334
25:30	230	20–23	90
26:1–33	230n50	20:5	317
27	230	20:25	317
27:1–4	219	22:25–26	308
27:18–26	230n52	24	9, 312, 319
27:18–29	224	24:4	312
27:30–38	230n52	24:7	319, 312
28	230	24:12	312, 313
28:1–9	231,	24:12–31:18	314
	231n58, 235	25–31	313
28:10–22	230n55	31:18	312, 313
28:13–15	224	32–34	334
29	230		

33:11	330	JOSHUA	
34	300–301		
34:1	256–57	8	9, 316
34:6–7	327	8:31	317

LEVITICUS

JUDGES

18:12–13	168	13:2–3	220n12
20:21, 17	168		
23:23–25	251		
23:40–42 MT	253–54	1 SAMUEL	

NUMBERS

		1:1	207
		2:5	220n12
1:2	58	18:6–7	189
5	9	21;12	189
5:16–30	316	29:5	189
6:24–26	147, 308		
22–24	92, 144	2 SAMUEL	
29:1–6	251n28		
		1–4	207
		2:19–25a	189
DEUTERONOMY		3:21	51
		6:12–19a	207
1:9	227	6:20b–23	207
2–3	229n34	8:16–18	76, 76n13
2:26–3:7	228	11:1a	207
2:26–3:7	228–29	12:26–31 MT	2, 207–9,
4	334		207, 211
7:1–3	256, 258	12:27–29	209–10, 212
7:	308	23:8–39	207
7:9–10	147		
7:25	168	1 KINGS	
16:11	251n28		
16:15	251n28	2	156
17:5	168	2:12	207
17:18–19	311	4:2–6	76
22:6	168	9:11	165
23	258	11:39	51
23:4–6	258	12:11	77
24:12–15	308	18:18	76
24:16	317	18–19	90
27:5–6	317	19	334
27–29	9, 315–16	19:16–19	22
31:9–13	259	20:20	90

22:12	76	Ezra	
25:19	77		
		1:1–5	243n10
2 Kings		3:2	247, 247n17
		3:4	247
2:15–18	226	4:7–24	243
9:2, 14	22	4:8–16	243n10
12:12	58	4:17–22	243n10
12:18	117	4:21	245
14:6	317	4:23–24	245
18	3	5:5	246
18–19	90	5:6–17	243n10
18:25	119	5:13–15	245n13
18:26	91	6:2–5	243n10
19:23	165	6:3–5	243n10
19–22	226	6:6–12	243n10
22–23	241n6	6:13–15	246n15
22:5, 9	58	6:18	247, 247n17
22:15–16	319	7:5	252
23:2	319	7:6	247n17
23:3	312	7:10	247n17
23–25	226	7:11–26	243n10
		7:12–16	241
1 Chronicles		7:21	247n17
		9:1–3	257
10:1–29:30	207	9:10–12	257–59
11:10–47	207	10:1–4	257
12	207, 209n38	10:2–4	258
15:25–16:3	297	10:3	247n17, 258
20:1b–3 MT	6, 207–9, 211	10:3–4	257–59
		10:10–11	257
20:2	209		
20:3	210	Nehemiah	
27	207		
		2:19–4:16	246
2 Chronicles		2:7–9	243nn10, 11
		8	240
9:11	165	8–10	247
24:11	77	8:1	247, 247n17, 252, 259
32:30	90	8:1–8	255
34:10	58	8:1–12	247, 248–51, 252
34:12	58	8:2	247n17
34:17	58	8:3	247n17

8:4–6	249	JOB	
8:5	247		
8:7	247n17, 261	24:1	220n12
8:8	247n17	27:10, 12–16	149
8:13	247n17, 261		
8:13–14	247	PSALMS	
8:13–17	251–57, 259		
8:14	247n17, 253	88	308
8:14–15 MT	254	89:22	51
8:15	247n17, 253–54, 256	103	308
8:18	247n17		
8:32	256	PROVERBS	
9–10	255–57		
9:1–3	255	1–9	310
9:3	247, 247n17	3:1–4	308
9:6–10	255	22:17–24:22	92
9:13	247n17	31:17	51
9:26	247n17		
9:29	247n17	ISAIAH	
9:34	247n17		
10:1	255	5:12	188
10:2–28	255	36–38	90
10:29	247n17	37:20	165
10:29–30	256, 258	37:24	165
10:29–40	257	54:1	220n12
10:30	247, 247n17		
10:30–41	259	JEREMIAH	
10:31	257–58		
10:31–41	257	8:8	318
10:35	247n17	36	10
10:35–37	256	36:11–20	77
10:36–37	257n39	36:12	77
10:37	247n17	37:15, 20	77
13:1–3	247–48, 257–59	52:25	77
13:1	247n17		
13:1–3	257	AMOS	
13:3	247n17, 258		
		8.5	256
ESTHER			
		NAHUM	
3:12	77		
8:9	77	2:2	51

Zephaniah

2:14–18	189

Early Jewish Texts

Ben Sira

38:24	71
38:24–39:11	82
38:26	71
38:27	71
38:28	72
38:29	72
38:31, 32	72
38:32, 33	72
39:1, 4, 9	72

Jubilees

19:15–31	219n8
22:1	219n9
22:10–23:2	219n8
23:6–7	219n9

Mishna

m. Hagigah 1:8	284

Qumran

Temple Scroll

11QT II, 1–15	168
11QT LII, 6–7	168
11QT LII, 7–21	168
11QT LXV, 4	168
11QT LXVI, 8–16	168
11Q19 LVI, 20–21	312

Ancient Near Eastern Sources

Gilgamesh

XI	
7	290
14	290
23–27	289
128–131	291
134–135	191
137–138	191
147ff	292
157–167	293

Ugarit

KTU

1.3.i	186
1.40	157
1.113	156

Inscriptions and Ostraca

Arad

Ad1–18	50
Ad1–40	50
Ad2	88
Ad16	89
Ad21	50, 89
Ad22	88
Ad24	50
Ad31	88
Ad33	88
Ad34	88
Ad40	50, 89
Ad41–74	50
Ad42	88
Ad46	88
Ad60	88
Ad65	88
Ad76	88
Ad76–81	49
Ad87	50
Ad88	50–52

Ad89–92	50	Lh5	89
Ad93	49	Lh6	89
Ad94–95	50		
Ad98	50	\multicolumn{2}{l}{Meṣad Ḥashavyahu}
Ad99	50		
Ad100–104	50	Mh3	88
Ad111	50	Mh4	88

CAI

Samaria

59	143	Sa22	88
		Sa27	88

Horvat ʿUza

		Sa28	88
		Sa34	88
1	54, 55	Sa58	88
2	53, 54, 55, 56	Sa61	88
3	53, 55, 56		
4	53, 55, 56	\multicolumn{2}{l}{Tel ʿIra}
5	53, 55, 56		
6	53, 55, 56	1	58
7	53, 56	2	58
8	55, 56	3	58
10	53, 55, 58		
11	53	\multicolumn{2}{l}{Tel Masos}
12	53		
14	53, 56	1	57
15	56	3	57
16	56		
17	53, 56	\multicolumn{2}{l}{Classical Works}
18	53, 56		
23	53	Lucian, *Dea Syr.* 15	187
24	53		
27	53		
28	53		
21	53		
22	53		
29	53		
34	53		

Lachish

Lh2	89
Lh3	64, 77, 89
Lh4	89

www.ingramcontent.com/pod-product-compliance
Lightning Source LLC
Chambersburg PA
CBHW030104010526
44116CB00005B/95